THE BROCK BIBLIOGRAPHY OF PUBLISHED CANADIAN PLAYS IN ENGLISH 1766-1978

Edited by Anton Wagner

Compiled by

Bonita J. Orosz Bryan
David R. Clark
Richard Cummings
Merle Doherty
Paula Eykelhof
Elizabeth Fajta
Christopher Johnson
Deborah Nathan
Patrick B. O'Neill
Richard Plant
Elizabeth Reynolds
Anton Wagner

PLAYWRIGHTS PRESS

THE BROCK BIBLIOGRAPHY OF PUBLISHED CANADIAN
PLAYS IN ENGLISH 1766-1978
Copyright © 1980 Playwrights Press

Published with the assistance of the Canada Council, the Canada Council Explorations Programme, the Ontario Arts Council, the Ontario Ministry of Culture and Recreation, Alberta Culture, Metropolitan Toronto and the City of Toronto.

Playwrights Press (a division of Playwrights Canada)
8 York Street
Toronto Canada M5J 1R2
416-363-1581

Playwrights Canada is a national association of professional playwrights. It was founded originally as Playwrights Co-op and reincorporated as Playwrights Canada in April 1979. It publishes plays and reference books for the theatre under the imprint Playwrights Press.

Typeset by Howarth & Smith Limited, Toronto
Printed in Canada by the Hunter Rose Company, Toronto
First Edition August 1980

CAUTION: This book is fully protected under the copyright laws of Canada and all other countries of the Copyright Union. No part of this book may be reproduced or transmitted in any form, by any means, electronic or mechanical, including photocopying, and recording, information storage and retrieval systems, without permission in writing from the publisher.

CANADIAN CATALOGUING IN PUBLICATION DATA
Main entry under title:
The Brock bibliography of published Canadian plays
  in English, 1766-1978
Includes index.
ISBN 0-88754-157-7 bd. ISBN 0-88754-155-0 pa.
1. Canadian drama (English)—Bibliography.*
I. Wagner, Anton, 1949-
Z1377.D7B758   016.812   C79-094758-7

CONTENTS

Introduction   i

A. The Seventeenth Century   1

B. The Eighteenth Century   5

C. The Nineteenth Century   9

D. The Twentieth Century   39

Drama Short Title Index   345

Resource List   373

INTRODUCTION

In any attempt to examine English-Canadian drama from its beginnings to the present, the bibliographic maxim "before books can be studied they must be known to exist" has been particularly appropriate. Until the early 1970s, artistic directors at several regional theatres across Canada maintained that there simply were no Canadian plays suitable for production at their theatres. In 1971, English-Canadian playwrights countered with a controversial manifesto demanding among other points a 50% Canadian content quota at government supported theatres.[1] The phenomenal growth of the alternate theatre movement and its championship of the Canadian play in the 1970s gradually has led to the realization that Canadian drama does indeed merit more concerted literary analysis and bibliographic enumeration.

This annotated bibliography takes as its departure Reginald Eyre Watters' *A Checklist of Canadian Literature and Background Materials 1628-1960*, W. S. Milne's annual drama bibliographies in *Letters in Canada*, between 1935 and 1942, the Canadian Association for Adult Education's 1957 *Canadian Plays and Playwrights* and greatly enlarges upon the work begun in *The Brock Bibliography of Published Canadian Stage Plays in English 1900-1972* and the 1973 *First Supplement to the Brock Bibliography of Published Canadian Plays*. Dorothy Sedgwick's *A Bibliography of English-Language Theatre and Drama in Canada 1800-1914* facilitated expanding the *Brock Bibliography* to include plays published before 1900. Patrick O'Neill's *Canadian Plays—A Supplementary Checklist to 1945* in turn provided a considerable number of titles not included in previous bibliographies. A resource list of the most useful sources in compiling and up-dating this bibliography can be found following the short-title index.

This present volume, *The Brock Bibliography of Published Canadian Plays in English 1766-1978*, is intended as a companion volume to *A Bibliography of Canadian Theatre History 1583-1975* and its 1975-1976 *Supplement* published by the Playwrights Co-op, and aims to record the growth and development of Canadian drama in English from its literary and live theatre origins. Because this bibliographic project marks the first time that the whole body of English-Canadian drama and French-Canadian drama in English translation has been read and annotated in its entirety, some observations regarding the development of English-Canadian drama over two centuries may be helpful to users of this bibliography.

Marc Lescarbot's "Le Théâtre de Neptune en la Nouvelle-France" published in his *Les Muses de la Nouvelle-France* in 1609 marks the beginning of dramatic writing and performance in French-Canada. Because Lescarbot's masque was not included in Pierre Erondelle's translation *Nova Francia* of 1609 or subsequent editions and was only published in translation in 1926, one must look to the plays of later British colonial soldiers and authors for the tentative beginnings of English-Canadian drama. We have nevertheless included "Le Théâtre de Neptune" as a separate seventeenth century item, (A 1), rather than listing it as a twentieth century title.

The starting date 1766 for this bibliography is derived from the works of two authors in British North America, George Cockings' *The Conquest of Canada; or, The Siege of Quebec*, (B 2), and Robert Rogers' *Ponteach; or, the Savages of America*, (B 3), published by their authors in London in 1766. It must be pointed out that, like Lescarbot, Cockings and Rogers can be considered to have produced Canadian plays only within the context of having resided briefly in Canada and having written about Canadian subject matter. Cockings is primarily an English author and Rogers is claimed by both the Americans and British as one of their nationals. Their plays, along with Adam Allan's *The New Gentle Shepherd* published in London in 1798, (B 1), are nevertheless representative of a British literary tradition that strongly influenced the many writers who emigrated from Britain to Canada in the eighteen hundreds.

Dramatic writing and live theatre in Canada in both the nineteenth and twentieth centuries have been, to a significant degree, a theatre and drama of immigrants. Charles Heavysege, Samuel James Watson, John Hutchinson Garnier, John Hunter-Duvar, Sarah Anne

Curzon, Eliza Lanesford Cushing, William Henry Fuller and Frederick Augustus Dixon are only the more prominent nineteenth century immigrant authors. Beginning with the 1820s, early immigrant writers such as Samuel Hull Wilcocke tentatively began to explore the literary and thematic possibilities of dramatic composition. The frequent publication of political satires and farces appearing in English Canada from Wilcocke's *The Scribbler* to "The Triumph of Intrigue" in *The New Brunswick Courier*, (C 50), Hugh Scobie's "Provincial Drama Called The Family Compact" in *The British Colonist*, (C 171), the dozens of satires appearing in J. W. Bengough's *Grip* from 1873 to 1894 and many other publications suggest a distinct genre of political satire scrutinizing society in colonial Canada and the post-Confederation new Dominion.

Side by side with the literary poetic drama in the nineteenth century and significant because of the frequency of its publication is the satirical literary parody from Wilcocke's "The Charrivarri", a "mixto-poetico-prose-comico-tragico-melo-dramatico-farrago", (C 187), to Sam Scribble's burlesques in the mid-1860s and the parodies of Gilbert and Sullivan operettas and grand opera by Frederick Augustus Dixon, J. W. Bengough and G. L. W. Broughall in the last quarter of the century. The frequency of parodies throughout the eighteen hundreds not only reflects the popularity of the burlesque in live theatre but also indicates an awareness on the part of writers of the comic artificiality of live stage and dramatic conventions without playwrights, at the same time, being able to develop a more theatrically credible dramatic style.

Contrasting with the stylistic sophistication of literary parodies in the nineteenth century are a number of dramatic compositions which can be catagorized as "naive" drama similar to the indigenous naive vernacular Canadian folk painting of the seventeen and eighteen hundreds. Although they represent the work of unskilled writers, compositions such as Robert McBride's "A Division Court and County Court Case", (C 147), John Robertson's "The Hamesick Wife and Consoling Husband", (C 167), and the anonymous "Saint Bartholomew's Day in Canada", (C 55), are of interest for the vigorous expression of their subject matter and their depiction of Canadian society. Such "naive" dramatic compositions, along with works of skilled poets such as Alexander McLachlan's "Fate", (C 154), and Samuel James Watson's "The Legend of the Roses", (C 185), force one to define what constitutes a play. Watson called his work "a poem" but includes in it long passages of dialogue assigned to various distinctly identifiable characters. In contrast, a similar mixture of poetry and poetic dialogue (but to a much lesser degree and therefore not annotated here) can be found in Charles Sangster's "Hesperus". For the purpose of this bibliography, a play has been defined as a dramatic composition containing dialogue or action by clearly delineated characters. The bibliography therefore annotates not only full length works but also compositions labelled by their authors as "a dramatic fragment", "a dialogue" and various other kinds of dramatic scenes. While no such individual dramatic sketch may be of great literary significance in itself, the overall pattern they indicate can be significant in pointing out various stylistic and thematic explorations. It is not farfetched, for instance, to suggest that William Henry Fuller's important "The Unspecific Scandal", (C 114), was influenced by the many brief political satires appearing in *Grip* and other publications.

This actual examination and thematic annotation of dramatic texts is one of the unique features of the *Brock Bibliography*. Title entries in other bibliographies, such as Watters' listing of John Underhill's *Damon and Pythias. A Drama of Quebec Liberalism.* Author, 1891 and *The Passing of the Buffalo* by Buckskin (pseud.). Vancouver, Selkirk, 1916 quickly reveal themselves as not being dramas at all. Similar title entries such as Arthur George Doughty's comic opera *Bonnie Prince Charlie.* Montreal, Desbarats, 1892 and Wilson MacDonald's musical comedy *In Sunny France.* Moose Jaw, 1924 reveal themselves, upon examination, as programs documenting the production of plays but not the printed text itself. Through the examination of texts, it also becomes possible to provide dates of first production of plays as well as act and cast breakdowns. (It should be noted that the usage of "act" varies widely among authors and that, particularly in the case of satires, a three or five act play does not necessarily indicate a full-length work.)

One additional significant feature of this bibliography is the way in which it facilitates, through the play annotations, the reduction of a massive number of drama titles into various thematic categories or more specific genres such as radio, television, and children's drama; comedy, musicals, operetta, opera, historical and poetic-drama; tragedy, masques, pageants, political satire and melodrama. By combining the previously separate author listings for radio and television drama of the 1972 and 1973 *Brock* bibliographies, a playwright's entire dramatic output in several media becomes apparent.

•

One of the challenges in compiling any bibliography of Canadian drama is the lack of sufficient biographical information on nineteenth and twentieth century authors. The frequent migration of writers to and from Canada makes it very difficult to determine Canadian nationality. To define what constitutes a Canadian play, we have maintained the definition set out in the 1972 edition of the *Brock Bibliography*, "plays written by Canadians, native, naturalized or landed immigrant. Therefore, plays written by an immigrant before he or she came to Canada are not Canadian, and presumably plays written by a native Canadian after he or she becomes a citizen of another country are not Canadian either". For nineteenth century authors, this definition means excluding the works of writers such as Isidore Gordon Ascher, Barnabas Bidwell, Frances Brooke, Clara Louise Burnham and Mary Anne Sadlier written before coming to Canada or after having emigrated from this country. Twentieth century writers similarly excluded are Nicholas Cosentino, Reby Edmond, Philip Freund, Simon Grey, Josephine Hammond, John Edward Hoare, George Vere Hobart, Amice Anna Botham Macdonell, Ronald Elwy Mitchell, George Frederick Mountford, Harvey Jerrold O'Higgins, Hubert Osborne, Bernard Slade and Anna Louisa Walker.

Besides determining Canadian citizenship of writers, one can also ask to what degree their works function within a Canadian theatrical and dramatic context. Do their plays contain Canadian subject matter or were they published or performed in Canada and thereby possibly influenced other writers? We have included Henry James Finn's *Montgomery; or, The Falls of Montmorenci*, (C 112), even though it was written after Finn moved to the United States from Canada because of the play's Canadian subject matter. George Hulme's *Displaced Affections*, (D 990), and *The Life and Death of Adolf Hitler*, (D 991), have been included because of their Canadian publications. Bernard Slade's *Same Time Next Year* has been excluded because he must be considered to be primarily part of the American, rather than the Canadian theatrical community.

Lacking detailed histories of English-Canadian theatre, the bibliographer of Canadian drama to a considerable degree assumes the function of a theatre historian who must verify his findings through a variety of sources. On occasion, simply determining whether a play announced for publication has in fact been published is difficult since sources such as publishers' catalogues or the annual *Canadian Books In Print* based on publishing projections are not always reliable. For this edition of the *Brock Bibliography*, we have listed only those plays of which copies can actually be located in Canadian or foreign libraries and collections.

In our research, one of the most useful sources in verifying the nationality of authors and other bibliographic information for pre-1951 *Canadiana* titles has been *The National Union Catalog, Pre-1956 Imprints*, a cumulative author list representing Library of Congress printed cards and titles reported by other American libraries. For example, plays published in Canada with Canadian subject matter such as the political satires *Our National Pie and What It Contained* by Paul Ford, Montreal, Drysdale, 1877 and *Commercial Courtship and Unselfish Union* by Oliver Leigh, (Geoffrey Quarles, pseud.), Toronto, Irving, 1888 are revealed by the *National Union Catalog* to be by prolific American authors. "Alice Chadwicke", the adaptor of Lucy Maud Montgomery's *Anne of Green Gables* published by French in New York in 1937, is similarly revealed to be a pseudonym for the prolific American playwright Wilbur Braun.

•

As section D indicates, there is a great proliferation of dramatic writing in the twentieth century. It reflects to a great extent, the state of live theatre, or lack of it, in English-Canada at various periods. Theatre and drama in the classroom constitute an important phenomenon throughout the century. They range from the drills and dramatic sketches issued for "school concerts" by Educational Publishing in Toronto during three decades at the beginning of the century, to play anthologies such as Ida Emma Baker's *Dialogues and Dramas for School and Home* of 1928, Alexander Stephen's *Classroom Plays from Canadian History* of 1929, to D. J. Dickie and E. M. Jones' *Canadian School Plays* of 1931 and 1948, up to and including the latest school drama anthologies published in the 1970s. Much of this pre-World War II educational output is didactic, moralistic and of poor literary quality and is frequently the work of authors largely unfamiliar with professional theatre and dramatic literature. The works of these unskilled authors (Sister Mary Agnes being the most prolific example) can be compared to the "naive" drama of nineteenth century writers and is of interest primarily for sociological and historical reasons. Nevertheless, because of the great frequency of its publication and widespread actual performance in schools, this pre-World War II educational drama constitutes a genre of its own which first introduced large numbers of children to live dramatic performances.

Of greater literary significance is the influence of the little theatre movement on dramatic writing from the 1920s to the post-World War II period. Authors such as Merrill Denison, Gwen Pharis Ringwood, Elsie Park Gowan and many others were encouraged by the possibilities of having their plays produced. At the same time, they were restricted in their dramatic writing by the limited production resources of the amateur theatre. For the first time, individual theatres, as exemplified by Vincent Massey's *Canadian Plays from Hart House Theatre* of 1926 and 1927, began to contribute to the rapidly growing body of published Canadian drama. Beginning with the 1930s, radio became an important training ground for several generations of writers. The re-establishment of professional theatres across Canada in the 1960s and 1970s, through funding from the Canada Council, has provided playwrights with the most extensive production opportunities in the history of English-Canadian theatre. That several dozen playwrights have emerged to create works of high literary excellence within only one decade is a very promising indication for the future development of Canadian drama. As Alexander Leggatt notes in "Letters In Canada: 1974", "the most encouraging sign is that the number of playwrights one wants to keep an eye on is growing steadily".

But the development of English-Canadian drama is not only related to the health of live theatre in Canada but also to that of Canadian publishing. The relatively small Canadian market for published drama makes anthologies such as the American ninety-five cent Dell mass-market paperback *Ten Canadian Short Plays* an economic impossibility. "Published for the Author" is therefore not only a time-honoured Canadian literary tradition in the nineteenth century but extends to the 1970s. The creation of the Playwrights Co-op in 1972 brought into existence an organization which W. S. Milne in "Letters in Canada: 1936" had already called for: a "manuscript clearing house for the handling, at a small fee, of Canadian scripts already produced by some reputable group". The Co-op's list of over 300 playscripts, representing the work of more than one hundred playwrights, has provided an economical link between live theatre production and literary publishing, while helping to keep plays alive for reading enjoyment and further theatre productions.

For the purpose of this bibliography, we have regarded a play as "published" as defined by the laws of copyright which state that a work is published when copies of it have been issued to the public. The great majority of dramas here annotated appear in regular hardcover or paperback editions or in periodicals. A large number, such as those issued by Robinson Plays, the University of Alberta Department of Extension plays of the 1940s, the Ottawa Little Theatre Workshop plays of the 1960s and Playwrights Co-op titles (with the exception of Henry Beissel's *Inook and the Sun, Playwrights In Profile: Carol Bolt, Four Plays by Larry Fineberg, Blitzkrieg* by Bryan Wade, George F. Walker's *Zastrozzi* and Sheldon Rosen's *Ned and Jack*) are mimeographed editions. A smaller number of titles, specifically scripts issued by the Alberta Ministry of Culture, the New Play Centre in Vancouver and the Dramatists Co-op in Halifax, also appear in xerox form. Because of the great number of titles contained in this bibliography, it has not been possible to provide listings for locations of plays at Canadian and foreign libraries. Locations for a large number of plays are provided in the Watters, Sedgwick and O'Neill bibliographies as well as by the American *National Union Catalog*. The largest single collections of Canadian drama have been assembled by the Theatre Department of the Metropolitan Toronto Library and the Cameron Library at the University of Alberta, Edmonton. The Ministry of Alberta Culture Library now holds the several dozen plays published in the 1940s by the Department of Extension, University of Alberta. The largest Canadian drama collections outside of Canada can be found at Brown University and the New York Public Library. Their title holdings are listed in Brown University's *Dictionary Catalog of the Harris Collection of American Poetry and Plays* of 1972 and its *First Supplement* of 1977, and *The New York Public Library Catalog of the Theatre and Drama Collections* of 1967 and its *First Supplement* of 1973. Since no complete collection of English-Canadian drama exists at present, researchers will invariably have to make use of the inter-library loan department of their local library.

One of the difficulties in compiling this bibliography has been the vast number of periodicals and the obscure or ephemeral nature of publications such as *Educational Review, Echoes, Canadian Red Cross Junior, Acadia Athenaeum* and many others which published Canadian plays at various periods. While many of these plays and "playlets" are of minimal literary interest, collectively they can provide us with theatrical and sociological insights about their authors and the theatre and society of their time. It is interesting to note, for instance, that T. M. Morrow, Mazo de la Roche, P. N. Jacobson and Don Wetmore were first published in *Echoes* and Gregory Doane in *Acadia Athenaeum*. Academic or university affiliated journals were often important dramatic outlets. *Acta Victoriana* at the University of Toronto Victoria College, for example, published plays or dramatic sketches by William Wilfred Campbell, E. J. Pratt, Margaret Atwood and Carol Bolt. This edition of the *Brock Bibliography* annotates plays published in a dozen nineteenth century and seventy-five twentieth century periodicals and newspapers. Periodicals will continue to be the major difficulty in up-dating the bibliography since coverage of published play texts by the *Canadian Periodical Index* is extremely limited.

•

This bibliographic project, including work on the 1972 and 1973 editions of the *Brock Bibliography*, now extends over a five year period in which we have become indebted to a great number of individuals and institutions for their assistance. My personal thanks go first of all to the compilers of the two previous editions of the *Brock Bibliography* who permitted us to incorporate their work in this current edition: Christopher Johnson, the project advisor, and Bonita J. Orosz Bryan, David R. Clark, Richard Cummings, Merle Doherty, Paula Eykelhof, Elizabeth Fajta and Elizabeth Reynolds. The bibliography was expanded to its present scope by Richard Plant, Deborah Nathan, Paula Eykelhof, Patrick O'Neill and myself through a grant from the Canada Council Explorations Program without whose assistance this project could not have been undertaken. We are also very grateful for the generous assistance of the numerous libraries and librarians in Canada and abroad who aided us in our work, particularly Heather McCallum and the staff of the Theatre Department of the Metropolitan Toronto Library, the University of Toronto libraries, the National Library of Canada, the Alberta Culture Library, Brown University, the New York Public Library, the British Museum, the Library of Congress and the many other individual Canadian and American institutions who made copies of Canadian plays available to us for annotation. Compilation of this bibliography would not have been possible without the great assistance of the inter-library loan departments of the University of Toronto Robarts Research Library, Brock University and the Metropolitan Toronto Library.

We would also like to express our gratitude to Professor Janet Dolman and the Brock University Drama Department and all the many other individuals who assisted in the compilation of the 1972, 1973 and 1980 editions of the *Brock Bibliography*. We are grateful to Tom Hendry, Heather McCallum and Professor Ann Saddlemyer for supporting our Canada Council Explorations application, to Shirley Gibson, director of Playwrights Canada, for her confidence and support, and to Dorothy Sedgwick for generously making her own bibliographic research available to us.

During the course of our work, we have become all too aware of the great chances for error in a bibliographic project of this nature and scope. We hope that any errors and omissions will be drawn to our attention for correction in future supplements to this volume. Correspondence should be addressed to The Brock Bibliographic Project in care of Playwrights Canada.

Because quantity cannot be equated with quality, a brief closing observation on the literary merit of the works contained in this bibliography is in order. That many of these plays succeeded in theatrical terms is indicated to a degree by the fact that a large percentage of them were performed on stage. The *Bibliography of Canadian Theatre History* lists the various sources documenting the critical reception to and relative popularity with their audiences of Canadian drama. To a great degree, literary criticism of English-Canadian drama must be based on contextual criticism, viewing a play within the context of the live theatre, audience and society of its time and the evolutionary nature of Canadian theatre and drama. As late as 1966, only a year before the Canadian Centennial celebrations which launched several of our large regional theatres as Centennial projects, W. S. Milne, in the Dominion Drama Festival's *Canadian Full-Length Plays in English*, provided the following advice to prospective dramatists: "What sort of play has the best chance of production by a Canadian Drama Group? Probably a play with one set; a relatively small cast; with women predominating—numerically at any rate; modern costume, and no intricate problems of effects, properties or lighting."[2] Fortunately, many of the dramas annotated in this bibliography transcend the live theatre production constraints of their time and are of sufficient literary quality to remain dramatically meaningful long after their composition.

But, as with dramatic writing in any country, many plays deserve to be forgotten. In Canada, however, the relative obscurity into which two centuries of English-Canadian drama have been relegated is less the result of critical evaluation than critical neglect. Frequently, this neglect has resulted from a lack of awareness, on the part of critics, of the extent of dramatic material on which literary evaluations must be based. The function of literary bibliographies is not to make critical judgements, but to enable sound critical judgements to be made on the basis of all the evidence available. If *The Brock Bibliography of Published Canadian Plays in English 1766-1978* stimulates and assists such an evaluation, it will have achieved its purpose.

Anton Wagner, Editor

[1] Report on a Playwrights Conference, Niagara-on-the-Lake, August 14, 15, 1971. Toronto, Canadian Theatre Centre, 1971. p. 6.

[2] *Canadian Full-Length Plays in English (II)*: a supplement to the preliminary annotated catalogue. W. S. Milne, ed. Ottawa, Dominion Drama Festival, 1966, p.vi.

ABBREVIATIONS USED IN THE TEXT

n.p.	No place of publication or publisher known.
n.d.	No date of publication known.
ed.	Editor.
trans.	Translator.
(pseud.)	Pseudonym.
fp:	First produced by.
p:	Produced by.

PUBLISHER'S NOTE

Playwrights Co-op was founded in 1972. In 1979 the name was changed to **Playwrights Canada**. When reading the text please keep in mind that they are the same organization.

Playwrights Press is the imprint under which Playwrights Canada publishes paperback books.

A
The Seventeenth Century

LESCARBOT, Marc 1570-1642

A1. "Le Théâtre de Neptune", Rivers Keith Hicks, trans. *Queen's Quarterly*, vol. 34, #2, October 1926 and *Neptune's Theatre*. Edna B. Holman, trans. New York, London, French, 1927 and *The Theatre of Neptune in New France*. Harriette Taber Richardson, trans. Boston, Riverside Press for Houghton Mifflin, 1927 and "Le Théâtre de Neptune", R.K. Hicks, trans. *Journal of Education for Nova Scotia*, series 4, vol. 10, March 1939 and *Theatre of Neptune*. R.K. Hicks, trans. Lower Granville, Nova Scotia, Abanaki Press, 1947 and *The Theatre of Neptune in New France*. Harriette Taber Richardson, trans. N.p., Canadian Association for Adult Education, 1957.
1 act. 13m. Extras.
A translation of his "Le Théâtre de Neptune en la Nouvelle-France" contained in his *Les Muses de la Nouvelle-France* published in Paris in 1609. A poetic masque in which Neptune, tritons and Indians praise the valour of de Poutrincourt and his companions whose return to Port Royal was the occasion for the original presentation in the bay.
fp: Port Royal, Nova Scotia, Nov. 14, 1606 and, English translation by Harriette Taber Richardson, Port Royal, Aug. 15, 1956.

B

The Eighteenth Century

ALLAN, Adam 1757-1823

B1. *The New Gentle Shepherd.* London, Richardson, 1798.
5 acts. 6m/5f. Extras.
A verse drama in pastoral comedy tradition. Adapted from *The Gentle Shepherd* (Allan Ramsay, 1758) with Scottish dialect "reduced to English" by Lieutenant Allan. Patie, son of Symon, a shepherd to Sir William, loves Peggy, daughter of another shepherd. Sir William, who fled fearing Cromwell, returns home and reveals Patie is his son. Peggy and Patie cannot get married because of differences in station until Mause, a poor old woman, reveals that Peggy is really Sir William's niece. Now they can marry as can a second pair, Roger and Jenny, since Roger has won Jenny's love by proving to her that men can be constant lovers.

COCKINGS, George -1802

B2. *The Conquest of Canada; or, The Siege of Quebec.* London, Author, 1766 and Baltimore, Hodge & Shober, 1772 and Philadelphia, Magill, 1772 and London, n.p., 1796.
5 acts. 11m/2f. Extras.
"A historical tragedy" in verse relating the tale of Wolfe's victory over Montcalm. The heroism of Wolfe and the skill and courage of outnumbered British troops are honoured.

ROGERS, Robert 1727-1795

B3. *Ponteach; or, The Savages of America.* London, Author, 1766 and Chicago, Caxton Club, 1914 and in *Representative Plays by American Dramatists,* vol. 1. Montrose Moses, ed. New York, Dutton, 1918.
5 acts. 19m/2f. Extras.
A poetic drama in blank verse in which Ponteach's ill-usage at the hands of reprehensible Englishmen forces him to urge an Indian confederation to drive the evil people from Indian lands. At the same time, disorder erupts within Ponteach's own household. In the war with the whites, Ponteach's warriors have captured and punished the evil English. But the good English, the garrison soldiers loyal to the crown, prove too much for the Indians. As the play ends, Ponteach is left without children and with his forces in defeat. Yet he remains heroic and defiant.

C
The Nineteenth Century

ANONYMOUS

C1. "The Beauties of the Jury System" in *Grinchuckle,* vol.1, Sept. 30, 1869.
1 scene. 4m. Extras.
A brief satiric sketch attacking the jury system in which a murderer is set free.

C2. "The Boycott" in *Grip's Almanac, 1881.* p.42.
3 acts. 8m. Extras.
"Probably by the author of 'The O'Dowd' ". A brief satiric sketch of a farmers' boycott in Scotland.

C3. "The Brighter World Above" in *The Canadian Quarterly Review and Family Magazine,* vol.1, #1, Oct. 1863.
1 scene. 2g.
A brief dialogue between two girls praising the beauty of God's universe.

C4. "The Canadian Club" in *Grip,* vol.3, nos. 11, 14, Aug. 8, 29, 1874.
2 scenes. 6m. Extras.
A satire of contemporary politics and journalism.

C5. "A Comedy in One Act" in *Grinchuckle,* vol.1, Nov. 25, 1869.
1 scene. 3m. Extras.
A brief satiric sketch of King Macdougall and Provencher.

C6. "The Commissioner and the Injun" in *Grip,* vol.9, #17, Sept. 15, 1877.
1 scene. 2m.
A brief satire of Mills, Sitting Bull and free trade.

C7. "The Crooked Tree" in *Light for the Temperance Platform.* George Maclean Rose, ed. Toronto, Hunter, Rose, 1874.
1 scene. 2g.
A pro-temperance dramatic sketch.

C8. *Culture.* A Drawing Room Comedietta, Adapted from a Foreign Source and Slightly Altered, by ****. Halifax, Halifax Printing, 1889.
3 scenes. 2m/3f.
A young Englishman who pretends to be a man of intellect tends to snub his Canadian-born wife. After his wife secretly begins classes at Dalhousie, the husband is soon overwhelmed by his wife's knowledge and his own ignorance. The mother-in-law solves the problem and the couple plan a new honeymoon to Europe.
p: Mount Saint Vincent University, Oct. 28, 1978.

C8A. *Extract From an Original and Unpublished Play, Lately Performed at the Prescott Municipal Amphitheatre!.* Prescott, Ont., n.p., (187-?).
1 scene. 5m.
A brief satire of the Prescott Municipal Council.

C9. "Fair Rosamond" in *Grip,* vol.17, #14, Aug. 20, 1881.
4 acts. 2m/3f. Extras.
A brief "tragedy in four acts by *Grip*'s own dramatist" parodying Swinburne.

C10. "The Fishery Commission at Halifax" in *Grip,* vol. 9, #8, July 14, 1877.
A brief satire of Uncle Yankee Jonathan and Pa John Bull's treatment of little Canada regarding their respective fishing rights.

C11. "Following Up a Clue" in *Grip,* vol.24, #19, May 9, 1885.
1 scene. 2m. Extras. Chorus.
A brief satirical "detectivish reportorial operetta" in Gilbert and Sullivan style.

C12. "The Great Land Bubble" in *Canadian Illustrated News,* vol.10, #8, Aug. 22, 1874.
2 acts. 5m.
"A little comedy" satirizing politicians involved in a land speculation incident in Quebec.

C13. *The Greatest Realistic Burlesque Farce of the Latter Part of the Nineteenth Century.* Justice Peg and his Justice Shop in the City of Winnipeg. (Winnipeg, 1897?).
4acts.
"A play issued by the saloon keepers against the temperance campaign of the time".

C14. "Grip in Council" in *Grip,* vol.2, nos. 16, 17, 19, 20, 21, 25, March 14, 21, April 4, 11, 18, May 16, 1874.
6 scenes. Multiple roles.
A series of comic scenes satirizing current political events.

C15. "H.M. Canadian Ship Blunderbore" in *Grip,* vol.12, #17, March 15, 1879.
1 scene. 3m. Extras. Chorus.
A fragment of a "new opera" satirizing Macdonald.

C16. "The Happy Return" in *Grip,* vol.6, #26, May 20, 1876.
1 scene. 4m.
A brief satire of Mackenzie and Blake.

C17. "John Bull and Jonathan" in *Grip,* vol.7, #13, Aug. 19, 1876.
1 scene. 2m.
A brief satiric dialogue regarding the treatment of Indians.

C18. "Labor and Capital" in *Grip,* vol.22, #7, Feb. 16, 1884.
1 scene. 2m.
"A conversation of the times" set in a saloon on King Street. Two Irish labourers conclude that, with the same government grants, labour could construct the Pacific railway as well as the Syndicate.

C19. "The Land of Liberty" in *Grip,* vol.9, #10, July 28, 1877.
2 scenes. Multiple roles.
A brief satire of political unrest in the United States.

C20. *The Land Swap.* Montreal, n.p., 1875.
4 parts. 15m. Extras.
A satire about land speculation and political intrigue in Quebec.

C21. "The Letellier Drama" in *Grip,* vol.13, #25, Nov. 8, 1879.
3 scenes. 3m.
A brief satiric attack against Letellier's dismissal in Quebec.

C22. "Local" in *Acta Victoriana,* vol.11, #6, March 1888.
2 scenes. 10m.
A brief satirical dramatic sketch about four students and six murderers.

C23. "Locals" in *Acta Victoriana,* vol.5, #2, November 1882.
4 scenes. 7m.
A brief parody of Shakespearian scenes and quotations involving a student prank in Alumni Hall.

C24. "The Moderate Drinker" in *Light for the Temperance Platform*. George Maclean Rose, ed. Toronto, Hunter, Rose, 1874.
1 scene. 4m.
A pro-temperance dramatic sketch.

C25. "Mr. Mackenzie at Buckingham" in *Grip*, vol.5, #8, July 17, 1875.
1 scene. 2m/1f.
A brief satire of Alexander Mackenzie.

C26. "The New Minister" in *Grip*, vol.7, #24, Nov. 4, 1876.
1 scene. 3m.
A brief satiric scene in which Mackenzie introduces a new member of the cabinet who turns out to be slightly mad.

C27. "Our Poet in the Council Chamber" in *Grip*, vol.1, #11, Aug. 9, 1873, #15, Sept. 6, 1873.
2 scenes. 7m.
A brief satire of the Toronto City Council.

C28. "The Popish Plot" in *Grip*, vol.27, #24, Dec. 18, 1886.
3 acts. 5m. Extras.
A brief farce about religious interference in Ontario schools.

C29. "Presbyterian General Assembly" in *Grip*, vol.6, #4, June 17, 1876.
1 scene. 8m. Extras.
A brief satire of the Macdonnell case.

C30. "Pro and Con" in *The Scribbler*, vol.2, #54, July 11, 1822.
1 scene. 2m.
A dramatic dialogue between a deacon and a reader of the *Albany Microscope* defending that paper's attack on religious bigotry and aristocratic libertines.

C31. *Pro and Con*. Quebec, n.p., 1828.
1 scene. 2m.
"A satirico-political dialogue in familiar rhyme partly imitated from the Latin of Horace and dedicated (without permission) to the late Grand Jury" between an editor and a friend discussing the responsibility of the press.
"To aid Religion and established Right,
To blend at once instruction and delight:
The truth diffuse, and men with knowledge bless,
These are the noblest uses of the Press."

C32. "The Pump and the Tavern" in *Light for the Temperance Platform*. George Maclean Rose, ed. Toronto, Hunter, Rose, 1874.
1 scene. 3m/1f.
A pro-temperance dramatic sketch.

C33. "The Queen's Oak" in *The Literary Garland,* new series, vol.8, #4, April 1850.
1 act. 1m/1f/2b.
"A dramatic sketch". A poetic drama concerning the initial meeting between Edward IV, the Yorkist victor of the Wars of the Roses, and Elizabeth Woodville, the widow he is to marry later.

C34. "Scene at Ottawa" in *Grip*, vol.7, #16, Sept. 9, 1876.
1 scene. 2m.
A brief satire of Mackenzie and Blake.

C35. "Scene at Ottawa" in *Grip,* vol. 12, #9, Jan. 18, 1879.
1 scene. 3m.
A brief satire of the National Policy.

C36. "Scene — City Hall" in *Grip,* vol. 7, #22, Oct. 21, 1876.
1 scene. 10m.
A brief satire of corruption at City Hall.

C37. "Scene in Ottawa" in *Grip,* vol.12, #3, Dec. 7, 1878.
1 scene. 2m.
A brief satire of Sir John and Tupper.

C38. "Scenes in Court" in *Grinchuckle,* vol.1, Sept. 23, 1869.
1 scene. 4m/1f.
A comic sketch demonstrating "the difficulties of being a witness".

C39. "Scenes in Court — The Deaf Female Witness" in *Grinchuckle,* vol.1, Sept. 30, 1869.
1 scene. 3m/1f.
A brief comic sketch.

C40. "Scenes from Unpublished Dramas" in *Diogenes,* vol.1, March 5, 1869.
2 scenes. 2m.
A brief satiric sketch of an impoverished representative of a foreign power attending a Canadian festival.

C41. "The Senator's Sensitive Daughter" in *Grip,* vol.15, #9, July 17, 1880.
3 acts. 2m/5f/1b.
A brief satirical "society drama" in which a senator's daughter advocates the abolishment of the useless Senate.

C42. "Short Drama" in *Grip,* vol.7, #20, Oct. 7, 1876.
1 scene. 3m.
A brief satiric sketch in which Mackenzie mourns his waning strength and the ascendency of Sir John A.

C43. *Sir John and Sir Charles; or, The Secrets of the Syndicate.* Montreal, Published by a Syndicate, 1881.
1 scene. 2m.
A satire of Sir John A. Macdonald, Sir Charles Tupper and the Pacific Railroad Scandal.

C44. "The Sleeping Beauty" in *Canadian Illustrated News,* vol.24, #26, Dec. 24, 1881.
2 acts. 4m/8f. Extras.
"An original drama for children". A retelling of the traditional tale of the princess who sleeps 100 years and is awakened by a prince's kiss.

C45. "Socrates and Xantippe" in *Grip-Sack,* vol.1, 1882.
1 scene. 1m/1f.
A comic argument in rhymed verse.

C46. "The Sweets of Office" in *Grip,* vol.11, #16, Sept. 7, 1878.
1 scene. 5m.
A brief satire of Mackenzie.

C47. "Temperance Dialogue" in *The Canadian Quarterly Review and Family Magazine,* vol.2, #2, April 1865.
  1 scene. 2m.
  A pro-temperance dialogue between Adam Drinkup and Doctor Searchall.

C48. "Theatricals at the Theatre" in *Grinchuckle,* vol.1, Dec. 16, 1869.
  3 scenes. 2m/1f.
  A brief satire of American actors.

C49. "The Tribulations of N.F.D." in *Grip,* vol.12, #16, March 8, 1879.
  1 scene. 8m. Extras.
  A brief satire of Nicholas Flood Davin unsuccessfully attempting to establish Industrial Schools for the Indians of Saskatchewan.

C50. "The Triumph of Intrigue" in *The New Brunswick Courier,* Saint John, vol.22, nos.43, 44, 45, Feb. 23, March 2, March 9, 1833.
  3 acts. 10m/1f. Extras.
  A thinly veiled political farce attacking the new British lieutenant governor who is shown being manipulated by members of his government for their private gain.

C51. "The Two Premiers" in *Grinchuckle,* vol.1, Jan. 27, 1870.
  1 scene. 2m.
  A brief critique of Quebec's financial extravagance.

C52. "Vol. One" in *Grinchuckle,* vol.1, Sept. 23, 1869.
  1 scene. 3m.
  A dialogue between Grinchuckle and the public announcing the new Montreal comic paper.

C53. "The Way They Manage It" in *Grinchuckle,* vol.1, Jan. 6, 1870.
  1 scene. 1m/1f.
  A comic sketch of a recently married "rising young barrister".

C54. "What Next! And Next!! And Next!!!" in *The Canadian Patriot,* vol.1, #5, May 2, 1864.
  1 scene. 2m.
  A dramatic dialogue in which the Montreal chief of police is sharply interrogated at the bar of justice for advocating the legal licensing of Montreal's 100 brothels.

A PROTESTANT (pseud.)

C55. "Saint Bartholomew's Day in Canada" in *Rhymes for the Times.* Montreal, n.p., 1857.
  1 scene. 2m.
  A dramatic dialogue in verse "between a Stranger and a Citizen of Montreal in reference to the Massacre of the 9th June, 1853".

A SPIRITUAL MEDIUM (pseud.)

C56. *The Comedy of Trade; or, Every Man for Himself:* as recently performed at Ottawa by a distinguished company of amateur legislators. Montreal, Dawson, 1876.
  1 act. 23m.
  A satirical reconstruction of "the great tariff debate in the Dominion Trade Congress, Ottawa, 1876".

ALLAN, Peter John 1825-1848

C57. "Pygmalion, Prince of Cyprus" in *The Poetical Remains of Peter John Allan, Esq.* Rev. Henry Christmas, ed. London, Smith, Elder, 1853.
1 act. 5m/2f. Extras. Chorus.
The first act of an incompleted "dramatic poem". A verse drama in which the virtuous Pygmalion ascends the throne of Cyprus to rescue his people from corruption.

ALLEN, Joseph Antisell 1814-1900

C58. *The True Romantic Love-Story of Col. and Mrs. Hutchinson.* London, Elliot Stock, 1883.
4 scenes. 7m/3f.
"A drama in verse" eulogizing the love and courtship of Hutchinson and Miss Apsley during the time of Charles I. Their precious love and decorous behaviour win out over "great hazard and many obstacles".

ANDERSON, William E.

C59. *A Roman Drama in Five Acts Entitled Leo and Venetia.* Pickering, Ont., Pickering Newsprint, 1895.
5 acts. 10m/5f.
Leo, a young nobleman, rescues the Duke's daughter, Venetia, from death at a lion's jaws. They quickly fall in love and Leo becomes embroiled in the evil Ronolo's plots to obtain control of the duchy and Venetia's hand. With the intervention of witches, Ronolo is foiled and the deserving Leo avenged.

BENGOUGH, John Wilson 1851-1923

C60. *Bunthorne Abroad; or, The Lass That Loved a Pirate.* Toronto, n.p., 1883.
2 acts. 7m/4f. Chorus.
A parody of Gilbert and Sullivan operettas. Bunthorne, last appearing in *Patience*, is travelling incognito aboard what he believes is a trader ship bound for America. The ship is actually a pirate vessel, the Pirates of Penzance presiding, and it was their hatred of Bunthorne, a sentimental aesthete, which drove them to piracy. Ethel, the captain's ward, falls in love with Bunthorne. The H.M.S. Pinafore appears and defeats the pirates with the help of Buttercup who has information regarding the pirate to whom Ethel is promised and Ethel's birth.
p. Templeton Star Opera Company, Hamilton, August 1886.

C61. "The Edison Doll" in *Grip*, vol.42, nos. 22, 23, 24, 25, 26, Dec. 1, 8, 15, 22, 29, 1894.
1 act. 1m/2f/1b.
A "farcical tragedy dramatised by J.W.B. from a humorous poem by F. Anstey" about a crazed bachelor pining for his lost love.

See also item D171.

BLENNERHASSETT, Margaret (Agnew) 1778-1842

C62. "How the Song was Made" in her *The Widow on the Rock and Other Poems*. Montreal, Sparhawk, 1824 and Ann Arbor, Michigan, University Microfilms, 1965.
1 scene. 2m.
A satirical dramatic dialogue in black and white southern dialect between Sambo and Massa Jonathan about a song the two will compose for the U.S. President, the text of which follows.

BORLAND, Rev. John 1809-1888

C63. *Dialogues Between Two Methodists*. Toronto, John Donogh, 1856.
2 scenes. 2m.
Two dialogues between Algernon Newways and Samuel Oldpaths "in which attendance at class meetings as a condition of church membership is shown to be both Wesleyan and scriptural and the relation of children to the visible church of Christ is explained and vindicated".

BROUGHALL, George Lewis William 1861-1927

C64. *The 90th on Active Service; or, Campaigning in the North West*. Winnipeg, Bishop, 1885.
2 acts. 26m. Extras.
This "musical and dramatic burlesque" was written by Staff Sergeant Broughall and rehearsed while the 90th Battalion, on a mission to quell the Metis rebellion, was stationed at Fort Pitt. It is a variety show made up of songs and satirical sketches about army life. Two war correspondents, a black cook and a fat English soldier receive special satirical attention. There is little mention of Riel, Big Bear or the rebellion.
fp: Princess Opera House, Winnipeg, July 19, 1885.

C65. *The Tearful and Tragical Tale of The Tricky Troubadour; or, The Truant Tracked*. Winnipeg, Manitoba Free Press, 1886.
4 acts. 6m/4f. Extras. Chorus.
"A topical and tuneful tradition told in travesty" constituting a satirical burlesque of grand opera, particularly Verdi's *Il Trovatore*.
fp: Princess Opera House, Winnipeg, Sept. 28, 1886.

BROWN, John Henry 1859-1946

C66. "A Mad Philosopher" in his *Poems: Lyrical and Dramatic*. Ottawa, Durie, 1892.
4 acts. 10m/6f. Extras.
A poetic drama. The mad philosopher is Corot, the author of an idealistic project to reform the world's thought. Corot intends to secure the assistance of Jefferson and Buonaparte and would have them implement laws compelling their people to adopt progressive scientific ideas.

BUSH, Thomas

C67. *Santiago.* Toronto, Rollo & Adam, 1866 and in *Canada's Lost Plays,* vol.1, *The Nineteenth Century.* Anton Wagner, Richard Plant, eds. Toronto, CTR Publications, 1978.
5 acts. 22m/3f. Extras.
A poetic drama in verse with a gothic South American setting. Vampries, a mysterious man with otherworldly powers, saves Credulous, a Spanish traveller, from a trio of cut-throats. Credulous and Vampries go on to Santiago where Vampries, through a disastrous church fire, punishes a group of corrupt priests who are maintaining idolatrous and fraudulent practices.

C.P.M. (pseud.)

C68. "Innocent Bigamy" in *Grip,* vol.18, #12, Feb. 4, 1882.
5 acts. 3m/2f/1g.
"A drama of the period by the author of 'The Planter's Wife' " parodying a domestic melodrama.

C69. "Lord Fitz Fraud" in *Grip,* vol.17, #7, July 2, 1881.
3 acts. 1m/2f. Chorus.
"A Toronto society drama as performed in *Grip's* Canadian Theatre, Adelaide Street" satirizing Torontonians with upper class pretensions.

C70. "Mrs. Tactician's Triumph" in *Grip-Sack,* vol.1, 1882.
5 acts. 4m/2f.
A brief farcical "tragedy of love and tobacco". Mrs. Tactician wins a husband for her daughter by causing her listless fiance to abjure tobacco.

C71. "Queen Eleanor and Fair Rosamond" in *Grip,* vol.24, #5, Jan. 31, 1885.
5 acts. 3m/2f. Extras.
A brief parody of *Becket,* "being a variation of Lord Tennyson's lately published drama".

C72. "Society Idyls" in *Grip,* vol.17, #11, July 30, 1881.
1 scene. 1m/1f.
Two lovers run away from home.

CAMERON, George Frederick 1854-1885

C73. *Leo, the Royal Cadet.* Kingston, Henderson, 1889.
4 acts. 14m/2f. Extras. Chorus.
A light "military opera" which praises the Royal Military College in Kingston, army life and the heroic future possible for cadets when they become soldiers. Its action centres around the love of Nellie and Leo, a Royal Cadet, sent off to fight the Zulus. He is believed killed but returns to her a hero with the Victoria Cross. Music by Oscar F. Telgmann.
fp: Martin's Opera House, Kingston, 1889.

CAMPBELL, William Wilfred 1858-1918.

C74. "The Brockenfiend" in *The Lounger,* n.d., p. 285.
5 acts. 12m/5f. Extras.
A charcoal burner is cursed by a friar and sells his earthly happiness to the Brockenfiend for his magic fire. He murders his brothers shortly afterwards.

C75. "Daulac" in *Acta Victoriana*, vol.22, #3, 1898 (act 5 only) and in his *Poetical Tragedies of Wilfred Campbell*. Toronto, Briggs, 1908.
5 acts. 8m/3f. Extras.
"An historical tragedy of French Canada". The play is an imaginative reconstruction of the events that led to the famous battle of the Long Sault in defence of Montreal.

C76. "Hildebrand" in his *Mordred and Hildebrand*. Ottawa, Durie, 1895 and in his *Poetical Tragedies of Wilfred Campbell*. Toronto, Briggs, 1908.
5 acts. 11m/4f. Extras.
"An historical tragedy founded upon the life and character of the great Pope Gregory VII". Gregory's refusal to compromise in spiritual and political matters leads to unhappiness and tragedy.

C77. "Mordred" in his *Mordred and Hildebrand*. Ottawa, Durie, 1895 and in his *Poetical Tragedies of Wilfred Campbell*. Toronto, Briggs, 1908.
5 acts. 11m/4f. Extras.
A tragedy based on Malory's rendering of the Arthurian legend. Mordred, Arthur's deformed son, the result of his unwitting incest, starts the series of deceptions and intrigues that lead to the splitting of the kingdom.

C78. *Morning*. Ottawa, Lounger Press, 1897 and in his *Poetical Tragedies of Wilfred Campbell*. Toronto, Briggs, 1908.
5 acts. 13m/2f. Extras.
In a "mythical time" in the city of Avos, the good citizen Leonatus maintains his belief in God and in the necessity for the virtues of faith and hope against the onslaught of the cynical and corrupt Vulpinus.

CANDIDUS, Caroli (pseud.)

C79. *The Female Consistory of Brockville*. Brockville, Ont., Author, 1856 and in *Canada's Lost Plays*, vol.1, *The Nineteenth Century*. Anton Wagner, Richard Plant, eds. Toronto, CTR Publications, 1978.
3 acts. 4m/8f.
Inspired by an incident at the time in the Brockville area, this satire in prose and verse attacks the female consistory for driving their innocent minister from the community on trumped-up charges of mistreating his wife.
p: (Public reading), NDWT Co., Toronto, Jan. 14, 1979.

CARLETON, John Louis 1861-1939

C80. *More Sinned Against Than Sinning*. New York, De Witt, 1883 and Chicago, Dramatic Publishing, 1883.
3 acts. 11m.
A stock "Irish" melodrama in which Alphonsus Belhaven, rejected by Mary O'Connor in favour of Marmaduke Hilton, seeks revenge. He turns Squire Hilton, who does not want his son marrying an Irish girl, against "Duke" but is then kidnapped by Belhaven. With help from Teddy O'Neill, Duke finds his father, good is rewarded and evil punished.
p: Dramatic Society of St. Michael's College, Toronto, Dec. 6, 1899.

See also items D349-351.

CARTER, William

C81. *Placida, The Christian Martyr.* Toronto, Globe Printing, (1873?).
2 parts. 4m/2f. Chorus.
"A cantata" concerning the conversion to Christianity of a nobleman's daughter who is rejected by her father and condemned to death on the grounds that, worshipping another king, the Christians disown the Emperor Nero and are guilty of treason.
fp: St. James Cathedral Sunday School Rooms, Toronto, Jan. 28, 1873.

CHESNUT, Thomas Herbert

C82. *Nina, or A Christmas in the Mediterranean.* Hamilton, Ont., David Bewicke, Caxton Press, (188-?).
2 acts. 9m/2f. Extras.
"A nautical comic operetta written for the Harmonic Club" in Gilbert and Sullivan style. Nina, daughter of Captain Taffrail, is abducted by pirates and her father, fiance and the crew of the H.M.S. Snowbird held prisoner by the pirate leader Antonio. A formerly captured maiden, Irene, is revealed to be Antonio's long lost daughter. The pirates are reformed and Nina marries her hero, Dick LeRoy.

CHRONONHOTONTHOLOGOS (pseud.). See SCOBIE, Hugh.

CURZON, Sarah Anne 1833-1898

C83. *Laura Secord, the Heroine of 1812.* Toronto, Robinson, 1887.
3 acts. 20m/7f. Extras.
A historical drama in verse praising Laura Secord's heroism in warning the British of an impending attack.

C84. "The Sweet Girl Graduate" in *Grip-Sack,* vol.1, 1882 and in *Laura Secord, the Heroine of 1812.* Toronto, Robinson, 1887.
4 acts. 3m/4f. Extras.
A short comedy attacking discrimination against women in the academic world. Kate Bloggs has been denied admission to university on the grounds that no women are permitted. She disguises herself as a boy and enters university where she becomes a distinguished scholar. She reveals her true identity and the gentlemen whose respect she has gained agree to petition for the admission of women.

CUSHING, Eliza Lanesford (Foster) 1794-1886

C85. "The Blind Pastor" in *The Literary Garland,* vol.3, #6, May 1841.
1 act. 2m/1f.
"A dramatic fragment". A poetic dialogue between a blind pastor and his devoted daughter concerning the different forms of love — filial, romantic and spiritual — and the ways in which these are properly connected to each other.

C86. "Charles the First in Spain" in *The Literary Garland,* new series, vol.1, #2, February 1843.
3 scenes. 2m/3f.
A poetic dramatic fragment. The proposed marriage between the Spanish Infanta and Charles I, prospective king of England, is threatened by the intrigues of their advisors. Because of religious differences, the marriage is delayed.

C87. "Dramatic Scene" in *The Literary Garland,* vol.2, #4, March 1840.
1 act. 2f.
A poetic dialogue based on Biblical incidents. In their shared grief, Ruth devotes herself to her mother-in-law Naomi.

C88. "A Dramatic Sketch" in *The Literary Garland,* vol.1, #5, April 1839.
1 act. 3m/2f.
A poetic drama. Encouraged by his vengeful sister Salome, Herod orders the death of his beautiful and righteous wife Marianne.

C89. "Dramatic Sketch" in *The Literary Garland,* vol.4, #8, July 1842.
1 act. 4m/1f.
A poetic drama. Alexander the Great indulges in a dalliance with a slave and commissions her portrait. When he discovers that she and the artist have fallen in love, he demonstrates the nobility of his character by condoning the match.

C90. "Dramatic Sketch from Scripture History" in *The Literary Garland,* new series, vol.2, #4, April 1844.
1 act. 3m/3f/1b. Extras.
A poetic drama recounting the triumph of David's line over the worshippers of Baal on the day the Hebrews "dispossess of her usurped rights,/the guilty murderess, who over Judah reigns".

C91. "Dramatic Sketch. The Intercepted Letter" in *The Literary Garland,* new series, vol.3, #8, August 1845.
1 act. 3m/2f.
A woman's grief at her husband's apparent death in battle is dispelled by her accidental discovery of his survival — his letters to her had been intercepted by another man, a rival for her love.

C92. "Esther" in *The Lady's Book,* vol.16, June 1838 and vol.17, July, August, November, December 1838 and in *Esther, a Sacred Drama; with Judith, a Poem.* Boston, Dowe, 1840.
5 acts. 8m/4f. Extras.
A poetic drama in blank verse about the Jews in Persia under King Ahasueras. Esther, a beautiful, virtuous Jewish woman, becomes Ahasueras' queen. Ambitious Haman, second to the king, coerces him into decreeing the death of Jews. Haman hates Mordecai, Esther's foster father, and plots his death. Esther reveals to Ahasueras that she is Jewish but he loves her still. Haman is defeated.

C93. "The Fatal Ring" in *The Literary Garland,* vol.2, nos. 8, 9, 10, July, August, September 1840.
3 acts. 8m/6f.
A poetic drama on the theme of love betrayed by woman's "frailty". Despite her husband's attempt to protect her from the wiles and seductions of court and the interest of King Francis, the "royal spoiler", a young countess succumbs to the temptation of power and ambition. Her disloyalty reduces the count to a frenzied wretch and her later repentance is insufficient to secure her from his vengeance.

C94. "Parting of Boabdil and Morayma" in *The Literary Garland,* vol.1, #10, September 1839.
1 act. 1m/2f.
A poetic drama set in the Alhambra. The Moorish king Boabdil prepares for battle against the Spaniards, with his mother urging him on toward military honour and his kingly duties, and his wife Morayma pleading that he forgo the possibility of death for the sake of their love.

C95. "Return to an Early Home" in *The Literary Garland,* new series, vol.1, #4, April 1843.
1 scene. 1f/1g.
A poetic dialogue in which a mother reminisces about her youth with her child.

DAVIN, Nicholas Flood 1843-1901

C96. *The Fair Grit; or, The Advantages of Coalition.* Toronto, Belford, 1876 and in *Canada's Lost Plays,* vol.1, *The Nineteenth Century.* Anton Wagner, Richard Plant, eds. Toronto, CTR Publications, 1978.
5 scenes. 11m/2f/ Extras.
A farcical political satire which attacks corruption and opportunism in Canadian government and makes fun of both political parties. George St. Clair, the son of a "relic of the Family Compact", a Tory, falls in love with "the fair Grit", the daughter of Senator Alexander McPeterson. Their marriage is opposed by both parties until George's father senses the "advantages of coalition" when offered a lucrative position in the Grit camp and joins the enemy party.
p: (Public reading), NDWT Co., Toronto, Dec. 3, 1978.

DIXON, Frederick Augustus 1843-1919

C97. *The Episode of the Quarrel Between Titania and Oberon from Shakespeare's A Midsummer Night's Dream.* Ottawa, Durie, 1898.
4 acts. 8m/6f. Extras.
Shakespeare's text "specially arranged for representation with the Mendelssohn music".

C98. *Fifine, the Fisher-Maid; or, The Magic Shrimps.* Ottawa, Woodburn, 1877.
1 act. 8m/8f.
A comic nonsense fantasy in rhyme. Fifine, a poor, frivolous fisher-maid, is granted the secret of the magic shrimps. Advertising enables Fifine to make her fortune. The play makes frequent satirical topical allusions to famous actors, advertising, fashions, romances, Darwinism and politics.
fp: Government House, Ottawa, New Year's Day, 1878.

C99. *Little Nobody.* Toronto, Adam, Stevenson, 1875.
4 scenes. 6m/3f. Extras.
"A fairy play for fairy people". Little Nobody and the King and Queen of the fairies help Tim the Tooter rescue Princess Sunnylocks from the Ogre and Ogress.
fp: Government House, Ottawa, New Year's Day, 1876.

C100. *Maiden Mona the Mermaid.* Toronto, Belford, 1877.
1 act. 6m/4f.
"A fairy play for fairy people". A comic-satirical fantasy in rhyme parodying fairy tale conventions. Prince Noodle and Prince Doodle were thrust from their kingdom by the wicked uncle who poisoned their father. Doodle is given impossible demands to fulfill if he is to return and Noodle falls under the power of the Gnome King who chains him to a rock. Mona the mermaid discovers Doodle shipwrecked and assists him in completing his tasks.
fp: Government House, Ottawa, New Year's Day, 1877.

C101. *The Maire of St. Brieux.* Ottawa, Bureau, (1875?).
1 act. 4m/2f. Extras.
A comic operetta set in Brittany in 1800 in which a young Englishman and the Comtesse de Beaudry, a disguised Royalist, escape the machinations of an amorous old mayor as they plot to restore the monarchy to France. Music by Frederick W. Mills.
fp: Her Excellency the Countess of Dufferin's Private Theatricals, Government House, Ottawa, February 1875.

C102. *A Masque Entitled "Canada's Welcome".* Ottawa, Citizen Print., 1879 and Ottawa, MacLean, Roger, 1879 and Ottawa, J.L. Orme, (1879?).
1 act. 7m/4f. Chorus.
A masque portraying the taming of the Canadian wilderness by immigrant pioneers under the benevolent protection of the British crown. Music by Arthur A. Clappe. "Shown before His Excellency the Marquis of Lorne and Her Royal Highness the Princess Louise".
fp: Grand Opera House, Ottawa, Feb. 24, 1879.

C103. *The Mayor.* Philadelphia, Ledger Job Print., 1879.
2 acts. 5m/2f. Extras.
"An English comic opera". A slightly expanded version of *The Maire of St. Brieux.* Music by Frederick W. Mills.

C104. *Pipandor.* Ottawa, Citizen Print., 1884.
3 acts. 6m/3f. Extras.
A farcical "comic opera" with a commedia dell'arte plot plus Gilbert and Sullivan style arias. In 1718, Pipandor, a Harlequin-like character and servant to the Marquis of Chateaugris, a Pantalone, becomes the Regent's instrument in foiling a plot by Philip of Spain to assume control of France. Music by S.F. Harrison.

C105. *Ye Last Sweet Thing in Corners.* Philadelphia, Duncan & Hall, 1880.
3 acts. 9m/6f. Extras.
"Being Ye Faithful Drama of Ye Artists' Vendetta". Gamboge and Moddle, two down-on-their-luck artists, contrive a scheme for bamboozling the town's major art critic, who knows nothing about art, and marrying his daughters.

DIXON, Sergeant L.

C105A. *Our Boys in the Riel Rebellion. Halifax to the Saskatchewan.* Halifax. Holloway, 1886.
3 acts. 17m. Extras. Chorus.
"A musical and dramatic burlesque" tracing the rather uneventful participation of the Halifax Regiment in fighting the Riel Rebellion.
fp: Academy of Music, Halifax, April 12, 1886.

DRUM, Titus A. (pseud.)

C106. "The Baron Bold and the Beauteous Maid" in *Grip,* vol.23, #1, July 5, 1884.
3 acts. 3m/1f. Extras.
A brief "Old Time Melodrama (Adapted)" parodying melodrama and its acting conventions.

C107. "Before and Behind the Curtain" in *Grip*, vol.27, #23, Dec. 11, 1886.
2 scenes. 3m/1f. Extras.
A brief "political farce" exposing a candidate for office allegedly in favour of the workers and universal suffrage.

C108. "The Mind Cure" in *Grip*, vol.25, #16, Oct. 17, 1885.
1 scene. 3m.
A brief farce in which a quack doctor robs a patient of his silver.

C109. "Such Is Life" in *Grip*, vol.24, #21, May 23, 1885.
3 acts. 2m/2f. Extras.
"An American drama of the affections". A brief parody of a domestic melodrama.

C110. "The Tuggers and the Toll-Gate" in *Grip*, vol.24, #7, Feb. 14, 1885.
1 scene. 2m. Extras. Chorus.
Farmers destroy a toll-gate in protest in this brief "operatic absurdetta" in Gilbert and Sullivan style.

ERVIN, John

C111. *Le Lucciole: A Tale of Genoa*. Halifax, Author, (186-?).
3 acts. 6m/4f. Extras.
"A tragedy". In this poetic drama of confused identities, Bianca, a nobly born peasant girl is loved by Marco and Fernando. Marco is being forced by his father to marry Beatrice, the base born substitute in the household of Count Marino. Fernando rescues Bianca who has been left for dead by Beatrice and confronts the families involved with the deception at the wedding festivities for Beatrice and Marco.

FINN, Henry James 1795-1840

C112. *Montgomery; or, The Falls of Montmorenci*. Boston, Wells & Lilly, 1825.
3 acts. 16m/2f. Extras.
Montgomery's siege of Quebec serves as a setting for this melodrama. A beautiful Indian girl is separated from her soldier husband by a villain seeking revenge. Helped by a motley crew of Americans and Canadians who make it clear that the war is between America and her British oppressor and that Canada and America are friends, the lovers are reunited. The villain dies when his canoe goes over Montmorenci Falls.
fp: Boston, Feb. 21, 1825.

FULLER, William Henry

C113. *H.M.S. "Parliament"; or, The Lady Who Loved a Government Clerk*. Ottawa, Citizen Printing, 1880 and in *Canada's Lost Plays*, vol.1, *The Nineteenth Century*. Anton Wagner, Richard Plant, eds. Toronto, CTR Publications, 1978.
2 acts. 6m/2f. Extras. Chorus.
A comic operetta of Canadian topical interest closely resembling its model, *H.M.S. Pinafore*. Sam Snifter, a government clerk, loves Angelina, the daughter of Captain MacA. Angelina is promised to Sir Samuel Sillery, chief financier of Parliament. But Mrs. Butterbun, purveyor of refreshments to Parliament, saves the day by revealing that Snifter is really Sir Samuel's nephew. Government folly of the time, particularly the "National Policy" of Sir Samuel Tilley, provides the satirical focus of attack.
fp: Academy of Music, Montreal, Feb. 16, 1880.

C114. "The Unspecific Scandal" in *Canadian Illustrated News,* vol.9, nos. 1, 2, Jan. 3, 10, 1874 and *The Unspecific Scandal.* Ottawa, Woodburn, 1874.
3 acts. 7m/1f. Extras. Chorus.
"An Original, Political, Critical, Grittical and likely to be Historical Extravaganza performed by Her Majesty's Servants at the Great Dominion Theatre, Ottawa, in the Year of Grace, 1873" satirizing John A. Macdonald and his role in the Pacific Railway Scandal.

GARNIER, John Hutchinson 1810?-1898

C115. *Prince Pedro.* Toronto, Belford, 1877.
5 acts. 18m/5f. Extras.
A poetic drama in blank verse set in Portugal in which Matteo and his sister Inez lose their ancestral lands through a will forged by Ludro, Abbot of Centra. They take to the forest where Prince Pedro meets and falls in love with Inez. Their marriage is opposed by the Queen, Pedro's mother, who, with help from Ludro, later murders Inez and her children. By the end of the play, Pedro has become king, banishes his mother and carries out a violent revenge on Ludro and the murderers.

(HALLIBURTON, Brenton) Paculet (pseud.).

C116. *Report of Mr. Bull's Jury, Ex-Officio, on the Late Conduct of his Servants, in a Certain Public Establishment.* Printed for Messrs. Lefax and Rurus, by Particular Desire of Mr. Public Opinion, Mr. Common Sense, and Others. (Halifax), 1829.
1 scene. 55m.
A political satire commenting on the expulsion of John Alexander Barry from the House of Assembly of Nova Scotia for his strong advocacy to reform the Militia Laws.

HAMMOND, George Arthur

C117. *The Crowning Test.* Kingsclear, N.B., Lahstok Rustic Press, 1901.
12 scenes. 11m/5f. Extras.
A verse drama of the testing of Abraham and Isaac by God. Nakach, the Dragon, is the symbol of evil but is finally defeated so that Abraham and Isaac triumph and stand in the good will of God.

C118. *Jassoket and Anemon.* Kingsclear, N.B., Lahstok Publishing, 1896.
18 scenes. Multiple roles.
A religious, theological and philosophic "ramble" about the origin of man and the meaning of life.

C119. "Knud Iverson" in *Canadian Illustrated News,* vol.3, #23, June 10, 1871 and in his *A Triad, Three Volumes in Miniature.* Lahstok Rural Press, 1887.
5 scenes. 1m/6b.
A moral tale in verse "based on an incident in an old America journal". Knud Iverson is a young boy who refuses to steal apples with his playmates because it is against his Christian principles. His playmates drown him and Knud is last seen in heaven, happy to be with his Maker.

C120. "Lamech" in his *The Two Offerings.* Kingsclear, N.B., Lahstok Publishing, 1890.
1 scene. 1m/2f.
Lamech attempts to pacify his jealous wives Ada and Zilla.

C121. *Rayon.* Kingsclear, N.B., Lahstok Publishing, 1898.
4 scenes. 3m/7f.
"An idyllic vagary" about the warrior Rayon who must choose a second wife.

C122. *Starborn the Conjurer.* Kingsclear, N.B., Lahstoq Rustic Press, 1903.
16 scenes. 17m/1f. Extras.
"A dramatic poem". Attracted by a vision of Lola, Starborn has renounced hunting and fishing to seek the meaning of the Spirit. He and his wife Elkona are dragged beneath the Cave of Bones by Beelzebub who has used a false image of Lola to capture Starborn.

C123. "The Two Offerings" in his *The Two Offerings.* Kingsclear, N.B., Lahstok Publishing, 1890.
4 scenes. 13m/14f. Extras.
A religious poetic play set in Paradise about Adam and Eve, their children and their fall from grace.

HAND, Thomas William and Walter Teale

C124. *Hand & Teale's Pyro-Spectacular Drama, The Bombardment of Pekin, By the British and French. Time 1860.* N.p., Author, 1899.
5m. Extras. multiple scenes.
A jingoist historical pageant showing the defeat of the Chinese by British and French colonial forces.

C125. *Hand & Teale's Spectacular Drama of "The Relief of Lucknow".* (Hamilton, Ont.?), 1895.
6 parts. 8m/1f. Extras. Doubling.
"An original, outdoor military spectacle designed to exhibit new pyrotechnic, scenic and spectacular effects". A description of a vast historical pageant showing the defeat of the King of Oude and his Indian mutineers and the relief of the English garrison at Lucknow.

C125A. **HANKS, J.M.** *Dermot McMurrough. The Fireworshippers.* See **NEWCOMB, C.F.**

HARDY, Abel

C126. "The Bachelors' Club" in *The Literary Garland,* new series, vol.2, #5, May 1844.
1 act. 5m. Extras.
A satire of the activities of the club dedicated to "the cause of single blessedness" and the formation of exclusive male friendships based on the renunciation of women and children.

HEAVYSEGE, Charles 1816-1876

C127. *Count Filippo; or, The Unequal Marriage.* Montreal, Author, 1860 and Montreal, Dawson, 1860 and Toronto, University of Toronto Press, 1973.
5 acts. 11m/3f. Extras.
A verse drama set in Italy concerning the consequences of a marriage between youth and old age. An evil counsellor to a prince tricks a young man into falling in love with the beautiful young wife of aging Count Filippo.
fp: Radio adaptation by Peter Haworth, CBC, 1968.

C128. *Saul.* Montreal, Henry Rose, 1857 and revised edition, London, Sampson Low, 1859 and Montreal, John Lovell, 1859 and Boston, Fields, Osgood, 1869 and New York, Lovell, 1876 and Toronto, University of Toronto Press, 1973 and in *Saul and Selected Poems.* Toronto, University of Toronto Press, 1976.
3 parts. 27m/3f. Extras.
A verse drama based on the biblical narrative of King Saul and his hatred of the next King of Israel, David.
fp: Radio adaptation by Peter Haworth, CBC, 1973.

HENDERSON, J. Duff

C129. "The Battle of Little Big Horn" in his *Alvira Alias Orea.* Toronto, Hunter, Rose, 1899.
4 acts. 10m/3f. Extras.
A rhymed-verse melodrama. Young Roy Buster from the east has wandered west seeking health, wealth and fame. He encounters Greta Custer, niece of the General and daughter of Captain Custer, who survived the battle and was taken captive but was rescued by a group of miners.

C130. "Millions for Her" in his *Alvira Alias Orea.* Toronto, Hunter, Rose, 1899.
4 acts. 8m/5f. Extras.
A rhymed-verse melodrama. The banker Sir Allfiston has been robbed by two men who then encounter him and his family in Paris and vie for the hand of his daughter Marvettia. She is prepared to accept whichever wins at duelling but it is discovered that they are the long-lost sons of Sir Allfiston and his secretary, Sir Mordant, also wealthy and recently deceased.

HUNTER-DUVAR, John 1830-1899

C131. *De Roberval.* Saint John, N.B., McMillan, 1888.
5 acts. 9m/3f. Extras.
A historical drama in blank verse which dramatizes Sieur de Roberval's attempt to establish a French colony at Quebec in the early 1840's. It chronicles his wars with the Indians, his search for a passage to Cathay and his love for Ohnawa, a beautiful and wise Indian maiden whom the French clergy try in vain to Christianize, and who is killed saving de Roberval from an Indian ambush.

C132. *The Enamorado.* Summerside, P.E.I., Graves, 1879.
5 acts. 10m/5f. Extras.
A poetic drama in blank verse set in Spain in 1405. The melodramatic plot concerns the "enamoured one", Mazias, a handsome nobleman, poet and soldier, who falls in love with Clara de Lope, who is betrothed to Tellez in a match arranged by her guardians. Mazias' uncontrollable passion forces him to hazard all in declaring his love for Clara. She resists at first but finally admits a similar feeling for him, but by then she has been married to Tellez, with tragic results.

C133. "Ten Years" in *The Maritime Monthly: A Magazine of Literature, Science, and Art,* vol.2, #2, August 1873.
3 acts. 5m/5f. Extras.
"A parlor drama". In this romantic melodrama, three merchant adventurers captured and enslaved by Barbary pirates for ten years are assisted in their escape by Zuleika, a Moorish princess who has fallen in love with William. Reaching England, Dobbio and Lubin are reunited with their wives and William marries Zuleika.

J.W.S. (pseud.)

C134. "Ambition; or, Be Sure You Are Off With the Old Hall Before You Are On With the New" in *Grip,* vol.24, #26, June 27, 1885.
1 scene. 9m. Extras. Chorus.
A brief "Hamilton operetta in one act" satirizing the decision to build a new city hall.

JOHNSON, George Washington 1839-1917

C135. "The Columbiad" in his *Maple Leaves.* Hamilton, Ont., Author, 1864.
2 scenes. 3m/1f. Extras.
A poetic drama in blank verse about Columbus' voyage to America. King Ferdinand of Spain, jealous of Queen Isabella's attention to Columbus and her support of his voyage, arranges for a stowaway to sabotage the voyage. But his plan fails, the saboteur is captured and Columbus arrives in America.

C136. "The Count's Bride" in his *Maple Leaves.* Hamilton, Ont., Author, 1864.
11 scenes. 6m/2f. Extras.
A poetic drama in verse set in gothic Hamilton with a melodramatic plot in which Carle Carter, an outlaw, corrupts, then kills the son of his old enemy to gain revenge. Lillian and her lover disguised as a "Mysterious Stranger" hunt down and capture Carter.

C137. "Grantly Granville; or, The Hag of the Mountain" in his *Maple Leaves.* Hamilton, Ont., Author, 1864.
4 acts. 7m/2f. Extras.
A poetic drama in blank verse with a complicated melodramatic plot set in gothic Spain. Viola, a beautiful gypsy girl, is rejected by her husband, Bernardo, a Spanish nobleman. She leaves their baby on a castle doorstep, becomes the Hag of the Mountain and vows revenge on Bernardo and his friend Granvillo. She finds Grantly Granville, Granvillo's young son, lost in the forest and teaches him to hate his evil father. After many complications, Bernardo and Viola finally stab themselves.

KAYELLE, Jay

C138. "Marmion" in *Grip,* vol.19, #20, Oct. 7, 1882.
2 acts. 12m. Extras.
A satire in which the Ontario Minister of Education is confronted by an archbishop demanding the removal of various literary texts from grammar schools because of their alleged immorality.

C139. "Underground Theology" in *Grip,* vol.18, nos. 4, 5, 6, Dec. 10, 17, 24, 1881.
3 acts. 2m/1f/1b. Extras.
An attack on freethinkers and a defence of Christians caring for the destitute of Toronto.

KEATING, James W.

C140. *The Shrievalty of Lynden.* St. Catharines, Ont., Sherwood, 1889.
1 act. 7m.
"A tragedy" set in the town of Arcona. Fred Dickson, cousin of the local Crown Attorney, has been appointed sheriff of Lynden County. Frank Dardanus is sentenced to be hanged for murder. At the last moment, after we see that the incompetent Dickson, against his own better judgement, was willing to hang Dardanus, an innocent man, a writ from the Governor General grants Dardanus his freedom.

KERR, William Warren Hastings 1826-1888

C141. *The Kidnappers.* Montreal, N.p., (1867?) and Montreal, n.p., 1868.
4 scenes. 11m.
Four scenes or acts of a projected "tragico-comical melodrama in ten acts about to be produced at one of the leading Theatres in London". A bitter farce about corruption in pre-Confederation Quebec set in "Splashville, the commercial centre of Skitzland" with the French-Canadian Hon. Mr. Gorilla, Attorney General of Skitzland, and T.K. Chimpanzee, the English Crown Prosecutor, the chief focus of attack.

LANIGAN, John Alphonsus 1854-1919

C142. *Eithne; or, The Siege of Armagh.* Buffalo, Express Steam Print., 1872.
4 acts. 13m/8f. Extras.
In an attempt to "raise the Irish character from the low, insipid burlesque that pervades the Irish drama", the author, in a poetic verse play, relates the heroic adventures of Teddy O'Hare, an uplifted stage Irishman, and Hugh O'Neill as they lead the Irish against the English during the reign of Elizabeth I.

LESPERANCE, John Talon 1838-1891

C143. *One Hundred Years Ago.* Montreal, "La Minerva" Steam Presses, 1876.
4 acts. 24m/5f. Extras.
"An historical drama of The War of Independence" championing the American fight for liberty. Eva Parker loves a royalist officer, her sister Nelly a rebel officer. Eva and her lover are killed but Nelly and her soldier triumph over the villainy of a jealous, evil man who seeks the sisters' fortunes and hands.

LINDLEY, Harry

C144. *"Chick" or Myrtle Ferns.* Peterborough, Ont., Times Publishing, 1893.
5 acts. 9m/4f. Doubling.
A melodrama in which Chick, a "mountain waif", clears her sister's fiance of having murdered Chick's father and apprehends the real murderer who has been trying to marry a wealthy heiress.

LONGLEY, Ernest G.

C145. *A Modern Romeo and Juliet.* Brockville, Ont., Gazette Printing, (188-?).
2 acts. 2m/3f.
An operetta in Gilbert and Sullivan style. Upper-class Mrs. Montague Smith refuses to let Juliet marry Romeo Robinson because he is poor. But all ends happily when Romeo receives an inheritance and Paris Brown decides he'd rather marry a more docile woman. "Written for the Prescott Dramatic Club".

McBRIDE, Robert

C146. "Dialogue Between the Client and the Lambton Ghost on Going From Court" in his *Poems, Satirical and Sentimental.* London, Ont., Dawson, 1869.
8 dialogues. Multiple roles.
"Several theatrical Acts and Dialogues showing how the people have been, and are now victimized. All tending to prove on the part of those indicated, a complete conspiracy set up by them for the purpose of enslaving the people of this country."

C147. "A Division Court and County Court Case" in his *Poems, Satirical and Sentimental.* London, Ont., Author, 1858 and London, Ont., Dawson, 1869.
9 scenes. 14m/1f/1b.
An honest merchant refusing to sell his vote in an election is brought to ruin by false lawsuits and a corrupt judicial system of packed juries, conniving lawyers and corrupt judges.

MacCULLOH, Lewis Luke. See WILCOCKE, Samuel Hull.

McDONNELL, William 1814-1900

C148. *Marina, The Fisherman's Daughter.* Toronto, Strange, 1883.
3 acts. 7m/3f. Extras.
"An operatic romance". Stephen, a young fisherman, loves Marina who does not return his affection. He enlists and is sent to India. Marina becomes a maid to Lady Ford whose son, Captain Ford, returns from India bringing Stephen with him. Ford falls in love with Marina and is wounded by the jealous Stephen. Stephen is court-martialled but wins a reprieve just before facing the firing squad.

McFARLANE, A.E.

C149. "The Beginning of the Scandal" in *Acta Victoriana*, vol.21, #8, May 1898.
1 scene. 1m/1f.
A dramatization of the romance between the journalist Jack Featherstone and the beautiful heiress Guendoline Vandewater.

McGEE, Thomas D'Arcy 1825-1868

C150. *Sebastian; or, The Roman Martyr.* New York, Sadlier, 1861.
4 acts. 16m. Extras.
"Founded on Cardinal Wiseman's celebrated tale of 'Fabiola' ". A poetic drama depicting Sebastian's martyrdom and the persecution of the Christians by emperor Maximian. Intended for production at a Christian Brothers' School.

MACHAR, Agnes Maule 1837-1927

C151. "The Winged Victory" in her *Lays of the True North.* London, Elliot Stock, 1899 and Toronto, Copp Clark, 1899 and Toronto, Musson, (1902).
3 acts. 2m/2f.
"A dramatic poem". Clara, Ernest and Philip are prompted to go off to the South Seas to bring Christianity to the natives by Gertrude's last wish.

McILWRAITH, Jean Newton 1859-1938

C152. *Ptarmigan; or, A Canadian Carnival.* Hamilton, Ont., Spectator Printing, 1895 and in *Canada's Lost Plays,* vol.1, *The Nineteenth Century.* Anton Wagner, Richard Plant, eds. Toronto, CTR Publications, 1978.
2 acts. 8m/4f. Extras. Chorus.
A satirical comic opera set at a winter carnival. Ptarmigan has returned from the United States where he signed papers to become an American citizen. His friends imprison him and decide that he be frozen into the Ice Palace as a warning to others. He is freed by Hepatica who argues that he was insane when he signed the documents. Music by John E.P. Aldous.
fp: Grand Opera House, Hamilton, Ont., Feb. 15, 1895.

MacKENZIE, James Bovell 1851-1919

C153. *Thayendanegea.* Toronto, William Briggs, 1898.
5 acts. 30m/3f. Extras.
"An historico-military drama" about Joseph Brant, the principal war-chief of the Six Nations Indians, written to refute "the charges of barbarity freely fabricated by American historians against Brant."

McLACHLAN, Alexander 1818-1896

C154. "Fate" in his *Poems.* Toronto, John Geikie, 1856.
1 scene. 4m.
"A fragment". A poetic discussion between a Mortal, Spirit, Oracle and Poet about man's existence and the world beyond.

McVICAR, William Mortimer 1851-1928

C155. *Imperial Britain.* Halifax, MacKinlay, 1894.
2 acts. 2m/5f/5b/7g.
"A patriotic drama suitable for public school exhibitions". A pageant in which Britannia's colonies pay homage to their mother country.

MAIR, Charles 1838-1927

C156. "The Capture of Detroit, 1812" in *Raise the Flag and Other Patriotic Canadian Songs and Poems.* Toronto, Rose Publishing, 1891.
1 act. 17m. Extras. Chorus.
"Being part of Act IV of Charles Mair's Drama of *Tecumseh*".

C157. *Tecumseh.* Toronto, Hunter, Rose, 1886 and London, Chapman, Hall, 1886 and Toronto, Briggs, 1901 and in *Master Works of Canadian Authors* vol.14. R. Norwood, ed. Toronto, Radisson Society, 1926 and in *Dreamland and Other Poems and Tecumseh: A Drama.* Toronto, University of Toronto Press, 1974.
5 acts. 26m/4f. Extras. Doubling.
Set just before the War of 1812, the play explores the conflicts between the Indians led by Tecumseh and the Americans which lead to the Indians' alliance with the British during the war. Rivalry between Tecumseh and his witch-doctor brother and a love affair between an Indian maiden and a white man provide sub-plots.
p: Toronto Truck Theatre, July 8, 1971. As "The Red Revolutionary", adaptation by Ken Gass, Factory Theatre, Toronto, July 28, 1971.

MAYNE, Daniel Haydn

C158. "The Lake of Killearny by Moonlight" in his *Poems and Fragments.* Toronto, Coates, 1838.
1 scene. 2m. Extras.
A brief dramatic fragment depicting an encounter between Lord Donochu and Lucifer.

C159. "Simon Black" in his *Poems and Fragments.* Toronto, Coates, 1838.
"Scene 3rd". 1m/1f.
"A fragment" of a domestic melodrama. Simon Black, "the Gore of Toronto", has a nightmare in which he sleepwalks and speaks to a sheep's head, fancying it a dollar, to the consternation of his despairing wife.

MERRITT, Catharine Nina 1859-1926

C160. *When George the Third Was King.* Toronto, Rowsell & Hutchison, 1897.
3 acts. 9m/4f.
The play chronicles how a prominent family of United Empire Loyalists are driven from their Albany home during the American Revolution, escape to Canada and settle in southern Ontario. The courage of the U.E.L.'s, their devotion to Britain and the part they played in building Canada are honoured.

MITCHELL, W.S.

C161. *The Klondike: or, The Experience of a Winter in the Klondike.* Vancouver, Author, 1898.
6 acts. 7m/4f/2b.
A closet stock melodrama about two young couples who journey to the Klondike to make a fortune so that they can marry.

MOYSE, Charles Ebeneezer 1852-1924

C162. *Shakespeare's Skull and Falstaff's Nose.* By Belgrave Titmarsh (pseud.).
London, Elliot Stock, 1889.
3 acts. 7m/2f. Extras.
"A fancy" ridiculing academic fanaticism when researching the works of Shakespeare. Dryasdustus believes himself to be a direct descendant of the Bard and robs Shakespeare's grave, making off with his skull.

MURDOCH, William

C163. "A Fireside Drama" in his *Discursory Ruminations, A Fireside Drama, Etc.,* Saint John, N.B., Chubb, 1876.
3 acts. 6m/3f. Chorus.
A double wedding in the last act summarizes the play's themes of contentment through proper wedded love between people suited in age and nature and the importance of decent, temperate living.

NEWCOMB, C.F. and J.M. Hanks

C164. "Dermot McMurrough" in *The Fireworshippers and Dermot McMurrough.* Toronto, Hunter, Rose, 1882.
4 acts. 17m/2f/ Extras.
A serious prose drama set in Ireland, 800 A.D. The oppressive rule of McMurrough, king of Ireland, has forced Ballynook and other nobles to become outlaws. With McMurrough totally mad and dying, Ireland is invaded by the Teague of Heath. Armagh, the king's man-at-arms, leads the Irish to victory. The coming of a new religion preached by a Christ-like old priest is a recurrent theme.

C165. "The Fireworshippers" in *The Fireworshippers and Dermot McMurrough.* Toronto, Hunter, Rose, 1882.
6 acts. 8m/3f. Extras.
A serious prose drama. King Potilihan has secretly murdered the former king and placed the heir, Saber, in prison. Saber's betrothed, Althea, believes him dead and enters a convent. With help from an old loyalist, Saber escapes to lead a revolt against Potilihan. Saber becomes king and saves Althea from her vows of convent celibacy.

C165A. **PACULET (pseud.).** *Report of Mr. Bulls' Jury.* See **(HALLIBURTON, Brenton).**

RAMSAY, Andrew -1907

C166. "French Chaos" in his *One Quiet Day, A Book of Prose and Poetry.* Hamilton, Ont., Lancefield, 1873 and (revised version) "Chaos" in his *Muriel the Foundling, and Other Original Poems.* Toronto, Hovey, 1886.
5 scenes. 6m/2f. Extras.
A poetic verse drama which discourses on the nature of Good and Evil in God's universe. On earth, an imminent war "fordoomed by France" under Napoleon IV, who appears as the Antichrist in the drama, is part of Lucifer and his compatriots' plan.

ROBERTSON, John

C167. "The Hamesick Wife and Consoling Husband" in *The Literary Garland,* vol.1, nos. 8, 9, July, August 1839 and in his *Warblings and Wailings of Leisure Hours.* By Scotus (pseud.). Three Rivers, Author, 1859.
2 parts. 1m/1f.
A verse dialogue in dialect between Jenny and Geordi "founded on the experience of Bush Life and intended to convey comfort and encouragement to newly arrived immigrants".

ROWAN, Roly (pseud.)

C168. "Woman Suffrage" in *Grip*, vol. 38, #13, June 4, 1892.
1 scene. 9f.
A brief satire of a women's suffrage meeting.

SANGSTER, Charles 1822-1893

C169. "Bertram and Lorenzo" in his *The St. Lawrence and the Saguenay and Other Poems*. Kingston, Creighton and Duff, New York, Miller, Orton, Mulligan, 1856 and Toronto, University of Toronto Press, 1972.
3 scenes. 2m. Extras.
"A dramatic fragment". A poetic drama in which a hermit takes a light-hearted youth on a spiritual journey into the mountains where he decides to abandon the distractions of the city and to take nature as his universal guide.

SCHUBART, William and Louisa Schubart

C170. *Ludwig, the Emigrant*. Buffalo, H. Wulff, 1896 and Toronto, Douglas Ford, 1896.
3 acts. 11m/4f. Extras.
A comedy-melodrama in which an honest German immigrant wins the hand of a wealthy miller's daughter and foils the machinations of an evil gambler.

SCOBIE, Hugh 1811-1853

C171. "Provincial Drama Called The Family Compact" by Chrononhotonthologos (pseud.) in *The British Colonist*, vol.2, nos. 20, 21, 23, 25, 26, June 19, June 26, July 10, July 24, July 31, 1839.
2 acts. 10m/3f. Extras.
A satirical drama in verse in which members of the Family Compact attempt to refute charges of malpractice and too powerful control over the affairs of Upper Canada. Their greatest opponent is Lord Durham and his report. Sir John Scot, clearly John Strachan, goes to England where, through political influence, he is made Bishop of Upper Canada. With his new powers and the ones already in the possession of Compact members, their reign is secure.

SCOTUS (pseud.). See ROBERTSON, John.

SCRIBBLE, Sam (pseud.)

C172. *Dolorsolatio*. Montreal, John Lovell, 1865 and in *Canada's Lost Plays*, vol.1, *The Nineteenth Century*. Anton Wagner, Richard Plant, eds. Toronto, CTR Publications, 1978.
3 scenes. 9m/3f.
"A local political burlesque" in which characters named after various cities and regions in Canada meet at Grandpapa Canada's house for Christmas. They bicker among themselves but a boisterous fight between their neighbours Abe North and Jeff South teaches them the virtues of a united family. A solution is found when Santa Clause arrives bearing the elixir "Dolorsolatio" whose sole ingredient is Federation.
fp: Theatre Royal, Montreal, Jan. 9, 1865.

C173. *The King of the Beavers*. Montreal, Longmoore, 1865.
4 scenes. 7m/3f. Extras.
"A new original, political, allegorical, burlesque, extravaganza". Britannia urges her "Maritime young friend" Azuline, the Queen of the Blue Noses, to marry the King of the Beavers. Together they defeat the Fenian conspirators attacking Beaverland.
fp: Amateurs of the Garrison, Theatre Royal, Montreal, Dec. 26, 1865.

C174. *"Not Dead Yet"; or, The Skating Carnival.* Montreal, John Lovell, 1865.
1 act. 7m/1f.
A farce about three revellers who return drunk from a masquerade believing they have killed a comrade and attempt to buy off all the witnesses to the supposed murder.
fp: Theatre Royal, Montreal, Feb. 22, 1865.

C175. *Orpheus and Eurydice.* Montreal, Longmoore, 1866.
3 scenes. 4m/5f. Extras.
A farcical "classical extravaganza". Orpheus wins the release of Eurydice from Pluto through his bad violin playing and Proserpine's jealousy.

SHARPE, Lynch Lawdon

C176. *The Viceroy's Dream; or, The Canadian Government Not "Wide Awake".*
London, Whittaker, 1838.
5 scenes. 9m. Extras.
"A mono-dramatico-political poem". A satire of Lord Durham who is visited by the ghosts of Brougham, Melbourne, Glenelg and John Russell opposed to his policies in Canada.

SIMPSON, John 1807-1878

C177. "Captain Plume's Courtship" by A Gentleman, One, Etc. (pseud.) in *The Canadian Forget Me Not for 1837.* J. Simpson, ed. Niagara, Thomas Sewell, 1837.
1 scene. 4m/1f.
A bankrupt officer gives up the independence of bachelorhood and marries a girl about to obtain a large inheritance in order to escape his creditors.

C178. "A Dramatic Sketch" in *The Canadian Forget Me Not for 1837.* J. Simpson, ed. Niagara, Thomas Sewell, 1837.
1 scene. 3m.
In the saloon of a Toronto hotel, three rogues discuss the lack of honest professions, including that of author, poet and playwright, available to them. "Very few arts or sciences can in Canada maintain their professors".

SKEY, Francis W.

C179. *Red Riding-Hood.* Quebec, Brousseau, 1854.
2 acts. 1m/3f. Extras.
An "operatic interlude" based on the tale of Red Riding Hood. In this version, the girl is hoping to be cheered as Queen of the May when the Wolf traps her at her grandmother's house. The Wolf attempts to kill Red Riding Hood but she is saved by the villagers. "The libretto by various hands".
fp: Music Hall, Quebed, Feb. 24, 1854 with an all male cast.

TELGMANN, Heinrich Bertram

C180. *Against the World; or, Life in London.* Kingston, Ont., British Whig Office, 1889.
4 acts. 9m/3f. Extras.
A stock melodrama in which John Harking, a wealthy English cotton mill owner whose son has been lost, arranges for his beautiful ward Pauline to marry James Harwood, a criminal posing as a lord.

THOMPSON, Elizabeth Jane (Sweetland) 1858-1927

C181. *A Double Life.* Toronto, Hill and Weir, 1884 and Louisville, Falls City Microcards, (1965?).
5 acts. 7m/4f.
A stage melodrama set in England in the seventeen hundreds in which a disguised villain kidnaps the daughter of a wealthy squire after apparently killing the man she loves.

(THOMPSON, John Sparrow?)

C182. *Cadets of Temperance, Entertainment for the Christmas Holidays.* Halifax, James Bowes, 1852.
2 acts. Multiple roles. Chorus.
An entertainment as performed by the Cadets of Temperance consisting of Christmas songs, short scenes and sketches extolling the virtues of abstinence from demon drink and pointing out the havoc created by drinking. (Attributed to John Sparrow Thompson by Reginald Eyre Watters).

TITMARSH, Belgrave (pseud.). See MOYSE, Charles Ebeneezer.

TOOTS (pseud.)

C183. "The Meal Club Plot" in *The Two Elders and the Sequel The Meal Club Plot.*
Toronto, Citizen, 1856.
3 acts. 11m. Extras.
A continuation of the satirical attack on Dr. Burns showing his old world authoritarianism and his refusal to accept the judgement of a church court appointed to investigate the strife within the Presbyterian congregation.

C184. "The Two Elders" in *The Two Elders and the Sequel The Meal Club Plot.*
Toronto, Citizen, 1856.
2 acts. 13m.
A satire in rhymed couplets of Dr. Robert Burns, pastor of Knox Church, Toronto, who is shown in bitter conflict with two elders of his session.

WATSON, Samuel James 1837-1881

C185. "The Legend of the Roses" in his *The Legend of the Roses — A Poem; Ravlan — A Drama.* Toronto, Hunter, Rose, 1876.
3 parts. 5m/1f.
A combination of poetry and poetic drama about a maiden falsely accused and convicted who is saved from death by burning through the grace of God.

C186. "Ravlan" in his *The Legend of the Roses — A Poem; Ravlan — A Drama*.
Toronto, Hunter, Rose, 1876.
5 acts. 7m/4f. Extras.
A poetic drama in blank verse set in Celtic Britain. Britomart, Chief Druidess, wishes to control the kingdom and has disposed of the elder Ravlan, the former king. The rightful heir, young Ravlan, searches for his father and is in love with Aidnai, Britomart's daughter. Britomart's crimes are discovered. Young Ravlan takes Aidnai for his queen but at the coronation celebrations Britomart attacks him. Aidnai intercepts the blow and dies. Grief-stricken, Ravlan commits suicide.

WILCOCKE, Samuel Hull (Lewis Luke MacCulloh, pseud.) 1766?-1833

C187. "The Charrivarri" in *The Scribbler*, vol.3, #104, June 26, 1823, vol.4, nos. 105, 106, 107, 108, 109, July 10, July 24, Aug. 7, Aug. 21, Dec. 4, 1823.
Multiple scenes and roles.
"A mixto-poetico-prose-comico-tragico-melo-dramatico-farrago". A literary parody in prose, poetry and drama attacking the Montreal police for attempting to suppress the charrivarri, or carnival, and causing the unpunished death of a participant.

C188. "Dialogue" in *The Scribbler*, vol.2, #58, Aug. 8, 1822.
1 scene. 3m.
The editor decides to publish "Lord Goddamnhim's Soliloquy on the Immortality of the Scribbler".

C189. "A Dialogue at M'Killaway-Lodge" in *The Scribbler*, vol.2, #74, Nov. 28, 1822.
1 scene. 4m/1f. Extras.
Sir Plausible Pompous M'Killaway and Lord Goddamnhim rant against the editor of *The Scribbler* in despair because he is satirizing them in his publication.

C190. "Economy" in *The Scribbler*, vol.4, #109, Sept. 4, 1823.
4 scenes. 6m. Extras.
A brief dramatic sketch about General Fleabite satirizing the military.

C191. "The Olympic Banquet" in *The Scribbler*, vol.2, #61, Aug. 29, 1822.
1 act. 9m/3f. Extras.
An account of a "pantomimical ballet interlude that was performed with so much satisfaction to the actors at the Hon. Tory Loverule's on the 6th instant" satirizing local British government officials and high society.

C192. "The Scribleromania" in *The Scribbler*, vol.3, #79, Jan. 2, 1823.
1 scene. Multiple roles.
"A farce in several acts as performed at the theatres royal, with general satisfaction". Scriblerians and anti-scriblerians eagerly await the latest issue of the publication.

WOOD, W.P.

C193. *Minnie Trail; or, The Women of Wentworth.* Hamilton, Ont., Evening Times Office, 1871.
3 acts. 5m/3f. Extras.
A melodramatic "tragedy" set in Wentworth County, Ontario. Minnie Trail is lured away from her husband Mungo by fraudulent letters implying he is unfaithful. The evil scheme is the work of Ned Grailing who seeks revenge on Mungo. In the end, Minnie returns and in remorse stabs herself. Mungo kills Grailing. As she is dying, Minnie is reconciled with Mungo, a small consolation since his life and family are ruined.

WORTH, Edward

C194. *Worth's Burlesque Ritual.* Kent Bridge, Ont., Author, 1896.
Multiple scenes. 16m. Extras.
A burlesque of rituals of secret societies (the Canadian Order of Foresters in the play), in which local topical references are to be inserted to create fun for a specific audience.

YOUMAN, J.W.

C195. "The Cantata of the Festival of the Rose; or, A Day in Arcadia" in his *Juvenile Songs*. Montreal, Becket, 1861.
1 act. Multiple roles. Chorus.
The pure Orphan Flower Girl of the Wild Moor is chosen as queen in an idyll only briefly clouded by the appearance of a pacifist Yankee tin merchant wounded in battle who has lost his way in the mountains of Arcadia.
fp: "As performed at his popular Juvenile Concerts".

D
The Twentieth Century

ANONYMOUS

D1. "The Alphabet Tragedy" in *Sketches and Plays*. Toronto, National Girls' Work Board, Religious Education Council of Canada. (192-?).
2 scenes. 4m/3f.
A brief spelling parody.
fp: Canadian Girls In Training camps.

D2. "The Baronets of Nova Scotia" in *Journal of Education for Nova Scotia,* series 4, vol.11, September 1940.
6 scenes. 7m. Extras.
"Prepared by the Government of Nova Scotia". An historical pageant presenting Sir William Alexander's application to King James in 1621 for a grant of land in Acadia. In 1625, King Charles appoints Sir Robert Gordon as the first Baronet of Nova Scotia.
fp: Garrison Grounds, Halifax, June 15, 1939.

D3. *Biblical Drama Esther.* Ottawa, Modern Press, 1914.
5 acts. 8m/4f. Extras.
The libretto for a musical drama based on the Old Testament book Esther about the beautiful Jewess who saves her people from destruction.
fp: "Given in oriental costume under "Belshazzar" management", Russell Theatre, Ottawa, April 1, 1914.

D4. "Britannia" in *Educational Review,* vol. 32, May 1918.
1 scene. 32b or g.
On Empire Day, Britannia's explorers, heroes and other subjects come to pay her homage.

D6. "Dialogue — Columbus and his Men" in *Educational Review,* vol.21, October 1907 and vol.49, #2, Oct. 1934.
1 act. 1m. Extras.
Columbus stands fast in his conviction that he should sail west despite doubt expressed by the crew.

D7. "Dominion Day Pageant" in *Journal of Education for Nova Scotia,* series 4, vol.13, April 1942.
10 scenes. Multiple roles.
An historical pageant stressing the importance of responsible government, Confederation and Canadian unity to all the provinces.

D8. "Everyfreshette" in *Acta Victoriana,* vol.46, #1, Oct. 1921.
3 acts. 5m/2f.
"A morality play". A brief comic sketch about a freshman who joins too many university societies to the detriment of her studies.

D9. "Everygirl" in *Educational Review,* vol.37, #2, Oct. 1922.
1 act. 4b/4g.
"A health play" for children. An allegory in which Dread Disease tries to carry off Everygirl but is stopped by Fresh Air, Good Food, Cleanliness, Sunshine and Strength.

D10. "The Fatal Quest" in *Sketches and Plays*. Toronto, National Girls' Work Board, Religious Education Council of Canada, (192-?).
3 scenes. 2m/2f. Extras.
A brief fairy tale romance parody.
fp: Canadian Girls In Training camps.

D11. "Getting Rid of an Agent" in *Two Comic Dialogues*. Toronto, Educational Publishing, (192-?).
1 scene. 1m/3f.
Mr. Duncan is just as unsuccessful as his wife in getting rid of unwanted salesmen.

D12. "Good-By" in *Three Dialogues*. Toronto, Educational Publishing, (190-?).
1 scene. 2f.
"For two girls to impersonate Mrs. Green and Mrs. Twining" who are visiting one another.

D13. "Hansel and Gretel" in *Puppetry*. Toronto, Sports and Recreation Bureau, Ontario Ministry of Community and Social Services, (197-?).
4 scenes. 2m/3f. Extras.
An adaptation of the fairy tale for finger or hand puppets about the two hungry children who outwit a witch.

D14. "Health Hints" in *Educational Review,* vol. 36, #10, June-July 1922.
1 act. 1m/1f/6b.
A children's play. Visitors to the nurse's office prove that "cleanliness is next to Godliness in what you eat and drink as well as in every other way".

D15. "Home from Young Ladies' College" in *Three Dialogues*. Toronto, Educational Publishing, (190-?).
1 scene. 2g.
Isabel returns from college, little smarter than she was before.

D16. "The Indian Huntresses" in *The Indian Huntresses and Jumping Rope Drill*. Toronto, Educational Publishing, 1909.
1 scene. 1g. Extras.
"A spectacular Bow and Arrow Drill for eight, ten, twelve or sixteen girls".

D17. *The Intelligence Office*. Toronto, Educational Publishing, (192-?).
1 act. 3m/4f.
A comedy about various persons unsuccessfully using an employment agency.

D18. "The Irish Philosopher" in *Three Dialogues*. Toronto, Educational Publishing, (190-?).
1 scene. 2m.
An Irishman tries to comprehend the revolution of the earth around the sun.

D19. *Jake Hayseed in the City*. Toronto, Educational Publishing, 1907.
1 act. 1m/1b/1g.
A brief comic sketch in which a green country boy causes chaos in a photographer's studio.

D20. "Jumping Rope Drill" in *The Indian Huntresses and Jumping Rope Drill*. Toronto, Educational Publishing, 1909.
1 scene. 7g.
A jumping rope drill to musical accompaniment.

D21. "The Knights and the Dragon" in *Treats and Treasures.* John McInnes, ed. Toronto, Thomas Nelson, 1964.
2 acts. 7m/1f.
A children's play. On Dragon Killing Day in Nonoland, a group of knights try to kill a dragon and win a princess in marriage.

D22. "A Minister's Mistake" in *Two Comic Dialogues.* Toronto, Educational Publishing. (192-?).
1 scene. 1m/2f.
Mrs. Smith, whose St. Bernard has just died, is visited by the new minister who believes she has lost her husband.

D23. "Mrs. Jones' Conversion" in *Educational Review,* vol.36, #9, May 1922.
1 act. 5m/2f/1g.
A play for children. Mrs. Jones learns the wisdom of regular dental check-ups.

D24. *The Mouse Trap.* Toronto, Educational Publishing, (19—?).
1 act. 1m/2f. Extras.
"A farce". Arguments supporting women's suffrage and the end of their privileged status are ridiculed by being attributed to a "feminine" woman who lacks logic and intellectual independence.

D25. "An Ounce of Prevention" in *Educational Review,* vol.37, #1, Aug. – Sept. 1922.
1 act. 1b/4g.
A play for children. Those who take the precaution of visiting Miss Sanitation when suffering from a headache or sore throat escape the villain Influenza.

D26. "A Place of Refuge" in *Voice and Vision.* Jack Hodgins, William H. New, eds. Toronto, McClelland & Stewart, 1972.
1 act. Multiple roles.
A radio documentary about contemporary Canadian Indian life on the reservation.

D27. *The Safety Court.* N.p., Canadian Red Cross Youth on the Move Supplement, February 1973.
1 scene. 15b/11g.
A brief comedy emphasizing various rules of safety for young people.

D28. "The Salvage Play" in *Christmas Mumming in Newfoundland.* Herbert Halpert, G.M. Story, eds. Toronto, University of Toronto Press, 1969.
1 scene. 9m/2f.
The combat, death and revival of St. George is presented in semi-dramatic form and simple verse.

D29. "Skit" in *Acta Victoriana,* vol.56, #1, Oct. – Nov. 1931.
1 scene. 2m.
A slick salesman tries to sell a new-fangled pen to an old fashioned city-editor of a Toronto newspaper.

D30. "Soldiers Acting at Christmas" in *Christmas Mumming in Newfoundland.* Herbert Halpert, G.M. Story, eds. Toronto, University of Toronto, Press, 1969.
1 scene. 11m.
St. George and the Turkish knight engage in combat. St. George is killed but is revived by a doctor.

D31. "Something Suitable for Him" in *Argosy Weekly,* (Sackville, N.B.), Christmas 1938.
1 act. 5m.
Wealthy John Craig perpetrates a practical joke by presenting each of his nephews with imitation Chinese figurines which together, he tells them, would be worth a fortune.

D32. "Theatre Our Weapon" in *Masses,* Dec. 1932 and in *Eight Men Speak and Other Plays from the Canadian Workers' Theatre.* Richard Wright, Robin Endres, eds. Toronto, New Hogtown Press, 1976.
1 scene. Chorus.
A choral recitation adapted from *New Red Stage* supporting the cause of workers rising against the establishment and against the class system. Theatre should be made of revolutionary anger and organized by the will of the workers.
fp: British Workers' Theatre Movement.

D33. "The Tragedy of St. George" in *Christmas Mumming in Newfoundland.* Herbert Halpert, G.M. Story, eds. Toronto, University of Toronto Press, 1969.
1 scene. 8m.
The combat, death and revivification characteristic of "Hero Combat" mumming plays is presented semi-dramatically in verse.

D34. *The Twins' Santa Claus.* Toronto, Educational Publishing, (191-?).
2 scenes. 3m/3f.
The twins' lost father returns just in time for Christmas.

D35. *United Church of Canada.* (Toronto, United Church of Canada, 1926?).
2 acts. Multiple roles.
A pageant commemorating the founding of the United Church of Canada.

D36. "Val and Tyne" in *McMaster University Monthly,* vol.20, #5, Feb. 1911.
3 acts. 4m/4f.
Tyne is offended when she receives a blotted valentine from Val but he explains the reason and is forgiven.

D37. *Writing Poetry.* Toronto, Educational Publishing, (190-?).
1 scene. 5b. Extras.
A comic sketch about a group of boys collectively composing a poem for the Literary Society.

ACORN, Milton 1923–

D38. "The Execution of William Abel, Rent Collector, by a Farmer Named Pierce" in his *The Island Means Minago.* Toronto, NC Press, 1975.
1 scene. 3m/1f.
Based on a legend and historical account of a man named Abel who was killed with a bayonet.

D39. "Hypothetical Meeting Between William Cooper and William Lyon MacKenzie" in his *The Island Means Minago.* Toronto, NC Press, 1975.
1 scene. 2m.
A fictional encounter between the two historical figures.

D40. "The Road to Charlottetown" in his *The Island Means Minago*. Toronto, NC Press, 1975.
1 scene. 5m/1f. Extras.
At the governor's ball, leading characters from Canada's history discuss the formation of a Dominion and the transcontinental railway.
p: The Island Players, Harbourfront Theatre, Toronto, Jan. 5, 1977.

D41. "To Write a Poem of Walter Patterson" in his *The Island Means Minago*. Toronto, NC Press, 1975.
1 scene. 2m.
An interview with Walter Patterson, first British governor of Minago, the island now called P.E.I.

ACTON, Jean Bonar

D42. "How to Get Your Man — In Three Parts" in *Curtain Call*, vol.9, #51, Feb. 1938.
1 act. 6f.
The members of a charm school discover they have all been practicing their art on the same man.

ADAMS, J. Philip

D42A. "Reverberations of Erostratus" in *York Theatre Journal*, vol. 5, #2, Winter 1976.
1act. 5m/2f. Extras.
A drama about "a man who hates".

ADELBERG, Marjorie

D43. *The Pied Piper*. Vancouver, New Play Centre, 1973.
2 acts. 5m/4f/1b/1g. Chorus.
A musical fantasy for children based on the classic tale of the Pied Piper.
fp: Holiday Theatre, Vancouver, 1961.

D44. *Pinocchio*. Vancouver, New Play Centre, (197-?).
2 acts. 6m/1f/3b.
A musical version of the children's story of Pinocchio.
fp: Holiday Theatre, Vancouver, 1964.

AIKINS, Charles Carroll Colby 1888–

D45. *The God of Gods*. British Columbia, Author, 1919 and in *Canadian Plays from Hart House Theatre* vol.2. V. Massey, ed. Toronto, Macmillan, 1927.
3 acts. 4m/3f.
Tragic consequences befall the lovers Suiva and Yellow Snake as a result of the Chief's son's jealousy.
fp: Birmingham Repertory Theatre, Birmingham, England, Nov. 8, 1919. Hart House Theatre, Toronto, April 17, 1922.

ALEXANDER, Enid

D46. "The Roads of Learning" in *Educational Review,* vol.51, #6, Feb. 1937.
1 scene. 1m/1f/1b.
A poetic dramatic sketch about a man whose son wants to quit school and who is visited by the Spirit of Progress.

ALEXANDER, Phyllis

D47. *An Evening in August.* Western Canada Theatre Conference. Edmonton, Dept. of Extension, University of Alberta, 1945.
1 act. 3m/3f. Extras.
An impressionistic view of life as seen by two generations as a young woman decides which of her boyfriends she will eventually marry.
fp: Banff School of Fine Arts, Aug. 22, 1945.

D48. *Kee Kee.* Edmonton, Dept. of Extension, University of Alberta, (194-?).
1 act. 1f/4b/3g. Extras.
A children's play in which a boy and a girl encounter the elves, fairies and dark people in their garden.

D49. *Scarlet Slippers.* Edmonton, Dept. of Extension, University of Alberta, (194-?).
1 act. 4m/2f.
A comedy in which a brother enables his forty year old sister to marry the man she loves.

ALIANAK, Hrant 1950–

D50. *Brandy.* Toronto, Playwrights Co-op, 1973 and in his *Return of the Big Five.* C. Brissenden, ed. Toronto, Fineglow, 1975.
1 act. 2m/2f.
A clearing in the jungle is the backdrop for a series of comic scenes between Jeremia, the native tribal chief with "lots of muscles", Hubert, "a spectacled, skinny nobody", the flat-chested Blonde and the well-endowed Brunette.
fp: Theatre Passe Muraille, Toronto, May 11, 1973.

D51. "Christmas" in his *Return of the Big Five.* Toronto, Fineglow, 1975.
1 act. 5m/1f.
A Christmas story without words from the point of view of the tree who is chopped down by the Lumberjack, spends Christmas brightening up the lives of a poor young couple and dies alone in the snow-covered street.
fp: Theatre Passe Muraille, Toronto, Dec. 1973.

D52. "Mathematics" in his *Western and Mathematics.* Toronto, Playwrights Co-op, 1973 and in *Now In Paperback.* C. Brissenden, ed. Toronto, Fineglow, 1973 and in his *Return of the Big Five.* C. Brissenden, ed. Toronto, Fineglow, 1975 and in *Transitions I: Short Plays.* Edward Peck, ed. Vancouver, Commcept Publishing, 1978.
1 act.
"A play for and by objects" without dialogue or characters. One man home from the office plus one woman doing housework equals two people in bed.
fp: Factory Theatre Lab, Toronto, Dec. 5, 1972.

D53. "Passion and Sin" in *Canadian Theatre Review,* #19, Summer 1978.
11 scenes. 3m/3f.
A surrealist satirical gangster drama set in a dilapidated shack on a Havana beach.
fp: Toronto Free Theatre, March 4, 1976.

D54. *Tantrums.* Toronto, Playwrights Co-op, 1972 and in his *Return of the Big Five.* C. Brissenden, ed. Toronto, Fineglow, 1975.
4 scenes. 14m/10f. Doubling.
Sexual and social myth is presented in a collage of four impressionistic scenes including a menacing countdown, sirens and a mechanistic soundtrack.
fp: Theatre Passe Muraille, Toronto, April, 1972.

D55. "Western" in his *Western and Mathematics.* Toronto, Playwrights Co-op, 1973 and in *Now In Paperback.* C. Brissenden, ed. Toronto, Fineglow, 1973 and in *Return of the Big Five.* C. Brissenden, ed. Toronto, Fineglow, 1975.
1 act. 2m/1f.
A black comedy and satire of Western heroes and movies depicting three travellers surrounded by 500 Indians in the Arizona Territory of 1874.
fp: Theatre Passe Murraille, Toronto, Sept. 29, 1972.

ALLAN, Andrew 1908–1974

D56. *Narrow Passage.* Toronto, Author, (1950?). (Mimeographed).
3 acts. 5m/3f.
The small Ontario town of Grantville represents for some "burial", a stifling of self. For others, it means warmth and protection from human changeability and confusion.
fp: New Play Society, Museum Theatre, Toronto, Jan. 13, 1950.

ALLAN, Marguerite Martha 1895–1942

D57. *Summer Solstice.* Toronto, French, 1935.
1 act. 4m/2f.
The play deals with conflicts between a patriotic father and his pacifist children. The father's ideas are shown to be irrelevant in a world of modern war but his stubbornness prevents his family from taking measures to save themselves.

ALLAN, Ted 1916–

D58. *Double Image.* By Ted Allan and Roger MacDougall. London, French, 1957.
3 acts. 5m/2f.
In order to obtain the family fortune, an insane composer poses as his long lost twin and murders his uncle.
fp: Savoy Theatre, London, England, Nov. 14, 1956.

D59. *My Sister's Keeper.* Toronto, University of Toronto Press, 1976.
2 acts. 1m/1f.
Sarah unexpectedly arrives at her brother's London flat and convinces him that he is the only one who can restore her to her senses. Through their encounter, Sarah's terrifying background of mental illness and Robert's guilt over betraying her emerge.
fp: As "I've Seen You Cut Lemons", Fortune Theatre, London, England, Dec. 5, 1969. Revised version as "My Sister's Keeper", Festival Lennoxville, Quebec, 1974 summer season.

ALLARD, K. Cameron

D60. "The Chinese Joss" in *Acadia Athenaeum,* vol.60, #5, March 1935.
1 scene. 2m/2f.
Believing in young love rather than ancestral ways, an aged Chinese servant disguised as a god directs her young mistress to follow her American lover.

D61. "Crocus Bulbs" in *Acadia Athenaeum,* vol.60, #7, May 1935.
1 scene. 2m/2f.
A dying man who has no faith in eternal life is persuaded by his daughter's account of the resurrection of a flower bulb and dies content. Having deceived him, she is left to wonder.

D62. "The Poet" in *Acadia Athenaeum,* vol.60, #6, April 1935.
1 scene. 2m/1f.
A young poet confronted by the unpleasant reality of overdue rent learns that a long-awaited cheque is payment not for his "art" but for a story written by his sensible wife.

ALLEN, George

D63. "Upon a Midnight Clear" in *Acadia Athenaeum,* vol.63, #2, December 1937.
2 scenes. 5m/1f. Extras.
The traditional Christmas story from the perspective of the three shepherds.

ANCEVICH, John

D64. *Castle Zaremba.* Toronto, Ontario Educational Communications Authority, 1970.
16 episodes. 27m/9f/1b.
Two volumes of television drama "designed to help you learn English". In soap-opera style, the drama revolves around the people who live at Castle Zaremba, a downtown Toronto rooming house; they are of various ethnic and cultural backgrounds and have been in Canada varying lengths of time.
fp: O.E.C.A. TV, 1969.

ANDERSON, Clara E. (Rothwell) –1958

D65. *Aunt Mary's Family Album.* Ottawa, Pattison Print., 4th edition, (19—?).
1 act. 1m/14f.
A humorous "character sketch entertainment for young people's societies, ladies' aids and associations, bible classes, choirs, women's institutes and other organizations" about social life in a small rural town fifty years ago.

D66. *Aunt Sophia Speaks.* Ottawa, Author, (1940?).
1 act. 12f.
Aunt Sophia is the centre of attention at her niece's tea. The guests, all former girlfriends of her niece Caroline, assume a great number of airs and Aunt Sophia puts them all in their proper places.

D67. *Aunt Susan's Visit.* Ottawa, Author, 1917.
4 acts. 3m/7f.
Aunt Susan's visit to her nephew John changes the lives of the people she meets. Rather than strive after money or society's airs, Aunt Susan instills a desire for the simple life and doing good works by helping one's neighbours.

D68. A Character Sketch Entertainment Entitled *Afternoon Tea in Friendly Village, 1862*. Ottawa, James Hope, 1912.
2 scenes. 1m/15f.
A group of women in a small rural village meet for a quilting bee.

D69. A Character Sketch Entertainment Entitled *The Young Village Doctor*. Ottawa, James Hope, 1915.
4 scenes. 6m/8f/1b.
A new young doctor comes to a village to start a practice and find a wife.

D70. *The Joggsville Convention*. Ottawa, Progressive Printers, (19—?).
2 acts. 16f/1b/1g.
A rather out of the ordinary convention held by the Women's Protective Association is the focus of this comedy. The business of the day is forever sidetracked by gossip, socializing and food.
p: Women's Aid of the Victoria Presbyterian Church, Toronto, March 1, 1926.

D71. *Let Mary Lou Do It*. Ottawa, n.p., (19—?).
4 acts. 3m/6f/1b.
Two sisters, one beautiful but helpless, the other plain but hardworking, try to find husbands and always come up with the same man.

D72. *Marrying Anne?*. Ottawa, Rothwell Anderson, (192-?).
3 acts. 3m/6f.
A great turmoil is created when a young "modern" girl is taken in by her stuffy Victorian step-grandfather and step-aunt.

D73. *Martha Made Over*. Ottawa, Pattison, 1923.
5 scenes. 4m/8f/1b.
Martha, who has devoted her life to her housework and her family, realizes that her family is unhappy and ashamed because she has ignored the more important things of life.
p: High Park Dramatic Club, High Park Presbyterian Church, Toronto, Feb. 25, 1924.

D74. *The Minister's Bride*. Ottawa, James Hope, 1913.
4 scenes. 6m/11f. Extras.
"A character entertainment for Young People's Societies, Bible classes and other church organizations". A village minister takes a new bride who must meet the approval of the members of the parish.

D75. *An Old Time Ladies' Aid Business Meeting at Mohawk Crossroads*. Ottawa, James Hope, 1912.
1 act. 16f.
A Ladies' Aid Society convenes to discuss business, women's suffrage and the local gossip.

D76. *Wanted — A Wife*. Ottawa, n.p., (19—?).
4 scenes. 4m/8f. Extras.
A young swinging bachelor must marry an old-fashioned girl, if he can still find one, in order to inherit $100,000 from his uncle.

D77. *The Young Country Schoolm'am.* Ottawa, James Hope, 1920.
4 scenes. 5m/8f/1b.
A new school teacher comes to board with a family. During her stay she helps the daughter to catch her boyfriend, becomes engaged to the minister and encourages the son to quit college to do what he wants to do — marry a country girl and run a farm.

ANDERSON, W.F.

D78. "Alone" in *Acadia Athenaeum,* vol.56, #4, February 1930.
1 scene. 3m/1f.
An historical vignette from the life of Mary Queen of Scots at the time of David Rizzio's murder.

ANGEL, Leonard 1945–

D79. *After Antietam.* Vancouver, New Play Centre, 1976 and Toronto, Playwrights Co-op, 1977 and in his *After Antietam/Isadora and G.B.* Toronto, Playwrights Co-op, 1978.
1 act. 1m/1f.
The idealism of the Confederacy is juxtaposed with the brutal reality of the War Between the States when, after the battle at Antietam, a Confederate soldier on a secret mission for General Jeb Stuart meets a young southern woman who is looking for an adventure.
fp: New Play Centre, Vancouver, April 29, 1976.

D80. *The Ballad of Etienne Brule.* Vancouver, New Play Centre, 1973.
2 acts. 11m/4f. Extras.
An account of the events leading up to the betrayal, judgement and eventual death of Etienne Brule.
fp: Frederic Wood Studio, Vancouver, 1968.

D81. *Forthcoming Wedding.* Vancouver, New Play Centre, 1973 and in *West Coast Plays.* C. Brissenden, ed. Vancouver and Toronto, New Play Centre – Fineglow, 1975.
1 act. 2m/1f.
An old man doesn't want to lose his daughter in marriage and tries to shoot the son-in-law to-be. He fails and everyone is reconciled. The father decides that maybe he should try to shoot the young man again.
fp: "Works" festival, Factory Theatre Lab, Toronto, Dec. 1972.

D82. *Isadora and G.B.* Vancouver, New Play Centre, 1976 and in his *After Antietam/Isadora and G.B.* Toronto, Playwrights Co-op, 1978.
1 act. 1m/1f.
G.B. Shaw visits Isadora Duncan's studio to see her dance in the nude but she tries to seduce him instead.
fp: Aladdin Theatre, Toronto, 1976.

D83. *A Play About How the Greeks Dealt With Their Military and Industrial Complex in 645 B.C.* Vancouver, New Play Centre, 1973.
1 act. 9m/3f.
Pisistratus seizes power aided by the theatre and ushers in the Golden Age of Athens.
fp: Simon Fraser University, Vancouver, 1969.

ANSTRUTHER, Ken

D84. "A Restoration Show for Strumpet and Fruit" in *York Theatre Journal,* #6, March 1974.
1 act. 1m/1f.
A brief comic verse play in which a gay man disguised as a woman and a gay woman disguised as a man attempt a sexual encounter under these mistaken impressions.

ARCHIBALD, Edith Jessie (Mortimer) 1854–1938

D85. *The Token.* Ottawa, Graphic, 1926 and Halifax, Royal Print, 1927.
3 acts. 11m/5f. Extras.
A play about "old days in Cape Breton". Sheila gives her communion token to Alan to give him strength to be good and her grandfather disowns her for this act.
fp: Majestic Theatre, Halifax, March 10, 1927.

ARCHIBALD, Olive

D86. "The Lost Queen" in *Acadia Athenaeum,* vol.52, #7, June 1925.
1 scene. 1m/2f.
A little girl who fantasizes a dance with Oberon, King of the Fairies, makes her father realize that he must reconcile himself with his estranged wife, the lost Queen.

ARCHIBALD, Rosamond Mansfield de Wolfe 1882–

D87. *During the Tea Hour.* N.p., (19—?).
2 scenes. 6f.
An educational play in which three women commit 96 grammatical errors during the course of a tea party. The second scene is a repeat of the first with their errors corrected.

ARMOUR, Stuart

D88. "The Maid" in *One Act Plays by Canadian Authors.* Montreal, Canadian Authors' Association, 1926.
1 act. 4m/1f.
Joan of Arc appears to British soldiers in France and castigates them for paying more attention to regulations than to the war.

D89. "The Newcomer" in *One Act Plays by Canadian Authors.* Montreal, Canadian Authors' Association, 1926.
1 act. 3m.
A derelict is made comfortable in a place we gradually learn is heaven.

ARMSTRONG, Louis Olivier 1874–

D90. *The Book of the Play of Hiawatha the Mohawk Depicting the Siege of Hochelaga and the Battle of Lake Champlain*. N.p., n.p., 1909 and in *The Champlain Tercentenary*. Albany, New York, Lake Champlain Tercentenary Commission, 1911.
2 acts. 19m/7f. Extras. Chorus. Doubling.
A pageant based on W.D. Lighthall's romance *The Master of Life* depicting the history of the Indian wars of the early 17th century and the formation of the Indian confederacy under Hiawatha.
fp: Lake Champlain Tercentenary, Quebec, 1908.

D91. *Hiawatha or Manabozho*. Boston, Rand Avery Supply Co., 1900 and Montreal, Desbarats, 1901.
Many scenes. 9m/4f. Extras.
"An Ojibway Indian play". An adaptation of Longfellow's *Hiawatha* enacted by 75 Ojibway Indians from the Shingwauk band.
fp: Desbarats Islands, Garden River Reserve, Sault Ste. Marie, Ont., Aug. 25, 1900.

ARMSTRONG, Margaret 1929–

D92. "The Haskill House" in *Callboard*, vol. 22, #4, June 1975 and Halifax, Dramatists Co-op, 1977.
1 act. 5m/5f.
When Jacob Haskill decides to sell his inn, Auntie Bess discourages prospective buyers with tales of ghosts and strange happenings.
fp: Annapolis District Drama Group, N.S., Order of Good Cheer, May 1973.

D93. "The Legend of the Light" in *Callboard*, vol.23, #1, Jan. – Feb. 1976 and Halifax, Dramatists Co-op, 1977.
1 act. 2m/4f.
Katie and Olivia are planning to renovate the haunted Haskill Inn for the tourist trade. A storm brings visitors seeking shelter and a complex situation develops to a startling climax.
fp: Annapolis District Drama Group, N.S., Nov. 1973.

D94. *Undercover*. Toronto, Playwrights Co-op, 1976.
3 acts. 2m/4f.
A woman writer and her male publisher discover that the last chapter of her book about a platonic relationship between a man and a woman needs to be re-written.
fp: Annapolis District Drama Group, Annapolis Royal, N.S. Dec. 1977.

D95. *Victoria 412*. Halifax, Dramatists Co-op, 1977.
3 acts. 2m/4f.
Diana Fleming advertises for a roommate and ends up with svelte, blond Rosemary Allen who brings a secret from her past and much confusion into Diana's already complicated life.

D96. "Where There's a Will — There's a Way" in *Callboard*, vol.25, #1, Spring 1978 and *Where There's a Will*. Halifax, Dramatists Co-op, 1978.
1 act. 3m/4f.
A comedy about a rich 79-year-old widow who assembles her relatives for the reading of her last will and testament.

ATKIN, G. Murray

D97. "Our Lady of the Moon" in *The Canadian Magazine,* vol.55, #6, Oct. 1920.
1 act. 1m/1f.
A young man searches for the ideal woman and ideal love.

ATKINSON, Lois

D98. *Waiting.* Vancouver, New Play Centre, 1975.
1 act. 1m/3f.
An evocative portrayal of two adolescents growing up in a small prairie town.
fp: New Play Centre, Vancouver, 1975.

ATWOOD, Margaret E. 1939–

D99. "The Moon-Tree" in *Acta Victoriana,* vol.85, #2, Jan. 1961.
1 scene. 1m/1f. Extras.
An encounter between a woman who has lost her lover in a war and an enemy soldier.

D100. "Oratorio for Sasquatch, Man, and Two Androids" in *Poems for Voices.*
Toronto, CBC, 1970.
1 act. 4m.
A radio play in which two androids and a man hunt and kill the Sasquatch, legendary half-man of the Canadian woods. "He would have given you knowledge of life, you chose instead the knowledge of death."
fp: CBC radio, February/March 1970.

D101. "The Triple Goddess" in *Acta Victoriana,* vol.84, #3, April 1960.
2 scenes. 1m/3f.
"A poem for voices" in which a blind man selling pencils hears snatches of conversation between a girl, a woman and a matron.

AYLEN, Elise 1904–1972

D102. "The Holy Crown" in *The Best One-Act Plays of 1937.* J.W. Marriott, ed.
London, George Harrap, 1938.
1 act. 7m/3f. Extras.
Misfortune befalls an Italian mountain village after a thief steals the crown of the blessed Virgin.

BABINEAU, Gordon

D103. *The Troublemaker.* Western Canada Theatre Conference. Edmonton, Dept. of Extension, University of Alberta, 1947.
1 act. 2m/1f/2b/1g.
In a prairie city in the late thirties, the children of an Ukrainian immigrant labourer come into conflict with a bigoted neighbour.

BAGLOLE, Harry 1942– and Ron Irving 1934–

D104. *The Chappell Diary.* Belfast, P.E.I., Ragweed Press, 1977.
1 act. 6m/2f. Extras. Doubling.
A drama about the struggle for survival in Prince Edward Island in 1775.
fp: Confederation Theatre Company, P.E.I., 1976.

BAIRD, Evelyn

D105. "Just Johnny" in *Acadia Athenaeum*, vol.56, #6, April 1930.
1 scene. 3m/2f.
An amnesiac returns to Ottawa after W.W. I and awakens after a storm to find himself reunited with his family.

BAKER, Dora

D106. "The Building of the Empire" in *Educational Review*, vol.35, #9, April 1921.
1 act. Multiple roles.
"A pageant for Empire Day" in which Britannia's colonies pay her court.
fp: Dramatic Club, Truro Normal College, N.S.

BAKER, Ida Emma (Fitch) 1858–1948

D107. "Adopting Sara" in her *Dialogues and Dramas for School and Home*. Toronto, Musson, 1928.
6 scenes. 3b/2g. Extras.
A rancher adopts a girl of twelve and marries her six years later.

D108. "Angelina Goes to Boarding School" in her *Dialogues and Dramas for School and Home*. Toronto, Musson, 1928.
4 scenes. 6b/4g.
A black family's daughter returns from college with "high-up notions".

D109. "Bill Holsinger from Cochrane" in her *Dialogues and Dramas for School and Home*. Toronto, Musson, 1928.
5 scenes. 4b/4g.
The rags-to-riches tale of a north country bumpkin and a fortune hunter's inability to trap him.

D110. "Complicated Courtship" in her *Dialogues and Dramas for School and Home*. Toronto, Musson, 1928.
6 scenes. 3b/3g.
A young language teacher learns that one of her students is in love with her.

D111. "The Domestics at Glenholme" in her *Dialogues and Dramas for School and Home*. Toronto, Musson, 1928.
3 scenes. 4b/3g. Extras.
Four servants disrupt a dinner party with their arguments caused by racial prejudice.

D112. "Ghosts" in her *Dialogues and Dramas for School and Home*. Toronto, Musson, 1928.
3 scenes. 6b/2g.
Two girls scheme to prove to the boys that they aren't afraid of ghosts.

D113. "Going to the North Pole" in her *Dialogues and Dramas for School and Home*. Toronto, Musson, 1928.
8 scenes. 8b/3g. Extras.
Two restless farm boys on their way to the North Pole encounter numerous hardships and are arrested for vagrancy.

D114. "Mr. Huntington, F.R.G.S." in her *Dialogues and Dramas for School and Home.* Toronto, Musson, 1928.
2 scenes. 4b/3g.
An inexperienced farmhand inherits a fortune and becomes his former employer's benefactor.

D115. "Old Times and Old Timers" in her *Dialogues and Dramas for School and Home.* Toronto. Musson, 1928.
1 scene. 7b.
Old timers learn that the only thing in the world that hasn't been modernized is Christmas.

D116. "The Pumpkinhead Family" in her *Dialogues and Dramas for School and Home.* Toronto, Musson, 1928.
2 scenes. 6b/2g.
The Pumpkinhead family stages a Halloween concert to pay for the church organ.

D117. "Rocky Mountain Bill" in her *Dialogues and Dramas for School and Home.* Toronto, Musson, 1928.
5 scenes. 6b/1g.
A lonely mountaineer saves the life of a young boy.

D118. "A School for Backwards" in her *Dialogues and Dramas for School and Home.* Toronto, Musson, 1928.
2 scenes. 9b/1g.
A teacher is confused by her "backwards" students.

D119. *The Story of Canada.* Toronto, Musson, 1927.
24 scenes. 19m. Extras.
A pageant presenting incidents from Canadian history from the time of Cartier to Confederation.
fp: Separate School children, Massey Hall, Toronto, May 26, 1927.

D120. "The Trial of Karl Von Bunker" in her *Dialogues and Dramas for School and Home.* Toronto, Musson, 1928.
1 scene. 5b/2g. Extras.
A man found guilty of having thirteen children and a house which smells is condemned to eat six barrels of sauerkraut within a fortnight.

D121. "The Tubtown Orchestra" in her *Dialogues and Dramas for School and Home.* Toronto, Musson, 1928.
3 scenes. 8b/3g. Extras.
An orchestra leader who specializes in "artistic conducting" leads his musicians in a disastrous concert.

BAKER, William King

D122. *Gabriel Lajeunesse.* London, Routledge, 1926.
13 scenes. 8m/3f.
The Acadian exile of 1755 separates two lovers who spend the remainder of their lives desperately searching the American continent for each other. They are reunited just before death.

D123. *George and Margaret Fox.* London, Routledge, 1926.
13 scenes. 25m/3f. Doubling.
Narrative passages link together scenes which portray the lives of George Fox, founder of the Quaker sect, and his wife Martha.

BALDRIDGE, Mary Humphrey 1937–

D124. *The Bride of the Gorilla.* Toronto, Playwrights Co-op, 1974.
1 act. 1m/2f.
A divorcee and her best friend spend an acerbic yet comic evening with the ex-husband, re-opening and re-patching old wounds.
fp: Factory Theatre West, Calgary, Feb. 1974.

D125. *The Photographic Moment.* Toronto, Playwrights Co-op, 1975.
3 acts. 2m/3f.
A group of brothers and sisters — unmarried and unhappy — are gathered on a failing Alberta ranch during the Depression for a stifling summer. The arrival of Bunny, the most outspoken of the reticent family, touches off a series of confrontations.
fp: Theatre 3, Edmonton, Oct. 23, 1974.

D126. *The Suicide Meet.* Toronto, Playwrights Co-op, 1977.
1 act. 2m/2f.
A series of satiric sketches examining Canadian life.
fp: City Stage, Vancouver, Feb. 1977 as "Canadian Skittish".

BALL, Alan Egerton 1944– and Paul Bradbury

D127. "Professor Fuddle's Fantastic Fairy-Tale Machine" in *A Collection of Canadian Plays* vol.4. R. Kalman, ed. Toronto, Simon & Pierre, 1975.
2 acts. 4m/2f. Extras. Doubling.
Professor Fuddle invents a computor which brings stories to life. In this instance, the story is Snow White and the Seven Dwarfs with a smattering of Shakespeare and an understanding that the invention is as befuddled as the inventor.
fp: Arts and Culture Centre, St. John's, Newfoundland, Dec. 27, 1974.

BALLANTYNE, Lereine (Hoffman) 1891–1962

D128. *Heroes of History.* Toronto, Educational Publishing, (192-?).
2 parts. Multiple roles.
A pageant for children presenting the exploits of Cartier, Champlain, Dulac, Madeleine Vercheres, Wolfe, Brock, Tecumseh, Laura Secord and the Empire Loyalists.

BANKSON, Douglas

D129. *Lenore Nevermore.* Vancouver, New Play Centre, 1972.
2 acts. 6m/2f.
Characters created by Edgar Allan Poe mix with people from his life as the writer searches for the lost Lenore.
fp: Troupe, Intermedia Hall, Vancouver, May 18, 1972.

D130. *Nature In the Raw Is Seldom.* Vancouver, New Play Centre, 1970.
1 act. 2m/1f.
"A farce". A Park Supervisor in the Rockies tries to show an American family how to commune with nature but they continue killing bugs and try to feed the local bear.

D131. *Rest Home or Many Happy Returns, Pratt.* Vancouver, Author, 1967 (mimeographed) and (revised version) as *Stonehenge, or Many Happy Returns, Pratt,* Vancouver, New Play Centre, 1972.
2 acts. 4m/7f.
Dr. Suture and his staff try to keep Frank Pratt, at 100 short a day the oldest resident of the rest home, alive and happy in order that the institution might be certified. Meanwhile, Pratt attempts to start a revolution and is involved in a love affair.
fp: Neptune Theatre, Halifax, 1972.

D132. *Shellgame.* Vancouver, New Play Centre, 1970.
2 acts. 2m/2f.
Two couples decide to switch wives and husbands, then to pair off husband with husband and wife with wife, then to form a foursome, and finally to masturbate.
fp: Playbox Studio, New York, July 17, 1968.

D133. *Shootup.* Vancouver, New Play Centre, 1970.
1 act. 2m/2f.
"A farce about the old west". The Sheriff of Shootup is determined to kill the Last Varmint who in turn is determined to kill the Sheriff. Lydia, the Painted Lady, is looking for her deserter-husband. Dulcimer, the eastern teacher, is looking for her mother, father, and brother. A recognition scene.

D134. *Vacation.* Vancouver, New Play Centre, 1970.
3 acts. 5m/4f.
An "average American family" wins a two week vacation underground. They plan to stay forever to avoid pollution and ecological danger but quarrel over whether or not to go to the surface.
fp: Montana, 1963.

BANNING, Gerard, et al.

D135. "An Unanswerable Collage. A Perhaps Answer to a Perhaps Question" in *York Theatre Journal,* #2, Spring 1972.
3 scenes. Multiple roles.
Brief satiric summaries of contemporary theatre styles and fads: "Brechtian Sequence", "Theatre of Cruelty Sequence" and "Theatre of the Past, Done 'Modern' " a la Brook.

BARBEAU, Jean 1945–

D136. *Bobolink.* Montreal, Centre d'Essai, 1971.
1 act. 2m.
Two men, unable to think of anything to do, spend a Saturday evening recalling the past and avoiding doing anything in the present.

D137. "Goglu", John Van Burek, trans., in *Canadian Theatre Review,* #11, Summer 1976.
1 act. 2m.
Goglu and Godbout do the same thing day in and day out. Goglu has many fantasies which he relates to Godbout because he is lonely, and because they don't know how to change their empty lives.
fp: Pleiade Theatre Company, Toronto, St. Nicholas Street Theatre, Jan. 1976.

D138. *Manon Lastcall.* Philip and Susan London, trans. Montreal, Centre d'Essai, 1972.
1 act. 2m/2f.
The director of an art museum is blackmailed by Manon; he hired her as a guide although she knows nothing about art. Her joie de vivre greatly increases attendance at the museum and convinces the director that he has been leading a pointless life.
fp: Conservatoire d'Art dramatique, May 1970.

D139. "Solange", John Van Burek, trans., in *Canadian Theatre Review,* #11, Summer 1976.
1 act. 1f.
Solange tells the story of her meeting with a stranger on a train. We discover she has been a nun defrocked for having an affair with one of the girls in her charge and that her meeting on the train resulted in the birth of a son whose father is a revolutionary now on trial.
fp: Pleiade Theatre Company, Toronto, St. Nicholas Street Theatre, Jan. 1976.

D140. *The Way of Lacross.* Laurence Berard and Philip London, trans. Montreal, Centre d'Essai, 1972 and Toronto, Playwrights Co-op, 1973.
2 acts. 2m/1f.
Lacross relates to the audience, with the help of two friends, the story of his arrest and torture. The action parallels the stations of the cross.
fp: Poor Alex Theatre, Toronto, summer 1972.

BARKER, Ken *et al.*

D141. *Origins.* (Toronto, United Church of Canada, 1975?).
1 act. Multiple roles.
"An historical pageant in celebration of the 50th anniversary of the United Church of Canada, Montreal-Ottawa Conference, Bishop's University, Lennoxville, Quebec, June 1st, 1975".

BARNARD, Leslie Gordon 1890–1961

D142. "The Midnight of Monsieur St. Jean" in *One Act Plays by Canadian Authors.* Montreal, Canadian Authors' Association, 1926.
1 act. 3m.
An elderly rogue is apparently haunted by the ghost of a woman he had betrayed in his youth.

D143. "The Traitor" in *One Act Plays by Canadian Authors.* Montreal, Canadian Authors' Association, 1926.
1 act. 3m/2f.
The officer-son of a military father turns traitor to "war . . . but not to England" by using on himself poison-gas intended to suppress a colonial uprising.
p: Brandon, Manitoba, 1928.

BARNARD, Mrs. Leslie Gordon. See ELLIOTT, Margaret E.

BAWTREE, Michael 1938–

D144. *The Last of the Tsars.* Toronto, Clarke, Irwin, 1973.
2 acts. 24m/6f. Extras. Doubling.
Russia, 1918, is the backdrop for this drama which traces the decision of Nicholas II to enter W.W. I, the defeat of the Russian army by the Germans, the rising revolutionary feeling among the Russian people, and the abdication and eventual murder of the Romanov family.
fp: Stratford Festival, Avon Theatre, July 12, 1966.

BAXTER, Arthur Beverly 1891–1964

D145. *It Happened In September.* London, Hutchinson, 1943.
3 acts. 6m/4f.
A young man, his girlfriend, and a young Nazi are caught in the social and political upheavals in Britain and Europe during World War II.
fp: St. James Theatre, London, England.

BAXTER, Vera and Kenneth Brown

D146. *Famous People Once Were Kids.* Toronto, Early Years Associates, 1978.
A collection of ten history "mini-plays for the classroom" from the landing of Cabot to the founding of the Hudson Bay Company.

BEAUCHESNE, Arthur 1876–

D147. *Talleyrand.* Ottawa, Author, 1937. (Mimeographed).
6 acts. 30m/15f. Extras.
"A Photoplay". A historical drama tracing the political career of Talleyrand in France from 1774 to his death in 1838.

BECKWITH, John 1927– and Jay MacPherson

D148. "Jonah" in *Alphabet,* #8, June 1964.
1 act. 7m. Extras.
"A cantata" concerning the Biblical story of Jonah and the whale.

BEDER, Edward Arthur

D149. "Hell" in *Canadian Forum,* vol.12, #143, Aug. 1932.
1 act. 4m/1f.
A young woman enters Hell and finds out what the afterlife is all about.

BEER, Marjorie and Doris McCarthy

D150. "A Fairy Play" in *Echoes,* June 1922.
Issue unavailable for annotation.

BEISSEL, Henry 1929–

D151. "For Crying Out Loud" in *Canadian Drama/L'Art Dramatique Canadien*, vol.1, #2, Fall 1975 and in *Cues and Entrances*. H. Beissel, ed. Toronto, Gage, 1977.
1 act. 4m/1f. Doubling.
A play for teenagers in which a young man experiences a realistic nightmare of teenage revolution to awaken bound to a bed in an asylum. Rocky struggles to learn if he is insane or if he harbours the truth of the future.
fp: Theatre Arts Class, Charlottenburg-Lancaster High School, Williamsburg, Ontario. 1975.

D152. *Goya*. Toronto, Playwrights Co-op, 1978.
2 acts. 4m/3f. Extras. Doubling.
A series of flashbacks charts the life of the Spanish painter caught up in political intrigue, including surveillance by the Inquisition, in old age.
fp: Montreal Theatre Lab, Oct. 26, 1976.

D153. *Inook and the Sun*. Toronto, Playwrights Co-op, 1973.
10 scenes. 10 Bunraku-style marionettes.
A young Eskimo boy sets off to capture the sun and return it to the land of his people so that they will no longer starve and freeze in winter. Suitable for presentation by live actors, 5m/4f.
fp: The Third Stage, Stratford, Ont., Aug. 1973.

D154. *A Trumpet for Nap*. Toronto, Playwrights Co-op, 1973.
11 scenes. 28 marionettes.
A marionette play adapted from the play by Tankred Dorst. Napoleon the dishwasher climbs to the top of the recording industry with the help of his magic trumpet. His innocence and gullibility allow him to be exploited. He loses everything and returns to his childhood sweetheart.
fp: Little Angel Marionette Theatre, London, England, May 17, 1968.

BELL, Anne Doris

D155. "Ships That Pass" in *Canadian Red Cross Junior,* November 1939.
2 scenes. 21 ships.
An encounter in the Panama Canal between the great explorer ships of the past.

BELL, Doris and Winifred Kerr

D156. "Angin Sama" in *Canadian Red Cross Junior,* April 1939.
1 act. 4b/4g.
Members of the Junior Red Cross in Japan prepare an exhibit for the World's Fair in Tokyo.

D157. "The Book of Marco Polo" in *Canadian Red Cross Junior,* October 1938.
1 act. 6b/6g.
In a Venetian antique shop, various antiques brought back by Marco Polo recall his exploits travelling to China.

D158. "Canada's Royal Feast" in *Canadian Red Cross Junior,* May 1939.
1 act. 10m/3f/1b/2g.
A pageant in which the Builders of the Nation pay homage to Miss Canada.

D159. "Captain Cook's Ship of Health" in *Canadian Red Cross Junior,* March 1939.
1 act. 13b/2g.
A dramatization of Captain James Cook's explorations of the South Pacific and his conquest of scurvy through proper nutrition.

D160. "Drake's Drum" in *Canadian Red Cross Junior,* February 1939.
1 act. 10b/4g.
A dramatization of Francis Drake's return from sailing around the world on the Golden Hind.

D161. "Ever Onward" in *Canadian Red Cross Junior,* January 1940.
1 act. 11b/1g.
A dramatization of the hazards and rewards faced by explorers Joliet and Marquette and La Salle and others travelling on the Mississippi.

D162. "The Great Company" in *Canadian Red Cross Junior,* February 1940.
1 act. 1f/4b/4g.
A dramatization of the exploits of the Hudson Bay Company.

D163. "The Lantern of Magellan" in *Canadian Red Cross Junior,* January 1939.
1 act. 11b/1g.
Magellan prepares to sail around the world in 1519. Three years later, one of his ships returns safely.

D164. "The Mystery of the Nile" in *Canadian Red Cross Junior,* June 1939.
1 act. 9b/5g.
A dramatization of the white man's exploration in Central Africa in the second half of the 19th century.

D165. "Noel in Old Quebec" in *Canadian Red Cross Junior,* December 1939.
1 act. 9b/5g.
In the Place d'Armes in Quebec City, Champlain's monument recalls Christmas time in Old Quebec.

D166. "The Norsemen in America" in *Canadian Red Cross Junior,* September 1939.
1 act. 2f/5b/3g.
A dramatization of how the Norsemen briefly settled in the Maritimes 500 years before Columbus' discovery of America.

D167. "Spanish Conquistadores" in *Canadian Red Cross Junior,* October 1939.
1 act. 9m/1f.
A group of Central and South American Indian chiefs relate the destruction of their peoples by Spanish explorers.

BELL-SMITH, F.M.

D168. "The Cratchits' Christmas Dinner" in *Scenes from Dickens.* J.E. Jones, ed. Toronto, McClelland & Stewart, 1923.
1 scene. 1m/1f/4b/2g.
An adaptation of an episode from the story "A Christmas Carol" by Charles Dickens. At Bob Cratchit's insistence, the family toasts Mr. Scrooge.

D169. "Scenes from 'The Old Curiosity Shop' " in *Scenes from Dickens.* J.E. Jones, ed. Toronto, McClelland & Stewart, 1923.
2 scenes. 3m/2f/1b.
An adaptation of an incident from Dickens' novel. It concerns the disappearance of a five pound note from the office of Sampson Brass.

BENEDICT, Nona 1951–

D170. "The Dress" in *The Only Good Indian.* Essays by Canadian Indians. Waubageshig, ed. Toronto, New Press, 1970.
1 act. 12m/3f/2b/2g.
Scenes dramatizing the displacement of Indians in white urban society are connected by the characters' memories of their common loss — the disintegration of the links with their people and their past.

BENGOUGH, John Wilson 1851–1923

D171. *The Breach of Promise Trial — Bardell vs. Pickwick.* Toronto, Dickens Fellowship, 1907 and as "Bardell vs. Pickwick" in *Scenes from Dickens.* J.E. Jones, ed. Toronto, McClelland & Stewart, 1923.
1 act. 15m/3f/1b. Extras.
An adaptation of an incident from Charles Dickens' *Pickwick Papers.* Pickwick is taken to court on a breach of promise suit when Mrs. Bardell misunderstands a request for advice on hiring a servant as a proposal of marriage.
fp: Dickens Fellowship Company of Players, Toronto, May 9, 1907.

See also items C60, C61.

BENNER, Richard

D172. "The Last of the Order" in *Drama at Calgary,* vol.4, #1, Fall 1969.
2 acts. 2m/1f. Extras.
A deranged matador brings strength to Abraham, an old and humourous priest, and to his sacriligious cook, Lucy. Abraham is able to realize his vision of the crucified Jesus and gives all to his order, the Order of the Blessed Hands, of which he is the last member.
fp: University of California, Santa Barbara, California, 1968. Tarragon Theatre, Toronto, Oct. 10, 1972.

D173. "The Love Feast" in *Drama at Calgary,* vol.3, #1, Fall 1968.
Many scenes. 3m/2f. Extras.
An adaptation of Euripides' *Medea* structured on contemporary society and ritual: race prejudice, the drug culture, and contemporary theatrical styles of audience participation and improvisational techniques.
fp: University of California, Santa Barbara, California, 1968.

BENNETT, Lawrence 1942–

D174. *Simon's Reason.* Toronto, Playwrights Co-op, 1973.
1 act. 2m/2f.
A four-sided argument about psycho-sexual perversities in the academic world of philosophy.

BENSON, Eugene 1928–

D175. *Gunner's Rope.* Toronto, Playwrights Co-op, 1973.
1 act. 2m.
Two old men decide that one of them should commit suicide so that the survivor can collect two pensions.
fp: Backdoor Theatre, Toronto, 1973.

D176. *Joan of Arc's Violin.* Toronto, Playwrights Co-op, 1972.
1 act. 1m/1f.
Noone, a writer, attempts to finish his work before his mysterious competitor who is writing exactly the same book.
fp: Backdoor Theatre, Toronto, Sept. 1972.

BENSON, Nathaniel Anketell Michael 1903–1966

D177. *Dollard.* Toronto, Nelson, 1933.
1 scene. 3m.
"A tale in verse". A poetic monologue in which a poet recounts the exploits of Adam Dollard and his death at the hands of the Iroquois while defending white settlements in New France in 1660.

D178. "The Leather Medal" in his *Three Plays for Patriots.* Ottawa, Graphic, 1930.
1 act. 5m/1f.
This play deals with the principle that promotions in the civil service are determined by who you know rather than what you know. The obvious man for the job is passed by and a less capable man with political connections is chosen.

D179. "The Paths of Glory" in the *Toronto Star Weekly,* July 14, 1928 and in his *Three Plays for Patriots.* Ottawa, Graphic, 1930.
1 act. 7m.
On the eve of the battle of Queenston Heights, General Brock dissuades a young soldier from deserting and reprimands his successor, Colonel Sheaffe, for his bestial treatment of soldiers.
fp: Players Guild of University College, Toronto, Feb. 15, 1927.

D180. "The Patriot" in his *Three Plays for Patriots.* Ottawa, Graphic, 1930 and in *Shining Skies.* F.C. Biehl, J.R. McIntosh, C.E. Lewis, eds. Toronto, Copp Clark, 1952.
1 act. 2m/1f/1b/1g.
Fleeing from the unsuccessful York rebellion, William Lyon Mackenzie stumbles upon the isolated home of John Waters. The Patriot Mackenzie, who identifies himself at the end of the play, justifies the need for reform in Upper Canada.
p: Players Guild of University College, University of Toronto, 1927.

BENSON, Winslow

D181. "Unemployed" in *Echoes,* #136, Oct. 1934.
1 act. 4m/1f.
Ed Ross is unemployed and won't accept charity but his infant daughter's illness makes him accept both the charity of a kindly doctor and a job.

BERTON, Pierre 1920–

D182. "Shakespeare Revises a Play" in *Canadian Humour and Satire.* Theresa Ford, ed. Toronto, Macmillan, 1976.
1 scene. 8m/2f.
Shakespeare reluctantly agrees to all the gory plot suggestions of his executive producer, director, script editor and others in writing *Hamlet.*

BETT, S.G.

D183. "The Eyewash Indians" in *Curtain Call,* vol.10, #4, Jan. 1939.
1 act. 10m/2f. Extras.
A tribe of Indians captures three college students and a chauffeur in an attempt to marry the Chief's daughter to one of them.

D184. "Higher Entrance Exam" in *Curtain Call,* vol.11, #4, Jan. 1940.
1 act. 4m/3f.
A comedy about five new arrivals at the main entrance to Heaven who must account for their lives to Saint Peter.

D185. *Nunc Dimittis.* Ottawa, Ottawa Little Theatre Workshop, #11.
1 act. 2m/3f.
An elderly lady on her deathbed awaits the birth of her great-grandchild. She dies peacefully and contentedly when she hears she is the great-grandmother of twins.

BICKNELL, Minnie Evans

D186. *Relief.* Toronto, Macmillan, 1938.
1 act. 2m/2f.
Relief comes too late for a Prairie farmer who takes his life when he loses faith in both God and man.
fp: Marshall Dramatic Club, Marshall, Sask., 1936.

BINNS, Agnes S.

D187. *Grande Finale.* Ottawa, Ottawa Little Theatre Workshop, #21.
1 act. 3m/2f.
Finally realizing that he can never fulfill his parents' expectations for him, Wayne defies their wishes and begins to lead his own life.
fp: Ottawa Drama League Workshop.

D188. *Mr. Thompson Retires.* Western Canada Theatre Conference. Edmonton, Dept. of Extension, 1950.
1 act. 3m/1f.
A comedy about a seventy-year-old retired white-collar worker who refuses to give up his independent life in the woods even though he has just received a large inheritance.

BIRNEY, Earle 1904–

D189. "Damnation of Vancouver" in his *Selected Poems 1940–1966.* Toronto, McClelland & Stewart, 1966 and *The Damnation of Vancouver.* Toronto, McClelland & Stewart, 1977.
1 act. 9m/2f. Doubling.
A revised adaptation for the stage of the radio play *Trial of a City.* A televised hearing is in progress at the request of the "Office of the Future" to decide whether Vancouver, in view of her frenzied urban growth, can continue to exist.
fp: U.B.C. Players, Vancouver, Feb. 10, 1957.

D190. "Trial of a City" in his *Trial of a City and Other Verse.* Toronto, Ryerson, 1952.
A radio play. See "Damnation of Vancouver".
fp: CBC, "Wednesday Night", Oct. 8, 1952.

BISSELL, Keith 1912–

D191. *His Majesty's Pie.* Waterloo, Ont., Waterloo Music, 1966.
3 acts. 8b/1g.
"An operetta for young people". The Chancellor and his secretary steal a pie baked specially for the King and then cast the blame on a wandering troubadour.

BLACKBURN, George G.

D192. *There Go I.* Ottawa, Ottawa Little Theatre Workshop, #37.
1 act. 4m/1f/1b/1g.
The problems of discrimination facing a white family that has become a black one in a dream are depicted.

D193. *A Walk Through the Valley.* Ottawa, Ottawa Little Theatre Workshop, #28.
1 act. 5m/1f/1g.
The contrast between the inhumanity of the bureaucratic mind and the warmth and love of the family is shown in a scene at the entrance to a shelter moments before a nuclear attack.

BLACKLOCK, Jack

D194. *A Time of Minor Miracles.* Boston, Baker's Plays, 1960.
1 act. 6m/3f.
On Christmas Eve, a group of travellers stranded by a bus breakdown seek shelter in the home of a cynical news commentator. Through them he recognizes the loneliness of his life because of his failure to believe in the values of Christmas.

D195. *Not All Who Grieve.* Ottawa, Ottawa Little Theatre Workshop, #12.
1 act. 2m/4f.
A small mining community falsely attributes a widow's strange behaviour to her grief at the sudden death of her husband.

BLAIS, Marie-Claire 1939–

D196. *The Execution.* D. Lobdell, trans. Vancouver, Talonbooks, 1976.
2 acts. 8m/3f.
A study of evil in which two schoolboys plot the murder of one of their classmates and then enact the crime.
fp: Théâtre du Rideau Vert, Montreal, March 15, 1968.

D197. "The Ocean", R. Chamberlain, trans., in *Exile,* vol.4, #3 & 4, Fall-Winter 1977.
1 act. 5m/4f.
An intricate examination of the difficulties of creating relationships within families, particularly between fathers and children, and of the emotional cruelty created by artists', in this case the fathers', needs.

BLANCHARD, C. Stewart

D198. *Miss Pebble (of New York).* Winnipeg, Wray's Music Store, 1911.
2 acts. 7m/6f. Extras.
The libretto to the comic opera about high society love intrigues in rural England. Music by William Dickmont.
fp: "Produced by Mr. Mowbray S. Berkeley", Winnipeg Theatre, April 21, 1910.

BLANKNER, Fredericka

D199. *The Face of Life.* Western Canada Theatre Conference. Edmonton, Dept. of Extension, University of Alberta, 1946.
1 act. 6m/1f. Extras.
An abstract poetic drama about a group of pilgrims searching for God.

BLISS, Amelia M.

D200. "Christmas Capers" in *Acadia Athenaeum,* vol.58, #2, December 1931.
3 scenes. 3m/2f.
Saint Nick has forgotten one corner of the world but the children search for him and bring him back.

D201. "Symbols" in *Acadia Athenaeum,* vol.57, #5, March 1931.
3 scenes. 3m/1f. Extras.
A short fantasy of two silhouette portraits on a wall which fall and break in their attempt to reach each other.

D202. "A Tale of a Tub" in *Acadia Athenaeum,* vol.57, #4, February 1931.
2 scenes. 2f.
Dormitory life is rendered bathetic in iambic pentameter as a young girl attempts to take a bath in Tully Residence.

D203. "Tulip Talks" in *Acadia Athenaeum,* vol.57, #6, April 1931.
2 scenes. 2m/2f.
Two tulips talk in a garden. One dies and the other is thrown away because of its colour.

D204. "The Way of a Man and a Maid" in *Acadia Athenaeum,* vol.58, #1, November 1931.
3 scenes. 3m/1f.
Three quick vignettes on the relationship of woman and man.

BLOSTEIN, David

D205. "Busride" in *Alphabet,* #6, June 1963.
1 act. 9m/6f/1g. Extras.
"Excerpts" from a poetic radio play which uses the metaphor of a bus ride to metaphysically explore the riders on the bus, particularly different forms of women.

BOISSONNEAULT, Lorette and Bernice Chapman

D206. "To What Purpose" in *Canadian School Plays,* Series 1. E.M. Jones, ed. Toronto, Ryerson, 1948.
1 act. 5f.
The contrast between the attitude of Dagon and that of her daughter-in-law in relation to the Biblical incidents incorporated in the plot illustrates the Christian ideals of charity and forgiveness.

BOLT, Carol 1941–

D207. *Buffalo Jump*. Toronto, Playwrights Co-op, 1972 and in *Playwrights In Profile: Carol Bolt*. Toronto, Playwrights Co-op, 1976.
2 acts. 4m/1f. Doubling.
A look at Canada and her problems during the Depression focusing on the supposed Communist conspiracy to organize the workers culminating in the Regina riot.
fp: Globe Theatre, Regina, March 1971 as "Next Year Country".

D208. *Cyclone Jack*. Toronto, Playwrights Co-op, 1972 and in *A Collection of Canadian Plays*, vol.4, R. Kalman, ed. Toronto, Simon & Pierre, 1975.
1 act. 8m/1f.
A children's musical which studies the exploitation of the Indian marathon runner Tom Longboat who represented Canada in the 1908 Olympics.
fp: Young People's Theatre, Toronto, Nov. 1972. CBC TV, 1977.

D209. *Gabe*. Toronto, Playwrights Co-op, 1973 and in *Playwrights in Profile: Carol Bolt*. Toronto, Playwrights Co-op, 1976.
2 acts. 3m/2f.
Gabe is a young Metis just out of jail who loves "talking and women and everything that takes all your mind and your time". He and his friends drink, fight and search for the spirit of Louis Riel.
fp: Toronto Free Theatre, Feb. 14, 1973.

D210. "I Wish" by Carol Johnson in *Causeway*, #1, 1966 and in *Upstage and Down*. D.P. McGarity, ed. Toronto, Macmillan, 1968.
1 act. 3m/1f.
A woman, accompanied by two men, commits what seems to be an illogical murder.
fp: Central Library Theatre, Toronto, Aug. 1966.

D211. "Maurice" in *Performing Arts In Canada*, vol.11, #4, Winter 1974 and Toronto, Playwrights Co-op, 1975 and in *Cues and Entrances*. H. Beissel, ed. Toronto, Gage, 1977.
1 act. 8m/1f.
A satirical musical for high school audiences dealing with living conditions under the Duplessis regime in Quebec focusing on the Chaplinesque Maurice's abuse of power. Music by Paul Vigna.
fp: Young People's Theatre, Toronto, April 1973.

D212. *My Best Friend Is Twelve Feet High*. Toronto, Playwrights Co-op, 1972.
1 act. 3b/2g.
A children's play about a neighborhood club where the main pastime is making up and performing adventure stories. Music by Jane Vasey.
fp: Ontario Youth Theatre, July 1972.

D213. *One Night Stand*. Toronto, Playwrights Co-op, 1977.
2 acts. 2f/1m.
A lonely young woman invites a stranger to her apartment to celebrate her birthday with unexpected deadly results.
fp: Tarragon Theatre, April 1977. CBC TV "Front Row Centre", March 8, 1978.

D214. *Red Emma.* Toronto, Playwrights Co-op, 1974 and in *Playwrights in Profile: Carol Bolt.* Toronto, Playwrights Co-op, 1976.
2 acts. 7m/2f.
The story of Emma Goldman, feminist, anarchist, whom J. Edgar Hoover called "the most dangerous woman in the world". The play centres on her youth in New York in the 1890s and the events leading up to the assassination attempt on Henry Clay Frick.
fp: Toronto Free Theatre, Feb. 5, 1974. CBC TV "Performance Series", 1976.

D215. *Shelter.* Toronto, Playwrights Co-op, 1975.
3 acts. 5f.
A comic account of a South Saskatchewan politician's widow who runs for office in order to retain her late husband's seat and make a new life for herself.
fp: Firehall Theatre, Toronto, Dec. 1974.

D216. "Star Quality" in *Acta Victoriana,* vol.102, #2, Fall 1978.
1 scene. 1m/1f.
An excerpt from a play set in a Winnipeg hotel room about the encounter between a young female singer and a hip American tourist.

D217. *Tangleflags.* Toronto, Playwrights Co-op, 1974.
1 act. 3f/1m.
A children's play about a town with no name. Mr. Rubinek from Czechoslovakia and Mrs. Nishimura from Japan would each like to name it in memory of their home country. Brownie, the dog, would like to name it in memory of himself.
fp: Young People's Theatre, Toronto, Sept. 1973.

BOLTON, Mada Gage

D218. "Dealer's Choice" in *Curtain Call,* vol.9, #3, Dec. 1937.
1 act. 2f/1m.
A successful Broadway designer gives up her way of life for her lover.

D219. "Her Affairs in Order" in *Three Prize One Act Plays and Two Others.* E. Everard, ed. London, Allen & Unwin, 1937 and in *Ten One-Act Plays for Women.* Elizabeth Everard, ed. London, Harrap, 1958.
1 act. 6f.
A woman sentenced to life imprisonment for murder is pardoned to return home to die with her family; each member of the family has a different attitude toward her.
fp: International One-Act Play Theatre at the Vaudeville Theatre, London, England, 1936.

BOND, F. Fraser

D220. *The Woolly Lamb of God.* Toronto, French, 1933.
4 scenes. 14m/2f/1b/1g.
A boy, his father, and his uncle are among the shepherds who greet the baby Jesus in the stable in Bethlehem.

BONVIE, Tom L. 1940–

D221. *Martha's Looking Glass.* Toronto, Playwrights Co-op, 1975.
2 acts. 6m/5f.
A sit-com about Jane Berlington, a college freshman, who lures the town's not-so-great lover Horrible Horace to her apartment where she must keep him overnight as part of her initiation.
fp: Nova Theatre Company, New Glasgow, N.S., 1976.

BORSOOK, Henry

D222. "The Feast of Belshazzar" in *The Canadian Forum,* vol.9, #107, Aug. 1929.
1 act. 7m/1f. Extras.
A presentation of the Biblical episode in which Belshazzar, king of Babylon, sees the writing on the wall.

D223. "Three Weddings of a Hunchback" in *Canadian Plays from Hart House Theatre,* vol.1. V. Massey, ed. Toronto, Macmillan, 1926.
3 acts. 10m/5f. Extras.
An ironic treatment of three successive marriages in a Jewish family and the fate of the youngest daughter, a hunchback.
fp: Hart House Theatre, Toronto, April 21, 1924.

BOSTON, Stewart

D224. *Butterball.* Elgin, Illinois, Performance Publishing, 1972.
1 act. 4m/3f.
An adaptation of de Maupassant's short story about a young prostitute and her upper class travelling companions who are retained at a French inn by an arrogant Prussian officer.

D225. *Counsellor Extraordinary.* Edmonton, Citadel Theatre, 1971 (mimeographed) and in *A Collection of Canadian Plays* vol.1. Rolf Kalman, ed. Toronto, Simon & Pierre, 1972.
2 acts. 17m/2f. Extras.
The play deals with the treason of the Earl of Essex and the role Francis Bacon played in it. The focus is on the trial of Essex.
fp: Citadel Theatre, Edmonton, March 24, 1971. CBC radio.

D226. *Cressida.* Edmonton, Alberta Dept. of Culture, 1970, and Elgin, Illinois, Performance Publishing, 1972.
3 acts. 4m/1f. Extras.
A retelling of the story of Troilus and Cressida. Cressida's sacrifice is to no avail; she loses both her father and Troilus and is cast off by the ruthless and victorious Diomede.
p: CBC radio.

D227. *The Cruise.* Edmonton, Alberta Dept. of Culture, 1969.
1 act. 6m/2f. Extras.
A man who takes a cruise for the good of his health discovers that the purpose of the journey is to fulfill the death wish of passengers and crew.
fp: Central Memorial H.S., Calgary, Alberta.

D228. *The Experiment*. Edmonton, Alberta Dept. of Culture, 1969.
1 act. 2m.
The history of mankind is seen through the eyes of God and Lucifer as they sit in their "heavenly" office and operate the computer.
fp: Alberta Play Festival.

D229. *The Sacrifice*. Chicago, Dramatic Publishing, 1969.
1 act. 9m/2f.
After a nuclear war, insane dictators establish a system of the "Elect" whereby most people are kept in ignorance and are treated as beasts.

D230. *School of Darkness*. Elgin, Illinois, Performance Publishing, 1972.
1 act. 7m/7f.
A former teacher threatens the principal of the high school from which he has been banned. Because of this and his opposition to the social system he is committed to a reprogramming centre. Set in 1993.
p: CBC radio.

BOTTING, Gary 1943–

D231. *The Box Beyond*. Edmonton, Harden House, 1972.
1 act. 4m/1f.
This play explores in allegorical form the system of "boxes" that either exist or that man himself creates and man's attempt to escape them.
fp: Crestwood Drama Group, Peterborough, Ont. as "Who Has Seen the Scroll?".

D232. *Harriott!*. Edmonton, Harden House, 1972.
1 act. 4m/1f.
A comedy about Harriott, the mad scientist who experiments with tobacco, rabbits and seaweed, and is visited by Sir Walter Raleigh and Christopher Marlowe.
fp: Crestwood Drama Group, Peterborough, Ont.

D233. "Perambulance" in his *Perambulance and Pipe Dream*. Edmonton, Harden House, 1972.
1 act. 4m/3f.
Black comedy which features two babies in a carriage and a grocer who stocks his shelves with garbage.
fp: University of Alberta Noontime Theatre, Edmonton.

D234. "Pipe Dream" in his *Perambulance and Pipe Dream*. Edmonton, Harden House, 1972.
1 act. 7m.
A black comedy. A timid clerk is victimized in a public washroom, a microcosm of the real world.
fp: University of Alberta Noontime Theatre, Edmonton.

D235. *Prometheus Rebound*. Edmonton, Harden House, 1972.
2 acts. 8m/1f.
Prometheus whispers to man the secrets of atomic energy and is again bound to a rock as punishment.
fp: People and Puppets Inc., Barricade Coffee House, Edmonton, June 30, 1971.

BOWERING, George 1935–

D236. "The Home for Heroes" in *Prism*, vol.3, #2, Winter 1962 and in *Ten Canadian Short Plays*. J. Stevens, ed. New York, Dell, 1975.
1 act. 4m.
A "parable" in which the rigidly conventional and unquestioning role of the hero is explored. The play deals with the pathetic inadequacy of pop-culture heroes.

BOWIE, Douglas 1944–

D237. "Moving Day" in *Callboard*, vol.23, #4, Winter 1977.
1 act. 3m/1f.
Reality and fantasy intertwine when a widowed English teacher reluctantly breaks off an affair with her building superintendent to marry a stuffy English professor.
fp: (Workshop), Factory Theatre Lab, Toronto, 1974.

BOWLES, N.W.

D238. "Scientific Socialism" in *Masses*, March/April 1933 and in *Eight Men Speak and Other Plays from the Canadian Workers' Theatre*. Toronto, New Hogtown Press, 1976.
1 act. 5m. Extras.
G.B. Shaw and H.G. Wells discuss their varied opinions about socialism, while the workers struggle for themselves.

BOYAR, Josephine

D239. "Walk Into Our Parlour" in *Canadian School Plays* Series 1. E.M. Jones, ed. Toronto, Ryerson, 1948.
1 act. 2m/2f.
Jack and Poppy's schemes to encourage a romance between their sister Gail and Vince misfire because the two have already eloped.

BOYCE, Conrad

D240. *A Few Hills Away*. Edmonton, Alberta, Dept. of Culture, 1971.
2 acts. 12m/1f. Extras.
This play is concerned with the hardships endured by the La Verendrye brothers and their companions: winter, starvation, Indian attacks and low morale.

BRADBURY, Paul and A.E. Ball

D241. *Professor Fuddle's Fantastic Fairy-Tale Machine*. See **BALL, Alan Egerton**.

BRADEN, Bernard 1916–

D242. "The Man Who Would Like to Forget" in his *These English*. Toronto, McClelland, 1948.
1 act. 8m/1f.
A radio drama in which Harold Le Druilenec recalls the suffering and horror of a German concentration camp during World War I.
fp: CBC radio, Toronto.

BRAID, Angus 1945–

D243. "Outport" in *Performing Arts in Canada,* vol.8, #4, Winter 1971.
3 scenes. 5m/2f.
Modern life comes to a Newfoundland outport. Sacrey loses his job as postmaster to his neighbour, who has a truck. His son Pleman wants to leave a poor life of fishing for the "good life" of St. John's.
fp: Studio Theatre, Toronto, March 1970.

BRANDERS, Heather

D244. "The New Deal" in *Acadia Athenaeum,* vol.60, #2, December 1933.
3 scenes. 1m/4f.
Athenaeum bemoans the scarcity of playwrights until a group of schoolgirls promise to start writing.

D245. "Roommates" in *Acadia Athenaeum,* vol.58, #4, February 1932.
1 scene. 3f.
A short comic look at domestic life at Acadia University.

BREWER, George McKenzie 1889–

D246. *The Holy Grail.* A Whitsuntide Mystery of the Quest of the Soul. Montreal, Herald Press, 1933.
1 act. 15m/7f. Extras. Chorus.
A verse play "founded on Ancient legends derived from various sources". The Grail legends concerning Joseph of Arimathea, the Fisher King and Percivale, are dramatized in chronological sequence and connected with one another.
fp: Church of the Messiah, Montreal.

BRICKENDEN, Catharine (McCormick) 1896–

D247. *According to the Rules.* N.p. Author, 1966. (Mimeographed).
3 acts. 4m/3f/2b/1g.
A childless widower, who wishes to adopt three handicapped children from an orphanage, meets vehement opposition from his relatives.

D248. *No Red Carpet.* N.p. Author, 1960. (Mimeographed).
3 acts. 3m/6f.
"A contemporary play". A small town's citizens' committee tries to "keep (its) Anglo-Saxon heritage inviolate". Betsy Barony opposes her friends by helping a young Hungarian find work and a new life.

D249. *A Pig in a Poke.* Toronto, French, 1948.
3 acts. 6m/4f.
"Farce-comedy". A sick pig, a broken-down bus, a suspected robber and murderer at an old farmhouse provide a confusing and exciting evening for its occupants.
fp: Simcoe Little Theatre, 1948.

D250. *Zanorin.* Toronto, French, 1958 and in *Canada on Stage,* Stanley Richards, ed. Toronto, Clarke Irwin, 1960.
1 act. 2m/3f.
One act play on which *No Red Carpet* is based.

BRITISH COLUMBIA CENTENNIAL COMMITTEE

D251. *From Wilderness to Wonderland.* Victoria, British Columbia, 1957 and (enlarged version) 1958.
2 acts. Multiple roles.
"A pageant of British Columbia history prepared by the British Columbia Centennial Committee for presentation in connection with this province's centennial celebrations — 1958".

BROADFOOT, Dave 1926–

D252. "The Senate" in *Canadian Humour and Satire.* Theresa Ford, ed. Toronto, Macmillan, 1976.
1 scene. 2m.
A conversation between a Senator and his son satirizing the Canadian Senate.

BROOKS, Mary Wallace

D253. "The Dream" in *One Act Plays by Canadian Authors.* Montreal, Canadian Authors' Association, 1926.
1 act. 1m/2f.
A girl falls asleep while reading *Ariel* and dreams she meets Shelley.

D254. "Voices" in *One Act Plays by Canadian Authors.* Montreal, Canadian Authors' Association, 1926.
1 act. 4m/5f.
A blind man knows people as "voices". Through voices, he discovers that his fiancee does not love him, but that another does.

D255. "Whirr of Wings" in *Echoes,* #127, June 1932.
1 act. 1m/3f.
The death of old Sarah Martin brings a new acceptance and understanding of life to her grand-daughter, Nell.

BROOMER, Stuart

D256. "When I Hear the Word 'Ear' I Reach for the Side of My Head" in *Exile,* vol.15, #1/2, 1978.
1 act. 2m/2f.
A musical performance piece, "speech therapy for inarticulate instruments", in which musical sounds are made to approximate human speech.

BROWN, Barbara et al.

D257. "Real Christmas Gifts" in *Echoes,* December 1935.
1 act. 2f/1b/1g.
Two children are rewarded for their charity towards others at Christmas time.
fp: Community Speech and Drama Club, Junior College Branch, University of Alberta, Calgary.

BROWN, Kenneth.

D257A. *Famous People Once Were Kids.* See **BAXTER, Vera.**

BROWN, Lennox

D258. *The Captive.* Ottawa, Ottawa Little Theatre Workshop, #34.
1 act. 6m/1f.
A southern bigot, suspected of being instrumental in the deaths of several civil rights workers in Mississippi, is held prisoner by five black men of various temperaments. They explore their reactions to real and imagined persecution.

D259. "Devil Mas' " in *Kuntu Drama.* P.C. Harrison, ed. New York, Grove, 1974.
3 acts. 5m/2f/1b/1g. Extras.
Set within the environment, physical and emotional, of Trinidad at carnival time. Mano not merely impersonates but becomes the devil, descending into the "Black Hole of the Past" and returning to enact a ritual that reveals the origins of the communal reality and renews its sources of strength.
fp: Trinidad Theatre Workshop.

D260. "I Have To Call My Father" in *Drama & Theatre,* vol.8, #2, Winter 1969.
1 act. 3m/2f.
An African mask speaks of destruction to Adam on New Year's Eve. The ancient tribal mask reveals in symbolic and grotesque vignettes the brutality and eventual nuclear holocaust of the white civilization. For Frieda, the mask says nothing, at least nothing she can hear or see.

D261. *Jour Ouvert* (or *Daybreak*). Ottawa, Ottawa Little Theatre Workshop, #56.
1 act. 3m/2f.
A white woman and a black man together on New Year's Eve discuss this "night of birth and death" and the ancestors who haunt them. The young man is alternately haunted by the woman's white sexuality and an African "talking mask". The crash of a nuclear bomber turns the wait for the New Year into a wait for annihilation.

D262. *The Meeting.* Ottawa, Ottawa Little Theatre Workshop, #49 and in *Performing Arts in Canada,* vol.7, #4, Winter 1970.
1 act. 3m/1f.
Concerned with illusion and reality, this play questions the wisdom of tampering with either, even for the purpose of justice when the one who judges is self-appointed and self-righteous.
fp: CBC TV "The New Majority", March 1969.

D263. "The Trinity of Four" in *Caribbean Rhythms.* James Livingston, ed. New York, Washington Square Press, 1974.
1 act. 3m/1f.
A drama about an attempted slave rebellion in Trinidad in 1800.

BROWN, Randy

D264. "The Landlord and Tenant Act" in *Acta Victoriana,* vol.97, #2, April 1973.
5 scenes. 3m.
Excerpts from a play about the hassles of two sisters and two friends with their landlord.
fp: New Vic Theatre, University of Toronto, 1973.

BRUCE, Harry

D265. *Word From an Ambassador of Dreams.* Halifax, Dramatists Co-op, 1977.
1 act. 2m/2f.
A radio play celebrating the ebb and flow of one family over several generations on a remote Nova Scotian shore.
fp: Radio, 1975.

BRUYERE, Christian 1944–

D266. *Walls.* Vancouver, New Play Centre, 1978 and Vancouver, Talonbooks, 1978.
2 acts. 11m/2f.
A prison drama based on the 1975 hostage-taking incident at the B.C. Oakalla Penitentiary in which Mary Steinhauser was killed.
fp: New Play Centre and the Arts Club Theatre, Vancouver East Cultural Centre, May 4, 1978.

BUCHAN, Susan (Lady Tweedsmuir)

D267. *Christmas Time.* London, French, 1936 and in *Canadian Red Cross Junior,* December 1936 and in *Country Guide,* December 1936.
1 act. 2f/1b/3g.
A Christmas Fairy gives the greedy aunt Sophonisba Grim one last chance to change her life and she brings gifts and love to her impoverished relatives.

D268. *Fortune.* London, French, 1936.
1 act. 1m/5f.
May Cane ran off with Pierre, a young street entertainer, leaving her mother and fiance. Five years later, she returns ill and tired thinking Pierre has left her only to learn that he had gone to see a solicitor about an inheritance.

D269. *Reindeer at Christmas.* Toronto, French, 1937.
1 act. 4m/1f/2b/2g.
A children's play in which the poor and deserving are brought unexpected Christmas joy by Father Christmas and his two amusing reindeer.

BUCHAR, Frank

D270. "A Miner's Wife" in *Boreal,* #11/12, 1978.
1 act. 3m/2f.
A drama about the brief infidelity of an immigrant miner's wife and the death of her lover in a mining accident.

BUCKLEY, Marjorie White 1907–

D271. *Five Thousand Years Mortgage.* Ottawa, Ottawa Little Theatre Workshop, #43.
1 act. 10m/6f.
A northern community, concerned with the possible dangers which might result from nuclear testing, tries to put a stop to a scheduled explosion.

D272. *Passport Please.* Ottawa, Ottawa Little Theatre Workshop, #57.
1 act. 12m/6f. Extras. Doubling.
A comedy. An elderly English lady is the cause of much concern among a group of tourists travelling in the Middle East.

D273. *Prologue.* Ottawa, Ottawa Little Theatre Workshop, #3.
1 act. 2m/6f.
An episodic reconstruction of Emily Bronte's school teaching days and her unhappy romance. Emily is presented as a strong-willed, very private individual with a strong sense of moral duty and great sensitivity.
fp: Ottawa Little Theatre, Oct. 1, 1959.

D274. *A Question of Perspective.* Ottawa, Ottawa Little Theatre Workshop, #54.
1 act. 6m/4f.
William Blake, poet and artist, and his wife Catherine must contend with a swindling art dealer and with a public unprepared for Blake's art and visions of inspiration.

BULLOCK, Michael 1918–

D275. *The Island Abode of Bliss.* Vancouver, New Play Centre, 1973.
2 acts. 2m/2f.
A young couple meet an old man with a house boat and together set out for an island. There, a new woman replaces the original and the partners change in symbolic transformations.
fp: New Play Centre, Vancouver, 1973.

D276. "Not to Hong Kong" in *Dialogue & Dialectic: A Canadian Anthology of Short Plays.* Alive Theatre Workshop, ed. Guelph, Alive Press, 1972.
3 scenes. 1m/1f/1b.
Bella and Mendel discuss the ownership of a coat, help their son read a book that hasn't been written, and discuss the swimming abilities of their invisible dog.
fp: Inter-Action Productions, Festival of London, England, 1972.

BULLOCK-WEBSTER, Llewelyn 1879–

D277. The Original Version of *The Curse of ChirraPoonje.* By Chareh Sultan El Osman (pseud.) Victoria, Acme Press, 1924.
Prologue. 5 scenes. 15m/5f/1b. Extras.
"An Al-Fresco drama." A soldier steals the great ruby from the temple of Chirrapoonje and his kingdom is cursed with famine and disease as a result. Thirty years later, princess Sundari lifts the curse by renouncing her royal position.
fp: Victoria Little Theatre, July 15, 1924.

D278. "He Passed Through Samaria" in *The Anvil,* vol.1, 1931 and *He Passed Through Samaria.* New York, Fitzgerald, 1932.
1 act. 2m/2f.
"A religious play." Gortyna, involved in a conspiracy to steal government tax money, is profoundly affected by her meeting with Christ. She leads the others to seek salvation.

D279. *Remorse.* Rock Island, Ill., Ingram, 1936.
1 act. 2m/2f.
Creela Stolwert thinks her mother wants to become a movie actress and tries to prevent this from happening. But Lady Maude has actually gone to Vancouver to fetch an orphan she has adopted; the trip ends in tragedy.

D280. *The Shadow of the Nile.* Toronto, French, 1935.
1 act. 1m/2f.
Psamtik, with the welfare of Egypt at heart, is forced to use devious means to quell a threatened uprising and marry the woman he realizes will be the better queen.

BUNDY, Freda Graham

D281. *Kaleidoscope.* Edmonton, Dept. of Extension, University of Alberta, 1946.
1 act. 7m/3f.
A comedy set in a prairie pioneer general store whose colourful customers portray the "spirit of the West".

BURGESS, Ivan 1938–

D282. *Horseshoe House.* Toronto, Playwrights Co-op, 1972.
2 acts. 2m/2f.
A black man and a drunk fight over a white girl in a boarding house.
fp: Garret Theatre, Toronto, Feb. 26, 1970.

BURKE, Derek

D283. " 'I Can't Go On.' World Too Big for Him Midget Slays 3, Himself" in *York Theatre Journal,* #8, Winter 1974.
1 act. 7m/1f.
A "work-in-progress". Hypothetical reconstruction of events and feelings leading to a tragic incident. Through poetry and the fellowship of other amateur poets, a midget tries to escape the destiny inherent in his flawed physique.

BURKHOLDER, Mabel Grace (Clare) 1881–1954

D284. *Mr. Scrooge on Main Street.* Chicago, Hope, 1928.
2 scenes. 5m/3f/6b. Extras.
"A pageant". A modern retelling of Dickens' *Christmas Carol.*

D285. *A Pageant of Bethlehem.* Mt. Hamilton, Ont., Author, 1922 and Chicago, Hope Publishing, 1925.
4 scenes. 1m/3f/1b. Chorus.
A Christmas pageant retelling the events surrounding the birth of Christ. The three wise Kings leave Jerusalem and are joined by a group of shepherds in searching out Christ's birthplace and protecting the child from Herod's designs.

D286. *A Prince in Egypt.* Mt. Hamilton, Ont., Author, 1922.
5 scenes. 8b/2g.
A children's play based on the Biblical story of Joseph who was sold by his brothers into slavery and rose to the station of Pharaoh's minister.

D287. *Striking for Higher Wages.* Mt. Hamilton, Ont., Author, 1923 and Toronto, Education Publishing, (1923).
2 scenes. 6m/3f. Extras.
A comedy in which the members of a farmer's family go on strike and withdraw their free labour until the farmer agrees to compensate them for their work and makes them partners in the business.

D288. *The Ten Virgins.* Mt. Hamilton, Ont., Author, 1922.
1 act. 11b or g. Chorus.
A morality play for children in which the five foolish virgins, Wealth, Beauty, Power, Fashion and Greed, disobey the orders of the Bridegroom and are denied entrance to the feast.

BURNETTE, Norman L. and Ella Monckton

D289. *The Angry Men.* Ottawa, Metropolitan Life Insurance, 1942.
4 episodes. 20m/2f. Doubling.
A health propaganda play to popularize nutrition depicting man's victory over disease.

BURRILL, Scott

D290. "Cynicism and Seclusion Meet at the Altar" in *McMaster University Quarterly,* vol.46, #3, March 1937.
1 act. 3m/2f.
A comedy in which a young English playwright meets a glamorous Swedish actress on board a luxury liner.

D291. "Il Penseroso" in *McMaster University Quarterly,* vol. 49, #1, Nov. 1939.
1 act. 2m/1f.
A philosophic encounter between a disillusioned wealthy young socialite and an ex-college student.

BURTON, Franklin Wicher

D292. *Achilles.* Toronto, University of Toronto Press, 1928.
1 act. 2m/2f.
Preceding the siege of Troy, Hector and Andromache discuss the political situation with Paris and Helen.

BUSCHLEN, John Preston 1888–

D293. *Assembly Call.* By A Flyer's Dad (pseud.). Hollywood, California, Murray & Gee, 1943 and Toronto, Macmillan, 1944.
3 acts. 14m/5f.
Noel Taylor, a young and exuberant pilot during W.W. II, crashes and is killed. Through supernatural powers, he is permitted to help his family and friends through their grief and they in turn help others.

D294. *The Catalogue Cowboy.* By Jack Preston (pseud.). Los Angeles, Wetzel Publishing, 1927.
4 acts. 6m/3f. Extras.
"A comedy of Montana" about a young Harvard man and romantic entanglements on the frontier.

D295. *Everybody's Troubles.* By Jack Preston (pseud.). San Francisco, Banner Play Bureau, 1932.
3 acts. 4m/7f. Extras.
A comedy about a young philanthropic California lawyer who attempts to force an unscrupulous realtor to make amends for cheating unsuspecting widows out of their savings.
fp: Beaux Arts Theatre, Los Angeles, Dec. 8, 1930.

D296. *The Pleasures of the World.* By John Preston (pseud.). Lamoni, Iowa, Herald, 1915.
3 acts. 5m/6f/1b.
"A religious comedy". A father with very narrow religious convictions drives his son from home and interferes with his daughter's engagement. A happy reunion takes place three years later.

D297. *Truants.* By John Preston (pseud.). Lamoni, Iowa, Herald, 1915.
1 act. 3m/3f.
"A comedy" in which a single girl disillusioned with the hypocrisy of modern life and the church meets an artist who had once, anonymously, sketched her picture.

BUSH, Stephen

D298. "Once a Giant" in *Performing Arts in Canada,* vol.11, #2, Summer 1974.
1 act. Narrator, 2m. Chorus.
"An Idealistic Parable in Dramatic Form for Young and Not-So-Young People". There are elements of fairy tale and of communal story-telling in this pacifist "parable". The good king of the North knows the words with which to disarm the war-seeking Giant of the South because he himself was "once a giant".

BUTT, Grace

D299. "Winter Scene" in *Winning Entries in the Newfoundland Government Sponsored Competition for the Encouragement of Arts and Letters, etc.* Newfoundland, 1965.
2 acts. 5m/2f.
A TV drama about a young man who must decide between two jobs: a lucrative position with a firm in Newfoundland or a chance to do meaningful work with the Eskimos for the Dept. of Northern Affairs.

C.E.J.C. (pseud.)

D300. "A Poulterer In Hell" in *Acta Victoriana,* vol.52, #5, Feb. 1928.
1 act. 4m. Chorus.
"A play of ancient Japan" in which the ghost of an old poulterer charms the king of hell into letting him return to earth.

CADOGAN, Elda Magill 1916–

D301. *The Invisible Worm.* Durham, Ont., Durham House, 1953.
1 act. 2m/1f.
This comedy explores the problem of finding something that is real in this age of the disposable, replaceable imitation.

D302. *The Other Half.* Durham, Ont., Durham House, 1954.
1 act. 2m/2f.
Two reporters get a lesson in life and a not so exclusive story from a family of hillbillies who live in a cave.
fp: Victoria Little Theatre, Victoria, B.C., December 17, 1954.

D303. *Rise and Shine*. Durham, Ont., Durham Chronicle, 1952 and Durham House, 1968.
1 act. 2m/2f.
A comedy. On Judgement Day, Philip and Hepzibah, who has been dead for over 100 years, are left behind in the graveyard and use the opportunity to fall in love, until it is revealed that he is her great great grandson.

CAHILL, Tom 1919–

D304. *As Loved Our Fathers*. Portugal Cove, Nfld., Breakwater, 1974.
2 acts. 4m/3f.
The play explores the motives that determined voting in the 1948 referenda. There is bitter dissension between the supporters of confederation, and the supporters of "responsible government", who feel that a vote for confederation is a betrayal of homeland and independence, "selling us up the St. Lawrence River" for a pension and a baby bonus.
fp: Avion Players of Gander, April 5, 1974.

CAIRNS, Mary G.

D305. *The King's Ugly Bride*. Cody, Wyoming, Pioneer Drama Service, 1964.
1 act. 3m/4f.
A King meets a beautiful, kind-hearted girl and wishes to marry her. The girl's stepmother, the sorceress Mag, wants the King to marry her real daughter and so attempts to fool the King.

CALDWELL, James Ernest 1862–1954

D306. *The Yellow Bag*. Ottawa, Thorburn, 1907.
5 acts. 11m/3f. Extras.
During the Cuban rebellion of 1895–98, Don Castro is falsely accused of being a traitor to the rebel cause.

CALLAGHAN, Barry 1937–

D307. "Politics of Passion" in *Performing Arts in Canada*, vol. 9, #2, Summer 1972.
1 act. 2m/1f.
A television interviewer is attempting to understand the struggle between Mary Stuart and John Knox, as they are together in a television studio for the first time since their confrontation in the 16th century.

CALLAGHAN, Francis

D308. "The Death of Sappho" in *The Reed and the Cross*. Toronto, Ryerson, 1923.
1 scene. 1m/1f.
A verse drama about the suicide of Sappho after her lover leaves.

CALLAGHAN, Morley Edward 1903–

D309. "Season of the Witch" in *Exile,* vol.2, #3 & #4, 1975, and (revised edition), Toronto, House of Exile, 1976.
3 acts. 4m/3f. Extras.
A father and son whose shattered relationship is at the centre of a crisis that is the culmination of the family's degeneration rediscover the deep permanence of kinship ties through the mediation of a woman who truly loves them.
fp: Peterborough Summer Theatre, Ont., July 1976.

CALLAN, J.B., T.C. Mulvihill, E.C. Scully

D310. *A Pageant of Canadian History.* Toronto, French, 1938.
13 scenes, 32m/5f. Doubling.
A pageant of important persons and events in Canadian history.

CAMERON, B.A. See HUBERT, Cam

CAMERON, Harcourt

D311. "Night Mail" in *Acadia Athenaeum,* vol. 60, #7, May 1935.
1 scene. 3m.
A young pilot, whose wife has just died, volunteers to replace another flyer during a Christmas Eve snowstorm.

D312. "The Opera of the Machine" in *Acadia Athenaeum,* vol. 61, #5, March 1936.
3 acts. 8m. Extras.
A libretto about machines revolting against their human taskmasters and achieving the peace they crave after a long struggle.

CAMERON, Ron 1944–

D313. "Masque", in *A Collection of Canadian Plays* vol. 4. R. Kalman, ed. Toronto, Simon and Pierre, 1975.
Many scenes, 3m/2f. Doubling.
An adaptation of James Reaney's *One-Man Masque,* presenting vignettes of life and death as viewed by Man.
fp: Riverdale Collegiate Drama Club, 1972.

CAMPBELL, Amy

D314. "The Cradle" in *Willison's Monthly,* vol. 4, #4, Sept. 1928.
1 act. 3m/3f.
An old couple is about to move off their farm, but the land is bought by their son-in-law and an old dream comes true.

CAMPBELL, Brian

D315. "The Measures" in *Matrix,* Spring 1976.
1 act. 7m.
Branko, a university student, is in the midst of writing an essay when he is arrested on a charge of treason. He is brought to trial and convicted on evidence presented by Professor Bullsand, an essay on a poem by Shelley. He is subsequently executed by order of the Prime Minister.
fp: University of Ottawa Drama Guild, March 1971.

CAMPBELL, Helen G.

D316. "An Argument in the Kitchen" in *A Collection of Plays Suitable for Use in Junior Red Cross Groups.* Toronto, Canadian Red Cross Society, (1927?).
1 act. 1m/2f/3b/6g. Extras.
A health playlet in which Betty falls asleep in the kitchen and dreams of the Good Health Fairies who testify on behalf of Mrs. Milk Bottle and against Mrs. Coffee Pot.
p: Dairy Branch, Department of Agriculture, Ottawa.

CAMPBELL, John Gounod 1910–

D317. "The Big Helpers" in his *Six Plays for Children.* Hamilton and Saskatoon, School Publications & Specialties, 1958.
1 act. 2b/2f.
Two boys discuss how difficult it is to help people who don't want help, while all the time their mothers have many chores for them to help with.
fp: Peterborough Children's Theatre, April 1957.

D318. "The Bleeding Heart of Wee Jon" in *Canada on Stage.* S. Richards, ed. Toronto, Clarke Irwin, 1960 and in his *Three One-Act Plays.* Toronto, Playwrights Co-op, 1975.
1 act. 4m/1f.
A "Chinese fantasy" about a young man in love with the daughter of a rich lord, and the trick he uses to win her hand in marriage.

D319. *Fox of a Thousand Faces.* Toronto, Playwrights Co-op, 1973.
11 scenes. 5m/4f.
"A musical fantasy for children". A foolish prince and a wiser minstrel vie for the hand of a beautiful princess. A contest is set to see who can find the most precious thing in the world.
fp: Peterborough Children's Theatre, 1958.

D320. *The Groanin' Board.* Ottawa, Ottawa Little Theatre Workshop, #32, and Toronto, Playwrights Co-op, 1973.
1 act. 6m/2f.
The play presents a backwoods family on Thanksgiving Day to whom God "didn't provide nothin' las' Thanksgivin' cause we wasn' readin' the Book".
fp: Ottawa Little Theatre, 1965.

D321. *The Heart Specialist.* London, Ont. Author, 1974. (Mimeographed).
1 act. 3m/2f.
A musical fantasy for young children about the surgeon who solves romantic entanglements at court with help from his "Abracadabrum Machine".

D322. "Little Monsters" in his *Six Plays for Children*. Hamilton and Saskatoon, School Publications & Specialties, 1958.
1 act. 7b/6g. Extras.
A group of children cure the loneliness and bitterness of a poor old blind man on Christmas by giving him a cake and remembering him in their thoughts.

D323. "The Love Potion" in his *Six Plays for Children*. Hamilton and Saskatoon, School Publications & Specialties, 1958.
1 act. 3b/2g.
The King's Magician prepares a love potion that will cause the army to fall in love with the enemy, ending war forever.
fp: Peterborough Children's Theatre, December 1956.

D324. *Midashasassesears*. Toronto, Playwrights Co-op, 1973.
1 act. 7m.
A children's play which involves King Midas, Apollo and Jupiter. An irreverent version of the old legend which explains why the bulrushes "whisper" in the wind.
fp: Peterborough Children's Theatre, 1962.

D325. "Nice Mice" in his *Six Plays for Children*. Hamilton and Saskatoon, School Publications & Specialties, 1958.
1 act. 14m or f.
A group of inventive mice, their numbers diminishing because of a hungry cat, decide to improve their lives by getting rid of the feline threat.

D326. *The Optimistic Dollar*. Ottawa, Ottawa Little Theatre Workshop, #14.
1 act. 4m/2f. Extras.
A farce in verse. Van Adrianazoon de Kupper finds that it is difficult to be wealthy and "saved" simultaneously. He eventually gives up and becomes a used-car salesman.
fp: Ottawa Little Theatre, 1959.

D327. *The Play Is The Thing, Tra La!*. Toronto, Playwrights Co-op, 1973 and in *Laomedon Review*, vol.2, #1, March 1976,
1 act. 5m/3f.
The Author has finished his masterpiece, but by the time the Agent, Producer, Directors and Stars are through with it, the play is good only to the Sweeper.

D328. "Spring Tea" in his *Six Plays for Children*. Hamilton and Saskatoon, School Publications & Specialties, 1958.
1 act. 6m/10f.
A group of girls dress up in their mothers' clothes, determined to have an elegant spring tea despite the lack of co-operation on the part of the boys.

D329. "Summit Conference" in *The Best Short Plays, 1960–1961*. Margaret Mayorga, ed. Boston, Beacon Press, 1961, and in his *Three One-Act Plays*. Toronto, Playwrights Co-op, 1975.
1 act. 2m/6f.
A beauty contest on Mount Olympus for the fairest of goddesses is the spark which begins the Trojan War.

D330. *Was She Sown or Was She Reaped?*. Toronto, Playwrights Co-op, 1973 and in his *Three One-Act Plays*. Toronto, Playwrights Co-op, 1975.
1 act. 2m/5f.
This melodramatic spoof gives the audience all the gossip, rumour and innuendo of the genre without any exchanges between the characters themselves. The plot: a widow with two daughters, both of whom have suitors. But, one suitor is father and the other suitor is brother to the girls.
p: Centennial Theatre Group, Harbourfront Theatre, Toronto, May 8, 1976.

D331. "Why Mice Leave Home" in his *Six Plays for Children*. Hamilton and Saskatoon, School Publications & Specialties, 1958.
1 act. 3m/1f.
A mouse runs into a lot of hard work attempting to get one small piece of cheese and decides to find a new home as a result.
fp: Peterborough Children's Theatre, April 1957.

CAMPBELL, Paddy 1944–

D332. *Chinook*. Toronto, Playwrights Co-op, 1973 and in *Chinook and Too Many Kings*, Toronto, Playwrights Co-op, 1977.
1 act. 3m/2f.
The audience gathers to hear the Old Man tell one of his famous stories only to discover that he has been kidnapped by Icewoman. Two children, Chinook and Starchild, set off to the rescue with their friend Rattle and the ensuing adventure turns into the story all came to hear.
fp: Arts Centre Company, Calgary, 1968.

D333. "Hoarse Muse" in *Popular Performance Plays in Canada* vol. 1. M. Wilson, ed. Toronto, Simon & Pierre, 1976.
2 acts. 7m/3f. Extras. Chorus.
A "musical play" about Bob Edwards, the outspoken editor of the *Calgary Eye-Opener* in the early 1900s. Edwards comes back to life at his funeral and re-enacts some of his past. Music by William Skolnik.
fp: Alberta Theatre Projects, Calgary, March 28, 1974.

D334. "Too Many Kings" in *Chinook and Too Many Kings*. Toronto, Playwrights Co-op, 1977.
1 act. 4m/1f.
Fudge, the assistant to the Master Story Maker Mendel, mixes up her master's magic conjuring three story kings at once. With the help of the audience, Mendel appeases the angry kings.
fp: Arts Centre Company, Calgary, 1969.

D335. "Under the Arch" in *Canadian Theatre Review*, #10, Spring 1976.
Many scenes. 33m/5f. Doubling.
A music hall presentation of Canadian history with glimpses of the Mounties, bootleggers, mail order brides, and a short melodrama depicting the arrival of "culture" in Calgary.
fp: Alberta Theatre Projects, March 6, 1972 as "The History Show".

CAMPBELL, Randy

D336. "The Quilt" in *York Theatre Journal,* #10, March 1975.
1 act. 6f.
In the Niagara peninsula circa 1860, a group of women gathered to make a wedding quilt reveal different responses to the narrowness of women's choices in a pioneer society.

CAMPBELL, Terry

D337. "Who Governs Canada" in *The Muse,* vol.2, 1964–1965.
1 scene. 5m.
A debate between Democrates, Credules and other characters about who really governs Canada.

CANALE, Raymond 1930–

D338. *The Jingo Ring.* Toronto, Playwrights Co-op, 1973 and in *The Factory Lab Anthology.* C. Brissenden, ed. Vancouver, Talonbooks, 1974.
1 act. 8m/1f.
Each year the Chief of Police of a poverty-stricken Mexican village orders his policeman to arrest someone. This event is disrupted when a stranger enters town and gives himself up. After that anything can happen, and it does.
fp: Factory Theatre Lab, Toronto, November 1971.

CANNON, Mona Kenney

D339. "Haliburton Farmer" in *The Disk,* A Magazine for Experimental Ideas, Toronto, Discus Press, (1935?).
1 act. 3m/2f.
A city-bred woman's spirit has been gradually eroded by the unprofitability of her family's Haliburton farm, its isolation and the unrelenting routine. Her discontent, incomprehensible to her husband and sons, verges on an insane despair that leads her sons to their deaths.

CAPSON, Louis 1944–

D340. *Everlasting Salvation Machine.* Toronto, Playwrights Co-op, 1972.
14 scenes. 8m/3f. Extras. Doubling.
When the massive Salvation Army Machine starts getting out of control, Captain Stephen Kessler tries to take it on single-handedly. Shades of 1984.
fp: Creation Two, St. Lawrence Centre for the Arts, Toronto, September 1972.

D341. *I Love You Billy Striker.* Toronto, Playwrights Co-op, 1972.
1 act. 5m/2f.
In a future where "all knowledge is quantitative", two members of the Royal Chemical Medical Police search the basement of the Museum of Public Freedoms for a runaway student.
fp: Creation Two, Toronto, 1971.

D342. *In Search of the Last Paradiddle.* Toronto, Playwrights Co-op, 1972, and in *Laomedon Review,* vol. 1, #2, April 1975.
1 act. 5m/2f.
The trial of "The Persons Jeremy Cline and Steven Kessler vs. The World" and other business of the World Council is presided over by Billy Striker, "the Perfect Number".
fp: Creation Two, Toronto, 1971.

D343. *Midway Priest.* Toronto, Playwrights Co-op, 1973.
47 scenes. 8m or f. Extras.
A priest/educator in the new country of Quebec goes into showbusiness against a background of political intrigue and "back-stabbing". The characters search for their new Quebecois identity.
fp: Creation Two, National Arts Centre, Ottawa, August 1972.

D344. *To Become a Drummer.* Toronto, Playwrights Co-op, 1972.
1 act. 6m/2f.
Episodic narrative of the early life of Billy Striker from artist into hero.
fp: Creation Two, Toronto, 1971.

D345. *The True North Blueprint.* A trilogy. Toronto, Playwrights Co-op, 1972.
see Part I: *To Become a Drummer.*
Part II: *I Love You Billy Striker.*
Part III: *In Search of the Last Paradiddle.*

CARD, Patricia

D346. *The Life of a Toy.* Toronto, Patricia Card Costumes, 1940.
1 act. 2m/2f.
A children's play set in a nursery. Through the conversation of her dolls, we learn that a little girl's collection of toys is about to be dispersed as she grows older and the circumstances in her life change.
p: Junior Drama Festival, Toronto, 1939.

CARD, Raymond William George 1893–

D347. *General Wolfe.* Toronto, Nelson, 1931 and in *Curtain Rising.* W.S. Milne, ed. Toronto, Longmans, Green, 1958.
1 act. 7m.
This play focuses on the last day in Wolfe's life, his plans for the conquest of Quebec, and his death in the pursuit of that victory.
p: The Chester Players, Theosophical Hall, Toronto, May 8, 1922.

D348. *The Mystery of Meaux; or, The Last Interlude of the Twenty Four Stone Statues of St. Etienne's.* Plays of the Month series. Rock Island, Illinois, Frederick Ingram, 1934.
1 act. 24m/4f/1b/1g. Extras.
A Christmas play set in the Cathedral of Meaux, 1280. The sacristan's children are trapped in the cathedral as its twenty four statues come to life to perform the Nativity story, the play within the play. The animation of the statues is the devil's work. However, a guardian angel intervenes to protect the children.
fp: Canadian Drama League, Deer Park United Church, Toronto, December 14, 1932.

CARLETON, John Louis 1861–1939

D349. *Coom-Na-Goppel.* Chicago, Dramatic Publishing, 1906.
5 acts. 13m/1f. Extras.
A young man's brother is accused of murder and diamonds are stolen in this play which deals with the problem of tenant-landlord rights: "Paternal shame and disgust flourishes" but the real murderer is found.

D350. *Hildebrand.* Saint John, N.B., Author, 1903.
5 acts. 18m/4f. Extras.
An historical drama concerning Henry IV's rebellion against the spiritual authority of Pope Gregory, the Hildebrand, in the matter of the king's divorce. Henry's corruption culminates in his attempt to have Gregory assassinated and to proclaim an Anti-Pope in his stead. The play concludes with his repentance at Canossa, following his excommunication by Gregory.

D351. *A Medieval Hun.* Boston, Cornhill, 1921 and Toronto, Goodchild, 1922.
5 acts. 16m/4f. Extras.
An historical drama based on the incidents that resulted in the repentance of Henry IV, king of Germany and Emperor of Rome, at Canossa, and the political and moral triumph of Pope Gregory, the Hildebrand.

More Sinned Against Than Sinning. See item C80.

CARMAN, Albert R.

D352. "Easter Week at Rome" in *Canadian Magazine,* vol. 32, April 1909.
1 scene. 6m/4f.
A group of tourists in Rome have a discussion on Italians in general and their religious practices in particular.

CARMAN, William Bliss 1861–1929 and Mary Perry King 1865–

D353. "Children of the Year" in their *Earth Deities and Other Rhythmic Masques.* New York, Mitchell Kennerley, 1914.
13m/13f.
A masque. The months of the year parade through the woods: each is a woman singing of her particular attributes.

D354. "Dance Diurnal" in their *Earth Deities and Other Rhythmic Masques.* New York, Mitchell Kennerley, 1914.
1 act. 1m/2f.
The progress of Day and Night.

D355. *Daughters of the Dawn.* New York, Mitchell Kennerley, 1913.
11 scenes. 12m/9f. Extras. Doubling.
"A lyrical pageant" in which nine immortal women are praised: Eve, Deborah, Balkis, Sappho, Izeyl, Mary, Zenobia, Jeanne d'Arc, and Vittoria Colonna.

D356. "Earth Deities" in their *Earth Deities and Other Rhythmic Masques.* New York, Mitchell Kennerley, 1913.
2m/9f. Chorus.
In this poetic masque, a student presents gifts to the Earth Deities, who appear before him.

D357. "Pas de Trois" in their *Earth Deities and Other Rhythmic Masques.* New York, Mitchell Kennerley, 1914.
2m/2f.
It is spring, the time of love, and the organ-grinder watches as Pierrot's two sweethearts each pull him a different way. They perform a lovers' dance, then all three go their separate ways.

CARRUTHERS, Charles Edwin

D358. "God-Forsaken" in *Six Canadian Plays.* H.A. Voaden, ed. Toronto, Copp Clark, 1930.
1 act. 5m/3f.
Mr. Bradley has died and because only a small funeral was held the family is ignored by its neighbours. But the eldest son, Rafe, fighting for the French Colonial Government, has been given a military funeral "like a king" and the family is again acceptable.
fp: Central High School of Commerce, Toronto, April 9, 1930.

CARSLEY, Sarah Elizabeth (Keatley) 1887–

D359. *Say What You Will.* Western Canada Theatre Conference. Edmonton, Dept. of Extension, University of Alberta, 1945.
1 act. 2m/4f.
A comedy about a young scientist who discovers a miracle drug and searches for a philanthropic businessman to market his discovery at cost.

CASEY, Frank J.

D360. "Original Child Bomb" in *Look Both Ways.* H. Voaden, ed. Toronto, Macmillan, 1975.
1 act. 7m/7f. Doubling.
"Open-stage adaptation of the poem 'Original Child Bomb' by Thomas Merton". The play is both a partisan documentary of the Hiroshima bombing based on the poem's "Points for Meditation" and an experiment in ensemble playing.
fp: St. Clair Secondary School, Sarnia, Ont., 1971, Collegiate Festival.

CASS-BEGGS, Barbara (Cass) 1904–

D361. *A Festival Pageant.* Waterloo, Ont., Waterloo Music, 1964.
Many scenes. Multiple roles.
A pageant "concerned with carols, Christmas and other kinds of Winter Festivals" exploring the folk and ritual origins of Christmas.

CATTLEY, Elizabeth

D362. "Down to the Sea" in *New Voices, Canadian University Writing of 1956.* Earle Birney *et al.* eds. Toronto, Dent. 1956.
2 scenes. 3m/3f.
A fisherman's wife and her mother-in-law are drawn closer together through their fear that one of their men may have been drowned in the storm.

CATTO, Marion

D363. "My Eyes Were Opened" in *Pathfinder,* March 1938.
1 act.
A religious play. Issue unavailable for annotation.

CECIL-SMITH, E.

D363A. *Eight Men Speak.* See **RYAN, Oscar.**

CERVELLO, Santo 1949–

D364. "Gordon Paul McCray" in his *Stephen Truscott. Pierre LaPorte. Gordon Paul McCray.* Smithers, B.C., Northern Comfort Communications, 1976.
1 act. 2m/1f/1g.
Gordon McCray dies as the result of another boy's jealousy — a pitiful death in squalid circumstances. The day of Gordon's death is dispassionately described, by Gordon, his brother Ernie and their sister Fay; their mother is past caring, absorbed in her memories.
fp: CBC radio, Calgary.

D365. "Pierre LaPorte. A Play for the French Canadian" in his *Stephen Truscott. Pierre LaPorte. Gordon Paul McCray.* Smithers, B.C., Northern Comfort Communications, 1976.
1 act. 3m.
"What happened to this man while he was being held captive, no one really knows except the FLQ." A prose poem that infuses a political situation with the concrete details of sensations and feelings.
fp: Chilliwack Players' Guild at B.C. One Act Finals, June 1975. CBC radio.

D366. "Stephen Truscott" in his *Stephen Truscott. Pierre LaPorte. Gordon Paul McCray.* Smithers, B.C., Northern Comfort Communications, 1976.
1 act. 1m/1f.
The play, a prose poem, provides a hypothetical reconstruction of the well-known Stephen Truscott case: not Peter/Stephen but a stranger, a "shadow", is responsible for the girl's murder and the "voices" of the authorities are responsible for the destruction of Peter/Stephen.
fp: Erewhon Players, Abbotsford, B.C. CBC radio.

CHADWICK, Vivienne Charlton

D367. *The Invisible Line.* Toronto, French, 1960.
1 act. 2m/3f.
Mona Law, recuperating from illness and the sudden disappearance of her fiance, is spending the summer near Sidney, B.C. A stranger who is running from the RCMP comes to the cottage and the whole truth about her fiance is brought to light.

CHADWICK, William R. 1934–

D368. *Dead Heat.* Toronto, Playwrights Co-op, 1974.
1 act. 2m/1f.
A play about the nature of competition. A hospitalized army officer, confined to a wheelchair, builds his life around preparing for a wheelchair Olympiad. His illusions are shattered when a fellow invalid, a former Olympic walker, accepts his challenge to a race around the hospital grounds.
fp: Drama Centre's Studio Theatre, Toronto, May 1973.

D369. *Statues.* Toronto, Playwrights Co-op, 1973.
1 act. 3m/1f.
A pair of unsuspecting tourists, admiring a square full of statues, attract the attention of a couple of "wide boys". The touts offer their services as photographers but seem to have something more menacing in mind.
fp: Drama Centre's Studio Theatre, Toronto, May 1973.

CHALMERS, Penny. See KEMP, Penny.

CHAMBERS, Jack 1931–1978

D370. "Toronto — London — One Way — Gray Coach Lines" in *Alphabet,* #8, December 1965–March 1966.
1 act. 3m/1f. Extras.
A conversation between a small town couple as they return from the big city.

CHAPMAN, Bernice.

D370A. "To What Purpose". See **BOISSONNEAULT, Lorette.**

CHAPMAN, Doris

D371. *Midnight and Christmas Eve.* Toronto, Tower Printing, (1932?).
1 act. 3b/2g.
On Christmas Eve, Lucien travels to see the Christ-child and in answer to his prayers his sister Angela is able to walk again.
fp: Christmas, 1932.

CHARITON, Morris

D372. *Conversations With Shakespeare.* N.p., Author, 1969.
1 act. Multiple roles.
Ordinary people are presented in poetic conversation with Shakespeare about life.

CHARLTON, Dick

D373. *Joe Christ.* Halifax, Dramatists Co-op, 1978.
2 acts. 16m/3f.
A modern adaptation of the story of Christ in which Joe Lemmings, a carpenter in a dockyard, leaves his work with six co-workers to preach.

D374. *Miss Pebble's Retreat.* Halifax, Dramatists Co-op, 1978.
1 act. 3m/3f.
Two ministers who arrive at a lonely Scottish retreat where a million pounds has been hidden practise a strange brand of theology.

CHISHOLM, Thomas

D375. *Dialogues on Canadian History.* Toronto, Best, 1916.
"For use in schools, colleges, dramatic societies, parlor entertainments, etc.". A collection of 14 short one act plays presenting "the bare facts of Canadian history".

D376. *Dialogues on English History.* Toronto, William Briggs, 1903.
Thirty dialogues "for use in schools, colleges, dramatic and literary societies, social gatherings, parlor entertainments, etc.".

CHUDLEY, Ron 1937–

D377. *After Abraham.* Vancouver, Talonbooks, 1978.
2 acts. 15m/1f.
On the Plains of Abraham, the ghosts of Wolfe and Montcalm discuss the future of Quebec.
fp: Bastion Theatre, Victoria, Oct. 7, 1977.

D378. *The Life of Jackson Piper, Episode 2.* Agincourt, Ont., Book Society, 1967.
7m/3f.
A television play about a high-school student accused of cheating on an exam who devises a way of clearing his name.

CHURCH, Elizabeth Jerrold

D379. "The Turn of the Road" in *One Act Plays by Canadian Authors.* Montreal, Canadian Authors' Association, 1926.
1 act. 3m/1f.
A girl finds what she thinks is evidence of her late father's involvement in fraud. After her suicide, it is discovered that the signature in question was forged.

CLARK, Isabel Squires

D380. *The Christmas Tree Forest (In the Great Walled Country).* Toronto, French, 1959.
1 act. 11m/1f/5b/6g. Extras.
A children's Christmas play adapted from the story by Raymond Alden, with a moral concerning the consequences of selfishness.

CLARK, Sally

D381. "Two Together" in *York Theatre Journal,* #6, March 1974.
1 act. 2f.
A short play in which "two old women . . . joined together on one side, forming one large woman with two heads" engage in absurdly logical dialogue. With silly verbal rivalries they attempt to disguise their isolation and loneliness.

CLARK, Stanley E. 1927–

D382. "Rewrite" in his *Rewrite and Frosted Icing.* Toronto, Playwrights Co-op, 1975.
1 act. 3m/2f.
A successful, philandering playwright turns up in his ex-wife's apartment and wreaks havoc with her would-be cynicism about him.
fp: Stage West, Mimico Library Theatre, Ont., Aug. 22, 1975.

D383. "Frosted Icing" in his *Rewrite and Frosted Icing.* Toronto, Playwrights Co-op, 1975.
1 act. 1m/2f.
Two charming old ladies reminisce about their past lives and about the romantic gentleman caller who visits them once a year. Are their memories dreams or reality?
fp: Stage West, Mimico Library Theatre, Ont., Aug. 22, 1975.

CLARKE, George Herbert 1873–

D384. "The Toll Gate" in his *Halt and Parley and Other Poems.* Toronto, Macmillan, 1934 and in *A Book of Plays.* H.A. Voaden, ed. Toronto, Macmillan, 1935 and in *Look Both Ways.* H.A. Voaden, ed. Toronto, Macmillan, 1975.
1 act. 3m or f.
"A Morality Play" based on his poem "Halt and Parley". For the first time, Body and Soul are separated by the Gatekeeper, Death.
fp: Convocation Hall, Queen's University, Kingston, Ont., August 9, 1934.

CLARKE, Canon Wilfred John 1896–1965

D385. "A Plea of Judas" in his *Two One Act Plays: St. Paul's Defence and A Plea of Judas.* Fredericton, Usbell, 1950.
1 act. 1m/2f.
Judas betrays Jesus for need of money to pay debts, thinking that the Son of God cannot be harmed by the mortal Pilate or the High Priests.

D386. "St. Paul's Defence" in his *Two One Act Plays: St. Paul's Defence and A Plea of Judas.* Fredericton, Usbell, 1950.
1 act. 7m/2f.
St. Paul defends himself to the Roman governor against the High Priests' charges of heresy and conspiracy.

CLAVELL, James

D387. *Countdown to Armageddon $E = MC^2$.* Vancouver, New Play Centre, (197?).
3 acts. 14m. Extras.
A day and a crisis in the lives of men manning one of the D.E.W. line posts.
fp: Vancouver Playhouse Theatre Company, November 1966.

CLAXTON, Norah Mary. See HOLLAND, Norah Mary.

CLAY, Charles

D388. "The Kingdom of the Sun" in *Canadian Red Cross Junior,* September 1936.
1 act. 10b/9g.
A health play dramatizing the virtues of fresh air, plain food and good hours over disease and bad disposition.

CLAYTON, R.D. See FINCH, Robert Duer Claydon.

CLINTON, Robert

D389. *Chautauqua*. Regina, Sask., Department of Culture and Youth, 1974.
9 scenes. 3m/3f. Doubling.
An historical look at a small community in Saskatchewan during the 1920s. The play provides a wide variety of characters and experiences for a vivid picture of a rural community in Canada's past.
fp: Saskatchewan Summer Players, 1973.

CLOUGH, George E. (Mohican, pseud.)

D390. "The Striker" in *Echoes,* #92, June 1923.
1 act. 6m/1f/1b/1g.
A white-collar worker helps his miner brother-in-law, who is involved in labour violence, and proves the point that those who work with their heads and those who work with their hands share "fifty-fifty".

CLUTE, Doris

D391. *Life Burns On.* Western Canada Theatre Conference. Edmonton, Dept. of Extension, University of Alberta, 1945.
1 act. 1m/3f/1b/1g.
A drama in which two sisters finally manage to accept the death of loved ones and find happiness in the present.

COATES, Carol

D392. *The Jade Heart.* New York, Junior League of America, 1946.
1 act. 8m/2f.
"A fantasy in the Chinese manner". A young princess uses a pair of magic ear-rings to wish for a peaceful and loving husband, rather than the warrior whom her parents arrange for her to marry.

COHEN, Leonard Norman 1934–

D393. "A Man Was Killed". See **LAYTON, Irving.**

D394. "The New Step" in his *Flowers for Hitler.* Toronto, McClelland and Stewart, 1964 and in his *Leonard Cohen: Selected Poems 1956-1968.* Toronto, McClelland & Stewart, 1968.
1 act. 1m/3f.
"A Ballet-Drama". Mary is freed from her search for eternal beauty when she learns of an ugly charity collector's happiness and of her beautiful roommate's disappointment in love.
fp: The Land of the Young, Ottawa, November 1972.

COHEN, Maxwell Charles 1926–

D395. *Joker in the Pack.* Agincourt, Ont., Book Society, 1969.
1 act. 9m/2f.
A radio play about the class clown who is given one month to "clean up his act" or he will be expelled. He finds this difficult though and ends up in a row with other members of his club.

D396. *The Member from Trois-Rivieres.* Montreal, Canadian Jewish Congress, 1959.
1 act. 17m/2f. Extras. Doubling.
A play written for the National Bicentenary of Canadian Jewry 1759-1959 about the difficulties during the election of Ezechiel Hart, the first Jew to be elected to office in Canada.

COLLEY, Peter 1949–

D397. "The Donnellys" in *Look Both Ways.* H. Voaden, ed. Toronto, Macmillan, 1975 ("mini-play") and in *Popular Performance Plays in Canada* vol. 1. M. Wilson, ed. Toronto, Simon & Pierre, 1976.
2 acts. 21m/6f. Extras.
"A drama with music" which traces the history of the legendary Donnelly family from their involvement in the Protestant-Catholic feud in Ireland through the events that led to their brutal murder near Lucan, Ontario in 1880. Music by Berthold Carriere.
fp: Theatre London, London, Ont., April 12, 1974.

COLQUHOUN, Kathryn E.

D398. *A Run for His Money.* Toronto, Robinson Plays, 1937.
1 act. 3m/3f.
A comedy set on a frog farm in which a nephew tries to outwit his millionaire uncle in order to keep him from marrying and to inherit his fortune.

COMEAU, Madeline

D399. "Rehearsal II" in *Callboard,* vol.24, #3, Fall 1977.
1 scene. 2m/1f. Extras.
"A play for Jody Briggs". A brief comic sketch about the director of a community theatre at a rehearsal.

CONACHER, William M.

D400. "In County Mayo" in *Queen's Quarterly,* vol.40, #4, Winter 1933.
1 act. 8m/2f.
This play, which ends in a surprise revelation about one of the "enemy", pokes fun at the IRA of 1916.

CONE, Tom 1947–

D401. "Beautiful Tigers" in *3 Plays by Tom Cone.* Vancouver, Pulp Press, 1976.
1 act. 6m/2f.
Picasso directs a group of artists in recreating a living picture of Rousseau's "The Dream" as a surprise present for Henri Rousseau.
fp: New Play Centre at Vancouver East Cultural Centre, du Maurier Festival, May 1, 1976. CBC radio, Feb. 6, 1977.

D402. "Cubistique" in *West Coast Plays*. C. Brissenden, ed. Vancouver-Toronto, New Play Centre-Fineglow, 1975 and in his *3 Plays by Tom Cone*. Vancouver, Pulp Press, 1976.
1 act. 2f.
Annie, an American coquette, and Francis, a sophisticated Parisian, have not seen each other for twelve years. Their luncheon meeting in 1920s Paris forces them to confront themselves as well as each other as they reminisce and act out their past.
fp: New Play Centre, Vancouver, du Maurier Festival, April 26, 1974.

D403. "Herringbone" in *3 Plays by Tom Cone*. Vancouver, Pulp Press, 1976.
1 act. 1m.
George Herringbone, in a solo night club act, explains how he became a performer.
fp: New Play Centre, Vancouver, du Maurier Festival, April 30, 1975.

D404. *The Organizer*. Vancouver, New Play Centre, 1974.
1 act. 4m.
A charity organizer meets a blind man in a bar for an amusing but harrowing encounter.
fp: New Play Centre, Troupe, Vancouver, March 1974.

D404A. *Stargazing*. Toronto, Playwrights Co-op, 1978.
1 act. 2m/2f.
Two couples explore their relationships while searching the evening skies for falling stars.
fp: Third Stage, Stratford Festival, August 1978.

D405. *There*. Toronto, Playwrights Co-op, 1973.
1 act. 2m.
Two middle-aged men, Ben and Alan, reminisce about their sexual experiences with the same woman on the same isolated beach.
fp: Simon Fraser University, Vancouver, 1972.

D406. "Veils" in *Performing Arts in Canada*, vol.11, #1, Spring 1974.
2 acts. 1m/1f.
A man and woman, 70 years of age, have been married and operating a dress-making shop for 48 years. Edith is immersed in reliving the beginning of her adult life; Irving at first is impatient and uninterested but becomes caught up in the memories, struggling to maintain the counterpoint of his own perspective on them.
fp: Playwrights' Workshop, Montreal, May 1974.

D407. *Whisper to Mendelsohn*. Vancouver, New Play Centre, 1975.
3 acts. 5m/3f.
A group of people meet for dinner in a closed subway station to celebrate the anniversary of their mysterious meeting a year before.
fp: New Play Centre-West Coast Actors, Vancouver, Sept. 11, 1975.

CONEYBEARE, Arthur Rodney 1928–

D408. "An Incident at Hornsdale Park" in *Four Short Plays by Rod Coneybeare*. Toronto. Author, (197–?). (Mimeographed).
1 act. 2m/1f.
A comedy concerned with sexual mores and motives, set in the future. A government agency exists to provide partners and places for "post-marital affairs"; Molly and Ed in their several years of marriage have never availed themselves of the service and are requested to appear for an interview to determine why.

D409. "The Man Who Wanted to Sing Like Sinatra" in *Four Short Plays by Rod Coneybeare*. Toronto, Author, (197–?). (Mimeographed).
1 act. 3m/2f.
Four successfully middle-class people are gathered at a Muskoka resort hotel to arrange a civilized divorce. But Jeff, the central character in the proceedings, is distracted by a bizarre science fiction occurrence. Meanwhile, his wife and mistress reach an amicable agreement to share him equally.

D410. "A Nice Girl Like You" in *Four Short Plays by Rod Coneybeare*. Toronto, Author, (197–?). (Mimeographed.)
1 act. 2m/1f.
A sexual comedy. Betty, an actress, is involved with two aspiring playwrights; she is the mistress of Jack, a successful, middle-aged businessman who supports her, and the lover of Bob, a 20-year-old "drop-out" who is supported by her.

D411. "Where's That Happy Ending?" in *Four Short Plays by Rod Coneybeare*. Toronto, Author, (197–?). (Mimeographed.)
1 act. 5m/1f.
A very old and very rich gentleman named Rufus Emery is entertained by scenarios created for him by paid performers; he himself participates in the fantasized recreation of his life.

CONKLE, E.P.

D412. "Lavender Gloves" in *Canada on Stage*. S. Richards, ed. Toronto, Clarke, Irwin, 1960.
1 act. 4m/3f.
A melodramatic and comic macabre mystery set in a remote English inn. Inspector Gassaway foils the plot of two religious fanatics who are looking for the perfect spheroid sinister head to offer to their Master.

CONNOR, Fredric Jarrett 1920–

D412A. *Galarian*. By Fredric Jarrett. Lake Guindon, P.Q., Hart Severance, 1953.
2 acts. 3m/3f. Extras.
A poetic drama about Galarian and his various loves set in the City of Lovers.

D413. *The States*. By Fredric Jarrett (pseud.). Shawbridge, P.Q., Hart Severance, 1949.
7 scenes. 7m/1f. Chorus.
A "poetic drama" dealing with the problems of maintaining peace between rival states, one a peaceful free state, the other an aggressive slave state.

CONOVER, Dora Smith

D414. "Turns Home Again" in *Canadian Stage, Screen and Studio*, vol.1, #4, March 1937.
1 act. 2m/2f.
Ten years after W.W. I, an invalid father dies believing his son, once listed as missing in action, has finally returned home.
fp: Canadian Radio Corporation, 1936.

D415. "Winds of Life" in *Six Canadian Plays*. H. Voaden, ed. Toronto, Copp Clark, 1930.
1 act. 3m/1f.
Concerns the personal battle of a man "drying up from the wind and the sun and the long, long cold" and his son who belongs to the wilderness.
fp: Central High School of Commerce, April 9, 1930.

COOK, Greg

D416. *Bonfire on the Beach*. Halifax, Dramatists Co-op, 1977.
1 act. 3f/2m.
A family waits through a heavy storm, hoping against hope that the boat their father was on hasn't been lost.
fp: Dominion Drama Festival, 1965.

D417. *The Prodigal Son*. Halifax, Dramatists Co-op, 1977.
1 act. 2f/1m.
A son waits and struggles by his mother's deathbed.
fp: Workshop, 1965.

COOK, Michael 1933–

D418. "Colour the Flesh the Colour of Dust" in *A Collection of Canadian Plays* vol.1. Rolf Kalman, ed. Toronto, Simon & Pierre, 1972.
2 acts. 11m/5f. Extras.
The outpost of St. John's is captured by the French, then recaptured by the English. The change of flag has little effect on merchants, common folk, whores or the fog.
fp: Neptune Theatre Company, National Arts Centre, Ottawa, Oct. 1972. CBC radio, St. John's, 1973.

D419. "The Gayden Chronicles" in *Canadian Theatre Review*, #13, Winter 1977.
3 acts. 9m/4f.
As William Gayden awaits execution for mutiny and murder, he recreates his past life and the events which led to his sentence of death. Changes are being made in the British naval system, but for Gayden they are too late.
fp: (Workshop), Festival Lennoxville, Lennoxville, Quebec, 1977.

D420. "The Head, Guts and Sound Bone Dance" in *Canadian Theatre Review*, #1, Winter 1974 and *The Head, Guts and Sound Bone Dance*. Newfoundland, Breakwater, 1974 and in his *Three Plays*. Newfoundland, Breakwater, 1977.
2 acts. 6m/1f.
Skipper Pete and his son-in-law John spend every day preparing for the return of the thousands of fish to the sea, the return of their old livelihood. John's wife tries to pry her husband away from Pete, tries to make him understand that they are living in a world of memories. John finally leaves when jarred by the reality of a drowning he could have prevented.
fp: Arts and Culture Centre, St. John's, Newfoundland, March 4, 1973. CBC TV "Opening Night", 1974.

D421. *Jacob's Wake.* Vancouver, Talonbooks, 1975.
2 acts. 5m/2f.
The Blackburn family is gathered for Easter, just as always. The three sons, Brad, Wayne and Alonzo have all gone separate ways but are alike in their corruption. Winston, the father of this brood, spends his time in a drunken rage, belittling all around him and successfully destroying the careful facades of his sons. As a storm gathers and eventually overpowers the house, so too are the family members overpowered by memories of son, brother, lover and daughter long since dead.
fp: Festival Lennoxville, Lennoxville, Quebec, July 11, 1975.

D422. "On the Rim of the Curve" in his *Three Plays.* Newfoundland, Breakwater, 1977.
1 act. 14m/3f. Extras.
A play about the destruction of the Beothuk Indians of Newfoundland by the white colonists.
fp: Newfoundland Drama Festival, 1977. CBC radio "Tuesday Night", 1977.

D423. "Quiller" in his *Quiller and Tiln.* Toronto, Playwrights Co-op, 1975 and in his *Tiln and Other Plays.* Vancouver, Talonbooks, 1976 and in *The Blasty Bough.* Clyde Rose, ed. Newfoundland, Breakwater, 1976 and in *Cues and Entrances.* Henry Beissel, ed. Toronto, Gage, 1977.
1 act. 2f/1m.
Quiller, aged 65, lives alone and carries on a running conversation with God trying to figure out what his life has been about. He tells of his life as a fisherman, a wife who died and a friend who was burned alive.
fp: Memorial University, St. John's, Newfoundland, April 1975.

D424. "Therese's Creed" in *Tiln and Other Plays.* Vancouver, Talonbooks, 1976 and in *Three Plays.* Newfoundland, Breakwater, 1977.
1 act. 1f.
The thoughts and memories of a middle-aged Newfoundland widow as she sees the changing world in the actions of her eight children and recollects her own simpler yet harder life as wife of a poor fisherman.
fp: Centaur Theatre, Montreal, 1977.

D425. "Tiln" in *Encounter: Canadian Drama in Four Media.* E. Benson, ed. Toronto, Methuen, 1973 and in his *Quiller and Tiln.* Toronto, Playwrights Co-op, 1975 and in his *Tiln and Other Plays.* Vancouver, Talonbooks, 1976 and in *Transitions I: Short Plays.* Edward Peck, ed. Vancouver, Commcept Publishing, 1978.
1 act. 2m.
An absurdist play about two lighthouse keepers stationed in a lighthouse for the winter. One of them dies but the other continues talking to him.
fp: CBC radio, Aug. 29, 1971.

COOKE, Britton B. –1923

D426. "Gloriana" in *The Canadian Magazine,* vol.46, #5, March 1916.
1 act. 1m/2f.
Through the conversation of Hilda and Pomona, backwoods midwives, we learn about the marriage of Gloriana and the preacher Simon Hadley who are unsuited to pioneer life, and later, of Gloriana's death.

D427. "The Sickle" in *Canadian Magazine,* #46, December 1915.
1 act. 3m/1f.
When a murder is committed in a small town, a foreigner, Denis Lammond, is accused. However, the real murderer is the young son of the jury foreman.
fp: Arts and Letters Club, Toronto, Feb. 6, 1924.

D428. "The Translation of John Snaith" in *Canadian Plays from Hart House Theatre* vol.1. V. Massey, ed. Toronto, Macmillan, 1926.
2 acts. 2m/2f.
This play presents the life philosophy of people in a small northern Ontario town, their feelings about the war and its effects on their lives.
fp: Hart House Theatre, Toronto, March 29, 1923.

COOMBS, Francis Lovell 1876–

D429. *One Day's Fun.* Ottawa, Canadian General Council, The Boy Scouts Association, (191–?).
2 acts. 1m/1f/7b. Extras.
A comic and educational entertainment by and for Boy Scouts.

COOPER, Douglas

D430. *Widows Learn Fast.* Toronto, Robinson Plays, 1950.
3 acts. 2m/5f.
A "farcical" comedy. A widow sets out to captivate a friend's bachelor brother on a bet. The brother discovers the plot through a misplaced diary and sets up a counter-strategy. Further complications arise when another woman with the same name arrives on the scene.

CORBETT, Maurice William 1900–

D431. *Lucky Dollars.* Rock Is., Ill., Fred K. Ingram, 1934.
3 acts. 5m/5f.
Jimmy Drake, a young man out of work, wins a large amount of money in a sweepstakes and tries to keep it a secret because he cannot abide "fair weather friends". He also wants to "test" the woman he loves.
fp: St. Jude's Dramaticians, St. Jude's Church Hall, Winnipeg, 1933.

D432. *Rolling Stone.* Dayton, Ohio, Paine Publishing, 1931.
3 acts. 3m/3f.
Tommy has been wandering around the world searching for some meaning in life. His reputation as an unsettled character makes Grace's parents uneasy when he returns to town and starts going out with her again. They would prefer her to marry Fred, an up-and-coming young man.
fp: Winnipeg Suburban Players, Scottish Hall, East Kildonan, Manitoba, 1930.

D433. *Woman Called "X".* Franklin, Ohio, Eldridge, 1951 and Toronto, Robinson Plays, 1951.
3 acts. 3m/4f.
A young man is hired to temporarily replace "Mrs. Jenkins", an advice columnist for *The Era*. He becomes entangled in events involving a missing will, a masquerade ball, a beautiful and mysterious woman and a romance.
fp: York Theatre, Victoria, B.C., April 1953.

CORNELL, Mary

D434. "The Fur Coat" in *Echoes,* March 1935.
1 act. 3m/2f.
A farm wife turns down her sister's offer of a gift of money and a used fur coat after learning that her brother-in-law made his fortune by selling short on the falling wheat prices which ruined her husband.

D435. "I Thank You" in *Canadian Forum,* vol.12, #144, Sept. 1932.
2 scenes. 3m/2f.
A play dealing with the idea of sharing. A dictator interferes when a man offers coats and blankets to people who are standing on the deck freezing.

COULTER, John William 1888–

D436. *The Crime of Louis Riel.* Toronto, Playwrights Co-op, 1976.
2 acts. 12m/2f. Extras. Doubling.
A recreation of the events leading to the arrest, trial and conviction of Louis Riel. The play explores the political, social and religious tenor of the times; the reasons behind Riel's Provisional Government and his purpose in confronting the British; the attitude of the Prime Minister and his council.
fp: Dominion Drama Festival, Grand Theatre, London, Ontario, 1966.

D437. "Dark Days of Ancient Hate" in *God's Ulsterman.* Toronto, Author, 1971. (Mimeographed).
1 act. 6m/1f. Extras.
In a Catholic church in Drogheda, Cromwell causes the murder of two priests for attempting to hide the Blessed Sacrament.

D438. *Deirdre.* Toronto, Macmillan, 1965. Souvenir Edition, 1966.
3 acts. 7m/2f. Extras.
"The revised version of Deirdre of the Sorrows". Music by Healey Willan.

D439. *Deirdre of the Sorrows.* Toronto, Macmillan, 1944.
3 acts. 8m/2f. Extras.
Libretto for an opera. This is the classic tale of Deirdre, the foundling girl, of those who love her, and of the fates which had been prophesied for them. The time is the beginning of the Christian era. The place is Ullah and Alba (Ulster and Scotland). Music by Healey Willan.
fp: Radio version by the Northern Ireland station of the BBC. CBC radio, 1946.

D440. *The Drums Are Out.* Irish Drama Series, vol.6. Wm. J. Feeney, ed. Chicago, DePaul University Press, 1971.
3 acts. 4m/2f.
A Protestant Ulster constable's life is complicated by his daughter's marriage to an IRA leader.
fp: Abbey Theatre, Dublin, July 12, 1948. Dominion Drama Festival, 1950. CBC radio "Wednesday Night", July 11, 1951. CBC TV "FM Theatre", May 4, 1969.

D441. *The Family Portrait.* Toronto, Macmillan, 1937 and in his *The House in the Quiet Glen and The Family Portrait.* Toronto, Macmillan, 1937.
3 acts. 8m/4f.
An aspiring young playwright writes an exposé about his family which becomes a hit in London. There is dissent in the family, aggravated by the jealous older brother, but it is resolved in the end.
fp: BBC Belfast Radio, 1935. CBC radio, Toronto, 1938 as "Stars of Brickfield Street". Hart House Theatre, Toronto, 1938. CBC TV "G.M. Theatre", March 6, 1956 as "The Sponger".

D442. *François Bigot.* Toronto, Hounslow Press, 1978.
2 acts. 12m/4f.
"A rediscovery in dramatic form of the fall of Quebec" in which an interviewer questions the contemporaries of François Bigot, the corrupt last Intendant of New France, about the causes for the conquest of Quebec in 1759.

D443. *Holy Manhattan.* Toronto, Author, 1940. (Mimeographed).
3 acts. 7m/4f.
A nostalgic depiction of the loneliness of an exiled Irishman in New York for his native country.
fp: Arts and Letters Club, Toronto, April 24, 1940. CBC radio, 1941, as "This Is My Country". CBC TV, 1955, as "Come Back to Erin".

D444. *The House in the Quiet Glen.* Toronto, Macmillan, 1937 and in his *The House in the Quiet Glen and The Family Portrait.* Toronto, Macmillan, 1937.
1 act. 3m/2f.
Mr. and Mrs. McCann arrange for Sally to marry Robert, not realizing she loves his son Hughie. All ends well when Robert gives his blessing to the young people.
fp: Toronto Masquers, Margaret Eaton Hall, Toronto, Feb. 1937. CBC radio "Theatre Time", Vancouver, July 22, 1940.

D445. "Red Hand" in *God's Ulsterman.* Toronto, Author, 1971. (Mimeographed).
2 acts. 7m/3f. Extras.
Liz McNeagh rebels against the bigotry of her minister father, an Ian Paisley type character, but dies in the violence resulting from student protests against naming a new campus building "Cromwell House".
fp: CBC radio, Toronto, Feb. 9, 1974.

D446. *Riel.* Toronto, Ryerson, 1962 and Hamilton, Ont., Cromlech Press, 1972.
Part 1: 15m/1f. Extras. Part 2: 21m/2f. Extras.
The action centres on the Riel Rebellion and is divided into two periods: 1869–70 and 1885–86, including Riel's execution. The issue is whether Riel is a hero attempting to lead an oppressed people to freedom or a religious maniac.
fp: New Play Society, Toronto, 1950. CBC radio "Wednesday Night", May 9, 1951. CBC TV "General Motors Presents", April 23, 1961.

D447. *This Glittering Dust* (A Capful of Pennies.) Toronto, Author, 1967. (Mimeographed).
3 acts. 8m/4f. Doubling.
A "portrait of an actor based on the life of Edmund Kean".
fp: Aries Productions, Central Library Theatre, Toronto, March 22, 1967 as "A Capful of Pennies".

D448. *Transit Through Fire.* Toronto, Macmillan, 1942.
5m/1f. Chorus.
Libretto for an opera by Healey Willan. "An Odyssey of 1942". A young soldier spending his leave with his wife in a ski cabin, recalls in reverie scenes from their lives. Although the idealism of youth is shattered, they have found "the clue to the good life in the community".
fp: Radio version, CBC, March 8, 1942.

D449. *The Trial of Louis Riel.* Ottawa, Oberon, 1968.
1 act. 39m/2f. Extras.
A dramatized transcript of the trial of Louis Riel. The defence attempted to prove Riel insane since justifying armed rebellion for the redress of grievances "is like trying the government".
fp: Saskatchewan House, Regina, June 1967.

D450. *While I Live.* Toronto, Author, 1971. (Mimeographed).
2 acts. 6m/4f. Extras.
The elderly Sara Gregor struggles in vain to prevent a highway from being built across her property and disrupting her life.
fp: CBC radio, Toronto, 1951.

COUPAL, Clare Foley

D451. "Cold Flame" in *Callboard*, vol.22, #6, Sept. 1975.
1 act. 5f/1m.
A concert pianist competing for a scholarship at a music festival discovers her missing fiance married to another woman and the sponsor of the festival.

D452. *The Empty Cornucopia.* Ottawa, Ottawa Little Theatre Workshop, #19.
1 act. 4m/3f.
Inez's jealous attitude towards an ornament which belonged to Jim's first wife causes problems when Jim refuses to talk about it.
fp: Dansk Amator Theater Samvirke, Copenhagen, Denmark, 1962.

D453. *A Penny's Worth of Power.* Ottawa, Ottawa Little Theatre Workshop, #45.
1 act. 4m/1f.
M. Normedin, an old Quebec farmer, believes only in the "state of Quebec" and has been ostracized by his children: Rene who wishes to buy farmland and young Denise who will move to Sarnia, Ont. when she marries.

D454. *Press Release.* Ottawa, Ottawa Little Theatre Workshop, #38.
1 act. 3m/3f.
A comedy. When a false engagement announcement is printed in the newspaper, it causes unforeseen difficulties for all involved.
fp: Dept. of National Defence Recreation Association, R.A. Festival, Clark Memorial Centre, Ottawa, April 1, 1963.

D455. *Time Running Out.* Ottawa, Ottawa Little Theatre Workshop, #40.
1 act. 2m/3f/2b/1g.
A comedy in which the old adage "familiarity breeds contempt" is shown to be true of people in a family situation.
fp: New Play Society, Museum Theatre, Toronto, Oct. 26, 1962.

D456. *The Valentine.* Ottawa, Ottawa Little Theatre Workshop, #58.
1 act. 6f/1m.
After forty years, two former lovers are reunited at the Hope Lodge and Geriatric Centre on Valentine's Day.

D457. *When the Bough Bends.* Ottawa, Ottawa Little Theatre Workshop, #5.
1 act. 3m/2f.
Jack Pelton is having great difficulty obtaining money to help his fiancee, whose father has become mentally ill due to alcoholism. The secret is divulged in the end but Jack's family comes to the rescue and a new sense of solidarity and unselfishness is discovered in each member.
fp: Ottawa Little Theatre, Ottawa, Nov. 18, 1949.

COWAN, John Bruce 1882–

D458. *Canuck.* Vancouver, Rose, Cowan & Latta, 1931.
3 acts. 5m/4f.
Ruth decides to marry a Canadian farmer despite the objections of her mother who wants her to marry an English financier.

D459. *Number Five Cheyne Row.* Vancouver, Rose, Cowan & Latta, 1950.
4 acts. 7m/7f.
This play concerns the life of Jane Carlyle, wife of the writer Thomas Carlyle, as she entertained the literary elite of 19th century London.

COX, Janet

D460. "The Coward" in *Acadia Athenaeum,* vol. 61, #2, December 1935.
1 scene. 3m.
During W.W. I, a young man who has given in once to fear proves that he was no coward by sacrificing himself for a friend.

COYNE, Virginia. See KNIGHT, Virginia C.

CRAW, Evelyn

D461. *The Christmas Ship.* Toronto, Educational Publishing, (192–?).
1 act. 4b/1g.
A well-off family which has temporarily lost its wealth learns from a poor family that love, not money, matters most.

D462. *Wanted — A Radio or The Christmas Gift.* Toronto, Educational Publishing, (192–?).
3 scenes. 2m/1f/3b/1g.
A family gets a much wanted radio for Christmas and shares Christmas with a new Canadian family from Norway.

CRAWFORD, Blanche

D463. "A Christmas Story" in *Cape Breton Mirror,* vol.2, #1, December 1952.
1 scene. 1m/2f. Extras.
A verse rendering of the Christmas story by a mother to her two children on Christmas Eve.

D464. "Fine Feathers" in *Cape Breton Mirror*, vol.1, #12, November 1952.
1 scene. 3f.
A play about women helping each other in which a girl becomes a successful model to earn money for her sister's operation.

CRAWFORD, M. Myrtle

D465. "Christmas Music" in *Educational Review*, vol. 51, #4, Dec. 1936.
1 scene. 4b/5g. Chorus.
A brief "Christmas exercise" celebrating Christmas.

D466. "Nativity Play" in *Educational Review*, vol.52, #4, Dec. 1937 and vol. 64, #2, Dec. 1949.
2 scenes. 10m/1f. Extras.
A mixture of scriptural passages and Christmas songs presenting the traditional story of the Nativity.

CRISP, Jack H. 1923–

D467. "A Wife in the Hand" in *Popular Performance Plays in Canada* vol.1. M. Wilson, ed. Toronto, Simon & Pierre, 1976.
3 acts. 3m/4f.
For his interview as Man of the Year, James Henderson borrows the use of his nephew's cottage. James arrives at Jeff's cottage early and Jeff has not time to get his girlfriend, Valerie, out of the cottage before Norman Drummond, the reporter, arrives.
fp: Montreal International Theatre at International Theatre, Hemisfair '68 in San Antonio, Texas, June 21, 1968.

CROCKER, Brian C.

D468. *Explosion.* Halifax, Dramatists Co-op, 1977.
2 acts. 5m/5f. Doubling.
A chronicle of the days of the Halifax Explosion of 1917 based on recollections of survivors, court transcripts and contemporary newspaper reports.
fp: Seaweed Theatre, Halifax, Dec. 1977.

CROSS, Eric William Blake 1904–

D469. *The Patriots.* Toronto, Ryerson, 1955.
3 acts. 13m/6f. Extras.
The play presents the dilemma of Robert Baldwin, the Upper Canada moderate, during and after the Rebellion of 1837.
fp: Queen's University Drama Guild, Kingston, Ont.

CROSSLAND, Jackie 1943– and Rudie Lavalle

D470. *Rinse Cycle.* Vancouver, Talonbooks, 1972.
12 scenes. 9m/6f.
A 1950s nostalgia play concerning the daily lives of the high school greaser gang who "hang out" with Al, their leader who "knows where it's at".
fp: Troupe, Intermedia Hall, Vancouver, March 16, 1972.

CROTHERS, Tom and John Madden

D471. *Speak for Life.* Saint John, New Brunswick, Author, 1965. (Mimeographed).
3 acts. 19m/4f. Extras. Doubling.
After a nuclear war has destroyed southern Ontario, two dozen survivors near a secret government fallout shelter try to convince a screening board why they should be chosen to help start a new society.

CROWELL, Edwin 1853–1926

D472. *Chevrose, the Hermit of Cape Sable.* Yarmouth, N.S., Yarmouth Herald, 1925.
1 act. 10m/1f. Extras.
British soldiers carry out their orders to deport the Acadians despite their own feelings about the situation.

CULJAK, John

D473. *Plus One Minus One Equals.* Halifax, Dramatists Co-op, 1977.
2 acts. 3m/3f.
An absurdist play about four people under the influence of a domineering woman who decide to trap an unsuspecting arrival at their weekly ritual.

D474. *The Rain Falls Harder.* Halifax, Dramatists Co-op, 1977.
17 scenes. 18m/4f. Doubling.
A surrealistic play focusing on three rapes and a rapist.

D475. *The Resurrection of Philip Jerome Michaels: Or How Can I Rest In Peace?.*
Halifax, Dramatists Co-op, 1977 and Toronto, Playwrights Co-op, 1978.
1 act. 2m.
A lonely urbanite signs over his body to a mortician who represents the forces which beautify death as a release from life's meaninglessness.
fp: La Mama Experimental Theatre Company, New York, October 1966.

CUNNINGHAM, Jack 1941–

D476. *Wisp in the Wind.* New York, French, 1965.
1 act. 1m/1f.
A man becomes deeply disturbed by the story a strange young woman tells him. She runs off without finishing it.
fp: Sir George Williams University, Canadian University Drama Festival, Montreal, Feb. 1965. CBC TV "Shoestring Theatre", 1965.

DAFOE, Christopher

D477. *The Frog Galliard.* Toronto, Playwrights Co-op, 1978.
1 act. 5m/1f.
An embittered Elizabethan poet who wants to die in peace is not amused when Shakespeare arrives to choreograph a magnificent death scene.
fp: New Play Centre at the Vancouver East Cultural Centre, May 14, 1977.

DAKIN, Laurence Bradford 1904–

D478. "The Golden Age" in his *A Promethean Trilogy*. Toronto, Dent, 1962.
3 acts. 2m/1f. Extras.
Prometheus' spirit has led Saturn to realize the goodness of man and Saturn thus brings in the Golden Age and declares man immortal, freeing him from subservience to the gods.

D479. *Ireneo: A Tragedy in Three Acts*. Portland, Maine, Falmouth, 1936.
3 acts. 8m/2f. Extras.
"A Tragedy" of forbidden love between a Jewish girl and a Roman Christian is played against a background of Jewish unrest against Roman rule in first century Syria.

D480. "The Liberator" in his *A Promethean Trilogy*. Toronto, Dent, 1962.
3 acts. 4m/3f. Extras.
The spirit of Prometheus assists Saturn in regaining his heavenly throne from the usurper, Jupiter.

D481. *Marco Polo*. Portland, Maine, Falmouth, 1946.
4 acts. 12m/3f. Extras.
A verse drama about the love between Marco Polo and Golden Bells, the Kubla Khan's daughter.

D482. *A Promethean Trilogy*. Toronto, Dent, 1962.
See *Prometheus, the Fire Giver*. "The Liberator", "The Golden Age".

D483. *Prometheus, the Fire Giver*. Paris, Obelisk Press, 1938 and as "The Firegiver" in his *A Promethean Trilogy*. Toronto, Dent, 1962.
3 acts. 1m/4f. Extras.
Urged by the spirits and aided by Minerva, Prometheus steals the fire from Olympus and gives it to man on earth.

D484. *Pyramus and Thisbe*. Portland, Maine, Falmouth, 1939.
3 acts. 10m/3f.
The legend of the lovers who kill themselves through error and for love is mixed with the Biblical story of the warning on the wall to Babylon.

D485. *Tancred, Prince of Salerno*. Toronto, Dent, 1948.
4 acts. 10m/2f. Extras.
A princess of medieval Salerno loves a common knight. The Duke of Capua also loves the princess Ghismonda and seeks revenge on the lady and her lover by turning the prince Tancred, her father, against her.

DALRYMPLE, Andrew Angus 1937–

D486. *The Hottest Bet in Town*. Toronto, Playwrights Co-op, 1978.
3 acts. 14m/3f.
The revised all-comedy version of his *Quiet Day In Belfast*.
fp: Theatre Workshop at the Theatre Royal, London, February 1978.

D487. *Quiet Day in Belfast*. Toronto, Playwrights Co-op, 1973.
3 acts. 11m/2f.
A betting shop is used by an IRA man and the BBC during a Protestant parade in Belfast. As a result, two men are killed and the shop is besieged by the police. Irish irony and whimsy.
fp: Tarragon Theatre, Toronto, May 1973.

DALTON, Kathleen

D488. "A Matter of Curious Chemistry" in *Rubaboo 1*. Toronto, Gage, 1962.
1 act. 3b/1g.
"A play to be performed by children for children". Jerry's formula enlarges and animates a proton, an electron, a neutron, a clown doll and a cat doll.

DANARD, Joan

D489. *The Interview*. Edmonton, Alberta Dept. of Culture, 1970.
1 act. 2f.
Constance Gilchrist meets her stepson's fiancee one afternoon shortly before the wedding. Each woman's facade cracks slightly during the encounter.

DANIELS, Dan Samuel 1921–

D490. *The Audition*. Outremont, P.Q., Author, 1967. (Mimeographed).
3 acts. 4m/2f.
The young actor, auditioning for the Director's "part", is unwittingly participating in an exchange, both ritually and actually — the aging Director habitually renews and sustains himself by assuming the youth and strength of the young actors who innocently hope to succeed him.
p: Western Quebec Regional D.D.F., March – April 1965.

D491. *The Inmates*. Montreal, Alternative Probes Presentations, 1971.
2 acts. 4m/3f.
"A sensual charade of the ridiculous" making social and sexual comment. Attacks daily life in the Western world through exaggeration, black humour and direct confrontation with the audience.
p: Revue Theatre, Montreal, 1968.

DARBY, Paul

D492. "Love Mime #5" in *Acta*, vol. 92, #2, Dec. 1967.
1 act. 1m/1f.
A man and a woman discuss the happy and sad side of love.

DARBY, Ray 1912–

D493. "Mad Flight" in *On Stage*. Herman Voaden, ed. Toronto, Macmillan, 1945.
1 act. 2m/1f.
A radio play in which Bill Gordon relates the story of the strange disappearance of Myra Lane and Paul Hanover in the hope that someone will believe him.
fp: CBC radio, Winnipeg, Aug. 5, 1943.

DAULT, Gary Michael

D494. "An Evening on Innell and Auden and Avedon" in *Saturday Night*, vol.92, #9, Nov. 1977.
1 scene. 3m.
A "dialogue on portraiture". The author and Reg Innell discuss the merits of Innell's portrait of Auden and the art of portrait photography.

DAVIDSON, Ida Marion

D495. *The Acadian Tragedy.* Winnipeg, Manitoba Text Book Bureau, 1932.
4 acts. 20m/4f/1b/2g. Extras.
A play based on Longfellow's historical poem *Evangeline,* which deals with the British deportation of the Acadians during the Seven Years' War.

D496. *Alexander Mackenzie.* Winnipeg, Manitoba Text Book Bureau, 1932.
3 acts. 11m. Extras.
A history play intended for production by juveniles. The play follows the journey of Alexander Mackenzie as he sets out overland across Canada to reach the Pacific Ocean which he does on July 22, 1793.

D497. "The Capture of Quebec" in her *The Capture of Quebec and Madeline de Vercheres.* Winnipeg, Manitoba Text Book Bureau, (1932?).
3 acts. 15m.
A children's play. General Wolfe's plan to take Quebec is successful.

D498. *Gentlemen Adventurers.* Winnipeg, Manitoba Text Book Bureau, 1932.
3 acts. 21m.
A children's play about Radisson and Groseilliers, the two coureurs-de-bois who were cheated by the French government and in retaliation helped the English found the Hudson Bay Company.

D499. "Laura Secord" in her *Sir Isaac Brock and Laura Secord.* Winnipeg, Manitoba Text Book Bureau, (1932?).
3 acts. 8m/2f/1b/1g.
A play for children. Laura Secord, learning of the American plan to attack Beaver Dam, journeys to the Canadian headquarters to warn Lt. Fitzgibbon.

D500. *Lord Selkirk.* Winnipeg, Manitoba Text Book Bureau, 1932.
5 acts. 34m/6f. Extras.
Concerns the importance of Lord Selkirk's establishment of the Red River Settlement in the early 1800s. The bitter struggle between Lord Selkirk and the North West Fur Company is the central issue.

D501. "Madeline de Vercheres" in her *The Capture of Quebec and Madeline de Vercheres.* Winnipeg, Manitoba Text Book Bureau, (1932?).
2 acts. 4m/3f/4b. Extras.
A children's play. The courage and endurance of young Madeline, daughter of the Seigneur de Vercheres, saves the settlers of the seigneury from an Iroquois attack. Music and lyrics selected and translated by J. Murray Gibbon.

D502. "Sir Isaac Brock" in her *Sir Isaac Brock and Laura Secord.* Winnipeg, Manitoba Text Book Bureau, (1932?).
3 acts. 10m/1b.
A play for children. General Brock prepares for the invasion of the American forces led by General Van Rensellaer and is killed leading the Canadians at Queenston Heights.

DAVIDSON, True 1901–

D503. *Canada in Story and Song.* Toronto, Dent, 1927.
1 act. 66b/18g. Extras.
A children's pageant describing the founding and growth of Canada.

D504. *La Claire Fontaine.* Toronto, Author, n.d. (Mimeographed).
1 act. 4f.
Three brides shipped to Quebec during the intendancy of Talon are happily married after surmounting several obstacles.
fp: Playmakers and the Victoria College Alumnae, Toronto.

DAVIES, William Robertson 1913–

D505. *At My Heart's Core.* Toronto, Clarke Irwin, 1950 and in his *At My Heart's Core and Overlaid.* Toronto, Clarke Irwin, 1966.
3 acts. 3m/5f.
Although the play in part concerns the Rebellion of 1837, its chief concern is people who suppress their inner dreams. Dreams of love, science and art would not seem possible in the wilderness, but the protagonists reject advice to leave.
fp: Peterborough Summer Theatre, 1950. CBC TV "Theatre", Nov. 10, 1953.

D506. "At the Gates of the Righteous" in his *Eros at Breakfast and Other Plays.* Toronto, Clarke Irwin, 1949 and in his *Four Favourite Plays.* Toronto, Clarke Irwin, 1968.
1 act. 4m/2f.
The misconception that all robbers are against the sacred laws of society is proved false when two young aspiring revolutionaries try to join a band of highwaymen in Upper Canada.

D507. **Et al.** *The Centennial Play.* Ottawa, Centennial Commission, (1967?).
2 acts. 13–25m or f. 11–25b and g.
A wry look at 100 years of Canada and Canadians. Regional sketches are presented in revue style within a plot involving the "spirit" of Canada and his sidekick. "The Eastern Scene" by Arthur Murphy; "The Quebec Scene" by Yves Theriault; "Prologue", "Epilogue", and "The Ontario Scene" by Robertson Davies; "The Prairie Scene" by W.O. Mitchell and "British Columbia Scene" by Eric Nicol.
fp: Academy Theatre, Lindsay, Ont., Oct. 6, 1966.

D508. "A Dialogue On the State of Theatre in Canada" in *Royal Commission Studies. A Selection of Essays Prepared for the Royal Commission on National Development in the Arts, Letters and Sciences.* Ottawa, Edmond Cloutier, 1951 and in *Canadian Theatre Review,* #5, Winter 1975.
1 act. 2m.
A discussion between Lovewitt and Trueman written for the Massey Commission about "what the Government of Canada can do about the theatre in Canada".

D509. "Eros at Breakfast" in his *Eros at Breakfast and Other Plays.* Toronto, Clarke Irwin, 1949 and in his *Four Favourite Plays.* Toronto, Clarke Irwin, 1968.
1 act. 4m/1f.
"A psychosomatic interlude" which explores the relationship between body and soul. Takes place inside Mr. P.S. who falls in love and upsets the daily routine of the internal departments of heart, liver, soul, and intelligence.
p: Dominion Drama Festival, 1948.

D510. *Fortune My Foe.* Toronto, Clarke Irwin, 1949 and in his *Four Favourite Plays.* Toronto, Clarke Irwin, 1968.
3 acts. 7m/3f.
The play presents the artist's and intellectual's struggle for recognition in a culturally barren Canadian society, and raises the question whether it would be better to leave the wasteland. Szabo, the puppeteer, replies, "This is my country now and I am not afraid of it . . . I shall be all right".
fp: International Players, Kingston, Ont., 1948. CBC radio "Stage" series, Oct. 17, 1948. CBC TV "Theatre", May 7, 1953.

D511. "General Confession" in his *Hunting Stuart and Other Plays.* Toronto, New Press, 1972.
3 acts. 5m/2f.
A comedy. Casanova, a librarian in his old age, conjures up Voltaire, Cagliostro and the Ideal Beloved (all aspects of himself), in order to judge his life.

D512. "Hope Deferred" in his *Eros at Breakfast and Other Plays.* Toronto, Clarke Irwin, 1949.
1 act. 3m/1f.
The clergy blocks Count Frontenac's proposal to stage Moliere's *Tartuffe,* using the talents of a young Indian actress. To have her art appreciated the young lady has to go to Paris. Hope that art will come to Canada must be deferred.
fp: Montreal Repertory Theatre.

D513. "Hunting Stuart" in his *Hunting Stuart and Other Plays.* Toronto, New Press, 1972.
3 acts. 3m/4f.
A comedy in which a minor civil servant in Ottawa is discovered to be a direct descendant of Bonnie Prince Charlie. With the aid of a new drug, he relives episodes from the life of his famous ancestor, to the consternation of his family.
fp: Crest Theatre, Toronto, Nov. 22, 1955.

D514. *A Jig for the Gypsy.* Toronto, Clarke Irwin, 1954.
3 acts. 10m/2f.
Welsh folklore links politics and fortune-telling. A gypsy tells a politician's fortune and is threatened with many difficulties if she does not withdraw her prophecy. She is defiant to the end, eventually joining forces, through marriage, with Conjuror Jones.
fp: Crest Theatre, Toronto, 1954.

D515. "King Phoenix" in his *Hunting Stuart and Other Plays.* Toronto, New Press, 1972.
3 acts. 6m/2f. Extras.
A speculative historical play about King Cole and intrigues against his life. Davies offers his explanation for why King Cole came down through the ages as "a merry old soul".
p: North Toronto Theatre Guild, 1950.

D516. *Love and Libel.* New York, Studio Duplicating, 1960. (Mimeographed).
3 acts. 8m/6f. Extras.
Tyrone Guthrie's production of the comedy adapted from Robertson Davies' novel *Leaven of Malice* about love and intrigue in a small town.
fp: Theatre Guild, Martin Beck Theatre, New York, Dec. 7, 1960. Royal Alexandra Theatre, Toronto.

D517. *A Masque of Aesop.* Toronto, Clarke Irwin, 1952.
1 act. 26m. Extras.
Aesop is brought before Apollo to defend his fables. Apollo views three fables in the form of short plays. He rejects the mob's demand for Aesop's death, but does rebuke the storyteller. "Perfect wisdom is an attribute of the gods alone."
fp: Upper Canada College, Toronto, May 2, 1952.

D518. *A Masque of Mr. Punch.* Toronto, Oxford University Press, 1963.
1 act. 15m/6f. Extras. Doubling.
Mr. Punch performs his traditional show for representatives of theatre in Canada. T.V. producers, the press, critics, two playwrights and a director of the Stratford Festival all fail to comprehend the performance and try to change it. In the end, Punch emerges victorious.
fp: Upper Canada College, Toronto, 1962.

D519. *Overlaid.* Toronto, French, 1948 and in his *Eros at Breakfast and Other Plays.* Toronto, Clarke Irwin, 1949 and in *Curtain Rising.* W.S. Milne, ed. Toronto, Longmans, Green, 1958 and in *Canada on Stage.* S. Richards, ed. Toronto, Clarke Irwin, 1960 and in his *At My Heart's Core and Overlaid.* Toronto, Clarke Irwin, 1966 and in *Encounter: Canadian Drama in Four Media.* E. Benson, ed. Toronto, Methuen, 1973 and in *Ten Canadian Short Plays.* J. Stevens, ed. New York, Dell, 1975 and in *The Artist in Canadian Literature.* Lionel Wilson, ed. Toronto, Macmillan, 1976 and in *Transitions I: Short Plays.* Edward Peck, ed. Vancouver, Commcept Publishing, 1978.
1 act. 2m/1f.
This comedy is concerned with "intellectual and cultural starvation". Pop, an "op'ry" buff, unexpectedly receives a large amount of money and decides to live extravagantly in New York. His daughter considers this selfish and he gives her the money to buy a gigantic tombstone for the family plot.
p: CBC TV "First Person", Dec. 14, 1960, CBC radio "Stage" series, March 6, 1964.

D520. *Question Time.* Toronto, Macmillan, 1975.
2 acts. 10m/5f. Extras.
Peter Macadam, Prime Minister of Canada, is the sole survivor of a plane crash in the Arctic. While his body lies in a shock-induced coma, the inner man wanders through the Land Unknown to answer the question, will Macadam live or die. The public statesman is separated from the private man in a final debate in the House of Commons, which explores such topics as: Who is the Prime Minister and what does he represent? What is Canada?
fp: Toronto Arts Productions, St. Lawrence Centre, Feb. 25, 1975.

D521. "The Voice of the People" in his *Eros at Breakfast and Other Plays.* Toronto, Clarke Irwin, 1949 and in his *Four Favourite Plays.* Toronto, Clarke Irwin, 1968 and *The Voice of the People.* Agincourt, Ont., Book Society, 1968 and in *Upstage and Down.* D.P. McGarity, ed. Toronto, Macmillan, 1968 and in *Cues and Entrances.* H. Beissel, ed. Toronto, Gage, 1977.
1 act. 2m/2f.
Shorty Morton never does much thinking or writing, but he decides to write a rebuttal to a letter in the editor's column of the local weekly. The result shakes Shorty's uninformed and inflated ego.

DAVIS, Rae 1927–

D522. *Daily News from the Whole World.* A Trilogy of Assemblages for the Theatre. London, Ont., Author, (1965?). (Mimeographed).
3 acts. 14m/5f. Extras.
Three short multi-media plays, "Transistor", "Projector" and "Dissector", concerned with the authority and authoritarianism of images, visual and aural, in a media world. They show modern urban people confronted with a barrage of simultaneous and multiplied images and impressions and regulations.
fp: Campus Players, London, Ontario, July 1965.

D523. *Five Fugues for Isaac Newton.* Toronto, Playwright Co-op, 1972.
1 act. 6m/5f.
The play consists of five separate but related pieces using dance, projections, monologue, improvisation, a scene from Act III of *Ghosts,* an electronic score. The unifying motif is light.

D524. *Muffler.* Toronto, Playwrights Co-op, 1972.
1 act. 1m/2f.
An idle conversation among three co-workers at noon hour is explored at different levels through the use of slides, film and tape.

D525. "Simple Activities" in *Region VII,* June 1964.
1 act. Multiple roles.
A brief scenario for an abstract performance piece.

DAVIS, W.B.

D526. "Down by the Sea" in *Acadia Athenaeum,* vol.55, #7, May 1929.
1 act. 3m/1f.
A brief play about a young rum-runner who is ambushed by the coast guard but is rescued from the sea by his father, a retired ship's captain.

DAWSON, F.

D527. "The Tempest" in *Acadia Athenaeum,* vol.63, #5, March 1938.
1 scene. 2m/2f. Extras.
A love-crazed young man is driven to murder his fiancee during a storm.

DAY, Stacey Biswas 1927–

D528. *By the Waters of Babylon.* Montreal, Three Star Printing, 1966.
3 acts. 4m/1f. Extras.
An allegorical play, partially in verse, concerning the life and judgement of Wainright, "a student of man".

D529. *The Music Box.* Montreal, Cultural and Educational Productions, 1967.
3 acts. 7m/2f/1g. Extras.
A famous surgeon has dedicated his life to his work and in the process has ruined the lives of his son and his wife.

DEAN, Mary Morgan

D530. *The Metaphysical White Cat.* New York, Shakespeare Press, 1912.
5 acts. 4m/5f. Extras.
A children's play in which young Jacko inherits his parents' kingdom after freeing a princess who had been turned into a white cat by a wicked fairy.
p: Amateurs, All Saints' Parish Hall, Toronto, April 29, 1920.

DECOTEAU, L. See WILSON, Lawrence Maurice.

DeFELICE, James 1940–

D531. "The Elixir" in *First Stage*, vol.3, #1, Winter 1963-64 and *The Elixir.* Toronto, Playwrights Co-op, 1973.
3 scenes, 6m/2f. Extras.
In Medieval Spain, a fool and his master set out to sell the elixir of life to the citizenry of a pious village. As he is about to leave with the money taken from the citizens, the charlatan is confronted by a strange man who provides an unexpected twist in the climax.
fp: University of Alberta Studio Theatre, Feb. 23, 1973.

D532. *Fools and Masters.* Toronto, Playwrights Co-op, 1975.
1 act. 5m.
Italy, 1930s. The Magnificent Salto is preparing for his next performance, diving from a height of 60 feet into two feet of water. However, the city has decreed new safety precautions for circus performers. In Salto's case, the tank will be filled with 12 feet of water. For Salto, this means certain death, for he cannot swim.
fp: Factory Theatre Lab, Toronto, April 22, 1975 as *The Jumper.*

D533. *Take Me Where the Water's Warm.* Toronto, Playwrights Co-op, 1978.
3 acts. 5m/3f.
A contemporary comedy set on Vancouver Island about a young man fleeing from the altar who gets caught up in a tangle over love and idealism.
fp: Playwrights Workshop, Saidye Bronfman Centre, Montreal, October, 1977.

de la ROCHE, Mazo Louise 1879–1961

D534. "Come True" in *One Act Plays by Canadian Authors.* Montreal, Canadian Authors' Association, 1926, and *Come True.* Toronto, Macmillan, 1927 and in her *Low Life and Other Plays.* Toronto, Macmillan, 1929 and Boston, Little, Brown, 1929.
1 act. 5m/2f.
An old man in a home for the aged meets his sweetheart of forty years before.
fp: Hart House Theatre, Toronto, May 16, 1927.

D535. "Low Life" in *Echoes,* #100, June 1925 and *Low Life.* Toronto, Macmillan, 1925 and in *One Act Plays by Canadian Authors.* Montreal, Canadian Authors' Association, 1926 and *Low Life.* Boston, Little, Brown, 1929 and in her *Low Life and Other Plays.* Toronto, Macmillan, 1929 and Boston, Little, Brown, 1929 and in *A Book of Plays.* Herman Voaden, ed. Toronto, Macmillan, 1935 and in *Transitions I: Short Plays.* Edward Peck, ed. Vancouver, Commcept Publishing, 1978.
1 act. 2m/1f.
Mrs. Benn, who objects to supporting her husband's impoverished friend Linton, finally relents because his gentlemanly manners are a good influence on her daughter.
fp: Trinity Players, Trinity Memorial Hall, Montreal, May 14, 1925.

D536. *Return of the Emigrant.* Boston, Little, Brown, 1929 and in her *Low Life and Other Plays.* Toronto, Macmillan, 1929 and Boston, Little, Brown, 1929.
1 act. 3f.
Maggie anxiously awaits her sister's arrival from America, little expecting that though she is gaining a sister, she is losing a daughter.
fp: Hart House Theatre, Toronto, March 12, 1928.

D537. *Whiteoaks.* London, Macmillan, 1936 and Boston, Little, Brown, 1936.
3 acts. 7m/4f.
The members of the Whiteoaks family struggle for the favour of the family matriarch, Adeline, a woman of immense wealth. The artistic black sheep of the family inherits her fortune.
fp: Little Theatre, The Adelphi, London, April 13, 1936. H.M. Theatre, Montreal, Feb. 23, 1938.

del GRANDE, Louis 1942–

D538. *42 Seconds from Broadway.* Toronto, Playwrights Co-op, 1973 and New York, French, 1973.
2 acts. 11m/5f.
A revised version of Maybe We Could Get Some Bach.
fp: Playhouse Theatre, New York, 1973.

D539. *Maybe We Could Get Some Bach.* Toronto, Playwrights Co-op, 1972.
9 scenes. 12m/5f.
A comedy about two young people who decide to share an apartment in New York in the late '50s. John thinks he is "a little bit fruity" but Robin is determined to start "a meaningful relationship".
fp: Factory Theatre Lab, Toronto, 1972.

D540. *So Who's Goldberg?.* Toronto, Playwrights Co-op, 1972 and in *Now In Paperback.* C. Brissenden, ed. Toronto, Fineglow Plays, 1973.
1 act. 2m.
A comedy in which two men, one a pianist and the other a drifter, talk about their lives and their sexual habits.
fp: Factory Theatre Lab, Toronto, Feb. 1973.

DEMPSTER, Marianna

D541. *The Box of Music.* Halifax, Dramatists Co-op, 1978.
1 act. 4m/3f.
A fantasy for children set in the Swiss mountains.

D542. *A Song for Sara.* Halifax, Dramatists Co-op, 1977.
1 act. 4m/2f.
A lonely lady in her sixties with a married daughter decides to advertise for a husband.
p: Stellarton, N.S., April 1978.

DENISON, Merill 1893–1975

D543. "Alexander MacKenzie" in his *Henry Hudson and Other Plays.* Toronto, Ryerson, 1931.
1 act. 14m.
A radio play about the explorer Alexander MacKenzie and his overland journey through Canada's vast West to the Pacific in 1793.
fp: CNRM radio, Montreal, April 23, 1931.

D544. *An American Father Talks to His Son.* New York, Council Against Intolerance In America, 1939.
1 act. 2m/2b.
A radio play recalling the American libertarian tradition and warning against the rise of religious and racial bigotry.
fp: Columbia Broadcasting System, July 1, 1939.

D545. "Balm" in *Canadian Plays from Hart House Theatre* vol.1. V. Massey, ed. Toronto, Macmillan, 1926.
1 act. 3f.
Sara, who lives with Uminie in a run-down boarding house, wants to adopt a child. As both are very old, a social worker refuses her request and suggests that instead Sara go to a home for the aged. In a futile gesture of independence Sara expells the social worker and rejects society as unjust.
fp: Hart House Theatre, Toronto, Aug. 1, 1923.

D546. "Brothers in Arms" in his *The Unheroic North.* Toronto, McClelland & Stewart, 1923 and *Brothers in Arms.* New York, French, 1923 and in *Twenty-Five Short Plays.* Frank Shay, ed. New York, Appleton, 1925 and in *Canadian Plays from Hart House Theatre* vol.1. Vincent Massey, ed. Toronto, Macmillan, 1926 and in *A Book of Plays.* Herman Voaden, ed. Toronto, Macmillan, 1935 and in *On Stage: Plays for School and Community.* Herman Voaden, ed. Toronto, Macmillan, 1945 and in *Brothers in Arms.* Toronto, French, 1948 and in *Nobody Waved Goodbye and Other Plays.* Herman Voaden, ed. Toronto, Macmillan, 1966 and in *Mugwump Canadian* by Dick MacDonald. Montreal, Content Publishing, 1973 and in *Ten Canadian Short Plays.* John Stevens, ed. New York, Dell, 1975.
1 act. 3m/1f.
Major Brown and his wife are in the north and must return to the city quickly but their driver is on a deer hunt. After an exasperating discussion with Syd, another backwoodsman, the Major learns Syd could have taken him but did not offer to do so because he was not asked.
fp: Hart House Theatre, Toronto, April 5, 1921. CBC radio "Wednesday Night", March 9, 1955.

D547. "The First Christmas" in *The Canadian Home Journal,* Dec. 31, 1931.
An earlier version of *On Christmas Night.*
fp: NBC radio, New York, 1931.

D548. "From Their Own Place" in his *The Unheroic North*. Toronto, McClelland & Stewart, 1923.
1 act. 5m/1f.
Larry and Harriet Stedman are city people on winter vacation in the backwoods. They have been swindled many times by the local people, including their caretaker. Enlisting the aid of the game warden, the Stedmans get the furs (which the backwoodsmen had been trying to sell to them for exhorbitant prices) for nothing.
fp: Arts & Letters Players, Toronto, April 25, 1922.

D549. *Haven of the Spirit*. New York, Dramatists Play Service, 1939.
1 act. 13m/1f. Extras.
This play is concerned with the right of religious freedom in Providence Plantation founded by Roger Williams, following the arrival of the Quakers, Mary Dyer and her son.

D550. "Henry Hudson" in his *Henry Hudson and Other Plays*. Toronto, Ryerson, 1931.
1 act. 7m. Extras.
A radio play concerning Hudson's belief in a northwest passage and his failure to discover it. He, his son, and the loyal members of the crew die when mutineers set them adrift with few provisions.
fp: CNRM radio, Montreal, Jan. 22, 1931.

D551. "Laura Secord" in his *Henry Hudson and Other Plays*. Toronto, Ryerson, 1931.
1 act. 14m/2f.
A radio play about the role Laura Secord played in warning the British Commander Fitzgibbon of a secret American attack on Beaver Dam during the War of 1812.
fp: CNRM radio, Montreal, March 25, 1931.

D552. "Marsh Hay" in his *The Unheroic North*. Toronto, McClelland & Stewart, 1923 and in *A Collection of Canadian Plays* vol.3. R. Kalman, ed. Toronto, Simon & Pierre, 1974.
4 acts. 8m/4f. Extras.
John and Lena Serang lead a difficult life in the backwoods. They do not love themselves, each other, or the children. Their daughter Tess has already left home. Sarilin is pregnant and deliberately miscarries. Hope is aroused by a new point of view, but also miscarries and all is the way it was.
fp: Hart House Theatre, Toronto, March 1974.

D553. "Montcalm" in his *Henry Hudson and Other Plays*. Toronto, Ryerson, 1931.
1 act. 25m.
A radio play concerning Montcalm's defense of Quebec when it was under siege by the English commanded by Wolfe.
fp: CNRM radio, Montreal, May 7, 1931.

D554. *On Christmas Night*. New York, French, 1934.
1 act. 8m/1f. Extras.
A radio play about Christ's birth told in music, song and poetry.
fp: NBC radio, New York, 1931.

D555. "Pierre Radisson" in his *Henry Hudson and Other Plays*. Toronto, Ryerson, 1931.
1 act. 12m/1f/2b.
A radio play in which Pierre Radisson recounts to the king and court of England some of his more dangerous adventures in Canada.
fp: CNRM radio, Montreal, April 16, 1931.

D556. *The Prizewinner.* New York, Appleton, 1928.
1 act. 9m/3f.
Ed of Rawling's Rolling Road Show is having a popularity contest in which each person who buys one cake of soap receives one vote. The contest rekindles the feud between two families. Justice comes when Ed's bankroll is stolen by a half-wit he had refused to pay for work done.
p: Hart House Theatre, Toronto, Feb. 28, 1928.

D557. "Seven Oaks" in his *Henry Hudson and Other Plays.* Toronto, Ryerson, 1931 and in *Mugwump Canadian* by Dick MacDonald. Montreal, Content Publishing, 1973.
1 act. 12m/1f. Extras.
A radio play about the massacre of Governor Semple and some of his followers by the Bois Brules led by Cuthbert Grant in June 1816 at Fort Douglas and the larger fur trade war between the Hudson Bay Company and the Northwest Company.
fp: CNRM radio, Montreal, Feb. 26, 1931.

D558. *The U.S. vs Susan B. Anthony.* New York, Dramatists Play Service, 1941.
1 act. 10m/1f.
Susan B. Anthony is on trial for voting in the election of November, 1872. Her crime — being a woman.

D559. "The Weather Breeder" in his *The Unheroic North.* Toronto, McClelland & Stewart, 1923 and in *Canadian Plays from Hart House Theatre* vol.1. V. Massey, ed. Toronto, Macmillan, 1926 and in *Fifty More Contemporary One-Act Plays.* Frank Shay, ed. New York, Appleton, 1928 and in *Curtain Rising.* W.S. Milne, ed. Toronto, Longmans, Green, 1958.
1 act. 4m/1f.
John Hawley is sure that beautiful weather breeds storms and rejoices when one occurs because it proves him right, even though it appears his crop has been ruined. However, the storm is brief, the harvest is not ruined, and John becomes sour again.
fp: Hart House Theatre, Toronto, April 21, 1924.

DesBARRES, Frederick William Wallet 1867–

D560. *The Song of Songs.* Saenville, Tribune Press, 1953.
5 acts. 1m/1f. Extras. Chorus.
A short adaptation from the Bible "arranged as a lyrical drama by F.W. DesBarres. Mount Allison University faculty seminar, Jan. 14, 1953".

DEVERELL, Rex 1941–

D561. *Boiler Room Suite.* Toronto, Playwrights Co-op, 1978 and Vancouver, Talonbooks, 1978.
2 acts. 2m/1f.
A comedy-drama about a couple of Skid Row winos who have taken shelter from winter in the basement of a derelict hotel.
fp: Globe Theatre, Regina, Jan. 21, 1977.

D562. *The Copetown City Kite Crisis.* Toronto, Playwrights Co-op, 1973.
3 scenes. 3m/4f. Extras.
A children's play about a small town with a famous kite factory. The town's people have to choose between prosperity or pollution.
fp: Globe Theatre, Regina, 1973–74 season.

D563. *The Invitation.* Toronto, Religion and Theatre Council, 1966.
1 act. 1m/1f.
An old couple talk about their telephone which they never use and for which they never receive any bills. The man receives a party invitation and is stabbed with a letter opener by the old woman.
fp: Robinson Memorial Theatre, McMaster University, Hamilton, Ont., March 1966.

D564. *Sarah's Play.* Toronto, Playwrights Co-op, 1975.
4 scenes. 2m/2f.
Ivan, a child prodigy, invents a computer but can't make it work. The outspoken young Sarah gets it working and finds that it confers the power to have her wishes come true. But she also finds that her new power can't win her the ability to make friends.
fp: Globe Theatre, Regina, Sept. 1974.

D565. "The Shinbone General Store Caper" in *Three Plays by Rex Deverell.* Toronto, Playwrights Co-op, 1977.
9 scenes. 4m/3f.
A mystery drama for children in which the general store of Shinbone disappears. The town's Mountie, Matty Harris, has her work cut out for her as she unravels the mystery and sifts through a group of likely suspects.
fp: Globe Theatre, Regina, Sask., Sept. 15, 1975.

D566. *Shortshrift.* Toronto, Playwrights Co-op, 1972.
1 act. 7m/2f.
A children's play. A small prairie town attempts to regain its life and importance after it is taken off the map.
fp: Globe Theatre, Regina, Sask., 1972.

D567. "A Truly Great Offer" by Rex and Rita Deverell in *The Fold out, Hang up Push out, Global, Think and Do Thing.* Series 2, #4. Toronto, United Church of Canada, 1973.
1 act. 3m/2f/1b/1g.
This play, printed in poster format, focuses on the dilemma of a family who have been offered, absolutely free and with no strings attached, a whale. Would you accept this "truly great offer"?

D568. "The Underground Lake" in *Three Plays by Rex Deverell.* Toronto, Playwrights Co-op, 1977.
1 act. 4m/3f.
A children's play showing how ignorance breeds prejudice. Tiffin relates an old tale to the bigoted Typhoon, a tale about the Undergrounders and Overgrounders, who reconcile their differences upon meeting each other.
fp: Globe Theatre, Regina, Sask., Sept. 15, 1975.

D569. "The Up-Hill Revival" in *Three Plays by Rex Deverell.* Toronto, Playwrights Co-op, 1977.
2 acts. 6m/4f. Extras.
When strange lights are seen in the sky over Up-Hill, the townspeople become celebrities. Richard Lord, a con artist, takes advantage of the situation by exploiting the fertile imaginations and dreams of the rural community's inhabitants and especially of the fantasies of Amelia Morley, who "speaks" for the aliens.
fp: Globe Theatre, Regina, Sask., Oct. 18, 1976.

DEVLIN, Edward Wade

D570. *Rose Latulippe.* Toronto, French, 1935.
1 act. 7m/5f.
"A Canadian folk-play". An adaptation of the legend, as rendered into a ballad by F.J.W. Harrison. This is the story of the good but slightly vain Rose Latulippe who dances with the devil at Mardis Gras. Told in rhyming couplets.

DICKIE, Donalda James 1888–

D571. "Canada's First Christmas Party" in *Canadian School Plays.* D.J. Dickie, *et al.* eds. New York, Dutton, 1931 and Toronto, Dent, 1931.
1 act. 11m.
A play for children. To brighten life at Christmas, Champlain, Lord of the Revels, plans a festive party at which the plays are performed by the soldiers. Rehearsals and performances are chaotic.

D572. "Christmas at the Circle A" in *Canadian School Plays.* D.J. Dickie, *et al.* eds. New York, Dutton, 1931 and Toronto, Dent, 1931.
1 act. 3m/1f/1b/1g.
A play for children. An RCMP ruse to catch a rustler mingles with a Christmas celebration for two children.

D573. "The Christmas Committee" in *Canadian School Plays.* D.J. Dickie, *et al.* eds. New York, Dutton, 1931 and Toronto, Dent, 1931.
1 act. 6m/2f/4b or g.
A play for children. An allegorical representation of Canada and the provinces celebrating Christmas.

D574. "The Christmas Log" in *Canadian School Plays.* D.J. Dickie, *et al.* eds. New York, Dutton, 1931 and Toronto, Dent, 1931.
1 act. 1f/2b/2g.
A play for children. Four children act out the tale of the wicked Baron whose conduct on Christmas Eve banished him to the Moon forever.

D575. "A Little Child Shall Lead Them" in *Canadian School Plays.* D.J. Dickie, *et al.* eds. New York, Dutton, 1931 and Toronto, Dent, 1931.
1 act. 2m/1f/1g.
A play for children. A joyful Christmas celebration results for a farm couple who adopt a little girl.

D576. "Where is Betsy" in *Canadian School Plays.* D.J. Dickie, *et al.* eds. New York, Dutton, 1931 and Toronto, Dent, 1931.
1 act. 6m/7f.
A play for children. A "light comedy" about a paternally "arranged" elopement.

DOANE, Gregory 1906–

D576A. "A Bird in the Bush" By G.D.H. Hatfield in *Acadia Athenaeum,* vol. 52 #2, December 1925.
1 scene. 4m/1f.
A popular professor with a poor publishing record is rescued by his students, who reveal to the college president that the professor's dismissal results from the jealous machinations of the Dean.

D577. "A Dead Woman Bites Not" in *One Act Plays by Canadian Authors.* Montreal, Canadian Authors' Association, 1926.
1 act. 4m/1f.
Walsingham tries to persuade Elizabeth I to sign the warrant for the execution of Mary, Queen of Scots, and the French ambassador attempts to dissuade her.

D578. "For the Empire" in *One Act Plays by Canadian Authors.* Montreal, Canadian Authors' Association, 1926.
1 act. 2m/2f.
Napoleon succumbs to the machinations of his Minister of Police and agrees to divorce Josephine "for the Empire".
p: Little Theatre Guild, University Hall, Wolfville, N.S.

DOHERTY, Brian 1906–1974

D579. *Father Malachy's Miracle.* New York, Dramatists Play Service, 1938 and New York, Random, 1938 and in *Embassy Successes 1945–46* vol.1. London, Sampson Low, Marston, 1947.
3 acts. 13m/3f. Extras.
"Adapted from the novel by Bruce Marshall". Father Malachy, a Scottish monk, performs a miracle to prove to a skeptical clergyman of another faith that God still works in wondrous and old-fashioned ways.
fp: St. James Theatre, New York, Nov. 17, 1937. Embassy Theatre, England, March 28, 1945.

DOLLARD, Rev. James Bernard 1872–1946

D580. *Clontarf (An Irish National Drama).* Dublin, Catholic Truth Society of Ireland, 1920.
4 acts. 20m/3f. Extras.
Brian, Ard Righ of Ireland, must fight the Vikings to save Christian Ireland. Prince Thorstein, a Viking, joins Brian, the Irish win and Thorstein marries Reinalt after being baptized a Christian.

DONALDSON, Andrew

D581. *The Ashes on Gold Avenue.* Cobalt, Ont., Highway Book Shop, 1975.
24 scenes. 19m/4f. Chorus. Extras.
The play, "set in Northern Ontario at the time of a gold rush", is based on documentary material: it relates the creation and disintegration of the town of South Porcupine, hurried into being to satisfy the demands of the miners and merchants.
fp: Creation Two, Hamilton Place Studio Theatre, February 6, 1974.

DORN, Rudi

D582. "One's a Heifer" in *Encounter: Canadian Drama in Four Media.* Eugene Benson, ed. Toronto, Methuen, 1973 and in *Transitions I: Short Plays.* Edward Peck, ed. Vancouver, Commcept Publishing, 1978.
18 scenes. 2m/1b.
A TV adaptation of the short story by Sinclair Ross. An old man and a boy sit playing checkers and we see the world through the young boy's eyes.
fp: CBC TV, March 25, 1971, "Program X".

DOUCET, Clive 1946–

D583. *Hatching Eggs.* Toronto, Playwrights Co-op, 1974.
2 acts. 6m/2f. Extras.
An office spoof offering a glimpse of the inner workings of the Ottawa bureaucracy where the chief concerns are coffee breaks, pension plans, secretaries and whether, for the purposes of Customs officials, hatching eggs are animal, vegetable or mineral.
fp: National Arts Centre, Ottawa, Jan. 26, 1976.

D584. *A Very Desirable Residence.* Toronto, Playwrights Co-op, 1978.
2 acts. 2m/3f.
An examination of modern life in which a young Ottawa couple are confronted by a variety of vicissitudes.
fp: Penguin Performance Company, Ottawa, Nov. 17, 1977.

DOWLING, Clifford

D585. "Le Bon Dieu" in *Canadian Forum,* vol.14, #166, 1934.
1 act. 5m/1f.
God, tired of his creation, tries to find someone who can dissuade Him from destroying the world. When a minister, an atheist, a cleaning woman and a writer all fail, God leaves man to be "a master of his own destruction".

DOWSETT, Rev. Geoffrey Nevil

D586. *The Betrayal.* Toronto, New York, French, 1942.
3 acts. 26m/2f. Extras.
"A Passion Play". Christus is seized in the Garden of Gethsemane, defended by Nicodemus before the Sanhedrin, and handed over for execution by Pilate.
fp: The Literary & Debating Society of St. Patrick's College, Ottawa, 1936.

DRESKIN, Nathan

D587. "A Tragedy Entitled 'Cantamantaloedis' in One Short Spasm" in *Acadia Athenaeum,* vol. 57, #6, April 1931.
1 scene. 2m. Extras.
The pursuit of love and its pitfalls are depicted as a male student attempts to learn the piano to impress his love.

DREWERY, John

D588. *The Professionals.* Ottawa, Ottawa Little Theatre Workshop, #22.
1 act. 11m/1f.
A former love triangle is the major influence in Brigadier Harry Day's decision to sign the demand for the court martial of Major Philip Scott.

DUBÉ, Marcel 1930–

D589. *The White Geese.* Trans. Jean Remple. Toronto, New Press, 1972.
2 acts. 3m/5f.
A tragedy on the Greek model about the uncovering of family skeletons. The central theme is incest, and confrontation with this theme leads to suicide.
fp: Théâtre de la Comédie Canadienne, Montreal, Oct. 21, 1966.

DUCE, Jean

D589A. *Airman's Forty-Eight*. See **GOWAN, Elsie Park**.

DUFRESNE, Guy 1915–

D590. *The Call of the Whippoorwill*. Trans. Philip London and Laurence Berard. Toronto, New Press, 1972.
3 acts. 3m/3f.
A young woman in a Quebec town leaves her family when she chooses to follow the man she loves. Her decision is prompted by her father's inability to accept the young man's recommendation to expand the town factory onto another farmer's land, causing her family to lose a hoped-for financial gain.
fp: (original version) Comédie Canadienne, Montreal, Feb. 1960, (as written) Nouvelle Compagnie Théâtrale, Montreal, Oct. 12, 1972.

DUNLAP, A.R.

D591. "Gold" in *Acadia Athenaeum*, vol.52, #1, November 1925.
1 scene. 4m.
Thieves kill a miser while attempting to discover his cache of gold. They discover the gold and the devil who binds them in his power.

DUNN, Theo M.

D592. "Maada and Ulka" in *Contemporary Canadian Drama*. J. Shaver, ed. Ottawa, Borealis Press, 1974.
1 act. 1m/1f.
The story of a young couple: the man struggling to forget his traditional Cree upbringing, the young woman fighting for the spirit of her people and for capturing the heart of the bitter young man.

D593. *Nightjar*. Ottawa, Ottawa Little Theatre Workshop, #39.
1 act. 6m/2f.
Script unavailable for annotation.

D594. *They're Burning Down the House*. Ottawa, Ottawa Little Theatre Workshop, #23.
1 act. 2m/3f.
A young woman, deeply disturbed after she miscarries, is guided to the realization that she must carry on her life with her husband despite her loss.

DURAND, Evelyn 1870–1900

D595. *Elise Le Beau*. Toronto, University of Toronto Press, 1921.
5 acts. 8m/4f. Extras.
"A Dramatic Idyll". Elise, an heiress blinded by lightning, and her lover, an English colonel, are victims of the greed of a French-Canadian seigneur.

DWYER, Peter M.

D596. *Hoodman Blind*. Ottawa, Ottawa Little Theatre Workshop, #7.
1 act. 1m/1f.
"High comedy". An adaptation of the Faust legend with an unexpected ending. Set in eighteenth century Paris.

EARLE, Kathleen

D597. "Tramp's Progress" in *Asides* (Dramatists Alliance of Stanford University), No. 3, 1942.
1 act. 3m/1f.
A comedy in which two tramps are invited to join a theatrical company, the Tiddly Winks.
fp: (Public reading), Dramatists' Forum, New York, Jan. 25, 1951.

EDGAR, Mary Susanne 1889–

D598. *The Christmas Tree Bluebird.* New York, Woman's Press, 1920.
3 acts. 16g.
A group of girls in search of the bluebird of happiness find it on top of a Christmas tree.
fp: Toronto Boys Club, Memorial Institute, Dec. 21, 1927.

D599. "The Coming of the Pale-Face" in *Sketches and Plays*. Toronto, National Girls' Work Board, Religious Education Council of Canada, (192-?).
1 scene. 4m. Extras.
A brief dramatization of Champlain's visit to the country of the Hurons.
fp: Canadian Girls in Training camps.

D600. "The Conspiracy of Spring" in her *The Conspiracy of Spring and The Scarlet Knight*. New York, Womans Press, 1920 and in *Plays For Our American Holidays*. Robert Haven Schauffler, A. P. Sanford, eds. New York, Dodd, Mead, 1929.
1 act. 4m/4f/6b or g. Extras.
The flowers and representatives of nature's beauty teach a little earth mortal that Spring is Queen of the land.

D601. *Everygirl.* New York, Woman's Press, 1920.
1 act. 1f/19g. Extras.
Everygirl goes on a quest for life, "health, friends, opportunities for work and play".

D602. *The Scarlet Knight.* New York, Woman's Press, 1920 and in her *The Conspiracy of Spring and The Scarlet Knight*. New York, Woman's Press, 1920.
1 act. 5m/5f.
A pageant "autumn play for children" about the change of seasons from summer to fall.

D603. *The Wayside Piper.* New York, National Board of the Y.W.C.A., 1915 and New York, Woman's Press, 1923.
4 scenes, 1m/21f or g.
Faith, Hope and Love breathe into the Piper's flute. He is then sent by Counsellors and the Spirit of Service to girls in the workshop, the fields and the campus.

EDGE, Kathleen W.

D604. "To the Dead Man" in *A Book of Plays*. H. Voaden, ed. Toronto, Macmillan, 1935.
1 act. 3m.
A dramatic adaptation of Charles Dickens' *The Lazy Tour of Two Idle Apprentices*. Arthur Halliday arrives in Doncaster to find all except one room taken. He agrees to share it; his room-mate is dead but comes to life, or so Halliday dreams.
fp: Hart House Theatre, Toronto, March 30, 1935.

EDGELL, Mimi

D605. *Beyond Our Time*. Ottawa, Ottawa Little Theatre Workshop, No. 29.
1 act. 3m/3f.
Claire Manton wishes to marry an East Indian doctor. She meets opposition from her grandparents and his parents.

D606. *A Quiet Half-Hour*. Ottawa, Ottawa Little Theatre Workshop, No. 16.
1 act. 5m/3f.
A "thriller". A suburban housewife tries to calm an escaped maniac until the police arrive.

EDGERTON, E. Maud

D607. *The Ruby of Melchoir*. Toronto, Robinson Plays, 1937.
2 acts. 10m/4f. Extras.
A Christmas play. The insignificant gift of a beggar makes the chimes of the cathedral ring, rather than the offerings of the wealthy, for it is "the gift of love".

EDWARDS, Margaret Bunel

D608. "Turnabout" in *Plays*, vol. 31, No. 3, December 1971.
1 act. 1m.3b/3g.
A young girl sets about proving to her boyfriend that her idealistic beliefs are not unreasonable.
fp: Young People's Group, MacKay United Church, Ottawa, December 1971.

D609. "When the Winds Stopped Blowing" in *Explore*, vol.1, No. 47, July 26, 1970.
1 act. 8b or g.
A kite, a windmill, and a sailboat reassure the four winds that they are really important.

ELLIOTT, Margaret E.

D610. "The Favours of My Lady Leone" in *One Act Plays by Canadian Authors*. Montreal, Canadian Authors' Association, 1926.
1 act. 3m/1f. Extras.
A coquette rejects a suitor only to discover that he is the prince she had hoped to captivate.

ESCOFFERY, C.A.

D611. "Lord Ullin's Daughter" in *Acadia Athenaeum*, vol.62, No. 2, December 1936.
2 scenes. 3m/1f. Extras.
Translating a Scottish ballad to stage form, the play presents the ill-fated story of two young lovers who flee from the girl's father.

EVANS, Cicely Louise

D612. "Antic Disposition" in *Eight New One Act Plays of 1935*. J. Bourne, ed. London, Lovat, Dickson & Thompson, 1935.
1 act. 4m/4f.
"A study in madness" about a disturbed young man who thinks his father's remarriage drove his mother to commit suicide.

EVERSON, R.G.

D613. "It's Great to Be Single" in *Acta Victoriana*, vol.50 No. 1, Oct. 1925.
1 act. 2m/1f.
A comedy about the young Freeda who has promised her hand to Delbert but is in love with Peter. Peter threatens to shoot Delbert when he returns from the North but the conflict is resolved since Delbert wants to remain single after all.

EVERY, van, Jane. See Van EVERY, Jane.

FADER, Catherine

D614. "The Test" in *Educational Review*, vol.39, No. 2, October 1924.
1 act. 2b/2g. Extras.
"A better English play". The Fairy Queen, guardian of the King's English, arranges a contest between Jerry and Dick to see who speaks more correctly.

FAIRBAIRN, Archibald Macdonald Duff

D615. "Ebb-Tide" in his *Plays of the Pacific Coast*. Toronto, French, 1935.
1 act. 2m.
Two white outcasts realize that life among the Haida is not the answer to their problems.

D616. "A Pacific Coast Tragedy" in his *Plays of the Pacific Coast*. Toronto, French, 1935.
1 act. 3m/2f.
Within a single family, white and Indian values clash.

D617. "The Tragedy of Tanoo" in his *Plays of the Pacific Coast*. Toronto, French, 1935.
1 act. 3m/2f.
This play is concerned with the harmful effects of European contact on the Haida, particularly smallpox.

D618. "The War Drums of Skedans" in his *Plays of the Pacific Coast*. Toronto, French, 1935.
1 act. 3m/1b.
A century-old curse falls on a white ethnologist for desecrating a Haida burial ground.

FAIRBAIRN, Robert Edis 1880-1951

D619. *When the King Smiled*. Toronto, French, 1935.
1 act. 8m/3f. Extras.
"A Drama of the Resurrection". The last of the Wise Men, Gaspar, has for thirty years wondered what became of the king he had found in Bethlehem. He travels with his son and grandson to Jerusalem and arrives on the day of the Crucifixion.

FAIRLEY, Barker 1887–

D620. "The Runaway" in *Canadian Forum*, vol.5, No. 54, March 1925.
1 act. 2m/2f. Extras.
A woman tricks a would-be seducer into curtailing the activities of her roving husband.

FAIRWEATHER, Alice Lucilla

D621. "The Allies' Christmas Party" in *Educational Review*, vol.29, November 1915.
8b or g. Extras. Chorus.
A pageant. Canada invites friends for a Christmas party on Mother Britannia's first visit.

D622. "For the Red Cross" in *Educational Review*, vol.30, April 1916.
1 scene. 7g.
"A dialogue for girls" honouring the international and Canadian Red Cross.

FALK, Rod 1949–

D623. *Bummy Peepee in the Toto*. Edmonton, Harden House, 1972.
1 act. 5f/3m.
A comedy about a mental patient who writes a play and becomes famous but returns to his former institution and the nurse who is crazy about him.
fp: People and Puppets, Edmonton, August 1972.

FARMILOE, Dorothy Alicia 1920–

D624. "What Do You Save from a Burning Building?" in *Dialogue & Dialectic: A Canadian Anthology of Short Plays*. Alive Theatre Workshop, ed. Guelph, Alive Press, 1972.
1 act. 2m/1f.
A conservative student and his radical wife argue over a demonstration. An analogy for English and French Canada.

FARNSWORTH, David 1943–

D625. *The King, the Sword and the Dragon*. Toronto, Playwrights Co-op, 1975.
2 acts. 7m/3f. Extras. Doubling.
A comic mixture of the King Arthur legend and *Macbeth*. A boorish, tyrannical knight and his wife trick their way onto the throne and make a shambles of the kingdom.
fp: Dalhousie University, N.S., 1972.

FARQUHARSON, Mary Frederica (McLean)

D626. "Fifty Faces Spring" in *Echoes*, No. 152, Autumn, 1938.
1 act. 3m/3f.
A comedy about a fifty year old husband believed to be deceiving his wife.

D627. *Sure of a Fourth*. Toronto, French, 1935.
1 act. 1m/5f.
"A satirical comedy". At a bridge game, four middle-aged women try to impress each other with their popularity with men. Each refuses to admit that she prefers the companionship of women.
fp: Hart House Theatre, Toronto.

D628. *They Meet Again*. Toronto, French, 1938 and Toronto, Macmillan, 1938.
1 act. 2m/2f.
A comedy of manners. Two unhappy middle-aged couples exchange spouses for the evening.
fp: Studio Guild at Hart House Theatre, Toronto, Nov. 28, 1936.

FARRELL, John

D629. *Christmas in Skunk's Misery*. Edmonton, Dept. of Extension, University of Alberta, (194-?).
1 act. 3m/2f/1b.
A rich prospector returns to the mining town of Skunk's Misery to throw a Christmas party for the only child in the town who is discovered to be his son.

FAULDS, Mary Jeffrey

D630. "Pa-Ke-Noh-Ka, 'The Winner'" in *That All May Be One*. F.C. Stephenson and Sara Vance, eds. Toronto, United Church of Canada, 1929.
1 act. 18m/4f. Extras.
"A Dramatization of the Life of Rev. John McDougall, D.D.", a missionary much respected by the Indians of Alberta.

FEATHER, Jean

D631. "The Boy Who Went To The North Wind" in *Plays*, vol.28, No. 4, January 1969.
1 act. 3m/2f.
A children's play. An innkeeper cheats Ned and steals the gifts he was given by the North Wind, a magic table-cloth and a magic goat. A third gift, a magic stick, helps Ned get his own back.

D632. "Cap o' Rushes" in *Plays*, vol.28, No. 8, May 1969.
1 act. 5m/10f.
An English folk tale adapted for children. The daughter of a Baron is cast out by her father and forced to assume a disguise in order to seek work as a kitchen maid at a neighbouring Duke's castle. The Duke's son falls in love with her and they marry when her true identity is revealed.

D633. "The Clever Cobbler" in *Plays*, vol.29, No. 4, January 1970.
1 act. 6m/3f.
A children's play about Ahmet, a poor cobbler, who purely by chance makes people believe he is a great astrologer and wins the job of Royal Astrologer.

D634. "The Dressmaker and the Queen" in *Plays*, vol.29, No. 4, January 1970.
1 act. 2m/5f.
A children's play. A dressmaker's honesty appears to deprive her of trade, but the Queen, after testing Mrs. Quickly, rewards her by making her the Royal Dressmaker.

D635. "If You Meet a Leprechaun" in *Plays*, vol.29, No. 6, March 1970.
1 act. 3m/3f.
A children's play. Three young girls lost in the woods leave presents for the leprechauns and are given help in finding their way home.

D636. "The Long Leather Bag" in *Plays*, vol.30, No. 6, March 1971.
2 scenes. 3m/3f.
Irish folk tale adapted for children. Isabel's consideration for others helps her to recover the stolen money and to free her sister from the spell cast by the witch.

D637. "One Wish Too Many" in *Plays*, vol.30, No. 5, February 1971 and in *Dramatized Folk Tales of the World*. Sylvia Kamerman, ed. Boston, Plays, 1971.
3 scenes. 2m/3f.
A children's play. A wish come true brings good fortune to the kind-hearted Van Hoeks, but the same wish brings only well-deserved misery to the greedy Peter and Gretchen.

D638. "The Poor Man's Clever Daughter" in *Plays*, vol.29, No. 8, May 1970 and in *Magic Windows*. William D. Sheldon and Mary C. Austin, eds. Boston, Allyn and Bacon, 1973.
1 act. 5m/2f.
A children's play. The wife of a magistrate uses her wits to both influence her husband's judgement in court and to save her marriage.

D639. "Quick-Witted Jack" in *Plays*, vol.30, No. 4, January 1971 and in *Dramatized Folk Tales of the World*. Sylvia Kamerman, ed. Boston, Plays, 1971.
2 scenes. 19m/12f. Extras.
An adaptation of a Scandinavian folk tale for children. Jack, a poor fisherman, completes the tasks set by the king and wins the hand of the princess in marriage.

D640. "Tom and the Leprechaun" in *Plays*, vol.31, No. 6, March 1972.
1 act. 7m.
A children's play. Danny the leprechaun outwits Tom who is after his pot of gold.

D641. "Who is Strongest?" in *Plays*, vol.28, No. 5, February 1969 and in *Involvement*. J.W. Greig *et al*. eds. Toronto, McGraw-Hill Ryerson, 1972.
1 act. 1m/10m or f.
A children's play adapted from a folk tale. Icicle, Sun, Cloud, Wind, Mountain, Mouse, Cat, Dog, Tree and Candle argue about who is strongest.

FENNARIO, David 1947–

D642. *Nothing to Lose*. Vancouver, Talonbooks, 1977.
2 acts. 9m.
The plight of exploited working people and the personal problems created by the frustrating conditions in which such people live are the central concerns. A group of workers with "nothing to lose" and advised by a young radical playwright begin a sit-in strike when one of them unconsciously leads the way by challenging their abusive foreman.
fp: Centaur Theatre, Montreal, Nov. 11, 1977.

D643. *On the Job*. Vancouver, Talonbooks, 1976.
1 act. 8m.
On Christmas Eve in the shipping room of a Montreal dressmaking factory, the young workers, frustrated by lack of job opportunities and emboldened by smuggled booze, stop working. Their "strike" is a futile gesture against big business and unfair economic practices and they are sent home unemployed with their Christmas bonuses.
fp: Centaur Theatre, Montreal, Jan. 29, 1975.

FERGUSON, Doris M.

D644. "A Bed-Time Story" in *Canadian Red Cross Junior*, November 1939.
3 acts. 3m/3f/2g. Extras. Doubling.
No one sleeps when the ruler of the Kingdom of Pleasure arrests the Sandman for interfering with his festivities.

D645. "The Cave in the Woods" in *Canadian Red Cross Junior*, November 1940.
3 acts. 8b/2g. Extras.
A prince rescuing his kidnapped sister is saved from drowning through artificial respiration.

D646. "Christmas Candles" in *Canadian Red Cross Junior*, December 1939.
1 act. 6b.
A boy who sets himself on fire with a Christmas candle is saved through another boy's knowledge of first aid.

D647. "The Ice-Box Speaks" in *Canadian Red Cross Junior*, May 1939.
3 acts. 5b/5g.
House utensils teach Dick Know-Better a lesson to cure him of his rude selfishness.

D648. "The Magic Candlestick" in *Canadian Red Cross Junior*, October 1940.
2 acts. 4b/2g.
A boy's wish comes true and the whole world is turned into candy leaving him without food or water.

FERGUSON, James P. 1900–

D649. *Courage Mr. Green*. Toronto, French, 1936.
1 act. 3m/2f.
A "farce-comedy". A gentleman burglar robs a meek little "wage slave" but also helps Mr. Green to stand up to his domineering wife and to his boss.

FERGUSON, Max 1924–

D650. "Remember the Good Old Days" in *Canadian Humour and Satire*. Theresa Ford, ed. Toronto, Macmillan, 1976.
1 scene. 3m.
A brief satire in which Sir John A. Macdonald, the ghost of Canada past, unsuccessfully warns Pierre Elliot Trudeau to mend his earthy tongue.

D651. *The Unmuzzled Max*. Toronto, McGraw-Hill-Ryerson, 1971.
A series of many of the very short one-act political and social spoofs that Max Ferguson did on his daily CBC radio show.
fp: CBC, 1966-1971.

FERRET, A.

D652. "Christmas in the Village or Running the Perfect Gift to Earth" in *Curtain Call*, vol.9, No. 3, December 1937.
2 scenes. 2f.
A small town matron shops in Toronto with a chic friend.

D653. **FIELD, B.A.** *Cinderella*. See **VIVIAN, George.**

FIELD, Jameson

D654. "The Impressionists" in *Canadian Stage, Screen and Studio*, vol.1, No. 3, Jan. 1937.
1 act. 2m/2f.
A comedy about an eccentric author, his wife and his literary agent.
fp: Centre Stage Productions, Toronto, March 1937.

FIELDEN, Charlotte 1932–

D655. *One Crowded Hour*. Women Write for Theatre, vol.2. Toronto, Playwrights Co-op, 1976.
3 acts. 1f.
Mabel Harrison is vacationing at the New Life Guest Lodge to try and renew herself following the death of her husband. She decides to strike out on her own and catch up with life's experiences.
fp: Melanie Theatre at Centaur Theatre, Montreal, Oct. 7, 1975.

FINCH, Robert Duer Claydon 1900–

D656. *A Century Has Roots*. Toronto, University of Toronto Press, 1953.
7 scenes. 15m/6f. Doubling.
A masque written to commemorate the 100th anniversary of the founding of University College. Personified Time takes students on a tour of scenes from the college's history.
fp: Hart House Theatre, Toronto, 1953.

FINDLAY, John

D657. *Puss in Boots*. Victoria, B.C., Author, 1968. (Mimeographed).
2 acts. 5m.
A dramatized adaptation of the Perrault story about the poor young man whose clever and magical cat rearranges his life, finding him a fortune and a princess for a bride.
fp: Touring Players Foundation, Toronto.

D658. *Snow White and Rose Red*. Victoria, B.C., Author, 1969. (Mimeographed).
2 acts. 3m/3f.
A dramatization of the fairy tale about the sisters Rose Red and Snow White and their respective suitors Prince Random and his brother who is under the spell of the Gnome King and transformed into a bear.
fp: Touring Players Foundation, Toronto.

FINDLEY, Timothy 1930–

D659. *Can You See Me Yet?*. Vancouver, Talonbooks, 1977.
15 scenes. 4m/7f.
On the eve of W.W. II, the inmates of an insane asylum in a small rural Ontario town, significantly named Britton, are believed by Cassandra Wakelin, another inmate, to be members of her own ill-fated family. Does the asylum harbour the insane or offer sanctuary from the real world of 1939 which is insane?
fp: National Arts Centre, Ottawa, March 1, 1976.

FINEBERG, Larry 1945–

D660. *Death*. Toronto, Playwrights Co-op, 1972 and in *Performing Arts in Canada*, vol.10, No. 2, Summer 1973 and in *Now In Paperback*. C. Brissenden, ed. Toronto, Fineglow Plays, 1973 and in *Four Plays by Larry Fineberg*. Toronto, Playwrights Co-op, 1978.
3 scenes. 2m/1f.
A play about an old man's distaste for his useless life and his resulting preoccupation with death. A 16 year old boy tries to learn from the situation while the old man's daughter just waits for his death.
fp: Factory Theatre Lab, Toronto, Dec. 6, 1972. CBC TV "Peepshow", Feb. 5, 1976.

D661. *Eve*. Toronto, Theatrebooks, 1977.
2 acts. 4m/2f.
Eva, wife, mother, and grandmother, leaves husband and family for an independent way of life. Tired of being at others' beck and call, Eva just disappears, takes up residence in a ratty basement apartment, and becomes involved with her upstairs neighbour, Johnny Horvath.
fp: Stratford Festival, Stratford, Ont., July 14, 1976.

D662. *Hope*. Toronto, Playwrights Co-op, 1972 and in *Four Plays by Larry Fineberg*. Toronto, Playwrights Co-op, 1978.
2 acts. 4m/3f/1b/1g.
Characters compete for the possession of a hidden will in this comedy of talking dogs and exploding croquet mallets.
fp: Toronto Free Theatre, June 1972.

D663. *Human Remains*. Toronto, Playwrights Co-op, 1976 and in *Four Plays by Larry Fineberg*. Toronto, Playwrights Co-op, 1978.
2 acts. 2m/1f.
In the aftermath of a failed suicide attempt, Billy, Olive and Jeremy are forced to face their mutual needs and individual capacities.
fp: New Theatre, Toronto, Oct. 14, 1975.

D664. *Medea*. Toronto, Theatrebooks, 1978.
1 act. 4m/2f.
A poetic adaptation of the play by Euripides.
fp: Third Stage, Stratford Festival, June 1978.

D665. *Stonehenge*. Toronto, Playwrights Co-op, 1975 and in *Four Plays by Larry Fineberg*. Toronto, Playwrights Co-op, 1978.
3 acts. 5f.
An extensive revision of *Stonehenge Trilogy*.
fp: Vancouver East Cultural Centre, July 1974.

D666. *Stonehenge Trilogy*. Toronto, Playwrights Co-op, 1972.
3 acts. 9f.
This comedy deals with a group of women in the suburb of Stonehenge, Long Island, and examines various aspects of their lives.
fp: Factory Theatre Lab, Toronto, January 1972.

D667. *Waterfall.* Toronto, Playwrights Co-op, 1974.
1 act. 4m/f. Doubling.
A musical for children in which Who, the magician, sets off in search of the enchanted waterfall which will bring him peace and contentment. Music by William Skolnik.
fp: Young People's Theatre, Toronto, 1973.

FINNIGAN, Joan 1925-

D668. "Songs for the Bible Belt" in her *Living Together.* Fredericton, Fiddlehead, 1976.
1 act. 2m.
A poetic radio play about the Kitchener-Waterloo area.
fp: CBC radio.

FIRKINS, Yvonne

D669. *The Alien Heart.* Vancouver, New Play Centre, (197-?).
1 act. 2m/3f.
A young girl and her brother are both engaged to be married but their mother decides that the family should return to Austria. Family conflict ensues.

D670. "Royal Suspect" in *Invitation to Drama.* Andrew Orr, ed. Toronto, Macmillan, 1956.
1 act. 8m/5f. Extras.
A comedy-adventure set in revolutionary France concerning the identity of a young woman travelling near the French frontier.

FISHER, O.M.

D671. "The Toy Shop" in *Canadian School Plays.* D.J. Dickie *et al.* eds. New York, Dutton, 1931 and Toronto, Dent. 1931.
1 act. 5m/2f/1b/2g.
A play for children. The toys come alive and talk to the children who will own them.

FITCH, I.E.

D672. *The Story of Canada.* See **BAKER, Ida Emma (Fitch).**

FITZGERALD, Geraldine

D673. *Cousin Charlotte's Visit.* Halifax, Halifax Printing, 1900.
3 acts. 7f.
Charlotte replaces her two cousins in their dying aunt's estimation but all conflicts are resolved by the end of this genteel melodrama.

FLAVELL, Anne B.

D674. *Back to the World.* Revised Edition. Ottawa, Ottawa Little Theatre Workshop, No. 20.
1 act. 2m/7f.
Henry VIII's six fading queens spend their time in hell self-righteously perpetuating his and each other's discomforts until Dorothy Malone, gangster's moll, is sent to join them. All are caught up in her vitality and exuberance.

D675. *Bobbie Pulls Up Her Socks*. Toronto, Robinson Plays, 1953.
1 act. 3m/3f.
"A comedy". Bobbie gets some help from her kid brother in attracting the attention of a rugby hero, despite competition from her older sister.

D676. "Like It or Not" in *Saskatchewan Writing*, November 1960. See her *Back to the World*.

FLEISCHMAN, Maxine

D677. *The Bird in the Box*. Montreal, Factum, 1967.
3 acts. 5m/3f.
A group of people involved with the production of a new play await its opening night and the critics' decision.
fp: Western Quebec Region Festival, 1967.

A FLYER'S DAD (pseud.). See BUSCHLEN, John Preston.

FOON, Dennis 1951-

D678. *Heracles*. Vancouver, Talonbooks, 1978.
1 act. 2m/3f.
A play for young people about the life of the legendary Greek hero from his birth and maturation to his eventual madness.
fp: Green Thumb Players-Axis Mime Theatre, Citystage, Vancouver, May 22, 1978.

D678A. "The Last Days of Paul Bunyan" in his *The Windigo & The Last Days of Paul Bunyan*. Toronto, Playwrights Co-op, 1978.
2 scenes. 6 puppets.
A puppet play about the mythic giant lumberman competing with man's chainsaws before leaving for the Land of Tall Tales.
fp: The Green Thumb Players, Arts Club Theatre, Vancouver, 1977.

D679. *Peach*. Vancouver, New Play Centre, 1976.
1 act. 2m/2f.
A musical about a boy sent to an island because of his anti-social smell who is cured by a doctor and a nurse.
fp: New Play Centre, Vancouver, du Maurier Festival, April 29, 1976.

D679A. *Raft Baby*. Vancouver, Talonbooks, 1978.
1 act. 4m/2f.
A children's play about a trapper who finds a baby floating down the Peace River in British Columbia in 1872.
fp: The Green Thumb Players, Arts Club Theatre, Vancouver, March 25, 1978.

D680. *Wawa*. Vancouver, New Play Centre, 1976.
1 act. 2m.
Two men lost in the Ontario bush encounter death.
fp: (Workshop), New Play Centre, Vancouver, 1976.

D681. "The Windigo" in his *The Windigo & The Last Days of Paul Bunyan*. Toronto, Playwrights Co-op, 1978 and *Windigo*. Vancouver, Talonbooks, 1978.
1 act. 3m/2f. Extras. Doubling.
A dramatization of the Ojibway legend about the spirit which attacks the unsuccessful hunter.
fp: The Green Thumb Players, Vancouver Heritage Canadiana Festival, 1977.

FOORD, Isabelle 1941-

D682. "The Beast in the Bag" in her *The Beast in the Bag & Wild West Circus*. Toronto, Playwrights Co-op, 1977.
1 act. 2m/2f. Doubling.
A children's play about two girls who try to tame a ferocious dragon.
fp: Citadel-On-Wheels, Edmonton, 1972.

D683. *A Dream of Sky People*. Edmonton, Author, 1969 (mimeographed) and Toronto, Playwrights Co-op, 1973.
1 act. 4m/3f.
A "Rock Myth" drawn from Indian legends. An old storyteller recounts the tale of the sky-people who were the first creatures to settle on the earth.
fp: Citadel-on-Wheels, Edmonton, 1970.

D684. *I Don't Care What It Looks Like, As Long As It's Warm*. Toronto, Playwrights Co-op, 1978.
1 act. 4m/2f.
A satiric review for young audiences about the fashion industry and its destruction of Canadian wildlife and the culture of the native peoples.
fp: Citadel-On-Wheels, Edmonton, 1977.

D685. *Junkyard*. Toronto, Playwrights Co-op, 1973.
1 act. 1m/1f/2b/1g.
Two boys and a girl attempt to protect their favourite playground, a junkyard, from a crusading "clean-city" committee who wish to do away with it.
fp: Edmonton, 1970.

D686. *Say Hi To Owsley*. Toronto, Playwrights Co-op, 1975 and in *Cues and Entrances*. Henry Beissel, ed. Toronto, Gage, 1977.
1 act. 5m/1f.
A science fiction play for children about two Martians whose faulty starship causes panic on earth.

D687. *Shaman*. Toronto, Playwrights Co-op, 1973.
1 act. 2m/2f.
A children's play in which Shaman's 'dark' rival, Ooktah, is changing all the Arctic animals into Naked Newts. Can Shaman's own white magic prevail?
fp: Edmonton Experimental Theatre, March 1972.

D688. "Wild West Circus" in her *The Beast in the Bag & Wild West Circus*. Toronto, Playwrights Co-op, 1977.
1 act. 4m/1f.
A children's play about the town of Brimstone, Alberta, invaded by a gunfighter and a one-man circus.
fp: Parachute Theatre, Edmonton.

FORD, Florence

D689. *Peppercorn's Magic.* Waterloo, Ont., Waterloo Music Company, 1975.
5 scenes. 3m/1f.
A musical fairy tale for children in which the leprechaun Peppercorn saves the kingdom of Not-at-All and teaches the greedy troll that wealth cannot buy love.
p: Colonnade Theatre, Toronto, Oct. 7, 1972.

FORMAN, Frieda and Margot Smith

D690. *A Play About Bread and Roses.* Toronto, Kids Can Press, 1973.
3 acts. 10m/8f. Extras.
A children's play encompassing themes of equality, especially those of women's rights and equal distribution of manual labour across society. Hope, Faith and Energy skip school and accompanied by Uncle Merlin search for a better world.

FORMAN, Joan 1919-

D691. *The End of a Dream.* Toronto, Holt, Rinehart and Winston, 1969 and London, Holt-Blond, 1969.
1 act. 9m/1b.
A crew member narrates the events surrounding the last voyage of Henry Hudson which ended in mutiny.

D692. *The Freedom of the House.* Toronto, Holt, Rinehart and Winston, 1971.
1 act. 15m/3f.
Based on facts surrounding the effects of the American Revolution on French Canada, this play focuses on the Lebrun family who are divided when each member takes a different side in the conflict.

D693. *The Turning Tide.* Toronto, Holt, Rinehart and Winston, 1971.
3 acts. 20m/1f/1b. Extras.
Captain George Vancouver lands in Nootka Sound attempting to regain the land that is now known as Vancouver Island from the Spanish.

D694. *Westward To Canaan.* Toronto, Holt, Rinehart and Winston, 1972 and London, Holt-Blond, 1972.
1 act. 12m/5f/5b. Doubling.
A play about 19th century Ukrainian migrations to Canada set within a play about Ukrainians arriving in Canada in the 1930s.

FOWKE, Helen Shirley 1914-

D695. *A Gift for Benjamin.* Fredericton, Brunswick Press, 1960.
1 act. 7m/2f/1b. Extras.
A children's Christmas play. Benjamin begs the Christ-child to heal his dog.

D696. *The Unreluctant Hostage.* Halifax, Dramatists Co-op, 1977.
3 acts. 10m/2f. Extras.
A South American archbishop with a keen sense of mission allows himself to be kidnapped by terrorists.

D697. *When the Cock Crows.* Halifax, Dramatists Co-op, 1978.
3 acts. 8m/7f.
A comic drama about newly weds set in ancient Athens.

D698. "A Wig For My Lady" in *Canadian School Plays* Series 1. E.M. Jones, ed. Toronto, Ryerson, 1948.
1 act. 4m/1f. Extras.
Hoping to elude British troops and to escape to France, Prince Charlie disguises himself as a Highlander.

FOX, Marion Wathen

D699. "The Burglars" in *Educational Review*, vol.50, No. 7, March 1963.
1 act. 4m.
A "health play" about two boys who are awakened by robbers who have come to "steal" their teeth.

D700. "The First Christmas" in *Educational Review*, vol.51, No. 3, November 1936.
1m or f/1g. Extras.
A Christmas pageant focusing on a tableau of the nativity scene.

D701. "Following the Star" in *Educational Review*, vol.50, No. 4, December 1935.
3 acts. 2m/1f/1b/2g.
"A Christmas playlet". Good luck befalls a family who are travelling to meet their father.

D702. "The Little Fir Tree" in *Educational Review*, vol.51, No. 3, November 1936.
1 act. 4m/3f.
"A Christmas playlet". A small fir tree finally gets his wish to be chosen as a Christmas tree.

FRANKLIN, June 1924-

D703. *Take Away My Shadow*. Ottawa, Ottawa Little Theatre Workshop, No. 30.
1 act. 1m/6f.
The empty lives of two elderly patients and the decline of a jaded movie queen are revealed when they meet in the same hospital ward.
p: New Play Society, Toronto, May 16, 1965.

D704. "Welcome, Baby Dear" in *Performing Arts in Canada*, vol 7, No. 3, Fall 1970.
1 act. 5f.
The liberal attitude which a group of women display by giving a baby shower for their unwed pregnant friend is a false front for their narrow-minded suspicions.

FRASER, Alan and Pauline Morrish

D705. "Our Dream House" in *Canadian School Plays* Series 1. E.M. Jones, ed. Toronto, Ryerson, 1948.
1 act. 3m/4f.
Kathleen is not fond of Chester Nutkins but she defends him against her family's ridicule. Her dismay at his proposal is matched by her anger at the family's attempt to drive Chester away by feigning madness.
p: Young People's Society of Norwood Church, Edmonton Little Theatre 4th Annual Drama Festival, April 26, (1944).

FRASER, Alan A.

D706. *To Meet the Chinooks*. Edmonton, Dept. of Extension, University of Alberta, 1946.
1 act. 5m/3f.
A comedy about the parents of an English remittance man who visit their supposedly wealthy rancher son in Calgary in 1895.
fp: Banff School of Fine Arts, Aug. 22, 1945.

FRASER, Allan

D707. *Innocent in Zion*. Cobalt, Ont., Highway Book Shop, 1974.
3 scenes. 1m/4f/1g. Extras.
"*Innocent in Zion* is the world before a looking glass and one human being standing self to self and asking 'What the hell an I doing?' " An allegory, the dialogue in poetry, the narration prose.

FRASER, Donald Andrew 1875-1948

D708. *The Potter's Dream*. Franklin, Ohio, Eldridge, 1928.
1 scene. 1b. Extras.
"A playlet for young folks". A potter believes that in his sleep he created a perfect pot after a series of failures.

FRASER, Donalda

D709. "They Were All Deceived" in *Acadia Athenaeum*, April 1937.
1 scene. 1m/2f.
A young man fails to deceive his aunt regarding the repayment of a small loan.

FRASER, Hermia (Harris) 1902-

D710. *Hob's Heaven*. Franklin, Ohio, Eldridge, 1937.
3 scenes. 6b/5g.
Several children who have lost the pets they mistreated find themselves on Mars where their pets are the Masters.

FREEMAN, David 1945-

D711. *Battering Ram*. Toronto, Playwrights Co-op, 1972 and Vancouver, Talonbooks, 1974.
2 acts. 1m/2f.
This play is concerned with the mutual sexual and emotional exploitation of a cripple and the two women with whom he is staying.
fp: Factory Theatre Lab, Toronto, April 1972.

D712. *Creeps*. Toronto, University of Toronto Press, 1972 and in (abridged version) *The Best Plays of 1973-74*. Otis L. Guernsey, ed. New York, Dodd, Mead, 1974 and *Creeps*. New York, French, 1975.
1 act. 6m/1f. Extras.
Cerebral Palsy victims revolt against their lives in a sheltered workshop and against a "pitying" society.
fp: Factory Theatre Lab, Toronto, Feb. 3, 1971. Playhouse 2, New York, Fall 1973.

D713. *You're Gonna Be Alright, Jamie Boy.* Vancouver, Talonbooks, 1974.
2 acts. 3m/2f.
A contemporary comedy in which Jamie has just returned home from the Clarke Institute of Psychiatry where he has been recuperating from a nervous breakdown.
fp: Tarragon Theatre, Toronto, Jan. 12, 1974.

FRENCH, David 1939-

D714. *Leaving Home.* Toronto, Playwrights Co-op, 1972 and Toronto, New Press, 1972, and New York, French, 1976.
2 acts. 4m/3f.
A study of a Newfoundland family in Toronto in the late '50s. On the eve of the youngest son's wedding the Mercer family disintegrates.
fp: Tarragon Theatre, Toronto, May 1972.

D715. *Of the Fields, Lately.* Toronto, Playwrights Co-op, 1973 and Toronto, New Press, 1975 and New York, French, 1977.
2 acts. 3m/1f.
Ben Mercer arrives home unannounced for his aunt's funeral to find that his presence rekindles tension between his parents who have become extremely close since the kids left home.
fp: Tarragon Theatre, Toronto, Sept. 1973.

D716. *One Crack Out.* Toronto, Playwrights Co-op, 1975 and Toronto, New Press, 1976.
3 acts. 8m/2f.
Charlie Evans is a hustler down on his luck. He owes Jack the Hat $3000 and if he doesn't pay up within 48 hours, Bulldog will break his fingers and arms. He tries several cons, but they are revealed. With the support of Suitcase Sam, Al, Wanda and Helen, Charlie regains his confidence and possibly the ability to beat Bulldog at his own game.
fp: Tarragon Theatre, Toronto, May 24, 1975.

FRENCH, Florence Felton

D717. *Listen to the Tall Wheat Singing.* Edmonton, Dept. of Extension, University of Alberta, (1950?).
1 act. 3m/1f.
A drama with a happy ending about a concert singer who sacrifices her career in Toronto to raise a family on a prairie farm while her husband struggles to find success as a poet.

FRENCH, Helen

D718. "Charlie Who?" in *Performing Arts in Canada,* vol.8, No. 2, Summer 1971.
1 act. 1m/2f.
An "absurd" play. Charlie appears to grow smaller and smaller to the other characters until at the end another character begins the same cycle.
fp: TV version, CBC, 1971.

FRIEDLANDER, Mira

D718A. "The Night Before: The Morning After" in *York Theatre Journal*, vol.5, #2, Winter 1976.
1 act. 1m/1f.
A brief sketch in which a young couple fantasize about sex.

FROST, Margery

D719. "The Future" in *Acadia Athenaeum*, vol.58, No. 6, April 1932.
1 scene. 3m. Extras.
The Ruler promises food and coal to his rioting subjects but the Clerk wonders about a future with no jobs.

FRUET, William 1933-

D720. "Wedding in White" in *A Collection of Canadian Plays* vol.2. Rolf Kalman, ed. Toronto, Simon & Pierre, 1973.
3 acts. 6m/5f. Extras.
A young girl is raped by a soldier on leave, finds that she is pregnant, and is forced by her family to marry an old friend of her father.
fp: Poor Alex Theatre, Toronto, 1970

FRY, Beatrice E.

D721. "National Service" in *Educational Review*, vol.31, August 1917.
1 scene. 2b/3g. Chorus.
A "patriotic playlet" in praise of national service in wartime.

FYLEMAN, Rose

D722. "Father Christmas Comes to Supper" in *Canadian Home Journal*, vol.27, No. 8, Dec. 1930.
1 act. 2m/1f/1b/2g.
Three children waiting for Father Christmas are rewarded with gifts along with their sceptical, sour governess.

G.G.B.Y. (pseud.)

D723. "Monday, the Thirteenth" in *Acta Victoriana*, vol.42, No. 7, June 1918.
3 acts. 7f.
A brief comic sketch about a group of university women students awaiting the results of their exam.

GAGNIEUR, Elizabeth

D724. *Conflict and Triumph*. Montreal, Canadian Messenger Press, 1908.
3 acts. 7m/5f. Extras.
A religious allegory in verse closely paralleling biblical events. Involves the struggle of Ecclisea (Faith) against Lucifer and other evil personages and her devotion to the Veiled King.

D724A. **GALBRAITH, Robert.** "Nuts & Bolts & Rusty Things". See **THURY, Fred.**

GALLANT, Tom

D725. *Amadee Doucette & Son.* Charlottetown, P.E.I., Square Deal Publications, 1971.
3 acts. 5m/3f.
A contemporary drama of the shattered hopes of Amadee Doucette and his family. Living on a cold, barren piece of land, each family member covets dreams of escape.

GALLEY, Lucile Vessot

D726. *Famous Women.* Ottawa, Author, 1916.
36 scenes, 37f. Extras.
"An historic entertainment character representation" consisting of biographical and anecdotal recitations by 36 famous women from Joan of Arc to Queen Victoria and Canada.

D727. **GARCIA, A.E. de.** *Canada, Fair Canada.* See **KNIGHT, Albert Ernest.**

GARD, Robert Edward 1910–

D728. *Johnny Dunn.* Edmonton, Dept. of Extension, University of Alberta, (194–?) and in *Adventures in Acting.* W.H. Kaasa, G. Peacock, eds. Edmonton, Institute of Applied Art, 1957.
1 act. 2m/1f. Chorus.
Johnny Dunn, "one percent man and 99% straight liar", tells the tall tales which form part of the folklore of Alberta.

GARNEAU, Michel 1939-

D729. "Four to Four", Christian Bedard, Keith Turnbull, trans., in *A Collection of Canadian Plays* vol.5. Rolf Kalman, ed. Toronto, Simon & Pierre, 1978.
1 act. 4f.
A translation of his *Quatre A Quatre.* A poetic depiction of four generations of Quebec women conversing with one another through time and space.
fp: Option-Théâtre, College Lionel-Groulx, Saint-Thérèse, Quebec, May 11, 1973. Tarragon Theatre, Toronto, March 30, 1974.

GARNER, Hugh 1913–1979

D730. "The Magnet" in his *Three Women.* Toronto, Simon & Pierre, 1973 and in *A Collection of Canadian Plays* vol.2. Rolf Kalman, ed. Toronto, Simon & Pierre, 1973.
4 scenes. 3m/3f.
A lonely widow becomes involved with the younger man whom she hires as a hand for her farm.
fp: Brockville Theatre Guild, Ont., November 1966. CBC TV "First Person", June 15, 1960.

D731. "Some Are So Lucky" in his *Three Women*. Toronto, Simon & Pierre, 1973 and in *A Collection of Canadian Plays* vol.2. Rolf Kalman, ed. Toronto, Simon & Pierre, 1973.
2 scenes, 5m/2f.
A man meets a girl he once idolized and invites her for a drink. A pleasant evening of reminiscing ends in disaster as the girl becomes increasingly drunk, loud and obnoxious. The man finally leaves feeling very glad that he was not the "lucky one" who married her.
fp: CBC TV "On Camera", Dec. 17, 1956. CBC radio "Stage" series, Feb. 21, 1964. Brockville Theatre Guild, November 1966.

D732. *Three Women*. Toronto, Simon & Pierre, 1973 and in *A Collection of Canadian Plays* vol.2, Rolf Kalman, ed. Toronto, Simon & Pierre, 1973.
See "Some Are So Lucky", "The Magnet", "A Trip for Mrs. Taylor".

D733. "A Trip for Mrs. Taylor" in his *Three Women*. Toronto, Simon & Pierre, 1973 and in *A Collection of Canadian Plays* vol.2. Rolf Kalman, ed. Toronto, Simon & Pierre, 1973.
4 scenes. 4m/3f/1b.
An elderly widow packs her suitcase and boards the Montreal train at Union Station. She only travels to the outskirts of Toronto because she cannot afford to go farther. Although she must now return to her lonely room, she enjoys the fantasy of "her trip".
fp: CBC TV "On Camera", June 3, 1957. Brockville Theatre Guild, Ont., November 1966.

GARRETT, Ronald 1936–

D734. *Autumn At Altenburg*. Toronto, Playwrights Co-op, 1973.
4 acts. 11m/2f.
Lust, intrigue, and homosexuality in Nova Scotia in 1931. A military household in which incest and brutality (mental and physical) abound.
fp: Centaur Theatre, Montreal, March 2, 1973.

GARVIE, Peter

D735. "Lemons and Hieroglyphs" in *The Tamarack Review*, No. 13, Autumn 1959.
3m/2f.
A radio play in which a man on his deathbed revisits in his mind incidents from his life. Music by Peter Racine Fricker.
fp: CBC "Wednesday Night", Sept. 2, 1959.

GASPARINI, Len 1941–

D736. *Enough Rope*. Toronto, Playwrights Co-op, 1973 and in *Alive*, No. 34, 1974 and (revised version) Toronto, Playwrights Co-op, 1976.
1 act. 6m.
A depiction of the last tortured minutes of a man condemned to hang.
fp: Beggars' Workshop Theatre, Montreal, May 4, 1976.

GASS, Ken 1945–

D737. "The Boy Bishop" in *Canadian Theatre Review*, No. 12, Fall 1976.
2 acts. 12m/4f. Doubling.
A historical pageant and burlesque on revolution in which a precocious street urchin blackmails his way into the robes of the decadent Bishop Laval for what is supposed to be one day of freedom for the peasants of New France.
fp: Factory Theatre Lab, Toronto, April 14, 1976.

D738. *Hurray for Johhny Canuck!*. Toronto, Playwrights Co-op, 1975 and in *Five Canadian Plays*. Toronto, Playwrights Co-op, 1978.
2 acts. 4m/1f. Extras.
Based on the popular war-time comic-book series, this freewheeling romp through nostalgia, cliche, propaganda and nationalist fantasy features the clean-cut, one-dimensional Johnny Canuck as he deals telling blows to the entire Fascist war machine.
fp: Factory Theatre Lab, Toronto, Nov. 30, 1974.

D739. *Winter Offensive*. Toronto, Playwrights Co-op, 1978.
2 acts. 7m/2f.
The controversial play in which Mrs. Adolf Eichmann invites a group of Nazi officials to a Christmas party for grisly games of sex and violence.
fp: Factory Theatre Lab, Toronto, November 1977.

GAUVREAU, Claude 1925-1971

D740. "The Good Life", Ray Ellenwood trans., in *Exile*, vol.1, No. 2, 1972.
1 scene. 1m/1f.
A surrealist play about the relationship between a man and a woman.

D741. "Three Dramatic Objects", Ray Ellenwood trans., in *Exile*, vol.3, No. 2, 1976.
1 act. Multiple roles.
Three brief surrealist sketches, "Prayer for Indulgence", "Glints of Night" and "The Dream of the Bridge".

GELINAS, Gratien 1909-

D742. *Bousille and the Just*. Trans. Kenneth Johnstone. Toronto, Clarke Irwin, 1961.
2 acts. 6m/4f.
Emotional reactions and relationships of men and women intimately involved in a murder trial. The issues include the duping of the innocent and an attack on the pseudo-religious.
fp: La Comédie Canadienne, Montreal, Feb. 23, 1961. CBC TV "Festival", Feb. 26, 1962.

D743. "The Conscript's Return", Sheila Fischman, trans., in *Literature in Canada* Volume 2. Douglas Daymond, Leslie Monkman, eds. Toronto, Gage, 1978.
1 scene. 1m/1f.
An excerpt from a "Fridolinons" sketch, consisting of a conversation between a waitress in a Montreal restaurant and a conscript about to be shipped overseas to fight in W.W. II, subsequently expanded into his *Tit-Coq*.
fp: "Fridolinons" revue, Monument National Theatre, Montreal, 1946.

D744. *Tit-Coq*. Montreal, Author, 1950 (mimeographed) and trans. Kenneth Johnstone. Toronto, Clarke Irwin, 1967.
2 acts. 5m/5f.
During W.W. II, a man's loneliness is lessened for a short time by a woman's love and the hope of respectability.
fp: (In English), Le Monument National, Montreal, May 1950.

D745. *Yesterday the Children Were Dancing*. Trans. Mavor Moore. Toronto, Clarke Irwin, 1967.
2 acts. 5m/3f.
A play set in the explosive Montreal of 1967 presenting the emotional and ideological views of Quebec and the French Canadian.
fp: Charlottetown Festival, P.E.I., July 5, 1967.

GELINAS, Marc F.

D746. *Mortier*. Montreal, Centre d'essai, 1968.
1 act. 1m/1f.
A man and a woman meet in an empty space, incapable of leaving each other or the place. Through interaction and despair, they come to love each other.
p: Factory Theatre Lab, Toronto, "Works II", Dec. 6, 1972.

GEORGE, Richard

D747. "Food for Thought" in *Journal of Education for Nova Scotia*, series 4, vol.6, December 1935.
1 act. 2m/2f. Extras.
Promoting good health habits among children, this play introduces Buster Pander as he receives a dismal dental check-up. In a dream sequence, Rickets and Hollow Tooth are driven away by Good Food.

D748. **GERVAIS, Charles Henry 1946–**. *Baldoon*. See **REANEY, James.**

GIBBON, John Murray 1875-1952

D749. *The Man Comes Down From the Moon*. Toronto, Gordon V. Thompson, 1937.
1 act. 4m/2f. Extras.
A "musical playlet" in which the man in the moon visits Canada and is entertained by "good Canadians who have come along/to hold to-night a festival of song".

D750. *The Order of Good Cheer*. Toronto, Dent, 1929.
1 act. 3m/13m Extras.
This play is a re-creation of a feast held at Port Royal in 1606. "From the French version of Louvigny de Montigny, Canadian-Historical-Ballad-Opera of the First Settlers in Canada".
fp: NBC radio, 1928. Empress Hotel, Victoria, B.C., January 1930.

D751. *Prince Charlie and Flora*. Toronto, Dent, 1929.
1 act. 3m/2f/1b.
"A ballad opera" in which Bonnie Prince Charlie is disguised as a young lady-in-waiting in order to evade the British troops and sail for France.
fp: NBC radio, 1928.

GILBERT, S. Reid 1948–

D752. "A Glass Darkly" in *Dialogue & Dialectic: A Canadian Anthology of Short Plays*. Alive Theatre Workshop, ed. Guelph, Alive Press, 1972 and in *Transitions I: Short Plays*. Edward Peck, ed. Vancouver, Commcept Publishing, 1978.
1 act. 4m.
A man, devoid of name or direction, is summoned to the strange world of bob and dod, mirror images, to regain his identity and his mirror reflection.
fp: The Oakleaf Masquers, Vancouver, September 1972.

GILBERT, Sky

D753. "The Window" in *York Theatre Journal*, vol.3, #1, March 1974.
1 act. 1m/1f.
A man and a woman appear to see a passionate romantic encounter through a window which seems to represent a barrier, perhaps of fear, between them.

GILLIS, Annie

D754. "Slang" in *Educational Review*, vol.39, No. 2, October 1924 and vol.39, No. 3, November 1924.
1 act. 4m.
When Clarence returns from a visit to New York, his schoolmates must convince him that his newly acquired slang vocabulary is vulgar.

GITHAE, Micere

D755. "The Long Illness of Ex-Chief Kiti" in *The Fiddlehead*, No. 90, Summer 1971.
4 acts. 6m/5f/3b/1g.
The relations within one family provide both a metaphor and a focus for this examination of the disintegration of traditional Kenyan society and its possibilities of regeneration.

GLASS, Joanna M. 1936-

D756. "American Modern" in her *Canadian Gothic and American Modern*. New York, Dramatists Play Service, 1977.
1 act. 1m/1f.
Pat and Mike are collectors of odd, wasted things, incidents, thoughts. With this activity, they fill the empty spaces carefully surrounded by their words.
fp: (Workshop), Manhattan Theatre Club, 1972. Centaur Theatre, Montreal, Nov. 27, 1975.

D757. "Canadian Gothic" in her *Canadian Gothic and American Modern*. New York, Dramatists Play Service, 1977, and in *The Best Short Plays 1978*. Stanley Richards, ed. Radnor, Pennsylvania, Chilton, 1978.
1 act. 2m/2f.
A recollection by a mother and her daughter of two women's lives punctuated by gothic passions and events in the setting of a small prairie town.
fp: (Workshop), Manhattan Theatre Club, 1972. Centaur Theatre, Montreal, Nov. 27, 1975.

GLASSCO, John 1909–

D758. "The Wild Plum" in *Canadian Forum*, vol.40, August 1960.
1 scene. 4m/2f.
A radio play providing a poetic description of all the follies and vices of the world and of mankind.

GLYNN HOWARD, Hilda. See GLYNN-WARD, Hilda.

GLYNN-WARD, Hilda 1887–

D759. "The Aftermath" in *Poet Lore*, vol.27, 1926.
1 act. 3m/1f.
During W.W.I, Andy had convinced Celeste to marry him by telling her that Mickey, whom she loved, was dead. But when Mickey finds them in an isolated part of Canada, Celeste feels she must follow him and leaves Andy heartbroken.

GODLOVITCH, Charles Z. 1921–

D760. *Thunder on a Distant Mountain*. Montreal, Playwrights Workshop, 1971.
1 act. 5m/1f. Extras. Chorus.
The play is a parable of the timeless and universal course of leaders, mobs, war, conquest and forbidden knowledge.
fp: Playwrights Workshop, Montreal, March 17, 1971.

D761. "Timewatch" in *Contemporary Canadian Drama*. Joseph Shaver, ed. Ottawa, Borealis Press, 1974.
3m/1f.
Roth is placed in an apartment of sorts by the Administrator. He works but is lonely and requests a companion; he is given Sabrina. The story progresses along Adam and Eve lines with contemporary overtones.

D762. **GOLDBERG, Mildred.** *Eight Men Speak*. See **RYAN, Oscar.**

GOODCHILD, Roland

D763. "The Grand Duchess" in *Canada on Stage*. Stanley Richards, ed. Toronto, Clarke Irwin, 1960 and Vancouver, New Play Centre, (197-?).
1 act. 2m/2f.
The charming but inept young Duke of Moberly is in love with a chorus girl but is afraid the Dowager Duchess will disapprove until it is revealed that she too was once a chorus girl.
fp: Vancouver Little Theatre, 1969.

GOODWIN, George

D764. "Keillor House Dialogue" by George Goodwin and Douglas Mantz in *Son et Lumiere in Atlantic Canada*. Douglas Mantz, ed. Canadian Playwrights Co-operative, 1974.
1 scene. 2m/4f.
An amusing dialogue between members of the Keillor family at tea time in 1845 Canada.

D765. "Tantramar" in *Son et Lumiere in Atlantic Canada*. Douglas Mantz, ed. Canadian Playwrights Co-operative, 1974.
1 act. 7m/2f. Extras.
A multi-media historical drama tracing the founding and development of Sackville, New Brunswick.
fp: Mount Allison University, Sackville, N.B., June 1973.

GOTLIBOWICZ, Risha

D766. "As You Want It!" in *York Theatre Journal*, No. 1, Winter 1971 and vol.5, #3, Spring 1976.
1 act. 2m.
"An early draft version of a potential multi-media play". Poetic expression of the "separation anxiety" suffered by two brothers, Samuel and Samuti.

GOTLIEB, Phyllis Bloom 1926–

D767. "The Contract" in *Applegarth's Folly*, #1, Summer 1973 and in her *The Works*. Toronto, Calliope Press, 1978.
1 act. 2m/1f.
A poetic, futuristic dramatic sketch about a hired killer.

D768. "Doctor Umlaut's Earthly Kingdom" in *Poems for Voices*. Toronto, CBC, 1970 and *Doctor Umlaut's Earthly Kingdom*. Toronto, Calliope Press, 1974 and in her *The Works*. Toronto, Calliope Press, 1978.
1 act. 2m/2f. Doubling.
A radio play about Doctor Umlaut, the ultimate con man, who arrives to victimize more people but learns something about himself.
fp: CBC radio, February 1970.

D769. "Garden Varieties" in her *The Works*. Toronto, Calliope Press, 1978.
1 act. 4m/2f. Extras. Doubling.
A modern verse drama roughly based on the miracle plays of York and Chester from the Creation to Noah's Ark.

D770. "Score/Score" in *Visions 2020*. Stephen Clarkson, ed. Edmonton, Hurtig, 1970 and in *Playback: Canadian Selections*. Jack David, Michael Park, eds. Toronto, McClelland & Stewart, 1978.
1 scene. 1m/1f.
A brief comic dialogue between a computer teaching machine and a communicator learning English.

D771. "Silent Movie Days" in her *The Works*. Toronto, Calliope Press, 1978.
1 act. 1m/2b/2g.
A comic, poetic recollection of children attending silent movies.
fp: CBC radio, 1971.

GOULD, C.R.

D772. "The Red Shawl" in *Acadia Athenaeum*, vol.51, #6, May 1925.
1 act.
A family wish to prevent a young girl from marrying a B.C. Indian until she learns that she is, in fact, half-Indian herself.

GOULDING, Dorothy Jane 1923–

D773. "The Adventure of Bob Cactus" in her *We're Doing a Play*. Toronto, Ryerson, 1969.
1 act. 6m/3f.
A play for children. Bob Cactus battles the villains and doesn't get the girl.

D774. "The Cat" in her *We're Doing a Play*. Toronto, Ryerson, 1969.
1 act. 3m/7f.
A play for children. A fairy-tale about seven princesses and a prince disguised as a cat.

D775. "The Coming of Spring" in her *We're Doing a Play*. Toronto, Ryerson, 1969.
2 acts. 3m/4f.
A play for children. Spring finally comes when the Enchanter, gentle husband of the malicious Witch, uses the wrong potion in a punch for guests at a party celebrating winter.

D776. "The Gallant Soldiers" in her *We're Doing a Play*. Toronto, Ryerson, 1969.
1 act. 3m. Extras.
A play for children. The play is based on the rhyme "ten gallant soldiers" (similar to "ten little Indians"). The soldiers decrease in number "until there are none".

D777. "The Gift of the Drum" in her *The Master Cat and Other Plays*. Toronto, Dent, 1955 and in her *We're Doing a Play*. Toronto, Ryerson, 1969.
1 act. 6m/2f. Extras.
A children's play. A ritualistic treatment of the Zuni Indian legend of the creation and man's search for happiness.

D778. "Junior Hero" in her *We're Doing a Play*. Toronto, Ryerson, 1969.
1 act. 9m/1f.
A play for children. Junior Hero, schoolboy, becomes fearless space crusader who struggles with the villain, Jupiter.

D779. "The Master Cat or Puss in Boots" in her *The Master Cat and Other Plays*. Toronto, Dent, 1955.
6 scenes. 4m/1b/1f. Extras.
A musical fantasy for children based on the story of Puss in Boots with one important difference: a humorous conflict between the Master of Ceremonies and Puss. Music by Elizabeth MacKay.

D780. "Mr. Bunch's Toys" in her *The Master Cat and Other Plays*. Toronto, Dent, 1955.
3 scenes. 7m/3f.
A children's play. A group of dolls in a toy shop work together to retrieve a one dollar bill from a crack in the counter so a little girl can buy both Hans and Katrinka, the Dutch twins, for her sister.

D781. "The Mummer's Play" in her *We're Doing a Play*. Toronto, Ryerson, 1969.
1 act. 6m.
A play for children. An up-to-date version of the classic Christmas mumming play concerning St. George and the Turkish knight.

D782. "The Nativity" in her *The Master Cat and Other Plays*. Toronto, Dent, 1955.
1 act. 6m/2f. Extras.
A children's play. A look at the nativity in verse and song, stressing man's need for peace and love.

D783. "The Old Lady and the Pig" in her *We're Doing a Play*. Toronto, Ryerson, 1969.
1 act. 1m/1f/11m or f.
A play for children. The folk tale of the old woman whose pig won't jump the stile is the basis of this play.

D784. "Pagan Magic" in her *The Master Cat and Other Plays*. Toronto, Dent, 1955.
1 act. 1m/1f. Extras.
A children's play. A stylized treatment of good and evil in pantomime and verse focusing on the love of a shepherd boy and girl.

D785. "Pirates!!" in her *The Master Cat and Other Plays*. Toronto, Dent, 1955.
1 act. 5m/2f/3b/2g.
A children's play. An adventure tale of pirates, a kidnapping and hidden treasure.

GOURLAY, Elizabeth

D786. *Andrea Del Sarto*. Vancouver, New Play Centre, 1971.
5 acts. 15m/6f/1g.
This play presents selected episodes in the life of Renaissance painter Andrea del Sarto, from his early apprenticeship with Piero di Cosimo to his death.
fp: CBC radio, 1972.

D787. *From A to V*. Vancouver, New Play Centre, (197-?).
1 act. 2m/1f/2b.
A wife plans to murder her husband with a bomb.
fp: (Workshop), New Play Centre, Vancouver.

D788. *Isabel, or, The Continuous Dream of the Former Prime Minister*. Vancouver, New Play Centre, (197-?).
3 acts. 5m/5f.
Mackenzie King receives a dream visitation from his departed mother and former fiancee.
fp: La Pensee at the Discovery Theatre, Seattle, January 1978.

D789. *The Lake*. Vancouver, New Play Centre, 1972.
1 act. 1m/1f/2b.
A young man and his wife move into a new house where the wife hears things and senses the presence of a lake.
fp: (Rehearsed reading), New Play Centre, Vancouver, 1972.

D790. *The One-Eyed Jack*. Vancouver, New Play Centre, 1973.
1 act. 1m/3f.
Two women meet in a "greasy spoon" and talk about their lives.
fp: (Rehearsed reading), New Play Centre, Vancouver, 1973.

D791. *Transport Survey*. Vancouver, New Play Centre, (197-?).
1 act. 4m/3f.
An absurd comedy which follows a Surveyor in his interviews with a number of characters.
fp: University of B.C., Vancouver.

GOVIER, Katherine 1949–

D792. "A Modest Proposal" in *Title Unknown*. Judith Merril, ed. Toronto, Festival of Women and the Arts, 1975.
1 scene. 1m/2f.
A boy and a girl about to marry discuss their future life together in a restaurant.

GOWAN, Elsie Park (Young) 1905–

D793. *Airman's Forty-Eight*. Jean Duce and Elsie Park Gowan. Edmonton, Dept. of Extension, University of Alberta, (194-?).
1 act. 3m/3f.
A comedy in which a Calgary family invites a young airman for supper in the hope of marrying off their middle-aged aunt Emily.

D794. *Back to the Kitchen, Woman!*. Edmonton, Extension Dept., University of Alberta, (194-?).
1 act. 2m/9f.
A comedy about a man who writes a book about what women really want in life. Fortunately for him there is one woman who does not desert him in the chaos he creates.
fp: Banff School of Fine Arts, Aug. 25, 1941.

D795. *Breeches from Bond Street*. Toronto, French, 1952.
1 act. 4m/2f.
Eliza, a mail order bride, is rejected by Charlie who sent for her because she is too respectable. But Brooks, a seemingly disreputable Englishman initially mistaken for Charlie marries Eliza and becomes respectable.
fp: Studio Theatre, University of Alberta Provincial Players, 1949. CBC radio "Buckingham Theatre". CBC TV "On Camera", (195?).

D796. "Confederation" in *Prose and Poetry for Canadians*. J.W. Chalmers, ed. Toronto, Dent, 1951.
1 act. 6m/2f. Extras.
A radio play about the Quebec conference of 1864 as seen through the eyes of a young newspaper reporter who is covering the event.

D797. *Maestro*. Edmonton, University of Alberta Department of Extension, 1942 and in *Curtain Rising*. W.S. Milne, ed. Toronto, Longmans, Green, 1958.
1 act. 3m/3f.
The secretary of the director of a music academy discovers that her boss is a tone-deaf phony who was formerly employed as a refrigerator designer. She doesn't give him away because he saved the local symphony from financial disaster and because she loves him.
fp: Banff School of Fine Arts, CBC radio, 1942.

D798. "One Who Looks at the Stars" in *The Alberta Golden Jubilee Anthology*. William George Hardy, ed. Toronto, McClelland & Stewart, 1955.
1 act. 2m/1f.
A radio play in which the painter Paul Kane helps to bring together in marriage a white fur trader and a beautiful Indian girl.
fp: Station CJCA, Edmonton and the CBC Western Network.

D799. *The Princess Who Dreamed Too Much.* Edmonton, University of Alberta, Department of Extension, (194-?) and Edmonton, Alberta Department of Culture, n.d.
1 act. 3m/4f.
A wicked witch tries to kidnap a day-dreaming princess but is foiled by the prince. The prince and princess become engaged.
fp: Queen's University Summer School, Kingston, Ont., 1946.

D800. "The Royal Touch" in *Curtain Call*, vol.6, #8, 1935 and in *Canadian School Plays*. E.M. Jones, ed. Toronto, Ryerson, 1948.
1 act. 2m/3f/1b. Extras.
"A Ruritanian Fable" in which Nata, a princess, must choose between fashionable exile in Paris and assuming the responsibilities of change.
fp: Edmonton Little Theatre.

D801. *The Shop in Toad Lane or Password to Liberty*. Edmonton, Alberta Co-operative Wholesale Association, 1940 and in *Co-op News* (as a serial in 4 (?) parts), (194-?).
4 scenes. 8m/3f. Extras.
Charles Howarth, an idealistic weaver, unites the poor of Rochdale, England, to open a co-operative store of their own where they are free to buy quality goods and reap the profits of their own hard work.
fp: Olds School of Agriculture.

D802. *You Can't Do That*. See **IRVINE, William.**

GRAFF, Tom

D803. "Why Can't Men Cry" in *The Capilano Review*, #11, 1977.
1 scene, 4m/1f. Chorus.
An abstract mixed media "movement art work" commissioned by the Vancouver New Music Society.
fp: Vancouver East Cultural Centre, June 20, 1977.

GRAINGER, Tom 1921–

D804. *The Action Tonight*. Ottawa, Ottawa Little Theatre Workshop, #31 and in *Prism International*, vol.4, #3, Spring 1965.
1 act. 5m/1f.
Golden Echo Lovejoy and George Graham share an apartment. To relieve police pressure on himself, Binky, a pusher, frames Lovejoy, Graham, and a woman he wishes to break with.
p: Ottawa Little Theatre, 1965. CBC radio, 1973.

D805. *The Agreement*. Vancouver, New Play Centre, 1973.
1 act. 2m.
An Inspector of Public Safety who covets a luxurious apartment belonging to a retired man engineers an identity transfer and murders him.

D806. *Daft Dream Adyin'*. Toronto, Nelson, 1969 and in *The Best Short Plays of 1969*. Stanley Richards, ed. Philadelphia, Chilton, 1969 and *Daft Dream Adyin'*. Vancouver, New Play Centre. (197-?).
1 act. 12m/2f.
This play is based on the unsuccessful miners' strike in Loston, Lancashire, in the 1920s. It is concerned with the dreams by which a man lives, and with his chance of survival if that dream dies.

D807. *Down There*. Vancouver, New Play Centre, 1975.
3 acts. 4m/3f.
After the death of a miner, his son is forced to re-evaluate his marriage to a woman who believes in Fabian socialism.
fp: Octagon, Bolton, England, 1975.

D808. *The Exile*. Vancouver, New Play Centre, 1977.
2 acts. 4m/3f.
A drama based on the life of the 19th century English novelist George Gissing.

D809. *The Great Grunbaum*. Vancouver, New Play Centre, 1974.
1 act. 2m/1f.
Three old circus performers meet to plan a new circus act.
fp: New Play Centre, Vancouver, du Maurier Festival, April 26, 1974.

D810. *The Helper*. Vancouver, New Play Centre, 1972 and in *West Coast Plays*. Connie Brissenden, ed. Vancouver and Toronto, New Play Centre-Fineglow Plays, 1975.
1 act. 4m/1f.
A tramp outwits one of the syndicate's counterfeiting operations.
fp: New Play Centre, Vancouver, August 1972.

D811. *In Arizona the Air Is Clean*. Vancouver, New Play Centre, 1970.
1 act. 2m.
An old, sick Jewish socialist rejects his capitalist son's offer to have him leave his rooming house and be cured.
fp: CBC TV, Montreal, 1970.

D812. *The Injured*. Vancouver, New Play Centre, 1974 and Toronto, Playwrights Co-op, 1976.
3 acts. 3m/3f/1g.
A contemporary gothic horror play set in Lancashire, England, portraying the relationship between Jud and Sarah since the death of their little girl. Locked together by their bizarre secrets, Jud and Sarah continue their frightening life together.
fp: Studio Theatre, University of Alberta, Edmonton, January 1975.

D813. *The Kill*. Ottawa, Ottawa Little Theatre Workshop, #35 and Vancouver, New Play Centre, (197-?).
1 act. 7m.
Feldtman, a Jew who escaped death at Auschwitz, correctly senses that the new help, Lindtner, was a special butcher in the concentration camps and proceeds, with the help of Molnar and Joe, to kill Lindtner as he would kill a pig at the meat plant.

D814. *The Last Death of Abraham Schurmann*. Vancouver, New Play Centre, (197-?).
2 acts. 2m.
An old man sits in an old boarding house waiting for his eldest son to come and take him to Arizona. The younger son whom the old man despises arrives to take his father south, but the old man prefers to wait for the other.
p: Savage God, Vancouver, 1969.

D815. *The Man from Wulfshausen*. Vancouver, New Play Centre, 1974.
1 act. 2m/1f.
A student encounters a man from his home village who has come to revenge his sister's death.

D816. *Roundabout*. Vancouver, New Play Centre, 1976.
3 acts. 5m/3f. Doubling.
A comedy about a young Lancashire drop-out who meets a number of English archetypal characters while searching for his long-lost mother.
fp: New Play Centre, Vancouver, 1976.

D817. *Slane*. Vancouver, New Play Centre, 1975.
2 acts. 2m/2f.
A middle-aged foreman of a cotton mill is caught up in domestic problems which clash with his fantasy world in which he sees a creature from outer space.
fp: (Workshop), New Play Centre, Vancouver, 1975.

GRANDE, del, Louis. See del GRANDE, Louis.

GRANNAN, Mary E.

D818. "A Toy Mutiny" in *Educational Review*, vol.43, #3, Nov. 1928.
2 acts. 3b/5g.
Christmas toys decide to go on strike against the thoughtless children who take care of them.

GRANT, Diane 1939– and company

D819. *What Glorious Times They Had*. Toronto, Redlight Theatre, 1975 (mimeographed) and in *Popular Performance Plays in Canada* vol.1. Marian Wilson, ed. Toronto, Simon & Pierre, 1976.
2 acts. 9m/10f. Extras.
A series of satirical vignettes illustrating and commenting on the activities of Nellie McLung in her fight for women's rights in Manitoba during the early 1900s.
fp: Redlight Theatre, Bathurst Street United Church, Toronto, May 8, 1974.

GRANT, Lynn

D820. *Growth*. Western Canada Theatre Conference. Edmonton, Dept. of Extension, University of Alberta, 1949.
1 act. 4m/4f.
The hatred between a B.C. farmer and his Polish neighbour is overcome by their children after a 40-year feud when a flood threatens to destroy their land.

GRAVES, Warren 1933–

D821. *Chief Shaking Spear Rides Again*. Toronto, Playwrights Co-op, 1975.
2 acts. 6m/6f. Extras.
A take-off on melodrama, the rugged West and theatre set in Nellie's House of Easy Virtue at the turn of the century.
fp: Waterdale Theatre Associates at Citadel Theatre, Edmonton, 1974.

D822. *The Hand That Cradles The Rock*. Toronto, Playwrights Co-op, 1972.
2 acts. 2m/3f.
The wife works and the husband stays home bringing up baby and going a little crazy. A loony mother-in-law and her boyfriend arrive on the scene.
fp: Backdoor Theatre, Toronto, August 1972.

D823. *The Mumberley Inheritance, or His Substance Frittered.* Toronto, Playwrights Co-op, 1972.
2 acts, 5m/3f.
"A goodtime melodrama" complete with dastardly villain, Marmaduke Mayhem, and gallant hero, Rodney Stoutheart. Will Rodney be able to save Daphne from the evil clutches of Marmaduke Mayhem?
fp: Citadel Theatre, Edmonton, July 1971.

D824. *The Proper Perspective.* Edmonton, Alberta Department of Culture, 1971 and in *Contemporary Canadian Drama.* Joseph Shaver, ed. Ottawa, Borealis Press, 1974 and in *Who's Looking After the Atlantic? & The Proper Perspective.* Toronto, Playwrights Co-op, 1978.
1 act. 4m/1f.
Using the situation of a play within a play, the author has posed the question: what is the nature of reality?
p: Original Lunchtime Theatre, Charlottetown, P.E.I., July 21, 1977.

D825. "Who's Looking After the Atlantic?" in his *Who's Looking After the Atlantic? & The Proper Perspective.* Toronto, Playwrights Co-op. 1978.
1 act. 2m.
A comic encounter between a psychiatrist and a slightly insane millionaire.

D826. *Yes, Dear.* Toronto, French, 1967.
1 act. 1m/2f.
On their daughter's 21st birthday, John and Marie suddenly feel very old.

GRAY, Jack 1927–

D827. *Chevalier Johnstone.* N.p., Author, 1964 (mimeographed) and Toronto, Playwrights Co-op, 1972.
3 acts. 15m/4f. Extras.
The play is a comedy about a Scottish officer who joined the French after Culloden and is present at the capture of Louisbourg in 1758.
fp: Neptune Theatre, Halifax, March 17, 1964 as "Louisbourg". Revised version, Neptune, 1966.

D828. *Emmanuel Xoc.* Author, 1965. (Mimeographed).
2 acts. 6m/1f.
Xoc, "a leader of men and a wielder of power", Xoc, the amoral manipulator ironically aware of the deceptions of appearance, metes out what is deserved by both the moral and the immoral.
fp: Crest Theatre, Toronto, 1965.

D829. *Striker Schneiderman.* Toronto, Author, 1969 (mimeographed) and Toronto, University of Toronto Press, 1973.
1 act. 13m/3f. Extras. Doubling.
Moishe Schneiderman must decide which side he is on during the General Strike of 1919 in Winnipeg. By various coincidences and quirks, Moishe joins the Strikers and is eventually their leader, opting for compromise and a settlement when violence erupts.
fp: St. Lawrence Centre, Toronto, Feb. 27, 1970.

D830. *Susannah, Agnes and Ruth*. Toronto, Playwrights Co-op, 1972.
3 acts. 9m/4f.
The theme of women and love is explored. A matriarchal grandmother learns to let her daughter and her grand-daughter manage their own lives.

GRAY, James Orman

D831. *Antichrist*. Vancouver, Thomson, 1912.
5 acts. 13m/8f. Extras.
Gladys, daughter of the Prince Vittorio, will marry Orrie once he has attained fame so Orrie embarks on a plan for conquering the world. He reveals that he is really Napoleon Bonaparte and the hence legitimate heir to Greece and Turkey which he uses as his base. He is successful and all nations call him God's Apostle.

GRAY, John 1927–. See GRAY, Jack.

GRAYSON, Ethel Kirk

D832. "Flower of the Storm" in *Willison's Monthly*, vol.2, #6, November 1926.
1 act. 4m/2f.
A girl's lover is killed, by chance, by the man her brother wants her to marry.

GRAYSON, Philip

D833. *No More Octobers*. Ottawa, Ottawa Little Theatre Workshop, #15.
1 act. 2m/4f.
A realistic portrait of the inhabitants of a Toronto rooming house, focusing on the middle-aged landlady and the fortunes and misfortunes attendant on her inheriting a farm.

GREEN, Harry A.V.

D834. *The Death of Pierrot*. Winnipeg, Community Players, 1923 and in *One Act Plays by Canadian Authors*. Montreal, Canadian Authors' Association, 1926.
1 act. 3m/2f.
"A trivial tragedy" in which Columbine leaves Pierrot after an encounter with Mrs. Grundy who convinces her that her skirts are too short.
fp: Community Players of Winnipeg, May 3, 1923.

GREEN, Jeff

D835. "Azort Starbolt—Space Android" in *Reading, Writing and Radio*. Winston G. Schell, Marstan E. Woolings. Don Mills, Ont., Longman Canada, 1977.
1 act. 8m.
A brief radio satire of a science fiction serial.
fp: Radio Carleton, Carleton University, Ottawa, 1973.

GREEN, Mary A.

D836. *The Thirty Dollar Wreath*. Ottawa, Ottawa Little Theatre Workshop, #46.
2 scenes. 2m/5f.
A dying woman wills her body to science but her family interferes after her death.
fp: Ottawa Little Theatre, Ottawa, November 1960.

GREEN, Wilma and William Smith

D836A. "Cornplanter" in Krieg, Robert Edward. *Forest Theatre: A Study of the Six Nations' Pageant Plays on the Grand River Reserve.* Ph.D. Thesis, University of Western Ontario, 1978.
7 scenes. 9m/2f. Extras.
A pageant about the Indian warrior at the time of the American Revolution.
fp: Grand River Reserve, Brantford, Ont., 1975.

GREENE, Barnet M.

D837. "The God-Intoxicated Man" in his *Woman, the Masterpiece.* Toronto, Ryerson, 1923.
3 acts. 8m/1f. Extras.
The life of the philosopher Spinoza whose "whole attitude towards life and the universe began, continued and ended with God".

D838. "Woman, the Masterpiece" in his *Woman, the Masterpiece.* Toronto, Ryerson, 1923.
4 acts. 19m/7f.
Da Vinci, Rembrandt, Reynolds and Whistler choose Woman for their expression of the ideal.

GREENE, Donald

D839. "The Organizer" in *Sheaf*, Literary Supplement (University of Saskatchewan), March 1941.
1 act. 4m/1f.
A farmer neglects his family and farm for politics.

GREENLAND, Bill

D840. "We Three, You and I" in *Prism International* vol.9, #1, Summer 1969 and Vancouver, New Play Centre, 1972 and in *The Factory Lab Anthology*. Connie Brissenden, ed. Vancouver, Talonbooks, 1974.
1 act. 2m/1f/1g.
The play deals with the concept of charity and explores the motives of the charity worker.
fp: University of B.C., Vancouver, 1969.

GREGG, Audrey

D841. "The Lie" in *Acadia Athenaeum*, vol.55, #6, April 1929.
1 scene. 1m/3f.
Two girls love the same man but Shirley denies her love when she recognizes his love for the other.

GREY, Francis William 1860–1939

D842. *Bishop and King.* Ottawa, Miller, 1931 and in his *Four Plays.* Ottawa, Miller, 1931.
3 acts. 7m/2f. Extras.
"An historical drama". Nobles conspire to turn Charles II against Blessed Oliver Plunkett. The bishop is tried and executed despite the Queen's appeal.

D843. *The Bridegroom Cometh.* Ottawa, Miller, 1931 and in his *Four Plays.* Ottawa, Miller, 1931.
1 act. 10f.
"A morality play". Five wise and five foolish virgins wait for the Bridegroom.

D844. *Love's Pilgrimage.* Ottawa, Miller, 1931 and in his *Four Plays.* Ottawa, Miller, 1931.
3 acts. 10m/3f. Extras.
"A Passiontide Mystery". A pilgrim from Babylon goes in search of the King of Israel. When he arrives in Bethlehem, Mary and Joseph have already left for Egypt. Thirty years later he passes that way again, and the crucified and risen Christ appears to him as a beam of light.

D845. *Sixteen Ninety. A Series of Historical Tableaux.* Ottawa, Mortimer, 1904.
3 acts. 21m. Extras.
An historical account of the attempts by Raoul de St. Laurent to sabotage Frontenac's term as Governor of Canada.

D846. *The Valiant Woman.* Ottawa, Miller, 1931 and in his *Four Plays.* Ottawa, Miller, 1931.
2 acts. 10m/10f/2b. Extras.
An "Epiphany Masque". Isaiah prophesies to King Ahaz that "Every age shall shew/a valiant woman", Deborah, Ruth, Esther, Judith and Mary.

GROVES, Edith (Lelean) 1870–1931

D847. *Britannia.* Toronto, McClelland, Goodchild & Stewart, 1917 and Toronto, Educational Publishing (1917?).
1 act. 19b or g.
The countries of the Empire come to pay homage to their patroness, Britannia. Foremost in the ranks is Canada and all her children, the provinces.

D848. *Canada Calls.* Toronto, McClelland, Goodchild & Stewart, 1918.
1 act. 6m/3f. Extras.
"A Timely Patriotic Play dedicated to the Children of Canada". Industries, enterprises, children and housewives pledge their support to "the dear boys overseas" in answer to the call of Canada and Good Fairy Thrift.

D849. *Canada, Our Homeland.* Toronto, William Briggs, 1900.
1 act. 11b/1g.
A brief pageant to be acted by children celebrating Canada and the richness of its natural resources.
p: Miss Lelean's Elocution Class, Pavillion, Toronto, March 23, 1900.

D850. *A Canadian Fairy Tale.* Toronto, William Briggs, 1916.
1 act. 1f/15b/15g.
The queen of the fairies teaches four little girls that Canada is a wonderful, beautiful, important country with fairies, leprechauns and pots of gold.

D851. *The Key of Jack Canuck's Treasure-House.* Toronto, Briggs, 1916.
1 act. 2m/3f. Extras.
An allegory in which Miss Canada loses the key entrusted to her by Jack Canuck. Friends of all sorts, fairies, Indians and an aviator, help to rescue it from an eagle. The moral is "Canada for Canadians".

D852. *The Making of Canada's Flag.* Toronto, Briggs, 1916 and Toronto, McClelland & Stewart, 1918.
1 act. 9g/7b. Extras.
A children's play in the Canadian Patriotism series. In a series of tableaux, Britannia is given five "good reasons" for adding Canada's emblem to the Union Jack, from the Loyalists to the Canadian soldiers in W.W.I.

D853. *A Patriotic Auction.* Toronto, McClelland, Goodchild & Stewart, 1918.
1 act. 5g/3b.
Dolls are auctioned to raise money for the Red Cross.

D853A. *A Spring Fantasy.* Toronto, McClelland, Goodchild, Stewart, 1918.
1 act. 3m/2f. Extras.
A play for children about the change of seasons.

D854. *The War on the Western Front.* Toronto, Briggs, 1916.
1 act. 16g/1b. Extras.
A children's play in the Canadian Patriotism series. Groups of Belgian, French, British and Canadian girls knitting socks for the Allies declaim on the part their countries have played in the war.

D855. *The Wooing of Miss Canada.* Toronto, McClelland, Goodchild & Stewart, 1917.
1 act. 4b/9g. Extras.
A patriotic allegory. Miss Canada is courted by several foreign powers but she chooses Jack Canuck because he loves her not for her wealth but for herself.

GURIK, Robert, 1932–

D856. *API 2967.* Trans. Marc F. Gelinas. Montreal, Centre d'Essai, n.d. and Toronto, Playwrights Co-op, 1973 and Vancouver, Talonbooks, 1974.
2 acts. 1m/1f.
Two members of a future society rediscover the meanings of life in 1970, when one of them is given an apple to research. He shares it with a young girl, and together they relearn the pain and pleasure of existence.
fp: L'Egregore, Montreal, 1967.

D857. *The Hanged Man.* Trans. Philip London and Laurence Berard. Toronto, New Press, 1972.
3 acts. 9m/1f/2b.
A beggar attempts to help the poor and oppressed of the neighbourhood by giving them, for luck, pieces of the rope with which he is to hang himself. He is acclaimed as a sort of saint, but when he attempts to better their lot without sacrifice, he fails. Music by Robert Charlebois.
fp: (in French) Gesu Hall, Montreal, March 24, 1967.

D858. *Hearts.* Trans. Marc Gelinas. Montreal, Centre d'Essai, 1969.
13 scenes. 19m/3f.
A comment on the future of our progressive free society. The Heart Bank, which is "authorized to levy hearts from citizens of condemnable social strata" for use in transplant experiments, is overthrown by the firemen who carry on the violent inhumane practices rather than stopping them.
fp: (in French) Théâtre de Quat'Sous, October 1969, as "A coeur ouvert".

D859. *The Trial of Jean-Baptiste M.* Trans. Allan Van Meer. Vancouver, Talonbooks, 1974.
2 acts. 7m/2f. Doubling.
J.B. finds himself a sales representative for one of the largest chemical companies of the world, Dutron. The work stifles him, depresses him, and when he is fired, he retaliates with a sawed-off rifle, killing three of his superiors.
fp: Théâtre du Nouveau Monde, Montreal, October 12, 1972. CBC radio, Nov. 1977.

GUSTAFSON, Ralph Barker 1909–

D860. *Alfred the Great.* London, Michael Joseph, 1937.
3 acts. 19m/3f.
A poetic drama in which the Danish king's desire for Alfred's ward leads to war.

HAGMAN, Mary Wilkinson

D861. *Mary and the Holy Thorn.* New York, Vantage Press, 1966.
3 scenes, 6m/3f. Extras.
At the home of Saeone, Mary's adopted daughter, John tells Mary of the persecution of Christians by Saul. Joseph of Arimethea, on his way to Britain, receives a piece of the Holy Thorn from Mary to carry with him.

HAILEY, Arthur 1920–

D862. "Course for Collision" in his *Close-up on Writing for Television.* Garden City, N.Y., Doubleday, 1960.
3 acts. 20m/1f. Extras.
The President of the United States and the Canadian Secretary for External Affairs fly to Russia in a last ditch effort to stop all-out war between the two super powers. They find that nuclear bombers have already been launched, and that the only way to avert war is to collide with the initial bomber.
fp: CBC TV, "General Motors Theatre", April 1957.

D863. "Death Minus One" in his *Close-up on Writing for Television.* Garden City, N.Y., Doubleday, 1960.
3 acts. 12m/2f/1b/1g. Extras.
A boy and girl are trapped in the basement of an old bombed-out building in London when the rubble collapses and uncovers an armed V2 rocket warhead from the end of the Second World War.

D864. "Diary of a Nurse" in his *Close-up on Writing for Television.* Garden City, N.Y., Doubleday, 1960.
3 acts. 10m/13f/1g.
An excellently qualified student nurse contemplates leaving nursing because she feels that she is not able to control her natural emotions and humanity toward her patients.
fp: CBS TV, "Playhouse Ninety".

D865. "Flight into Danger" in his *Close-up on Writing for Television*. Garden City, N.Y., Doubleday, 1960 and in *Four Plays of Our Time*. H. Voaden, ed. Toronto, Macmillan, 1960 and in *Drama TV*. H. Voaden, ed. Toronto, Macmillan, 1966 and in *Ten Canadian Short Plays*. J. Stevens, ed. New York, Dell, 1975.
3 acts. 20m/3f.
An ex-fighter pilot attempts to land a large jetliner when the Captain, the First Officer and a number of the passengers are stricken with food poisoning.
fp: CBC TV, "General Motors Theatre", April 3, 1956.

D866. "Shadow of Suspicion" in his *Close-up on Writing for Television*. Garden City, N.Y., Doubleday, 1960.
3 acts. 16m/5f/3g.
A small child is raped and murdered by an unknown assailant. Frank Mason, a salesman and father, is mistakenly charged with the crime, until he proves that he was a hundred miles away at the time. However, after front page news coverage of the arrest, he and his family are persecuted by those in the city who do not believe his innocence.
fp: CBC TV, "Drama Theatre".

D867. "Time Lock" in his *Close-up on Writing for Television*. Garden City, N.Y., Doubleday, 1960 and in *Entertainment for All*. Ronald K. Side, ed. Toronto, Macmillan, 1968.
3 acts. 11m/2f/1b. Extras.
A young boy is accidentally locked inside a bank vault which will not open again for sixty-three hours. He only has ten hours of air left.
fp: Kraft Television Theatre.

HALLMAN, Eugene S.

D868. "Survival" in *Ways of Mankind*. W.R. Goldschmidt, ed. Boston, Beacon Press, 1954.
1 act. 4m.
A radio play about four men who try to make a 100-mile journey across the tundra after their plane crashes. Arvik, the Eskimo, helps the other three to survive the ordeal.

HAMBLETON, Ronald 1917–

D869. *The Luck of Ginger Coffey*. (Toronto?), n.p., 1967.
3 acts. 15m/6f. Extras.
Libretto for an opera based on the novel of the same name by Brian Moore. An immigrant nearing 40 and out of work almost runs out of his Irish luck. Music by Raymond Parnell.
fp: Canadian Opera Company, Toronto, Sept. 15, 1967.

HAMEL, Guy 1931–

D870. *The Pawnshop*. Toronto, Playwrights Co-op, 1972.
1 act. 8m/2f. Doubling.
An assortment of bizarre people visit the pawnshop and have dealings with the equally bizarre Keeper and his assistant. We find that there are patterns of sorts in all their chaotic and obsessed lives and that the Keeper plays God because "somebody has to".
fp: University of Toronto Studio Theatre, December 1971.

HAMEL, Guy F. Claude 1935–

D871. *Deadline F.L.Q.* Toronto, Hamel Theatre Productions, 1972.
3 acts. 11m/4f.
A drama about the Laporte and Cross kidnappings and the imposition of the War Measures Act.
fp: Theatre Passe Muraille, April 21, 1972.

D872. *Hearing Committee.* Toronto, Author, 1973. (Mimeographed).
2 acts. 5m/2f.
A drama examining the dismissal of a civil servant.

HAMER, Mamie and Helen Lustig

D873. "A Living Thing" in *Women Write For Theatre* vol. 1. Toronto, Playwrights Co-op, 1976.
1 act. 4f.
An ethnic comedy with three older women, one of whom has been recently widowed. With the spectre of her daughter's mother-in-law cooking the gefilte fish, Mrs. Gold manages to reactivate herself back into life.
fp: Smile Company, Toronto, 1976.

HAMILTON, Margaret M.

D874. "Golden Secrets" in *Educational Review,* vol, 61, #2, December 1946.
1 act. 12g.
A "health playlet" in which a little girl is visited by fairies who tell her the ten secrets of keeping fit.

D875. "Summer's Rehearsal" in *Educational Review,* vol. 48, #9, May-June, 1934.
1 act. 1g. Extras.
"A playlet" in which nature welcomes the arrival of summer.

HAMMOND, George Arthur. See Section C.

HANCOCK, W.C.

D876. "Black Precipitate" in *Acadia Athenaeum,* April 1937.
1 scene. 2m/2f.
Two young chemists discover love in the laboratory assisted by bottles of sulphuric acid and saccharine.

D877. "Fate" in *Acadia Athenaeum,* vol. 61. #7, May 1936.
1 scene. 2m/1f. Extras.
A Belgian child newly orphaned during W.W. I notices that her favourite doll — the only tie she retains to a happy past — was made in Germany.

D878. "We've Won" in *Acadia Athenaeum,* vol. 61, #6, April 1936.
1 scene. 3m/1f. Extras.
A striking electrical worker learns too late that the power strike has caused the death of his baby daughter.

HARDIN, Herschel 1936–

D879. "Esker Mike and His Wife Agiluk" in *The Drama Review,* vol. 14, #1, Fall 1969 and Vancouver, New Play Centre, 1972 and (revised version) Toronto, Playwrights Co-op, 1973 and Vancouver, Talonbooks, 1973.
14 scenes. 9m/6f. Extras.
An Innuit woman refuses to bear any more children by her white husband until she is assured that the children won't starve or be taken from her by the government.
fp: Factory Theatre Lab, Toronto, June 4, 1971.

D880. *The Great Wave of Civilization.* Vancouver, Talonbooks, 1976.
2 acts. 8m/6f. Doubling.
The destruction of the people of the Blackfoot Confederacy by the liquor trade in 19th century Montana and Alberta is depicted.
fp: Festival Lennoxville, Lennoxville, Quebec, July 28, 1976.

HARDWICK, H.C. 1896–

D881. "James and the Ogre" in his *None But the Brave.* Agincourt, Ont., Book Society, 1968.
1 act. 1m/1f/7b.
A children's play. Four boy scouts encounter Mr. and Mrs. Ogre.

D882. "Lost a Smallish Brown Dog" in his *None But the Brave.* Agincourt, Ont., Book Society, 1968.
1 act. 6m/4f.
A children's play. A dog is lost and found again in the forest.

D883. "None But the Brave" in his *None But the Brave.* Agincourt, Ont., Book Society, 1968.
1 act. 8m/1f. Extras.
A children's play. Manfred, a hero, wins the lady Ingrid for his bride.

D884. "Perseus and Andromeda" in his *None But the Brave.* Agincourt, Ont., Book Society, 1968.
1 act. 4m/2f. Extras.
A children's play. Perseus slays the sea monster and wins Andromeda for his bride.

D885. "Robin Hood and Friar Tobias" in his *None But the Brave.* Agincourt, Ont., Book Society, 1968.
1 act. 12m.
A children's play. Robin Hood and Friar Tobias rescue a poor shepherd from a greedy land owner.

D886. "Romantic Royalty" in his *None But the Brave.* Agincourt, Ont., Book Society, 1968.
1 act. 5m/2f. Extras.
A children's play. Prince Basilio wins the princess Sabrina for his bride.

D887. "The Sleeping Beauty" in his *None But the Brave.* Agincourt, Ont., Book Society, 1968.
1 act. 7m/3f. Extras.
A children's play. An adaptation of the Grimm fairy tale.

D888. "The Wishing Well" in his *None But the Brave*. Agincourt, Ont., Book Society, 1968.
1 act. 7m/1f/5b.
A children's play. A young boy meets the king and queen with the help of a wishing well.

HARKER, Lizzie Allen 1863– and F.R. Pryor

D889. *Marigold.* London, French, 1928.
4 acts. 8m/6f.
"An Arcadian comedy". Marigold has been brought up by Mrs. Pringle, and the identity of her real mother is kept from her. However, Marigold eventually discovers who her mother is, breaks off the marriage arranged by her father, and becomes engaged to the man she loves.

HARPER, John Murdoch 1845–1919

D890. *Champlain.* Toronto, Briggs, 1908 and Toronto, Trade Publishing, 1908 and London, Warne, 1908 and New York, Lane, 1908 and Toronto, T.J. Moore, n.d.
3 acts. 23m/5f. Extras.
An account of the history of Quebec City from its establishment to its capture by the English. The focus is on the animosity between trading interests and the colonists but also includes the conspiracy against Champlain's life and the riots against Beauchasse's policies.

HARRIS, James G.

D891. *Money for Jam.* Montreal, Author, 1965. (Mimeographed).
3 acts. 4m/2f.
Hugh, motivated purely by greed and by his envy of the sanctimonious Donny, murders him, consummating the perfect crime by marrying his accomplice, Donny's wife. But there's no honour among thieves and Hugh becomes more and more ensnared in the results of his treachery.
fp: La Poudriere, Montreal International Theatre, (1965?).

HARRIS, Marcia

D892. *The Wind on the Heath,* Western Canada Theatre Conference. Edmonton, Dept. of Extension, University of Alberta, 1945.
1 act. 3m/2f.
A blind girl and a crippled young man facing a lay-off in the war factory they have been working in discover their love for each other.

HARRIS, Neil

D893. *The Dream Unwinds.* Toronto, French, 1953.
1 act. 4m/2f.
After five years away, Joe returns home and his fantasized recollections of what home was like are shattered.

HARRIS, Walter Eric 1889–

D894. *Such Harmony.* Toronto, French, 1936.
1 act. 4m/3f. Extras.
A family picnic becomes the framework for a play concerned with the growth of socialism in the 1930s and the opposition's authoritarian reaction to it.

D895. *Twenty-five Cents.* Toronto and New York, French, 1936 and in *The Best One Act Plays of 1937.* M. Mayorga, ed. New York, Dodd, Mead 1938 and in *Eight New One-Act Plays of 1938.* William Armstrong, ed. London, Lovat Dickson, 1938 and Toronto, Macmillan, 1938.
1 act. 3m/3f.
This play, set in the Depression, deals with the demoralizing effects of the money shortage on a working class family.
fp: Sarnia Drama League, n.d. and London Little Theatre, D.D.F. Festival, 1936.

HARRISON, Susie Frances (Riley) 1859–1935

D896. "A Phantom Born of Song" by Seranus (pseud.) in her *Four Ballads and a Play.* Toronto, Haddon, 1933.
1 act. 7m/2f.
An evil miner attempts to murder a fellow worker in order to get a woman, but he is driven to madness and suicide by the hallucination of a tune his supposed victim used to whistle.

HARRON, Donald Hugh 1924–

D897. *Anne of Green Gables.* New York, French, 1972.
2 acts. 6m/11f/6b/6g.
The musical adapted from L.M. Montgomery's novel about the orphan girl adopted by a spinster and her old bachelor brother in turn-of-the-century Prince Edward Island. Music by Norman Campbell.
fp: City Centre 55 Street Theatre, Charlottetown, December 1971.

D898. *Private Turvey's War.* N.p., n.p. (1970?). (Mimeographed).
2 acts. 19m/3f. Doubling.
The musical comedy about a private's adventures in W.W. II adapted from Earle Birney's novel *Turvey.* Music by Norman Campbell.
fp: Charlottetown Festival, P.E.I., 1970.

HART, Jean T.

D899. "Butterflies in Bloom" in *Educational Review,* vol. 44, #10, June 1930.
1 act. 1g/3b. Extras.
Mother Nature reminds the caterpillars that it is time to build cocoons and turn into butterflies.

D900. "The Play-Room Closet Door" in *Educational Review,* vol. 44, #8, April 1930.
1 act. 4b/4g. Extras.
"A playlet for young children". The closet door is locked from the inside and no one can figure out how to open it.

HATFIELD, Gregory Doane Haliburton 1906-. See DOANE, Gregory.

HATTON, G.R., Mr. and Mrs.

D902. "Mr. Bumble's Proposal" in *Scenes from Dickens*. J.E. Jones, ed. Toronto, McClelland & Stewart, 1923.
1 act. 1m/1f. Extras.
An adaptation of an incident from Charles Dickens' *Oliver Twist*. When Mr. Bumble has tea with Mrs. Corney, he uses the opportunity to propose to her.

HAUSVATER, Alexander

D903. *The Crime and Punishment Show*. Toronto, Playwrights Co-op, 1978.
2 acts. 4m/3f. Extras. Doubling.
A dramatic adaptation of Dostoyevsky's classic novel.
fp: Montreal Theatre Lab at the Centaur Theatre, Nov. 5, 1975.

HAVARD, Lezley

D904. "Claws" in *Victims*. Women Write For Theatre, vol. 4. Toronto, Playwrights Co-op, 1976.
1 act. 1m/1f.
Jeff finds his cat frozen to death and the shock has strange repercussions on both Jeff and his wife, Paula. Jeff slowly becomes his pet and reduces Paula to admitting that she left Puss outside, causing its death.

D905. "Despair" in *Victims*. Women Write for Theatre, vol. 4. Toronto, Playwrights Co-op, 1976.
1 act. 1f.
The guilt and frustration following a woman's abortion ends in tragedy.

D906. "Forfeits" in *Victims*. Women Write for Theatre, vol. 4. Toronto, Playwrights Co-op, 1976.
1 act. 1m/2f.
Cass plays a deadly game with her childhood companion in which the loser must pay a forfeit, a tragic forfeit that neither Emma nor George suspect.

HAWKINS, Albro

D907. *To Get Off the Street*. Halifax, Dramatists Co-op, 1978.
1 act. 3m/2f.
A 40-year-old pregnant woman tries to find a solution for her predicament and that of her son Joey.

HEARN, John

D908. *A Festival of Carol's*. Don Mills, Ont., Author, 1967. (Mimeographed).
3 acts. 7m/3f. Doubling.
An absurdist comedy about three couples, their various entanglements and the obsessions which imprison them, metaphorically and physically.
fp: Royal Alexandra Theatre, Toronto, March 20, 1968.

HEIDE, Christopher 1951–

D909. *On the Lee Shore.* Halifax, Dramatists Co-op, 1977 and Toronto, Playwrights Co-op, 1978.
2 acts. 2m/2f.
David and Vicky return to the East Coast after three years at University of Toronto. The day before they are to be married, David has a change of heart having made several discoveries about himself, his parents and his fiancee.
fp: Tarragon Theatre, Toronto, May 8, 1977.

D910. *The Stamp Lady's Miracle.* Halifax, Dramatists Co-op, 1977.
1 act. 4m/3f.
Wheelchair-bound Jennie struggles to maintain the happiness of her adopted daughter Katie through her stamp collection.

D911. *Two Sisters/The Scream.* Halifax, Dramatists Co-op, 1977 and in *Event,* vol. 6, #1, 1977.
1 act. 2f.
An expressionist play in which two sisters, completely dependent upon each other, explore the boundaries of the world in which they are trapped.
fp: Noon Hour Theatre, Halifax, December 1976.

HELWIG, David 1938–

D912. "The Dancers of Colbek" in his *Figures in a Landscape.* Ottawa, Oberon, 1967.
1 act. 3m/3f.
"A play based on a medieval legend". A group of raggle-taggle young people and the priest's daughter dance and play in the churchyard, and when they will not stop their sacrilege are cursed to dance for a whole year.

D913. "The Dreambook" in his *Figures in a Landscape.* Ottawa, Oberon, 1967.
1 act. 2m/2f.
An allegory about a poet who has never been able to write a poem and a woman whose daughter he loves. To see the daughter he must reveal his dreams to the mother and this he cannot do.

D914. "A Time of Winter" in his *Figures in a Landscape.* Ottawa, Oberon, 1967.
3 acts. 4m/3f.
In this examination of a family's disintegration, which is paralleled by the financial failure of the town, the focus is on the youngest daughter Clare and her relationships with her father, her sister and her lover.
fp: Domino Theatre, Kingston, Ont., March 10, 1967.

HENDRY, Tom 1929–

D915. "Fifteen Miles of Broken Glass" in *A Theatre Happening.* Toronto, Nelson, 1968 and *Fifteen Miles of Broken Glass.* Toronto, Playwrights Co-op, 1972 and Vancouver, Talonbooks, 1975.
2 acts. 7m/3f. Extras.
Alec McNabb turns 18 during the last days of W.W. II. He has been looking forward to being a fighter pilot and finds it hard to accept that the war is over. Returning veterans and others try unsuccessfully to convince him that war is ugly and that he should be grateful not to have to go.
fp: CBC TV, "Festival", Sept. 21, 1966. CBC radio "Stage", Oct. 15, 1967. Central Ontario Drama Festival, Hart House Theatre, Toronto, 1970.

D916. *Gravediggers of 1942.* Toronto, Playwrights Co-op, 1973 and in *Canadian Theatre Review,* #15, Summer 1977.
1 act. 4m/2f.
A musical-comedy-documentary account of the Dieppe Raid in which an amateur theatre group get their wish for a backer and a chance to do their bit for the war effort. However, things don't quite turn out as planned as they find fantasy becoming an undesirable reality of decadence, violence and bloodshed.
fp: Toronto Free Theatre, June 26, 1973.

D917. *Friends and Lovers.* Toronto, Playwrights Co-op, 1972.
"Two One Act Plays suitable for performing together or separately." See *You Smell Good to Me* and *The Missionary Position.*

D918. *How Are Things With the Walking Wounded?.* Toronto, Playwrights Co-op, 1972.
3 acts. 4m/4f.
The painful and tangled emotional relationships of a group of people are revealed at a party celebrating the anniversary of two homosexuals.
fp: Toronto Free Theatre, June 1972.

D919. *The Missionary Position.* Toronto, Playwrights Co-op, 1972.
1 act. 2m/2f.
The play takes place in the New York apartment of a homosexual professional man and his lover, a painter. A black girl, a model for the painter, lives there as well while she waits for her "big chance" in theatre.
fp: Noon-hour Theatre, Vancouver, Fall 1972.

D920. "That Boy, Call Him Back" in *Performing Arts in Canada,* vol. 9, #4, Winter 1972.
1 act. 5m/1f.
An old man, dying in hospital, is visited by his younger son, a successful businessman, whose success and whose life the father is unable to understand.
fp: Michigan State University.

D921. *You Smell Good to Me.* Toronto, Playwrights Co-op, 1972.
1 act. 2m/1f.
Six years of being treated like "a convenience" provokes a secretary to examine her relationship with her lover.
fp: (Workshop), Factory Theatre Lab, Toronto, April 1972.

HENRY, Ann 1914–

D922. *Lulu Street.* Toronto, Playwrights Co-op, 1972 and Vancouver, Talonbooks, 1975.
3 acts. 9m/3f.
Set in Winnipeg during the General Strike of 1919, this play focusses on the characters who live in a boarding house on Lulu Street. Owned by Mathew Alexander, a "platform man" in the strike and run by his daughter Elly, the house harbours a cross-section of strike supporters, from Sadie, "sometime whore", to Big Isaac, "master of the pipes".
fp: (original), Manitoba Theatre Centre, Winnipeg, March 1967; (revised), Festival Lennoxville, P.Q. Summer 1972. CBC TV, September 1975.

HENSLEY, Sophia Margaret (Almon) 1866–

D923. *Princess Mignon.* By Almon Hensley. New York, Kenworth, 1900.
3 acts. 10m/4f. Extra.
A musical based on the fairytale by Andrew Lang about the search of a young king for a worthy wife who will help him solve his country's problems. Music by Hubert A. Hensley.

HERBERT, John 1926–

D924. "Beer Room" in *Some Angry Summer Songs.* Vancouver, Talonbooks, 1976.
1 act. 6m.
In a downtown Toronto gay bar, various characters banter with one another and philosophize about life.
fp: Forest Hill Chamber Theatre, Forest Hill Library, Toronto, May 30, 1974.

D925. "Close Friends" in *Some Angry Summer Songs.* Vancouver, Talonbooks, 1976.
1 act. 2m.
A ritualistic encounter in which two former lovers are briefly reunited, explore their failed relationship and drift apart again like fading memories.
fp: Forest Hill Chamber Theatre, Forest Hill Library, Toronto, May 30, 1974.

D926. "The Dinosaurs" in *Some Angry Summer Songs.* Vancouver, Talonbooks, 1976.
1 act. 1m/1f.
The world famous Canadian actress Monique Dominique confronts and vanquishes Rudolph Nabob, Canada's most influential drama critic, who has once again destroyed her career in Canada with his hostile reviews.
fp: Forest Hill Chamber Theatre, Forest Hill Library, Toronto May 30, 1974.

D927. *Fortune and Men's Eyes.* New York, Grove Press, 1967 and in *Open Space Plays.* Charles Marowitz, ed. Harmondsworth, England, Penguin, 1974.
2 acts. 5m.
A boys' reformatory in Canada receives a new inmate who is provoked by the violence and strangeness into abandoning his plans to become a mechanic and becomes instead an outcast.
fp: Actors' Playhouse, New York, Feb. 23, 1967. (Workshop), Stratford Festival, Oct. 1965.

D928. "Omphale and the Hero" in *Canadian Theatre Review,* #3, Summer 1974.
3 acts. 3m/1f.
A sensitive drama concerning a whore, Antoinette, who takes in a wanderer, Mac, angering her usual customers, the sadistic chief of police and the reticent mayor. In retaliation for locking him out, the police chief kills Antoinette and moves a new woman into her room to become the new town whore.
fp: Forest Hill Chamber Theatre, Toronto, 1974.

D929. "Pearl Divers" in *Some Angry Summer Songs.* Vancouver, Talonbooks, 1976.
1 act. 3f/1m.
Despite his flamboyance and opposition from the management, Queenie lands a job as a dishwasher in a restaurant with the help of Irish Mary.
fp: Forest Hill Chamber Theatre, Forest Hill Library, Toronto, May 30, 1974.

D930. "Variations on a Schizoid Interview" in *Stage Voices.* Geraldine Anthony, ed. Toronto, Doubleday, 1978.
1 act. 2m.
John interviews Herbert about John Herbert's life and art.

HERFORD, Beatrice

D931. "The Telegram" in *Echoes,* March 1925.
1 scene. 2f.
A brief comic sketch about a woman with a cold phoning a telegram message.

HEZZELWOOD, Oliver 1861-1933

D932. "The Invisible Urge" in his *Poems and a Play.* Toronto, Ontario Press, 1926.
3 acts. 6m/3f. Extras.
"A Canadian drama of the Great War". The play deals with the fates of the young men who enlist in the army.

HILL, Frederick T.

D933. *The Adventures of Moses.* Riverhurst, Saskatchewan, Weekly Courier, (1935?).
1 act. 1m/1f.
A farce in which a newlywed couple find their love turned to antagonism when Tom brings home a cat which destroys many of their valuable possessions.

D934. *The Day of Redemption.* London, Ont., Peter Morris, (1935?).
1 act. 4m/1f.
"A Christian drama". On Christmas Eve, the Wandering Jew warns the cold hearted Adam and Barbara Fane of the results of their greed and cruelty, and they undergo a change of heart.

D935. *The Eleventh Hour.* London, Ont., Peter Morris, 1935.
4 acts. 5m/2f.
A melodrama in which a scheming lawyer is foiled in his attempt to take over a blind grandfather's Saskatchewan farm during the Depression and to force his grand-daughter to marry him.

HILL, Kathleen Louise 1917–. See HILL, Kay.

HILL, Kay 1917–

D936. "Cobbler, Stick To Thy Last" in *Encounter: Canadian Drama in Four Media.* Eugene Benson, ed. Toronto, Methuen, 1973 and in *Ten Canadian Short Plays.* J. Stevens, ed. New York, Dell, 1975 and in *Transistions 1: Short Plays.* Edward Peck, ed. Vancouver, Commcept Publishing, 1978.
1 act. 2m/3f.
A man faces the problem of having a new wife before the older, previous one is dead. Other problems arise when a young man cannot be convinced that he should love the charming Susanna Comfort rather than his dog.
p: Instant Theatre, Montreal, December 1965.

D937. "Midnight Burial" in *Blue-Ribbon Plays for Girls.* Sylvia Kamerman, ed. Boston, Plays 1955 and in *Favourite Plays for Classroom Reading.* Donald Durrell and B. Alice Crossley, eds. Boston, Plays, 1965 and in *One Hundred Plays for Children.* A.S. Burack, ed. Boston, Plays, 1970.
1 act. 8g.
A young girl at a summer camp is sent a poisoned cake which she has difficulties getting rid of.

D938. "Three to Get Married" in *Beyond the Footlights.* Hugh McKellar, ed. Toronto, Macmillan, 1963 and *Three to Get Married.* New York, French, 1964.
3 acts. 6m/4f.
A comedy set in Nova Scotia about the successful attempts of an absent-minded clergyman to find husbands for his three daughters by temporarily turning his house into an inn.
fp: CBC TV "On Camera", Feb. 17, 1958. CBC radio "Summer Stage", Oct. 2, 1964.

HINE, Daryl

D939. "Defunctive Music" in *Tamarack Review,* vol. 38, Winter 1966.
1 act. 2m/1f.
A radio play. A young man and his wife discuss their lives together and their ideas of life, love, trust and faithfulness.
fp: CBC radio "Wednesday Night", June 28, 1961.

HIRSCH, John Stephen 1930–

D940. *The Dybbuk.* Winnipeg, Peguis Publishers, 1975.
2 acts. 15m/6f. Extras. Doubling.
An adaptation of S. Ansky's classic about the greedy Sender whose daughter becomes possessed by an evil spirit as punishment.
fp: Manitoba Theatre Centre, Winnipeg, Jan. 11, 1974.

HITCHINS, William English 1910–

D941. *Even Our Faith.* Toronto, General Board of Religious Education, (1952?).
3 acts. 47m/2f. Extras.
"A pageant depicting the story of the Anglican Church in Canada" from the Rev. Wolfall, companion to Martin Frobisher, to Bishop Bompas of the Yukon.
fp: General synod, London, Ont., September 1952.

HODKINSON, Ken

D942. "How Long" in *Prism,* vol. 2, #3, Spring 1961.
1 act. 5m/2f. Extras.
A play in which people are representatives of functions and ideologies, focusing on the idea that man must show concern for the welfare of others. A discussion of the playwright's act of creation is an underlying theme.
fp: Frederic Wood Theatre, U.B.C., Nov. 25, 1960 as "Look Bound in Apathy."

HOLDEN, Lyle P.

D943. "A Spring Flower Garden" in *Educational Review,* vol. 35, #11, June-July 1921.
1 act. 7m/7f.
Miss Springtime wakens all her flowers and they introduce themselves.

HOLLAND, Norah Mary 1876–1925

D944. "The Awakening of the Lily" in her *When Half Gods Go and Other Poems*. Toronto, Macmillan, 1924.
1 act. 9m/17f. Extras.
"A fairy phantasy". The witch Winter places a spell on the Lily Fairy which is broken by a kiss from the unselfish Bee.

D945. "When Half Gods Go" in her *When Half Gods Go and Other Poems*. Toronto, Macmillan, 1924.
1 act. 6m/3f. Extras.
"A mystery play". Greek gods come to worship "the God-made man" in Bethlehem.
p: Eaton Girls Club, Margaret Eaton Hall, Toronto, Dec. 15, 1930.

HOLLINGSHEAD, Greg

D946. "Straight Man" in *Acta*, vol. 92, #2, December 1967.
1 act. 3m.
A man attempts to be a poet but is overwhelmed by the comments of his companions.

HOLLINGSWORTH, Margaret

D946A. *Alli Alli Oh*. Vancouver, New Play Centre, 1977.
1 act. 2f.
Set in a farmhouse on an island off the coast of B.C., this psychological drama offers a disturbing look at the relationship between two women. Alli must choose between reality, which includes a healthy relationship with Muriel, and a relapse into madness.
fp: New Play Centre at the Vancouver East Cultural Centre, duMaurier Festival, May 12, 1977.

D946B. "The Apple in the Eye" in *Branching Out*, vol.4, #5, Nov./Dec. 1977.
1 act. 1m/1f.
A radio play in which a young married woman contemplates her marriage with Martin, a computer scientist.
fp: CBC radio.

D947. *Bushed*. Vancouver, New Play Centre, 1973.
1 scene. 2m/4f.
Two old men sit telling tales of past experiences and planning to rape the manageress of the laundromat. When she arrives they leave.
fp: New Play Centre, March 1973.

D948. *Dance for My Father*. Vancouver, New Play Centre, 1976.
2 acts. 5m/4f.
The story of one girl's growth and her attachment to her absent father and the women in his life.

D949. *Islands*. Vancouver, New Play Centre, 1978.
1 act. 3f.
A sequel to her *Alli Alli Oh*. Rose, who plans to re-marry, visits her daughter Muriel on her farm. Old conflicts over disparate expectations are intensified when Muriel's ex-lover Alli returns from treatment in an asylum, adding her problems to the situation and, ultimately, renewing Muriel's determination to become self-reliant.

D950. *Mother Country.* Vancouver, New Play Centre, 1978.
2 acts. 2m/5f.
A family gathering in an eccentric house on a Gulf Island is interrupted by the arrival of the absent father's prospective young wife. Levels of role-playing are provided by the interaction of British, American and Canadian characters.

D951. "Operators" in *West Coast Plays.* C. Brissenden, ed. Vancouver and Toronto, New Play Centre-Fineglow Plays, 1975.
1 act. 3f.
Jerri, 28 and independent mother of two, is the new woman on the night shift working with Sara, a mild and introverted middle-aged mother of five, and Christmas, an abrasive sixty-year-old mystery. They question, cajole and badger one another into revelations which have disquieting consequences.
fp: New Play Centre, Vancouver, du Maurier Festival, April 27, 1974.

HOLLINGSWORTH, Michael

D952. *Clear Light.* Toronto, Playwrights Co-op, 1973 and Toronto, Coach House Press, 1976.
1 act. 3m/2f.
A graphic and violent satire on the social mores of the 1970s. Host, Hostess, Boy Friend and Girl Friend are spending a Saturday night playing cards. But the evening becomes an indulgence in forbidden and revolting activities.
fp: Toronto Free Theatre, October 1973.

D953. *Strawberry Fields.* Toronto, Playwrights Co-op, 1973 and in *The Factory Lab Anthology.* C. Brissenden, ed. Vancouver, Talonbooks, 1974 and as *Fields.* Toronto, Playwrights Co-op, 1974.
2 scenes. 3m.
In the aftermath of a rock festival, three men talk, scrounge food, contemplate eating a dog, and eventually murder one of their number.
fp: Factory Theatre Lab, Toronto, December 1972.

D955. **HOLMES, John.** *The Fair Country. The Loyalists.* See **PARKHILL, Francis.**

HONEYSETTE, Anne C.

D956. *The Last Chapter.* Ottawa, Ottawa Little Theatre Workshop, #13.
1 act. 5m/1f.
A comedy about a spare-time writer of murder mysteries who can never manage the last chapter. Heeding his wife's advice that a writer should write about what he knows, he attempts to work himself up to murder the milkman.

HOOD, Hugh John Blagdon 1928–

D957. "Friends and Relations" in *The Play's the Thing.* Tony Gifford, ed. Toronto, Macmillan, 1976.
4 acts. 6m/4f.
A television drama. Mrs. Bird, the widow of the town's doctor and most popular citizen, was treated with pity and condescension by many of his family while he lived. After his death, she begins to assert a new decisiveness and independence of action.
fp: CBC TV series "The Play's the Thing", September 1973–May 1974.

HOOKE, Hilda Mary 1898–

D958. "Brown Lady Johnson" in her *One Act Plays from Canadian History*. Toronto, Longmans, Green, 1942.
1 act. 5m/5f. Extras.
This is the story of Molly Brant, the Indian wife of Sir William Johnson, and her role as peacemaker between whites and Indians.

D959. "Helene of New France" in her *One Act Plays from Canadian History*. Toronto, Longmans, Green, 1942.
1 act. 3m/3f/1b/1g.
The story of the marriage and life together of Samuel de Champlain and his young wife Helene of New France.

D960. "Here Will I Nest" in her *One Act Plays from Canadian History*. Toronto, Longmans, Green, 1942.
1 act. 4m/2f.
This play concerns Colonel Talbot's desire for settlers at Castle Malahide on Lake Erie and their arrival in 1809.
p: London Little Theatre, London, Ont., 1938.

D961. "More Things in Heaven" in her *One Act Plays from Canadian History*. Toronto, Longmans, Green, 1942.
1 act. 4m/3f.
Several young people, including Dr. Troyer's grand-daughter Margaret, are playing games and as a penalty for losing Marg is forced to demonstrate her grandfather's magic divining rod which has the power to summon spirits. A spirit descends in the form of a hawk which draws away the soul of the doctor.

D962. "On the King's Birthday" in her *One Act Plays from Canadian History*. Toronto, Longmans, Green, 1942.
1 act. 6m/4f.
This play is the story of Thomas Talbot's unsuccessful courtship of the half Indian daughter of Sir William Johnson.

D963. "The Princess of the Snows" in her *One Act Plays from Canadian History*. Toronto, Longmans, Green, 1942.
1 act. 2m/2f.
This play presents the friendship of Thomas Talbot and Amelia, youngest daughter of George III.

D964. *The Streamlined Madonna*. Western Canada Theatre Conference. Edmonton, Dept. of Extension, University of Alberta, 1946.
1 act. 4m/2f.
A drama about a minister at a clinic who talks a bank robber into surrendering and to change his life of crime.

D965. "Widow's Scarlet" in her *One Act Plays from Canadian History*. Toronto, Longmans, Green, 1942.
1 act. 2m/1f.
Michael Troyer falls in love with the widow Rosa Monroe and together they foil Dr. Troyer's plan to prove her a witch.
p: London Little Theatre, London, Ont., 1939.

D966. "The Witch House of Baldoon" in her *One Act Plays from Canadian History.* Toronto, Longmans, Green, 1942.
1 act. 4m/3f.
The famed German physician Dr. Troyer removes a curse placed by an Indian witch on the home of John McDonald.
p: London Little Theatre, London, Ont., 1939.

HOOKE, Samuel H.

D967. "The Tyrants of Toronto" in *The Canadian Forum,* vol. 9, #102, 1929.
3 acts. 5m. Extras. Chorus.
"A (very) Light Opera, by Gullem and Silliman. (No rights reserved.)" Makes fun of the anti-Bolshevik feeling in Toronto in the '20s.

HOOPER, Dora M.

D968. *Where the Buffalo Roam.* New York, French, 1940 and in *Twenty Short Plays on a Royalty Holiday* vol. 2. M. Mayorga, ed. New York, French, 1940.
1 act. 3m/2f/1g.
Not wishing to disillusion a visiting aunt from England, the family of a prairie farmer decides to live up to her expectations of the wild and rugged west.

HOPKINS, Marion

D969. "The Spirit of Giving" in *Educational Review,* vol. 35, #4, November 1920.
1 act. 1m/1f/4b. Extras.
Jack wins the contest and displays the spirit of giving to his friends who so generously helped him.

HORNBY, Richard

D970. "The Kidnappers" in *The Kidnappers and Two Pollution Sketches.* Drama at Calgary, Playscript Number One. Philip McCoy, ed. Calgary, University of Calgary, 1974.
1 act. 3m/1f.
A satirical play in which three members of an extremist "radical" group bungle the kidnapping of a government official.
fp: Department of Drama, University of Calgary, 1971.

HORNE, Florence

D971. "Mother Canada's Christmas Tree" in *Canadian Thinker,* December 1937.
Issue unavailable for annotation.

HOSEIN, Jennifer

D972. "Chanson Pour Rene Claude" in *Event,* vol. 6, #2, 1977.
1 act. 1m.
A play about a mentally disturbed young man in a Montreal slum.

HOSIE, Herbert– 1966

D973. "Photograph" in *West Coast Review,* vol. 12, #3, January 1978.
1 act. 1m/1f.
An experimental play in which an old photograph recalls the encounter between a man and a woman 30 years earlier.
fp: CBC radio, 1965. Revised version, CBC radio, 1973 and July 19, 1976.

HOWARD, Hilda (Glynn) 1887–. See GLYNN-WARD, Hilda.

HOWARD, Wilbur

D974. "Murder in the University" in *Acta Victoriana,* vol. 61, #2, Nov. 1936.
1 scene. 4m. Chorus.
A satire of university life.

HUBERT, Cam 1938–

D975. *Echoes of Other Things.* Vancouver, New Play Centre, (197-?).
3 acts. 5m/2f.
Through its focus on the marriage of a middle-aged couple, a depiction of how city life affects and alters people from a small town.

D976. *Rites of Passage.* Vancouver, New Play Centre, 1975.
2 acts. 2m/2f/1g.
The humorous story of three generations of a mining family from Nanaimo, B.C. as seen through the eyes of the youngest child.
fp: Vancouver, New Play Centre, Nov. 4, 1975.

D977. *The Trouble With the Women's Movement Is, It Has No Sense of Humour At All.* Vancouver, New Play Centre, 1976.
1 act. 2m/2f. Chorus.
An improvisational play using nursery rhymes to satirize the Women's Movement.
fp: West Vancouver, 1976.

D978. *The Twin Sinks of Allan Sammy.* Toronto, Playwrights Co-op, 1973 and in *Five Canadian Plays.* Toronto, Playwrights Co-op, 1978.
1 act. 4m/3f.
Allan Sammy is an Indian cut loose in the big city — out of work, out of money, and for a moment, almost out of pride as he finds himself tempted to trade in his cultural heritage for survival on the White Man's terms.
fp: Tillicum Theatre, Nanaimo, B.C., 1973.

D979. *We're All Here Except Mike Casey's Horse.* Toronto, Playwrights Co-op, 1974.
2 acts. 5m/4f.
Old friends gather to welcome Joe back to the small western town of his childhood. Together they re-enact their most luminous memories, including the saga of Old Mike Casey's horse.

HUGHES, Alan

D980. "Aquarium" in his *Aquarium, The Kibitzer, Requiem for a Mensh.* Toronto, Playwrights Co-op, 1978.
1 act. 2m/1f.
Revelations are forthcoming when a trio gathers at a public aquarium.

D981. "The Kibitzer" in his *Aquarium, The Kibitzer, Requiem for a Mensh*. Toronto, Playwrights Co-op, 1978.
1 act. 2m/1f.
While spending time on a riverbank, a couple is visited by an interfering stranger.

D982. "Requiem for a Mensh" in his *Aquarium, The Kibitzer, Requiem for a Mensh*. Toronto, Playwrights Co-op, 1978.
1 act. 3m.
Two men building a scaffold find themselves unemployed when the death penalty is suddenly abolished.

HUGHES, E. Llewellyn

D983. "The Recoil" in *Canadian Magazine*, #54, December 1919.
1 act. 1m/2f.
A young woman who has lost her fiance and her baby turns to liquor to forget her problems. This only causes her the loss of her best friend as well.

HUGHES, John

D984. "The Ship of Dreams" in *Canada on Stage*. Stanley Richards, ed. Toronto, Clarke Irwin, 1960.
1 act. 4m/3f.
Tom Daley, a young Welsh boy full of dreams about the exciting life of the sea, overcomes his father's efforts to mould him into a businessman and follows his own vision.

HULL, Raymond Horace 1919–

D985. "The Bunker" in his *Profitable Playwriting*. Don Mills, Ont., Longmans, 1968.
1 act. 2m/3f.
"A comedy". After a nuclear war, a provincial premier tries to carry on without any word from Ottawa despite the desertion of almost all his staff and the appearance of the People's Militia.

D986. *The Drunkard.* Denver, Colorado, Pioneer Drama Service, 1967.
2 acts. 3m/2f.
A young man drinks himself and his family into ruin and starvation, while an evil lawyer attempts to drive him further into despair and gain possession of his estate.

D987. *Men Were Deceivers Ever or The Curse of the Ginger Tipple.* Cody, Wyoming, Pioneer Drama Service, 1969.
3 acts. 3m/2f.
A reformed drunkard, owner of a temperance hotel, is tempted from the "straight and narrow path" by the evil Lushmoor who convinces him that Ginger Tipple is a non-alcoholic beverage.
A sequel to *The Drunkard*.

D988. *Roast Pig.* Chicago, Dramatic Publishing, 1967.
1 act. 7m/5f.
The Chinese legend of how man learned to roast pig meat. Based on the essay "A Dissertation upon Roast Pig" by Charles Lamb.

D989. *Wedded to a Villain or Locked in a Living Tomb.* Cody, Wyoming, Pioneer Drama Service, 1967.
1 act. 3m/3f.
"An olde-time melodrama" in which Murgatroyd Flashington marries Bonnie, imprisons her in an asylum, forges her death certificate and then tries to collect her insurance money. Jack Manley, the milkman, saves the day.

HULME, George 1932–

D990. *Displaced Affections.* Toronto, Canadian Theatre Centre, 1967.
3 acts. 6m/3f.
Sharon, an alcoholic widow who has built up a prosperous restaurant business, marries Eddy, an ineffectual, grasping and much younger man. More and more she shuts her son Mike out of her life and gradually acquiesces to Eddy in everything.
p: Royal Court Theatre, London.

D991. *The Life and Death of Adolf Hitler.* London, Colin Smythe, 1975 and Toronto, Macmillan, 1976.
5 parts. 70m/20f/5b. Doubling.
A vast documentary drama beginning with Hitler's christening and ending with his death in the Berlin bunker, showing the forces that shaped Hitler and the death and destruction he wreaks upon the world.

HUMPHRYS, Ruth

D992. *No Trouble At All.* Toronto, French, 1959.
1 act. 2m/3f. Extras.
Domestic comedy concerning the mishaps caused by a movie actress' dinner visit with a first cousin whose husband, a professor of English at the local university, brings the dean home for dinner the same evening.

HUNTER, Charlotte

D993. "Mercedes Bends" in *Reading, Writing and Radio.* Winston G. Schell, Marstan E. Woollings. Don Mills, Ont., Longman Canada, 1977.
1 scene. 2m.
A one-minute radio play consisting of an argument between a Mercedes and an Austin based on puns of car names.
fp: CBC radio "Sunny Days", summer 1975.

HUNTER, Martin 1933–

D994. *Charisma.* Toronto, Playwrights Co-op, 1972.
2 acts. 12m/6f.
The play traces the career of the irascible and irrepressible Alkibiades from the time of his uncle Pericles' death to his exile to Thrace.
fp: University of Toronto Summer Centre Theatre, July 1972.

D995. *Flowers of Paradise.* Toronto, Playwrights Co-op, 1972.
14 scenes. 7m/7f.
A downtown church trying to revitalize itself opens its doors to a group of young people who start a commune there. Music by Jeffrey Cohen.
fp: University College Playhouse, Toronto, February 1971.

D996. *Out Flew the Web and Floated Wide.* Toronto, Playwrights Co-op, 1972.
3 acts. 6m/7f.
An old established family goes through several crises when the younger set throws a party.
fp: Hart House Theatre, Toronto, 1967.

D997. *Young Hunting.* Toronto, Playwrights Co-op, 1972.
2 acts. 2m/2f.
Chaos results when Jeannie returns home after a 13 year absence and tries to reorganize the lives of her family and friends.
fp: Hart House Theatre, Toronto, 1969.

HURLEY, Christopher 1949– and Randy Woods

D998. *The Fat Clown at the Circus and Other Plays for Puppets.* Winnipeg, Prairie Publishing, 1977.
A collection of eleven short puppet plays for children developed by the Manitoba Puppet Theatre.

HURLEY, Joan Mason

D999. *Death Seat.* Vancouver, New Play Centre, (197-?)
1 act. 2m/3f/1b.
A woman goes into a bar after an accident in which her son was severely injured and his friend killed. As she and the other characters speak, we realize that all are dead or dying and that the bartender is a representation of death.

D1000. "Fugue for Female Voices" in *Canadian One Act Plays for Women.* Victoria, A Room of One's Own Press, 1975.
1 act. 5f. Extras.
Solo voices are revealed as personalities in overheard bus-depot conversations.

D1001. *Get Away Somewhere Quiet.* Vancouver, New Play Centre, (197-?).
3 acts. 4m/5f.
A comedy about life at a guest house on the Gulf Islands.

D1002. *The Grandmother.* Vancouver, New Play Centre, (197-?).
1 act. 3m/3f.
"A period melodrama" about a girl whose father wants her to marry an ugly old lecher. She is saved by her grandmother who has sewn her dowry into a shawl. Set in Vancouver, 1887.
fp: Victoria Theatre Guild, 1971.

D1003. *Our Own Particular Jane.* Victoria, A Room of One's Own Press, 1975.
2 acts. 2m/2f. Doubling.
"A piece of theatre based on the life, letters and literature of Jane Austen".
fp: Phoenix Theatre, University of Victoria for the Jane Austen Bicentenary Commemoration, April 3, 1975.

D1004. "Parents' Day" in *Canadian One Act Plays for Women.* Victoria, A Room of One's Own Press, 1975.
1 act. 8f.
A private girls' school seen at a time of crisis for both the school and one of its older teachers.

D1005. *Passacaglia.* Vancouver, New Play Centre, 1973 and in *Canadian One Act Plays for Women.* Victoria, A Room of One's Own Press, 1975.
1 act. 6f.
A young girl starts to work at a nursing home with altruistic motivations and to put her boyfriend through university. After encountering the problems of the residents, the girl realizes that "eight hours is a long day".
fp: Gallery Players, Victoria, B.C., 1973.

D1006. *Piggy Back.* Vancouver, New Play Centre, (197-?).
1 act. 3m/3f.
A comedy concerning a bet that has the actors playing piggy back in order to win a flowering cherry tree.

D1007. *Play and By Play.* Vancouver, New Play Centre, (197-?).
1 act. 3m/3f.
A theatrical company encounters problems after deciding to produce a ghastly play. They chose the play because it was Canadian and written by the theatre owner's boyfriend.
fp: University of Victoria Players Club, November 1969.

D1008. *The Seedling.* Victoria, Author, (196-?). (Mimeographed).
3 acts. 4m/7f/1b/1g.
Diana and Stuart Hartley emigrated to Vancouver Island in 1920 and created a family and a house, a "link from the past to the future". The play depicts their lives in the carefree 1920s, the grim war years and in the very changed world of 1967.

HUSTON, Mervyn J.

D1009. "The Grey Cup Murder Trial" in his *The Great Canadian Lover and Other Commentaries.* Toronto, Musson, 1964.
2 acts. 7m/1f.
A football referee who dies when he is strung up on the goal post by angry fans finds himself in the Court of Absolute Justice, where he witnesses the trial of Homosap. Mephistopheles claims he has the right to Homosap's soul, but Homosap doesn't have one.

HUTCH, Basil

D1010. *A Man for Mathilde.* Ottawa, Ottawa Little Theatre Workshop, #41.
1 act. 4m/2f. Extras.
A farce. M. Chaput outwits the village merchant and so gets a husband for his plain eldest daughter.

HUXTABLE, Horace Leslie

D1011. *The Fountain.* Ryerson Poetry Chapbooks, #41, Toronto, Ryerson, 1929.
1 act. 1m/2f.
"A dramatic fantasy". Pierrot mistakes his love of poetry for the love of the Mistress Muse herself.
fp: Women's Art Association of Canada, Toronto, June 26, 1929.

IBBITSON, John 1956–

D1012. "Catalyst" in *A Collection of Canadian Plays* vol. 4. Rolf Kalman, ed. Toronto, Simon & Pierre, 1975.
1 act. 5m/4f.
Two men dressed in formal attire play a game of chess in the street. The players are a catalyst, remaining static while others change for better or worse.
fp: Young People's Theatre, 1975.

D1013. "The Ritual" in *Performing Arts in Canada,* vol. 11, No. 3, Fall 1974.
1 act. 4m/4f.
Three young college men and a fourth who is unfamiliar with the "ritual" set a scene for the seduction of four young women.

INGRAHAM, Mary (Kinley) 1874–1949

D1014. *Acadia.* Wolfville, N.S., Davidson, 1920.
5 acts. 2m/3f.
An allegorical pageant in which the Coming of Acadia, her Sorrow, the place of Woman in Acadia and War and Peace are depicted in verse.

IRVINE, William 1885–1962

D1015. *The Brains We Trust.* Toronto, Nelson, 1935.
3 acts. 12m/9f. Extras.
"Backroom" politics is the main concern here. The two old parties — the Loyalists and the Patriots — are well supported by business interests; the Socialists have little monetary support, only their beliefs in a better society.
fp: Strand Theatre, Toronto, March 1935.

D1016. *You Can't Do That.* William Irvine and Elsie Park Gowan. Toronto, Nelson, 1936.
3 acts. 12m/4f.
A comedy set in Ottawa. The Prime Minister's niece is prompted by her love for a young M.P. as well as by her concern for the welfare of Canada when she instigates a plan to "kidnap" her uncle and his cabinet.

D1017. **IRVING, Ron.** *The Chappell Diary.* See **BAGLOLE, Harry.**

ISRAEL, Charles Edward 1920–

D1018. *The Labyrinth.* Toronto, Macmillan, 1969 and New York, St. Martin's Press, 1970.
Many scenes. 10m/9f. Extras.
A TV drama. The labyrinth is an institution for emotionally disturbed girls. The play focuses on Abbie, her therapy and the people who made her what she is: parents, Kenneth and Mark.
fp: CBC TV "Festival".

IWASUK, James 1949–

D1019. *Treasure Island.* Toronto, Playwrights Co-op, 1972.
1 act. 10m.
An adaptation of Robert Louis Stevenson's classic about Long John Silver, Jim Hawkins and the search for buried treasure.
fp: Colonnade Theatre, Toronto, March 1972.

JACK, Donald Lamont 1924–

D1020. "Exit Muttering" in *A Collection of Canadian Plays* vol. 1. Rolf Kalman, ed. Toronto, Simon & Pierre, 1972.
2 acts. 3m/4f.
A man searches for and achieves a unity of the soul, mind and body.
fp: Grenville St. Playhouse, Vancouver, January 1962.

JACKSON, Dorothy

D1021. "Jack and Jill and the Tree Fairies" in *Journal of Education for Nova Scotia*, series 4, vol. 6, March 1935.
1 scene. 2m/2f. Extras.
After Jack and Jill tumble down the hill, tree fairies appear to teach them the value of trees.

JACKSON, Elva

D1022. "The Barred Door" in *Acadia Athenaeum*, vol. 58, #2, December 1931.
1 scene. 3m/2f. Extras.
An historical vignette depicting the death of King James I of Scotland.

D1023. "Recompense" in *Acadia Athenaeum*, vol. 59, #2, December 1932.
1 scene. 2m/1f.
A couple who eloped on Christmas Eve 20 years earlier are faced with a similar situation when their daughter duplicates their action.

JACKSON, Graham 1949–

D1024. "Peter & John — Two Cameos" in *Acta,* vol. 94, #1, Nov. 1969.
1 scene. 2m.
A brief portrait of a friendship.

D1025. "Sisters of Mercy" in *Acta*, vol. 93, #3, Feb. 1969.
1 scene. 2m/1f.
The second scene of the play about a young man who has defrauded his employer and asks his sister and brother-in-law to repay the money.
fp: New Vic Theatre, University of Toronto, 1968.

D1026. "To the Hollow" in *Acta Victoriana*, vol. 94, #3, Feb. 1970.
1 scene. 1m/2f.
An excerpt from a play about two former lesbian lovers.
fp: New Vic Theatre, University of Toronto, Feb. 4, 1970.

JACOB, Fred B. 1882–1926

D1027. "And They Met Again" in his *One Third of a Bill*. Toronto, Macmillan, 1925.
1 act. 3m/1f.
This comedy presents the reunion of two people who had romanced years before; each thinks he/she is maintaining the other's illusions.
p: Hart House Theatre, Toronto, Jan. 25, 1926.

D1028. "Autumn Blooming" in his *One Third of a Bill*. Toronto, Macmillan, 1925.
1 act. 2m/4f.
Mrs. Spiller is finally going to do exactly what she wants to, in the face of her children's selfish disapproval.
fp: Arts and Letters Players Club, Toronto, February 6, 1924.

D1029. "The Basket" in his *One Third of a Bill*. Toronto, Macmillan, 1925.
1 act. 2m/2f.
What is in the basket brought by the strange woman from Carlos' past? Whatever it is has very curious effects on the people concerned: Carlos, his wife, and his father-in-law.
fp: Hart House Theatre, Toronto, March 8, 1929.

D1030. "The Clever One" in his *One Third of a Bill*. Toronto, Macmillan, 1925.
1 act. 2m/3f.
This "satiric trifle" exposes the self-conscious and self-indulgent cleverness of young people who think they can see through everything but in reality don't see anything at all.
p: Sarnia Drama League, 1928.

D1031. "Man's World" in his *One Third of a Bill*. Toronto, Macmillan, 1925.
1 act. 4m/3f.
The men at their weekly card game complain that the world is being controlled by women and resolve to do something about it.
p: Hart House Theatre, January 25, 1926.

JACOBSON, Percy Nathanial 1886-1952

D1032. "Accident" in *Echoes*, #132, October 1932 and *Accident*. Rock Island, Ill., Ingram, 1935.
1 act. 2m/3f.
Arthur Sands, who can no longer afford to maintain his family's style of living during the Depression, is prevented by his daughter from committing suicide.

D1033. *... And Sendeth Rain*. Rock Island, Ill., Ingram, 1934.
1 act. 4m/2f.
A young man's wife is poisoned by bad milk, leading to a confrontation between the husband and his boss on the subject of business ethics.

D1034. *Not Only the Guppy*. Rock Island, Ill., Ingram, 1934.
1 act. 1m/4f/1b.
Set in Montreal. A bitter, possessive old lady, an invalid, learns that she has a grandson.

D1035. *Ridiculous and Sublime*. Boston, Baker's Plays, 1948.
1 act. 2m/3f.
The dilemmas of the young are perplexing to Arthur Burton but his wife helps him to understand their son and daughter.

D1036. *The Usual Three.* Toronto, French, 1948.
1 act. 3f.
When Carol Foster discovers that her husband, a successful professor, is having an affair with the college's new librarian, she decides to break it up by discussing the situation with the young woman.

JACOT, Michael

D1037. *The Man With the Red Hat.* N.p., Author, 1957. (Mimeographed).
3 acts. 10m/4f/1b. Extras.
Set in a fictitious totalitarian republic in 1985 following W.W. III. A few people who have refused to accept the new order are held prisoner in a disused cathedral. A former cardinal, the last major rebel and the leader of an underground ecclesiastical movement, appears among them and their lives depend on whether or not he recants.

JACQUES (pseud.)

D1038. "The English Essay" in *Acta Victoriana,* vol. 43, #5, March 1919.
2 scenes. 3m.
A comic sketch about a student's attempt at originality.

JAMESON, Sheilagh

D1039. *Irish Plays Cupid.* Edmonton, Dept. of Extension, University of Alberta, 1946.
1 act. 4m/3f.
An Irish store owner in Calgary in the 1890s manages to marry off his daughter to a local rancher and to reconcile an Englishman in the process of being Westernized to his newly arrived English bride.

JARRETT, Fredric. See CONNOR, Fredric Jarrett.

JARVIS, Marjorie Mountain

D1040. "The Most Lamentable Tragedy of the Topless Tower" in *Echoes,* December 1928.
Issue unavailable for annotation.

JENNINGS, Fabian 1942–

D1041. *The Bacchants.* Toronto, Playwrights Co-op, 1974.
2 acts. 7m/4f. Extras.
A modern reworking of *The Bacchae* in which Dionysus comes to Thebes to teach his countrymen a lesson in worship.

D1042. *Charles Manson a.k.a. Jesus Christ.* Toronto, Playwrights Co-op, 1972.
2 acts. 10m/7f.
"A rock-musical tragedy". Within the frame of his trial, the story of the enigmatic Charles Manson and its implications concerning the North American way of life are explored. Music by Alan Rae.
fp: Theatre Passe Muraille, Toronto, December 1971.

D1043. **JOHNSON, Carol.** "I Wish". See **BOLT, Carol.**

JOHNSON, Chris 1944–

D1044. *Duet for a Schizophrenic.* Vancouver, Pulp Press, 1973.
3 scenes. 1m/1f or 3m/3f.
A man and a woman are involved in three separate conversations which explore identity.

D1045. "Mirrors" in *Poesis*, vol. 1, 1971.
1 act. 1m/1f.
The Chinese legend of the war between men and their reflections is retold in a room full of mirrors.

D1046. *Sex, Cold Cans, and a Coffin.* Toronto, Playwrights Co-op, 1972.
1 act. 2m/2f.
Black comedy set in an old folks' home. Two old men who sustain themselves with the thought of sexual rejuvenation put their fantasy to the test when a young woman arrives to do a sociological survey of the home.
fp: Frederic Wood Theatre, Vancouver, December 1967.

D1047. *Trips.* Toronto, Playwrights Co-op, 1972 and Vancouver, New Play Centre, 1973.
2 acts. 9m/12f. Extras. Doubling.
"A folk-rock musical". The small town boy goes to the big city encountering girls and myths all the way. Music by Barry Dowden.
fp: Brock University, St. Catharines, Ont., March 1972.

JOHNSTON, G.B.

D1048. "Coffee at 12:30" in *Acta Victoriana*, vol. 60, #5, Feb. 1936.
1 act. 2m/1f.
A conversation at a soda-fountain between a young man and woman and the soda-jerker.

D1049. "Mr. Miggles" in *Acta Victoriana*, vol. 59, #6, April-May 1935.
1 scene. 1m/1f.
A one-sided conversation between the pseudo-sophisticated Bubbles and Archibald Miggles, the tennis player.

JONES, James Edmund 1866-1939

D1050."Sam Weller's Walentine" in *Scenes from Dickens*. J.E. Jones, ed. Toronto, McClelland & Stewart, 1923.
1 act. 2m. Extras.
An adaptation of an incident from *Pickwick Papers*. Sam Weller's father advises him on the valentine he has just composed.

D1051. "Tony Weller's Beneficence" in *Scenes from Dickens*. J.E. Jones, ed. Toronto, McClelland & Stewart, 1923.
1 scene. 3m. Extras.
An adaptation of a scene from *Pickwick Papers*. Pickwick is engaged in providing for Sam so that Sam can marry, but Sam refuses to leave Pickwick.

D1052. "The Trial of John Jasper for the Murder of Edwin Drood" by J.E. Jones *et al.* in *Scenes from Dickens.* J.E. Jones, ed. Toronto, McClelland & Stewart, 1923.
1 act. 9m/4f/1b. Extras.
An adaptation of an incident from Dickens' *The Mystery of Edwin Drood.* The counsel for the prosecution and the counsel for the prisoner call witnesses.
fp: Dickens Fellowship, Masonic Hall, Toronto, Nov. 18, 1921.

JONES, Sandra

D1053. *Ready, Steady, Go.* Toronto, Playwrights Co-op, 1975.
1 act. 6m/6f.
The adventures and romances of a group of dolls in an attic.
fp: Cameo Productions, Flare Square Theatre, Calgary, July 1973.

JORDAN, F. Marjorie

D1054. "The Street Cleaner" in *Curtain Call*, vol. 9, #6, March 1938.
1 act. 1m/2f.
A London street cleaner finds a valuable strand of pearls in the park but his family thinks it is imitation.

JOUDRY, Patricia 1921–

D1055. *The Song of Louise in the Morning.* New York, Dramatists Play Service, 1960.
1 act. 1m/2f.
The marriage of Stanley and Louise deteriorates until it ends in Louise's death.
fp: BBC TV, January 1960.

D1056. *Teach Me How to Cry.* New York, Dramatists Play Service, 1955.
3 acts. 3m/7f. Extras.
In a small American town, Melinda and Will struggle against their parents and society for the right to love each other.
fp: CBC radio "Stage", April 19, 1953. CBC TV "Theatre", Oct. 13, 1953. Theater de Lys, New York, April 5, 1955. D.D.F., 1956.

D1057. *Three Rings for Michelle.* New York, Dramatists Play Service, 1960.
3 acts. 2m/3f.
The story of an orphan girl who enters the lives of a family rather unexpectedly and brings meaning and love into their existence.
fp: Avenue Theatre, Toronto, Nov. 15, 1956.

JULIANI, John

D1058. *The Magic Donkey.* Vancouver, New Play Centre, (197-?).
2 acts. 5m/3f. Extras.
A children's play. A fat, ugly king wants to marry a beautiful but reluctant princess. Adapted and translated from the play by Luan Asllani.
fp: Holiday Theatre, Vancouver, May 1967.

K.O. (pseud.)

D1059. "Overcrowding in the Desert" in *Acta Victoriana*, vol. 52, #2, Nov. 1927.
1 scene. 1m.
A parable consisting of a dialogue between Abdul-El-Vic and a camel about the camel's future in life.

KARDISH, Larry 1945–

D1060. *Brussels Sprouts.* Toronto, Playwrights Co-op, 1972, and in *The Factory Lab Anthology.* C. Brissenden, ed. Vancouver, Talonbooks, 1974.
1 act. 2m/1f.
Two young Americans on a holiday in Brussels end up in bed with a young woman who becomes one third of a very odd love triangle.
fp: Factory Theatre Lab, Toronto, February 1972.

D1061. *Little Steps to Heaven.* Toronto, Playwrights Co-op, 1972.
3 scenes. 2m/2f.
An unstable marriage is complicated by memories, a family death and the fact that the husband is a draft dodger.

KARSTON, Celia

1062. *Triptych.* Vancouver, New Play Centre (197-?).
3 acts. 2m/1f.
An allegorical drama about three young people living in a forest and their discovery of an Indian cave.

KEEN, A.G.

D1063. *When Sin Rides High.* London, Ont., Peter Morris, 1933.
4 acts. 8m/2f. Extras.
A melodrama in which a corrupt New York City detective and his "dope fiend" accomplice ruin a man's life by implicating him in a crime he didn't commit, then murder him, manipulating the evidence to effect the conviction of the victim's daughter and her fiance.

KEENAN, Anne

D1064. *Dragon Lady or the King's Servant.* Halifax, Dramatists Co-op, 1978.
7 scenes. 6m/6f.
An adaptation for children of the Arthurian tale "Sir Gawain and Dame Ragnell".

KELLER, Betty

D1065. "Bridgework" in *Trick Doors and Other Dramatic Sketches.* Vancouver, November House, 1974.
1 act. 2m.
In an encounter on a bridge, a tramp loses his coat as well as his life.

D1066. "Down on Your Knees" in *Trick Doors and Other Dramatic Sketches.* Vancouver, November House, 1974.
1 act. 2m/1f.
Martha returns home to gloat at the death of her father. She is confronted by two burglars as she is about to set the house ablaze.

D1067. "Fortunes" in *Trick Doors and Other Dramatic Sketches.* Vancouver, November House, 1974.
1 act. 2m/1f.
A woman has waited many years for her husband's return, but when her son enters with an Old Man, the woman denies the man is her husband, unwilling to accept the fact that she had been deserted all those years ago.

D1068. "Holed Up" in *Trick Doors and Other Dramatic Sketches*. Vancouver, November House, 1974.
1 act. 1m/1f.
A young reporter comes to interview Mrs. Burkin, the cleaning lady of the bank, who caught some bank robbers by shutting them in the vault.
p: CBC radio "Hornby Collection", Oct. 22, 1977.

D1069. "In the Middle of the Night" in *Trick Doors and Other Dramatic Sketches*. Vancouver, November House, 1974.
1 act. 1m/1b.
Gerry, aged 65, tells Leo, aged 10, a bedtime story of fire and destruction which left them together and alone.

D1070. "Love Scene: Dominic and Sadie" in *Trick Doors and Other Dramatic Sketches*. Vancouver, November House, 1974.
1 act. 1m/1f.
A love scene between a fastidious garbageman and the owner and cook of Sadie's Diner.

D1071. *Minnie*. Vancouver, New Play Centre, (197-?).
1 act. 3m/3f.
A black comedy about a mentally retarded woman living on skid row in Vancouver who accidentally kills her common-law husband.

D1072. "Mr. Excelsior" in *Trick Doors and Other Dramatic Sketches*. Vancouver, November House, 1974.
1 act. 2m.
While giving a lecture on saws, Mr. Excelsior becomes absorbed in his subject, giving Sonny the opportunity he needs to load up on the shop's wares.

D1073. "Perfect Perley" in *Trick Doors and Other Dramatic Sketches*. Vancouver, November House, 1974.
1 act. 2m.
A science fiction one-act in which Delegate Rhal from the planet Zond conducts an interview with Lionel Perley, an over protected and immature young man who succeeds in committing himself to death.

D1074. "Sophie" in *Trick Doors and Other Dramatic Sketches*. Vancouver, November House, 1974.
1 act. 1f.
Sophie is directed by a voice — she is obviously the servant and the voice is master.

D1075. "Tea Party" in *Trick Doors and Other Dramatic Sketches*. Vancouver, November House, 1974.
1 act. 2f/1m.
Alma and Hester, two lonely elderly ladies, await the one bright spot in their week: the arrival of the paperboy.

D1076. "Trick Doors" in *Trick Doors and Other Dramatic Sketches*. Vancouver, November House, 1974.
1 act. 1m/1f.
A mother's overindulgent behaviour towards her vulgar and gross son comes to a dramatic halt when she decides to run away from home.

D1077. "The Victim" in *Trick Doors and Other Dramatic Sketches.* Vancouver, November House, 1974.
1 act. 1m/1f.
The scene is South America and the victim is a kidnapped foreign businessman kept prisoner by his female abductor.

D1078. "Walking Back" in *Trick Doors and Other Dramatic Sketches.* Vancouver, November House, 1974.
1 act. 1m/1f.
A soldier separated from his company wanders into an eerie situation in which he comforts mother, lover and child who all disappear as he continues walking.

D1079. "Winnifred and Grace" in *Trick Doors and Other Dramatic Sketches.* Vancouver, November House, 1974.
1 act. 2f.
Winnifred and Grace discuss Philip's death and the events leading up to their individual decisions to kill him: one for love and one for fame.

KELLY, John

D1080. *Fantasy, Flight and Feathers.* Vancouver, New Play Centre, (197-?).
3 acts. 5m/2f.
A play which follows the life struggles of two men.
fp: Prince Rupert, B.C., Pacific Players, 1969 regional D.D.F. Festival.

D1081. *Fireweed.* Vancouver, New Play Centre, (197-?)
3 acts. 3m/5f. Extras.
A middle-aged logger and his wife have problems when an old "friend" of the wife appears looking for the $10,000 she owes him.
fp: (Reading), New Play Centre, Vancouver, 1972.

D1082. *I'll Remember You Love, In My Prayers.* Vancouver, New Play Centre, (197-?).
3 acts. 7m/3f/1b.
Problems erupt when a young Indian girl comes home to her boyfriend whose mother despises her.
fp: Prince Rupert Community Theatre, B.C., 1968.

D1083. *Loggerheads.* Vancouver, New Play Centre, (197-?).
1 act. 2m/2f.
Wink and Plank, two loggers, argue over who is going to make it with the camp cook.
fp: CBC TV, Vancouver, 1969.

D1084. *One Hundred Feet Up.* Vancouver, New Play Centre, 1973.
1 act. 1m/1f.
A man and a woman are trapped one hundred feet up a tree because the man has been cutting off all the branches below them to protect the couple from some unidentified threat.
fp: (Reading), New Play Centre, Vancouver, 1973.

D1085. *The Way Out.* Toronto, French, 1965.
1 act. 3m/1f.
An Old Yukon trapper disarms two city criminals on the run, sends them on a wild goose chase, and sets an RCMP officer on their trail.

KELLY, Wilfred C.

D1086. "Faith" in his *Second Random Thought.* Cumberland, B.C., Author, 1937.
Title unavailable for annotation.
fp: Comox District Theatre Club, 1937.

KEMP, David

D1087. "King Grumbletum and the Magic Pie" in *A Collection of Canadian Plays* vol. 4. Rolf Kalman, ed. Toronto, Simon & Pierre, 1975.
1 act. 4m/3f.
An audience participation play for children concerning King Grumbletum who has a pain and rumbling in his tummy that his faithful servants cure with a magic pie.

KEMP, Penny 1944–

D1088. *Angel Makers.* Toronto, Playwrights Co-op, 1978 and in *Canadian Drama,* vol. 4, #1, Spring 1978.
1 act. 7f/1b.
A drama bringing together a group of women in an abortion ward and examining the despair and joys which define their lives.
fp: Red Light Theatre, Toronto, Oct. 13, 1976.

D1089. *The Epic of Toad and Heron.* Coatsworth, Ontario, Black Moss, 1977.
2 acts. 3f/2m. Doubling.
A political fantasy about a prince and princess whose marriage cannot take place until insurmountable obstacles have been overcome.
fp: Pendas Productions, Ward's Island Clubhouse, Toronto, Sept. 3, 1977.

KENNY, George 1952–

1090. *October Stranger.* Toronto, Chimo, 1978.
1 act. 3m/2f.
A play based on his *Indians Don't Cry* about a young Ojibwa torn between a sense of duty to his people and the lure of fame as a writer in the city.
fp: Association for Native Development in the Performing and Visual Arts, Todmorden Mills Theatre, Toronto, July 29, 1977.

KERR, James Stolee 1928–

D1091. *As Grace Is Given.* Camrose, Alberta, Camrose Lutheran College, 1961.
3 parts. 15m/7f/1b/1g. Extras. Doubling. Choir.
"A Golden Anniversary pageant" celebrating the founding and history of Camrose Lutheran College and its contribution to the people of Alberta.

KERR, Lois Reynolds 1908–

D1092. "Among Those Present" in *Curtain Call,* vol. 10, #1, October 1938.
1 act. 3m/4f.
An Irish poet and a British heiress, previously engaged, rediscover each other in Canada.
fp: Hart House Theatre, Toronto.

D1093. *Nellie McNabb.* Toronto, French, 1937.
1 act. 2m/4f.
"A farce-comedy". Three women write for advice to the love-lorn column and follow the advice given.
fp: Hart House Theatre, Toronto, October 20, 1934.

D1094. *No Reporters Please.* Vancouver, New Play Centre, (1971).
2 acts. 4m/3f.
Two reporters try to scoop each other in invading the privacy of a prominent politician.
fp: University Women's Club, Vancouver, Oct. 28, 1969.

D1095. *O Woman!.* Vancouver, New Play Centre, (1973).
3 acts. 2m/5f.
A mosaic showing the fragmented life of preliberated woman in contrast with today's liberated woman.
fp: University Women's Club, Vancouver, 1972.

D1096. "Open Doors" by Lois Reynolds in *Echoes,* June 1930.
2 scenes. 5m/2f.
A steel industry owner imports foreign labour rather than hiring unemployed Canadians. His daughter opposes his illegal activities when she becomes involved with one of the Canadian families affected by the owner's policy.
fp: Little Playhouse, Toronto, Jan. 27, 1931.

D1097. *Summer Hotel.* Chicago, Denison, 1936.
1 act. 1m/4f.
"A tragedy". A young school teacher has a summer romance with a wealthy man from "society".
fp: Playwrights' Studio Group, Hart House Theatre, Toronto, 1935.

KERR, Winifred and Doris Bell. See BELL, Doris.

KEY, Archibald F.

D1098. "The Mother Lode" in *Six Canadian Plays.* H.A. Voaden, ed. Toronto, Copp Clark, 1930.
1 act. 5m.
This play presents the prospector's life during the gold rush in Northern Ontario and his hopes for striking it rich.

D1099. *Routine.* Western Canada Theatre Conference. Edmonton, Dept. of Extension, University of Alberta, 1946.
1 act. 7m/1f.
The daily routine of a hospital is undisturbed by either the birth of a baby or the death from burning of a homesteader's wife.
p: Allied Arts Festival, Western Canada Auditorium, May 27, 1947.

KILIAN, Crawford

D1100. "Little Legion" in *The Capilano Review,* vol. 1, #3, Spring/Summer 1973.
1 act. 5m.
A radio play satirizing CBC sports coverage of the 1992 Little Legion Finals from Fort Calley, California in which the Canadian and American teams use real machine guns and laser weapons in all-out infantry war games.

KINCH, Martin 1943–

D1101. *Me?*. Playwrights Co-op, Toronto, 1973 and Toronto, Coach House, 1976.
2 acts. 3m/2f.
Set in Toronto. The problems of a young Canadian novelist who can't decide what he wants and why he wants it. His wife, mistress, best friend, and younger brother all try to help him.
fp: Toronto Free Theatre, May 1, 1973.

KING, Alan 1930–

D1102. *A Man at Westminster*. Toronto, CBC, 1967.
14 scenes. 16m/5f. Extras. Doubling.
A radio chronicle of the growth of the British Parliament as seen through the eyes of Thomas Common, who is reincarnated century after century as an M.P.
fp: CBC radio, Vancouver.

D1103. "Reluctantly Last Summer" in *Actra*, vol. 3, #3, Fall 1966.
1 act. 2m/1f.
A radio play. A script writer's ego and alter ego argue about why the script he is writing isn't working.

KING, David 1949–

D1104. *Gesture of Concern*. Toronto, Playwrights Co-op, 1973.
1 act. 2m/1f.
A young man attempts unsuccessfully to rape a girl and she visits him the next day to return his wallet.
fp: Factory Theatre Lab, Toronto, Dec. 6, 1972.

KING, Mary Perry 1865–

D1105. *Daughters of the Dawn* and *Earth Deities and Other Rhythmic Masques*. See **CARMAN, William Bliss.**

KINGSMAN, I.M.

D1106. "The Tiger from Zanzibar" in *Nunny Bag 2*. Scarborough, Ont. Gage, 1963.
1 act. 3m/2f/4g.
A play for children. The Lion, King of the Beasts, learns a lesson in modesty and unselfishness from an upstart tiger.

KINLEY, Margaret

D1107. "The Guest" in *Acadia Athenaeum*, vol. 61, #2, December 1935.
1 scene. 2m/2f.
An aged innkeeper desperate for money kills her rich American guest only to learn that he was her son who had intended to take her to his new home.

KIRKCONNELL, Watson 1895–1977

D1108. "Let My People Go" in his *Centennial Tales and Selected Poems*. Toronto, University of Toronto Press, 1965.
1 act. 3m/2f. Extras. Chorus.
"A dramatic poem" set in Egypt the evening before the Exodus. The Pharaoh attempts to arrest Moses but the death of the Pharaoh's firstborn son convinces him of the power of Moses' god and the Hebrews are allowed to depart.

D1109. *The Mod at Grand Pre*. Wolfville, N.S., Author, 1955. (Mimeographed).
2 acts. 3m/3f. Chorus.
Celeste Leblanc, an Acadian widow from Louisiana, has brought her 18 daughters on a bicentennial pilgrimage to the scene of the 1755 expulsion. They meet 18 engineering students from Acadia University, all of them Highland Scotch, out on a field trip at Grand Pre. After some misunderstandings, they fall in love and stage the events of 1755 as they would have been if the British troops had been Highlanders.
p: Nova Scotia Drama League, 1956.

D1110. *Sixteen Decades of Parsonages*. Wolfville, N.S., Davidson, 1964.
1 act. 6m/6f.
"A series of dramatic dialogues" between six pastors and their wives describing the 168 year long history of the parsonages of Wolfville Baptist Church in an "anniversary pageant" of their homes.

KLAIMAN, Nina F.

D1111. "Two Pollution Sketches" in *The Kidnappers and Two Pollution Sketches*. Drama at Calgary, Playscript Number One. Philip McCoy, ed. Calgary, University of Calgary, 1974.
2 acts. 3m/3f.
Two separate short plays. In "What Did You Have for Breakfast" a woman carries on a discussion of other people entirely in terms of what their garbage reveals about them. In "Never . . . Never . . ." one character gradually instills in the others her fear and terror of a vast invisible force that is intent on consuming them.

KLEIN, Abraham Moses 1909-1972

D1112. "Hershel of Ostropol" in *Canadian Jewish Chronicle*, vol. 26, March 31, 1939 and vol. 27, September 13, 1939.
3 acts. 22m/2f/1b. Extras.
Hershel, a renowned clown, comes to Medziboz to be a court jester for a melancholy rabbi and ends up marrying a girl who has been jilted on her wedding day. They have six children but a less than idyllic marriage.

KNIGHT, Albert Ernest (A.E. de Garcia pseud.)

D1113. *Canada, Fair Canada*. Montreal, Montreal Shorthand Institute and Business College, 1902.
4 acts. 11m/7f. Extras.
A "modern romantic tragedy" in which Alice Chopineau and George Kingheart's love is opposed by their families.

KNIGHT, David

D1114. "Wind of Power" in *Acta Victoriana*, vol. 71, Dec. 1946.
1 scene. 2m.
Two men discuss the formation of an individual's identity.

KNIGHT, Mary A.

D1115. "Christmas Eve in Santa Claus Land" in *Pageants and Plays*. Mary A. Knight and Marguerite Letson. Toronto, Nelson, 1935.
1 act. 9m/1f. Extras.
A children's play. Santa Claus leaves three Christmas trees behind when he starts off on his annual voyage, and Mrs. Claus and the elves must solve the problem.

D1116. "A Day at Mother Nature's Court" in *Pageants and Plays*. Mary A. Knight and Marguerite Letson. Toronto, Nelson, 1935.
1 act. 5m/1f. Extras.
A children's play about the importance of forest conservation.

D1117. "The Dream of Glooscap" in *Journal of Education for Nova Scotia*, series 4, vol. 5, December 1934 and in *Plays and Pageants*. Mary A. Knight and Marguerite Letson. Toronto, Nelson, 1935 and in *Educational Review*, vol. 50, #8, April 1936.
1 act. 5m/2f. Extras.
A children's play. Glooscap dreams of Canada's future and her potential for growth as a part of the British Commonwealth.

KNIGHT, Virginia Coyne

D1118. "Cupid on the Wire" in *Curtain Call*, vol. 9, #7, April 1938.
1 act. 2m/1f.
A telephone lineman, listening in, helps to reunite an arguing couple.
p: Dickens Fellowship, Toronto, 1936.

D1119. "The Mighty Mr. Samson" in *Curtain Rising*. W.S. Milne, ed. Toronto, Longmans, Green, 1958.
1 act. 4m/1f.
This play was "faintly suggested by a Russian animal tale". It deals with the unsuccessful efforts of the widow Maroosia Ivanova to win a second husband.
p: Play Workshop, Toronto, 1936.

KNISTER, Raymond 1899-1932

D1120. "Youth Goes West" in *Poet Lore*, vol. 39, 1928.
1 act. 3m/2f.
Just after Garland discovers his father is allowing him to go west to visit relatives, he is killed in an accident while doing the chores.

KNOX, Alexander 1907–

D1121. *Old Master*. London, Constable, 1940 and Toronto, Macmillan, 1940.
3 acts. 10m/5f. Extras.
A situation comedy about an English painter who fakes his own death to drive up the prices of his paintings.
fp: Malvern Theatre, England, 1939.

KNOX, Olive Elsie

D1122. "Fresh Water from the Sea" in her *Penicillin and Fresh Water from the Sea.* Toronto, Macmillan, 1945.
1 act. 4m/1f.
A dramatized science lesson for radio in which a pilot and his companions discover how to extract drinking water from the sea after their plane has crashed.
fp: CBC radio, Winnipeg, Station CKY.

D1123. "How We Hear" in her *How We Hear and Sewing Seams with Steel.* Toronto, Macmillan, 1945.
1 act. 16m. Extras.
A radio play. A young man who wishes to enlist in the army during World War II must first pass a high school science test on sound.
fp: CBC radio, station CKY, Winnipeg.

D1124. "Penicillin" in her *Penicillin and Fresh Water from the Sea.* Toronto, Macmillan, 1945.
1 act. 5m/3f. Extras.
A radio documentary on the discovery and uses of penicillin in wartime.
fp: CBC radio, station CKY, Winnipeg.

D1125. "Sewing Seams with Steel" in her *How We Hear and Sewing Seams with Steel.* Toronto, Macmillan, 1945.
1 act. 3m/1f/2b.
A radio play. Two boys take a bicycle to be repaired and are given an impromptu lesson on the scientific principles involved in welding.
fp: CBC radio, station CKY, Winnipeg.

D1126. "Sulfa Drugs" in her *Wheels and Friction/Sulfa Drugs.* Toronto, Macmillan, 1945.
1 act. 4m. Extras. Doubling.
A radio play about the discovery of the life-saving sulfa drugs and their use in war and peacetime.
fp: CBC radio, station CKY, Winnipeg.

D1127. "Wheels and Friction" in her *Wheels and Friction/Sulfa Drugs.* Toronto, Macmillan, 1945.
1 act. 2m/1f. Extras.
A radio play about the invention, history, and uses of the wheel to reduce friction in travel and transportation.
fp: CBC radio, station CKY, Winnipeg.

KOCH, Eric and Vincent Tovell, with John T. Saywell

D1128. *Success of a Mission.* Toronto, Clarke Irwin, 1961.
3 acts. 18m/1f.
A TV drama about Lord Durham's mission to reform constitutionally the governments of Upper and Lower Canada.
fp: CBC TV, Dec. 14, 1960.

KOLIC, Markus F.

D1129. "The Invisible Dogs" in *Callboard,* vol. 22, #3, May 1975.
1 act. 4f/2m.
A comedy about Le Mat, the joker, who sells imaginary dogs.

KROEKER, Phyllis

D1129A. "Eve" in *York Theatre Journal*, vol.5, #1, Fall 1975.
1 act. 4m/3f. Extras.
A brief poetic dramatic sketch about the fall of man.

KROETSCH, Robert 1927–

D1130. "The Man in the Winter Catalogue" in *Creation*. Robert Kroetsch, ed. Toronto, New Press, 1970.
2 acts. 3m/1f. Extras.
"An anti-TV TV play for the Canadian imagination". Schmidt is obsessed with catalogues and the long underwear depicted therein.

KUPCHENKO, Oleh

D1131. *Brigadier Thompson, O.B.E. and Teresa's Old Canoe*. Edmonton, Alberta, Dept. of Culture, 1971.
1 act. 4m/1f.
Arthur Thompson, member of parliament, his irascible brother, and his daughter wait for news of his son who is known to have taken part in an anti-American demonstration which jeopardizes the M.P.'s career.

D1132. *A Cold Winter and a Dead Spring*. Edmonton, Alberta, Dept. of Culture, 1971.
1 act. 2m/2f.
This play portrays the anguish of East European immigrant parents in north-western Canada who cannot save their son from conscription.

LAGER, Martin

D1133. *The Magnificent Slowpoke*. Toronto, Playwrights Co-op, 1977.
2 acts. 5m/3f.
A comedy in which bungling Ubby Ellison is haunted by his mother's ghost.
fp: Kawartha Summer Theatre, Lindsay, Ontario, July 20, 1976.

LAMBERT, Betty 1933–

D1134. "The Good of the Sun" in *West Coast Review*, vol. 10, #1, June 1975.
1 act. 2m/1f.
A study of infidelity in which the wife of a Canadian recuperating in a Mexican village falls in love with the local doctor.

D1135. *Once Burnt, Twice Shy*. Vancouver, New Play Centre, 1972.
1 act. 2m/3f.
A radio play. When a man seemingly dies in a forest fire, his wife, his son, his sister-in-law and his mistress all meet for the first time.
p: CBC radio.

D1136. *The Riddle Machine*. Vancouver, New Play Centre, (197-?) and in *Contemporary Children's Theatre*. Betty Jean Lifton, ed. New York, Avon, 1974.
2 acts. 6m/3f.
"A children's play". Children from another world have been sent to Earth with a robot.
fp: Holiday Theatre, Vancouver, February 1966.

D1137. *The Song of the Serpent.* Vancouver, New Play Centre, 1972 and Toronto, Playwrights Co-op, 1973.
1 act. 7m/2f. Extras.
An adventure melodrama set during the Gold Rush days in British Columbia.
fp: Holiday Playhouse, Vancouver, May 1967.

D1138. *Sqrieux-De-Dieu.* Toronto, Playwrights Co-op, 1975 and Vancouver, Talonbooks, 1976.
2 acts. 3m/5f.
A sex farce set in Vancouver about a husband, his wife, his mistress and their interrelated lives.
fp: New Play Centre, Vancouver, August 1975.

LAMBIE, Alexander 1870–

D1139. *The Lady of Lodore.* Vancouver, Author, 1928.
5 acts. 14m/10f. Extras.
After many adventures, Conval rescues the Lady of Lodore from Tullis' castle where he has imprisoned her to obtain her hand in marriage in this "fantasy of the Cumberland Lakes".

LAMPMAN, Archibald 1861-1899

D1141. "David and Abigail" in *The Poems of Archibald Lampman.* Duncan Campbell Scott, ed. Toronto, Morang, 1900 and Toronto, Musson, 1900.
3 scenes. 5m/3f.
Abigail goes to King David to plead for the life of her husband. In doing so she becomes enamoured with the King and discovers that she no longer loves her husband.

LANDER, Jan

D1142. "A Wake" in her *Space Baby.* Edmonton, Tree Frog, 1971.
1 act. 1m/1f. Doubling.
A surrealistic and potentially allegorical play about Sunripe, a young woman who is in the peculiar state of being simultaneously dead and alive, and the men who both exploit and are threatened by her strange condition.
fp: Students' Union, University of Alberta, Edmonton, Students' Arts Festival, (1968?).

LANE, Myrtle E.

D1143. "Of Course I Never Get Excited" in *Western Recorder*, (Victoria, B.C.), December 1936.
1 scene. 1f. Extras.
A brief monologue by an eccentric woman leaving by bus for the city.

LANE, Wilmot Burkmar 1872–

D1144. *Quebec.* Toronto, Macmillan, 1936.
1 act. 11m/1f.
A poetic drama which "recalls the great incidents of courage, endurance and sacrifice in the taking of Quebec" when Wolfe met Montcalm on the Plains of Abraham.

LANGFORD, Ernest

D1145. "The Snake" in *Prism,* vol. 1, #2, Winter 1959.
1 act. 12m/5f. Extras.
Peter, a bank teller continually prodded by his wife about his lack of financial success, finds a snake and interprets it as the divinity which will find success for him.

LANGLEY, Rod 1942–

D1146. *Bethune.* Vancouver, Talonbooks, 1975.
3 acts. 19m/10f. Extras. Doubling.
An historical drama about the life of Dr. Norman Bethune.
fp: Globe Theatre, Regina, Nov. 5, 1974.

D1147. *The Station.* Toronto, Playwrights Co-op, 1972.
1 act. 2m.
A young man attempts to escape his ineptitude by catching a train at a station where no trains stop.
fp: Frederick Wood Theatre, University of British Columbia, Dec. 7, 1967.

D1148. *Tales from a Prairie Drifter.* Toronto, Playwrights Co-op, 1974.
2 acts. 7m/1f. Doubling.
Focusing on homesteading, the building of the CNR, and the Metis Rebellion, the play presents an epic panorama of the Canadian West.
fp: Globe Theatre, Regina, February 1973.

LANGUIRAND, Jacques 1930–

D1149. *The Departures.* Albert Bermel, trans. N.p., Author, 1961 (stencil) and in *Gambit,* #5, 1966.
3 acts. 3m/2f.
A comedy about a failed writer, his exploited wife, her paralytic father and hypochondriac sister who must move to a smaller apartment because they can't afford the rent.
fp: English Stage Society, Royal Court Theatre, London, England, May 1961. Canadian Players, Toronto, 1966.

D1150. *The Gallows.* Albert Bermel, trans. N.p., Author, (1959?). (Stencil).
3 acts. 11m/4f.
A comedy about a man setting a world endurance record for living on a pole and his effect on his neighbours.
fp: Comédie Canadienne, Montreal, Nov. 10, 1958.

D1151. *Keyhole.* Albert Bermel, trans. Paris, Author, 1962. (Mimeographed).
1 act. 1m/1f.
Two neighbours are unable to overcome their inhibitions to communicate with one another.
fp: Canadian Players, Central Library Theatre, Toronto, Feb. 17, 1966. (In French), Théâtre de la Place, Montreal, 1966.

D1152. *Louis Riel.* See **MOORE, Mavor.**

D1153. *The Partition.* Albert Bermel, trans. Paris, Author, 1962. (Mimeographed).
1 act. 1m/1f.
The same play, with only the title different, as his *Keyhole.*

D1154. **LAST, Terry.** *The Night They Raided Truxx.* See **LEDOUX, Paul.**

D1155. **LAVALLE, Rudie 1947–.** *Rinse Cycle.* See **CROSSLAND, Jackie.**

LAVIGNE, Louis-Dominique 1949–

D1156. "Are You Afraid of Thieves?", Henry Beissel, trans., in *A Collection of Canadian Plays* vol. 5. Rolf Kalman, ed. Toronto, Simon & Pierre, 1978.
2 acts. 3m/3f.
A translation of his *As-Tu Peur des Voleurs?*. A comedy about three couples and how they act in the games they invent to amuse themselves.
fp: La Troupe Brind'si, Université du Québec, Montreal, Dec. 20, 1973.

LAWRENCE, Margaret E.

D1157. "A Flag of Empire" in *A Collection of Plays Suitable for Use in Junior Red Cross Groups.* Toronto, Canadian Red Cross Society, (1927?).
1 act. 2b/3g.
A group of children pledge their "love and toil in the years to be" to their country on Empire Day.

LAWRENCE, Wendy

D1158. "On Streisand: A Fictional Dialogue" in *Acta,* vol. 92, #3, February 1968.
1 act. 3m or f.
Three characters, Scepticism, Enthusiasm, and Detached Analysis discuss the pros and cons of Barbra Streisand and her art form.

LAWSON, Jessie I.

D1159. "The Empire Calls" in *Educational Review*, vol. 46, #9, May, 1932.
1 act. 17b or g.
A pageant in which the colonies and dominions pledge allegiance to Britannia.

LAYTON, Irving 1912– and Leonard Cohen 1934–

D1160. "A Man Was Killed" in *Canadian Theatre Review,* #14, Spring 1977.
6 scenes. 7m/1f.
An absurdist comedy set in Montreal in which a former professor and Mafia figures prepare to shoot pedestrians on the street.

LAZARUS, John 1947–

D1161. *Babel Rap.* Toronto, Playwrights Co-op, 1972 and in *Five Canadian Plays.* Toronto, Playwrights Co-op, 1978.
1 act. 2m.
Two men contemplate the thoughts and actions of God while building a tower to heaven.
fp: Troupe of Vancouver, Intermedia Hall, Vancouver, April 1972. CBC radio and television.

D1162. *Chester, You Owe My Bird an Apology.* Toronto, Playwrights Co-op, 1972 and in *Transitions I: Short Plays.* Edward Peck, ed. Vancouver, Commcept Publishing, 1978.
3 scenes. 1m/2f.
The hero is bullied by his sister and her parrot. Encouraged by his girlfriend, he kills the bird and sets out to be a new man.
fp: West Vancouver Little Theatre Guild, Community Centre, Jan. 29, 1972. CBC radio, 1972.

D1163. *Classroom Theatre.* Vancouver, Cedar House, 1972 and New York, Young Readers Press, 1974.
A collection of ten short tales adapted from sources such as Aesop's *Fables* in such a way as to permit young children to act them.

D1164. *A Cold Beer With a Warm Friend.* Vancouver, New Play Centre, 1973.
1 act. 1m.
A monologue in which a man in a beer parlour tells of his life speaking to an imaginary friend.

D1165. *How We Killed the Moose.* Vancouver, New Play Centre, 1975.
1 act. 4m/3f. Doubling.
A depiction of how people in a small town react to a wild moose in their midst.
fp: New Play Centre, Vancouver, du Maurier Festival, April 30, 1975.

D1166. *Screwaround.* Vancouver, New Play Centre, 1973.
1 act. 3m/3f.
A revue about the different types of people in life.

D1167. *You Remind Me of Me.* Vancouver, New Play Centre, (197-?).
1 act. 2m/1f.
A famous dancer and his friend exchange roles for a magazine interview.

LEACOCK, Stephen Butler 1869-1944

D1168. "Beauty and the Boss or The Sacrifice of a Stenographer" in his *Funny Pieces: A Book of Random Sketches.* New York, Dodd, Mead, 1936 and Toronto, McClelland & Stewart, 1936 and London, John Lane, 1937.
1 act. 4m/2f. Extras.
A tongue-in-cheek version of the story of the country girl who goes to New York to find work and true love.

D1169. "Behind the Beyond" in *Behind the Beyond and Other Contributions to Human Knowledge.* London and New York, John Lane, 1913 and Toronto, Bell & Cockburn, 1913 and Toronto, S.B. Gundy, 1915 and New York, Dodd, Mead, 1923 and Toronto, McClelland & Stewart, 1937 and 1969.
3 acts. 5m/3f.
"A modern problem play" with tongue-in-cheek. Lady Cicely leaves her husband Sir John to live in Paris with her lover Jack Harding, Sir John's secretary and son by Mrs. Harding.
fp: Cambridge University Amateur Dramatic Society, 1922.

D1170. "Damned Souls" in his *Over the Footlights*. Toronto, S.B. Gundy, 1923 and New York, Dodd, Mead, 1923 and in his *Over the Footlights and Other Fancies*. London, John Lane, 1923.
1 act. 5m/2f.
"A bright little tragedy of Russian home life". Satire of the "new style" of Russian drama.

D1171. "Des Deux Choses L'Une" in his *Over the Footlights*. Toronto, S.B. Gundy, 1923 and New York, Dodd, Mead, 1923 and in his *Over the Footlights and Other Fancies*. London, John Lane, 1923 and in *Harper's Magazine*, vol. 147, July 1923 and in his *Laugh with Leacock*. New York, Dodd, Mead, 1930 and Montreal, Pocket Books of Canada, 1947 and in his *The Leacock Roundabout*. New York, Dodd, Mead, 1946 and in *Laugh With Leacock*. Toronto, Montreal, McClelland & Stewart, (1966?).
1 act. 14m/2f. Extras.
Satire of the plays of "Dumas, Sardou, Hugo, Racine, Corneille and all others who ever wrote of Napoleon".

D1172. "Forging the Fifteenth Amendment" in his *Over the Footlights*. Toronto, S.B. Gundy, 1923 and New York, Dodd, Mead, 1923 and in his *Over the Footlights and Other Fancies*. London, John Lane, 1923 and in *Harper's Magazine*, vol. 147, July 1923 and in his *Laugh with Leacock*. New York, Dodd, Mead, 1930 and Montreal, Pocket Books of Canada, 1947 and in his *The Leacock Roundabout*. New York, Dodd, Mead, 1946 and in *Laugh With Leacock*. Toronto, Montreal, McClelland & Stewart, (1966?).
1 act. 4m.
Satire of plays written about the American Civil War.

D1173. "Mettawamkeag" in his *Over the Footlights*. Toronto, S.B. Gundy, 1923 and New York, Dodd, Mead, 1923 and in his *Over the Footlights and Other Fancies*. London, John Lane, 1923 and in *Harper's Magazine*, vol. 147, July 1923 and in his *Laugh with Leacock*. New York, Dodd, Mead, 1930 and Montreal, Pocket Books of Canada, 1947 and in his *The Leacock Roundabout*. New York, Dodd, Mead, 1946 and in *Laugh With Leacock*. Toronto, Montreal, McClelland & Stewart, (1966?).
1 act. 3m/1f.
Satire of blank verse tragedies about North American Indians.

D1174. "Q". By Stephen Leacock and Basil MacDonald Hastings. London, French, 1915.
1 act. 3m/1f.
"A farce". A young gentleman and his lady friend join forces to dupe George Gnoff, a spiritualist.
fp: London Coliseum, London, England, November 1915.

D1175. "The Raft: An Interlude" in his *Over the Footlights*. Toronto, S.B. Gundy, 1923 and New York, Dodd, Mead, 1923 and in his *Over the Footlights and Other Fancies*. London, John Lane, 1923 and in *Ten Canadian Short Plays*. John Stevens, ed. New York, Dell, 1975.
1 act. 1m/1f.
A satire of romantic adventures. A "story tale adventurer" fishes a girl out of the sea.
p: Player's Guild of University College, Hart House Theatre, Toronto, Oct. 1, 1924.

D1176. "Red Riding Hood Up to Date" in his *Funny Pieces: A Book of Random Sketches*. New York, Dodd, Mead, 1936 and Toronto, McClelland & Stewart, 1936 and London, John Lane, 1937.
1 act. 2m/3f. Extras.
A farcical version of "Red Riding Hood" in which Miss Hood and the wolf are secret lovers.

D1177. "The Russian Drama: Old Style" in his *Over the Footlights*. Toronto, S.B. Gundy, 1923 and New York, Dodd, Mead, 1923 and in his *Over the Footlights and Other Fancies*. London, John Lane, 1923.
1 act. 13m/1f.
Satire of the kind of play that deals with "dear old Russia".

D1178. "The Sub-Contractor" in his *Over the Footlights*. Toronto, S.B. Gundy, 1923 and New York, Dodd, Mead, 1923 and in his *Over the Footlights and Other Fancies*. London, John Lane, 1923 and in *The Leacock Book*. Ben Travers, ed. London, John Lane, 1930 and in *A Book of Canadian Humour*. J.D. Robins and M.V. Ray, eds. Toronto, Ryerson, 1951.
1 act. 4m/4f.
A satire of Ibsen's plays.

D1179. "Sunshine in Mariposa" in *MacLean's*, vol. 30, May, June, and July, 1917.
4 acts. 10m/3f.
When a Mariposa barber makes a fortune on a silver mine, New York con-artists come to town to fleece him and other gullible citizens.

D1180. **LEARNING, Walter.** *Frankenstein. The Incredible Murder of Cardinal Tosca.* See **NOWLAN, Alden A.**

LEAVITT, Jean T.

D1181. "Christmas Bells and Fairies" in *Educational Review*, vol. 30, December 1916.
1 act. 6b/6g.
"A play for little children". The bells from the Christmas tree in the house on the hill play with the little men from the woods on Christmas Eve.

D1182. "A Christmas Eve in the Forest" in *Educational Review*, vol. 27, Nov. 1913.
3 scenes. 2b/2g. Extras.
A tiny baby fir tree finds happiness when a boy takes him home for Christmas.

D1183. "Our Flags" in *Educational Review*, vol. 28, May 1915.
1 scene. 1b/1g. Extras.
"An Empire Day play for children". A group of children honour the Union Jack.

D1184. "The Red Cross Badge" in *Educational Review*, vol. 31, Nov. 1917.
2b. Extras.
A brief sketch relating the founding of the Red Cross by Dunant and Dufour in Switzerland in 1865.

LECLAIR, Larry

D1185. "Prince Edward Island" in *Son et Lumiere in Atlantic Canada*. Douglas Mantz, ed. Canadian Playwrights Co-operative, 1974.
1 act. 6m/2f. Extras.
A multi-media historical drama about the settling of Prince Edward Island.
fp: Prince Edward Island Centennial Commission, Charlottetown, P.E.I., July 1973.

LEDOUX, Paul

D1186. *The Dada Show.* Halifax, Dramatists Co-op, 1978.
2 acts. 5m/1f.
A cabaret musical about the life and times of a group of avant-garde artists and writers sitting out W.W. I in Zurich. Music by Sam Boskey and Bruce Ried.
fp: aTheatrical Co., Montreal, April 1977.

D1187. "The Electrical Man" by Paul Ledoux and Bill Power in *Callboard*, vol. 24, #4, Winter 1977 and *The Electrical Man.* Halifax, Dramatists Co-op, 1978.
1 act. 3m/1f.
A rock and roll comedy about Johnny K, the all-night DJ, who creates an electrical man to be his number one fan. They are both destroyed by the schizoid Angel who out-manipulates their fantasies for her own ends.
fp: aTheatrical Co., Quebec Drama Festival, Saidye Bronfman Centre, Montreal, Feb. 4, 1976.

D1188. *Kill Them.* Halifax, Dramatists Co-op, 1978.
2 parts. 2m/1f.
A violent look at captivity and death as seen through the eyes of a prisoner awaiting execution.
fp: aTheatrical Co., Toronto, 1976.

D1189. *The Night They Raided Truxx.* Paul Ledoux and Terry Last. Halifax, Dramatists Co-op, 1978.
2 acts. 8m.
A cabaret musical based on the police raid on the Montreal gay bar in October 1977. Music by Sam Boskey.
fp: bTheatrical Co., Halifax, June 1978.

D1190. *North Mountain Breakdown.* Halifax, Dramatists Co-op, 1978.
6 scenes. 7m/2f.
A kitchen sink satire about the owners of a dying farm on North Mountain in Nova Scotia's Annapolis Valley.

1191. *Rag Doll.* Halifax, Dramatists Co-op, 1978.
1 act. 1m/1f.
A horror story about a pregnant girl who is denied a legal abortion and is forced to bear a child she doesn't want.
fp: aTheatrical Co., Montreal, December 1976.

LEIMAN, Brad

D1192. *For Love & Chicken Soup.* Toronto, Playwrights Co-op, 1978.
2 acts. 2m/2f.
A comedy about the unconventional romance between the 68-year-old Sammy and Sarah, 64.
fp: Warehouse Theatre of the Manitoba Theatre Centre, Winnipeg, May 1978.

LELEAN, Edith. See GROVES, Edith Lelean.

LE MAY, Bonnie

D1193. *Boy Who Has A Horse.* Toronto, Playwrights Co-op, 1974.
9 scenes. 4m/1f.
This play for children concerns the story of a Sioux boy growing up during the years when Sitting Bull's people took refuge in Southern Alberta.
fp: Canmore Opera House, Alberta Theatre Projects, Heritage Park, Calgary, October 1972.

D1194. *Hit and Run.* Ottawa, Ottawa Little Theatre Workshop, #52.
1 act. 1m/1f.
This play examines the stereotype of the Indian; does white society force the Indian into the mould it has created?
p: CBC radio, 1967. CBC TV, Montreal, May 1, 1967.

D1195. *Roundhouse.* Toronto, Playwrights Co-op, 1977.
2 acts. 4m/3f.
A comedy about two harassed couples in 1920s Calgary focusing on the attempted sabotage of a silk train.
fp: Alberta Theatre Projects, Calgary, Feb. 25, 1975.

LEMM, Richard

D1196. *Remembrance Day.* Vancouver, New Play Centre, 1976.
2 acts. 3m/2f.
A young woman who has lost her husband in a war is visited by his ghost.

LEPAGE, Roland 1929–

D1197. *In a Lifetime.* Sheila Fischman, trans. Vancouver, Talonbooks, 1978.
2 acts. 5m/1f.
A translation of his *Temps d'une vie.* An old woman, ending her days in a city apartment, reflects on her life, beginning with her childhood on a farm.
fp: Tarragon Theatre, Toronto, May 13, 1978.

LETSON, Marguerite

D1198. "The Totem" in *Plays and Pageants.* Mary A. Knight and Marguerite Letson. Toronto, Nelson, 1935.
1 act. 3m/2f.
A drama of life in colonial Canada in which the settlers and Indians put aside their differences and celebrate Thanksgiving together.

LEVINE, Andy

D1198A. "Peepshow" in *York Theatre Journal,* vol. 5, #2, Winter 1976.
1 act. 1m/1f.
A brief conversation between two alienated young people.

LIBMAN, Carol

D1199. "Follow the Leader" in *Dialogue & Dialect: A Canadian Anthology of Short Plays*. Alive Theatre Workshop, ed. Guelph, Alive Press, 1972.
1 act. 3m.
Three men, a leader and two followers, build an imaginary war and empire for righteousness.
fp: The Theatre Club of the Playwrights' Workshop, Montreal, Nov. 13, 1968.

D1200. *The Reluctant Hero*. Ottawa, Ottawa Little Theatre Workshop, #4.
1 act. 3m/1f.
This play deals with the problem of heroism: is it determined by intention or by the result?
fp: Ottawa Little Theatre, 1956.

LINKLATER, John R. 1904–

D1201. *Champlain*. Orillia, Ont., Author, 1970.
5 scenes. 5m/1f. Chorus. Doubling.
"An historical pageant" about Champlain and the Hurons, celebrating the 400th anniversary of Champlain's birth.
fp: Ontario Youth Theatre, Couchiching Park, Orillia, July 18, 1970.

LIPPMAN, Anna

D1202. *The Babies*. Chicago, Dramatic Publishing, 1969.
1 act. 1m/1f.
Two babies live out their whole lives in highchairs, symbolic of the confining roles society forces on them from the time of birth.

LITCHEN, Stephen D.

D1202A. "When at Unawares" in *York Theatre Journal*, #14, Feb. 1977.
1 act. 3f.
A bitter, elderly woman, robbed of her one love in her youth, murders her husband.

LIVESAY, Dorothy (MacNair) 1909–

D1203. *Call My People Home*. Toronto, Ryerson, 1950 and in her *The Documentaries*. Toronto, Ryerson, 1968 and in her *Collected Poems: The Two Seasons*. Toronto, McGraw-Hill Ryerson, 1972 and in *The Evolution of Canadian Literature in English: 1914-1945*. George Parker, ed. Toronto, Holt, Rinehart and Winston, 1973 and in *The West Coast Experience*. Jack Hodgins, ed., Toronto, Macmillan, 1976.
1 act. 5m/1f. Chorus.
"A documentary poem for radio" about the life of Japanese immigrants in B.C. before and after Pearl Harbour.
fp: CBC radio "Listening Room Only", Montreal, March 1949.

D1204. "Joe Derry" in *Masses*, September 1933 and in *Eight Men Speak and Other Plays from the Canadian Workers' Theatre*. Richard Wright and Robin Endres, eds. Toronto, New Hogtown Press, 1976.
1 act. 4b or g. Extras.
A narrated pantomime about the career of Joe Derry, a worker's boy, who became an organizer for the workers labouring for better conditions during the Depression.
p: Workers' Experimental Theatre, Ontario tour, summer 1933.

D1205. "Struggle" in her *Right Hand Left Hand*. Erin, Ont., Press Porcepic, 1977.
1 scene. 2 groups.
"A mass chant" about class struggle in Germany and Canada and the international solidarity of workers.

D1206. "The Times Were Different" in her *Right Hand Left Hand*. Erin, Ont., Press Porcepic, 1977.
1 act. 7f/3m/1b/1g.
A radio play with strong autobiographical elements. Through shifting time frames, Margaret is shown growing up and becoming politicized.

LLWYD, Rev. John Plummer Derwent 1861–1933

D1207. *The Vestal Virgin*. Halifax, n.p., 1920.
4 acts. 6m/5f. Extras.
"A Dramatic Poem." Nysia becomes a vestal when she is falsely told by a priest that her fiance has been unfaithful. The lovers are caught together and tried but an earthquake saves them from execution and they leave for Parthia to become Christians.

LOGAN, Gloria

D1208. "Twenty-one Trolls and a Dragon" in *Rubaboo 3*. Scarborough, Ont., Gage, 1964.
1 act. 24m.
A children's play about Twenty-one Terrible Trolls who are convinced by George, a brave boy from the village, and by their usually mild-mannered gingerbread dragon to stop harassing the villagers.

LOGIE, Ray and Jane Logie

D1209. *The Strange Disappearance of Princess Gloriana*. Vancouver, New Play Centre, 1970.
8 scenes. 5m/2f. Extras.
On her birthday, Princess Gloriana is kidnapped by the Troll King but is rescued by the Royal Forester, the Court Jester, the Royal Cook and her dog, Randolf.
fp: Vancouver Little Theatre, 1970.

LOGIE, Ray, Myles F. Murchison and Peter Wilson

D1210. *Gilliam*. Vancouver, New Play Centre, (197-?).
2 acts. 5m/1f.
"A grotesquerie". Gilliam looks to his past and into various fantasy worlds to discover if he has any real friends or a real self.
fp: Vernon Powerhouse Theatre, Vernon, B.C., 1966.

LOHAN, Patrick

D1211. *Irish Grannie*. Vancouver, New Play Centre, (197-?).
1 act. 1m/2f.
Two German women meet their cousin on leave from the Navy during W.W.II.

LOOMER, L.S.

D1212. *Abolishing the Monarchy.* Halifax, Dramatists Co-op, 1977.
1 act. 5m/3f.
A satire about the monarchy in Canada based on the Mad Hatter's Tea Party.

D1213. *Festival of the Arts.* Halifax, Dramatists Co-op, 1977.
1 act. 6m/3f.
A satire set at a cocktail party following a folk concert at the Nova Scotia Festival of the Arts.

D1214. *Ye Gunne Pouder Plott.* Halifax, Dramatists Co-op, 1977.
10 scenes. 12m/4f.
A comedy loosely based on the Guy Fawkes plot to blow up the British Parliament.

LOVE, Frank

D1215. *Eight Men Speak.* See **RYAN, Oscar.**

D1216. "Looking Forward" in *Eight Men Speak and Other Plays from the Canadian Workers' Theatre.* Richard Wright and Robin Endres, eds. Toronto, New Hogtown Press, 1976.
1 act. 1m/2f.
An agitprop play concerning the struggles of a family to survive poverty.
fp: Progressive Arts Club, Toronto, 1932.

LUGSDIN, L.J.

D1217. "Something Wrong Somewhere" in *Scenes from Dickens*, J.E. Jones, ed. Toronto, McClelland & Stewart, 1923.
1 scene. 1m/1f/1g. Extras.
An adaptation of an incident from Charles Dickens' *Little Dorrit.* Mr. Dorrit consults Mrs. General on how to make Amy "one of ourselves".

LUNNEY, J.H.

D1218. "Au Revoir" in *Tuesday Night.* Regina, University of Saskatchewan, Regina College Writers' Club, 1935.
1 act. 3m/1f.
"A dramatic incident" in which a sculptor's son and daughter enlist in the military.

D1219. **LUSTIG, Helen** and Mamie Hamer. "A Living Thing". See **HAMER, Mamie.**

LYNAS, Edward

D1220. "The Movers" in *Alive*, vol. 2, #8, July/August 1971.
1 act. 3m.
An absurdist play in which two movers deprive an old man of all his possessions for non-payment of rent.

McALISTER, Alexander 1920–

D1221. *The V.P.* Toronto, Playwrights Co-op, 1975.
2 acts. 7m/2f. Doubling.
American Electric of Canada has just appointed its first token Canadian vice-president, Doug Marshall, who has some peculiarly uppity notions about how our corporations should be managed and what their interests should be.
fp: Citadel Theatre, Edmonton, November 1972.

McALLISTER, Ross W.

D1222. *Flowers in the City.* Toronto, Author, 1970. (Mimeographed).
3 acts. 6m/2f.
A rooming house is on the verge of being destroyed to make room for another parking lot. The play focusses on the tenants in the last few days of its existence, their fears and fantasies, needs and affections, disguises and mistaken identities.
fp: Central Library Theatre, Toronto, Oct. 8, 1970.

McANUFF, Des 1952–

D1223. *Leave It To Beaver Is Dead.* Toronto, Playwrights Co-op, 1976.
2 acts. 4m/1f.
Dennis leaves university and returns to his old haunt to pick up the reins of his drug clinic he began in the sixties. He finds the environment and his friends changed and the clinic replaced by a self-indulgent fantasy palace devoted to games of violence.
fp: Theatre Second Floor, Toronto, Feb. 12, 1975.

MacARTHUR, Mary

D1224. "A Garden for Recompense" in *Acadia Athenaeum,* vol. 57, #4, February 1931.
1 scene. 4m/1f.
An historical play in which Bonnie Prince Charlie is urged to take the boat to France by Flora MacDonald.

McATHY, George

D1225. *New Laff-Tested Dialogues.* Calgary, Mickey Hades Enterprises, 1967.
Includes 24 brief comic dialogues and routines.

McBEATH, Allan

D1226. "Many Days and Holidays" in *Educational Review,* vol. 49, #8, April–May 1935.
1 act. 3b/2g. Extras.
A group of children review the civic holidays and what they stand for.

MACBETH, Madge Hamilton (Lyons) 1878–1965

D1227. *Curiosity Rewarded.* Ottawa, Graphic Publishers, 1926.
1 act. 1m/1f.
"A dialogue between Gilbert Knox (pseudonym for Madge Macbeth) and the curious public", regarding the author's true identity and his or her purpose in writing novels.

D1228. *The Goose's Sauce.* Toronto, French, 1935.
1 act. 3m/1f.
A comedy set in the Canadian northwoods, in which a man and a woman are prevented from beginning an affair by the unexpected presence of the lady's husband.

MacCABE, Zoa J.

D1229. "Aunt Sara Expects Company" in *Acadia Athenaeum*, vol.52, #5, April 1926.
1 scene. 2m/2f.
Mistaken for his master, Jenks the valet impersonates the Hon. Archibald Roland and creates temporary confusion in the home of Miss Sara Holmstead.

D1230. "The Coming of Susan" in *Acadia Athenaeum*, vol. 52, #3, January 1926.
1 scene. 2m/4f.
An aged couple who cannot remember the names of their grandchildren but are preparing for the impending arrival of one of them, discover that Susan is a pet rabbit.

MacCALLUM, Jean A. See SWEET, Jean MacCallum.

MacCALLUM, Russell

D1231. *Cornflowers.* Ottawa, Ottawa Little Theatre Workshop, #24.
1 act. 2m/3f.
Star-crossed lovers are reunited in this city-country farce.

McCONKEY, Hugh T. 1922–

D1232. *Trilogy in a Garden.* New York, Exposition Press, 1955.
3 acts. 4m/1f.
"A play for voices". Allegory in which two lovers and their fathers wait in a garden which is Limbo. They are faced with an important choice between the pleasures of the moment and acceptance of God.

McCONNELL, Peter J. 1940–

D1233. *The Cool Constable or More About Moses in a Minute.* Toronto, Playwrights Co-op, 1972.
2 acts. 5m/4f. Doubling.
A farce about a bumbling police officer who is trying to decide whether to leave the force for a life on the stage.
fp: Belmont Production, Toronto.

MacDONALD, Helen C.

D1234. "Margaret MacLeod" in *Cape Breton Mirror*, vol.2, #8, #10, July, September 1953.
5 acts. 5m/4f.
An historical play recounting the story of the MacLeod migration from Saint Ann's, Cape Breton, to New Zealand through the eyes of Margaret MacLeod, daughter of the minister who led the expedition.

MacDONALD, Marjorie

D1235. "By a Romany Camp Fire" in *Sketches and Plays.* Toronto, National Girls' Work Board, Religious Education Council of Canada, (192-?).
1 act. 3m/4f. Extras.
A Gypsy lass and lad tell Canadian Girls in Training about their people.
fp: Canadian Girls in Training camps.

D1236. "The Legend of Echo and Narcissus" in *Sketches and Plays.* Toronto, National Girls' Work Board, Religious Education Council of Canada, (192- ?).
3 scenes. 3m/3f. Extras.
A brief dramatization of the legend of Echo's love for Narcissus.
fp: Canadian Girls in Training camps.

MacDONALD, Zillah Katherine

D1237. *A Royal Romance.* Western Canada Theatre Conference. Edmonton, Dept. of Extension, University of Alberta, 1946.
1 act. 5m/1f. Extras.
A historical drama about the relationship of the Duke of Kent with Madame St. Laurent in Halifax and their parting when he is recalled to England to marry and ascend the throne.

McDONOUGH, John Thomas 1924–

D1238. *Charbonneau and Le Chef.* Toronto, McClelland & Stewart, 1968.
3 acts. 9m/1f. Extras.
The play concerns the bitter conflict between the government of Maurice Duplessis and the strikers in Asbestos, P.Q. who were supported by Archbishop Charbonneau of Montreal.
fp: CBC radio, June 30, 1968.

MacDOUGALL, James Brown 1871–1950

D1239. *Miss Canada's Reception.* Toronto, McClelland, Goodchild & Stewart, 1917.
1 scene. 5m/10f.
Miss Canada meets her allies who pledge their willingness to beat "the Hun".

McEVOY, Bernard 1842–1932

D1240. "Anselmo and Bernadine" in his *Away from Newspaperdom and Other Poems.* Toronto, Morang, 1897 and in *Verses for My Friends.* Vancouver, Cowan Brookhouse, 1923 and in his *Elvira and Fernando and Other Selections.* Montreal, Southam Press, 1927.
1 act. 3m/4f. Extras.
A short dramatic romance in blank verse concerning the mature love of a gypsy-like niece of an imperious duke.

D1241. *The Spratts.* Montreal, Southam Press, 1927 and in his *Elvira and Fernando and Other Selections.* Montreal, Southam Press, 1927.
3 acts. 4m/4f. Extras.
Follows the Spratt family from affluence through stock market losses to poverty. Although they lose material possessions, they gain a daughter.

MacEWEN, Gwendolyn 1941–

D1242. "Terror and Erebus" in *Tamarack Review,* #63, October 1974.
1 act. 4m.
A verse play for radio in which the explorer Rasmussen follows the trail of death of the Franklin expedition and its over 100 men who perished in the Arctic searching for the Franklin Strait.
fp: CBC radio "Sunday Night", Jan. 10, 1965.

McFADDEN, Isobel

D1243. "A Dreamer in Moab" in *Canadian Poetry Magazine,* vol. 15, #2, Winter 1951.
1m/4f/1g.
A short scene from the play in which Orpah confides to her sister her dreams of leaving Moab for a better land.
fp: CBC radio, Winnipeg, Dec. 27, 1951.

McFARLANE, Leslie 1902–1977

D1244. "Alias Mr. Pollard" in *Life and Literature.* M. Spence, ed. Toronto, McGraw-Hill, 1966 and in *The Play's the Thing.* Jack Blacklock, ed. Toronto, McGraw-Hill, 1965.
2 acts. 7m/2f.
A TV drama. A young man is sentenced to death for murder. His friend, an older man, tries to prove the youth's innocence.
fp: CBC TV, April 21, 1958.

D1245. "Chicago Property" in *Literature for Enjoyment.* Murray K. Spence, ed. Toronto, McGraw-Hill, 1967.
3 acts. 7m/2f/3b/1g. Extras.
A TV drama. A father with "convictions" discovers that his young son's hockey team is part of a pre-farm system sponsored by the Chicago Blackhawks. He challenges the hockey system.
fp: CBC TV "Playdate", March 29, 1963 as "The Man Who Cheered the Leafs".

D1246. *Fire In the North.* Cobalt, Ontario, Highway Book Shop, 1972.
1 act. 31m/5f. Extras. Doubling.
A radio drama recreating the Haileybury fire of October, 1922 as related by the people of Haileybury.
fp: CBC radio, "The Bush and the Salon", Oct. 3, 1972.

McGOUGAN, Norma

D1247. *Marjorie's WeddingDress.* Edmonton, Dept. of Extension, University of Alberta, (194-?).
1 act. 1m/3f.
A comedy about the confusion arising from the delayed arrival of Marjorie's mail-order wedding dress.

McGOVERN, John Ward

D1248. "The Purple Seal" in his *Plays to Ponder*. New York, Vantage Press, 1970.
3 acts. 12m/1f. Extras.
Concerns the opposition which a dedicated physician encounters from a number of unscrupulous colleagues during his career.

D1249. "The Red Hand" in his *Plays to Ponder*. New York, Vantage Press, 1970.
3 acts. 11m. Extras.
Set in Ireland, 1921, during the British occupation. The play deals with the "problems of British officials and soldiers" trying to sustain "the Imperial regime".

D1250. "Reformation and Reward" in his *Plays to Ponder*. New York, Vantage Press, 1970.
3 acts. 12m.
"The meaning of life and the mystery of death" are explored in this play which concerns a merchant sailor on a cargo ship.

MacINTOSH, Claire (Harris) 1882–

D1251. "Flowers" in her *Two Plays for Child Actors*. N.p., n.p., 1934.
3 scenes. 6g.
Little girls playing in a woodland clearing decide to pretend they are flowers.
fp: The Young Pretenders of the Theatre Arts Guild, Halifax, March 3, 1934.

D1252. "The Tea Party at the Shoe" in *Two Plays for Child Actors*. N.p., n.p., 1934.
2 scenes. 7b/8g.
An old woman tells nursery rhymes to some visiting children. When they leave she falls asleep and dreams of being the old lady who lived in a shoe.
fp: The Young Pretenders of The Theatre Arts Guild, Halifax, April 20, 1934.

MacINTYRE, Annie

D1253. "The Silver Jubilee" in *Journal of Education for Nova Scotia*, series 4, vol.6, April 1935.
1 scene. 4m/1f. Extras.
In honour of George V's Silver Jubilee, the Empire children join the arts, sciences and technology to pay tribute to the king and the accomplishments of the past quarter century.

MacKAY, Eileen E.

D1254. "Mr. and Mrs." in *Acadia Athenaeum*, vol.55, #3, January 1929.
1 scene. 1m/1f.
Her bad cooking ends the honeymoon stage of their marriage until a young bride gives up a business trip with him to take cooking lessons.

MacKAY, Isabel Ecclestone (Macpherson) 1875–1928

D1255. *Goblin Gold*. New York, French, 1933.
3 acts. 4m/5f.
"A comedy-drama". When Uncle Simon comes to stay with the Beamer family he does not appear to be the rich relative they expected but they grow fond of him nonetheless.

D1256. *The Last Cache.* New York, French, 1927 and in *One-Act Plays for Stage and Study* 3rd series. New York, French, 1927.
1 act. 8m/1f.
When Ned returns from the mining claim without his partner Ben, he manages to conceal his treachery from all but Amelia and her father.
p: Hart House Theatre, Toronto, May 16, 1927.

D1257. "The Second Lie" in *Canadian Plays from Hart House Theatre* vol.1. V. Massey, ed. Toronto, Macmillan, 1926.
1 act. 3m/2f.
A well planned suicide within a love-triangle. "He wants to part our souls . . . to blacken and smirch the thing he has never been able to touch."
fp: Hart House Theatre, Toronto, April 5, 1921.

D1258. *Treasure.* New York, French, 1927 and in *Echoes,* #105, October 1938.
1 act. 4m/2f/2g.
Although all have heard that the old couple left a hidden treasure, none but the gypsy recognize it when it appears.
p: Brandon, Manitoba, 1928.

D1259. *Two Too Many.* Philadelphia, Pennsylvania Publishing, 1927.
3 acts. 4m/6f.
Sophia Winkworth must select an heir to her estate. She informs her three nephews that the one of them will be her successor who at the end of six months presents the most suitable fiancee, together with the best reason for his choice.
fp: Hart House Theatre, Toronto, 1928.

MacKAY, Louis Alexander 1901–

D1260. "The Freedom of Jean Guichet" in *Canadian Plays from Hart House Theatre* vol.2. V. Massey, ed. Toronto, Macmillan, 1927.
3 acts. 3m/6f.
A man is encouraged by his cousins to rebel against the tyranny of his wife and mother. Tragedy results.
fp: Hart House Theatre, Toronto, April 20, 1925.

McKENNA, Robert Ivan 1942–

D1261. *Middleman.* Toronto, Playwrights Co-op, 1973.
1 act. 5m.
A modern morality play about society and social change set in a representative office.

MACKENZIE, Alwilda Frances

D1262. "The King of the Golden Mountain" in *Canadian School Plays.* D.J. Dickie *et al.* eds. New York, Dutton, 1931 and Toronto, Dent, 1931.
3 acts. 35b/28g. Doubling.
A play for children. A merchant loses all his money but has his fortune restored by a magic dwarf in exchange for the merchant's son.

MacKENZIE, Brenda

D1263. "Tiny's Story" in *Callboard,* vol.25, #2, Summer 1978 and *Tiny's Story.*
Halifax, Dramatists Co-op, 1978.
1 act. 4m.
A comedy about a town drunk building exquisite model trains in a Saskatchewan saloon during the Depression.

MacKENZIE, Lee 1936–

D1264. *Rear View.* Prince George, B.C., Caledonia Writing Series, 1974.
2 acts. 21m & f. Doubling.
An irreverent history of B.C., specifically the Prince George area.
fp: Vanier Hall, Prince George, B.C., 1971.

MacKENZIE, Malcom

D1265. *Canada Forever or Home Is the Roamer.* Boston, Baker's Plays, 1950.
2 acts. 9m/6f.
When Angus John returns to Nova Scotia, he brings with him a Texan "smoothie" who apparently has a strange hold over Angus. The Texan turns out to be a con-man who almost succeeds in cheating the people of the community.

McKENZIE, Poppy

D1266. *The Error of Our Ways.* Vancouver, New Play Centre, (197-?).
1 scene. 5m/1f.
A young Scottish girl is to be married to an old storekeeper by her fanatically religious father but she refuses. In the end she runs away to join her brother.
fp: CBC radio and TV. One-act play festival, 1954.

D1267. *The Magic Nugget.* Vancouver, New Play Centre, (197-?).
2 acts. 6m/1f/1b.
Two miners are accused of attacking and robbing a fur trader. While they are being brought to trial, the real scoundrel is tricked into confessing.
fp: Holiday Theatre, Vancouver, 1958.

MACKENZIE, Stanley E.

D1268. "An Incident" in *Acadia Athenaeum,* vol.61, #4, February 1936.
1 scene. 1m/3f.
A chance incident reveals that a wealthy spinster's new maid is, in fact, her niece.

McKIM, Audrey

D1269. "New Horizons for Rolling Prairie" in *A Playette Quartet.* New York, Friendship Press, 1958.
1 act. 3m/3f.
A Saskatchewan farm family is faced with the problems of living with other racial and ethnic groups. A student missionary from Trinidad helps them to accept the "new Canadian" family next door.

MacLEAN, Mary H.

D1270. "Tea for Two" in *Curtain Call,* vol.10, #2, November 1938.
1 act. 1m/3f.
Tom mistakes the boss's daughter for his sister's roommate who he knows is posing as a maid to play a practical joke on him, and he treats her accordingly.

MacLENNAN, J. Munro 1900–

D1271. "Pipistrelle of Aquitaine" in *Canadian School Plays* series 1. E.M. Jones, ed. Toronto, Ryerson, 1948.
1 act. 7m/2f.
"An historical impertinence". Richard Coeur-de-lion is imprisoned by Count Alberic of Katzenblitzendom with whom he is now quite friendly. When the pest Princess Pipistrelle of Aquitaine is brought to the Count as another prisoner, Richard decides that his comfortable confinement should end.
p: Ottawa Drama League Workshop, 1938.

D1272. *Seven Caesar's Ransoms.* New York, Exposition Press, 1952.
3 acts. 15m/3f. Extras.
The Christian princess, betrothed to a prefect, falls in love with a centurion while the Visigoths, led by Alaric, besiege Rome.
p: Ottawa Branch, C.A.A., 1940.

McLENNAN, Winnifred

D1273. *Yea, Though I Walk.* Western Canada Theatre Conference. Edmonton, Dept. of Extension, University of Alberta, 1945.
1 act.
Title unavailable for annotation.

MacLEOD, Robert

D1274. *Flood.* Ottawa, Ottawa Little Theatre Workshop, #18.
1 act. 1m/3f.
During a flood, a woman can only accuse her son-in-law of incompetence in choosing the site of the house, forgetting her own role in its acquisition.
fp: Ottawa Little Theatre Workshop, 1953.

D1275. *Kate.* London, Deane, 1955.
1 act. 3m/4f.
A retiring cleaning lady gives gifts to her various employers by exchanging their valuable possessions until one day her system is discovered.
fp: England, 1955.

D1276. *The Ladies of Camelot.* London, Deane, 1957.
1 act. 3f.
Women in an old folks' home who knit for charity discover that their organizer is selling what they produce.
fp: England, 1957.

McMACKIN, Annie

D1277. "What Price?" in *Acadia Athenaeum*, vol.56, #5, March 1930.
1 scene. 4m/1f.
A minister's wastrel son is reclaimed after he implicates his younger brother for his own crime.

McMASTER, Beth 1935–

D1278. "Put On the Spot" in *Popular Performance Plays in Canada* vol.1. Marian Wilson, ed. Toronto, Simon & Pierre, 1976.
1 act. 5m/5f/1g.
A play for children in which Janie dreams her stuffed animals come to life in a wonderful zoo which is threatened by the evil mayor Krumpt and his accomplice, the zoo inspector Gonda Seed.
fp: Peterborough Theatre Guild, Ont., June, 1975.

D1279. *Stick With Molasses*. Toronto, Playwrights Co-op, 1973.
10 scenes. 5m/2f.
A children's play. When the owner of a circus dies, the nasty ring master and his girlfriend, the fortune teller, take over and mistreat the rightful heir, young Charles Holbrook. Lyrics by Monica Palmer.
fp: Peterborough Theatre Guild, Ont., 1971.

D1280. "When Everybody Cares" in *Popular Performance Plays in Canada* vol.1. Marian Wilson, ed. Toronto, Simon & Pierre, 1976.
1 act. 5m/2f.
A futuristic play for children about prejudice. Richard Robot is the subject of ridicule until an appreciation of his unique features dispels the prejudice of his neighbours.

D1281. "Which Witch Is Which?" in *A Collection of Canadian Plays* vol.4. Rolf Kalman, ed. Toronto, Simon & Pierre, 1975.
1 act. 1m/4f. Doubling.
A play on words for children. The underlying message is the desirability of being oneself rather than being one of a group.
fp: Peterborough Theatre Guild, Ont., 1972.

McMILLAN, Arvo 1940–

D1282. *Concerning a Temporary Permit*. Halifax, Dramatists Co-op, 1977.
1 act. 4m/1f.
Three people in a small Ontario planning office get a chance to explore their bizarre fantasies.

D1283. *New Maurry's Lunch*. Halifax, Dramatists Co-op, 1977.
1 act. 7m/5f.
A surrealistic play about the killing of an ex-RCAF pilot by an Italian restaurateur.
fp: Pier 1 Theatre, Halifax, 1973.

D1284. *Pope John VIII*. Halifax, Dramatists Co-op, 1977.
9 scenes. 16m/3f. Extras. Doubling.
A drama about a young and ambitious woman in the ninth century who becomes Pope.

D1285. *The Sad Story of Billy Max*. Halifax, Dramatists Co-op, 1977.
1 act. 8m/1f.
An examination of the insurance business in Cape Breton.

D1286. *A Toronto Hotel Room*. Halifax, Dramatists Co-op, 1977.
2 acts. 8m/3f.
In a fancy Toronto hotel, several characters confront their past including a childhood prank and its emotional repercussions.
fp: Seaweed Theatre, Halifax, 1978.

MacMILLAN, Kenneth

D1287. "The Adventures of Nicholas Nickleby" in *Scenes from Dickens*. J.E. Jones, ed. Toronto, McClelland & Stewart, 1923.
3 acts. 12m/10f. Extras.
An adaptation of Dickens' novel *Nicholas Nickleby* which follows the career of Nicholas from the time of his father's death until the reunion with his mother, sister, and friends.
p: Dickens Fellowship Players, Central Technical School, Toronto, March 8, 1922.

McMULLIN, R.

D1288. "And One Will Betray" in *Saskatchewan Writing 1965*. Saskatchewan Jubilee and Centennial Corporation, 1965.
1 act. 7m. Extras.
A small force of the German Resistance Movement meet in the basement of a warehouse. They have discovered that there is an informer among them and go about finding who it is.

McMURRY, Dorothy E.

D1289. *Jessie, the Nymph of the Foot-hills*. Vancouver, M.L. Jewell, 1908.
1 scene. 9m/1f.
The libretto to a pioneer romance set in Salmal Marie, B.C. Two boys love the same girl but a "sweet-voiced ragamuffin" ensures that the true love triumphs.

MACNAGHTEN, Professor R.E.

D1290. "Ruth" in *Westminster Hall Magazine and Farthest West Review*, (Vancouver, B.C.), vol.3, #1, #2, #3, January, February, March 1913.
5 acts. 10m/8f. Extras.
A poetic drama about the Biblical Ruth and her devotion to her widowed mother Naomi.

MacNAUGHTON, Isabel Christie

D1291. "The Crickets Must Sing" in her *Wood Fires*. Oliver, B.C., Oliver Chronicle and Osoyoos Observer, 1942 and Oliver, B.C., Chronicle Publishing, 1948.
1 scene. 1m. Chorus.
"Adapted from an Okanagan Indian folk tale as told by Josephine Shuttleworth". The carefree crickets explain to the industrious ant, "we have need of singing as you have need of work".

D1292. "The Greasewood Tree" in her *Wood Fires*. Oliver, B.C., Chronicle Publishing, 1948.
1 act. 1f/1g. Extras. Chorus.
"A fantasy played in verse and mime" relating the Indian tale of the old woman who becomes a gnarled greasewood tree rather than go with the spirit braves to spirit land.

D1293. "Why the Ant's Waist Is Small" and "Why the Chipmunk's Coat Is Striped". See **RENYI, Elizabeth.**

MacNAUGHTON, John A.

D1294. "Final Edition" in *Canadian School Plays* series 1. E.M. Jones, ed. Toronto, Ryerson, 1948.
1 act. 5m/1f.
The editor of a small town newspaper decides to quit his position but not before he gives the gossipy, phony townspeople the real truth about themselves.
p: Banff School of Fine Arts, 1940.

MacNEILL, Mary

D1295. "Too Late" in *Acadia Athenaeum*, vol. 58, #6, April 1932.
1 scene. 1m/3f.
Queen Guinevere learns too late that she loves Arthur rather than Lancelot.

MACPHAIL, Sir Andrew 1864–1938

D1296. "Company" in *Saturday Night*, May 9, 1936.
1 act. 3f.
While waiting for her sons to return, a mother is visited by a mysterious old woman.

D1297. "The Land" in *The University Magazine*, Montreal, 1914.
1 act. 8m/2f.
"A Play of Character". A woman who expects to inherit her father's fortune finds herself suddenly penniless and is forced to examine her former lifestyle.

D1298. "The Last Rising" in *Queen's Quarterly,* vol.37, Spring 1930.
1 act. 2m/1f/1b/1g.
"A melodrama" displaying a family's willingness to fight for "God, King and country" at the outbreak of W.W. I.

D1299. "The New House" in *Saturday Night,* June 12, 1937.
1 act. 2m/2f/2b.
An old woman tries to trick a neighbour into building a house for her.

McPHEE, Janet Alexandra

D1300. "Divinity in Montreal" in *Curtain Call,* vol.11, #3, December 1939.
1 act. 5m/4f.
"Divine Sarah" (Bernhardt) is rescued from a mob of fans by a man wanted for murder. He falls in love with her sister Jeanne, but is caught before they elope.
p: Dominion Drama Festival, 1939.

MacPHERSON, Jay.

D1301. "Jonah". See **BECKWITH, John.**

MacSWAIN, James

D1302. *The Big Catch.* Halifax, Dramatists Co-op, 1977.
1 act. 1m/5 puppets.
A rod and hand puppet play about two elves who catch the King of the fish while fishing.
fp: Gargoyle Puppet Troupe, Nova Scotia.

D1303. *The Prime Minister's Golden Wig.* Halifax, Dramatists Co-op, 1977.
1 act. 10 puppets.
A political satire about the PM's wig which is stolen by Dracula.
fp: Gargoyle Puppet Troupe, Nova Scotia.

MADDEN, John

D1304. *Adam Malt Defrosted.* Saint John, N.B., Author, 1966. (Mimeographed).
1 act. 4m/3f. Extras.
A science-fiction television or stage play set in 2367 A.D. in which an alcoholic refrigerator mechanic, winner of the Irish Sweepstakes, is brought back to life.

D1305. *Speak for Life.* See **CROTHERS, Tom.**

MADDEN, Peter

D1306. *The Night No One Yelled.* Toronto, Playwrights Co-op, 1975.
1 act. 18m.
In a prison cell block, a group of inmates banter back and forth: the tough, frustrated, ultimately lonely talk of men doing time, stuck with each other and with themselves.
fp: Beggars' Workshop at the Playwrights' Workshop Theatre, Montreal, May 9, 1974.

MAGUIRE, Trevor

D1307. "Unemployment" in *The Canadian Labour Monthly,* May/June, 1928 and in *Eight Men Speak and Other Plays from the Canadian Workers' Theatre.* Richard Wright and Robin Endres, eds. Toronto, New Hogtown Press, 1976.
1 act. 5m/2f.
Arthur Dickson can't find work and has no means by which to support his wife, daughter Nellie, and baby. The family's belongings are repossessed and they face eviction. Nellie, driven by hunger, leaves her home for the streets.

MAHON, James 1910–

D1308. *The Imaginary Line.* Toronto, Author, 1946.
3 acts. 18m/6f. Extras.
"A play of substance". A comedy about a young artist living in Windsor on the Detroit River who wishes to live in the U.S.A. but rejects offers of assistance by both government and business interests.

MALCOLM, Ian 1927–

D1309. *God Save McQueen.* Toronto, Religion and Theatre Council, n.d. and in *Performing Arts in Canada,* vol.6, #4, 1969.
1 act. 4m.
McQueen has achieved nothing in life, not even individuality. Outside forces discourage him from deviating from the accepted norm.
fp: CBC TV "Shoestring Theatre".

D1310. "A Moment of Existence" in *Canada on Stage.* Stanley Richards, ed. Toronto, Clarke Irwin, 1960 and in *Voice and Vision.* Jack Hodgins and William H. New, eds. Toronto, McClelland & Stewart, 1972.
1 act. 5m.
Is man a human being or an object to be manipulated, a specimen to be examined clinically? A man examines his life by speaking to four visitors.
fp: New Play Society, Toronto, May 9, 1965. CBC radio "Stage", Dec.5, 1965 as "A Dream Within Time".

D1311. "This, Gentlemen, is Justice" in *The Best Short Plays of 1960–1961.* Margaret Mayorga, ed. Boston, Beacon Press, 1961.
1 act. 1m/2f. Extras.
Three people, each experiencing a different life style, are confronted by a murderer. All, including the murderer, are killed, and arrive in heaven. The judge clears up a mix-up, and each receives his lot.

MANDEL, Eli 1922–

D1312. "Mary Midnight" in *Alphabet,* #8, June 1964.
1 act. 5m/1f. Extras.
"An oratory." A prostitute and her clients journey through phases of reality.

MANN, Vida

D1313. "Riz Flowers" in *Acadia Athenaeum,* April 1937.
1 scene. 3m/3f.
A dialect comedy about life on a black homestead in the Gaspe and Sarah's efforts to win first prize for her hooked rugs at the local fair.

D1314. **MANTZ, Douglas.** "Keillor House Dialogue". See **GOODWIN, George.**

MARCOTTE, Danielle *et al.*

D1315. "Fort Beausejour" in *Son et Lumiere in Atlantic Canada.* Douglas Mantz, ed. Canadian Playwrights Co-operative, 1974.
1 act. 12m/2f. Extras.
An historical pageant about the border area of Nova Scotia and New Brunswick which became an area of great controversy between the British and French in the 18th century.

MARCUS, Felicity Coleman

D1316. *George, Gertie and the Garbage Grabbers.* Toronto, Playwrights Co-op, 1973.
2 acts. 3m/2f.
George and Gertie, junkshop proprietors, combine forces with a singing garbage can to thwart the Great Garbage Conspiracy.
fp: Edmonton Experimental Theatre, October 1972.

MARKLE, Fletcher 1921–

D1317. "Sometime Every Summertime" in *Radio's Best Plays.* Joseph Liss, ed. New York, Greenberg, 1947.
1 act. 3m/3f. Extras.
A radio play about a brief summer romance on an island off Vancouver recalled from three different points of view.
fp: CBC "Radio Folio", Aug. 5, 1945.

MARKOWITZ, Harvey 1933–

D1318. *Branch Plant.* Toronto, Playwrights Co-op, 1972.
2 acts. 9m/1f.
This play attacks the "branch plant mentality" of the management level in Canadian business by presenting the shutdown of a subsidiary plant of a foreign-owned rubber processing company.
fp: Factory Theatre Lab, Toronto, 1971.

D1319. *Lovemaking for Profit and Taxes.* Toronto, Playwrights Co-op, 1972.
3 acts. 6m/5f.
A very proper civil service accountant gains a new outlook on life when he is put in charge of a government-operated brothel.
fp: Central Library Theatre, Toronto, April 1972.

MARSHALL, Tom

D1320. "Words for an Imaginary Future" in *Poems for Voices.* Toronto, CBC, 1970.
1 act. 2m/1f.
A radio play. A woman, her husband, and her lover talk about their past and present lives and try to decide upon a future.
fp: CBC radio, February 1970.

MARY Agnes, Sister –1939

D1321. *The Arch of Success.* Winnipeg, St. Mary's Academy, 1919.
1 act. 15g.
"A dialogue for commencement day". Each of eight students places a block representing a specific character trait necessary for success in the framework of an arch symbolic of success.

D1322. "At the Court of Isabella" in her *The Last of the Vestals and Other Dramas.* Winnipeg, St. Mary's Academy, 1914.
3 acts. 7m/4f/1b. Extras.
"An historical drama" concerning the saintly Queen Isabella's faith in Columbus' missionary voyage to the East and his subsequent discovery of America.

D1323. "The Best Gift" in her *The Best Gift and Other Short Plays*. Winnipeg, St. Mary's Academy, 1923.
1 act. 1f/8g. Extras.
The members of the "Little Missionaries Club" are preparing for their bazaar in aid of foreign missions. Lilian, the vain and worldly actress, learns a lesson, and her sister Mary finally receives their mother's permission to become a missionary.

D1324. *Better Than Gold*. Winnipeg, St. Mary's Academy, 1922.
2 acts. 11f. Extras.
Rosemary finds love and true satisfaction when her real mother is revealed to her and willingly gives up her luxurious life to go and live with her because "a mother's love is better than gold".

D1325. "The Birthday of the Divine Child" in her *The Best Gift and Other Short Plays*. Winnipeg, St. Mary's Academy, 1923.
1 act. 3m/11b. Extras.
"A Christmas play for boys" in which a special Christmas entertainment is being rehearsed. A former student, now studying to be a doctor, is persuaded to use his skills in the mission.

D1326. *Children of Nazareth*. Winnipeg, St. Mary's Academy, 1926.
1 act. 6m/3f.
The child Jesus makes a gift for His Mother's birthday.

D1327. "Choosing a Model" in her *The Last of the Vestals and Other Dramas*. Winnipeg, St. Mary's Academy, 1914.
1 act. 17f/1g.
Girls preparing for commencement exercises try to choose an historical theme. Various historical figures appear to plead their suitability.

D1328. "Christmas Guests" in her *Queen of Sheba and Other Dramas*. Winnipeg, St. Mary's Academy, 1915.
1 act. 1f/26g.
A group of young girls get a lesson in the meaning of true Christian charity.

D1329. *Cross and Chrysanthemum*. Winnipeg, St. Mary's Academy, 1922.
2 acts. 18m/6f/3b/1g. Extras.
"A story of missionary labours and the persecution of Christians in Japan", centered on the martyrdom of Christian Japanese rulers by non-Christian Japanese.

D1330. *A Day with Peggy*. Winnipeg, St. Mary's Academy, 1927.
1 act. 2f/5g.
An unwanted young girl convinces her aunt to take her in.
p: "Works I", Factory Theatre Lab, Toronto, Dec. 5, 1972.

D1331. "The Divine Guest" in her *The Best Gift and Other Short Plays*. Winnipeg, St. Mary's Academy, 1923.
1 act. 1f/7g/1b.
"A Christmas play for girls". Madeleine confuses the formalities of worship with the charitable activities required by a truly Christian life.

D1332. *The Empress Helena or The Victory of the Cross*. Winnipeg, St. Mary's Academy, 1915.
2 acts. 11g.
"An historical drama for girls". Empress Helena, mother of Constantine, journeys from Rome to Jerusalem in search of the Holy Cross.

D1333. *A Happy Mistake.* Winnipeg, St. Mary's Academy, 1924.
1 act. 7m/3f/4b/3g.
In the face of her employer's opposition, a young maid and a policeman scheme to get married.

D1334. "How St. Nicholas Came to the Academy" in her *The Last of the Vestals and Other Dramas.* Winnipeg, St. Mary's Academy, 1914.
1 act. 14b or g. Extras.
St. Nicholas comes to visit some good little girls who are sick in the Academy at Christmas time. He brings with him a group of jolly little "Esquimaux" to help entertain the girls.

D1335. *An Irish Princess.* Winnipeg, St. Mary's Academy, 1917.
2 acts. 2m/11f. Extras.
The English invade Ireland and Princess Eva must marry in order to save the Irish people from slaughter.

D1336. *Katy Did.* Winnipeg, St. Mary's Academy, 1926.
1 act. 3m/2f.
Katy's generosity, her cleverness in foiling a thief, and a case of mistaken identity result in happiness and romance.

D1337. "The Last of the Vestals" in her *The Last of the Vestals and Other Dramas.* Winnipeg, St. Mary's Academy, 1914.
3 acts. 4m/23f/1b/1g. Extras.
"An historical drama" for girls, based on the ruling of Constantine, Christian Roman Emperor, that the Temple of Vesta be closed.

D1338. "Little Cinderella" in her *Short Plays and Recitations.* Winnipeg, St. Mary's Academy, 1922.
1 act. 4f/1b/8g.
The Cinderella story which Maud and her friends act out is paralleled in real life by the unexpected good fortune of Annie, an orphan child.

D1339. *Little Saint Teresa.* Winnipeg, St. Mary's Academy, 1923.
1 act. 5m/3f/3b/4g.
Young Teresa of Avila and her brother Rodrigo journey to the land of the Moors seeking martyrdom but both learn that they must "wait till it is clear that God asks this sacrifice".

D1340. *Mary Magdalen.* Winnipeg, St. Mary's Academy, 1918.
3 acts. 4m/18f. Extras.
Mary Magdalen refuses to listen to Ruth, the daughter of Jairus, and become a follower of Christ. Mary enjoys her life of luxury and the possibility of becoming the wife of Herod. She is converted, however, when she sees Ruth raised from the dead.

D1341. *Mary Stuart and her Friends.* Winnipeg, St. Mary's Academy, n.d.
3 acts. 4m/8f. Extras.
The daughter of the Earl of Morton betrays Mary.

D1342. "A May Festival" in her *The Best Gift and Other Short Plays.* Winnipeg, St. Mary's Academy, 1923.
1 act. 8b/7g. Extras.
The Mission Club holds a festival and picnic to make money for the foreign missions.

D1343. "The Millionaire's Daughter" in her *The Queen of Sheba and Other Dramas*. Winnipeg, St. Mary's Academy, 1922.
2 acts. 3f/8g.
The girls at a boarding school are expecting a millionaire's daughter to arrive for the new term but they are unsuccessful in detecting her identity.

D1344. *Mother's Birthday*. Winnipeg, St. Mary's Academy, 1921.
2 acts. 1f/1b/8g. Extras.
A group of children preparing to celebrate their mother's birthday criticize the deleterious effect of the movies.

D1345. "The New Governess" in her *Short Plays and Recitations*. Winnipeg, St. Mary's Academy, 1922.
1 act. 3f/1b/5g.
Marjorie schemes to trick her aunt into hiring Gertrude for the post of governess.

D1346. "New Year's Eve" in her *Short Plays and Recitations*. Winnipeg, St. Mary's Academy, 1922.
1 act. 4m/3g.
On New Year's Eve, the older girls enact the parts of the Old Year and the New Year for the benefit of the sleepy children.

D1347. *Old Friends and New*. Winnipeg, St. Mary's Academy, 1917.
1 act. 1m/12f/5g. Extras.
"A dialogue for commencement day". The graduates say goodbye to childhood visions and joys and welcome those of the adult.

D1348. *Our Japanese Cousin*. Winnipeg, St. Mary's Academy, n.d.
4 acts. 5f/1b/2g.
Mrs. Somerville's brother has died in Japan and his daughter Suki comes to live with the Somerville family. She teaches them about "giving" to help those less fortunate.

D1349. "A Patriot's Daughter" in her *The Last of the Vestals and Other Dramas*. Winnipeg, St. Mary's Academy, 1914.
3 acts. 6f/2g. Extras.
A melodrama concerning the tribulations of a young lady whose father does not support the Royalist cause in Boston after the "tea-party" of 1773.

D1350. *Pearls for the Missions*. Winnipeg, St. Mary's Academy, 1923.
1 act. 8f/1g. Extras.
A former president of the Foreign Missions Club decides to leave the bulk of her fortune to it.

D1351. "Plans for the Holidays" in her *The Queen of Sheba and Other Dramas*. Winnipeg, St. Mary's Academy, 1915.
1 act. 27g. Extras.
"A school play for closing exercises in the grammar grades". The older schoolgirls disguised as gypsies give their younger friends a lesson in the appreciation of learning.

D1352. *Queen Esther*. Winnipeg, St. Mary's Academy, 1924.
3 acts. 3m/2f. Extras.
Esther pleads with the king of Persia to save the Jewish people from extinction.

D1353. "The Queen of Sheba" in her *The Queen of Sheba and Other Dramas.*
Winnipeg, St. Mary's Academy, 1915.
3 acts. 7m/19f/1g. Extras.
A Biblical drama concerning the conversion of the Queen of Sheba and her visit to King Solomon.

D1354. *The Red Cross Helpers.* Winnipeg, St. Mary's Academy, 1918.
2 acts. 2f/1b/13g.
During W.W. I, the graduating class of an American academy takes up a collection for a hospital for wounded soldiers. When the money disappears suspicion falls in turn on a Chinese laundry boy, a German student, and her half-sister, before the real culprit is found.

D1355. *Schoolgirl Visions.* Winnipeg, St. Mary's Academy, 1923.
1 act. 11g. Extras.
The graduates recall incidents from their pasts and remember the struggle to attain what knowledge they now have.

D1356. *Sense and Sentiment.* Winnipeg, St. Mary's Academy, 1920.
3 acts. 1f/8g.
A few girls set out to cure a friend of her sentimentality.

D1357. "A Shakespeare Pageant" in her *The Queen of Sheba and Other Dramas.*
Winnipeg, St. Mary's Academy, 1915.
1 act. 20g. Extras.
"A dialogue for commencement day". Short scenes from "the lives of Shakespeare's women" illustrating "lessons of wisdom" are performed for a graduating class.

D1358. *The Step-Sisters.* Winnipeg, St. Mary's Academy, 1917.
3 acts. 1m/11f.
To overcome her daughter Mabel's prejudice against Eva, the step-sister she has never met, Mrs. Temple arranges for both girls to go to the same boarding school where Mabel and Eva become fast friends.

D1359. *The Taking of the Holy City.* Winnipeg, St. Mary's Academy, 1918.
1 act. 8m or f. Extras.
"Recitation with song and pantomime" of the conquest by the Turks of Jerusalem and later its deliverance by "The Allied Nations".

D1360. *Their Class Motto: Duty First.* Winnipeg, St. Mary's Academy, 1925.
1 act. 2f/6g. Extras.
Young schoolgirls devise an entertainment to honour the graduating class.

D1361. "Those Shamrocks From Ireland" in her *The Last of the Vestals and Other Dramas.* Winnipeg, St. Mary's Academy, 1914.
1 act. 3f/11g. Extras.
A play within the rehearsal of a St. Patrick's entertainment at a girls' school, in which an orphaned Irish girl is almost kidnapped before she finds her sister and safety.

D1362. "The Trial of the Weather" in her *Short Plays and Recitations.* Winnipeg, St. Mary's Academy, 1922.
1 act. 4m/5f/4b/4g.
Mother Earth's servant, Weather, tries but is unable to satisfy everybody.

D1363. "Uncle Jerry's Silver Jubilee" in *The Best Gift and Other Short Plays*. Winnipeg, St. Mary's Academy, 1923.
"A play in two acts for boys". Text at British Museum unavailable for annotation.

D1364. *The Young Professor*. Winnipeg, St. Mary's Academy, 1927.
1 act. 16b. Extras.
Young students decide on a way to honour their teacher.

D1365. *Zuma, The Peruvian Maid*. Winnipeg, St. Mary's Academy, 1922.
3 acts. 7m/3f/2g/4b. Extras.
In return for the kindness which they show towards the Peruvian natives, Zuma gives the Count and Countess of Spain the secret drug to cure malaria. This action brings peace between the two peoples.

MASON, Harold Campbell 1895–

D1366. *Smith Broadens Out*. Toronto, Author, 1923.
2 acts. 4m/1f.
An ex-soldier-writer, who flirted with communism in Toronto in order to change the misery of urban society, finds contentment in the hard work and self-dependence of farm life.

MASON, Marjorie H.

D1367. "Interrupted Plans" in *Acadia Athenaeum*, vol.52, #9, May 1926.
1 scene. 3m/2f.
A telegram delivered to the wrong house disrupts everyone's plans until the confusion is righted.

D1368. "Preparations" in *Acadia Athenaeum*, vol.52, #1, November 1925.
1 scene. 5m.
A brief sketch of college humour in which a man races to get ready for a date only to learn that his watch had been set fast.

MASON, Michael 1924–

D1369. *The Oasis*. Toronto, Playwrights Co-op, 1973.
3 acts. 19m/3f. Extras.
A radio play. English professors teaching in a free university in Africa are caught in the middle of a bloody revolution, accused by both the ruling white government and the black majority of causing all the trouble.
fp: Australian Broadcasting Commission, Feb. 21, 1972.

MATHER, Barry

D1370. "Dirty Work At the Crosswalks" in *A Treasury of Canadian Humour*. Robert Thomas Allen, ed. Toronto, McClelland & Stewart, 1967.
1 act. 2m/1f.
A policeman dresses in civilian clothes to capture jaywalkers.

MATHEWS, Robin 1931–

D1371. *Selkirk*. Toronto, Steel Rail Educational, 1977.
2 acts. 18m/2f. Doubling.
A portrayal of Lord Selkirk's struggle to establish the Red River settlement in the early eighteen hundreds against the violent opposition of the fur trading North West Company.
fp: Great Canadian Theatre Company and the Carleton University Fine Arts Committee, Alumni Theatre, Carleton University, Ottawa, Oct. 28, 1976.

MATTHEWS, Don

D1372. *The Deviates*. Parry Sound, Ontario, Author, 1967. (Mimeographed).
3 acts. 3m/3f.
The play concerns four people sharing a room in a cheap London boarding house; it describes the dynamics of their relationships and the strategies they have devised to protect themselves from harsh personal truths and uncertainties.

MAURA, Sister (née Mary Power) 1881–1957

D1373. "A Coronation Pageant" in *Journal of Education for Nova Scotia*, series 4, vol.8, September 1937.
1 scene. 7m/7f. Extras.
Various countries, including Canada, proclaim their allegiance to the Empire and the new king, George VI.

D1374. "Dramatization of Civics Lesson: What is Democracy?" by A Sister of Charity (pseud.) in *Educational Review*, vol.55, #4, Dec. 1940.
1 act. 2b/2g.
A group of school children discuss the meaning of democracy.

D1375. "Pageant of the Years" in *Journal of Education for Nova Scotia*, series 4, vol.5, December 1934.
1 scene. 13f.
A pageant for the fiftieth anniversary of St. Patrick's Girls' High School in Halifax.

D1376. *Via Vitae: a Morality Play*. A Sister of Charity (pseud.). London, Humphrey Milford, 1923.
5 scenes. 1f/12m. Extras.
Psyche resists the temptations of Satan and the world with the help of Faith, Hope and Charity, and reaches Heaven with the guidance of her guardian angel.

MAZUMDAR, Maxim 1953–

D1377. *Oscar Remembered*. Toronto, Personal Library, 1977.
2 acts. 1m.
A monodrama about the life and love of Oscar Wilde and Lord Alfred Douglas.
fp: Quebec Drama Festival, 1974; revised version, Stratford Festival, Aug. 16, 1975.

MEDD, Nellie

D1378. *The Crowning of Canada.* Exeter, Ont., Author, (193–?).
1 act. 13m/12f. Extras.
"A Jubilee Confederation Pageant." The provinces, territories, Indians and Canadian historical figures celebrate Canada's diamond jubilee.
p: Pupils of the Orthopedic School, Toronto, June 23, 1927.

MELNICK, Peter 1943–

D1379. "The Empress of China" in his *Nu-Style Plays.* Toronto, Playwrights Co-op, 1978.
1 act. 1f.
A comic monodrama in which the exiled Empress of China reminisces about her life with the Emperor.
fp: Theatre Passe Muraille at the New Theatre, Toronto, June 1977.

D1380. *Monomania.* Toronto, Playwrights Co-op, 1976 and in his *Nu-Style Plays.* Toronto, Playwrights Co-op, 1978.
1 act. 2m/1f.
An experimental multi-media play in which three performers enact situations in which their identities and relationships to each other are hinted at but are constantly in flux in what is essentially a musical structure.
fp: Theatre Passe Muraille, St. Paul's Centre, Toronto, May 15, 1975.

D1381. "Sitting in the Audience" in his *Nu-Style Plays.* Toronto, Playwrights Co-op, 1978.
1 act. 2m/2f.
An experimental play examining the dramatic potential of time, sound and space.
fp: Unified Theatre at A Space and CEAC, Toronto, August 1976.

D1382. "The Wringing of Hearts" in his *Nu-Style Plays.* Toronto, Playwrights Co-op, 1978.
11 scenes. 2m/2f.
An experimental play about two pairs of lovers.
fp: Theatre Passe Muraille, Toronto, May 25, 1976.

MENDRITZKI, Wolf

D1383. "Iggy Makes an End" in *The River City Tribune,* vol.3, #2, June 8, 1971.
1 act. 7m. Extras.
A satirical play about plays which use "cheap symbolism".

MERCIER, Serge 1944–

D1384. "A Little Bit Left", Allan van Meer, trans., in *A Collection of Canadian Plays* vol.5. Rolf Kalman, ed. Toronto, Simon & Pierre, 1978.
3 scenes. 2m/1f.
A translation of his *Encore Un Peu.* A comedy about an old Quebec couple living a life of impotence and monotony.
fp: P'tits Enfants Laliberté, 1972. Ontario educational television network.

MERTEN, Elizabeth

D1385. "The Boy with Green Fingers" in Merten, George. *The Hand Puppets.* Toronto, Nelson, 1957.
2 acts. 3m/3f/1b.
A play for hand puppets. An old gardener gives a young boy the gift of "green fingers", a way with plants, in consolation for the ugliness and stupidity with which a cruel witch has cursed him.

D1386. "Sea Legend" in Merten, George. *The Marionette.* Toronto, Nelson, 1957.
2 acts. 4m/3f.
A marionette play. A Chinese fisher-boy goes beneath the sea to seek the reason for the scarcity of fish on which his village depends.

D1387. "Welcome, Stranger" in Merten, George. *The Marionette.* Toronto, Nelson, 1957.
1 act. 2m/2f/1b.
The father monkey is constantly interrupted in his attempts to sleep and irritably sends away a stranger who turns out to be his father-in-law.

MERTEN, George 1910–

D1388. "A Head for Peppino" in his *The Hand Puppets.* Toronto, Nelson, 1957.
1 act. 2m/1b.
Peppino, a newly-made puppet who dislikes his face without even having seen it, learns to be satisfied with the way he was created.

MIDDLETON, Helen E.

D1389. "At a Cross-Roads' Schoolhouse" in *Educational Review*, vol.55, #3, Nov. 1940.
1 act. 1m/4b/5g. Extras.
A group of children marooned in a schoolhouse by a blizzard the day before Christmas are cheered by the Christmas Fairy and Santa Claus.

MIDDLETON, Jesse Edgar 1872–1960

D1390. "Boots and His Brothers" in *Willison's Monthly*, vol.4, #1, June 1928.
1 act. 4m/1f.
Boots, the Canadian architect, competes with his brothers, Yank and Frenchy, to get a commission for an important building contract. He succeeds with the help of his fairy godmother who looks remarkably like Premier Ferguson.

D1391. "Lake Dore" in *Six Canadian Plays*. H.A. Voaden, ed. Toronto, Copp Clark, 1930.
1 act. 2m/1f.
Stella Kirkman accepts her late husband's guilt in a robbery in the only way she can, with her own death.
fp: Central High School of Commerce, Toronto, April 9, 1930.

D1392. *A Pageant of Nursing in Canada.* (Toronto?), Canadian Nurses Association, (1934?).
23 scenes. 32m & f.
"Specially written for the Twenty-fifth Anniversary of the founding of the Canadian Nurses' Association". A pageant, in prose and poetry, recounting the history of nursing as a profession, its development in terms of world medicine, as well as its unique history in Canada.
fp: Royal York Hotel Concert Hall, Toronto, June 29, 1934.

D1393. *Pilgrims and Strangers.* Toronto, Crocker Printing, 1914.
2 acts. 3m/3f. Extras.
"A picture in two lights". A comedy in which the initial trepidations of a Methodist minister's family about the new congregation to which he has been posted are dispelled by the kindheartedness of the Ladies' Aid Auxilliary.

MILLAR, Kenneth

D1394. "Little Theatre" in *Saturday Night*, October 21, 1939.
1 scene. 6m/1f.
A director struggles through a rehearsal of *Macbeth*.

MILLAR, Maude

D1395. "Too Much Plum Pudding" in *Curtain Call*, vol.9, #3, Dec. 1937 and in Ness, Margaret E. *Practical Play Production for Canadian Schools and Communities.* Toronto, Curtain Call Publishing, 1938.
1 scene. 1g. Extras.
A little girl dreams her dolls come to life.

D1396. "The Toy Shop" in *Curtain Call*, vol.9, #3, Dec. 1937 and in Ness, Margaret E. *Practical Play Production for Canadian Schools and Communities.* Toronto, Curtain Call Publishing, 1938.
1 scene. 1m/1f/1g. Extras.
A children's play. Toys try to console a doll separated from its twin.

MILLER, Hanson Orlo 1911–

D1397. *This Was London.* London, Ontario, Author, 1955. (Mimeographed.)
3 acts. 17m/4f. Extras.
The history of the southwestern Ontario city of London reflected in the rising and falling fortunes of the Parker family from 1855 to 1926.

MILLER, Jean

D1398. "The Man in the Moon" in *Acadia Athenaeum*, vol.55, #4, February 1929.
1 scene. 1m/1f.
Two lovers meet in the moonlight. She laughs at his love for her and returns to her husband and her other lovers.

D1399. "Years Afterward" in *Acadia Athenaeum*, vol.55, #6, April 1929.
1 scene. 4m/1f.
A young lawyer decides to represent the wife in a divorce action rather than her wealthy husband because of a kindness done him by the wife's father.

MILLER, Lily Poritz 1938–

D1400. *The Proud One*. Toronto, Playwrights Co-op, 1973.
3 acts. 2m/6f.
A Jewish girl who has "made it" as a writer in New York returns home for her sister's wedding. Her family and friends find her baffling and mystifying, but they do not realize she is often lonely and insecure despite the facade of bravura.
p: Backdoor Theatre, Toronto, March 13, 1974.

MILLER, Roscoe R.

D1401. *Amerigo and the Naming of America*. New York, Carlton Press, 1968.
28 scenes.
A diary-format play which describes the travels of Amerigo Vespucius to the new world and his discovery of America.

MILLIGAN, James Lewis 1876–

D1402. *Judas Iscariot*. Toronto, Ryerson, 1929.
1 act. 16m/2f. Extras.
"A poetical play" of the betrayal of Christ by Judas Iscariot in the Garden of Gethsemane and Christ's trial before Pontius Pilate.
fp: Westminster Central United Church, Toronto, March 21, 1929.

MILNE, William Samuel 1902–1979

D1403. *The Failure*. Toronto, Robinson Plays, 1937 and in *Curtain Rising*. W.S. Milne, ed. Toronto, Longmans, Green, 1958 and in *Transitions I: Short Plays*. Edward Peck, ed. Vancouver, Commcept Publishing, 1978.
1 act. 3m/2f.
Three sons, two successful and one who is not, are in love with their widowed mother's ward. Although she could have married any of them she accepts the "failure" because "I felt that I simply couldn't marry . . . a successful man".
p: Hart House Theatre, Toronto, April 7, 1923.

D1404. *The Lampshade*. Toronto, French, 1936.
1 act. 3m/1f.
"A Guignol Piece". When Thomas Wye keeps an appointment to play a game of chess with a friend he becomes involved in a strange murder.
fp: Hart House Theatre, Toronto, May 28, 1925 as "The Cuckoo Clock".

MILLS, John

D1405. "The Wind on the Heath" in *Evidence*, #5, 1962.
2 acts. 12m/1f.
Set in an insane asylum, "a masque" about soldiers trying to get a discharge by "the course of the wise" — medical grounds.

MIROLLA, Michael

D1406. *Gargoyles*. Vancouver, New Play Centre, (197-?).
1 act. 3m/1f.
An old man and an old woman talk about their previous lives, his job, sex, their son, their daughter-in-law, and death.
fp: University of British Columbia, Vancouver.

D1407. *A Revised Experiment*. Vancouver, New Play Centre, (197-?).
1 act. 4m/1f.
An illustrated lecture on mental disorders goes awry and it becomes clear that the doctor himself is not at all well.
fp: (Reading), New Play Centre, Vancouver, May 1971.

MIRVISH, Robert Franklin 1921–

D1408. *Margo*. New York, Author, (196-?). (Mimeographed).
2 acts. 10m/6f. Chorus.
A musical adapted from his novel *A House of Her Own*. Margo is the "number one girl" at the Hotel International, most opulent and patronized of the brothels in Las Piedras, the oilfield country of Venezuela.

MITCHELL, George

D1409. "Telemachus" in *Acadia Athenaeum*, vol.58, #3, January 1932.
1 scene. 3m/2f. Extras.
A recounting of Ulysses' return and the slaughter of Penelope's suitors.

MITCHELL, Ken 1940–

D1410. *Cruel Tears*. Regina, Saskatchewan, Pile of Bones, 1976 and Vancouver, Talonbooks, 1977.
3 acts. 8m/3f. Chorus.
A "country opera" about love and rivalry among Saskatchewan truckdrivers based on the plot of Shakespeare's *Othello*. Music by Humphrey and the Dumptrucks.
fp: Persephone Theatre, Saskatoon, Sask., March 15, 1975. CBC radio, 1976.

D1411. *Heroes*. Toronto, Playwrights Co-op, 1973 and in *Five Canadian Plays*. Toronto, Playwrights Co-op, 1978.
1 act. 3m/1f.
Satiric black comedy about the everyday lives of Superman, the Lone Ranger, Tonto, and Lois Lane.
fp: Centre Bilingue, University of Saskatchewan, Regina, August 1971.

D1412. *The Medicine Line*. Regina, Saskatchewan, Dept. of Culture and Youth, 1974.
Many scenes. 21m/2f. Extras.
An historical drama about the Sioux under Chief Sitting Bull and his fight for a treaty with the British. The pressure of politics removes the Indians' one friend, Major Walsh, and the tribe start back across the border to certain death in the U.S.
fp: Moose Jaw, 1976.

D1413. "Showdown at Sand Valley" in *Cues and Entrances*. Henry Beissel, ed. Toronto, Gage, 1977.
1 act. 8m/1f. Doubling.
A tale of the wild west in which Montana Bill, American gunslinger, invades the quiet town of Sand Valley, Saskatchewan. The irascible Mrs. McAllister saves the town from her son's temper tantrums and gun-blazing bravado.
fp: University of Regina, Summer 1975. CBC radio, Regina, 1968.

D1414. *This Train*. Toronto, Playwrights Co-op, 1973 and in *Performing Arts in Canada*, vol.10, #1, Spring 1973.
1 act. 1m/1f.
A comedy. The postmaster and the stationmaster's wife sit outside the depot and wait for the train to make its weekly stop.
fp: Tarragon Theatre, Toronto, March 1973. CBC radio, 1973. CBC TV, 1977.

MITCHELL, William Ormond 1914–

D1415. "The Black Bonspiel of Willie MacCrimmon" in *Three Worlds of Drama*. John Powell Livesley, ed. Toronto, Macmillan, 1966.
3 acts. 14m/2f.
Willie strikes a bargain with the Devil who turns out to be an avid curler. He wants to win the Celestial Brier.
fp: CBC radio "Stage", Feb. 25, 1951. CBC TV "Playdate", Jan. 19, 1962.

D1416. *The Centennial Play*. See **DAVIES, Robertson.**

D1417. "The Devil's Instrument" in *A Collection of Canadian Plays* vol.2. Rolf Kalman, ed. Toronto, Simon & Pierre, 1973.
23 scenes. 12m/5f.
A young Hutterite boy rebels against the restrictions of his religion and after much inner struggle leaves the community as had his brother before him.
fp: CBC radio "Stage", March 27, 1949. CBC TV "Folio", Nov. 21, 1956. Ontario Youth Theatre, 1972.

D1418. "Ladybug, Ladybug" in *Edge*, #5, Fall 1966.
1 act. 7m/2f.
A radio play. The number of Hutterite communities in Alberta increases, revealing the prejudices of people living in the surrounding area.

MOHER, Frank 1955–

D1419. *Pause*. Toronto, Playwrights Co-op, 1975.
1 act. 3m/3f.
Crootoo and Kurdell are delivering a carpet to a mountaintop in Banff National Park. Their customer, apparently, is the Almighty, and the end of the world is at hand.
fp: Forty-ninth Street Theatre, Calgary, August 1974.

MOHICAN (pseud.) See CLOUGH, George E.

MONCKTON, Ella.

D1420. *The Angry Men*. See **BURNETTE, N.L.**

MONTINGNY, Louvigny Testard de 1876–1955

D1421. "I Love You" in *Short Plays from Twelve Countries*. Winifred Katzin, ed. London, Harrap, 1937.
1 act. 1m/1f.
A vacationing lawyer finally declares his love to a young girl from the resort town.

MOORE, Alexander

D1422. *A Celebration Indeed.* Halifax, Dramatists Co-op, 1977.
1 act. 6 puppets.
A rod puppet play about forest spirits, a prince and a moon goddess.
fp: Gargoyle Puppet Troupe, Nova Scotia.

MOORE, James Mavor 1919–

D1423. "The Argument" in *Performing Arts in Canada*, vol.10, #4, Winter 1973.
1 act. 1m/1f.
An argument between a man and a woman which begins as a domestic situation widens as they disparage each other's methods of argument, understanding of truth and honesty of motive.
fp: CBC radio, 1971.

D1424. "Come Away, Come Away" in *Encounter: Canadian Drama in Four Media.* Eugene Benson, ed. Toronto, Methuen, 1973.
1 act. 1m/1f.
A "recreation of the traditional image of death" in which an old man and a young girl meet and talk about the man's life.
fp: CBC radio, Fall 1972. CBC TV "Program X", 1973.

D1425. "Customs" in *Cues and Entrances.* Henry Beissel, ed. Toronto, Gage, 1977.
1 act. 3m/2f.
A young professor returning from Europe passes through Canadian Customs where, during an inspection, he is literally stripped of his clothes and possessions, his invented histories and roles, in sum, of his identities.

D1426. *Getting In.* Toronto, French, 1969.
1 act. 2m.
A man applies for admission to an ambiguous organization. His facade and his confidence are shattered when the interview takes an unexpected direction.
fp: CBC radio, 1968. CBC TV "Program X", 1973 as "The Interview".

D1427. "Inside Out" in *Three One-Act Plays by Mavor Moore.* Toronto, Simon & Pierre, 1973 and in *A Collection of Canadian Plays* vol.2. Rolf Kalman, ed. Toronto, Simon & Pierre, 1973.
1 act. 1m/1f.
A father and daughter learn to bridge the generation gap and communicate through their profession, acting.
fp: CBC TV "Program X", 1971. CBC radio, 1972.

D1428. *Louis Riel.* By Mavor Moore and Jacques Languirand. Toronto, n.p., 1967.
3 acts. 15m/3f. Extras. Chorus.
The libretto for Harry Somers' opera about the North-West Rebellion and Riel's trial and execution.
fp: Canadian Opera Company, O'Keefe Centre, Toronto, Sept. 23, 1967.

D1429. *The Ottawa Man.* Toronto, Canadian Writers' Service, 1958.
3 acts. 10m/4f. Extras. Doubling.
An adaptation of Gogol's *The Inspector General* set in a small town in Manitoba in the 1870s.
fp: Crest Theatre, Toronto, May 21, 1958.

D1430. "The Pile" in *Three One-Act Plays by Mavor Moore*. Toronto, Simon & Pierre, 1973 and in *A Collection of Canadian Plays* vol.2. Rolf Kalman, ed. Toronto, Simon & Pierre, 1973.
1 act. 2m.
An engineer and a businessman create a worthless pile and then attempt to dispose of it.
fp: CBC radio, 1969.

D1431. "The Roncarelli Affair" in *The Play's the Thing*. Four Original Television Dramas. Tony Gifford, ed. Toronto, Macmillan, 1976.
4 acts. 26m/3f. Extras.
A documentary-drama describing the Roncarelli affair: the unjust revocation of the restaurateur's licence on the grounds of "sedition" through an order given by Duplessis himself, and the ensuing fight, on Roncarelli's behalf and in the interest of "human rights . . . and the Rule of Law", by lawyers A.L. Stein and F.R. Scott.
fp: CBC TV "The Play's the Thing", September 1973 — May 1974.

D1432. "The Store" in *Three One-Act Plays by Mavor Moore*. Toronto, Simon & Pierre, 1973 and in *A Collection of Canadian Plays* vol.2. Rolf Kalman, ed. Toronto, Simon & Pierre, 1973.
1 act. 2m/2f.
A department store manager goes mad from the pressure of handling complaints.
fp: CBC radio, 1971. CBC TV "Program X", 1972.

D1433. "Togetherness" in *A Treasury of Canadian Humor*. Robert Thomas Allen, ed. Toronto, McClelland & Stewart, 1967.
1 scene. 4m.
A brief excerpt from a Spring Thaw revue satirizing Canadian ecumenism.

D1434. *"Who's Who"*. Toronto, Author, 1949. (Mimeographed).
3 acts. 3m/2f. Extras. Doubling.
A comedy about the advertising business and theatre as a means of expression.
fp: New Play Society, Museum Theatre, Toronto, Sept. 16, 1949.

MOORE, John

D1435. "The Consumer Goes to the Drug Store" in *McMaster University Quarterly*, vol.45, #4, April 1936.
1 scene. 2m.
A conversation between a clerk and a consumer revealing the false advertising and price-fixing in the pharmaceutical industry.

MORAY, Elspeth

D1436. *The Dream of the Months*. Toronto, McClelland, Goodchild & Stewart, 1918.
1 scene. 15b/17g. Extras.
"A New Year Pageant". The Sandman leads Billy and Betty into the Enchanted Wood where they meet the months of the year.

D1437. *The Festival of the Wheat*. Toronto, McClelland, Goodchild & Stewart, 1918.
1 act. 17m/1f/1b/1g. Extras.
"A play for the little folk" celebrating the harvesting and uses of wheat.

MORGAN, Dorothy 1901–

D1438. *The Witch of Plum Hollow*. Cornwall, Ont., Vesta Publications, 1977.
1 act. 5m/5f.
"A one-act play on a Canadian legend". At Plum Hollow north of Brockville, Ont. in the 1870s, Mary Elizabeth Martin tells the fortunes of her neighbours and solves many of their problems.

MORIN, Victor 1865-1960

D1439. "Operetta-Dinner" in his *La Chanson Française*. Toronto, University of Toronto Press, 1939.
2 acts. 6m/4f. Doubling.
"A gastronomico-musical fantasy". A dinner-play of parodies of French operas and musical comedies to accompany a dinner service in the French tradition.
fp: (In French), Chateau de Ramezay, 1930 and (in English), Royal Society, Mount Royal Hotel, Montreal, May 23, 1939.

MORLEY, David

D1440. *"Good Morning, Mr. Bell!"*. Aylmer East, Quebec, Author, 1965. (Mimeographed).
2 acts. 12m/9f. Chorus.
A musical comedy recounting the attainment of personal and professional success by the young Alec Bell. His involvement with the wealthy Hubbard family of Boston provides the possibilities of both — in his love for the deaf elder daughter and in her father's financial support of his experiments.
fp: Ottawa Little Theatre, May 17, 1967.

MORRIS, Marjorie

D1441. *One Plus One = ? (Knock, Knock, Who's There?)*. Ottawa, Ottawa Little Theatre Workshop, #51.
1 act. 2m/2f.
Two women, one passionate and clinging, the other rigid and independent, discover truths about themselves, the man they love and the nature of love itself.

D1442. *Requiem For a Small Boy*. Vancouver, New Play Centre, 1973.
1 act. 6m/5f.
A requiem-play for five year old Johnny Greene who has been run over by a truck. A look at the people surrounding Johnny and their relationship to the boy.
fp: Vancouver Little Theatre, 1973.

MORRIS, Richard and Ted Wood.

D1443. *Mr. Scrooge*. Chicago, Dramatic Publishing, 1963.
2 acts. 10m/9f. Extras.
A musical comedy based on Charles Dickens' "A Christmas Carol". Music by Dolores Claman.
fp: Crest Theatre, Toronto, Dec. 4, 1963.

MORRISH, Pauline.

D1444. "Our Dream House". See **FRASER, Alan.**

MORRISON, Frank

D1445. *Tzinquaw.* Vancouver, J.W. Bow, 1950.
4 scenes, 13m/6f. Extras.
"A musical dramatization of the Cowichan Indian Legend". It depicts the ancient Indian belief in the supreme power of the Great Spirit and the native faith that the observance of traditional ceremony will bring the desired divine intervention.
fp: Georgia Recreations Ltd., Vancouver, 1950.

MORROW, T.M.

D1446. "The Blue Pitcher" in *One Act Plays by Canadian Authors.* Montreal, Canadian Authors' Association, 1926.
1 act. 2m/2f.
A realistic portrait of two unmarried sisters who have grown old looking after their domineering father. The blue pitcher of the title is "a symbol . . . of all the petty tyrannies" but no one has the courage to smash it.

D1447. "Coincidence" in *Echoes,* #96, June 1924.
1 act. 4m/2f/16m or f.
A coroner's inquiry hears evidence which suggests that a woman shot her sleeping husband in his bed. We later learn that he had already committed suicide.
p: Trinity Players of Montreal.

D1448. "Manitou Portage" in *Six Canadian Plays.* H.A. Voaden, ed. Toronto, Copp Clarke, 1930.
1 act. 9m.
The play revolves around the confrontation between "Big Jack" O'Connors, riverman, and The Great Manitou, spirit of the Indian nations. Music by Charles Rice.

MORRY, Virginia

D1449. *Train Town.* Western Canada Theatre Conference. Edmonton, Dept. of Extension, University of Alberta, 1950.
1 act. 6m/5f.
A comedy about gossip in a small train town somewhere in Canada.

MORTIMER, Jane Wallace

D1450. "Billy and Floss" in *Educational Review,* vol.30, November 1916.
1 act. 2b/2g.
A play for children. Two poor children are given proof that there is a Santa Claus.

MORTON, Ralph Kelly

D1451. *My Father Was a Doctor.* Halifax, Dramatists Co-op, 1977.
2 acts. 15m/5f.
A drama about a Halifax country doctor and his family from the early 1900s through W.W. II.

MORTON, Ralph S.

D1452. "Gold-Mad" in *Echoes*, #120, June 1931.
1 act. 5m/1f.
One of the characters strikes gold in a mine in Nova Scotia that has been considered barren for years. A young man and his fiancee leave for a new life in western Canada, thereby hoping to escape the effects of the gold fever that had possessed his father.

MOSER, Marguerite

D1453. *The Dumbfounding*. Edmonton, Alberta Dept. of Culture, 1970.
1 act. 5m/1f.
A young girl arbitrates a dispute between her fiance and her father.

MOTYER, Arthur

D1454. *Poets for Lunch*. St. John, N.B., The Purple Wednesday Society, 1972.
1 act. 3m/2f.
David Ashton and his friend Michael eagerly await the arrival of their honoured guest, Mr. Chumley, the poet. Conversations amongst the poet and young people are metaphysical and metaphorical, but Mrs. Ashton, David's mother, misinterprets these sentiments in a very literal manner.

MUIR, Olive (Evitt)

D1455. *Women and War*. Bridge of Weir, N.B., Scottish Castles, 1928.
3 acts. Multiple roles.
An anti-war play moving from the battle between the Israelites and the Philistines to the fulfillment of David's prophecy in London in 1932: a warless world is created at last.

THE MULGRAVE ROAD CO-OP

D1456. *Let's Play Fish*. Halifax, Dramatists Co-op, 1978.
3 acts. 2m/2f.
A portrayal of the development of a family through three decades in a small fishing community in Guysborough County, Nova Scotia.
fp: Mulgrave Road Co-op, Star of the Sea Parish Hall, Canso, N.S., July 1, 1978.

D1457. *The Mulgrave Road Show*. Halifax, Dramatists Co-op, 1978.
1 act. 3m/1f.
A collection of songs and stories based on life in Guysborough County over the past 200 years including a satirical look at the present political scene.
fp: Mulgrave Road Co-op.

MULVIHILL, T.C.

D1458. *A Pageant of Canadian History*. See **CALLAN, J.B.**

MUNRO, Alice 1931–

D1459. "How I Met My Husband" in *The Play's the Thing*. Four Original Television Dramas. Tony Gifford, ed. Toronto, Macmillan, 1976.
4 acts. 3m/4f/1b/1g.
Amid the restrictive propriety of a rural Ontario town in the late 1940s, an adolescent girl discovers romantic feelings and their disappointment for the first time.
fp: CBC TV, "The Play's the Thing", September 1973 — May 1974.

MURCHISON, Myles F.

D1460. *Gilliam*. See **LOGIE, Ray.**

MURPHY, Arthur L. 1906–

D1461. *The Breadwinner*. Halifax, Dramatists Co-op, 1977.
3 acts. 2m/2f.
A comedy about a young wife who puts her husband through college.
p: Rothesay Players, Rothesay Playhouse, N.B., Sept. 12, 1967.

D1462. *The Centennial Play*. See **DAVIES, Robertson.**

D1463. "52 North by 21 West" in his *Three Bluenose Plays*. Halifax, Dramatists Co-op, 1977.
1 act. 5m.
Based on a Nova Scotia folk-tale. A superstitious crew mutinies against a captain's decision to set sail on Christmas Day.

D1464. *The First Falls on Monday*. Toronto, University of Toronto Press, 1972.
3 acts. 8m/4f.
This play deals with the crucial 48 hours before the final agreement on Canada's first cabinet and the compromising sacrifice which makes Confederation a reality.
fp: Kawartha Summer Theatre, Academy Theatre, Lindsay, Ont., June 26, 1967.

D1465. "Keeper of the Gold" in his *Three Bluenose Plays*. Halifax, Dramatists Co-op, 1977.
1 act. 8m.
Based on a Nova Scotia folk-tale. Three Halifax men set out to find if there is pirate treasure buried on Goose Island.

D1466. *The Sleeping Bag*. Halifax, Dramatists Co-op, 1977.
2 acts. 2m/1f.
A play about an inhibited young woman marooned in the Arctic with two men.
fp: Neptune Theatre, Halifax, July 19, 1966.

D1467. *Thy Sons Command*. Halifax, Dramatists Co-op, 1977.
3 acts. 8m/4f.
A drama about French-English Canadian conflict.

D1468. *A Virus Called Clarence*. Toronto, Playwrights Co-op, 1972 and Halifax, Dramatists Co-op, 1977.
3 acts. 5m/2f.
Denys Adam, M.D., working in the research lab of a hospital, discovers the virus responsible for breast cancer, but at great cost to his emotional life and to that of the whole research team.

D1469. *What to Do After You've Done Doing What You Did.* Halifax, Dramatists Co-op, 1977.
2 acts. 6m/2f.
The sixty-year-old Anthony Bruce is unprepared for retirement from the Bankers' Syndicate.

D1470. "Witch Doctor" in his *Three Bluenose Plays*. Halifax, Dramatists Co-op, 1977.
1 act. 3m/1f.
Based on a Nova Scotia folk-tale. In Herring Cove in 1865, a man is convinced his ailing son was bewitched by the midwife.

MURPHY, Aubrey L.

D1471. "The Crucifixion" in *Acadia Athenaeum*, vol.63, #6, April 1938.
3 scenes. 2m/5f.
An Easter play with Joseph of Arimathea as the central character.

MURRAY, David Graham 1926–

D1472. *The Line.* Durham, Ont., Durham House, 1954.
1 act. 7m/6f. Extras.
A number of people are queued up in a line though no one is sure for what purpose.

MURRELL, John 1945–

D1473. *Memoir.* New York, Avon, 1978.
2 acts. 1m/1f.
During the last summer of her life, Sarah Bernhardt dictates her memoirs to her secretary and relives parts of her life.
fp: Guelph Spring Festival of the Arts, Ontario, May 1977.

D1474. *Metamorphosis.* Edmonton, Alberta, Dept. of Culture, 1970.
1 act. 2m/1f.
This play deals humorously with the relationship between Nero and his mother, the Empress Agrippina.

MUTCH, David 1924–

D1475. *And at Night We Dream.* Toronto, Playwrights Co-op, 1972.
1 act. 2m/1f.
"Everything's all right in Toronto" but Jerry and Susan who live there are haunted by sounds of suffering apparently coming from nowhere.
fp: Backdoor Theatre, Toronto, March 1973.

NABLO, Jan Pierre

D1476. *Another Piece of Crust.* Vancouver, New Play Centre, 1973.
3 acts. 9m/5f/1g.
A play about the problem of striking workers during the 1930s.
fp: (Workshop), New Play Centre, Vancouver, 1973. CBC radio.

D1477. *The Stick Men.* Vancouver, New Play Centre, (197-?).
2 acts. 4m/3f.
A farce about long-lost children, mixed identities and confused sexual roles.

NEMO (pseud.)

D1478. "The Ghost" in *Prince Edward Island Magazine*, vol.3, #10, December 1901.
1 act. 5m.
A man hurriedly enters a house to tell to his friends a tale of his ghostly encounter with Billy the Kid that night.

NESS, Margaret

D1479. "Enter the Prince" in *Curtain Call*, vol.9, #4, January 1938 and in her *Practical Play Production for Canadian Schools and Communities*. Toronto, Curtain Call Publishing, 1938.
1 act. 7m/5f. Extras.
A princess pretends to be her lady-in-waiting so she can gauge the true character of a prince she has never met but is to marry.

NEWSON, Jeremy

D1480. *Bull Durham*. Vancouver, New Play Centre, (1970).
1 act. 18m. Extras.
A Western about two "sanitary engineers", a giant cow dung, a corrupt mayor, a German social scientist, and Bull Durham tobacco.
fp: University of British Columbia, 1970.

NEWTON, Christopher

D1481. *Where Are You When We Need You, Simon Fraser?*. Vancouver, Playhouse Theatre Centre of B.C., 1971. (Mimeographed).
1 act. 3m/2f.
A documentary musical based on the early history of British Columbia. Music by Allan Rae.
fp: Vancouver, Holiday Theatre, 1972.

NEWTON, Norman Lewis

D1482. *The Lion and the Unicorn*. Vancouver, New Play Centre, (197-?).
3 acts. 6m/3f. Extras.
A play in blank verse about the mythical tale of Hercules' encounter with a queen.

D1483. *The Rehearsal*. Ottawa, Ottawa Little Theatre Workshop, #17.
1 act. 6m/3f.
A "theatre" play satirizing verse drama. The rehearsal of a new play by Phipps, an opportunist playwright, is punctuated by comments favourable (from himself) and unfavourable (from his angel's wife).

NEWTON-WHITE, Muriel E.

D1484. "Yet Shall He Live" in *Boreal*, #3, 1975.
1 act. 4m/2f.
"A story of the in-finality of death". An old farming couple reluctantly accept the drowning death of their son who had been running their farm.

NICHOL, James W. 1940–

D1485. *The Book of Solomon Spring.* Toronto, Canadian Theatre Centre, 1966.
2 acts. 6m/3f/3g. Extras.
An Upper Canada farmer falsely implicates his hired man in the murder of a young girl in order to shield his mentally disturbed son whom he knows to be guilty of the crime and to break up the relationship which is starting between his daughter and the man.
p: Factory Theatre Lab, Toronto, June 9, 1972.

D1486. *Gwendoline.* Toronto, Playwrights Co-op, 1978.
2 acts. 4m/2f.
A half-crazed young woman manages to escape the oppressiveness of a small Ontario town and her own haunting family past.
fp: Blyth Summer Festival, Ontario, August 1978.

D1487. "Him: A Play for Voices" in *Exile*, vol.3, #1, 1975.
1 act. 3m/2f/1b.
A surrealist play about a man's physical and mental disintegration.

D1488. *The House on Chestnut Street.* Toronto, Playwrights Co-op, 1972.
2 acts. 2m/4f.
This play deals with an average family in rural Canada of 1900 who turn out to be not so average.
fp: Theatre Calgary, 1972.

D1489. "The House on Chestnut Street" in *Performing Arts in Canada*, vol.10, #3, Fall 1973 and in *Isolation in Canadian Literature*. David Arnason, ed. Toronto, Macmillan, 1975.
1 act. 3f/1m.
The half-hour radio play version of the longer stage work.
fp: CBC radio.

D1490. "Purr: A Play for Voices" in *Exile*, vol.2, #2, 1974.
1 act. 4m/3f.
A disturbed adolescent protects himself from his intense sensitivity by refusing to communicate. His disgust with his family transforms them into grotesque, dehumanized caricatures and he becomes increasingly absorbed in nurturing a fantasy of power and destruction.

D1491. *Sainte-Marie Among the Hurons.* Toronto, Playwrights Co-op, 1977.
2 acts. 7m. Extras.
Father Rejean comes to the new land to save the heathens. However, as the Hurons convert to Christianity, their nation perishes from a foreign fever. The Iroquois massacre the remnants of the Hurons, now deserted by their Christian saviours.
fp: Theatre London, Nov. 22, 1974.

D1492. *Sweet Home Sweet.* Toronto, Canadian Theatre Centre, 1967.
2 acts. 2m/2f.
The tensions in a family in which the woman is white, the man black, arise from her alcoholism and her husband's and son's reaction to it.
fp: Second Stage, Halifax, 1972.

D1493. "Tub" in *Performing Arts in Canada*, vol.7, #1, 1970 and Toronto, Playwrights Co-op, 1972.
1 act. 2m/1f/1b.
Alienated from each other early in their marriage, Christine and Rip have been unable to lend each other the mutual support they needed in times of stress. The result is spiritual death.
fp: Stratford Theatre Workshop, 1969.

NICHOLL, Freeman

D1494. "Week End" in *Tuesday Night*. Regina, University of Saskatchewan, Regina College Writers' Club, 1935.
1 act. 2m/2f.
A radio play revealing Kurt's inner thoughts about his first encounter with Grace.

NICHOLSON, Don

D1495. "The Folks Next Door" in Kruk, Mark. *Come in and Take Your Clothes Off*. Toronto, Gateway Press, 1971.
1 act. 2m/2f.
Joe and Melinda, neighbours, are in bed in the basement while their respective spouses are making it upstairs in the bedroom. Meeting later with suitable alibis, they all feel safe and well satisfied until the surprise ending.

NICOL, Eric Patrick 1919–

D1496. *Beware the Quickly Who*. Vancouver, New Play Centre, (197-?) and Toronto, Playwrights Co-op, 1973.
2 acts. 8m/1b/1g.
A play for children about a young boy who is given the choice between finding out who he is or becoming a non-entity. An analogy for Canada.
fp: Holiday Theatre, Vancouver, 1967.

D1497. *The Centennial Play*. See **DAVIES, Robertson**.

D1498. "The Citizens of Calais" in *Canadian Theatre Review*, #7, Summer 1975.
2 acts. 7m/2f.
A comic look at the problems of national unity as Ted English attempts to direct a multi-cultural theatre production in Quebec amidst arguments between francophones, anglophones, Italians, Americans, and Ted's wife, Donna.
fp: Department of Theatre, York University, Downsview, Ontario, Nov. 27, 1974.

D1499. *The Clam Made A Face*. Vancouver, New Play Centre, (197-?) and Toronto, New Press/Firebrand Press, 1972 and in *A Collection of Canadian Plays* vol.4. Rolf Kalman, ed. Toronto, Simon & Pierre, 1975.
1 act. 3m/1f.
A participation play for children which dramatizes West Coast Indian legends.
fp: Holiday Theatre, Vancouver, Dec. 16, 1967.

D1500. *The Fourth Monkey*. Vancouver, New Play Centre, 1973 and in his *Three Plays*. Vancouver, Talonbooks, 1975.
3 acts. 6m/4f.
A Canadian poet, who is being "kept" by an American couple who consider themselves patrons of the arts, finds his island retreat invaded by a creative writing teacher, her class, and a famous Russian poet who decides to defect.
fp: Vancouver Playhouse Theatre Company, October 10, 1968.

D1501. *Like Father, Like Fun*. Vancouver, New Play Centre, 1973 and in his *Three Plays*. Vancouver, Talonbooks, 1975.
2 acts. 3m/3f.
A father gets his senior public relations man to find a woman to seduce his overly business-like son in the hopes of getting the son to enjoy more of the "finer" things in life.
fp: Playhouse Theatre Company, Vancouver, March 24, 1966.

D1502. "The Man from Inner Space" in *The Play's the Thing*. Four Original Television Dramas. Tony Gifford, ed. Toronto, Macmillan, 1976.
4 acts. 2m/1f.
A satirical comedy about the encounter of three characters, each of whom responds differently to the complexity and impersonality of urban life.
fp: CBC TV series "The Play's the Thing", September 1973 – May 1974.

D1503. "Pillar of Sand" in his *Three Plays*, Vancouver, Talonbooks, 1975.
2 acts. 10m/2f. Extras.
A debate between spirit and intelligence as embodied in Daniel Stylite, the Christian saint, and Titus, soldier of Rome.
fp: Playhouse Theatre, Vancouver, 1972-73.

NOBLE, Dennis E.

D1503A. "Recollections of a Civilized Man" in *Canadian Drama*, vol. 3, #2, Fall, 1977.
1 act. 1m/1f.
An ordinary, middle-aged married couple, unable to communicate with each other, reflect on their past and present in silence.

D1503B. "Mary Tudor" in *Canadian Drama*, vol.4, #2, Fall 1978.
1 act. 17m/7f. Extras.
An historical drama about the unfortunate reign of Queen Mary Tudor and her attempts to impose Catholicism on England.

NOBLSTON, Allen

D1504. "Sacrifice" in *One Act Play Magazine*, September, 1937.
1 act. 5m/1f.
A poetic drama about an astronomer and his wife waiting for the appearance of a rare comet who are trapped by an escaped murderer.

NON DE SCRIPT (pseud.)

D1505. "The Masque of Learning" in *Acta Victoriana*, vol.50, #3, December 1925.
1 act. Chorus.
A satire of a commission set up by the university board of regents to discover the true state of learning in the Halls of Higher Education.

NORWOOD, Gilbert 1880-1954

D1506. "The Silent Customer" in *The Canadian Forum*, vol.9, #98, November 1928.
1 act. 5m.
A farce. An escaped criminal comes into a barber shop and the other patrons play a trick on him. The tables are turned however before the end of the play.

NORWOOD, Rev. Robert Winkworth 1874-1932

D1507. *The Man of Kerioth*. New York, Doran, 1919 and Toronto, McClelland, Goodchild & Stewart, 1919.
5 acts. 27m/5f/1b/1g. Extras.
Judas Iscariot is the central figure in this religious work. Christ, more human than spiritual, is presented as a man coping with his "Betrayer".

D1508. *The Witch of Endor*. Toronto, McClelland, Goodchild & Stewart, 1916 and New York, Doran, 1916.
5 acts. 8m/5f. Extras.
Loruhamah, priestess of Astoreth, renounces her love for Saul so that he might be king. But Samuel's curse is fulfilled; the kingdom is torn asunder and Saul goes mad. In the end, Loruhamah and Saul find peace together.

NOWLAN, Alden A. 1933–

D1509. "Gardens of the Wind" in *Poems for Voices*. Toronto, CBC, 1970.
1 act. 4m.
A radio play. Part of a farm is expropriated for an airfield during W.W.II. The old farmer resists, but loses. After the war, the grasses and flowers take back the land.
fp: CBC radio, February/March 1970.

D1510. *Frankenstein: The Man Who Became God*. Alden A. Nowlan and Walter Learning. Toronto, Clarke, Irwin, 1976.
3 acts. 13m/2f/1b.
The play is "a Victorian melodrama written in the 1970s", the classic "thriller"/allegory of Victor von Frankenstein's god-like presumption in taking science to its limits to create a living being.
fp: Theatre New Brunswick at the Playhouse, Fredericton, N.B., July 17, 1974.

D1510A. *The Incredible Murder of Cardinal Tosca*. Alden A. Nowlan and Walter Learning. Fredericton, N.B., Learning Productions, 1978.
2 acts. 8m/2f. Doubling.
"A Sherlock Holmes Adventure" in which Holmes is arrested for murder before defeating the evil Moriarty and temporarily preventing W.W.I.
fp: Theatre New Brunswick, Fredericton, Jan. 16, 1978. CBC radio "Festival Theatre", July 31, 1978.

NOXON, Gerald 1910–

D1511. "Pete Goes Home" in *On Stage*. Herman Voaden, ed. Toronto, Macmillan, 1946.
1 act. 7m/2f.
A radio play. The best friend of a Canadian soldier killed in Italy during W.W. II returns to Canada and marries his friend's sweetheart.
fp: CBC radio "Stage 44", Toronto, March 12, 1944.

NUGENT, Olive

D1512. *Hey, Mister, Are You a Stranger?*. Vancouver, New Play Centre, 1973.
1 act. 1m/1f/1b.
A young construction worker and a middle-aged housewife meet in a park and talk about the life of a little boy they encounter and debate whether the young man should return to his pregnant girlfriend.
fp: (Rehearsed reading), New Play Centre, Vancouver, 1973.

D1513. *Through the Glass*. Vancouver, New Play Centre, (197-?)
1 act. 1m/1f.
A depiction of a middle-aged husband and his wife on the final day of their marriage.

NYBERG, Morgan

D1514. *Crazy Horse Suite*. Vancouver, Intermedia, 1978.
1 act. 3m/1f.
"A series of poems for four voices" about the life of the Indian leader Crazy Horse.

O'HAGEN, Denis

D1515. *The Wisdom Tooth*. Vancouver, New Play Centre, 1973.
1 act. 1m/2f. Doubling.
A comedy in which two servants discuss the younger one's search for a more rewarding life.

O'MEARA, Martin

D1516. *Sitting Bill*. Toronto, French, 1949.
1 act. 5m/2f/1b/2g.
A comedy in which Bill, a university student, discovers that babysitting is not "easy money".

ORCHARD, Betty

D1517. "Joe's Lunch" in *Acadia Athenaeum*, vol.63, #1, February 1938.
1 scene. 3m. Extras.
A policeman is deceived by an honest-faced crook and eats his afternoon snack while the owner of the lunch counter is tied and gagged.

D1518. "Pair of Rubbers" in *Acadia Athenaeum*, November 1937.
1 scene. 3m/2f.
In a Depression setting a woman chooses the comfortable life rather than return to the poverty which is all her first love can offer her.

ORTON, Maurine

D1519. *5BX in History*. Ottawa, Ottawa Little Theatre Workshop, #25.
1 act. 4m/2f. Extras.
A bizarre, humorous look at mankind and the inevitable problems inherent in human nature.
fp: Ottawa Little Theatre.

OSBORNE, C.

D1520. "And This Is Life" in *Acadia Athenaeum*, vol.55, #2, December 1928.
1 scene. 2m/3f.
Two girls revise their estimate of a drunken farmer when his son's illness galvanizes him into action.

OSBORNE, James 1943–

D1521. *By the Sea*. Toronto, Playwrights Co-op, 1973.
1 act. 1m/1f/1b.
A middle-aged man and his wife, while on a seashore picnic, meet a young Japanese boy who tells them old Oriental tales. Conflict arises among the three over the understanding of the meaning of life.
fp: Theatre 3, Edmonton, February 1973.

OSBORNE, Marian (Francis) 1871–1931

D1522. "The Point of View" in *Canadian Plays from Hart House Theatre* vol.1.
V. Massey, ed. Toronto, Macmillan, 1926.
1 act. 3m/1f.
"Comedie de moeurs" about a burglar who interrupts a woman and her lover and threatens to tell her husband. The husband returns after having missed his train for an important meeting. The woman, the lover and the burglar then go into an act to get them all out of their predicament.
fp: Hart House Theatre, Toronto, March 29, 1923.

D1523. *Sappho and Phaon*. Toronto, Macmillan, 1926.
2 scenes. 2m/8f.
"A Lyrical Drama". The lovers Sappho and Phaon incur the wrath of the jealous Aphrodite with tragic results.

OUZOUNIAN, Richard

D1524. *British Properties*. Vancouver, New Play Centre, 1978.
2 acts. 3m/3f.
A farce in which a wittily acrimonious family gathering in the posh north shore Vancouver area, British Properties, is interrupted when mafiosi besiege the house.
fp: New Play Centre and City Stage at City Stage, Vancouver, Nov. 5, 1977.

OWENS, Charles R.

D1525. *Tattered Roses*. Mimico, Ont., Epworth Press, 1928.
1 act. 3m/3f/1g. Extras.
St. Nicholas sends gifts to aid a family in distress but they appreciate only the monetary value of the gold rather than the spirit of giving.
p: Metropolitan Church, Toronto, Dec. 22, 1929.

PACAUD, George Washington 1879–

D1526. *Social Idolatry*. London, New York, French-Toronto, Musson, 1920 and Montreal, G.W. Pacaud, 1920.
3 acts. 9m/5f.
A play about a penniless French duke who comes to the States to find a rich wife satirizing the ruthless social ambitions of the American nouveau riche.

PALMER, George Alfred 1869–1954

D1527. *Exit Columbine*. Regina, Sask. Author, 1930.
1 act. 3m/2f.
"With apologies to Harry Green's 'Death of Pierrot' ". Mrs. Grundy causes Columbine to abandon both her identity and traditional costume for more fashionable "modern" dress.

D1528. *Hail*. Regina, Sask., Author, 1933.
2 acts. 3m/2f.
Kate and Wilbur Blake face a hard life on the Canadian prairies. Kate finds solace in the snappy chatter of ex-Londoner Fred Woodley, the hired man. With the coming of a devastating hailstorm, Wilbur accuses his wife and Woodley of having an affair.

D1529. *Madam Verite at Bath*. Regina, Sask., Author, 1932 and Toronto, French, 1935.
1 act. 1m/2f.
Lady Pettiwood feels that her husband has been unfaithful and he thinks that she has. Peggy the maid knows all and resolves the quarrel.
fp: Balfour Grill, Regina, Sept. 22, 1932.

PALMER, John 1943–

D1530. *Bland Hysteria*. Toronto, Playwrights Co-op, 1972.
2 acts. 1m/1f. Doubling.
A farce about Sally who meets Jeff at a bus stop. The two develop into several different characters.
fp: St. Lawrence Centre, Toronto, April 1, 1971.

D1531. *The End*. Toronto, Playwrights Co-op, 1972.
2 acts. 4m/3f.
"A fast-paced farce". On their first anniversary, Webster and Belinda, who we later learn are brother and sister, are visited by one of Webster's old boyfriends, a psychologist looking for a mother, a butch Girl Guide leader, a school-boy and a nymphomaniac.
fp: Toronto Free Theatre, Aug. 4, 1972.

D1532. *Henrik Ibsen On the Necessity of Producing Norwegian Theatre*. Toronto, Playwrights Co-op, 1976 and "Henrik Ibsen on the Necessity of Producing Norwegian Drama" in *Canadian Theatre Review*, #14, Spring 1977 and in *This Magazine*, vol.11, #6, Dec. 1977.
1 act. 2m/1f.
A thinly-veiled contemporary satire in which Henrik Ibsen champions the development of an indigenous theatre and drama.
fp: Factory Theatre Lab, Toronto, Oct. 10, 1976. CBC radio "Festival Theatre", January 1978.

D1533. *Memories for My Brother: Part 1 — Before the Guns*. Toronto, Playwrights Co-op, 1972.
20 scenes. 6m/3f. Extras.
A collection of incidents — some comical, some satirical, some serious — presenting a view of life.
fp: Canadian Place Theatre, Stratford, Ont., 1969.

D1534. *A Touch of God in the Golden Age.* Toronto, Playwrights Co-op, 1972.
3 acts. 2m.
Gene and David both try to escape frustration and despair through the use of alcohol and drugs.
fp: Factory Theatre Lab, Toronto, Dec. 22, 1971.

PALUK, William

D1535. "Back Door" in *The Immigrant Experience.* Leuba Bailey, ed. Toronto, Macmillan, 1975.
1 act. 2m/3f.
A Ukrainian-Canadian girl must choose between Peter Kritiuk, the baker, and Henry Smith, a college student unfamiliar with her cultural origins.
fp: CBC radio "Prairie Playhouse", May 12, 1961.

PANY, Lily

D1536. *Quid et Quare.* Montreal, Factum, 1967.
2 acts. 1m/1f. Doubling.
A multi-media drama attempting to explore the psychology of a woman's emotional decisions.
fp: Western Quebec Region Festival, 1967.

PAOLOZZI, Anne

D1537. *The Castle Builders.* Ottawa, Ottawa Little Theatre Workshop, #33.
1 act. 4m/6f/1b/1g.
Two young children find strength and tenderness in each other when their parents deny them love.
fp: Ottawa Little Theatre.

PARKHILL, Francis and John Holmes

D1538. *The Fair Country.* Toronto, Author, 1965 (mimeographed) and (revised edition) Toronto, Author, 1967. (Mimeographed).
3 acts. 6m/3f/1b.
Based on an historical incident, the rivalry between two Frenchmen for the possession of land in Acadia. Music by Douglas Major.

D1539. *The Loyalists.* Toronto, Author, 1967. (Mimeographed).
3 acts. 15m/4f/4b/2g. Extras.
A musical comedy about the landing of the Loyalists in the Maritimes and their attempt to establish an economically successful and self-governing community. Music by Douglas Major.

PASCH, Irene 1916–

D1540. *The Gift of the Sun.* Waterloo, Ont., Waterloo Music, 1971.
2 acts. 5m/3f.
"A play with music based on North American Indian folklore" for children. Not until the Coyoteman brings fire to warm the people he loves do they appreciate the other gifts of the animals: wood, weaving, apples. Music by Silvio Pasch.
fp: Cornell School, Scarborough, Ont., 1967.

PATTERSON, Pat and Dodi Robb

D1541. *Dandy Lion. The Popcorn Man. Red Riding Hood.* See **ROBB, Dodi.**

PAYSON, Stella P.

D1542. "Canada" in *Educational Review*, vol.41, #8, April 1927.
1 scene. 3b/3g.
A brief "exercise for Empire Day" in praise of Canada.

D1543. "Canada Welcome" in *Canadian School Plays*. D.J. Dickie *et al.* eds. New York, Dutton, 1931 and Toronto, Dent, 1931.
1 act. 2m/1f/3b/4g.
A play for children. A pageant about the builders of Canada, explorers and settlers.

D1544. "The Farmer and the Birds" in *Canadian School Plays*. D.J. Dickie *et al.* eds. New York, Dutton, 1931 and Toronto, Dent, 1931.
1 act. 2m/1f.
A play for children. A farmer must cut his grass, but not until the young birds hidden there can fly.

D1545. "Good-bye Books" in *Canadian School Plays*. D.J. Dickie *et al.* eds. New York, Dutton, 1931 and Toronto, Dent, 1931.
1 act. 5m/1b.
A play for children. A child's relationship with his books is explored.

D1546. "Pot of Gold" in *Canadian School Plays*. D.J. Dickie *et al.* eds. New York, Dutton, 1931 and Toronto, Dent, 1931.
1 act. 2m/3f. Extras.
A play for children. A young Irish girl seeks the proverbial "pot of gold" with the help of leprechauns and fairies.

D1547. "The Same Old Santa Claus" in *Canadian School Plays*. D.J. Dickie, *et al.* eds. New York, Dutton, 1931 and Toronto, Dent, 1931.
1 act. 1m/1f/5b/4g.
A play for children. Santa thinks "children are tired of the old things and want something more modern". Mrs. Santa and visiting children prove him wrong.

D1548. "The Tea-Party" in *Canadian School Plays*. D.J. Dickie *et al.* eds. New York, Dutton, 1931 and Toronto, Dent, 1931.
1 act. 3g.
A play for children. Dorothy and Jennie invite poor Denise to their tea-party and she receives her first doll from them.

PEARSON, Harry Mitchell 1891–1938

D1549. *The Love Gift.* Toronto, Ryerson, 1923.
3 acts. 15m/3f. Extras.
"A religious Mystery play". The Christ-child's chimes will only ring if a true love gift is placed on the altar. Pedro's small coin succeeds where all rich gifts fail.
fp: Young People's Assoc., St. Enoch's Church, Toronto, December 1922.

PEGASUS (pseud.) See BENSON, Nathaniel.

PENDERGRAST, William 1925–

D1550. *The Secret of the Spyglass.* Toronto, Playwrights Co-op, 1975.
3 acts. 6m/8f.
A melodrama in which female pirates based in the Thousand Islands threaten the existence of Kingston in 1824.
fp: Moonlight Melodrama, Thunder Bay, Ont., 1972.

PENMAN, Margaret

D1551. "Wheelchair" in *Women Write for Theatre* vol. 1. Toronto, Playwrights Co-op, 1976.
1 act. 2m/1f.
An old woman sits at the top of a hill in a park in her wheelchair, mingling the past and present in her doddering mind. Two buoyant young men, angels of death, approach her and while they play roles in her remembrances, strip her of her accoutrements of old age.

PERRIGARD, Pauline Bradley

D1552. "All Hallows' Eve" in *One Act Plays by Canadian Authors.* Montreal, Canadian Authors' Association, 1926.
1 act. 5m/2f.
An adventure play about an aristocratic couple captured by pirates, in a contemporary frame. The adventure is enacted by ghostly portraits on All Hallows' Eve.
fp: Miss Edgar's and Miss Cramp's School, Montreal, Feb. 20, 1926.

D1553. "The King" in *One Act Plays by Canadian Authors.* Montreal, Canadian Authors' Association, 1926.
1 act. 5m/2f.
A peasant family gives food and shelter to a stranger lost on a winter night. The stranger is either a king or a madman.

PERRY, Helen M.

D1554. "City Street" in *Acadia Athanaeum*, vol.59, #4, February 1933.
1 scene. 3m/2f.
A delivery boy struck by a chauffeured limousine is brought home to his widowed mother who is presented with $100 in compensation for his destroyed hand.

D1555. "Our House" in *Acadia Athenaeum*, vol. 58 #6, April 1932.
1 scene. 3m/1f.
Two real estate agents have sold the same house separately to a man and a woman who decide to marry and live there together.

PETCH, Steve 1952–

D1556. *The General.* Toronto, Playwrights Co-op, 1973 and in *Now In Paperback.* C. Brissenden, ed. Toronto, Fineglow Plays, 1973.
1 act. 1m/1f.
A soldier is left behind in an inn by his unit. In his conversation with the woman who runs the inn, the possibility is raised that there are no rebel forces and that the officers are picking off their own army.
fp: (Workshop), Factory Theatre Lab, Toronto, 1972.

D1557. *Passage*. Toronto, Playwrights Co-op, 1974.
8 scenes. 4m/2f.
A play centring on the disintegration of order and civilization in the aftermath of war.
fp: (Workshop), Factory Theatre Lab, Toronto, 1974.

D1558. *Turkish Delight*. Toronto, Playwrights Co-op, 1975.
10 scenes. 3m/2f.
Madame and Mademoiselle arrive in the steaming city of Istanbul in 19th century Turkey and are greeted by a mysterious native, Aslan, who frightens them with his silence.
fp: Theatre Second Floor, Toronto, March 10, 1976.

PETERS, J.R.

D1559. *I Can't Afford It*. St. Thomas, Ont., Sutherland Press, 1921.
Text unavailable for annotation. Described as a comedy-drama for eight men and seven women illustrating what happens to those who are penny wise and pound foolish.

D1560. *Money and Mud*. St. Thomas, Ont., Sutherland Press, 1927.
1 act. 4m/3f.
A tight-fisted farmer refuses to allow his wife and children any money or freedom on the farm until he is sick and has a vision of his unpleasant future.

PETERSON, Leonard 1917–

D1561. *Adolescent Rebellion*. (#4 in pamphlet series *In Search of Ourselves*). Toronto, McClelland & Stewart, 1949.
1 act. 1m/2f/1b/1g.
A short play about the importance of responsibility and freedom for teenagers.
fp: CBC radio "In Search of Ourselves", 1947–49.

D1562. *All About Us*. Toronto, Author, 1964. (Mimeographed).
1 act. Multiple roles.
A cynical, embittered look at Canada's history intended to dispel "our aura of innocence"; a history of joylessness and vindictiveness, of always being a pawn in other countries' games.
fp: Manitoba Theatre Centre, Oct. 28, 1964.

D1563. *Almighty Voice*. Agincourt, Ont., Book Society, 1974.
1 act. 3m/1f. Doubling.
A dramatization for children of the government's hunt for Almighty Voice, a Cree Indian who was forced into hiding for the crime of stealing a cow to feed his starving people.
fp: Young People's Theatre, Toronto, August 1970.

D1564. "Billy Bishop and the Red Baron" in *A Collection of Canadian Plays* vol.4. Rolf Kalman, ed. Toronto, Simon & Pierre, 1975.
1 act. 3m/1f. Doubling.
A children's play about the flying aces of W.W.I, Billy Bishop and the Baron von Richthofen, otherwise known as the Red Baron.
p: Young People's Theatre, Toronto, Fall 1975.

D1565. *Brotherly Hatred.* (#2 in pamphlet series *In Search of Ourselves*). Toronto, McClelland & Stewart, 1949.
1 act. 3m/1f/2b.
A short play about sibling jealousy and the importance of parental understanding of the child's motives and his need for reinforcement.
fp: CBC radio "In Search of Ourselves", Jan. 11, 1949.

D1566. *Burlap Bags.* Toronto, Playwrights Co-op, 1972.
1 act. 3m. Extras. Doubling.
The theme of the world's absurdity and man's insensitivity is presented by the dramatization of a tramp's diary. The tramp, who has recently died in a rooming house "transformed for awhile to Limbo", is the narrator.
fp: CBC radio "Stage", Feb. 3, 1946. CBC TV "Quest", Jan. 3, 1960.

D1567. *The Careful Boy.* (#3 in pamphlet series *In Search of Ourselves*). Toronto, McClelland & Stewart, 1949.
1 act. 2m/1f/1b.
A short play advising parents of the importance of tempering strictness with understanding.
fp: CBC radio "In Search of Ourselves", 1947-49.

D1568. "Desert Soliloquy" in *Ways of Mankind*. W.R. Goldschmidt, ed. Boston, Beacon Press, 1954.
1 act. 1m.
A radio play. A young Hopi Indian boy, sitting alone on a desert night tells us of his childhood and explains something of Hopi religion and society.

D1569. *The Great Hunger.* Agincourt, Ont., Book Society, 1967.
3 acts. 7m/5f. Extras.
A tragedy set in the Arctic. Retribution is demanded for a past murder and inevitably the unknowing and innocent are caught up in the unfinished pattern and the entire community is affected.
fp: Arts Theatre, Toronto, November 1960. CBC radio "Wednesday Night", March 20, 1962 as "Tomorrow We Hunt".

D1570. *The Grin on the Moon.* New York, Friendship Press, 1966.
1 act. 7m/2f.
A look at American prejudice towards different cultures and the American tradition of violence as a means of settling disputes.

D1571. "Home Sweet Home" in *Ways of Mankind*. W.R. Goldschmidt, ed. Boston, Beacon Press, 1954.
1 act. 5m/2f.
A radio play. Two men have a discussion about family ties and one, a Chinese-American, tells the other how he learned to respect the old family system of China.

D1572. *Let's Make A World.* Toronto, Playwrights Co-op, 1973.
1 act. 3m/1f.
A children's participation play in which four myth-makers explore Greek, Nordic and scientific creation myths.
fp: Young People's Theatre, Toronto, 1971.

D1573. *Sex Education.* (#1 in pamphlet series *In Search of Ourselves*). Toronto, McClelland & Stewart, 1949.
1 act. 4m/1f.
A short play about the importance of sex education for young people. The dramatic situation involves a young high school girl who discovers that she is pregnant.
fp: CBC radio "In Search of Ourselves", Jan. 25, 1949.

D1574. "Stand-in For a Murderer" in *Ways of Mankind.* W.R. Goldschmidt, ed. Boston, Beacon Press, 1954.
1 act. 6m
A radio play. A retelling of a Tlingit legend showing clan ritual, honour, and social demands.

D1575. "Sticks and Stones" in *Ways of Mankind.* W.R. Goldschmidt, ed. Boston, Beacon Press, 1954.
1 act. 10m/1f/1b or g. Doubling
A radio play showing the Arunta (Australian aborigines) answers to the eternal questions of man: life, love, death, possession, social organization, religion.

D1576. *Women in the Attic.* Toronto, Playwrights Co-op, 1972.
3 acts. 14m/7f. Doubling.
A newspaperman covering the funeral of an old and legendary lady of pleasure becomes fascinated by his subject. While reading her diary, written on rolls of wallpaper stored in an attic, he moves into the reality of the story of her life—she appears on stage, accompanied by her younger self.
fp: Globe Theatre, Regina, Nov. 11, 1971.

PHARIS, Gwen. See RINGWOOD, Gwen Pharis.

PHELPS, Arthur L. 1887–

D1577. "A Woman's Heart" in *Canadian Magazine*, vol.46, April 1916.
3 scenes. 5m/2f.
A young Newfoundland girl receives a proposal of marriage but hesitates to accept because she cannot forget her former lover.

PHILLIPS, Dorrie

D1578. *The Apple.* Halifax, Dramatists Co-op, 1977.
1 act. 1m/3f.
Based on the play by Lope de Rueda about the tiny apple tree that causes a giant commotion.
fp: Mermaid Theatre, Wolfville, N.S.

D1579. *Killarney's Return.* Halifax, Dramatists Co-op, 1977.
1 act. 5m/2f. Extras.
A ghost story in which Nell O'Hara is troubled by the ghost of her first lover.
p: CBC radio, Halifax.

D1580. *Night of Betrothal.* Halifax, Dramatists Co-op, 1977.
1 act. 3m/5f.
A comedy about Joshua and Genessa's progress toward marriage.

D1581. *Salt in the Blood.* Halifax, Dramatists Co-op, 1977.
1 act. 6m/2f.
A drama about the fisherman Caleb Smith who wants a better future for his son than the sea.

D1582. *Three Sheets in the Wind.* Halifax, Dramatists Co-op, 1977.
3 acts. 5m/5f.
An expanded version of *Night of Betrothal.*
fp: Dominion Drama Festival, 1966.

PICHETTE, Wayne

D1583. "February 25, 1972" in *Acta Victoriana,* vol.98, #1, December 1973.
1 scene. 1m/1f.
A conversation about life between a professor and a whore.

PICKTHALL, Marjorie Lowrey Christie 1883–1922

D1584. "Mons Angelorum" in her *The Complete Poems of Marjorie Pickthall.* Toronto, McClelland & Stewart, 1926.
1 act. 2m/3m.
A short poetic drama based on the last days of Moses' life. At the boundary of the Promised Land from which he is excluded Moses prepares Joshua, his successor, to lead the Israelites and waits for his own death.

D1585. "The Woodcarver's Wife" in *University Magazine,* vol.19, #2, 1920 and in *The Woodcarver's Wife and Later Poems.* Toronto, McClelland & Stewart, 1922 and in The *Complete Poems of Marjorie Pickthall.* Toronto, McClelland & Stewart, 1927.
1 act. 3m/1f.
Jean Marchand, the woodcarver, is carving a pieta for which his wife, Dorette, is posing. She is not able to achieve the required sorrowing intensity of expression until Shagonas, her husband's Indian helper, discovers her unfaithfulness to Jean, and her lover Louis is slain on the order of her jealous husband.
p: Montreal Community Players, Hart House Theatre, Toronto, Nov. 19, 1921. CKCK radio, Regina, December 1928.

PINSENT, Gordon 1930–

D1586. *John and the Missus.* Toronto, Playwrights Co-op, 1977.
2 acts. 13m/5f. Extras. Doubling.
An evocative portrayal of a dying Newfoundland community.
fp: Neptune Theatre, Halifax, Feb. 2, 1976.

PITT, Sidney H.

D1587. "Burglars for Love" in *Acadia Athanaeum,* vol.60, #3, January 1934.
1 scene. 2m/2f.
A penniless young man convinces his sweetheart's father of his finer qualities after an aborted attempt at theft.

D1588. "Faithful" in *Acadia Athanaeum,* vol.58, #3, January 1932.
1 scene. 4m/1f.
A Virginia belle promises eternal faithfulness to her dying Yankee sweetheart having already rejected a Confederate suitor who had brought news of the Yankee's death — actually his twin brother.

D1589. "Guilty or not Guilty" in *Acadia Athenaeum*, vol.58, #1, November 1931.
1 scene. 5m/1f.
A courtroom playlet in which the evidence was wrongly interpreted because "you Mounties don't always get your man."

D1590. "Paid in Full" in *Acadia Athenaeum*, vol.58, #2, December 1931.
2 scenes. 11m.
A man kills two thieves who claim to have lost his diamond that they stole and then receives a telegram announcing its recovery.

D1591. "The Promise" in *Acadia Athenaeum*, vol.58, #6, April 1932.
1 scene. 3m/1f.
Jeanette's faithfulness to her Acadian lover is rewarded when he returns to Grand Pre seven years after the Expulsion.

D1592. "What Price Love" in *Acadia Athenaeum*, vol.58, #4, February 1932.
1 scene. 1m/3f.
In the year following W.W. I, a young French girl chooses her German count over her own family.

PITTMAN, Al 1940–

D1593. *A Rope Against the Sun*. Newfoundland, Breakwater Books, 1974.
1 act. 7m/6f. Extras.
This play portrays life in a small outport community. The characters, including widows, children and old folks, all must come to grips with the outside world in a slowly petrifying social setting.
fp: Festival Production, Eastport Summer Festival, 1970.

PLOURDE, Marc

D1594. "The Clean End" in his *The White Magnet*. Montreal, DC Books, 1973.
1 act. 1m/1f.
Madeline and Kryss are thrashing out a break-up. Madeline wants Kryss to go without a fuss, but Kryss has other ideas.

PLUNKETT, Captain Merton W. 1888–1966

D1595. *Captain M.W. Plunkett, Manager and Owner, Presents "The Dumbells" In Biff-Bing-Bang*. N.p., n.p., 1921.
2 acts. 2m/1f. Extras.
An entertainment about the Armistice as celebrated in Paris by two young air force non-coms.
fp: Grand Opera House, Toronto, Oct. 28, 1919.

D1596. *The New Dumbells Play, "Carry On"*, N.p., n.p., 1923.
2 acts. 12m/3f. Extras.
In this two part revue, a French family entertains the Canadian boys on leave during W.W.I, and the patients of an army hospital try to cure a fellow patient of "melancholia".
fp: Grand Opera House, Toronto, January 1923.

PLUTA, Leonard 1937–

D1597. "Little Guy Napoleon" in *Dialogue & Dialectic: A Canadian Anthology of Short Plays.* Alive Theatre Workshop, ed. Guelph, Alive Press, 1972.
6 scenes. 4m/1f.
In Poland at the end of W.W.II, Martha, a schoolteacher and collaborator, and her son Augustine are mentally tortured for the role they played in the execution of four boys for stealing a horse.
fp: English Stage Company, Royal Court Theatre, London, March 27, 1966.

POCOCK, Wilfred

D1598. "Heroes of Health" in *Canadian Red Cross Junior*, November 1936.
1 act. Multiple roles.
The Goddess of Health shows Bobby the many contributions men and women have made to modern medicine.

POIRIER, Leonie

D1599. *A Night With a Stranger.* Halifax, Dramatists Co-op, 1977.
1 act. 2m/2f.
A play about Indian lore showing a contrast in values.

D1600. *The White Night.* Halifax, Dramatists Co-op, 1977.
1 act. 9m/7f.
A drama about the son of an Acadian widow who fails to return from a hunting trip.

POLLOCK, Sharon

D1601. *Compulsory Option.* Edmonton, Alberta Dept. of Culture, 1970 and Vancouver, New Play Centre, 1972.
3 acts. 3m.
A comedy about paranoia and how one person's view of life can irrationally spread to "normal" people.
fp: New Play Centre, Vancouver, 1972.

D1602. *The Komagata Maru Incident.* Toronto, Playwrights Co-op, 1978.
1 act. 3m/3f.
A drama about the racism which kept the ship Komagata Maru carrying East Indian immigrants from landing in Vancouver in 1914.
fp: Vancouver Playhouse, Jan. 20, 1976.

D1603. *Walsh.* Vancouver, New Play Centre, 1972 and Vancouver, Talonbooks, 1974.
3 acts. 11m/1f.
The story of the flight of the Sioux Nation to Canada after the massacre at Little Big Horn and of the murder of Sitting Bull and his son Crowchild.
fp: Theatre Calgary, Nov. 7, 1973.

POLOWY, Hannah

D1605. *Adam's Sons.* See **SAGO, Mitch.**

POMEROY, Stanton B.

D1606. "The Lady Sees Red" in *Acadia Athenaeum*, vol. 57, #1, November 1931.
1 scene. 3m/1f.
A wife persuades her husband to leave the country after he kills the Mafia bootlegger who was apparently her lover. She is thus free to continue her real affair with the red-headed butler.

PORTER, Helen

D1607. *Forte Fortissimo*. Edmonton, Alberta Dept. of Culture, 1970.
1 act. 2m.
A conversation between two hobos leads to a discussion about the existence of God and the good in mankind.

POTTER, Ida Elizabeth

D1608. *Annabel's M.I. Club*. Winnipeg, Hull Printing, 1931.
3 acts 4m/10f.
A play of moral instruction in which Mrs. Moreton learns a lesson about judging people by their appearances. Annabel, her daughter, founds a mutual improvement club for the neighbourhood children and her generosity pays off handsomely.

D1609. *At Hopper's Corners*. N.p., Author, 1927.
2 acts. 2m/15f.
A play of moral instruction in which the minister's wife together with her friend teach the people of Hopper's Corners to be more generous and not think so much of their own needs.

D1610. *Farmer Maxwell's City Niece*. N.p., Author, 1926.
3 acts. 8m/7f/1b.
A rural play with a moral lesson. Marion, a spoiled girl from the city, visits her country cousin, Chrissie, and learns the meaning of generosity and happiness.

D1611. *Wanted — a Chauffeur*. N.p., Author, 1928.
1 act. 5m/4f/1g. Extras.
A temperance play about the tragic results of drinking and driving.
fp: Manitoba Provincial Temperance Convention, May 1928.

D1612. *We Are Coming*. Portage la Prairie, Author, 1923.
5 acts. 6m/5f/1g.
A drama about temperance and class struggle. Mrs. Meredith learns she has been snobbish and selfish, and pledges to use her wealth to the advantage of the future of Canada.

POVEY, George

D1613. *The Gook*. Vancouver, New Play Centre, 1973.
1 act. 6m/2f.
A play set in Vietnam revealing the moral problems faced by men at war.
fp: New Play Centre, Vancouver, March 1973.

POWER, Bill

D1614. *The Electrical Man*. See **LEDOUX, Paul**.

POWER, Mary. See MAURA, Sister.

POWICKE, Hilda Benson

D1615. *Barrier.* New York, Friendship Press, 1971.
1 act. 5m/3f/1g.
A young Nigerian scholarship student in an American university experiences his first encounter with racial prejudice.

D1616. *Coffee House.* Toronto, Board of Evangelism and Social Service, United Church of Canada and Dept. of Christian Social Service, Anglican Church of Canada, 1965.
1 act. 4m/3f.
A view of church workers in "Cabbagetown" and the work of the church in helping people in trouble.
fp: Luke's Drama Group.

D1617. *No Certain Harbour.* New York, Friendship Press, 1962.
1 act. 3m/2f/1b/1g.
An American-educated son of refugees from Communist China decides to return to the mainland to work on a river project, employing the skills which are not being used in Hong Kong.

D1618. *No Longer At Ease.* Boston, Baker's Plays, 1968.
1 act. 3m/4f.
Kate, a volunteer at a church drop-in centre, is faced with a situation which ultimately reveals how her own personal inadequacies make her unable to meet the needs of the people who frequent the centre.

PRATT, Edwin John 1883–1964

D1619. "The Greater Sacrifice" in *Acta Victoriana*, vol.41, #6, June 1917.
1 scene. 1m/1f.
A dialogue between A Mother of France and An Unseen Messenger who asks her to sacrifice her son for her country.

PRESTON, John. PRESTON, Jack. See BUSCHLEN, John Preston.

PREVOST, Arthur. 1910–

D1620. *French and Langlais of Wakanda.* Sorel, Quebec, Editions Princeps, (194-?).
1 act. 4m/2f.
A feud between the French and the Langlais families is resolved when the children make their parents see the detrimental effects which it will cause in the village economy. French version included.

PRICE, Marjorie

D1621. *God Caesar.* Toronto, French, 1935.
1 act. 2m/3f.
Cleopatra tries to lure Caesar from Rome to Egypt while Calpurnia's slave, posing as a statue, observes.
fp: Playmakers, Mousetrap Theatre, Toronto, February 1935.

D1622. *The Six Queens of Henry*. Toronto, French, 1937.
1 act. 2m/6f.
"An historical fantasy" in which Henry VIII and his wives return as ghosts to Hampton Court for a banquet. The ladies do not always get along.
p: Shakespeare Society, Toronto, 1936 as "The Six Wives of Henry VIII".

PRICELESS, Inc. (Pseud.)

D1623. "Gimme Yeast, or Bound to Rise" in *Acta Victoriana*, vol.53, #6, March–April 1929.
2 acts. 3m/2f. Extras.
A brief parody.

PROCUNIER, Edwin Robert 1927–

D1624. "Appassionata" in his *A Knife To Thy Throat and Nine Other One Act Plays*. Agincourt, Ont., Book Society, 1962.
1 act. 1m/2f.
A middle-aged woman interferes in the friendship between her younger brother and a married woman because the neighbours are gossiping.

D1625. "The Beginning of Summer" in his *A Knife to Thy Throat and Nine Other One Act Plays*. Agincourt, Ont., Book Society, 1962.
1 act. 2m/2f.
When Phillip returns from school, he has plans which don't fit his mother's expectations.

D1626. "Granite and Oak" in his *A Knife to Thy Throat and Nine Other One Act Plays*. Agincourt, Ont., Book Society, 1962 and in *Plays from Modern Media*. J.C. Saxton, J.W. MacDonald, eds. Toronto, Longmans, 1964 and in *Upstage and Down*. D.P. McGarity, ed. Toronto, Macmillan, 1968 and *Granite and Oak*. Agincourt, Ont., Book Society, 1974.
1 act. 6m/1f.
Wilfrid Laurier's dilemma as the French Canadian leader of a national party was that he was both liberal and Catholic at the time when it was difficult to be either. John A. Macdonald encourages him to persevere.

D1627. "Incident at the Poseidon" in his *A Knife to Thy Throat and Nine Other One Act Plays*. Agincourt, Ont., Book Society, 1962.
1 act. 5m/2f.
"There's idealism where you never expect to find it." The derelicts discuss their hopes and dreams of "Utopia".

D1628. "A Knife to Thy Throat" in his *A Knife to Thy Throat and Nine Other One Act Plays*. Agincourt, Ont., Book Society, 1962.
1 act. 4m/2f. Extras.
This play is concerned with the final confrontation between Queen Elizabeth I and the Earl of Essex on the eve of his execution: as ruler, she is less free than any of her subjects.

D1629. "The Moonless Nights" in his *A Knife to Thy Throat and Nine Other One Act Plays*. Agincourt, Ont., Book Society, 1962.
1 act. 3m/3f.
A successful businessman who has severed all ties with his family returns to the house of his childhood and regains a sense of the values he had lost.

D1630. *The Second Duchess.* Agincourt, Ont., Book Society, 1962 and in *A Knife to Thy Throat and Nine Other One Act Plays.* Agincourt, Ont., Book Society, 1962.
1 act. 4m/3f.
The duchess, realizing that her predecessor was a close school friend, becomes instrumental in her husband's murder.

D1631. "The Strength of Love" in his *A Knife to Thy Throat and Nine Other One Act Plays.* Agincourt, Ont., Book Society, 1962.
1 act. 2m/2f.
Friends and relatives try to comfort a woman whose husband has been lost at sea.

D1632. "Two Sides of Darkness" in *The Best Short Plays 1958-1959.* Margaret Mayogra, ed. Boston, Beacon Press, 1959 and in his *A Knife to Thy Throat and Nine Other One Act Plays.* Agincourt, Ont., Book Society, 1962 and in *Beyond the Footlights.* H.D. McKellar, ed. Toronto, Macmillan, 1963.
1 act. 3m/5f/1b.
The play deals with the ageless misery war inflicts on the individual and the family.

D1633. "Voices of Desire" in *Canada on Stage.* Stanley Richards, ed. Toronto, Clarke Irwin, 1960 and in *A Knife to Thy Throat and Nine Other One Act Plays.* Agincourt, Ont., Book Society, 1962 and *Voices of Desire.* Agincourt, Ont., Book Society, 1974.
1 act. 3m/3f.
Along with Emile the waiter, we see both the comic and the pathetic aspects of humanity in a Parisian cafe. On this particular morning Emile encounters a Canadian tourist couple. He sees Ethel Potter's love for Nicholas Mantochuk thwarted by her sister's trickery.

PROUDFOOT, Lucy South

D1634. "A Christmas Festival of Play" in *Educational Review*, vol.36, #4, Dec. 1921.
6 scenes. Multiple roles.
A dramatization of children's Christmas games around the world.

D1635. **PRYOR, F.R.,** and A.L. Harker, *Marigold.* See **HARKER, Lizzie Allen.**

PURDY, Al 1918–

D1636. "The Myth Includes" in *Poems for Voices.* Toronto, CBC, 1970.
1 act. 4m/1f.
A radio play. A middle-aged man, while travelling across Canada (literally or metaphorically) remembers when he crossed the country as a young man, "riding the rails".
fp: CBC radio, February/March 1970.

QUINCE, Peter

D1637. *To-Night of all Nights.* Western Canada Theatre Conference. Edmonton, Dept. of Extension, University of Alberta, 1949.
1 act. 3m/5f.
A comedy about an amateur drama group thrown into confusion on opening night when one of the cast leaves town to play in a hockey game.

RABOURNE, Erma

D1638. *Hannah, Come Back.* Edmonton, Alberta Dept. of Culture, 1971.
1 act. 2m/1f.
The play focuses on the relationship between Hannah, her husband John and their neighbour Matt as Hannah, a victim of the flu epidemic, deliriously relives the terrifying moments of her past.

RAMSAY, Alexander

D1639. *Coercion.* Toronto, French, 1935.
1 act. 2m/2f.
John and Lois support the revolution despite the fact that Susan thinks they are "all brainsick with these new-fangled Red notions".
fp: Sarnia Little Theatre, April 23, 1934.

RANKIN, Nancy

D1640. "The Hardhead" in *One Act Plays by Canadian Authors.* Montreal, Canadian Authors' Association, 1926.
1 act. 2m/1f.
A young man goes home to the backwoods to borrow money from his father to buy a weekly newspaper.

RAVEL, Aviva 1938–

D1641. "Black Dreams" in *Contemporary Canadian Drama.* Joseph Shaver, ed.
Ottawa, Borealis Press, 1974.
1 act. 1m/1f.
Leona, a white, married socialite, tries several approaches to begin an affair with Eugene, a black musician.

D1642. *Dispossessed.* Women Write for Theatre vol.3. Toronto, Playwrights Co-op, 1976.
1 act. 2m/1f.
An absurdist comedy about a hopeless old couple and their 40 year old imbecile son who live out an endless existence of repetitive conversation and dreams.
fp: Saidye Bronfman Centre, Montreal, 1977.

D1643. "Horns" in *Callboard*, vol.23, #3, Fall 1976.
1 act. 1m/1f.
A look at the prejudices which separate people from different backgrounds and religions.

D1644. *Shoulder Pads.* Agincourt, Ont., Book Society, 1967.
1 act. 1m/2f.
A middle-aged woman outwits herself in an attempt to make her daughter content with a middle-class life.
fp: Instant Theatre, Montreal.

D1645. "Soft Voices" in *A Collection of Canadian Plays* vol.3. Rolf Kalman, ed. Toronto, Simon & Pierre, 1974 and in her *Twisted Loaf and Soft Voices*. Toronto, Simon & Pierre, 1976.
1 act. 2f.
Toby and Carol spend an evening together discussing old times; they haven't seen each other in fifteen years.
fp: St. John's Players, Newfoundland.

D1646. "The Twisted Loaf" in *A Collection of Canadian Plays* vol.3. Rolf Kalman, ed. Toronto, Simon & Pierre, 1974 and in her *The Twisted Loaf and Soft Voices*. Toronto, Simon & Pierre, 1976.
1 act. 4m/6f. Extras.
Bessie lies dying in hospital and is besieged by memories as well as by the reality of her daughters' unfulfilled lives.
fp: Saidye Bronfman Theatre, Montreal.

REANEY, James Crerar 1926–

D1647. "Apple Butter" in his *Apple Butter and Other Plays for Children*. Vancouver, Talonbooks, 1973.
1 act. 3m/4f.
A marionette play about the irreverent orphan Apple Butter on an Ontario farm in the 1890s.
fp: Western Fair, London, Ont., September 1965.

D1648. *Baldoon*. By C.H. Gervais and James Reaney. Erin, Ont., Porcupine's Quill, 1976.
2 acts. 6m/5f. Doubling.
Based on events at the Baldoon settlement near Wallaceburg, Ontario in the 1830s, this play relates a tale of a house haunted by mysterious apparitions and the attempt by a witch-finder to locate the source of their occurrence.
fp: NDWT Co., Bathurst Street Theatre, Toronto, Nov. 20, 1976.

D1649. *Colours in the Dark*. Toronto, Centennial Planning Branch, Ontario Dept. of Tourism and Information, 1967 (stencil), and Vancouver, Talonbooks, 1969. Revised Edition. Vancouver, Talonbooks, 1971.
2 acts. 3m/3f. Extras.
A "playbox" of impressions on growing up in south-western Ontario.
fp: Avon Theatre, Stratford Festival, 1967.

D1650. "The Death and Execution of Frank Halloway or The First Act of John Richardson's *Wacousta*" in *Jubilee*, #4, 1978.
1 act. Multiple roles, Chorus.
The first act of Reaney's dramatization of the novel by Richardson.
fp: St. Paul's Public School, Timmins, Ont., March 1, 1977.

D1651. *The Dismissal, or Twisted Beards and Tangled Whiskers*. Erin, Ont., Press Porcepic, 1978.
3 acts. 14m/5f. Extras. Doubling.
A satiric dramatization of historical events surrounding a student strike protesting the firing of Professor William Dale from the University of Toronto for exposing nepotistic hiring practices.
fp: NDWT Co., Hart House Theatre, Toronto, Nov. 7, 1977.

D1652. *The Easter Egg* (London, Ont.?), Author, (1962?) (mimeographed) and in his *Masks of Childhood*. Brian Parker, ed. Toronto, New Press, 1972.
3 acts. 3m/2f.
A middle-aged woman and a young one are engaged in a struggle over Kenneth, an "attic child": one seeks to keep him an idiot, the other wants to help him find maturity.
fp: Coach House Theatre, Toronto, Nov. 13, 1962.

D1653. "Geography Match" in his *Apple Butter and Other Plays for Children*. Vancouver, Talonbooks, 1973.
1 act. 2m/2f. Extras. Doubling.
A play about a thirty day transit of Canada based on a geography contest between schoolchildren.
fp: Broughdale Public School at Middlesex College Theatre, May 19, 1967.

D1654. *Handcuffs: The Donnellys, Part III*. Erin, Ont., Press Porcepic, 1977.
3 acts. 10m/4f. Doubling.
The conclusion of the Donnelly trilogy culminating in the massacre of the Donnellys on Feb. 3, 1880.
fp: Tarragon Theatre, Toronto, March 29, 1975.

D1655. "Ignoramus" in his *Apple Butter and Other Plays for Children*. Vancouver, Talonbooks, 1973 and in *Cues and Entrances*. Henry Beissel, ed. Toronto, Gage, 1977.
1 act. 4m/2f. Extras. Doubling.
A comedy about theories of progressive child education.
fp: York Mills Collegiate Institute, Toronto, February 1967.

D1656. "The Killdeer" in his *The Killdeer and Other Plays*. Toronto, Macmillan, 1962 and (revised version) in his *Masks of Childhood*. Brian Parker, ed. Toronto, New Press, 1972.
3 acts. 7m/7f.
A play built around the survivors of a macabre family slaying, exploring the complexity of love-hate relationships in a small south-western Ontario farm community.
fp: University College Alumnae Society, Coach House Theatre, Toronto, Jan. 13, 1960. CBC TV "Festival", Jan. 12, 1961. BBC radio, 1966.

D1657. *Let's Make A Carol*. Waterloo, Ont., Waterloo Music, 1965.
1 act. 2m/2f.
"A play with music for children". A group of children earn money so that their music teacher can finish his symphony. Music by Alfred Kunz.

D1658. *Listen to the Wind*. Toronto, Canadian Theatre Centre, 1967 and Vancouver, Talonbooks, 1972.
3 acts. 4m/2f/1b/3g. Chorus.
The children of a south-western Ontario town in 1936 stage a play of their own creation. By means of this adaptation of a Victorian novel about Caresfoot Court, Owen, the sick boy, hopes to bring his parents back together.
fp: Althouse College Auditorium, London, Ont., July 26, 1966.

D1659. "Names and Nicknames" in *Nobody in the Cast.* Robert Barton, *et al,* eds. Toronto, Longmans, 1969 and *Names and Nicknames.* New York, New Plays for Children, 1969 and in his *Apple Butter and Other Plays for Children.* Vancouver, Talonbooks, 1973 and in *Contemporary Children's Theatre.* Betty Jean Lifton, ed. New York, Avon, 1974.
1 act. 4m/2f/2g. Extras.
An old man gets revenge on children by giving them hateful nicknames.
fp: Manitoba Theatre Centre, Winnipeg, October 1963.

D1660. "Night-Blooming Cereus" in his *The Killdeer and Other Plays.* Toronto, Macmillan, 1962.
1 act. 2m/6f.
Libretto for a chamber opera. "It will be the Kingdom of Heaven/When this shy flower blooms." Music by John Beckwith.
fp: Hart House Theatre, Toronto, April 5, 1960. CBC radio "Wednesday Night", March 4, 1959.

1661. "One-Man Masque" in his *The Killdeer and Other Plays.* Toronto, Macmillan, 1962 and in *The Evolution of Canadian Literature in English: 1945-1970.* Paul Denham, ed. Toronto, Holt, Rinehart and Winston, 1973.
1 act. 1m.
The speaker leads the audience "through the worlds of life, of life and death", a mixture of associations.
fp: Hart House Theatre, Toronto, April 5, 1960.

D1662. *The St. Nicholas Hotel: The Donnellys, Part II.* Erin, Ont., Press Porcepic, 1976.
3 acts. 11m/4f. Doubling.
The story of William and Mike Donnelly and their stage line, the Opposition Stage. In the battle for mastery of the road, William and Mike make powerful enemies.
fp: Tarragon Theatre, Toronto, Nov. 16, 1974.

D1663. "Sticks and Stones: The Donnellys, Part I" in *Canadian Theatre Review,* #2, Spring 1974 and *Sticks and Stones.* Erin, Ont., Press Porcepic, 1976.
3 acts. 9m/3f. Doubling.
James Donnelly moves his family from the old country to Canada in order to escape prejudice and violence. However, the new country is itself divided and the old societies of Whitefoot and Blackfoot reappear.
fp: Tarragon Theatre, Toronto, Nov. 24, 1973.

D1664. "The Sun and The Moon" in his *The Killdeer and Other Plays.* Toronto, Macmillan, 1962.
3 acts. 9m/11f.
A woman comes to a small Ontario town specifically to destroy the reputation of a minister.
p. London, Ont., 1964.

D1665. "Three Desks" in his *The Masks of Childhood.* Brian Parker, ed., Toronto, New Press, 1972.
8 scenes. 4m/1f. Extras.
This play is a macabre view of English departments and teaching at a small liberal arts college on the prairies.
fp: London Little Theatre, Grand Theatre, London, Ont., Feb. 3, 1967.

REEVES, John 1926–

D1666. *The Arithmetic of Love.* Toronto, 68 Publishers, 1975.
Many scenes. 4m/4f. Extras.
A radio play giving the chronological history of Czechoslovakia and its constant struggle for justice and freedom.
fp. (In Czech), Oct. 28, 1975 at the Town Hall, St. Lawrence Centre, Toronto. In English, CBC radio, 1975.

D1667. *A Beach of Strangers.* Toronto, Oxford University Press, 1961.
3 acts. 21m/21f.
A verse drama in which three separate sets of characters relate their very different views of a summer's day at a holiday beach.
fp: CBC radio "Wednesday Night", April 15, 1959.

D1668. *Triptych.* Toronto, CBC, 1972.
3 acts. 12m/4f. Extras. Doubling.
A trilogy which takes the form of a series of contrasts, showing the three major days of the Christian calendar, Christmas, Good Friday and Easter, in both a religious and secular light.
fp: CBC radio, 1971.

REID, Leslie

D1669. "Trespassers" in *Canadian Plays from Hart House Theatre* vol.2. V. Massey, ed. Toronto, Macmillan, 1927.
3 acts. 6m/4f.
Sir Benjamin Parlowe, M.P., though a conservative in family matters and on woman's place in society, spearheads a bill to stop right of way over property, closing century-old roads and disrupting the community's way of life.
fp: Hart House Theatre, Toronto, May 2, 1923.

REILLEY, Robert McAmis 1920–

D1670. "The Door" in his *The Constant Factor.* Montreal, Factum, 1967 and in his *Collected Plays.* New York, Vantage Press, 1970.
1 act. 3m/1f.
Thieves discuss ways of breaking down the door — they discover it is unlocked.
fp: Lakeshore Players, Ste Anne de Bellevue, P.Q., March 17, 1967.

D1671. "Express" in his *The Constant Factor.* Montreal, Factum, 1967 and in his *Collected Plays.* New York, Vantage Press, 1970.
1 act. 3m/1f.
The action of the play centres around priority disputes in the line-up at a bus stop.
fp: Lakeshore Players, Ste Anne de Bellevue, P.Q., March 17, 1967.

D1672. "The Road" in his *Collected Plays.* New York, Vantage Press, 1970.
1 act. 2m/2f.
Everyman's journey through life is linked with the creation of Adam and Eve.
fp: Playwrights' Workshop, Montreal, March 1969.

D1673. *A Tower for Tommy*. Ottawa, Ottawa Little Theatre Workshop, #48 and in his *Collected Plays*. New York, Vantage Press, 1970.
1 act. 2m/2f.
"An allegorical play" in which three characters exhort the fourth to make use of the gift of life and live.
fp: Saidye Bronfman Workshop, Montreal, Dec. 7, 1967.

D1674. "Vignette #5: Charlie, Charlie" in his *The Constant Factor*. Montreal, Factum, 1967 and in his *Collected Plays*. New York, Vantage Press, 1970.
1 act. 2m/2f.
Charlie is the leader of four ghoulish murderers who express their blood lust in rhyming couplets. When one of them fails to rhyme they make him the next victim.
fp: Lakeshore Players, Ste Anne de Bellevue, P.Q., March 17, 1967.

D1675. "Vignette #1: Jump, Jump" in his *The Constant Factor*. Montreal, Factum, 1967 and in his *Collected Plays*. New York, Vantage Press, 1970.
1 act. 2m/2f.
A crowd gathers to watch a man on the ledge of a tall building who is about to jump.
fp: Lakeshore Players, Ste Anne de Bellevue, P.Q., March 17, 1967.

D1676. *The Wheel*. Montreal, Factum, 1967 and (revised version) in his *Collected Plays*. New York, Vantage Press, 1970.
2 acts. 3m/1f.
In a limbo region, a character named Zor cracks a whip to put other characters through their paces. When they are granted their freedom, they don't know how to handle it and willingly return to bondage.
fp: Our Town Theatre Club, Lethbridge, Alta., March 8, 1967.

RENYI, Elizabeth

D1677. "Little Chipmunk and the Owl Woman" in *The Carolina Play-Book*, vol.13, #4, December 1940.
1 act. 3f/2m.
Little Chipmunk is pursued by the Owl Woman who scratches her coat and tears out her heart. But Meadow Lark brings Chipmunk back to life.
fp: Fourth bill of experimental productions of new Canadian folk plays, Banff School of Fine Arts, Aug. 28, 1940.

RENYI, Elizabeth and Isabel Christie MacNaughton

1678. "Why the Ant's Waist Is Small" in *The Carolina Play-Book*, vol.12, #4, December 1939 and in MacNaughton, Isabel Christie. *Wood Fires*. Oliver, B.C., Oliver Chronicle and Osoyoos Observer, 1942 and Oliver, B.C., Chronicle Publishing, 1948.
1 act. 2f/2m.
"An Okanagan Indian fold legend" recorded by the authors. An ant mourns the death of Little Partridge and pulls tight the belt of her buckskin dress in grief.
fp: Rustic Theatre, Banff School of Fine Arts, Aug. 15, 1939.

D1679. "Why the Chipmunk's Coat Is Striped" in *The Carolina Play-Book*, vol.12, #4, December 1939.
1 act. 3m/1f.
"An Okanagan Indian folk tale" recorded by the authors. Little Chipmunk escapes the Owl's claws but his coat is permanently marked by three great stripes.
fp: Music Theatre, Banff School of Fine Arts, Aug. 15, 1939.

REOCH, Richard

D1680. *Songs for the Coal Forest Children*. Toronto, Anansi, 1970.
2 acts. 7m/5f. Extras.
A poetic drama about a group of people living a primitive existence in a cave.
fp: Prospero Productions and the Trinity College Dramatic Society, Central Library Theatre, Toronto, Dec. 16, 1969.

REYNOLDS, Lois. See KERR, Lois Reynolds.

REYNOLDS, Mary

D1681. "And the Answer Is..." in *New Frontier*, March 1937 and in *Eight Men Speak and Other Plays from the Canadian Workers' Theatre*. Richard Wright, Robin Endres, eds. Toronto, New Hogtown Press, 1976.
1 act. 4m/5f.
A drama about apathy and prejudice of the wealthy towards the poor. Ladies discuss their club's Christmas entertainment while the unemployed struggle against starvation and disease.
p: Theatre of Action, Toronto, April 1937.

D1682. *The Bequest*. One-Act Plays No.26. London, Muller, 1939.
1 act. 2m/1f.
"A Grotesque". In mediaeval Germany, a dying philosopher's attempt to return from the dead through a magic potion is foiled by the greed of his loutish son.
fp: Vancouver Little Theatre, 1938, as "Dust Into Gold".

D1683. "The Waxen Man" in *Fifty One-Act Plays*. Constance Martin, ed. London, Gollancz, 1934.
1 act. 2m/1f.
A Cornish girl puts a curse on the man who had rejected her. Her secret is discovered and she is forced to flee with her half-wit brother from the angry villagers.
fp: Little Theatre, Vancouver, 1924.

RICHARDSON, Alan 1946–

D1684. *Wozzeck*. Toronto, Theatrebooks. 1977.
20 scenes. 7m/4f. Extras. Doubling.
An adaptation of Georg Buchner's *Woyzeck* set in 20th century Toronto about an alienated German immigrant who murders his common-law wife.
fp: Theatre Compact, Toronto, Sept. 26, 1977.

RICHARDSON, Grace

D1685. "You Are the Only WASP I Know" in *Performing Arts in Canada,* vol.6, #3, Summer 1969.
1 act. 1f/1m.
A young man and woman spend an accustomed evening together and a good deal of their personalities and of their relationship is revealed.
p: Jonas-Malcolm Productions, Central Library Theatre, Toronto, Nov. 6, 1968.

RICHLER, Mordecai 1931–

D1686. "The Bells of Hell" in *Toronto Life*, February 1974.
4 acts. 11m/5f/1g. Extras.
A TV comedy about Manny, a successful, middle-aged Jewish lawyer who finds life increasingly hard to understand. Threats of violent sexuality, conspiracy and death seem to be everywhere isolating him from his family and friends.
fp: CBC TV, January 24, 1974.

RIDOUT, Denzil G. 1887–1954

D1687. *United to Serve.* Toronto, United Church Of Canada, 1927.
2 parts. Epilogue. 30m/15f. Extras. Doubling.
"A pictorial presentation" produced and written by Denzil Ridout, assisted by E.J. Pratt, Ernest Macmillan and others. The history and heritage of the United Church of Canada and its mission of Christian service is depicted in pageant form.
fp: Simpson Avenue United Church, Toronto, Feb. 10, 1927.

RINGWOOD, Gwen Pharis 1910–

D1688. "The Courting of Marie Jenvrin" in *The Carolina Play-Book*, vol.14, #4, Dec. 1941 and in *Best One-Act Plays of 1942*. M. Mayorga, ed. New York, Dodd, Mead, 1943 and in *Canadian School Plays* series 1. E.M. Jones, ed. Toronto, Ryerson, 1948 and in *International Folk Plays*. Samuel Selden, ed. Chapel Hill, N.C., University of North Carolina Press, 1949 and *The Courting of Marie Jenvrin*. Toronto, French, 1951 and in *Adventures in Reading*. J.M. Ross, B.J. Thompson, eds. New York, Harcourt, Brace, 1952 and in *Canada On Stage*, Stanley Richards, ed. Toronto, Clarke Irwin, 1960.
1 act. 5m/2f.
A comedy about the young Marie who promises to marry any man who will transport a cow to her in Yellowknife so that she can have fresh cream.
fp: Banff School of Fine Arts, Aug. 25, 1941. CBC radio.

D1689. *Dark Harvest.* Toronto, Nelson, 1945 and (revised version) in *Canadian Theatre Review*, #5, Winter 1975.
3 acts. 5m/2f.
"A tragedy of the Prairies". For Gerth Hansen, wheat farmer, God is in the land and he struggles against it, alone.
fp: University of Manitoba Dramatic Society, Winnipeg Auditorium, Jan. 17, 1945. CBC radio "Wednesday Night", Sept. 12, 1951.

D1689A. *The Dragons of Kent*. Edmonton, Dept. of Education, Province of Alberta, 1936.
1 act. 5m/1f/3b. Extras.
"A fantastic comedy" about the encounter between a family of dragons and a descendant of St. George.
fp: Banff School of Fine Arts, 1935.

D1690. *The Jack and the Joker*. Edmonton, Extension Dept., University of Alberta, 1944.
1 act. 3m/4f.
In this comedy, Bob Edwards, the pioneer Albertan newspaperman, punctures a particularly pompous and dishonest politician by uncovering a fraud.
fp: Banff School of Fine Arts, 1944.

D1691. *Lament for Harmonica. (Maya)*. Ottawa, Ottawa Little Theatre Workshop, #10 and in *Ten Canadian Short Plays*. John Stevens, ed. New York, Dell, 1975.
1 act. 2m/5f.
Maya, an Indian girl who has had a child by a white man, kills her Indian lover to save the child's father.
fp: Ottawa Little Theatre, 1959. CBC TV "Shoestring Theatre", Montreal, Feb. 14, 1960.

D1692. *The Lodge*. Vancouver, New Play Centre, 1976.
3 acts. 7m/4f.
A family gathers at an old interior B.C. hunting lodge to celebrate their eccentric grandmother's birthday.
fp: West Vancouver Little Theatre, West Vancouver Recreational Centre, 1976.

D1693. "Pasque Flower" in *The Carolina Play-Book*, vol.12, #1, March 1939.
1 act. 2m/1f.
An earlier version of *Dark Harvest*. Three years after the death of their child, a gift of spring flowers reunites Lisa with Jake and helps her forget her feelings for Jake's brother David.
fp: Carolina Playmakers, Playmaker Theatre, University of North Carolina, March 2, 1939.

D1694. *The Rainmaker*. Edmonton, Extension Dept. University of Alberta, 1946 and Vancouver, New Play Centre, 1973 and Toronto, Playwrights Co-op, 1975.
1 act. 13m/8f.
Hatfield the rainmaker saves the inhabitants of Medicine Hat, Alberta from a several year long drought.
fp: Banff School of Fine Arts, Aug. 22, 1945.

D1694A. *Red Flag at Evening*. Edmonton, Dept. of Extension, University of Alberta, 1940.
1 act. 2f/1m.
A comedy. After a thirteen year courtship Bessie finally puts the question to the fussy Elmer Engletree and starts a new life.
fp: Youth Training Schools, Edmonton, 1939.

D1694B. *Saturday Night*. Edmonton, Dept. of Extension, University of Alberta, 1940.
1 act. 5m/2f.
A comedy in which four teenagers and their parents argue about the use of the family car.
fp: Youth Training Schools, Edmonton, 1939.

D1695. "The Sleeping Beauty" in *My Heart Is Glad* Book II. G.P. Ringwood, ed. Cariboo Indian School, Williams Lake, B.C., 1965.
1 act. 12f/6m. Chorus.
An adaptation of the classic fairy tale in an Indian setting.
fp: Cariboo Indian School, Williams Lake, B.C., April 1965.

D1696. *Stampede*. Edmonton, Extension Dept., University of Alberta, 1946.
3 acts. 9m/2f. Extras. Doubling.
A drama about the last years of the ranching era in Alberta.
fp: University of Alberta Drama Society, March 1946.

D1697. "Still Stands the House" in *The Carolina Play-Book*, vol.11, #2, June 1938 and in *American Folk Plays*. F.H. Koch, ed. New York, Appleton-Century, 1939 and in *Argosy to Adventure*. C.L. Bennet, ed. Toronto, Ryerson, 1950 and *Still Stands the House*. New York, French, 1955 and in *Eight One-Act Plays*. Toronto, Dent, 1966 and in *Encounter: Canadian Drama in Four Media*. Eugene Benson, ed. Toronto, Methuen, 1973 and in *The Prairie Experience*. Terry Angus, ed. Toronto, Macmillan, 1975 and in *Transitions I: Short Plays*. Edward Peck, ed. Vancouver, Commcept Publishing, 1978 and in *Literature in Canada* volume 2. Douglas Daymond, Leslie Monkman, eds. Toronto, Gage, 1978.
1 act. 2m/2f.
"A drama of the Canadian frontier". Bruce wishes to sell the family farm and move closer to town with his wife. But his sister Hester feels the family property should not be sold, and to keep the land, allows both her brother and his wife to perish in a blizzard.
fp: Carolina Playmakers, University of North Carolina, March 3, 1938. Edmonton and Medicine Hat Little Theatres, 1938. CBC radio.

D1698. *Widger's Way*. Toronto, Playwrights Co-op, 1976.
4 scenes. 9m/2f.
A melodrama-farce set in Alberta about a miserly farmer, his innocent daughter, hidden gold, oil, and a murderer on the loose.
fp: University of Alberta Studio Theatre, March 1952.

RIPPINGTON, D.J.

D1699. *Let Swords Slash for Freedom*. Edmonton, Institute of Applied Art, 1970.
1 act. 11m/6f. Extras.
"An historical drama" about the revolt of the "Roundheads", led by Oliver Cromwell, against Charles I of England, and the support given to them by Lady Aubrey.

RITTER, Erika 1948–

D1700. *The Splits*. Toronto, Playwrights Co-op, 1978.
2 acts. 3m/1f.
A contemporary comedy in which a young harried woman writer tries to sort out her life and the men in it.
fp: Toronto Free Theatre, January 1978.

D1701. *A Visitor from Charleston*. Toronto, Playwrights Co-op, 1975.
2 acts. 4m/1f.
Eva, a disillusioned divorcee, increasingly lives in a fantasy world based on repeated viewings of *Gone With the Wind*.
fp: Loyola College, Montreal, 1974.

ROBB, Dodi and Pat Patterson

D1702. *The Dandy Lion.* Toronto, New Press, 1972.
1 act. 5m/2f/1b.
"A musical play for children". A young boy and his gentle pet lion try to join the "greatest little show on earth" only to find that the circus already has a ferocious lion and a conceited, jealous lion tamer. Music by Pat Patterson.
fp: Museum Children's Theatre, Toronto, 1965.

D1703. *The Popcorn Man.* Toronto, New Press, 1972.
1 act. 6m/3f/1b.
"A musical play for children". A happy-go-lucky popcorn man teaches the grumpy park superintendent and a too-busy businessman that life should be happy and gay. Music by Pat Patterson.
fp: Young People's Theatre, Toronto, 1970.

D1704. *Red Riding Hood.* Toronto, New Press, 1972.
1 act. 4m/1f/1g.
"A musical play for children". While off to visit her sick grandmother, Little Red Riding Hood is confronted by the Great White Wolf in many disguises. Music by Pat Patterson.
fp: Young People's Theatre, Toronto, 1968.

ROBB, Wallace Havelock 1888–

D1705. "Radio Script" in *The Crucible*, vol.6, #4, Summer 1940.
1 act. 2m/1f. Extras.
"A broadcast by 'The Abbé of Abbey Dawn' ". After an evening in a New York nightclub, a disillusioned poet calls on the world's peoples to march and fight for freedom.

ROBERTS, Lloyd 1884–1966

D1706. "Syrinx — A Fantasy" in *Willison's Monthly*, vol.1, #2, April 1926.
1 act. 2m/1f.
A youth travels north in search of Syrinx accompanied by a guide who is somewhat sceptical of the youth's idealistic fantasies.

ROBERTSON, Kenneth A.

D1707. *Duet for Three.* Edmonton, Dept. of Extension, University of Alberta, (1947?).
1 act. 4m/1f. Extras. Doubling.
An experimental play about the trial of a soldier accused of murdering his wife's lover in London.

D1708. *Forever till Friday.* Western Canada Theatre Conference. Dept. of Extension, University of Alberta, 1950.
1 act.
Title unavailable for annotation.

ROBERTSON, Paddy

D1709. *No Moon — No Son.* Ottawa, Ottawa Little Theatre Workshop, #27.
1 act. 4m/7f.
Katherine Carr McLeod must choose between her own career and helping her husband in his and is influenced by her family in making what she eventually considers to be the right decision.

ROBINSON, Hazel Alberta 1913–1955

D1710. "The Perilous Dream" in her *Poems and a Play*. Toronto, Ryerson, 1955.
1 act. 6m/2f/1b.
In "The Perilous Dream" the world turns its back on the rumblings of war because people were told that W.W.I was the end of all war. To mankind's dismay, the threat grows, until, at the last moment, the free people of the world answer the alarms of war.
fp: CBC radio Trans-Canada Network, Nov. 11, 1949.

ROCHE, Evita

D1711. *The Velvet Rut.* Edmonton, Alberta Dept. of Culture, 1971.
1 act. 3m/1f.
Two young people on their way to Toronto are forced to spend some time in the railway town of Capreol and so learn what keeps some people in such a small place.

RODD, P.G.

D1712. "Noot-chee and the Paddle" in *Nunny Bag 1*. Toronto, Gage, 1962.
1 act. 7m/3f.
A play for children. The totem helps the son of a West Coast Indian chief recover the tribe's magic paddle stolen by the Beaver.

RODDICK, Amy (Redpath) 1869–1954

D1713. "The Birth of Montreal" in her *The Birth of Montreal, a Chronicle Play, and Other Poems*. Montreal, Dougall, 1921.
4 acts. 10m/6f. Extras.
Concerns the founding of Montreal and the trials of the young settlement: the flooding of the St. Lawrence River and the Iroquois. The Church is everywhere present, converting young Indians like Jeanne, a Huron girl who can never fully commit herself to the new religion.

D1714. "In a Venetian Garden" in her *In a Venetian Garden and St. Ursula*. Montreal, Dougall, 1926.
1 act. 11m/3f.
Massaccio's story about the debt which the duke owes him is corroborated by the appearance of the monkey.

D1715. "The Key That Unlocks" in her *The Birth of Montreal, a Chronicle Play, and Other Poems*. Montreal, Dougall, 1921.
3 acts. 4m/4f.
A poet writing in his Montreal attic on Christmas Eve travels far in his mind, learns much, and finally dies.

D1716. "The Romance of a Princess" in her *The Romance of a Princess, a Comedy, and Other Poems*. Montreal, Dougall, 1922.
5 acts. 7m/3f/1b. Extras.
Emma, daughter of Charlemagne, is in love with her father's secretary, Eginhardt. In anger, Charlemagne banishes both, but in six years he finds them living in the forest and is reconciled to their love.

D1717. "St. Ursula" in her *In a Venetian Garden and St. Ursula*. Montreal, Dougall, 1926.
4 acts. 12m/5f. Extras.
Princess Ursula renounces a worldly way of life and spends her life in God's service attended by her maidens who do likewise. She is martyred when murdered by Atilla the Hun.

D1718. *The Seekers*. Montreal, Dougall, 1920.
5 acts. 15m/4f. Extras.
"An Indian mystery play" retelling the legend of a group of Hochelagan youths who search for the Lord of Man and Beasts, each to ask of the Divinity one gift.

D1719. *Tharbis*. Montreal, Dougall, 1937.
4 acts. 10m/2f. Extras.
A poetic drama. A princess of Ethiopia falls in love with Moses, commander of the Egyptian army besieging the capital Sheba.

D1720. "The Tomahawk" in her *The Tomahawk, A Playlet, and Other Poems*. Montreal, Dougall, 1938.
1 act. 4m/4f. Extras.
"A playlet" in which a woman writer transcribes a scene which is conjured before her depicting the origin of the tomahawk.

RODGERS, Charles Gordon

D1721. "Out of the Past" in *Canadian Magazine*, #30, December 1907.
1 act. 2m.
Twenty years ago, Laplante's wife was stolen away by another man. The man's son returns to the old cabin by mistake, and mistaking the visitor for the father, Laplante attempts to get revenge.

RODRIGUEZ, Patricia

D1722. "The Pobble People" in *Nunny Bag 4*. Toronto, Gage, 1965.
1 act. 5b/4g.
A children's play. Homemade cut-out dolls introduce a newcomer to the hazards of life. They all await rescue from spring cleaning and they go off to find refuge on the planet Papyrus.

ROOKE, Leon 1943–

D1723. *Evening Meeting of the Club of Suicide*. Vancouver, New Play Centre, (197-?).
1 act. 2m/4f. Doubling.
An abstract comedy about suicide victims and the conflicts that lead to their actions.

D1724. *Krokodile*. Toronto, Playwrights Co-op, 1973.
15 scenes. 3m/1f. Extras.
Two explorers, Gore and Osko, set about to discover Canada and murder a whole Indian family in their conquest.

D1725. *Sword/Play*. Vancouver, New Play Centre, 1973 and Toronto, Playwrights Co-op, 1974.
1 act. 2m/2f.
Four people meet to talk, to play jokes on each other, and to perform for each other.
fp: New Play Centre, Vancouver, March 26, 1973.

D1726. **ROSEN, Beverley.** "Twisted Roots". See **SIMONS, Beverley.**

ROSEN, Sheldon 1943–

D1727. "The Box" in *West Coast Plays*. C. Brissenden, ed. Vancouver and Toronto, New Play Centre-Fineglow Plays, 1975.
1 act. 2m.
Two men play out their separate fantasies over an unopened gift-wrapped box.
fp: New Play Centre and Troupe, Vancouver, March 1974.

D1728. *Frugal Repast*. Vancouver, New Play Centre, 1974 and in his *Frugal Repast/The Grand Hysteric*. Toronto, Playwrights Co-op, 1978.
1 act. 1m/1f.
A play based on the Picasso painting of the same name.
fp: New Play Centre, Vancouver East Cultural Centre, April 1974.

D1729. *The Grand Hysteric*. Vancouver, New Play Centre, 1975 and in his *Frugal Repast/The Grand Hysteric*. Toronto, Playwrights Co-op, 1978.
1 act. 1m/1f.
A drama about a young man's final meeting with his psychiatrist.
fp: New Play Centre, Vancouver East Cultural Centre, May 1975 as "Like Father, Like Son".

D1730. *Love Mouse*. Toronto, Playwrights Co-op, 1972 and in *A Collection of Canadian Plays* vol.1. Rolf Kalman, ed. Toronto, Simon & Pierre, 1972.
1 act. 2m/1f.
A comedy in which a man and his wife create their own version of original sin aided by a mouse who turns into a rat who turns into a wolf and helps to bring them back together.
fp: Learning Resources Centre, Toronto Public Library, June 21, 1971.

D1731. *Meyer's Room*. Toronto, Playwrights Co-op, 1972 and in *A Collection of Canadian Plays* vol.1. Rolf Kalman, ed. Toronto, Simon & Pierre, 1972.
1 act. 3m.
A surrealistic look at society which presents Rock Hudson as prey, Madeline and Meyer, the blind man, as predators and Rock's anti-homosexual attitude.
fp: Poor Alex Theatre, Toronto, August 1971.

D1732. *Ned and Jack*. Toronto, Playwrights Co-op, 1978.
2 acts. 3m.
A drama about an encounter between the actor John Barrymore and the playwright Edward Sheldon.
fp: New Play Centre, Vancouver, November 1977.

D1733. *Waiting to Go.* Vancouver, New Play Centre, (197-?).
1 act. 3m.
A comedy about a young commercial artist whose life is changed by a meeting with a janitor in a men's room at Lincoln Centre during a performance of The Nutcracker.

D1734. *The Wonderful World of William Bends Who is Not Quite Himself Today.* Toronto, Playwrights Co-op, 1972.
2 acts. 6m/3f.
A black comedy about the doctors and patients in an insane asylum.
fp: Tarragon Theatre, Toronto, April 19, 1972.

ROSENFELD, David

D1735. *Hasid.* Toronto, Playwrights Co-op, 1978.
1 act. 1m.
A poetic recollection of the Holocaust.
fp: Actor's Lab (Théâtre de l'Homme), Hamilton, Ont., May 1974.

ROSS, Dorothea Lucile

D1736. "Neighbours' Business" in *Willison's Monthly*, vol.2, #7, December 1926.
1 act. 1m/1f/1b/3g.
Neighbours send help to a poor farmer so his children can have a Christmas after all.

ROSTANCE, Mrs. A.J.

D1737. "David at Aunt Betsy's" in *Scenes from Dickens*. J.E. Jones, ed. Toronto, McClelland & Stewart, 1923.
2 scenes. 1m/1f/1b. Extras.
An adaptation of an incident from *David Copperfield* in which David, running away from Murdstone, arrives at his aunt's house in Dover.

D1738. "Wardle's Christmas Party" in *Scenes from Dickens*. J.E. Jones, ed. Toronto, McClelland & Stewart, 1923.
3 scenes. 8m/3f/1b. Extras.
An adaptation of the Christmas at Dingley Dell sequence in *Pickwick Papers*.

ROULSTON, Keith

D1739. *The Shortest Distance Between Two Points.* Toronto, Playwrights Co-op, 1978.
3 acts. 6m/1f.
A comedy about a small town's reaction to a proposed super-highway.
fp: Blyth Summer Festival, Ontario, 1977.

ROUSSIN, Claude 1941–

D1740. "Looking for a Job", Allan van Meer, trans., in *A Collection of Canadian Plays* vol.5. Rolf Kalman, ed. Toronto, Simon & Pierre, 1978.
1 act. 10m/10f.
A translation of his *Une Job*. A drama about a Quebec family in which the son of a passive father and domineering mother looks for a job in a world in which he has no control.
fp: l'Option-Théâtre de la Magdeleine, Brassard, Quebec, May 8, 1972.

ROWAN, Beverley

D1741. *Floating Homeland.* Edmonton, Dept. of Extension, University of Alberta, 1947.
1 act. 2m/2f. Extras.
A poetic drama about a group of Jewish refugees from Europe on board ship trying to illegally enter the port of Haifa, Palestine.

ROY, James Alexander 1884–

D1742. *The Breaking of the Bridge.* Kingston, Jackson Press, 1923.
1 act. 3m/3f. Extras.
Life in a small, poor Irish family before and after the drunken father dies.

D1743. *The Recognition.* Kingston, Jackson Press, (192-?).
1 act. 8m/4f.
A gentleman, walking through the slums of London, takes pity on a young woman, only to discover that she is his former girlfriend.

RUGGLES, Ruth

D1744. *The Cross.* Toronto, Religion and Theatre Council, (196-?).
1 act. 3m/2f. Extras.
A dramatization of the passion and death of Christ designed to be performed in church as part of the religious service.
fp: Cathedral Players of Ottawa.

D1745. *The Moon for a Candle.* Ottawa, Ottawa Little Theatre Workshop, #2.
1 act. 1m/3f.
Margaret wants to elope with William but fears she must marry Mr. Anderson to fulfill the promise she made to him and to her parents.

RUSSELL, Frances Foster

D1746. "Down the Years" in *Journal of Education for Nova Scotia*, series 4, vol.14, March 1943.
12 scenes. Multiple roles.
"An historical pageant of Nova Scotia" tracing its history from Glooscap through the reign of the French and the English conquest to Confederation and the war effort.

RUSSELL, Lawrence 1941–

D1747. "The Beautiful Woman and The Bleeding Man" in *Canadian Fiction Magazine*, #16, Spring 1975 and in his *Mystery of the Pig Killer's Daughter.* Seattle, Washington, Angst World Library, 1975.
1 act. 5m/1f.
A surrealist science-fiction play.

D1748. "Deep Sea" in his *Penetration.* Mission City, B.C., Sono Nis, 1972.
1 act. 2m/2f.
A surrealist play about a retired surgeon who is paranoid about dust and his wife, and his daughter who picks up a diver with a buzz in his head.
fp: Factory Theatre Lab, Toronto, Sept. 20, 1972.

D1749. "Foul Play" in *The Cougar City Gazette*, March 1970 and *Foul Play*. Toronto, Playwrights Co-op, 1972 and in his *Penetration*. Mission City, B.C., Sono Nis, 1972.
1 act. 4m/1f.
A short play concerning the sexual difficulties of a dude with a heart pacemaker which runs on solar energy.
fp: Factory Theatre Lab, Toronto, Sept. 20, 1972.

D1750. *I Remember Dali When He Was Just a Little Kid and Couldn't Keep His Nose Clean.* Toronto, Playwrights Co-op, 1972 and in *The Malahat Review*, #26, April 1973 and in his *Mystery of the Pig Killer's Daughter*. Seattle, Washington, Angst World Library, 1975.
1 act. 2m/1f.
Absurdist play about love, lust, death, indecision, and the importance of toenails.
fp: Factory Theatre Lab, Toronto, September 1972.

D1751. "Magic Juice" in *Canadian Fiction Magazine*, vol.1, #2/3, Spring/Summer 1971 and in his *Penetration*. Mission City, B.C., Sono Nis, 1972.
"Theatre of the invisible" in which the "environment becomes a metaphor for the unconscious". A child loses all her/his illusions as he/she grows up into a perverted world.
fp: Vancouver Art Gallery, August 1971.

D1752. "Monster" in his *Mystery of the Pig Killer's Daughter*. Seattle, Washington, Angst World Library, 1975.
1 act. 3m/1f.
An absurdist comedy about a man's obsession with storing meat in his house.
fp: (Dramatized reading), Stratford Festival, October 1972.

D1753. "Mystery of the Pig Killer's Daughter" in his *Mystery of the Pig Killer's Daughter*. Seattle, Washington, Angst World Library, 1975.
11 scenes. 4m/3f.
A gothic murder mystery about the disappearance of a pig killer's daughter.
fp: Toronto Free Theatre, Nov. 26, 1975.

D1754. *Penetration*. Toronto, Playwrights Co-op, 1972 and in *Dialogue & Dialectic: A Canadian Anthology of Short Plays*. Alive Theatre Workshop, ed. Guelph, Ont., Alive Press, 1972 and in his *Penetration*. Mission City, B.C., Sono Nis, 1972.
1 act. 2m/1f.
A mysterious woman arrives at the home of two bachelor brothers and subtle, peculiar things begin to happen.
fp: Phoenix Theatre, University of Victoria, December 1969.

D1755. "Time Warp" in *Tuatara*, vol.1, #4, March 1971 and *Time Warp*. Toronto, Playwrights Co-op, 1972 and in his *Penetration*. Mission City, B.C., Sono Nis, 1972.
1 act. 1m/1f.
A man and his wife cannot sleep because the man has recurring nightmares of living human torsos without eyes, ears, or noses.
fp: Chilliwack, B.C., June 1971.

RUSSELL, Ted 1904–1977

D1756. "The Hangashore" in *Baffles of Wind and Tide*. Clyde Rose, ed. Newfoundland, Breakwater, 1976 and in *Transitions I: Short Plays*. Edward Peck, ed. Vancouver, Commcept Publishing, 1978.
1 act. 5m/2f.
A radio play in which Grampa Walcott explains the meaning of "hangashore" by telling the story of the lazy fisherman who stole his neighbour's fishing holes in the ice.
fp: CBC radio "Summer Fallow", Aug. 2, 1954.

D1757. *The Holdin' Ground*. Toronto, McClelland & Stewart, 1972.
1 act. 6m/2f.
A stranger arrives at an "outport" in Newfoundland asking questions about previous inhabitants. Slowly it becomes apparent that the man is the son of a person that once lived there.
fp: CBC radio, "Wednesday Night", July 27, 1955.

RYAN, J. Alexander

D1758. *Parallels*. Toronto, Playwrights Co-op, 1972.
2 acts. 2m/1f. Extras. Chorus.
"A pop opera" about Tom Solomon, a young songwriter, who has died in a freak accident and is now in "purgatory to be judged". Music by Rick Jones.

RYAN, Josephine

D1759. *The Mirrored Countenance*. Ottawa, Ottawa Little Theatre Workshop, #47.
4 scenes. 4m/2f.
Dolly, a London prostitute, leaves poet Francis Thompson after he becomes successful.

RYAN, Oscar

D1760. "Unity" in *Masses*, May-June 1933 and *Unity*. New York, International Labour Defense, n.d. and in *Eight Men Speak and Other Plays from the Canadian Workers' Theatre*. Richard Wright, Robin Endres, eds. Toronto, New Hogtown Press, 1976.
1 act. 8m or f. Extras.
An agitprop play whose message asks the workers to unite in the struggle against the capitalists.
fp: Workers' Experimental Theatre, Hygeria Hall, Toronto, May 1, 1933.

RYAN, Oscar, E. Cecil-Smith, Frank Love and Mildred Goldberg

D1761. *Eight Men Speak*. Toronto, Progressive Arts Club of Canada, 1934 and in *Eight Men Speak and Other Plays from the Canadian Workers' Theatre*. Richard Wright, Robin Endres, eds. Toronto, New Hogtown Press, 1976.
6 acts. 44m/8f. Doubling.
A play about the trial and imprisonment of Tim Buck and his seven comrades who were "especially singled out for persecution" because of their political beliefs.
fp: Toronto Progressive Arts Club, Standard Theatre, Toronto, Dec. 4, 1933.

RYERSON, Stanley

D1762. "War in the East" in *Masses*, March-April 1934 and in *Eight Men Speak and Other Plays from the Canadian Workers' Theatre*. Richard Wright, Robin Endres, eds. Toronto, New Hogtown Press, 1976.
1 act. 12m.
An anti-war, anti-capitalist play in which Japanese soldiers meet and join their enemies, the advancing Chinese Soviets.
p: Workers' Experimental Theatre, Ontario tour, summer 1933.

RYGA, George 1932–

D1763. *Captives of the Faceless Drummer*. Vancouver, Talonbooks, 1971.
2 acts. 5m/2f. Chorus.
Confrontation between kidnapper and victim, the revolutionary and the diplomat. The play deals with the exploitation of the French Canadians by the English, and the exploitation of the poor by the rich.
fp: Vancouver Art Gallery, April 16, 1971.

D1764. *The Ecstasy of Rita Joe*. Vancouver, Talonbooks, 1970 and in *The Demanding Age*. R. Side and R. Greenfield, eds. Toronto, McGraw-Hill, 1970 and in his *The Ecstasy of Rita Joe and Other Plays*. Toronto, New Press, 1971.
2 acts. 6m/5f. Extras.
The gradual destruction of the Indian woman Rita Joe for whom there is no real place in Canadian society is shown.
fp: Playhouse Theatre, Vancouver, Nov. 23, 1967.

D1765. "Grass and Wild Strawberries" in his *The Ecstasy of Rita Joe and Other Plays*. Toronto, New Press, 1971.
3 acts. 9m/4f.
Allan is caught between alternative attitudes, between the disenchanted radicalism of his Uncle Ted and the childish mysticism of his lover, Susan, and the Group. Music by "The Collectors".
fp: Playhouse Theatre, Vancouver, April 10, 1969.

D1766. "Indian" in *Maclean's*, vol.75, #24, Dec. 1, 1962 and in *Tamarack Review*, #36, Summer 1965 and *Indian*. Agincourt, Ont., Book Society, 1967 and in *Performing Arts in Canada*, vol.8, #3, Fall 1971 and in his *The Ecstasy of Rita Joe and Other Plays*. Toronto, New Press, 1971 and in *The Oxford Anthology of Canadian Literature*. Robert Weaver and William Toye, eds. Toronto, Oxford University Press, 1973 and in *Ten Canadian Short Plays*. John Stevens, ed. New York, Dell, 1975 and in *Native Peoples in Canadian Literature*. William and Christine Mowat, eds. Toronto, Macmillan, 1975 and in *Cues and Entrances*. Henry Beissel, ed. Toronto, Gage, 1977 and in *Literature in Canada* volume 2. Douglas Daymond, Leslie Monkman, eds. Toronto, Gage, 1978.
1 act. 3m.
An examination of the deep personal despair of the Indian as a victim of Canadian society in which he has no acknowledged identity.
fp: CBC TV "Quest", Nov. 25, 1962. CBC radio "Late Night Theatre", Montreal, Oct. 18, 1963.

D1767. "Laddie Boy" in *Transitions I: Short Plays*. Edward Peck, ed. Vancouver, Commcept Publishing, 1978.
1 act. 2m/1f.
A wealthy middle-aged man spends a night in a Nova Scotian jail with a bum and the jail's cleaning woman.

D1768. *Nothing But a Man*. Vancouver, New Play Centre, (197-?).
3 acts. 16m/5f/2b.
A wandering man heads west in search of the things previously denied him — love, friendship, and a home.

D1769. "Paracelsus" in *Canadian Theatre Review*, #4, Fall, 1974.
2 acts. 3m/1f. 20 Extras.
A history of the career of Paracelsus, the Renaissance healer and practitioner of black arts. The motivations and emotions behind his quest for ultimate healing power are juxtaposed with those of two contemporary physicians who discuss the medical profession.

D1770. *Ploughmen of the Glacier*. Vancouver, Talonbooks, 1977.
2 acts. 3m.
Philosophical questions are the focus of this vaguely *Godot*-like play in which an old prospector and an old newspaperman with opposing life styles argue about how life should be lived.
fp: Western Canada Theatre Co., Kamloops, B.C., April 1976. CBC radio, Nov. 19, 1977.

D1771. *Seven Hours to Sundown*. Vancouver, Talonbooks, 1977.
3 acts. 6m/2f.
This play reveals the viciousness and damage that result from small town bigotry and political intrigue. A leather craftsman whose non-conformist teaching career was ended by an intolerant school board chairman, now the town's mayor, becomes a political football, as does the mayor himself, when two local power brokers pursue their own ambitions.
fp: Theatre Network, University of Alberta, Edmonton, May 27, 1976.

D1772. *Sunrise on Sarah*. Vancouver, Talonbooks, 1973.
2 acts. 8m/6f. Doubling.
Sarah cannot come to terms with herself. Confronted by the Man, who is at times the doctor and at times an insensitive, possessive and all-consuming force, Sarah's life unfolds.
fp: Banff School of Fine Arts, July 29, 1972.

SABLOFF, Robert

D1773. "The Critics" in *Performing Arts in Canada*, vol.3, #1, Fall 1964.
1 act. 6m.
A satirical look at literary critics trying to review the Bible.

SADRO, Marie E.

D1774. *Judith of Bethulia*. Nelson, B.C., Author, 1975.
4 acts. 12m/4f. Extras.
A dramatic recreation of the story of Judith of the Old Testament.

SAGO, Mitch 1914–

D1775. *Adam's Sons.* By Hannah Polowy and Mitch Sago. Toronto, Ukrainian Canadian, 1969.
2 acts. 7m/5f. Extras.
"Based on Olga Kobylyanska's *Zemlya* (Land)."
The land-hungry younger son Sava kills his brother in order to inherit all his father's property.
fp: Theatre 100, Playhouse Theatre, Winnipeg, Feb. 1971.

D1776. "The Builders" in *The Ukrainian Canadian*, Sept. 1974.
5 scenes. Multiple roles. Chorus.
The narration to a series of scenes celebrating the contribution of progressive immigrants, labour and youth in the 100 year history of Winnipeg.
fp: Festival Winnipeg 100, Winnipeg, May 1974.

D1777. "Little Taras" in *The Ukrainian Canadian,* March 1973.
1 act. 2m.
Scenes "based on the children's storybook by Hannah Polowy" about the Ukrainian poet and painter Taras Shevchenko.
fp: Theatre 80, Heritage 73 Festival, Student Union Building Theatre, University of Alberta, Edmonton, May 6, 1973.

D1778. "The Pencil" in *The Ukrainian Canadian,* July/August 1973.
1 act. 2m/1f/2b. Extras.
"Based on the autobiographical short story by Ivan Franko" about a Ukrainian schoolboy who finds another boy's pencil.

D1779. "The Signature" in *The Ukrainian Canadian,* Feb. 1974.
1 act. 6m/2f.
"Based on the short story by Wasyl Stefanyk" about a young girl who teaches four peasants to write their name.

D1780. "The Stone Cross" in *The Ukrainian Canadian,* July/August 1971.
4 scenes. Multiple roles. Chorus.
An adaptation of the short story by Wasyl Stefanyk and three additional scenes dramatizing 80 years of Ukrainian immigration to Canada.
fp: Festival 80, Jubilee Auditorium, Edmonton, May 23, 1971.

SAILBAD SINNER, PLAYWRIGHT (pseud.)

D1781. "One Act Is Plenty" in *Acta Victoriana,* vol.53, #3, Dec. 1928.
1 act. 1m/2f.
A satire of the "just healthful, wholesome play".

ST. PIERRE, Paul 1923–

D1782. "The Education of Phyllistine" in *Invitation to Drama.* Andrew A. Orr, ed. Toronto, Macmillan, 1967.
1 act. 5m/4f. Extras.
A TV drama. A young West Coast Indian girl is brought to school in town resulting in conflict between red and white society.
fp: CBC TV "Cariboo Country", March 10, 1964.

D1783. *How to Run the Country.* Vancouver, New Play Centre, (197-?).
3 acts. 10m/4f. Extras.
Organizers for the Liberal Party choose a man from Chilcotin with Socred sympathies to run in an important provincial election.
fp: Playhouse, Vancouver, 1966–67.

D1784. *Sister Balonika.* Agincourt, Ont., Book Society, 1973.
2 acts. 5m/6f. Extras.
A TV drama. Sister Veronica arrives at the Dunjek Ridge school to teach the Indian students. She is young and permissive and does not adhere to the strict schedule established by the Superior with tragic results.
fp: CBC TV, Vancouver, 1969.

D1785. "The Strong People" in *Voice and Vision.* Jack Hodgins, William H. New, eds. Toronto, McClelland & Stewart, 1972.
1 act. 9m/2f. Extras.
A TV drama about a rancher in northern B.C. who is married to both an Indian woman and an English bride. Forced by his Indian son, he raises two families side by side.

SAISSELIN, Remy G.

D1786. "A Language Game in Limbo" in *Queen's Quarterly,* vol.69, #4, Winter 1963.
1 act. 4m.
Hume, Voltaire and Fontenelle converse on the nature of philosophy and conclude that it is the very imprecision of language which permits thought.

SALT, Jim

D1787. "The Bird" in *Edge,* #3, Autumn 1964.
1 act. 6m.
An allegorical verse play. Phoroneus the Rich Man spends his life searching for the identity of an extraordinary bird once stoned by his gardener.

D1788. "The Worm" in *Edge,* #1, Autumn 1963.
1 act. 4m/1f. Chorus.
A stylized verse play in which Yehl the transformer sets loose the "worm of illiteracy" in the city of Edmonton where it eats everything made of paper.

SALUTIN, Rick 1942–

D1789. *Les Canadiens.* Vancouver, Talonbooks, 1977.
2 acts. Multiple roles. Doubling.
An examination of the significance of the legendary Canadiens hockey team as it relates to hockey and to intellectual and social life in Quebec and Canada. Written with the assistance of Ken Dryden.
fp: Centaur Theatre, Montreal, Feb. 10, 1977.

D1790. "1837: The Farmers' Revolt" in *Canadian Theatre Review,* #6, Spring 1975 and *1837.* Toronto, James Lorimer, 1976.
2 acts. Multiple roles. Doubling.
A collective creation of the historical events of 1837 sharing humorous and dramatic looks at the Canada of the time, the events leading to the revolt and the revolt itself.
fp: Theatre Passe Muraille, Toronto, Jan. 1972; revised version, June 7, 1974.

SALVERSON George 1916–

D1791. "Hero at Hatch's Mill" in *Invitation to Drama*. (Revised edition). Andrew A. Orr, ed. Toronto, Macmillan, 1967.
4 acts. 8m/2f. Extras.
A thief on the run inadvertently helps Dr. Blount, Mackenzie's lieutenant in the Rebellion of 1837, to escape pursuing militiamen.
fp: CBC TV.

D1792. "You Are Not Alone" in *Ways of Mankind*. W.R. Goldschmidt, ed. Boston, Beacon Press, 1954.
1 act. 8m/3f.
A radio play. Gregarious proves to Solo that no human being is alone. He always carries with him the attitudes of the social groups which have shaped his personality and values.

SAMUELS, Arthur

D1793. *The Whistler in the Whirlwind*. Montreal, Factum, 1967.
2 acts. 3m/4f.
A study of an unconventional relationship between the libertarian Cully and Rita.
fp: Western Quebec Region Festival, 1967.

SANDIFORD, Betti Primrose

D1794. "The Bone Spoon" in *Six Canadian Plays*. Herman Voaden, ed. Toronto, Copp Clark, 1930.
1 act. 5m/3f.
A division separates "different happenings in a setting which has been unchanged through the centuries". Gaston Souflot dies to allow his comrades to escape from the Indians and young Prudence relives her past.

D1795. "Crows" in *The Canadian Magazine,* vol.58, #5, March 1922.
1 act. 2m/1f/1b.
A young widow schemes to put her blind father-in-law in a "home" but is thwarted by her son.
fp: Rosedale Community Club, Toronto, 1923.

SAROSSY, Via

D1796. "Dinner Party" in *Women Write for Theatre* vol.1. Toronto, Playwrights Co-op, 1976.
1 act. 3m/3f.
A farce in which Mama Griselda attempts a last stand against technology.

SAYWELL, John T.

D1797. *Success of a Mission*. See **KOCH, Eric**.

SCHLICK, Karen

D1798. *The Pearl Without Price.* Halifax, Dramatists Co-op, 1977.
1 act. 10 puppets.
A rod and shadow puppet play for adults about a boy and a dragon who search for the pearl of wisdom.
fp: Gargoyle Puppet Troupe, Halifax.

D1799. *The Philosopher's Stone.* Halifax, Dramatists Co-op, 1977.
1 act. 21 puppets.
A wood-cutter's son goes in search of a magic stone that will free an old man's daughter from the ogre's spell.
fp: Gargoyle Puppet Troupe, Halifax.

SCHULL, Joseph 1910–

D1800. "The Ladies" in *Willison's Monthly,* vol.4, #2, July 1928.
1 act. 2m/2f.
A homesteader's wife and Dynamite Jane convince him that he shouldn't abandon his farm and return to school teaching.

D1801. "The Land of Ephranor" in *Nobody Waved Good-bye and Other Plays.* Herman Voaden, ed. Toronto, Macmillan, 1966.
1 act. 5m/1f. Extras.
A young lord attempts to cure the ills of mankind only to find the task foolish and hopeless.
fp: CBC radio "Stage", 1966.

D1802. "Pardon" in *Willison's Monthly,* vol.4, #6, Nov. 1928.
1 act. 3m. Extras.
A murderer arranges for the apprehension of his accomplice.

D1803. "The Vice President" in *A Collection of Canadian Plays* vol.3. Rolf Kalman, ed. Toronto, Simon & Pierre, 1974.
Many scenes. 9m/3f. Extras.
Conflict results when an English Canadian company builds a new French Canadian plant and promotes Jean-Pierre Allard to the position of the first French Canadian vice president.
fp: CBC radio.

SCHWARZ, Ernest 1934– and Studio Lab Theatre

D1804. *Pig Tales.* Toronto, Playwrights Co-op, 1973.
1 act. 3m/2f.
A children's play. The big bad wolf attempts to eat two little piglets only to be foiled by Miss Penelope Pickles who is secretly Wonder Pig.
fp: Studio Lab Theatre, Toronto, July 1971.

SCOTT, Duncan Campbell 1862–1947

D1805. "The Flight" in his *Beauty and Life.* Toronto, McClelland & Stewart, 1921 and in *The Poems of Duncan Campbell Scott.* Toronto, McClelland & Stewart, 1926.
1 act. 1m/1f.
Two lovers are on a narrow cliff during a thunderstorm. He allays her fears by telling her that love can conquer death.

D1806. "A Mystery Play" in his *Lundy's Lane and Other Poems.* New York, Doran, 1916 and in *The Poems of Duncan Campbell Scott.* Toronto, McClelland & Stewart, 1926.
1 act. 6m/1b.
A poor man and his son bravely meet death with thoughts of heaven to comfort them.

D1807. "Pierre" in *Canadian Plays from Hart House Theatre* vol.1. Vincent Massey, ed. Toronto, Macmillan, 1926.
1 act. 2m/8f. Extras.
On New Year's Eve, Pierre Durocher returns to his family after 11 years of wandering. He is the same "bad egg" as ever.
fp: Hart House Theatre, Toronto, April 5, 1921.

D1808. "Prologue" in *The Poems of Duncan Campbell Scott.* Toronto, McClelland & Stewart, 1926.
1 act. 2f.
A dedication for the opening of a new playhouse. The Spirit of Drama wanders poor and homeless until the Spirit of the House offers her a home.
fp: The Little Theatre, Ottawa, Jan. 18, 1923.

D1809. *Prologue.* Ottawa, Modern Press, 1928.
1 scene. 1f.
A brief monologue about the purpose of the theatre "spoken by Dorothy White at the opening of The Little Theatre, Ottawa, Jan. 4, 1928".

D1810. "Spirit and Flesh" in *The Poems of Duncan Campbell Scott.* Toronto, McClelland & Stewart, 1926.
1 act. 1m/1f.
A woman forsakes her lover in her pursuit of pleasure and too late realizes the error of her ways.

D1811. "Variations on a Seventeenth Century Theme: Part Five" in his *Beauty and Life.* Toronto, McClelland & Stewart, 1921 and in *The Poems of Duncan Campbell Scott.* Toronto, McClelland & Stewart, 1926.
1 act. 2m/1f.
A playwright commits suicide following the successful opening of his new play because he imagines the leading lady has rejected his love.

SCOTT, Mrs. Duncan Campbell. See AYLEN, Elise.

SCOTT, Rev. Frederick George 1861–1944

D1812. *The Key of Life.* Quebec, Dussault, 1907 and n.p., n.p., 1913 and Quebec, n.p., 1917 and n.p., n.p., 1927.
5 scenes. 12m/9f. Extras.
"A Mystery Play". A retelling of the Christmas story with the addition of an allegorical scene in which Death and the Seven Deadly Sins are vanquished by God's love of man.

SCOTT, Munroe 1927–

D1813. "Wu-feng" in *A Collection of Canadian Plays* vol.1. Rolf Kalman, ed. Toronto, Simon & Pierre, 1971.
2 acts. 11m/2f. Extras.
Based on the legendary exploits of the Formosan folk hero. As governor of the Mount Ali tribe, Wu-feng maintains a delicate balance between return to barbarism and imperial suppression from Peking.
fp: St. Lawrence Centre, Toronto, Oct. 22, 1974.

SCUDAMORE, H.B., R.W. Downie, W.L. McGeary and H.R. Dillon

D1814. "The P.B.I. or Mademoiselle of Bully Grenay" in *The Canadian Forum*, vol.1, #12, vol.2, #13, #14, #15, Sept., Oct., Nov., Dec. 1921.
4 acts. 14m/f.
A comedy about the Canadians in the trenches in 1918. The 16th Platoon of the "Poor Bloody Infantry" is placed under a new lieutenant.
fp: Hart House Theatre, Toronto, March 10, 1920.

SCULLY, E.C.

D1815. *A Pageant of Canadian History.* See **CALLAN, J.B.**

SEAMAN, Barbara

D1816. *It Happened Only Yesterday.* Toronto, Religion & Theatre Council, (196-?).
1 act. 4m/2f.
The life and death of Christ are made relevant to modern man and the 20th century church.

SELLAR, Robert 1841–1919

D1817. *The Tragedy of Wallace.* Huntingdon, P.Q., Gleaner Book, 1919.
4 acts. 13m/4f. Extras.
Wallace, leader of the Scots, is captured, tried and executed by the invading English.

SERANUS (pseud.) See HARRISON, Susie Frances Riley.

SERVANT, Catherine H.

D1818. "Escape" in *Acadia Athenaeum,* vol.57, #7, October 1931.
1 scene. 1m/1f.
After losing one daughter in an automobile accident, a father overprotects his younger daughter, but life must go on.

D1819. "For All Eternity" in *Acadia Athenaeum,* vol.56, #7, May 1930.
1 scene. 1m/1f.
Francesca and Paolo, two characters from Dante's *Divine Comedy,* discover in eternity that they no longer love each other.

SETON, Ernest Thompson 1860–1946

D1820. *The Wild Animal Play for Children.* New York, Doubleday, 1900 and Toronto, Morang, 1901.
1 act. 1f/10b/6g.
The animals of the forest are being killed off by the evil sportsman until the Angel of the Wild Things rids the woods of the danger.

SEYMOUR, Emma Carter

D1821. *Final Rehearsal.* Niagara Falls, Ont., Frontier Printing, 1910.
1 act. 2m/1f.
A "musical sketch". Three actors rehearse their musical numbers before a mock audience and discuss the next evening's performance.
fp: Anglican Club of Niagara Falls, Ont., Dec. 19, 1909.

SHAND, Beatrice

D1822. "The Blue Willow Plate" in *Canadian School Plays* series 1. E.M. Jones, ed. Toronto, Ryerson, 1948.
1 act. 5m/2f.
A parody of traditional Chinese stage methods. Two lovers, though victims of a vengeful murder, live happily in their reincarnation as doves.

D1823. "The Gift of the Nile" in *Sketches and Plays.* Toronto, National Girls' Work Board, Religious Education Council of Canada, (192-?).
1 act. 3f. Extras.
A dramatization of the Biblical story of Moses' adoption by the Pharaoh's daughter.
fp: Canadian Girls In Training camps.

D1824. "Lost — a Temper!" in *Nunny Bag 1.* Toronto, Gage, 1962.
2 acts. 4m/7f. Extras.
"A fairy fantasy" for children. Little Princess Primrose has lost her temper but it is restored by a peddler and the Fairy Queen's magic charm.

D1825. "Strong Wind's Choice" in *Sketches and Plays.* Toronto, National Girls' Work Board, Religious Education Council of Canada, (192-?).
1 act. 1m/4f.
"Adapted from the Canadian folk tale 'The Indian Cinderella' ." An Indian brave chooses a bride.
fp: Canadian Girls In Training camps.

SHARMAN, Abbie Lyon 1872–

D1826. *A Somersault to Love.* Toronto, Macmillan, 1926.
1 act. 3m/7f.
Jade Maiden and Tu Fast fall in love in this "comedy of changing manners in China".
fp: Ottawa, Nov. 14, 1925.

SHARP, Edith Lambert

D1827. "The Little People of Crazy Mountain" in *Treats and Treasures.* John McInnes, ed. Toronto, Thomas Nelson, 1964.
1 act. 1m/3b/1g. Chorus.
A children's play. Three Indian children recover food stolen by the angry Dwarf People.

SHAW, Beatrice M. Hay

D1828. "The Passing Hours" in *Echoes,* March 1925.
1 act. 5m/3f. Extras.
While on a visit to Annapolis Royal, the Duke of Kent turns the head of a flirtatious young woman engaged to marry a local gentleman.

SHAY, Timothy

D1829. "The Song of James and John" in *Nebula,* #5, 1977.
1 act. 3m/2f.
A poetic account of the escape, recapture and hanging of John and James Young for the murder of Abel McDonald of Haldimand County in 1875.

SHEIN, Brian 1947–

D1830. *Cowboy Island.* Toronto, Playwrights Co-op, 1972 and in his *Theatrical Exhibitions.* Vancouver, Pulp Press, 1975 and in *Five Canadian Plays.* Toronto, Playwrights Co-op, 1978.
13 scenes. 2m/1f.
A ritual set around the betrayal of Billy the Kid by Paulita Maxwell and his subsequent shooting by Pat Garrett.
fp: Vancouver Art Gallery, Sept. 1972.

D1831. "An Entertainment at the Cafe Terminus" in his *Theatrical Exhibitions.* Vancouver, Pulp Press, 1975.
1 act. 3m/1f. Doubling.
A script intended for radio and stage production about the trial of Emile Henry accused of exploding two bombs in a crowded nightclub and a police station.
fp: CBC radio, Feb. 1, 1975.

D1832. "Ground Zero" in his *Theatrical Exhibitions.* Vancouver, Pulp Press, 1975.
1 act. 4m/1f.
A radio play adapted from a total theatre science fiction stage play in which a man seeks refuge at Salutex, a shelter compound for selected members.
fp: CBC radio, Feb. 16, 1975.

D1833. "Kafka" in *Prism International,* vol.7, #3, Spring 1968 and in his *Theatrical Exhibitions.* Vancouver, Pulp Press, 1975.
1 act. 4m/2f.
"A ritual" which makes use of iambic pentameter verse, chant and computer programming.
fp: Frederic Wood Theatre, University of British Columbia, Dec. 7, 1967.

D1834. "Rex Morgan, M.D." in his *Theatrical Exhibitions*. Vancouver, Pulp Press, 1975.
1 act. 1m/1f.
A satire of the comic serial of the same name emphasizing the sameness of dialogue and characters of the strip.
fp: Vancouver Art Gallery, May 12, 1972.

SHIP, Reuben 1915–

D1835. *The Investigator*. London, Sidgwick and Jackson, 1956.
22m/1f. Extras. Doubling.
A radio play. "A narrative in dialogue" commenting satirically on the McCarthy investigations of the 1950's.
fp: CBC radio "Stage", May 30, 1954.

SHIRLEY, Robert

D1836. *Alpha and Omega*. Ottawa, Ottawa Little Theatre Workshop, #36.
1 act. 3m.
The dreams of two old men are shattered by a callous and money-hungry intruder.

SHOVELLER, Brock 1935–

D1837. "Westbound 12:01" in *A Collection of Canadian Plays* vol.2. Rolf Kalman, ed. Toronto, Simon & Pierre, 1973.
2 acts. 8m/1f/1g.
The paranoid stationmaster of a train depot which is no longer used is plagued by cryptic telegraph messages and two men trying to deliver an empty coffin.
fp: St. Lawrence Centre, Toronto, April 15, 1971.

SIDE, Ronald K.

D1838. "A Christmas Carol" in his *Entertainment for All*. Toronto, Macmillan, 1968.
1 act. 10m/4f/2b. Extras.
An adaptation of the story by Charles Dickens which can be played by children. Ebenezer Scrooge repents.

D1839. "D'Artagnan" in his *Entertainment for All*. Toronto, Macmillan, 1968.
2 acts. 10m/1f. Extras.
"A musical play", an adaptation of an episode in Dumas' novel in which d'Artagnan meets to duel with the three Musketeers and ends in league with them. Music by Ralph Greenfield.

D1840. "Oliver Twist" in his *Entertainment for All*. Toronto, Macmillan, 1968.
1 act. 6m/5f/3b.
An adaptation of the novel by Charles Dickens which can be performed by children.

D1841. "Robin Hood" in his *Entertainment for All*. Toronto, Macmillan, 1968.
1 act. 10m/1f. Extras.
The play presents the initial meeting of Robin Hood, Little John and Friar Tuck, and several incidents in which the Merry Men of Sherwood outwit the Sheriff of Nottingham.

SIMARD, André 1949–

D1842. "Waiting for Gaudreault", Henry Beissel, Arlette Franciere, trans., in *A Collection of Canadian Plays* vol.5. Rolf Kalman, ed. Toronto, Simon & Pierre, 1978.
1 act. 4m.
A translation of his *En Attendant Gaudreault*. A group of house painters renovating the facade of a Canada Manpower office discuss working conditions and the weariness of their lives.

SIMINOVITCH, Elinore 1922–

D1843. *Big X, Little Y*. Toronto, Playwrights Co-op, 1975.
1 act. 4m/4f. Doubling.
Women and their roles as seen through nursery rhymes, songs, dance, games and typical situations: love, marriage, childbirth, child-rearing, discrimination in politics and employment.
fp: Playwrights Workshop Theatre, Montreal, Feb. 1974.

D1844. *Tomorrow and Tomorrow*. Toronto, Playwrights Co-op, 1972.
2 acts. 1m/3f.
A married woman experiences schizophrenic fantasies while her husband is at work.
fp: Theatre Aquarius, Ottawa, July 1972.

SIMONS, Beverley 1938–

D1845. *Crabdance*. Vancouver, In Press, 1969 and (revised edition) Vancouver, Talonbooks, 1972.
2 acts. 3m/1f. Extras.
An absurdist comedy in which the middle-aged Sadie Goldman occupies herself with the ritual of salesmen's visits and consumer sexuality.
fp: A Contemporary Theatre, Seattle, Washington, Sept. 16, 1969.

D1846. "The Crusader" in her *Preparing*. Vancouver, Talonbooks, 1975.
1 act. 2m/1f.
A soldier brutally rapes and dismembers a woman only to have the same done to him by the Crusader, a masked dancer representing the forces of freedom.

D1847. *The Elephant and the Jewish Question*. Vancouver, New Play Centre, (197-?).
3 acts. 7m/5f.
A young Jewish man decides to break with tradition and leave his family in order to find himself.
fp: Vancouver Little Theatre, 1968.

D1848. *Green Lawn Rest Home*. Toronto, Playwrights Co-op, 1973 and in her *Preparing*. Vancouver, Talonbooks, 1975.
1 act. 1m/2f. Extras.
Three old people in a "rest home" on the prairies discover that the serenity of old age is a myth. Each finds, in his own way, death.
fp: Savage God, Simon Fraser University, Burnaby, B.C., 1969.

D1849. "Leela Means to Play" in *Canadian Theatre Review*, #9, Winter 1976.
2 acts. 9m/3f.
In this unorthodox comedy, the title is taken from a Sanskrit word, the characters try to adapt to a new order, relearning how to play the game of life.

D1850. "Preparing" in *The Capilano Review*, #6, Fall 1974 and in her *Preparing*. Vancouver, Talonbooks, 1975.
1 act. 1f.
Jeannie lives in a constant state of preparation: birth, adolescence, marriage, giving birth, nervous breakdown, politics, business, society matron, death.
fp: Tamahnous, Simon Fraser University Theatre, Burnaby, B.C., Sept. 12, 1973.

D1851. "Prologue" in her *Preparing*. Vancouver, Talonbooks, 1975 and in *Transitions I: Short Plays*. Edward Peck, ed. Vancouver, Commcept Publishing, 1978.
1 act. 1m/2f.
A satiric apologia for the playwright.

D1852. "Triangle" in her *Preparing*. Vancouver, Talonbooks, 1975.
1 act. 3m or f.
An actor is accosted with a bombardment of questions by two others representing left-wing and right-wing views. The confused victim is killed in the struggle.

D1853. "Twisted Roots" by Beverley Rosen in *First Flowering, A Selection of Prose and Poetry by the Youth of Canada*. Anthony Frisch, ed. Toronto, Kingswood House, 1956.
1 act. 2m.
A verse drama. A bitter farmer resents and abuses his sister's half-wit son.

SINCLAIR, Lister Shedden 1921–

D1854. "All About Emily" in *A Play on Words and Other Radio Plays*. Toronto, Dent, 1948 and in *A Theatre Happening*. Sheila Maurer, Gordon McLeod, eds. Toronto, Nelson, 1968.
1 act. 12m/3f.
The story of Emily, the goose that laid the golden egg, which shows that people are never very grateful for what they have.
fp: CBC radio "Stage", Feb. 25, 1945.

D1855. "All the World's a Stage" in *Ways of Mankind*. W.R. Goldschmidt, ed. Boston, Beacon Press, 1954.
1 act. 8m/2f. Extras.
A radio play. HERE and THERE take examples from various parts of the world to show the ways in which status and role differ in each society.

D1856. "Any Woman Is a Lady. A Study in American Manners" in *Democracy in America*. George Probst, ed. New York, National Educational Television and Radio Center, 1962.
1 act. 9m/5f.
A radio play. Beaumont and Tocqueville, attending social functions, are impressed by the attitude of respect and deference towards women, regardless of their social position.
fp: NBC radio, Jan. 17, 1962. CBC radio, Jan. 18, 1962.

D1857. "The Aristocrats of Democracy. A Study in American Law and Lawyers" by Lister Sinclair and George E. Probst in *Democracy in America*. George Probst, ed. New York, National Educational Television and Radio Center, 1962.
1 act. 11m.
A radio play. Tocqueville likens the authority and influence of lawyers in American political life to that of a conservative aristocracy.
fp: NBC radio, Jan. 17, 1962. CBC radio, Jan. 18, 1962.

D1858. "The Ark of Civilization. A Study in American Character" by Lister Sinclair and George E. Probst in *Democracy in America*. George Probst, ed. New York, National Educational Television and Radio Center, 1962.
1 act. 14m/1f.
Tocqueville and Beaumont journey through the forests of Michigan territory to the frontier and realize that "the great fact of America is the presence of the wilderness — the frontier".
fp: NBC radio, Jan. 17, 1962. CBC radio, Jan. 18, 1962.

D1859. "The Blood Is Strong" in *A Play on Words and Other Radio Plays*. Toronto, Dent, 1948.
1 act. 6m/2f.
Alan MacDonald thinks back on his life with his family from the time they emigrated to Canada from Scotland when the English expropriated their land in the early 1800s.
fp: CBC radio "This Is Our Canada", Feb. 2, 1945.

D1860. *The Blood Is Strong*. Agincourt, Ont., Book Society, 1956.
3 acts. 7m/4f.
"A drama of early Scottish settlement in Cape Breton" showing the various degrees with which members of a family of Highland immigrants adapt to the "new country".
fp: CBC TV "General Motors Theatre", Jan. 25, 1955.

D1861. "But I Know What I Like" in *Ways of Mankind*. W.R. Goldschmidt, ed. Boston, Beacon Press, 1954.
1 act. 13m/1f. Extras.
A radio play. HERE and THERE conduct a tour of the world and show the importance of art to society.

D1862. "The Case Against Cancer" in *A Play on Words and Other Radio Plays*. Toronto, Dent, 1948.
1 act. 9m/4f.
A short play explaining the treatment of cancer and advising regular check-ups.
fp: CBC radio, April 3, 1946.

D1863. "The Case of the Sea Lion Flippers" in *Ways of Mankind*. W.R. Goldschmidt, ed. Boston, Beacon Press, 1954.
1 act. 4m/2f. Extras.
A radio play. A Yurok Indian legend (Northern California) which illustrates their belief that to live a correct life one must place material wealth before all else.

D1864. "The Cement of Democracy. A Study in American Religion" in *Democracy in America*. George Probst, ed. New York, National Educational Television and Radio Center, 1962.
1 act. 10m/1f.
A radio play. Tocqueville and Beaumont examine the nature of religious tolerance in America.
fp: NBC radio, Jan. 17, 1962. CBC radio, Jan. 18, 1962.

D1865. "The Chief Instrument of Freedom. A Study of the American Press" in *Democracy in America*. George Probst, ed. New York, National Educational Television and Radio Center, 1962.
1 act. 11m.
A radio play. Beaumont and Tocqueville observe the operation of the American free press.
fp: NBC radio, Jan. 17, 1962. CBC radio, Jan. 18, 1962.

D1866. "The Cold Water Army. A Study in American Progress" in *Democracy in America*. George Probst, ed. New York, National Educational Television and Radio Center, 1962.
1 act. 21m.
A radio play. Beaumont and Tocqueville are astonished at the number and the power of voluntary associations in America.
fp: NBC radio, Jan. 17, 1962. CBC radio, Jan. 18, 1962.

D1867. "Common Sense and Moonshine. A Study in American Education" in *Democracy in America*. George Probst, ed. New York, National Educational Television and Radio Center, 1962.
1 act. 13m.
A radio play. Intrigued by the success of public schooling, Beaumont and Tocqueville evaluate the condition of American education.
fp: NBC radio, Jan. 17, 1962. CBC radio, Jan. 18, 1962.

D1868. "Day of Victory" in *A Play on Words and Other Radio Plays*. Toronto, Dent, 1948.
1 act. 7m/3f.
Examines what people should and shouldn't do after they've won a war.
fp: CBC radio, May 8, 1945.

D1869. "Epitaph on a War of Liberation" in *A Play on Words and Other Radio Plays*. Toronto, Dent, 1948.
1 act. 1m.
A voice speaks to the god of war, Mars, giving an epitaph for W.W.II.
fp: CBC radio "Stage 46", Jan. 13, 1946.

D1870. "The Faithful Heart" in *A Play on Words and Other Radio Plays*. Toronto, Dent, 1948.
1 act. 6m/3f.
The story of the life of Sebastian Bach told by members of his family.
fp: CBC radio "Stage 46", Dec. 16, 1945.

D1871. "Final Chorus From 'Ill-Met By Moonlight' " in *Canadian Poetry Magazine*, vol.11, #1, Sept. 1947.
1 scene. Chorus.
A brief excerpt from the radio drama in which the chorus mourns the death of the hero.
fp: CBC radio "Stage", 1947.

D1872. "The Fourth of July in Albany, 1831. A Study in American Independence" in *Democracy in America*. George Probst, ed. New York, National Educational Television and Radio Center, 1962.
1 act. 9m. Extras.
A radio play. The French observers are honoured with a request to join the Independence Day Parade.
fp: NBC radio, Jan. 17, 1962. CBC radio, Jan. 18, 1962.

D1873. "The Governor in the Boarding House. A Study in American Equality" in *Democracy in America.* George Probst, ed. New York, National Educational Television and Radio Center, 1962.
1 act. 8m/8f. Extras.
A radio play. Tocqueville and Beaumont receive the hospitality of the Governor of New York, resident in a boarding house.
fp: NBC radio, Jan. 17, 1962. CBC radio, Jan. 18, 1962.

D1874. "The Happy Republic. A Study in American Values" by Lister Sinclair and George E. Probst in *Democracy in America.* George Probst, ed. New York, National Educational Television and Radio Center, 1962.
1 act. 9m/2f.
A radio play. At a farewell gathering, Tocqueville, Beaumont and their American friends discuss the meaning of democracy, its advantages and disadvantages and recollect images of America.
fp: NBC radio, Jan. 17, 1962. CBC radio, Jan. 18, 1962.

D1875. "The Heavenly Prison. A Study in American Reform" in *Democracy in America.* George Probst, ed. New York, National Educational Television and Radio Center, 1962.
1 act. 9m.
The French observers discuss the theoretical basis of the American approach to the reformation of criminals and its consequences in practice.
fp: NBC radio, Jan. 17, 1962. CBC radio, Jan. 18, 1962.

D1876. "Legend of the Long House" in *Ways of Mankind.* W.R. Goldschmidt, ed. Boston Beacon Press, 1954.
1 act. 6m/1f. Extras.
A radio play. An Iroquois legend about the beginnings of their confederation through the work of two heroes, Dekanawida and Hiawatha.

D1877. "Museum of Man" in *Ways of Mankind.* W.R. Goldschmidt, ed. Boston, Beacon Press, 1954.
1 act. 1m.
A radio play. An analysis of man, his history, his needs, fears, ethics and pleasures through the metaphor of a museum tour.

D1878. "The New Canada" in *A Play on Words and Other Radio Plays.* Toronto, Dent, 1948.
1 act. Multiple roles.
The story of what Canada is really like, designed to explode American myths about Canada.
fp: CBC radio, March 7, 1946.

D1879. "No Scandal in Spain" in *A Play on Words and Other Radio Plays.* Toronto, Dent, 1948.
1 act. 1m.
A Spanish soldier is locked in a room with a gun and told he should kill himself in order to avoid a scandal over what he has said about the government.
fp: CBC radio, June 6, 1945.

D1880. "Oedipus the King" in *A Play on Words and Other Radio Plays.* Toronto, Dent, 1948.
1 act. 9m/1f.
An adaptation of Sophocles' play.
fp: CBC radio "Stage 47", Oct. 20, 1946.

D1881. "A Play on Words" in *A Play on Words and Other Radio Plays*. Toronto, Dent, 1948.
1 act. 10m/3f.
Sinclair's ideas on how language came to be.
fp: CBC radio "Stage 45", Nov. 12, 1944.

D1882. "Return to Colonus" in *Canadian Anthology*. C.F. Klinck, R.E. Watters, eds. Toronto, Gage, 1955.
1 act. 7m/2f.
A radio play. A literary treatment, modelled on the Greek tragedies, of the human consequences of atomic research.
fp: CBC radio, Toronto, Feb. 21, 1954.

D1883. *Socrates*. Montreal, Author, 1952 (mimeographed) and Agincourt, Ont., Book Society, 1957.
3 acts. 23m/5f. Extras.
When the oracle names Socrates the wisest man in the world, the Athenians listen to him with increased respect. Government officials conspire to silence him by falsely convicting him of sedition.
fp: CBC radio "Stage", Feb. 16, 1947. Jupiter Theatre at the Royal Ontario Museum Theatre, Toronto, Feb. 1952. CBC TV "Folio", May 29, 1958.

D1884. "These Precious Premises. A Study in Political Optimism" in *Democracy in America*. George Probst, ed. New York, National Educational Television and Radio Center, 1962.
1 act. 6m.
A radio play. Twenty years after his return to France, Tocqueville and the other members of the French legislature are imprisoned by Louis Napoleon in a popular move.
fp: NBC radio, Jan. 17, 1962. CBC radio, Jan. 18, 1962.

D1885. "The Tyranny of the Majority. A Study in American Freedom" in *Democracy in America*. George Probst, ed. New York, National Educational Television and Radio Center, 1962.
1 act. 18m.
A radio play. Beaumont and Tocqueville question the American faith in public opinion.
fp: NBC radio Jan. 17, 1962. CBC radio, Jan. 18, 1962.

D1886. "We All Hate Toronto" in *A Play on Words and Other Radio Plays*. Toronto, Dent, 1948 and in *A Treasury of Canadian Humour*. Robert Thomas Allen, ed. Toronto, McClelland & Stewart, 1967.
1 act. 9m/2f.
Charlie goes to Toronto and discovers that it is a major unifying influence in Canada because everybody hates Toronto.
fp: CBC radio "Panorama", Jan. 17, 1946.

D1887. "When Greek Meets Greek" in *Ways of Mankind*. W.R. Goldschmidt, ed. Boston, Beacon Press, 1954.
1 act. 14m/2f.
A radio play. The contrasting life styles and ideologies of the Athenians and the Spartans of the 5th century B.C. are shown.

D1888. "Where Could I Be Better Off? A Study in Jacksonian America" in *Democracy in America*. George Probst, ed. New York, National Educational Television and Radio Center, 1962.
1 act. 26m/6f/1g.
A radio play. Desiring to "make out the image of Democracy itself ", Beaumont and Tocqueville determine to investigate the American experiment in New York City in 1831.
fp: NBC radio, Jan. 17, 1962. CBC radio, Jan. 18, 1962.

D1889. "A Word in Your Ear" in *Ways of Mankind*. W.R. Goldschmidt, ed. Boston, Beacon Press, 1954 and in *The Best Short Plays of 1953-54*. M. Mayorga, ed. New York, Dodd, Mead, 1954.
1 act. 23m/8f.
A radio play. HERE and THERE discuss the languages of the world with their peculiar differences and the relationships of different societies to languages.
fp: CBC radio, Toronto.

D1890. "You Can't Stop Now" in *A Play on Words and Other Radio Plays*. Toronto, Dent, 1948.
1 act. 10m/1f.
An anti-atomic bomb play.
fp: CBC radio "Stage 46", Nov. 11, 1945.

SIROIS, Serge 1953–

D1891. "Dodo", John van Burek, trans., in *A Collection of Canadian Plays* vol.5. Rolf Kalman, ed. Toronto, Simon & Pierre, 1978.
2 acts. 4m/2f.
A translation of his *Dodo L'Enfant Do*. A drama about the disintegration of a family as a result of the frustration and boredom of their lives.
fp: Centre d'Essai de l'Université de Montréal, Jan. 25, 1973. Playwrights Workshop, Montreal, February 1974.

A SISTER OF CHARITY. See MAURA, Sister.

SLATER, Ian

D1892. *Black Lion*. Vancouver, New Play Centre, (197-?).
1 act. 6m.
A drama about the new IRA and the recent struggles in Ireland.

D1893. *Far Garden*. Vancouver, New Play Centre, (197-?).
1 act. 1m/3f.
A gothic tale set on the Canadian prairies in which conflict between two families leads to murder.

SMILEY, Charles Wesley 1940–

D1894. *George Johnson is a Son-of-a-Bitch.* Garson, Ont., Theatre Arts Productions, (197-?) and Toronto, Playwrights Co-op, 1972 and in his *Three Plays.* Toronto, Playwrights Co-op, 1976.
1 act. 2m/1f.
Marianna Hill wishes to transfer into Mr. Johnson's class and uses sexual blackmail to get her way.
fp: (Workshop), Factory Theatre Lab, Toronto, June 1972.

D1895. *The Horticulturist.* Garson, Ont., Theatre Arts Productions, 1973 and in his *Three Plays.* Toronto, Playwrights Co-op, 1976.
1 act. 2m/1f/1g.
A man is troubled by the observation that everything and everyone is becoming frigid and devoid of emotions.
fp: (Workshop), Espanola Little Theatre, Ont., March 1973.

D1896. *The Magician.* Garson, Ont., Theatre Arts Productions, 1973.
1 act. 5m.
While a sceptical yet concerned audience looks on, a magician tries to escape from a locked box which contains only a five minute supply of air.
fp: (Workshop), Espanola Little Theatre, Ont., March 1973.

D1897. *The Valedictorian.* Garson, Ont., Theatre Arts Productions, 1973 and in his *Three Plays.* Toronto Playwrights Co-op, 1976 and in *Transitions I: Short Plays.* Edward Peck, ed. Vancouver, Commcept Publishing, 1978.
1 act. 2m/1f.
A farce about a young man who discovers a girl hiding under the sink in the men's room and his attempts to convince her to leave.
fp: (Workshop), Espanola Little Theatre, Ont., March 1973.

SMITH, Mrs. H.M. See HOOKE, Hilda Mary.

D1898. **SMITH, William."Cornplanter". See GREEN, Wilma.**

SMYTH, Donna Ellen

D1899. *A.D.'s Dead.* Halifax, Dramatists Co-op, 1977.
1 act. 2m/3f.
A comedy in which Pascal and Adelle Davis comment on a modern domestic triangle from the afterlife.

D1900. *Jerome.* Halifax, Dramatists Co-op, 1977.
1 act. 4m/3f. Extras.
An injured man found on the seashore becomes a sounding board for the tensions and restrictions of life in an isolated Nova Scotian community in the 19th century.

D1901. *The True Believer.* Halifax, Dramatists Co-op, 1977.
1 act. 1m/2f.
A play set in a mental hospital dramatizing the confrontation between the rational and irrational.

SNUKAL, Sherman

D1902. *Talking Dirty.* Vancouver, New Play Centre, 1978.
2 acts. 2m/3f.
A comedy in which a young man and his old-fashioned lady discuss the consequences of his attempts to avoid "outmoded conventions that stunt our growth and impede our development" and to sleep around.

D1903. *The Whispering Time.* Vancouver, New Play Centre, 1976.
1 act. 1m/1f.
A discussion between a young married couple about whether their marriage has come to an end.
fp: New Play Centre, Vancouver, Du Maurier Festival, 1976.

SOCIAL CREDIT BOARD

D1904. *Alice in Blunderland.* Edmonton, Social Credit Board, 1941.
1 act. 1m/1f.
Alice, a social creditiste, arrives in Blunderland and tries to convince the Mad Hatter that social democracy is far better than imperialism or capitalism.

SPECK, Frank Gouldsmith 1881–

D1905. *The False Face Legend.* Waterloo, Ont., Waterloo Music, 1972.
1 act. 4m. Extras.
The brief libretto of the musical account "adapted from mid-winter rites of the Cayuga" about the creation of the world. Music by Paul W. Sweetman.

SPENSLEY, Philip 1940–

D1906. "Hell's Bells" in *Dialogue & Dialectic: A Canadian Anthology of Short Plays.* Alive Theatre Workshop, ed. Guelph, Alive Press, 1972 and in *Transitions I: Short Plays.* Edward Peck, ed. Vancouver, Commcept Publishing, 1978.
1 act. 19m or f.
"A mime". Two loner figures, one meek and one self-confident, are eventually forced into the mold of society.
fp: Drama Workshop, University of Guelph, Ont., Oct. 19, 1967.

SPUNDE, Walter G. 1944–

D1907. "The Mercenary" in *Contemporary Canadian Drama.* Joseph Shaver, ed. Ottawa, Borealis Press, 1974.
1 act. 4m.
Four very different men serving as mercenaries are stationed in a small trench for their tour of duty. The clashes amongst the soldiers lead to tragedy for the youngest member of the unit.

STACKHOUSE, Perry J.

D1908. "The Babe of Bethlehem: A Christmas Drama" in his *Bible Dramas in the Pulpit*. Philadelphia, Judson Press, 1926.
4 scenes. 10m. Extras.
A dramatization of the story of the three wise men and the three shepherds and their journey to pay homage to the Christ-child.

D1909. "The Conversion of a Dishonest Tax-Collector" in his *Bible Dramas in the Pulpit*. Philadelphia, Judson Press, 1926.
4 scenes. 4m/1f. Extras.
The Biblical story of the dishonest tax-collector who repents his sins, gives away half his worldly goods, and receives salvation from Jesus of Nazareth.

D1910. "The Disciple of the Night: A Drama Sermon" in his *Bible Dramas in the Pulpit*. Philadelphia, Judson Press, 1926.
4 scenes. 6m.
Nicodemus, a Pharisee, is won over to the teachings of Jesus and attempts to save his life when all the other members of the Sanhedrin vote for his execution.

D1911. "Facts Are Stubborn Things" in his *Bible Dramas in the Pulpit*. Philadelphia, Judson Press, 1926.
4 scenes. 6m/1f.
Jesus returns sight to a man who was born blind.

D1912. "Joseph the Dreamer" in his *Bible Dramas in the Pulpit*. Philadelphia, Judson Press, 1926.
4 scenes. 10m/1f. Extras.
Joseph is sold into slavery by his brothers because their father loves him and favours him over the others.

D1913. "Joseph, the Interpreter of Dreams" in his *Bible Dramas in the Pulpit*. Philadelphia, Judson Press, 1926.
3 scenes. 6m. Extras.
Joseph is released from prison and becomes the Pharaoh's chief advisor because of his ability to interpret dreams.

D1914. "Joseph's Dreams Come True" in his *Bible Dramas in the Pulpit*. Philadelphia, Judson Press, 1926.
4 scenes. 9m/1f.
A dramatization of the story of how Joseph was reunited with his father Jacob and his brothers after many years of separation.

D1915. "The Man of Kerioth: A Tragedy" in his *Bible Dramas in the Pulpit*. Philadelphia, Judson Press, 1926.
4 scenes. 4m/1f. Extras.
A dramatization of the story of how Judas became one of Christ's disciples and why he later betrayed him.

D1916. "A Queen Who Saved A Nation From Death" in his *Bible Dramas in the Pulpit*. Philadelphia, Judson Press, 1926.
4 scenes. 3m/2f.
Queen Esther of Persia saves her people from death when the Prime Minister convinces the King that all Jews are trouble-makers.

D1917. "The Rich Young Ruler" in his *Bible Dramas in the Pulpit.* Philadelphia, Judson Press, 1926.
3 scenes. 4m/2f.
A rich young man dies when he gives up everything, including food, to prove his belief in God and Christ. Jesus brings him back to life.

D1918. "Thomas, the Twin: An Easter Drama" in his *Bible Dramas in the Pulpit.* Philadelphia, Judson Press, 1926.
3 scenes. 5m/2f.
Thomas, one of Christ's disciples, is sceptical of the reports of the resurrection and decides he must see for himself.

STANBROOK, Ralph, Fred Phillips and Lawrence Cohen

D1919. "A Biting Election Satire from the Comic-Revue Stage" in *Maclean's Magazine,* vol.76, #7, April 1963.
1 act. 4m/4f.
The first act finale of the 1963 "Spring Thaw" satirizing the naive complacency of the electorate.
fp: Spring Thaw, Toronto, 1963.

STANBURY, Charles

D1920. "Play" in *Outset.* Montreal, Sir George Williams University, 1973.
1 act. 1m/2f.
An excerpt of a play about a new guest arriving at a mysterious boarding house.

STANFORD, J. Hunt

D1921. "Sam Weller Visits His Mother-in-law" in *Scenes from Dickens.* J.E. Jones, ed. Toronto, McClelland & Stewart, 1923.
1 scene. 3m/1f.
An adaptation of an incident from *Pickwick Papers.* Sam Weller visits his stepmother and finds a sanctimonious preacher present.
p: Players' Guild of University College, University of Toronto, Feb. 17, 1926.

STEIN, David Lewis 1937–

D1922. *The Hearing.* Toronto, Playwrights Co-op, 1978.
2 acts. 10m/6f. Extras. Doubling.
An examination of urban politics as a group of homeowners fight off a high-rise development.
fp: Open Circle Theatre, St. Paul's Centre, Toronto, Feb. 11, 1976.

STEIN, Miriam

D1923. "Retribution" in *Echoes,* #131, June 1933.
1 act. 4m. Extras.
A lumber camp store manager falls in with a plan to kill an old prospector and steal his bankroll.

STEPHEN, Alexander Maitland 1882–1942

D1924. "Across the Great Divide" in his *Classroom Plays from Canadian History.* Toronto, Dent, 1929.
1 act. 2m. Extras.
Alexander Mackenzie and his company borrow canoes from the Bella Coola Indians to complete their journey to the Pacific.

D1925. "Adam Daulac" in his *Classroom Plays from Canadian History.* Toronto, Dent, 1929.
1 act. 2m/2f.
A young woman in love with a young soldier blames the governor for sending him into danger and death.

D1926. "After Queenston Heights" in his *Classroom Plays from Canadian History.* Toronto, Dent, 1929.
1 act. 2m.
Two American prisoners-of-war discuss the battle of Queenston Heights.

D1927. "Before Quebec" in his *Classroom Plays from Canadian History.* Toronto, Dent, 1929.
1 act. 6m.
Wolfe prepares to take Quebec.

D1928. "The Bridge" in his *Classroom Plays from Canadian Industry.* Toronto, Dent, 1931.
1 act. 1m/1f/1b.
An engineer is comforted by his family after the bridge which he designed collapses due to an error made by the company for which he worked.

D1929. "Building Railroads" in his *Classroom Plays from Canadian Industry.* Toronto, Dent, 1931.
1 act. 3m.
The cook for a railway construction gang plays a joke, stirring up bad feelings among the men as a result.

D1930. "Canada — A Pageant" in his *Classroom Plays from Canadian History.* Toronto, Dent, 1929.
1 act. 10m/20f.
A pageant in which the past, present and future of Canada is celebrated.

D1931. "Canada in Flanders" in his *Classroom Plays from Canadian History.* Toronto, Dent, 1929.
1 act. 5m/2f.
An allegory in which Honour and Duty defeat Fear and Thirst and Death in the mind of a young soldier fighting for Canada in W.W.I.

D1932. "Captain Cook" in his *Classroom Plays from Canadian History.* Toronto, Dent, 1929.
1 act. 5m. Extras.
Captain Cook trades with the Indians before continuing his attempt to find the Northwest Passage.

D1933. "The Cattle Rancher" in his *Classroom Plays from Canadian Industry.*
Toronto, Dent, 1931.
1 act. 6m/1f. Extras.
A cattleman apologizes for damage done to a neighbouring farmer's land and acknowledges that "when you farmers come in, it's time for the cattleman to move on".

D1934. "Champlain at Quebec" in his *Classroom Plays from Canadian History.*
Toronto, Dent, 1929.
1 act. 6m/2f.
After a little boy claims that Joan of Arc told him that Canada would one day belong to France, Champlain surrenders to the English for the immediate present.

D1935. "The Coal Miner" in his *Classroom Plays from Canadian Industry.* Toronto, Dent, 1931.
1 act. 4m/1f.
A young man from the Prairies comes east to find work as a coal miner.

D1936. "Cod Fishing" in his *Classroom Plays from Canadian Industry.* Toronto, Dent, 1931.
1 act. 3m/1f.
When a fisherman's son rescues a girl from drowning, the grateful father offers him the opportunity to learn navigation.

D1937. "Columbus" in his *Classroom Plays from Canadian History.* Toronto, Dent, 1929.
1 act. 3m/1f.
Columbus has persuaded Isabella of his dream and she gives him ships; a young page who wishes to know where the sun sets joins him.

D1938. "Confederation" in his *Classroom Plays from Canadian History.* Toronto, Dent, 1929.
1 act. 1m/1f/1b/1g.
Mr. Perry explains the meaning of Confederation to his wife and children.

D1939. "Dairying" in his *Classroom Plays from Canadian Industry.* Toronto, Dent, 1931.
1 act. 1m/1f/1b/1g.
A farmer convinces his wife that it would be profitable to go into dairying.

D1940. "The Discovery of Canada" in his *Classroom Plays from Canadian History.* Toronto, Dent, 1929.
1 act. 8m. Extras.
A priest and Jacques Cartier convince an Indian chief to send his two sons to France.

D1941. "An Evening in a Loyalist Household" in his *Classroom Plays from Canadian History.* Toronto, Dent, 1929.
1 act. 2m/1f/1b/1g.
Mrs. Horton's husband is away selling their produce and the family is visited by a Yankee peddler and a friendly Indian.

D1942. "The Fruit Rancher" in his *Classroom Plays from Canadian Industry*. Toronto, Dent, 1931.
1 act. 2m/3f.
A fruit rancher and his wife decide to move to the city to give their children better educational opportunities.

D1943. "The Habitant" in his *Classroom Plays from Canadian History*. Toronto, Dent, 1929.
1 act. 2m/1f/1b/1g.
A coureur-de-bois brings money so that his farmer-father can pay the rent as the crops have failed because the son has not been there to help.

D1944. "Halibut Fishing" in his *Classroom Plays from Canadian Industry*. Toronto, Dent, 1931.
1 act. 3m/1f.
While an Indian fisherman explains to his blind sister how halibut are caught, news arrives that a white woman wishes to pay for an operation which will restore the girl's sight.

D1945. "Henry Hudson" in his *Classroom Plays from Canadian History*. Toronto, Dent, 1929 and in *Under the North Star*. Lorne Pierce, ed. Toronto, Ryerson, 1957.
1 act. 5m.
Minutes before his crew's mutiny, Henry Hudson proclaims, "if there is danger, there is also glory".

D1946. "The Homesteaders" in his *Classroom Plays from Canadian Industry*. Toronto, Dent, 1931.
1 act. 1m/1f/1b/1g.
A mother's worries are dispelled when her children return safely from a prairie thunderstorm.

D1947. "Hydro-Electric" in his *Classroom Plays from Canadian Industry*. Toronto, Dent, 1931.
1 act. 2m/1f/1g.
While changing a fuse, Harry explains to his sister how electricity is generated.

D1948. "In a Lumber Camp" in his *Classroom Plays from Canadian Industry*. Toronto, Dent, 1931.
1 act. 5m.
The lumberjacks devise a ruse to prevent their older comrade from riding the logs down the river to the mill.

D1949. "In the Oil Fields" in his *Classroom Plays from Canadian Industry*. Toronto, Dent, 1931.
1 act. 3m.
A man who holds stock in a drilling company arrives at the field just as they strike oil.

D1950. "The King of New Albion" in his *Classroom Plays from Canadian History*. Toronto, Dent, 1929.
1 act. 6m. Extras.
Francis Drake is crowned king of New Albion by the Indians whom he has treated kindly.

D1951. "The Last Spike" in his *Classroom Plays from Canadian History*. Toronto, Dent, 1929.
1 act. 4m/5f.
Oread, Spirit of the Mountains, recounts the story of the building of the Canadian Pacific Railway to her Mother Earth and other spirits.

D1952. "Laura Secord" in his *Classroom Plays from Canadian History*. Toronto, Dent, 1929.
1 act. 4m/1f. Extras.
Laura Secord informs Lt. Fitzgibbon of the planned American attack.

D1953. "Lief the Lucky" in his *Classroom Plays from Canadian History*. Toronto, Dent, 1929.
1 act. 6m.
Lief the Lucky and his Vikings leave North America because they are sailors, not farmers, and because the Indians are hostile.

D1954. "Madeleine de Vercheres" in his *Classroom Plays from Canadian History*. Toronto, Dent, 1929.
1 act. 5m/1f.
Madeleine almost single-handedly protects the fort until reinforcements arrive.

D1955. "Making Maple Sugar" in his *Classroom Plays from Canadian Industry*. Toronto, Dent, 1931.
1 act. 1m/2f/2b.
A family prepares for the annual sugaring-off.

D1956. "The Man Who Read the Stars" in his *Classroom Plays from Canadian History*. Toronto, Dent, 1929.
1 act. 3m.
Thompson reads the stars to find his bearings so he can make a map of Canada but an Indian thinks that what he sees is the future.

D1957. "The Miner" in his *Classroom Plays from Canadian Industry*. Toronto, Dent, 1931.
1 act. 1m/1f/1b/1g.
A miner reassures his family that his job is secure as a result of the discovery of a rich, new vein of ore.

D1958. "A Mission School" in his *Classroom Plays from Canadian History*. Toronto, Dent, 1929.
1 act. 2m. Extras.
A Jesuit father refuses to leave the Hurons despite a friend's warning of the impending massacre by the Iroquois.

D1959. "Paper Making" in his *Classroom Plays from Canadian Industry*. Toronto, Dent, 1931.
1 act. 1m/1f/1b/2g.
Jack explains to his visiting cousin the method of making paper.

D1960. "The Passing of the Red Man" in his *Classroom Plays from Canadian History*. Toronto, Dent, 1929.
1 act. 2m/1f.
After the surrender of Poundmaker at Battleford, the Crees realize that "we shall only have a memory of the time when we were free".

D1961. "Peace with Pontiac" in his *Classroom Plays from Canadian History*. Toronto, Dent, 1929.
1 act. 4m. Extras.
Sir William Johnson makes peace with the powerful Pontiac and his tribe and allies.

D1962. "A Play for Labour Day" in his *Classroom Plays from Canadian Industry*. Toronto, Dent, 1931.
1 scene. 24m/3f. Extras.
A pageant in which the workers of Canada tell of their labours and give thanks for the opportunities afforded them.

D1963. "The Prospector" in his *Classroom Plays from Canadian Industry*. Toronto, Dent, 1931.
1 act. 3m.
A prospector leads two city men to the site of a rich claim.

D1964. "Radisson" in his *Classroom Plays from Canadian History*. Toronto, Dent, 1929.
1 act. 5m.
Prince Rupert persuades Charles II to give Radisson a ship.

D1965. "Rebel and Patriot" in his *Classroom Plays from Canadian History*. Toronto, Dent, 1929.
1 act. 5m/1f.
William Lyon Mackenzie and Andrew Milne, a fellow rebel, hide in the Milnes' home because they are being pursued by soldiers.

D1966. "The River of White Flowers" in his *Classroom Plays from Canadian History*. Toronto, Dent, 1929.
1 act. 3m. Extras.
Simon Fraser and his men turn back before they have finished the course of the river because of the Musqueam Indians' fear that they are malicious Sky-People.

D1967. "Salmon Fishing" in his *Classroom Plays from Canadian Industry*. Toronto, Dent, 1931.
1 act. 3m/1f/1b.
A fisherman's wife anxiously awaits the return of her husband and son.

D1968. "The Sawmill" in his *Classroom Plays from Canadian Industry*. Toronto, Dent, 1931.
1 act. 3m/1f.
The son of a mill owner returns from university and expresses the desire to learn his father's business.

D1969. "The Seigneur" in his *Classroom Plays from Canadian History*. Toronto, Dent, 1929.
1 act. 3m/1f.
A young man decides to give up his life as coureur-de-bois for a position as seigneur.

D1970. "The Silver Chief" in his *Classroom Plays from Canadian History*. Toronto, Dent, 1929.
1 act. 2m. Extras.
Selkirk gathers colonists and prepares the way for his settlement.

D1971. "Trapping" in his *Classroom Plays from Canadian Industry*. Toronto, Dent, 1931.
1 act. 2m.
A trapper has difficulty convincing his partner that to break the law and set a beaver trap would be ill-advised.

D1972. "Vancouver and Quadra" in his *Classroom Plays from Canadian History*. Toronto, Dent, 1929.
1 act. 2m. Extras.
Captain Vancouver meets with Don Bodega y Quadra in order to reclaim the West Coast from Spain, though Quadra wants to delay the proceedings.

D1973. "Whaling" in his *Classroom Plays from Canadian Industry*. Toronto, Dent, 1931.
1 act. 2m/2b.
Two boys, ordered by the health officer to bury a dead whale, go to a retired sea captain for advice on how to cut it up.

D1974. "Where Wheat Is King" in his *Classroom Plays from Canadian Industry*. Toronto, Dent, 1931.
1 act, 1m/2f/1b/1g.
A good harvest makes it possible for a farmer to send his invalid daughter to recuperate in California.

D1975. "The White Peaks" in his *Classroom Plays from Canadian History*. Toronto, Dent, 1929.
1 act. 3m. Extras.
The Indians who have been guiding the La Verendrye brothers on their way to the sea return to their villages because they fear the Snake tribe.

D1976. "With the Seal Hunters" in his *Classroom Plays from Canadian Industry*. Toronto, Dent, 1931.
1 act. 6m/1b.
Two Indians accuse a member of a sealing crew of stealing their pelts. The captain of the crew repays the Indians and fires the thief.

D1977. "The Woolen Mill" in his *Classroom Plays from Canadian Industry*. Toronto, Dent, 1931.
1 act. 1m/2f.
A young mill worker, while home on the weekend, explains to a neighbour how the wool is processed by machine.

STERN, Sandy

D1978. "Check, Mate and Murder" in *Two Plays for Television: Camera One*. Toronto, Holt, Rinehart & Winston, 1972.
21m/6f/1b. Extras.
A script for the "Ironside" series concerning terrorism in Montreal.
fp: October 1970.

D1979. "Does Anybody Here Know Denny?" in *The Demanding Age*. Ronald Side, ed. Toronto, McGraw-Hill, 1970.
8 scenes. 17m/11f.
A TV drama. A young woman under psychiatric care inherits her family's wealth. She also falls in love with her psychiatrist but still cannot cope with the world around her.

STEWART, Cherie Thiessen 1947–

D1980. *Dandelion.* Vancouver, New Play Centre, 1972.
2 acts. 2m/2f/1g.
Five people meet in a field to make dandelion wine in an effort to destroy the mechanized society surrounding them and to bring back nature and all it stands for.
fp: New Play Centre, Vancouver, 1972.

D1981. "Elevator" in her *One Spring Morning/Elevator.* Toronto, Playwrights Co-op, 1975 and in *The Malahat Review,* #39, July 1976.
1 act. 2f.
Two old women meet in an apartment building elevator and decide to turn it into a "Koffee and Kocktail Korner".
fp: New Play Centre, Vancouver, 1973. CBC radio "Playhouse", 1975.

D1982. *The Extraverted Suicide.* Vancouver, New Play Centre, 1974.
1 act. 1m/2f/2g.
A comedy about a girl and boy, both planning suicide, who meet on a park bench.

D1983. *The Fall of Man.* Vancouver, New Play Centre, (197-?).
3 scenes. 8m/1f/1b/1g.
A brief description of the effects of the common out-house on everyday life.

D1984. *One Spring Morning.* Vancouver, New Play Centre, 1973 and in *One Spring Morning/Elevator.* Toronto, Playwrights Co-op, 1975.
1 act. 1m/2f/1g.
A middle-aged man is accosted verbally by an old lady, a little girl, and a young woman.
fp: Gallery Players, Victoria, 1973.

D1985. *Pass the Salt Peter.* Vancouver, New Play Centre, (197-?).
2 acts. 4m/5f.
Four women living together advertise for a husband for one of them.

D1986. *Revolutions.* Vancouver, New Play Centre, (197-?) and in her *Willie and the Watchers/Revolutions.* Toronto, Playwrights Co-op, 1978.
1 act. 2m/2f.
A comedy about four misfits outlawed from society.
fp: New Play Centre, Vancouver, 1975. CBC radio.

D1987. *Who's Pauline.* Vancouver, New Play Centre, (197-?).
2 acts. 3m/3f.
A play portraying Pauline Johnson's relationships with her sister and her friends during her last recital in Kamloops, B.C.

D1988. *Willie and the Watchers.* Vancouver, New Play Centre, (197-?) and in her *Willie and the Watchers/Revolutions.* Toronto, Playwrights Co-op, 1978.
1 act. 6m/1f. Extras.
Willie is mistaken by the Watchers for the new Messiah. When he kills himself, they look for yet another new Messiah.
fp: Vancouver Little Theatre, 1969.

STEWART, Luke

D1989. *Andrew McMurty, Immigrant.* Toronto, French, 1938.
1 act. 4m/2f.
An irascible old Scotsman creates pandemonium when he refuses to submit to the indignities of an immigration interview.

D1990. *Daft Danny.* Toronto, French, 1947.
1 act. 3m/1f.
Molly made a date with Howard after she and Danny quarrelled. Danny pretends to be Molly's simple-minded brother to scare off his rival.

D1991. *Release.* Toronto, French, 1937.
1 act. 7m/1f.
Rescue efforts are under way to free miners in a cave-in. One of the trapped men is an escaped convict who has been working under an assumed name.
fp: Ottawa Little Theatre, Feb. 10, 1937.

D1992. *The Revolt of the Puppets.* Ottawa, Ottawa Little Theatre Workshop, #6.
1 act. 4m/3f.
The study of a mediocre author of soap opera scripts is invaded by personifications of storybook heroes and heroines who are assigned by a celestial bureau to inspire him to write his particular brand of literature.

STOKES, Charles W.

D1993. "The Door" in *Canadian Magazine,* #58, April 1922.
1 act. 3m/1f.
A factory worker, an RCMP officer and a fat rich man all want to marry the same woman. She cannot decide between them so they flip a coin.

STONE, A.B. See BINNS, Agnes S.

STRATFORD, Phyllis (Coate) 1900–

D1994. *Bright and Glorious.* Toronto, French, 1938.
1 act. 2m/5f.
Mrs. Eberts, knowing she is soon to die, passes on to her granddaughter her philosophy of life and death with the hope that she can comfort her children through the innocence of a younger generation.
p: Western Ontario Drama League, 1937.

D1995. "Nets of Silver" in *Willison's Monthly,* vol.5, #1, July 1929.
1 act. 3m/2f.
A mother is visited by the ghost of her child on Hallowe'en, the anniversary of his birth and death.

STRATTON, Allan 1951–

D1996. "The Rusting Heart" in *Alphabet,* #15, Dec. 1968.
1 act. 6m/3f.
When George's transformation into the "perfect metal brain in the perfect metal body" is complete, the sun and moon die and the train stops.
fp: Alpha Centre, London, Ont., 1968.

D1997. *72 Under the 0.* Toronto, Playwrights Co-op, 1978.
2 acts. 3m/2f.
A farce mixing academia and sex about thwarted seductions and premature passions.
fp: Playhouse Theatre Centre, Vancouver, May 1977.

STRINGER, Arthur John Arbuthnot 1874–1950

D1998. *Alexander Was Great.* Toronto, French, 1937 and in *Tournament Plays.* New York, French, 1937 and in his *The Cleverest Woman in the World and Other One Act Plays.* New York, Bobbs-Merrill, 1939.
1 act. 3m/1f.
"A Greek burlesque". Thalestris, the Amazon queen, comes to Alexander for a son but it is really just a ruse while her warriors steal the Greek treasure barge.

D1999. "The Angle of Adventure" in his *The Cleverest Woman in the World and Other One Act Plays.* New York, Bobbs-Merrill, 1939.
1 act. 4m/1f.
Laurence Bentley wishes to divorce his wife and arranges matters so he will be caught in a compromising situation with another woman, a good friend of his.

D2000. "The Blot" in *Canadian Magazine,* vol.35, #3–6, July–Oct. 1910.
4 acts. 6m/2f.
A young girl takes a novel to New York after the author, for whom she copies it, shoots himself. She becomes an instant success.

D2001. "The Cleverest Woman in the World" in his *The Cleverest Woman in the World and Other One Act Plays.* New York, Bobbs-Merrill, 1939.
1 act. 2m/2f.
A newsman breaks up an illegal wiretapping and horse betting ring with the help of Claire, one of its members, who flees to Europe for safety and whom he follows to make his wife.

D2002. "The Death Cup" in his *The Cleverest Woman in the World and Other One Act Plays.* New York, Bobbs-Merrill, 1939.
1 act. 2m/1f.
Andrei and Olga face a winter of near-starvation on their prairie farm. The only solution is to poison the wealthy stranger who visits one afternoon. Unfortunately, the stranger was their only son who had left home years before.

D2003. "A Dialogue in Spring" in his *The Woman in the Rain and Other Poems.* Boston, Little Brown, 1907 and Toronto, McClelland & Stewart, 1949.
1 act. 1m/1f.
A monk questions an old woman whom he meets in a garden as to the reason for her sadness and discovers it is because she had no children.

D2004. "Evidence" in his *The Cleverest Woman in the World and Other One Act Plays.* New York, Bobbs-Merrill, 1939.
1 act. 2m/5f.
A policeman has been murdered and four women romantically involved with the killer are questioned in an attempt to find him.

D2005. "The Firebrand" in *Canada Monthly,* vol.9, Dec. 1910 to March 1911.
4 acts. 10m/2f.
The leader of the Nihilists, a terrorist group, attempts to blow up a big businessman.

D2006. "The House of Oedipus" in *Canadian Magazine,* vol.38, #4–6, Feb., March, April 1912.
3 acts. 22m/7f.
A modernization of the tragedy of Oedipus adapted and put into blank verse from the Italian of Ferdinando Fontana.

D2007. "On the Roof" in his *The Cleverest Woman in the World and Other One Act Plays.* New York, Bobbs-Merrill, 1939.
1 act. 4f. Extras.
Four white women are trapped on a hospital roof during the war in China in 1927. One must sacrifice herself to save the others.

D2008. "The Oyster" in his *The Cleverest Woman in the World and Other One Act Plays.* New York, Bobbs-Merrill, 1939.
1 act. 3m/2f.
Alice and Alan are in love but their respective aunt and uncle, former lovers, are terribly unhappy.

D2009. "Sappho in Leucadia" in his *Hephaestus, Persephone at Enna and Sappho in Leucadia.* Toronto, Methodist Book and Publishing, 1903 and London, Grant Richards, 1903.
1 act. 1m/1f. Extras.
A verse drama in which Phaon pleads with Sappho to return to Lesbos with him though they have been separated for many years. She says it is too late and leaps from a cliff into the sea.

D2010. *Sappho in Leucadia.* Boston, Little Brown, 1907 and in his *The Woman in the Rain and Other Poems.* Boston, Little Brown, 1907 and Toronto, McClelland & Stewart, 1949.
4 acts. 5m/5f. Extras.
A completely revised and expanded version of the one act play following the love of Sappho and Phaon from its beginnings and showing how the treachery of Pittacus, the tyrant of Mytilene, separates them.

D2011. "The Spotted Veil" in his *The Cleverest Woman in the World and Other One Act Plays.* New York, Bobbs-Merrill, 1939.
1 act. 2m/3f.
A young widow wishes to be with her children but complicated affairs in the Far East necessitate their continuing separation.

D2012. "Weathered Oak" in his *The Cleverest Woman in the World and Other One Act Plays.* New York, Bobbs-Merrill, 1939.
1 act. 4m/5f.
A doctor and his nurse love each other but can't marry because they have no money. One of the nurse's patients whom she has befriended inherits $30,000 which he uses to back the doctor's practice.

D2013. **STUDIO LAB THEATRE** and Ernest Schwarz. *Pig Tales.* See **SCHWARZ, Ernest.**

SUTHERLAND, Maxine

D2014. *Morning Glory.* Edmonton, Dept. of Extension, University of Alberta, 1946.
1 act. 4m/1f.
A house is haunted by the ghosts of a farming couple killed by the drought during the Depression.

SWEET, Jean MacCallum

D2015. "Christmas, 1940" in *Educational Review,* vol.55, #4, Dec. 1940.
1 act. 7b.
A group of children preparing to put on a Christmas play discover the true meaning of Christmas.

D2016. "The Green Glass Beads" in *Educational Review,* vol.48, #9, May–June 1934.
1 act. 4m/2f.
A princess held captive by evil King Murdo is rescued by Prince Charming when he finds the "key" to unlock the gate.

D2017. "Once in a Blue Moon" in *Educational Review,* vol.47, #4, Dec. 1932.
1 act. 3m/1f/2g. Extras.
Earth people who enter the Kingdom of Blue Moon "where the impossible may happen and all things come true" find happiness.

D2018. "Small Potatoes" in *Curtain Call,* vol.10, #5, Feb. 1939.
1 act. 3m/1f.
In 1950, ten years after the revolution, the state refuses two lovers permission to marry. Because of repeated crop failures, the man is jailed. The girl goes back in time to 1938, two years before the revolution, to warn of the impending disaster.
p: Theatre Guild of St. John, N.B., 1938.

SWERDLOW, Robert 1941–

D2019. *Copper Mountain.* Toronto, Playwrights Co-op, 1973.
6 scenes. 2m/1f/1b. Extras.
A children's play which teaches that being oneself and being nice to everyone else is best.
fp: Global Village, Toronto, Dec. 1969.

D2020. *Love Me, Love My Children.* Toronto, Playwrights Co-op, 1973.
2 acts. 5m/8f.
A contemporary musical about a young dancer who leaves home to go live with her hippie cult-leader sister in "fat city".
fp: Global Village, Toronto, 1969 as "Justine". New York, 1972.

SWIETLINSKI, Roman

D2021. "Untitled" in *York Theatre Journal,* #6, March 1974.
1 act. 3m.
A comedy in which two men become victims of their own ethnic prejudices.

SZABLOWSKI, Jerzy

D2022. "The Subsidiary Vice-President" in *Dialogue & Dialectic: A Canadian Anthology of Short Plays.* Alive Theatre Workshop, ed. Guelph, Alive Press, 1972.
1 act. 3m/1f.
A president of a Canadian division of an American corporation fires his son for going over his head. The son is reinstated in a better position, so the father quits.
fp: CBC TV, Montreal, Jan. 13, 1969.

SZANTO, George H. 1940–

D2023. *After the Ceremony.* Toronto, Playwrights Co-op, 1978.
3 acts. 3m/3f.
A drama about a Vietnam veteran's adjustment to civilian life in a lower-middle class section of Montreal in 1973.
fp: (Workshop), Playwrights Workshop, Montreal, May 1977.

TAIT, George E.

D2024. "Tommy and His Grandfather" in *Canadian Red Cross Junior,* February 1939.
1 act. 1m/1f/2b.
A dramatization of the advances in modern education methods.

TAIT, Michael S.

D2025. *Mountjoy and the Flower Children.* Toronto, Canadian Theatre Centre, (1968?).
2 acts. 6m/4f. Extras.
A middle-aged teacher has an acid-flashback in which he is tried for "stodginess" and is forced to take fifty hits of acid.
fp: McMaster University, Hamilton, spring 1969.

TALLMAN, James 1947 –

D2026. "Trans-Canada Highway" in *Contemporary Canadian Drama.* Joseph Shaver, ed. Ottawa, Borealis Press, 1974.
1 act. 1m/1f.
A professional hitchhiker is befriended by a first-timer and they join forces going down the road.

TARVER, Ben

D2027. *The Savage Dream.* Toronto, Playwrights Co-op, 1972.
2 acts. 5m/2f. Extras.
"Freely adapted from *La Vida Es Sueno* by Calderon", a fantasy parable about illusion and reality.
fp: Theatre Three, Edmonton, Oct. 20, 1971.

TAYLOR, Christopher

D2028. *The Wings of the Dove.* London and Toronto, French, 1964 and London, Elek Books, 1966.
4m/5f.
The adaptation of Henry James' novel about the love intrigues of a sensitive American woman who sets up a residence in Venice in 1900 with an aunt and her young niece.
fp:Lyric Theatre, London, England, 1963.

TAYLOR, Ron 1931–

D2029. "Ride to the Hill" in *Encounter: Canadian Drama in Four Media.* Eugene Benson, ed. Toronto, Methuen, 1973.
16 scenes. 2m/1f.
A TV drama in which a young girl at the beginning of puberty is forced to make a decision between her old life style and a new one.
fp: CBC TV, Jan. 20, 1972.

D2030. "The Unreasonable Act of Julian Waterman" in *A Collection of Canadian Plays* vol.3. Rolf Kalman, ed. Toronto, Simon & Pierre, 1974.
3 acts. 3m/1f.
Barb Waterman is looking for excitement and thinks she'll find it in resuming an old romance with Hank whom she invites to live with her and her husband Julian.
p: Citadel Theatre, Edmonton, Jan. 6, 1973.

TEMBECK, Robert 1940–1976

D2031. "Baptism" in *Contemporary Canadian Drama.* Joseph Shaver, ed. Ottawa, Borealis Press, 1974.
1 act. 3m/1f. Chorus.
The life and artistic pursuits of Antonin Artaud as portrayed by an asylum inmate who believes himself to be Artaud.
fp: McGill University, Montreal, May 16, 1972.

D2032. *Double.* Vancouver, New Play Centre, 1973.
1 act. 5m/3f. Doubling. Chorus.
An attempt to create an Artaudian theatre of cruelty play exploring the theory of "life as the double of the theatre".
fp: Montreal and Theatre 1, Vancouver.

D2033. "Fish Bowl" in *Jaws in a Fishbowl: Olympic Fiction Games* by Raymond Filip and Robert Tembeck. Ecowi (Labelle), Quebec, Manitou Community College, 1976.
2 acts. 6m/4f. Extras.
A drama about international politics and terrorism at the Munich and Montreal Olympics.
fp: Theatron Montreal, St. Gregory the Illuminator Armenian Cathedral, October 1973.

TEMPLETON, Frank

D2034. "The Appointed Hour" in *Acadia Athenaeum,* vol.60, #4, February 1934.
1 scene. 1m/2f.
Believing that her condemned husband has been reprieved, Mrs. Marshton rushes to greet him but instead meets his ghost since the evidence did not reach the prison in time to save him.

D2035. "Company or Voices of the Dead" in *Acadia Athenaeum,* vol.60, #5, March 1934.
1 scene. 2m/2f.
Aunt Hester knows her nephew is not dead as announced because the Voices of the Drowned Dead have been calling the name of the boy's father.

THEATRE PASSE MURAILLE

D2036. *Doukhobors.* See **THOMPSON, Paul.**

D2037. "1837: The Farmers' Revolt". See **SALUTIN, Rick.**

D2038. *Far As the Eye Can See.* See **WIEBE, Rudy.**

D2039. *The Farm Show.* Toronto, Coach House Press, 1976.
2 acts. 3m/3f. Doubling.
A collective creation presenting the inhabitants of the farming community near Clinton, Ontario.
fp: Theatre Passe Muraille at Ray Bird's barn, Clinton, Ont., 1972.

D2040. *I Love You, Baby Blue.* Erin, Ont., Press Porcepic, 1977.
2 acts. 3m/5f. Doubling.
A collective theatre piece exploring and exposing sex as practised in Toronto from Yonge Street body rub parlours to Rosedale living rooms.
fp: Theatre Passe Muraille, Toronto, Jan. 16, 1975.

D2041. **THERIAULT, Yves 1915–.** *The Centennial Play.* See **DAVIES, Robertson.**

THIESSEN, Cherie Stewart. See STEWART, Cherie Thiessen.

THOMAS, Lillian (Beynon) 1874–1961

D2042. *Jim Barber's Spite Fence.* Toronto, French, 1935.
1 act. 2m/2f.
A marriage of convenience resolves the long-standing feud between two old cronies.
fp: Winnipeg Little Theatre, 1933.

THOMPSON, Bob

D2043. "Good Morning Dear" in *Ryersonian,* 1973.
1 act. 1m/1f.
A husband refuses to respond to his wife's demands that he get up and go to work and instead dwells on his state of being.

THOMPSON, Glen

D2044. *Liquid Gold.* Vancouver, New Play Centre, 1978.
2 acts. 10m/2f.
An independent fisherman's widow and a flamboyant rum-runner join forces in an attempt to defeat a grasping shop-keeper who controls the economy of a small B.C. fishing village in the 1920s.
fp: Tamahnous Theatre, Vancouver East Cultural Centre, March 1, 1978.

THOMPSON, Hilary

D2045. *Anancy and Lizard.* Halifax, Dramatists Co-op, 1977.
1 act. 5 puppets.
Based on a West Indian folk-tale in which Anancy the Spider wins his princess despite a cheating lizard and a voracious chicken.

D2046. *Anansi the Spider.* Halifax, Dramatists Co-op, 1977.
1 act. 10 puppets.
Based on an Ashanti folk-tale from Ghana about Anansi who is rescued by his six spider sons and his dilemma in how to reward them.

D2047. *Madam Fou-Fou and the Apricot Mousse or Cinderella Comes of Age.* Halifax, Dramatists Co-op, 1978.
1 act. 7 puppets.
A play for children or puppets about Mother Goose who is more interested in telling stories than in little Sonja and her birthday party.

D2048. *The Quarrelling Quails.* Halifax, Dramatists Co-op, 1977.
1 act. 5 puppets.
Based on an Indian tale. The quail are safe from the hunter while they are not arguing. Unfortunately, the quails are by nature quarrelsome.

THOMPSON, Joan T.

D2049. *Par for the Course.* Edmonton, Alberta Dept. of Culture, 1971.
3 acts. 6m/1f.
An examination of one man's self-righteous, conventional and hypocritical attitude towards people who are "different" in any way.

THOMPSON, Paul 1940– and Theatre Passe Muraille

D2050. *Doukhobors.* Toronto, Playwrights Co-op, 1973.
25 scenes. 5m/3f. Doubling.
An interpretation of the history of the Doukhobors in Canada.
fp: Theatre Passe Muraille, Toronto, April 2, 1971.

THOMPSON, Ruth C.

D2051. *Beyond the Skyline.* Toronto, Committee on Missionary Education, United Church of Canada, 1937.
1 act. 9b/6g.
"A play of modern China". A young Chinese student finds strength and meaning for her life through the church.

THORLAKSON, Edward J.

D2052. "Father Lacombe" in his *Pioneer Theatre Series* Book 1. Edmonton, Institute for Applied Art, 1936.
1 act. 5m/2f.
Father Lacombe, a French priest in Canada, attempts to negotiate peace between warring tribes of Indians.

D2053. "The King's Girls" in his *Pioneer Theatre Series* Book 1. Edmonton, Institute of Applied Art, 1936.
1 act. 3m/3f. Extras.
"A comedy of New France." The King of France sends a boatful of women to the new world as wives for the soldiers of New France.

D2054. "Marie Hebert" in his *Pioneer Theatre Series* Book 1. Edmonton, Institute of Applied Art, 1936.
1 act. 4m/2f.
"A drama of Canada's first White Woman". Marie Hebert and her husband and daughter attempt to make a permanent home for themselves in the harsh new world of Canada.

D2055. "Poet of the Plains" in his *Pioneer Theatre Series* Book 1. Edmonton, Institute of Applied Art, 1936.
1 act. 3m/1f.
The story of the early life of Pauline Johnson and the struggles of her parents to preserve the Indian heritage in Canada.

THORNE, Steven

D2056. "Wild Goose Chase" in *York Theatre Journal*, #9, Feb. 1975.
1 act. 3m.
"A playlet" satirizing the inefficiency and paranoia of government and military bureaucrats.

THRELFALL, Merton Stafford 1887–

D2057. "The Happiest Place" in *One Act Plays by Canadian Authors*. Montreal, Canadian Authors' Association, 1926.
1 act. 3m.
A Cockney goes to the happiest place in all creation but since there is no beer or fish and chips there he decides that he prefers Whitechapel.
fp: Players Club, St. Lambert, P.Q., 1925.

D2058. "Two Tricks in Diamonds" in *Echoes*, #108, June 1927.
1 act. 4m/3f.
Two women decide to have their diamonds appraised. The one with the valuable diamonds is tricked into cheating herself of them.

THURY, Fred 1945– and Robert Galbraith 1934–

D2059. "Nuts & Bolts & Rusty Things" in *A Collection of Canadian Plays* vol.4. Rolf Kalman, ed. Toronto, Simon & Pierre, 1975.
1 act. 7m/1f. Doubling.
A children's musical in which Mr. Beans takes Sammy on a journey through the Forest of Illusion where they must solve the riddle of the Master of Illusion and find the golden key.
fp: Global Village Theatre, Toronto.

TIDLER, Charles

D2060. "Pan's Damn Lamb: A Dithyramb" in *Nebula*, #7, 1978.
1 act. 2m/1f. Chorus.
A parody in which the God Pan gives Omphale a lamb in order not to be castrated by her.

TINDALE, William A.

D2061. "The Statue and the Bust" in *McMaster University Quarterly*, vol.48, #2, Jan. 1939.
1 act. 2m/2f. Extras.
A dramatization for radio of Browning's poem about two unrequited lovers in sixteenth century Florence.

TIPE, David 1948–

D2062. *Diamond Cutters*. Toronto, Playwrights Co-op, 1972.
1 act. 2m/1f.
Two old diamond cutters remember their past and their youth yet never forget the present.
fp: Tarragon Theatre, Toronto, Dec. 29, 1971.

D2063. *Snow Birds*. Toronto, Playwrights Co-op, 1972 and in *Performing Arts in Canada*, vol.9, #1, Spring 1972.
1 act. 2m.
The relationship between Sid and Luke is established in the loneliness of a park in winter.
fp: Tarragon Theatre, Toronto, Dec.29, 1971.

D2064. *Three Cabbagetown Plays*. Toronto, Playwrights Co-op, 1972. See *Diamond Cutters. Snow Birds. The Travesty and the Fruit Fly*.

D2065. *The Travesty and the Fruit Fly*. Toronto, Playwrights Co-op, 1972.
1 act. 2m.
Two young men share their lives with the usual frustration of those in love.
fp: Tarragon Theatre, Toronto, Dec. 29, 1971.

TODD, Campbell

D2066. *Captain Reece of the "Mantelpiece"*. Halifax, n.p., 1904.
3 acts. 11m/5f. Chorus.
"A nautical extravaganza founded on W.S. Gilbert's ballads of 'Captain Reece' and the 'The Martinet' in 'Bab Ballads' ". In this satiric look at Halifax's naval society, Captain Reece proclaims a holiday picnic on McNab's island. Mock weddings unite the wrong people but the captain's daughter is pledged to her true love.

TOMS, Jim

D2067. "Hacta Nicotiana or Poetry in the Simplest Things" in *Acta Victoriana*, vol.88, #1, 1963
1 act. 1m/2f.
A satire of the typical campus literary rag.

TOPPING, C.W.

D2068. *Jesus Christ, Rabble Rouser*. Vancouver, College Printers, 1975.
3 acts. 11m/4f. Extras.
A portrayal of moral and political corruption in Jerusalem during the Roman Empire.

TOREN, C.K.

D2069. *Rosa.* Edmonton, Dept. of Extension, University of Alberta, (1948?).
1 act. 5m.
A drama about a sailor on board ship in Vancouver whose love for his girl on shore is too great for him to see her.

TOVELL, Vincent

D2070. *Success of a Mission.* See **KOCH, Eric.**

TOWNSHEND, Adele

D2071. *For the Love of a Horse.* Ottawa, Ottawa Little Theatre Workshop, #26.
1 act. 2m/4f.
Pat Pearce's obsessive love for his thoroughbred horse leads him to neglect his family and eventually to endanger his own life and theirs by committing a crime.

D2072. *Forgotten Heritage. (Be My Wedding Guest.)* Ottawa, Ottawa Little Theatre Workshop, #44.
1 act. 3m/3f.
An Englishwoman married to a Canadian Indian chief finally realizes why her attempts to improve the Indians' situation on the reservation have failed.

TREMAYNE, William Andrew 1864–1939

D2073. *Find the Thief.* Minneapolis, Minn., Northwestern Press, 1933.
1 act. 2m/1f.
A short mystery melodrama in which two supposed thieves are searching a country house when the owner returns.

D2074. *A Legal Puzzle.* New York, Dick & Fitzgerald, 1911.
3 acts. 8m/4f. Doubling.
"A farcical comedy" about a young spendthrift lawyer and his professional and romantic entanglements as he attempts to establish a career for himself.

D2075. *The Man Who Went.* Boston, Baker's Plays, 1918.
4 acts. 7m/3f. Extras.
"A melodramatic comedy". A ne'er-do-well young man turns out to be a British secret agent who foils the plans of two German spies.
fp: Grand Opera House, Toronto, Sept. 11, 1916 as "The Black Feather".

D2076. *A Question of Clothes.* Minneapolis, Minn., Northwestern Press, 1933.
3 acts. 11f.
A comedy for women with a Shakespearian twist. Madge Lawson impersonates her brother during an interview and sustains the deception long enough to get him a job lecturing to the Literary Idealists.

D2077. *A Runaway Couple.* New York, Fitzgerald, 1910.
2 acts. 4m/4f.
A stock romantic comedy in which a young woman elopes from a seminary and is discovered by her guardian and the seminary mistress at the house of her lover's friend. The friend is accused of bigamy by his wife and the others but finally the truth is revealed and all ends in connubial bliss.

D2078. *A Woman's Wager*. Philadelphia, Penn Publishing, 1926.
1 act. 2m/1f.
A comedy in which a liberated woman tricks an anti-suffragette writer into a donation to the suffrage cause.

TREMBLAY, Michel 1942–

D2079. *Les Belles-Soeurs*. Montreal, Centre d'Essai, n.d. and John Van Burek, Bill Glassco, trans. Vancouver, Talonbooks, 1974.
2 acts. 15f.
A Montreal housewife wins a million trading stamps and invites neighbours and relatives to help her stick the stamps in books. Comedy and biting satire arise when the women talk of their lives and start to steal some of the books.
fp: (in French), Théâtre du Rideau Vert, Montreal, Aug. 28, 1968. (in English), St. Lawrence Centre, Toronto, Feb. 1973. CBC TV "Front Row Centre", March 15, 1978.

D2080. "Berthe" in his *La Duchesse de Langeais & Other Plays*. Vancouver, Talonbooks, 1976.
1 act. 1f.
Berthe, ticket-taker at a chic cabaret, spends her time dreaming up the life of a great actress, the life she never attained.
fp: French-language CBC TV, Dec. 21, 1969.

D2081. *Bonjour, là, Bonjour*. John Van Burek, Bill Glassco, trans. Vancouver, Talonbooks, 1975.
31 scenes. 2m/6f.
Serge returns from Europe and visits the members of his family: four sisters, two aunts and his father.
fp: Compagnie des Deux Chaises, National Arts Centre, Ottawa, Aug. 22, 1974. Tarragon Theatre, Toronto, Feb. 1, 1975.

D2082. "La Duchesse de Langeais" in his *La Duchesse de Langeais & Other Plays*. John Van Burek, trans. Vancouver, Talonbooks, 1976.
2 acts. 1m.
The reminiscences and despair of a sixty-year-old transvestite who was the toast of four continents in her day.
fp: Les Insolents de Val d'Or, Val d'Or, Quebec, spring 1969.

D2083. *En Pièces Détachées*. Allan Van Meer, trans. Vancouver, Talonbooks, 1975.
7 scenes. 3m/6f. Extras.
A drama about the life and problems of middle-class French Canadians living in tenements in Montreal.
fp: Manitoba Theatre Centre, Winnipeg, Jan. 1973.

D2084. *Forever Yours, Marie-Lou*. John Van Burek, Bill Glassco, trans. Vancouver, Talonbooks, 1975.
1 act. 1m/3f.
Carmen visits Manon who has remained at their family home following the death of their parents. She finally leaves her sister to the ghosts of her parents and returns to her life in the outside world.
fp: Théâtre de Quat'Sous, Montreal, April 29, 1971. Tarragon Theatre, Toronto, Nov. 4, 1972.

D2085. "Gloria Star" in his *La Duchesse de Langeais & Other Plays*. John Van Burek, trans. Vancouver, Talonbooks, 1976.
1 act. 2m/7f.
A glimpse backstage at the Coconut Inn cabaret where the artists gossip about one another and await the appearance of the "star".
fp: French language CBC TV, Dec. 21, 1969.

D2086. *Hosanna*. John Van Burek, Bill Glassco, trans. Vancouver, Talonbooks, 1974.
2 acts. 2m.
The sad and bitchy world of Claude-Hosanna, an aging transvestite, who finds herself the centre of a destructive joke at Sandra's annual Hallowe'en ball.
fp: Théâtre de Quat'Sous, Montreal, May 10, 1973. Tarragon Theatre, Toronto, May 15, 1974.

D2087. "Johnny Mangano and His Astonishing Dogs" in his *La Duchesse de Langeais & Other Plays*. John Van Burek, trans. Vancouver, Talonbooks, 1976 and Arlette Franciere, trans. in *Cues and Entrances*. Henry Beissel, ed. Toronto, Gage, 1977.
1 act. 3m/1f.
Carlotta forces Johnny to face what he is, the inept trainer of a third-rate dog act.
fp: French language CBC TV, Dec. 21, 1969.

D2088. *Like Death Warmed Over*. Allan Van Meer, trans. Toronto, Playwrights Co-op, 1973. See *En Pièces Détachées*.

D2089. "Surprise, Surprise" in his *La Duchesse de Langeais & Other Plays*. John Van Burek, trans. Vancouver, Talonbooks, 1976.
1 act. 3f.
Jeannine has planned a surprise party for Madeleine but trouble occurs when Laurette phones the wrong Madeleine and throws an organized party into chaos.
fp: Théâtre-Midi du Maurier at Théâtre du Nouveau Monde, Montreal, April 1975. St. Lawrence Centre, Toronto, Oct. 22, 1975.

TREMBLAY, Renald 1943–

D2090. "Greta, the Divine", Allan Van Meer, trans., in *A Collection of Canadian Plays* vol.5. Rolf Kalman, ed., Toronto, Simon & Pierre, 1978.
2 acts. 4m/3f. Extras. Doubling.
A translation of his *La Celeste Greta*. A satiric look at Quebec's history as seen through the eyes of Greta, an angel who descends from heaven to view events in Quebec.
fp: La Compagnie de Quat' Sous, Montreal, Nov. 15, 1973.

TRILLO, Florence

D2091. *Among His Peers*. Halifax, Dramatists Co-op, 1977 and in *Callboard*, vol.24, #3, Fall 1977.
1 act. 5m/2f. Extras.
The friendship of a white man and a black man is put to the test in the ultimate discrimination of eternity.

D2092. *A Change Is As Good As*. Halifax, Dramatists Co-op, 1977.
1 act. 3m/2f.
A sex farce in which the battle of the sexes is brought to what may be its only possible conclusion.
fp: Nova Scotia Festival of the Arts.

D2093. "Pussy's in the Well" in her *Little Boy Blue, Wake Up!*. Halifax, Dramatists Co-op, 1977.
1 act. 4m/3f.
A farce in which wealthy summer residents of a small community dominate and exploit the year-round residents.
p: Dartmouth Players, N.S., 1971.

D2094. *Wagging Their Tails Behind Them.* Ottawa, Ottawa Little Theatre Workshop, #55 and in her *Little Boy Blue, Wake Up!*. Halifax, Dramatists Co-op, 1977.
1 act. 4m/5f. Extras.
In the confines of an airport terminal, a man is led through the frightening stages of being stripped of his individuality.
p: Dartmouth Players, N.S., 1971.

D2095. "What a Good Boy Am I" in her *Little Boy Blue, Wake Up!*. Halifax, Dramatists Co-op, 1977.
1 act. 1m/3f.
A man is castrated by three women.
p: Dartmouth Players, N.S., 1971.

TRIMMER, Ellen McKay

D2096. *Christmas Wonders.* Waterloo, Ont., Waterloo Music, 1957.
3 scenes. 24b/30g. Chorus.
A children's presentation of the three Christmas wonders: the star, the manger and the wise men.

TROTTER, Marjorie

D2097. "Scenes of World Fellowship" in *Sketches and Plays.* Toronto, National Girls' Work Board, Religious Education Council of Canada, (192-?).
1 act. 13f.
A dramatization intended to show that "of all the problems of human life the greatest, the most perilous today, is the problem of race".
fp: Canadian Girls In Training camps.

TRUSS, Jan

D2098. *Attack.* Edmonton, Alberta Dept. of Culture, 1970.
1 act. 17m/9f. Extras.
A teacher who is forced to defend himself and his students against a gang of hoodlums is condemned for his actions by those whom he saved.

D2099. "Ooomerahgi Oh" in her *Ooomerahgi Oh and A Very Small Rebellion.*
Toronto, Playwrights Co-op, 1978.
1 act. 2m/1f/1b/2g.
A children's play about a prairie family and their encounter with a mysterious stranger.
fp: Studio Theatre, Calgary Hall, University of Calgary, February 1974.

D2100. "A Very Small Rebellion" in her *Ooomerahgi Oh and A Very Small Rebellion.*
Toronto, Playwrights Co-op, 1978.
1 act. 6m/1f. Extras. Doubling.
A dramatization for children of Louis Riel and the Northwest Rebellion.
fp: Alberta Theatre Projects, Canmore Opera House, Calgary, Oct. 1, 1974.

TWARDOWSKI, Astrid

D2101. *The Curse of the Lost Lemon Mine.* Ottawa, Ottawa Little Theatre Workshop, #50.
1 act. 7m. Extras.
A comedy. All who seek the Lost Lemon Mine come to an untimely end.

TWEED, Thomas William 1908–1971

D2102. *The Dream.* Ottawa, Centennial Commission, 1965.
1 act. 15m.
"An entertainment concerning the events leading up to Confederation". In 1864, the Fathers of Confederation discuss the dream of a "Dominion from Sea to Sea".

D2103. "A Foretaste of Hindsight" in *A Treasury of Canadian Humour.* Robert Thomas Allen, ed. Toronto, McClelland & Stewart, 1967.
1 act. 10m/1f.
A satire on the difficulty of getting all the Canadian provinces to agree on anything, even a TV broadcast of Little Red Ridinghood.
fp: CBC radio, 1946.

TWEEDSMUIR, Lady. See BUCHAN, Susan.

TWENTY-FIFTH STREET HOUSE THEATRE

D2104. "Paper Wheat" in *Canadian Theatre Review,* #17, Winter 1978.
2 acts. 3m/2f. Doubling.
A collective creation about the sod-busting immigrants to the prairies and the formation of the Saskatchewan Co-operative Movement.
fp: 25th Street House Theatre, Memorial Hall, Sintaluta, Saskatchewan, March 18, 1977.

UDAHOV, Edward

D2105. (Untitled work) in Kruk, Mark. *Come in and Take Your Clothes Off.* Toronto, Gateway Press, 1971.
1 act. 2m/2f.
Twists and turns in the game of sexual mores. Joe, who has been fooling around on his wife, is confronted by his lover and her angry boyfriend.

URSELL, Geoffrey

D2106. "The Park" in *Performing Arts in Canada,* vol.9, #3, Fall 1972.
1 act. 9m/1f. Extras. Doubling.
A man and his cat cope with the world which is literally coming down around their ears.

van EVERY, Jane

D2107. *Mary.* Waterloo, Ont., Waterloo Music, 1932.
6 scenes. 12m/2f/1b/1g. Extras.
"A nativity play." Joseph and Mary are preparing for the coming of Jesus. Music by Mabel Mortimer.

VEAZEY, Emma

D2108. "A Christmas Tree for Mother Goose's Children" in *Educational Review*, vol.36, #4, Dec. 1921.
1 act. 7b/7g.
A children's play. Nursery rhyme characters decide to celebrate Christmas like other children.

D2109. "The Making of Our Flag" in *Educational Review*, vol.35, #9, April 1921.
1 scene. 6g.
An Empire Day exercise about the making of the Union Jack.

D2110. "When Santa Needed Help" in *Educational Review*, vol.35, #4, Nov. 1920.
1 act. 2b/3g. Extras.
A children's play. Santa surprises two children who thought he would not know their new address.

VIVIAN, George and B.A. Field

D2111. *Cinderella*. Toronto, Douglas, 1922.
2 acts. 7m/6f/1b/2g. Extras.
A modernized musical "Vaughan Glaser's Christmas pantomime" of the traditional story of the magic slipper. Music by Roy Webb.
fp: Uptown Theatre, Toronto, December 1922.

VIVIEN, Geoffrey

D2112. *How History Is Made*. Western Canada Theatre Conference. Edmonton, Dept. of Extension, University of Alberta, 1948.
1 act. 4m/2f.
While most of the Department of External Affairs is out at a party, a minor official is left to conduct business with the ambassador of Bazarenia.

VOADEN, Herman 1903–

D2113. *Earth Song*. Toronto, Playwrights Co-op, 1976.
5 scenes. 1m/1f. Extras.
A poetic drama tracing the legend of mankind through Adam and Eve, from innocence through experience to wisdom and beauty.
fp: Sarnia Drama League, Ont., Dec. 1932.

D2114. "Esther" in *Edward Johnson Building, Faculty of Music, Opening Ceremonies*. Toronto, Royal Conservatory of Music, University of Toronto, 1964.
5 parts. 1m/1f. Chorus.
A brief libretto arranged from the Bible for the dramatic symphony by Godfrey Ridout.
fp: Royal Conservatory of Music Chorus and Orchestra, Massey Hall, Toronto, April 29, 1952.

D2115. "Murder Pattern" in *Canadian Theatre Review*, #5, Winter 1975.
1 act. 8m. Extras. Doubling.
"An experiment toward a symphonic theatre". An expressionist presentation relating the story of a north Ontario farmer who murders the neighbourhood bully and is sent to Kingston Penitentiary.
fp: Play Workshop, Central High School of Commerce, Toronto, Jan. 24, 1936.

D2116. "Wilderness" in *Boreal,* #11/12, 1978.
1 act. 3m/2f.
"A play of the North" in which a school teacher waits in vain for the return of her lover who has perished in a blizzard.
fp: (Workshop), Department of Drama, Yale University, 1931. Faculty Players, Queen's University, Kingston, 1932.

D2117. **VOYER, Juli.** *Pickles and Puppets.* See **YOUNG, Noreen.**

WADE, Bryan 1950–

D2118. "Alias" in his *Alias and Antigravitational Menopause.* Toronto, Playwrights Co-op, 1974.
1 act. 2m/1f.
On their way to the Wasteland for a fresh supply of silver bullets, the Lone Ranger and Tonto meet Rebecca, a woman in distress, and a silent stranger.
fp: University of Guelph, Guelph, Ont., 1975.

D2119. *Aliens.* Toronto, Playwrights Co-op, 1975.
1 act. 1m/2f.
A back alley is transformed into a mysterious zone of shifting time and realities in which a power struggle between two women and a man is acted out.
fp: Factory Theatre Lab, Toronto, April 8, 1975.

D2120. "Antigravitational Menopause" in his *Alias and Antigravitational Menopause.* Toronto, Playwrights Co-op, 1974.
1 act. 2m.
A nightmare look at the world of middle-aged Sid and the sexually-frustrated barber, Dick, who cuts Sid's hair.

D2121. *Blitzkrieg.* Toronto, Playwrights Co-op, 1974.
1 act. 2m/2f.
At the Berghof, his chalet in the Bavarian alps, Adolf Hitler and Eva Braun live secluded from the devastation of war and spend their time indulging in fantasies and horrible dreams under the observation of Martin Borman and Gretl Braun.
fp: Tarragon Theatre at the Poor Alex Theatre, Toronto, Feb. 16, 1974.

D2122. "Coffee Break" in *Karaki,* 1971.
1 act. 2m.
A bus driver almost at retirement age finds out that after thirty years the company is about to change his route. His best friend went beserk because he was threatened with the same thing.

D2123. "Electric Gunfighters" in his *Lifeguard/Electric Gunfighters/Nightshift.* Toronto, Playwrights Co-op, 1976.
1 act. 2m.
Pete and Bob enact cliche routines from Western movies in this exploration of the impact of the media on our lives.
fp: Tarragon Theatre, Toronto, March 26, 1973.

D2124. *Lifeguard.* Vancouver, New Play Centre, 1973 and in his *Lifeguard/Electric Gunfighters/Nightshift.* Toronto, Playwrights Co-op, 1976 and in *Karaki,* #6, 1977.
1 act. 3m/2f.
A surrealistic encounter between a man, his wife and a lifeguard on a beach.
fp: New Play Centre, Vancouver Art Gallery, 1973.

D2125. "Nightshift" in *Absolute Cannon Review*, vol.3, #1, 1971 and in his *Lifeguard/Electric Gunfighters/Nightshift*. Toronto, Playwrights Co-op, 1976 and in *Karaki*, #6, 1977.
1 act. 2f.
An intense look at a young woman, Gail, whose fantasy world with a mannequin collides with the reality of Isobel, an older woman.
fp: Space Tool Company, Ottawa, June 29, 1973.

D2126. "Off the Freeway" in *Uvic Writing*. Victoria, Creative Writing Program, University of Victoria, April 1970.
1 act. 1m/2f.
A couple and their mother on vacation are delayed in a motel by thick fog. They intend to put her in an old folks' home, and she is afraid.

D2127. "Strobe" in *Martlet Magazine*, Dec. 1972.
1 act. 3m.
Three youths smoke marijuana after a baseball game and see a space capsule signalling to them.

D2128. *Tanned*. Toronto, Playwrights Co-op, 1976 and (revised version) 1977.
3 acts. 3m/3f.
A drama about three women at a summer cottage attempting to deal with the men in their troubled lives.
fp: Factory Theatre Lab, Toronto, Oct. 7, 1976.

D2129. *This Side of the Rockies*. Toronto, Playwrights Co-op, 1977.
7 scenes. 5m/1f.
Three young men emerge changed from their weekend camping expedition, having encountered two psychopathic hunters, a dead body, and an unearthly woman.
fp: Factory Theatre Lab, Toronto, Jan. 19, 1977.

D2130. *Underground*. Toronto, Playwrights Co-op, 1975.
3 acts. 2m/1f.
Claire, Al and Gerry share a bizarre relationship which is slowly unmasked in the three interrelated scenes culminating in a ritualistic suicide.
fp: Factory Theatre Lab, Toronto, May 20, 1975.

D2131. "Vacuum" in *Introductions from an Island 1971*. Victoria, University of Victoria, 1971.
1 act. 2m/1f.
Jones, Anne, and Anne's son Ed, a 20-year-old in a stroller, discuss the fine art of colouring, ambition, frustration, life, and snakes in toilet bowls.
fp: Players' Club, University of Victoria, April 1971.

WAGAR, Les

D2132. "Alley at the Back of Things" in *Rubaboo 2*. Scarborough, Ont., Gage, 1964.
1 act. 3b/2g.
A play for children. Robin has a butterfly in a bottle and the other children all want it. After various strategies, the butterfly is released.

WAIGHT, Quentin 1894–

D2133. "Tamerlane" in his *Prelude to Glory*. Seattle, Superior Publishing, 1951.
11 scenes. 7m/4f.
During his conquest of Moscow, Tamerlane falls in love with a beautiful Christian girl and carries her back to Samarkand to be his queen.

WAGNER, Phillip C.

D2134. *Murder in the Empress*. Toronto, Playwrights Co-op, 1978.
3 acts. 2m/3f.
A comic mystery play set in Victoria's Empress Hotel.
fp: Vancouver Island Players, Victoria, B.C., August 1977.

WALKER, George F. 1947–

D2135. *Ambush at Tether's End*. Toronto, Playwrights Co-op, 1972 and in *The Factory Lab Anthology*. Connie Brissenden, ed. Vancouver, Talonbooks, 1974.
2 acts. 4m/1f.
A comedy in which Bush and Galt are confronted with the corpse of their friend Max who has hanged himself.
fp: Factory Theatre Lab, Toronto, Dec. 1971. CBC radio, Vancouver, 1974.

D2136. *Bagdad Saloon*. Toronto, Playwrights Co-op, 1973 and in his *Three Plays*. Toronto, Coach House, 1978.
16 scenes. 7m/4f. Extras.
"A cartoon". A group of legendary characters in a western saloon in the middle of the Arabian desert suffer from the slow death and impotence of old age.
fp: Factory Theatre Lab, Toronto, March 1973.

D2137. *Beyond Mozambique*. Toronto, Playwrights Co-op, 1975 and in his *Three Plays*. Toronto, Coach House, 1978.
6 scenes. 4m/2f.
On the porch of a decaying colonial house in the midst of the Mozambique jungle, an ex-Nazi doctor, his murderous assistant, a porno movie star, an RCMP corporal, a junkie priest and a Chekhov-obsessed Russian act out real and imagined roles as the chaos of the surrounding jungle engulfs them.
fp: Factory Theatre Lab, Toronto, May 11, 1974.

D2138. *The Prince of Naples*. Toronto, Playwrights Co-op, 1972 and in *Now In Paperback*. Connie Brissenden, ed. Toronto, Fineglow Plays, 1973.
1 act. 2m.
A "cerebral farce" in which contemporary teaching is satirized and learning becomes more and more absurdly reduced and meaningless.
fp: Factory Theatre Lab, Toronto, July 1971. CBC radio, Vancouver, 1973.

D2139. "Ramona and the White Slaves" in his *Three Plays*. Toronto, Coach House, 1978.
1 act. 2m/3f. Doubling.
An exotic comedy-fantasy set in Hong Kong in 1919 in which a former nun, now the madam of a sinister brothel, experiences an opium nightmare in which she reduces her lovers and children to slavish humiliation.
fp: Factory Theatre Lab, Toronto, Jan. 13, 1976.

D2140. *Sacktown Rag.* Toronto, Playwrights Co-op, 1972.
2 acts. 6m/4f.
Max Barrett presents his "Indictment of Authority": a series of distorted and fantasized memories of growing up in a big city slum.
fp: Factory Theatre Lab, Toronto, April 5, 1972.

D2141. *Zastrozzi.* The Master of Discipline. Toronto, Playwrights Co-op, 1977.
2 acts. 4m/2f.
A revenge melodrama inspired by Shelley's novel in which Zastrozzi, the satan of Europe, engages in a never-ending quest of retribution with his double, the saintly, deluded Verezzi.
fp: Toronto Free Theatre, Nov. 2, 1977.

WALLACE, Robert 1943–

D2142. *'67.* Toronto, Playwrights Co-op, 1974.
2 acts. 5m/4f. Extras. Doubling.
A depiction of a tempestuous relationship between David Child, a successful university professor and master games-player and a new student, Paul.

WALLEY, M. Grace

D2143. "Simple Dramatization of History" in *Educational Review,* vol.35, #11, June–July 1921.
1 scene. 4b/3g. Extras.
A dramatization of the exploits of early North American explorers and the Pilgrims.

WALMSLEY, Tom 1948–

D2144. *Something Red.* Vancouver, New Play Centre, 1978.
2 acts. 2m/2f.
Bobby, ex-thief and hard-core unemployed, spends months on end watching TV, drinking and despising his lady and his friends who work. Self-destruction turns outward, passivity becomes violence, and sexual masochism becomes sadism, "something red".
fp: New Play Centre, Vancouver East Cultural Centre, Oct. 6, 1978.

D2145. *The Jones Boy.* Vancouver, Pulp Press, 1978.
1 act. 3m/2f.
A drama about heroin and sex.
fp: Toronto Free Theatre, Jan. 20, 1977.

D2146. *The Workingman.* Vancouver, Pulp Press, 1976.
1 act. 3m/1f.
Tom, Gene and Charlene rent a sleazy apartment for the purpose of filming themselves in sexual acts.
fp: New Play Centre, Vancouver, du Maurier Festival, May 2, 1975.

WALSH, F.G.

D2147. *The Trial of Louis Riel.* Fargo, N.D., North Dakota Institute for Regional Studies, 1965.
2 acts. 21m/1f. Extras.
A balladeer gives narrative comment presenting the historical trial for treason of the leader of the 1885 Metis uprising in Saskatchewan.
fp: The Little Country Theatre, North Dakota State University, Fargo, N.D., Oct. 16, 1963.

WALSH, Norman

D2148. "Let There Be Farce" in *The Best Short Plays of 1955-56.* Margaret Mayorga, ed. Boston, Beacon Press, 1956.
1 act. 1m/2f.
A new woman in the neighbourhood tries to follow her neighbour's creed — if you want something, go out and get it any way you can.
fp: Ottawa Little Theatre, Oct. 13, 1955.

D2149. *Number One.* New Haven, Connecticut, James Granady, 1956.
1 act. 1m/2f.
A comedy. In a slum district, two middle-aged women hanging wash and a thief discover ways of taking care of "number one".
fp: Ottawa Little Theatre, Oct. 15, 1955.

WALSH, Patrick F.

D2150. *Mad Shelley.* Antigonish, N.S., n.p., 1971 and in *Callboard,* vol.24, #1, Spring 1977.
3 acts. 11m/9f. Extras. Doubling.
A picturesque portrayal of Shelley's life covering the period 1803 to 1822.

WARD, James Edward 1883-1958

D2151. *The Cradle in the Hills.* Toronto, William Tyrrell, 1941.
4 acts. 12m/1f/1b.
"A play of the Nativity". The Gospel story of the journey to Bethlehem, the visit of the shepherds and the wise men is enacted.

D2152. *God's Plenty.* Toronto, Longmans, 1945.
3 acts. 5m/2f. Extras. Doubling.
"A pastoral idyll founded on the Book of Ruth with incidental lyrics". The widows Ruth and Naomi come to Bethlehem where Naomi dreams of another child "in a manger".
fp: As "The Gleaners", St. Stephen's Church, Toronto, Nov. 1, 1944.

WARMAN, Marie

D2153. *Kingdom of Kinkapoo.* (London, Ont. ?), 1906.
3 acts. 5m/3f. Extras.
An operetta in which fairies and opium dreams work their beautiful madness on everyone who lands on an enchanted island — traders, natives and American military cadets.

WARREN, Eileen

D2154. *Throw Sand Against the Wind.* Ottawa, Ottawa Little Theatre Workshop, #42.
1 act. 5m/1f.
An insecure, sensitive young man is driven away from any chance for happiness when his fellow cowhands and circumstances attest to his being guilty of raping a young girl.

D2155. *Whatever the Guise.* Ottawa, Ottawa Little Theatre Workshop, #1.
1 act. 2m/4f.
A small town, ignorant of the truth, blindly condemns a young schoolteacher for his involvement with a student. She refuses to tell the truth, fearing the consequences.
fp: Ottawa Little Theatre, Oct. 1, 1959.

WATMOUGH, David 1932–

D2156. "A First Death" in his *Ashes for Easter and Other Monodramas.* Vancouver, Talonbooks, 1972.
1 act. 1m.
Davey Bryant examines the ugliness of old age when his great aunt dies.

D2157. "A First Job" in his *Ashes for Easter and Other Monodramas.* Vancouver, Talonbooks, 1972.
1 act. 1m.
Young Davey Bryant takes his first job with a Cornwall newspaper as a junior reporter and finds his first love.

D2158. "Ashes for Easter" in his *Ashes for Easter and Other Monodramas.* Vancouver, Talonbooks, 1972.
1 act. 1m.
Davey Bryant returns to England to visit his mother shortly after his father's death, scattering his father's ashes over the Cornish countryside.

D2159. "Black Memory" in his *Ashes for Easter and Other Monodramas.* Vancouver, Talonbooks, 1972.
1 act. 1m.
Upon arriving in New York, Davey Bryant is robbed and threatened with death in an attempted homosexual encounter.

D2160. "Do You Remember One September Afternoon" in his *Names for the Numbered Years.* Vancouver, Bau-Xi Gallery, 1967.
3 acts. 4m. Extras.
Three aging and rather mad sisters, continually speaking of the past, persist in mistreating and nagging each other.

D2161. "Friedhof" in his *Names for the Numbered Years.* Vancouver, Bau-Xi Gallery, 1967.
1 act. 4m/1f.
The peacefulness of a graveyard seems to increase the horrors of life. A youth must learn to accept life as well as death.
fp: Frederic Wood Theatre, University of British Columbia, Vancouver.

D2162. "In the Mood" in his *Ashes for Easter and Other Monodramas.* Vancouver, Talonbooks, 1972.
1 act. 1m.
A youth of fifteen has his first homosexual encounter with a soldier at a community dance.

D2163. "My Mother's House Has Too Many Rooms" in his *Names for the Numbered Years.* Vancouver, Bau-Xi Gallery, 1967.
3 acts. 6m/2f.
Mr. and Mrs. Heirsworthy have much to cope with: their homosexual son Baby and their nymphomaniac daughter Hespera who murders the visiting Mr. Pellegrini.

D2164. *Plen-An-Guary.* Vancouver, Author, (197-?). (Mimeographed).
2 acts. 3m.
An absurd encounter set in the Bodwin Moors between a vacuous painter, a crazy photographer and the political activist Causely, the "Voice of Free Cornwall".

D2165. "Sacred and Secular" in his *Ashes for Easter and Other Monodramas.* Vancouver, Talonbooks, 1972.
1 act. 1m.
A young boy staying with his aunt begins having sexual fantasies, while his parents are involved with the war effort in Britain.

D2166. "Scar Tissue" in his *Ashes for Easter and Other Monodramas.* Vancouver, Talonbooks, 1972.
1 act. 1m.
Davey Bryant recalls his first encounter with the law and his three-week imprisonment during the war.

D2167. "Shipwreck" in his *Ashes for Easter and Other Monodramas.* Vancouver, Talonbooks, 1972.
1 act. 1m.
After many years in Canada, Davey Bryant returns to his English home to bury his father.

D2168. "Trading in Innocence" in his *Ashes for Easter and Other Monodramas.* Vancouver, Talonbooks, 1972.
1 act. 1m.
Three young boys trade an aunt's birthday gift for three pet rats.

D2169. "Wickanninish Memory" in his *Ashes for Easter and Other Monodramas.* Vancouver, Talonbooks, 1972.
1 act. 1m.
Davey Bryant recalls the life and death of a German friend.

WATSON, Wilfred 1911–

D2170. "The Canadian Fact" in *White Pelican,* vol.2, #1, Winter 1972.
1 act. 2m.
Two theatrical gentlemen discuss the advantages and disadvantages of staging an anti-American play.
fp: Waterdale Playhouse, Edmonton, May 1967.

D2171. "Over Prairie Trails to the Just Society" in *White Pelican,* vol.3, #1, Winter 1973.
12 scenes. 3m/1f.
Two horses try to get rid of the Prime Minister because of the cruel treatment he gives these "dumb" animals while travelling west to visit his wife, Lotte von Heimtal.

D2172. "Wail for Two Pedestals" in *Humanities Association Bulletin,* vol.16, #2, Fall 1965.
3 acts. 4m/3f.
"Theatre of the Absurd". The chorus wails to Godot while the daughter of Lefty, Mama Lolita and her son wander in and out.
fp: Yardbird Suite, Edmonton, Nov. 3, 1964.

WATT, Gladys Cameron

D2173. *Sawdust.* Ottawa, Ottawa Little Theatre Workshop, #9.
1 act. 3m/3f.
A dynamic woman of 74 lends her support and her controlling interest in the family lumber company to aid her nephew and his conservation project against the narrow views of his father.

WATTS, Irene N. 1931–

D2174. "A Blizzard Leaves No Footprints" in her *A Blizzard Leaves No Footprints.* Toronto, Playwrights Co-op, 1978.
1 act. 1m/3f/2b/1g. Extras.
Two Innuit children rescue their mother who has been captured by the Blizzard Spirit because of their negligence.

D2174A. *A Chain of Words.* Vancouver, Talonbooks, 1978.
1 act. 3m/2f.
A collection of six brief dramatic adaptations of Japanese folk-tales for young people.
fp: Green Thumb Players, Vancouver East Cultural Centre, Oct. 22, 1978.

D2175. "Listen to the Drum" in her *A Blizzard Leaves No Footprints.* Toronto, Playwrights Co-op, 1978.
1 act. 3m/2f. Extras. Doubling.
A children's play based on Innuit legends of how the Raven made the world.
fp: Citadel On Wheels/Wings, Alberta tour, September 1973.

D2176. "Patches" in her *A Blizzard Leaves No Footprints.* Toronto, Playwrights Co-op, 1978.
1 act. 15m/1f.
A play for children based on storytelling.
fp: Citadel On Wheels/Wings, Edmonton, September 1975.

D2177. "The Rainstone" in her *A Blizzard Leaves No Footprints.* Toronto, Playwrights Co-op, 1978.
1 act. 5m/1f.
A play for children based on a Japanese folk-tale about an old woman who finds a child near a river.
fp: Citadel On Wheels/Wings, Edmonton, 1974.

WATTS, Reg 1926–

D2178. *In the Blood.* West Vancouver, Watts, R.J. & Associates, 1974 and (second enlarged edition) 1977.
2 acts. 9m/4f. Extras.
The play portrays the cultural heritage of Canada's native people and the strength and spirit of the early pioneers in a West Coast fishing village in the 1870s.
fp: Centennial Theatre, Vancouver, 1971.

WAYGOOD, John

D2179. *Like as Two P's.* N.p., n.p., n.d. (Bound with Alexander Begg's *Practical Handbook and Guide to Manitoba).*
4 scenes. 8m/3f. Extras.
A comedy in which two unrelated men who are exact doubles are mistaken for each other. When no one believes the truth, they are locked up in an insane asylum by a vengeful doctor.

WEALES, Gerald

D2180. "The Western Hero" in *Nobody Waved Good-bye and Other Plays.* Herman Voaden, ed. Toronto, Macmillan, 1966.
1 act. 5m/1f/1b. Extras.
A documentary on how a Western works as seen through the eyes of the Western hero.
fp: CBC TV "Explorations", Oct. 5, 1960.

WELLWOOD, Ric

D2181. "Liberation" in *Jubilee,* nos.1 and 2, 1974 and 1975.
3 acts. 3m/3f.
"A comedy of morals" in which a young woman helps a repressed young man liberate himself from his oppressive mother and guilt feelings.

WENNER, Edward A.

D2182. *Bohunk.* Edmonton, Dept. of Extension, University of Alberta, (1948?).
1 act. 14m. Extras.
A drama about discrimination against foreign immigrants set in a B.C. logging camp.

WERRY, Wilfred Watson 1897–

D2183. *The Bag of Earth.* Ottawa, Ottawa Little Theatre Workshop, #53.
1 act. 5m/2f.
An old respected Jewish tailor waits for his grandson to return with a bag of earth from Israel. An old friend brings him the news of his grandson's death in the Arab-Israeli war and the bag of earth which was found with the body.

D2184. "Breakdown" in *Canada on Stage.* Stanley Richards, ed. Toronto, Clarke Irwin, 1960 and in *Ten Canadian Short Plays.* John Stevens, ed. New York, Dell, 1975.
1 act. 3m/1f.
John Bridgman has had a nervous breakdown and now tries to re-establish himself in the business world.

D2185. "Breakfast" in *Canadian Stage, Screen and Studio*, vol.1, #2, Oct. 1936.
1 act. 2m/1f.
Before an unemployed man contemplating suicide because he cannot support his wife and children can kill himself, he learns that he can have his old job back.
fp: Playwriting Group, Montreal Repertory Theatre, 1936.

WESTRAY, John

D2186. *God So Loved the World.* London, Arthur Stockwell, 1931.
3 acts. 3m/7f/2g. Extras.
A simple play of the Passion and Resurrection.

WETMORE, Andrew

D2187. *Andante and Variations.* Halifax, Dramatists Co-op, 1977, and in *Callboard*, vol. 25, #3, Fall 1978.
1 act. 3m/4f.
A young couple in the 1930s set up housekeeping while a young couple in the present visit a junk shop.

D2188. *Burwash, Site 3.* Halifax, Dramatists Co-op, 1977 and Toronto, Playwrights Co-op, 1978.
6 scenes. 2m/2f.
A comedy about love and archeology in backwoods Nova Scotia in which Marti McAndrews tries to dig up evidence to support a sagging thesis.
fp: Seaweed Theatre, Halifax, April 1978.

D2189. *The Gracchi.* Halifax, Dramatists Co-op, 1977.
3 acts. 13m/3f. Extras.
In Rome, 121 B.C., Gaius Gracchus tries to reform the republic without falling into demagoguery.

D2190. "The Great Religious Stir" in *Callboard*, vol.24, #2, Summer 1977.
1 act. 4m/1f. Extras.
In 1781, the revivalist Henry Alline brings the "new light" to the people of Yarmouth, N.S. The local minister objects to his message and methods, dividing the town.

D2191. *The Haunted House.* Halifax, Dramatists Co-op, 1977.
5 acts. 8m/4f. Extras.
A loose adaptation of Plautus' *Mostellaria* about a wastrel son and his self-serving servant.

D2192. "Man in the Basement" in his *Short Plays.* Halifax, Dramatists Co-op, 1977.
1 act. 1m/1f.
An elderly lady finds an intruder who claims to be the meter reader.

D2193. "Rendezvous" in his *Short Plays.* Halifax, Dramatists Co-op, 1977.
1 act. 1m/1f.
Nancy and Walter conduct a reluctant reunion outside the Nova Scotian Hotel in Halifax.

D2194. "Stand" in his *Short Plays.* Halifax, Dramatists Co-op, 1977.
1 act. 1m/1f.
A macabre encounter between a lonely hot-dog salesman and a lost woman on the beach.

WETMORE, Don

D2195. *The Highland Heart in Nova Scotia.* Halifax, Dramatists Co-op, 1977.
2 parts. 12m/9f/4b/4g. Extras. Doubling.
A nostalgic recollection of rural life in Cape Breton at the turn of the century and just prior to W.W. I.
p: Theatre Arts Guild, Halifax, 1967.

D2196. "The House of Laval" in *Echoes,* #115, March 1929.
1 act. 3m/1f.
Set in 1646 in the house of Francois de Laval in Montigny-sur-Avre, France. Francois decides to join the church instead of carrying on the tradition of the family name.

WHITE, Vincent A.

D2197. "Exit Son" in *Acadia Athenaeum,* vol.55, #6, April 1929 and vol.60, #4, February 1935.
1 scene. 3m/1f.
A man shoots a burglar in a dark room and learns that he has killed his returning son.

WHITMAS, E. Ardis

D2198. "There Little Girl, Don't Cry" in *Acadia Athenaeum,* vol.52, #4, March 1926.
1 scene. 1m/2f.
Hollyhocks mean contentment with the boy next door after roses from a romantic stranger prove to be a temporary infatuation.

WHYTE, Thomas 1938–

D2199. *Dismissal Leading to Lustfulness.* Toronto, Playwrights Co-op, 1974.
1 act. 4m/3f.
On the day of his dismissal from his latest job, a middle-aged dreamer is caught up in the fantasies of his rooming house neighbours.
fp: Little Theatre Club, London, England. BBC TV, 1967.

D2200. *Free Beer.* Toronto, Playwrights Co-op, 1972.
1 act. 2m/1f.
One bottle of free beer plus a song and dance routine are part of Cyriack's madcap scheme to get his daughter Hortensia and his son-in-law to move into his house.
fp: St. Martin's Gallery, London, England, Aug. 2, 1965.

D2201. *That Time of the Month.* Toronto, Playwrights Co-op, 1972.
2 acts. 1m.
"An ironical satire" in which the leader of the "Society of Rejects", a group of artists denied financial support by the "National Council", wins power when he includes a policy on menstrual periods in his platform.
fp: Theatre West, Edmonton Experimental Theatre, Oct. 1972.

WIEBE, Rudy Henry 1934– and Theatre Passe Muraille

D2202. *Far As the Eye Can See.* Edmonton, NeWest Press, 1977.
3 acts. 13m/4f. Doubling.
A contemporary drama about the Dodds-Round Hill Power Development Project near Edmonton and the Agricultural Protective Society set up by farmers to try to stop the project.
fp: Theatre 3, Edmonton, April 12, 1977.

WIESENFELD, Joe 1947–

D2203. *Spratt.* Vancouver, Talonbooks, 1978.
2 acts. 4m/3f.
A scathing portrait of a man locked into a macho world.
fp: Vancouver Playhouse, Jan. 28, 1978 as "Jack Sprat".

WIGGINS, Chris 1931–

D2204. *Please Don't Sneeze.* Toronto, Arrowig, (1966?).
2 acts. 6m/3f.
A musical play for children. Squire Tom and the other servants of Blunderbuss castle attempt to rid the baron of an overbearing housekeeper who intends to become the baroness. Music by John Sims.
fp: Museum Theatre, Toronto, Jan. 29, 1966.

D2205. *Sinbad and the Mermaid.* Toronto, Arrowig, 1965.
2 acts. 6m/1f. Extras. Doubling.
A play for children. Sinbad and a young boy and a mermaid defeat the Caliph's nephew and an ancient magician.
p: Fredericton Playhouse, Dec. 26, 1966.

D2206. *Sleeping Beauty.* Toronto, Arrowig, 1965.
2 acts. 5m/4f.
A musical retelling the children of the story of Briar Rose. The narrator is an apprentice magician and a former elf. Music by Chris Wiggins and John Fenwick.
fp: Museum Children's Theatre, Toronto, 1963.

WILLIAMS, Frances Fenwick

D2207. "Which" in *One Act Plays by Canadian Authors.* Montreal, Canadian Authors' Association, 1926.
1 act. 1m/9f.
While sleeping, a young man encounters the seven aspects of his fiancee's character and decides he wants all of them.

WILLIAMS, Minnie (Harvey)

D2208. *The Romance of Canada.* Toronto, Ryerson, 1923.
1 act. 25m/45f. Extras.
"An historical pageant of Canada". The Goddess of Fame recalls the past to remind Canadians of their obligations to the pioneers.
fp: Parkdale Methodist Church Choir, Toronto, April 25, 1923.

WILLIAMS, Norman 1923–

D2209. *A Battle of Wits.* Toronto, French, 1956 and in his *Worlds Apart.* Toronto, Copp Clark, 1956 and in *Invitation to Drama.* A.A. Orr, ed. Toronto, Macmillan, 1956 and (revised edition) 1967.
1 act. 5m/2f.
Silver Lotus and Sun Chu had always tried to outwit each other from childhood onward; as adults, the "battle of wits" continues but Sun Chu wins the final contest.
fp: Ottawa Little Theatre, Nov. 18, 1953.

D2210. *Don't Touch That Phone.* Toronto, Playwrights Co-op, 1972.
1 act. 2m/2f.
A man suddenly finds that he cannot understand how things work and feels he cannot live in such a world. Fortunately his mother resolves everything for him.
fp: (Workshop), Learning Resources Centre, Toronto, May 1972.

D2211. "Dreams" in his *Worlds Apart.* Toronto, Copp Clark, 1956.
1 act. 3m/3f.
Experience in this life and faith in the life after leads Mrs. Cullan to kill both herself and her son.
fp: West End Players, Arts and Letters Club, Toronto, Oct. 27, 1955.

D2212. *He Didn't Even Say Goodbye.* Toronto, Playwrights Co-op, 1972.
1 act. 4m/1f.
Ben's life has reached a turning point: people who make him sick literally disappear from his sight.
fp: CBC TV, 1966.

D2213. "The King Decides" in his *Worlds Apart.* Toronto, Copp Clark, 1956.
1 act. 4m/2f.
For both personal and political reasons, an exiled king refuses to return to the throne.
fp: Ottawa Little Theatre, Oct. 13, 1955.

D2214. "The Mountain" in his *Worlds Apart.* Toronto, Copp Clark, 1956.
1 act. 4m/1f. Extras.
The true nature of an aging matinee idol is exposed when he visits the site of an accident in which a famous actress, his former wife, was killed and there meets an old acquaintance.
fp: Ottawa Little Theatre, Nov. 24, 1955.

D2215. "Night of Storm" in his *Worlds Apart.* Toronto, Copp Clark, 1956.
1 act. 4m/2f.
Philip II, King of Macedonia, is the target of much enmity when he makes Eurydice his queen, superceding Olympias, his first wife and mother of his son, Alexander the Great.
fp: Ottawa Little Theatre, Nov. 18, 1954.

D2216. "Protest" in his *Worlds Apart.* Toronto, Copp Clark, 1956 and in *Curtain Rising.* W.S. Milne, ed. Toronto, Longmans, Green, 1958 and in *Beyond the Footlights.* H.D. McKellar, ed. Toronto, Macmillan, 1963 and in *Short Plays For Reading And Acting.* Bruce Vance, ed. Toronto, Clarke, Irwin, 1970 and in *Ten Canadian Short Plays.* John Stevens, ed. New York, Dell, 1975.
1 act. 1m/3f.
Modern Western thought challenges traditional Japanese beliefs in the Japan of the early 20th century, complicating the conflict between generations.

D2217. *Take to the Trees.* Toronto, Playwrights Co-op, 1972.
1 act. 3m/1f.
A comedy in which the members of the unconventional Midge family assert their right to individuality by pursuing their own interests and obsessions.

WILLIAMSON, C.N. and Alice Maude Williamson

D2218. "Motors That Pass in the Night" in *The Canadian Magazine,* vol.28, #6, April 1907.
1 act. 1m/1f.
A comedy about "how two motor cars 'act up' purposely and succeed in bringing two estranged lovers to a happy understanding".

WILLIAMSON, Ina

D2219. *A Christmas Dream.* Waterloo, Ont., Waterloo Music, 1950.
1 act. 3m/4f.
A Christmas play for young children featuring Santa Claus, Donald Duck and Red Riding Hood.

WILSON, David S.

D2220. "The Child" in *Acadia Athenaeum,* vol.59, #3, January 1935.
1 scene. 2m/3f.
A mother travelling by train in the Balkans hides the fact of her child's death so that she can keep the body with her until reaching her destination.

D2221. "Madame Leclaire" in *Journal of Education for Nova Scotia,* series 4, vol.6, January 1935.
1 scene. 4m/3f.
Madame Leclaire hides a French soldier fleeing from the British during the conquest of Acadia despite threats to her life and those of her two children.

WILSON, Ernest James

D2222. *The Release of Allen Danvers.* N.p., n.p., 1907.
3 acts. 8m/3f.
A play about ill-fated love on the Canadian prairies and in an English sitting-room. A famous Canadian actress pursues a young English actor who resists her love because of a fatal medical condition.

WILSON, G.B.

D2223. "Sis" in *Acadia Athenaeum,* vol.60, #6, April 1935.
3 scenes. 2m/2f.
A boy discovers he really loves someone else, someone whom he treated like a sister.

D2224. "Twenty Years" in *Acadia Athenaeum,* vol.60, #3, January 1935.
1 scene. 2m/3f.
During the Depression, a medical researcher and former nurse reestablish an acquaintance. Although both are unhappy in their present lives, neither is ready to resume their former relationship.

D2225. "Wanted — A Wife" in *Acadia Athenaeum,* vol.60, #4, February 1934.
1 act. 4m/2f.
An overeducated young man advertises for a wife, but the applicant his aunt forces him to accept had come to the house on other business.

D2226. "The Woman Haters' Club" in *Acadia Athenaeum,* vol.60, #5, March 1935.
1 scene. 8m/3f.
A group of mysogynists hire a housekeeper and are converted by her twenty-one-year-old daughter.

WILSON, Lawrence Maurice 1896–1963

D2227. *The Hiders.* L. Decoteau (pseud.). Westmount, P.Q., n.p., 1963.
1 act. 7m/2f.
An historically based play which concerns the experiences of four young French Canadians who remained hidden in an underground dugout to evade conscription during W.W. I.

WILSON, Peter

D2227A. *Gilliam.* See **LOGIE, Ray.**

WINLOW, Alice Maude (Dudley) 1885–

D2228. *The Broken Flower.* London, Fowler Wright, 1927.
1 act. 3m/3f.
A young woman who is both physically and emotionally exhausted is befriended by a family who reunite her with her long lost husband.

D2229. "The Miracle of Roses" in her *The Miracle of Roses and Poems.* Vancouver, Chalmers, 1926.
1 act. 3m/4f/1b.
Jean Picard has six beautiful red roses for the flower show but he gives them away to needy people. He gives the last rose to a carpenter, a Christ figure, and is rewarded for his generosity.

WINTER, Ashton

D2230. "Samuel de Champlain" in *McMaster University Quarterly,* vol.46, #2, Dec. 1936.
1 act. 8m. Extras.
A radio play celebrating Champlain's contribution to New France on the 300th anniversary of his death.
fp: CBC radio, Dec. 24, 1935 as "A Great Canadian".

WINTER, Jack 1936–

D2231. "15 U.B." in *Canadian Forum,* April 1961.
1 act. 7m/2f.
"A Pantomime" about the imminence of nuclear war.

D2231A. *Party Day.* Toronto, Playwrights Co-op, 1972.
1 act. 3m/1f. Doubling.
An exploration of the relationship between politics and the arts. Joseph Goebbels, the Minister of Propaganda, presents a "selective documentary" of the Nurnberg Party Day of 1934 and the Berlin Olympics of 1936.
fp: Studio Theatre, National Arts Centre, Ottawa, June 4, 1969.

D2232. "Who Am I?" in *Performing Arts in Canada,* vol.7, #4, Winter 1970.
1 act. 2m.
"A play on playwriting", a dialogue between the author and the magazine on aspects relating to the problem of what is a play.

D2233. "The Wrecked Blackship" in *Performing Arts in Canada,* vol.7, #2, Summer 1970.
1 act. 9m.
A pointed comment on international relations and the rewriting of history.
fp: TV version, CBC TV, Dec. 17, 1970 as "Blackship".

WOODCOCK, George 1912–

D2234. *Gabriel Dumont and the Northwest Rebellion.* Toronto, Playwrights Co-op, 1976 and in his *Two Plays.* Vancouver, Talonbooks, 1978.
16 scenes. 9m.
Gabriel Dumont has come to the U.S. seeking asylum and explains to the American officers the causes behind the rebellion. Through a series of flashbacks, the fight of the Metis nation comes to life.
fp: CBC radio, Feb. 21, 1975 as "Six Dry Cakes for the Hunted".

D2235. "Island of Demons" in his *Two Plays.* Vancouver, Talonbooks, 1978.
13 scenes. 7m/2f. Extras.
An adaptation for radio of the historic tale of Sieur de Roberval's niece and her forbidden love of a commoner. Set ashore on an island in the St. Lawrence, the lovers come face to face with the demons of Regret, Doubt and Discord.
fp: CBC radio "Vancouver Theatre", March 20, 1960.

D2236. "Maskerman" in *Prism,* vol.2, #2, Winter 1961.
9 scenes. 5m/3f.
A verse drama about the trials and tribulations of romance. Use is made of the Lorelei, the siren luring Maskerman to his downfall.
fp: CBC radio "Summer Stage", Aug. 28, 1960.

D2237. "Six Dry Cakes for the Hunted" in his *Two Plays.* Vancouver, Talonbooks, 1978. See *Gabriel Dumont and the Northwest Rebellion.*

WOODHEAD, W.D. 1885–1957

D2238. "Fragment of a Comedy on Prohibition" in *The Canadian Forum,* vol.9, #108, Sept. 1929.
1 act. 3m.
A prohibitionist and an anti-prohibitionist present their views to a student in an effort to persuade him to join their separate ranks. Based on the argument in Aristophanes' *Clouds.*

WOODLEY, Edward Garruthers 1878–

D2239. *A King's Girl.* Regina and Toronto, School Aids and Text Book Publishing, (19—?).
1 act. 5m/2f. Extras.
"An historical play for Social Studies (Senior Grades)". The Intendant Talon corresponds with Colbert, requesting wives for the soldier-settlers of New France.

WOODS, Grahame 1934–

D2240. "12 1/2 Cents" in *Camera Three: Three Plays For Television.* Toronto, Holt, Rinehart & Winston, 1972.
A TV drama. A school teacher tries to help a child who is beaten by her mother; "an attempt to illustrate the great problem known as the battered baby syndrome".

D2241. "Vicky" in *A Collection of Canadian Plays* vol.3. Rolf Kalman, ed. Toronto, Simon & Pierre, 1974.
2 acts. 3m/6f. Extras.
This drama follows Vicky's struggle to make a new life for herself after being discharged from a mental institution where she had been confined after being found guilty of murdering her children.
fp: CBC TV, 1974.

WREN, Frances

D2242. *Consquamcook to the Micmacs, Saint Andrews to You.* St. Andrews, N.B., n.p., 1942.
14 scenes. Multiple roles.
An outline for a series of historical tableaux depicting the early history of Saint Andrews, New Brunswick.
fp: Saint Andrews Historical Pageant, (1942?).

WRIGHT, Charles William

D2243. *The Man Who Played Judas.* Western Canada Theatre Conference Plays. Edmonton, Dept. of Extension, University of Alberta, 1948 and London, Religious Drama Society, 1950.
1 act. 3m/1f.
A play about a Mexican youth who plays Judas in the Passion Play. He has betrayed his best friend to the military and is about to hang himself in remorse when Judas himself appears and convinces him of Christ's compassion.

D2244. *The Rowley Band.* Ottawa, Ottawa Little Theatre Workshop, #8.
1 act. 3m/3f.
Mr. Rowley unsuccessfully attempts to reform his vagabond musician cousin and his wife by offering them a retirement cottage.

WYLIE, Betty Jane 1931–

D2245. "Kingsayer" in her *The Old Woman and the Pedlar/Kingsayer.* Toronto, Playwrights Co-op, 1978.
1 act. 4m/3f.
A depiction of the joyous world of childhood and the maturity which threatens it.
fp: Manitoba Theatre Centre, Winnipeg, December 1967.

D2246. "The Old Woman and the Pedlar" in her *The Old Woman and the Pedlar/Kingsayer*. Toronto, Playwrights Co-op, 1978.
1 act. 2m/2f. Extras. Doubling.
A group of concerned citizens help an old woman find her lost identity.
fp: Young People's Theatre, Toronto, Sept. 19, 1977.

WYNNE-JONES, Tim

D2247. "Elephant Dust" in *The Maker*, vol.1, #2, March 1973.
1 act. 3m/3f.
A young man's mind is destroyed and rebuilt through family loyalties and the habit of giving and expecting something in return.

YATES, J. Michael 1938–

D2248. "The Abstract Beast" in his *The Abstract Beast*. Port Clements, B.C., Sono Nis, 1971.
1 act. 5m/2f.
A radio play. A writer's mind argues with his body over whether they should go to bed with a woman or work on a novel in progress.
fp: CBC radio, May 1969.

D2249. "The Border" in his *The Abstract Beast*. Port Clements, B.C., Sono Nis, 1971 and in *The Soft Review*, #1, 1973.
1 act. 1m/1f.
A radio play. A woman pursues a man, informing him that he is about to cross a border. We learn that the border she refers to is the border between a man and a woman.
fp: CBC radio, Feb. 1971.

D2250. "The Broadcaster" in his *Abstract Beast*. Port Clements, B.C., Sono Nis, 1971.
1 act. 3m/2f.
A radio play. A broadcaster on a top-forty radio station discovers that he is being taken over by the mechanical instruments in the broadcast booth — he is becoming a tool of the system.
fp: CBC radio, Vancouver, Feb. 1968.

D2251. "The Calling" in *Fiddlehead*, #84, March/April 1970 and in his *The Abstract Beast*. Port Clements, B.C., Sono Nis, 1971 and in his *Quarks*. Toronto, Playwrights Co-op, 1975.
1 act. 1m/1f.
A radio play. A man and a woman attempt to discuss their lives together but the man's obsession with a broken telephone eventually destroys their capacity for communication completely.
fp: CBC radio "Tuesday Night", June 1968.

D2252. "The Net" in *Interstate Magazine*, (1974?) and in his *Quarks*. Toronto, Playwrights Co-op, 1975.
1 act. 3m/1f. Extras.
A radio play. A young man for whom fishing has become an all-encompassing metaphor finds himself literally trapped in an enormous gill-net, its strands growing into his flesh.
fp: CBC radio "Stage", 1975.

D2253. "Night Freight" in *Performing Arts in Canada,* vol.8, #1, Spring 1971 and in his *The Abstract Beast.* Port Clements, B.C., Sono Nis, 1971 and *Night Freight.* Toronto, Playwrights Co-op, 1972.
1 act. 1m/1f.
This play looks at how human beings define their own functions and purpose by means of other people. Even a corpse will do for a while.
fp: CBC radio, Toronto, Nov. 1968. Scarborough Players, Toronto, April 22, 1972.

D2254. "The Panel" in his *The Abstract Beast.* Port Clements, B.C., Sono Nis, 1971.
1 act. 5m/1f.
Distinguished Philosopher, Excellent Housewife, Prize-Winning Journalist and Successful Businessman try to determine the identity, or existence, of the Mystery Voice on a panel show.
fp: CBC radio, Vancouver, Feb. 1969.

D2255. "Search for the Tse Tse Fly" in his *Quarks.* Toronto, Playwrights Co-op, 1975.
1 act. 3m/2f. Extras.
A hypnotist obsessed with his power over sleep and the will of others devises his own perfect suicide.
fp: CBC radio.

D2256. "Smokestack in the Desert" in his *The Abstract Beast.* Port Clements, B.C., Sono Nis, 1971 and in *Edge,* #3, (New Zealand), 1972.
A radio play. Number One comes down from the mountain to the smokestack in the desert (civilization?) and there confronts a choice between several futile careers.

D2257. *Subjunction.* Vancouver, New Play Centre, (197-?).
2 scenes. 4m/4f.
A young man's friends act out various ways in which he might react to the news that he is to become a father.
fp: Fairbanks Drama Association, University of Alaska, Dec. 1965.

D2258. "Theatre of War" in his *The Abstract Beast.* Port Clements, B.C., Sono Nis, 1971.
1 act. 9m/1f.
A radio play. A juxtaposition of war and a child's game of war. The Minister of War, in an address to the children/troops, argues that "War is Man".
fp: CBC radio, Vancouver, April 1968.

YOUNG, David Leonard 1886–

D2259. *The Light.* Boston, Baker's Plays, 1943.
1 act. 5m/1f.
Mary reconciles Peter and Saul a few years after Christ's crucifixion.

YOUNG, Noreen 1939–

D2260. *Pickles and Puppets.* By Noreen Young and Juli Voyer. Toronto, Playwrights Co-op, 1975.
2 acts. 7m/5f. Extras.
A musical for children about the travelling puppeteers Henry and P.J. Pickles who arrive in a town where laughter has been outlawed and offenders are de-giggled.
fp: Ottawa Little Theatre, Feb. 1975.

D2261. *The Valiant Tailor.* Toronto, Playwrights Co-op, 1975.
2 acts. 7m/5f. Extras.
A musical for children adapted from the Grimm fairy tale. Killing seven flies with one swat induces the mild-mannered tailor to set off in search of greater adventures.
fp: Ottawa Little Theatre for Children, Feb. 1974.

YOUNGBLUD, Robert

D2262. "Offense and Defense" in *McMaster University Quarterly,* vol.48, #2, Jan. 1939.
1 scene. 1m/1b.
A brief anti-war sketch involving a lecturer in defense systems and a young student.

ZACHARKO, Larry 1951–

D2263. "Land of Magic Spell" in *A Collection of Canadian Plays* vol.4. Rolf Kalman, ed. Toronto, Simon & Pierre, 1975.
1 act. 5m/2f. Doubling.
While prospecting, Bill crosses into the Land of Magic Spell where Mountain Man will grant him one wish for returning five missing letters from his scrabble game.
fp: Young People's Theatre, Toronto, Oct. 1974.

D2264. *Maximilian Beetle.* Toronto, Playwrights Co-op, 1977.
1 act. 7m/4f. Doubling.
A musical for children about the adventures of a dapper beetle in love with a butterfly. Music and lyrics by G.K. Swanson.
fp: Young People's Theatre, Arts and Culture Program, June 24, 1976 Montreal Olympiad.

ZAPF, Carolyn

D2265. "The Eskimo People" in *Look Both Ways.* Herman Voaden, ed. Toronto, Macmillan, 1975.
1 act. 3m/2f.
A retelling of an Innuit legend about Awa and her old grandmother Tuki who dies but is reincarnated as a handsome young man who hunts for Awa until he is exorcised by the Shaman.
fp: Company One, Victoria, B.C., Jan. 1972.

ZILBER, Jacob

D2266. *The Award.* Vancouver, New Play Centre, (197-?).
1 act. 3m/1f. Extras.
A worker given an award for years of dependable service discovers it carries sinister effects.
p: CHAN TV, Vancouver. Vancouver Vagabond Players.

D2267. *Family Circle.* Vancouver, New Play Centre, (197-?).
1 scene. 2m/1f.
A harassed wife and husband try to follow marriage instructions from Family Circle Magazine.

D2268. *How to Make a Decent Revolution.* Vancouver, Mother Earth, n.d. and Vancouver, New Play Centre, 1971.
11 scenes. 8m.
A "stage entertainment" covering the history of the Industrial Workers of the World from 1905 to 1919 in the Pacific Northwest.
fp: (Rehearsed reading), New Play Centre, Vancouver, Sept. 1971.

D2269. "A Matter of Life and Death" in *Evidence,* #7, 1963.
1 act. 4m/1f.
A radio play. A man who has been awarded the title "Most Efficient Filing Clerk of the Decade" must prove his loyalty to the organization to be immortalized, even if it means killing himself.

D2270. "Verbrennte Soup" in *West Coast Review,* vol.3, #3, Winter 1969 and Vancouver, New Play Centre, 1973.
1 act. 3m/1f.
A young writer's characters come to life and take his play away from him.
fp: CBC radio. Vagabond Players, New Westminster, B.C.

Drama Short Title Index

A

A.D.'s Dead   *D1899*
Abolishing the Monarchy   *D1212*
The Abstract Beast   *D2248*
Acadia   *D1014*
The Acadian Tragedy   *D495*
Accident   *D1032*
According to the Rules   *D247*
Achilles   *D292*
Across the Great Divide   *D1924*
The Action Tonight   *D804*
Adam Daulac   *D1925*
Adam Malt Defrosted   *D1304*
Adam's Sons   *D1605, D1775*
Adolescent Rebellion   *D1561*
Adopting Sara   *D107*
The Adventure of Bob Cactus   *D773*
The Adventures of Moses   *D933*
The Adventures of Nicholas Nickleby   *D1287*
After Abraham   *D377*
After Antietam   *D79*
After Queenston Heights   *D1926*
After the Ceremony   *D2023*
The Aftermath   *D759*
Afternoon Tea in Friendly Village   *D68*
Against the World   *C180*
The Agreement   *D805*
Airman's Forty-Eight   *D589A, D793*
Alexander MacKenzie   *D496, D543*
Alexander Was Great   *D1998*
Alfred the Great   *D860*
Alias   *D2118*
Alias Mr. Pollard   *D1244*
Alice in Blunderland   *D1904*
The Alien Heart   *D669*
Aliens   *D2119*
All About Emily   *D1854*
All About Us   *D1562*
All Hallows' Eve   *D1552*
All the World's a Stage   *D1855*
Alley at the Back of Things   *D2132*

Alli Alli Oh   *D946A*
The Allies' Christmas Party   *D621*
Almighty Voice   *D1563*
Alone   *D78*
Alpha and Omega   *D1836*
The Alphabet Tragedy   *D1*
Amadee Doucette & Son   *D725*
Ambition   *C134*
Ambush at Tether's End   *D2135*
An American Father   *D544*
American Modern   *D756*
Amerigo and the Naming of America   *D1401*
Among His Peers   *D2091*
Among Those Present   *D1092*
Anancy and Lizard   *D2045*
Anansi the Spider   *D2046*
And at Night We Dream   *D1475*
And One Will Betray   *D1288*
And Sendeth Rain   *D1033*
And the Answer Is   *D1681*
And They Meet Again   *D1027*
And This Is Life   *D1520*
Andante and Variations   *D2187*
Andrea Del Sarto   *D786*
Andrew McMurty, Immigrant   *D1989*
Angel Makers   *D1088*
Angelina Goes to Boarding School   *D108*
Angin Sama   *D156*
The Angle of Adventure   *D1999*
The Angry Men   *D289, D1420*
Annabel's M.I. Club   *D1608*
Anne of Green Gables   *D897*
Another Piece of Crust   *D1476*
Anselmo and Bernadine   *D1240*
Antic Disposition   *D612*
Antichrist   *D831*
Antigravitational Menopause   *D2120*
Any Woman Is a Lady   *D1856*
API 2967   *D856*
Appassionata   *D1624*
The Apple   *D1578*
Apple Butter   *D1647*
The Apple in the Eye   *D946B*
The Appointed Hour   *D2034*
Aquarium   *D980*
The Arch of Success   *D1321*
Are You Afraid of Thieves?   *D1156*

The Argument *D1423*
An Argument in the Kitchen *D316*
The Aristocrats of Democracy *D1857*
The Arithmetic of Love *D1666*
The Ark of Civilization *D1858*
As Grace Is Given *D1091*
As Loved Our Fathers *D304*
As You Want It! *D766*
Ashes for Easter *D2158*
The Ashes on Gold Avenue *D581*
Assembly Call *D293*
At a Cross-Roads' Schoolhouse *D1389*
At Hopper's Corners *D1609*
At My Heart's Core *D505*
At the Court of Isabella *D1322*
At the Gates of the Righteous *D506*
Attack *D2098*
Au Revoir *D1218*
The Audition *D490*
Aunt Mary's Family Album *D65*
Aunt Sara Expects Company *D1229*
Aunt Sophia Speaks *D66*
Aunt Susan's Visit *D67*
Autumn At Altenburg *D734*
Autumn Blooming *D1028*
The Awakening of the Lily *D944*
The Award *D2266*
Azort Starbolt *D835*

B

The Babe of Bethlehem *D1908*
Babel Rap *D1161*
The Babies *D1202*
The Bacchants *D1041*
The Bachelors' Club *C126*
Back Door *D1535*
Back to the Kitchen, Woman! *D794*
Back to the World *D674*
The Bag of Earth *D2183*
Bagdad Saloon *D2136*
Baldoon *D748, D1648*
The Ballad of Etienne Brule *D80*
Balm *D545*
Baptism *D2031*
The Baron Bold and the Beauteous Maid *C106*
The Baronets of Nova Scotia *D2*
The Barred Door *D1022*

Barrier *D1615*
The Basket *D1029*
Battering Ram *D711*
The Battle of Little Big Horn *C129*
A Battle of Wits *D2209*
A Beach of Strangers *D1667*
The Beast in the Bag *D682*
The Beauties of the Jury System *C1*
Beautiful Tigers *D401*
The Beautiful Woman and The Bleeding Man *D1747*
Beauty and the Boss *D1168*
A Bed-Time Story *D644*
Beer Room *D924*
Before and Behind the Curtain *C107*
Before Quebec *D1927*
The Beginning of Summer *D1625*
The Beginning of the Scandal *C149*
Behind the Beyond *D1169*
Les Belles-Soeurs *D2079*
The Bells of Hell *D1686*
The Bequest *D1682*
Berthe *D2080*
Bertram and Lorenzo *C169*
The Best Gift *D1323*
Bethune *D1146*
The Betrayal *D586*
Better Luck Next Time *D1091*
Better Than Gold *D1324*
Beware the Quickly Who *D1496*
Beyond Mozambique *D2137*
Beyond Our Time *D605*
Beyond the Skyline *D2051*
Biblical Drama Esther *D3*
Biff-Bing-Bang *D1595*
The Big Catch *D1302*
The Big Helpers *D317*
Big X, Little Y *D1843*
Bill Holsinger from Cochrane *D109*
Billy and Floss *D1450*
Billy Bishop and the Red Baron *D1564*
The Bird *D1787*
The Bird in the Box *D677*
A Bird in the Bush *D576A*
The Birth of Montreal *D1713*
The Birthday of the Divine Child *D1325*
Bishop and King *D842*
A Biting Election Satire *D1919*

The Black Bonspiel of Willie MacCrimmon D1415
Black Dreams D1641
Black Lion D1892
Black Memory D2159
Black Precipitate D876
Bland Hysteria D1530
The Bleeding Heart of Wee Jon D316
The Blind Pastor C85
Blitzkrieg D2121
A Blizzard Leaves No Footprints D2174
The Blood Is Strong D1859, D1860
The Blot D2000
The Blue Pitcher D1448
The Blue Willow Plate D1822
Bobbie Pulls Up Her Socks D675
Bobolink D136
Bohunk D2182
Boiler Room Suite D561
Le Bon Dieu D585
The Bone Spoon D1794
Bonfire on the Beach D416
Bonjour, là, Bonjour D2081
Bonnie Prince Charlie C95
The Book of Marco Polo D157
The Book of Solomon Spring D1485
The Book of the Play of Hiawatha the Mohawk D90
Boots and His Brothers D1390
The Border D2249
Bousille and the Just D742
The Box D1727
The Box Beyond D231
The Box of Music D541
The Boy Bishop D737
Boy Who Has A Horse D1193
The Boy Who Went To The North Wind D631
The Boy with Green Fingers D1385
The Boycott C2
The Brains We Trust D1015
Branch Plant D1318
Brandy D50
The Breach of Promise Trial D171
The Breadwinner D1461
Breakdown D2184
Breakfast D2185
The Breaking of the Bridge D1742
Breeches from Bond Street D795

The Bride of the Gorilla D124
The Bridegroom Cometh D843
The Bridge D1928
Bridgework D1065
Brigadier Thompson D1131
Bright and Glorious D1994
The Brighter World Above C3
Britannia D4, D847
British Properties D1524
The Broadcaster D2250
The Brockenfiend C74
The Broken Flower D2228
Brotherly Hatred D1565
Brothers in Arms D546
Brown Lady Johnson D958
Brussels Sprouts D1060
Buffalo Jump D207
The Builders D1776
The Building of the Empire D106
Building Railroads D1929
Bull Durham D1480
Bummy Peepee in the Toto D623
The Bunker D985
Bunthorne Abroad C60
The Burglars D699
Burglars for Love D1587
Burlap Bags D1566
Burwash, Site 3 D2188
Bushed D947
Busride D205
But I Know What I Like D1861
Butterball D224
Butterflies in Bloom D899
By a Romany Camp Fire D1235
By the Sea D1521
By the Waters of Babylon D528

C

Cadets of Temperance C182
Call My People Home D1203
The Call of the Whippoorwill D590
The Calling D2251
Can You See Me Yet? D659
Canada D1542, D1930
Canada Calls D848
Canada, Fair Canada D727, D1113
Canada Forever D1265
Canada in Flanders D1931

Canada in Story and Song   *D503*
Canada, Our Homeland   *D849*
Canada Welcome   *D1543*
Canada's First Christmas Party   *D571*
Canada's Royal Feast   *D158*
The Canadian Club   *C4*
The Canadian Fact   *D2170*
A Canadian Fairy Tale   *D850*
Canadian Gothic   *D757*
Les Canadiens   *D1789*
The Cantata of the Festival of the Rose   *C195*
Canuck   *D458*
Cap o' Rushes   *D632*
Captain Cook   *D1932*
Captain Cook's Ship of Health   *D159*
Captain M.W. Plunkett   *D1595*
Captain Plume's Courtship   *C177*
Captain Reece of the Mantelpiece   *D2066*
The Captive   *D258*
Captives of the Faceless Drummer   *D1763*
The Capture of Detroit, 1812   *C156*
The Capture of Quebec   *D497*
The Careful Boy   *D1567*
Carry On   *D1596*
The Case Against Cancer   *D1862*
The Case of the Sea Lion Flippers   *D1863*
The Castle Builders   *D1537*
Castle Zaremba   *D64*
The Cat   *D774*
The Catalogue Cowboy   *D294*
Catalyst   *D1012*
The Cattle Rancher   *D1933*
The Cave in the Woods   *D645*
A Celebration Indeed   *D1422*
The Cement of Democracy   *D1864*
The Centennial Play   *D507, D1416, D1462, D1497, D2041*
A Century Has Roots   *D656*
A Chain of Words   *D2174A*
Champlain   *D890, D1201*
Champlain at Quebec   *D1934*
A Change Is As Good As   *D2092*
Chanson Pour Rene Claude   *D972*
The Chappell Diary   *D104, D1017*
Charbonneau and Le Chef   *D1238*
Charisma   *D994*
Charles Manson a.k.a. Jesus Christ   *D1042*

Charles the First in Spain   *C86*
Charlie Who?   *D718*
The Charrivarri   *C187*
Chautauqua   *D389*
Check, Mate and Murder   *D1978*
Chester   *D1162*
Chevalier Johnstone   *D827*
Chevrose, the Hermit   *D472*
Chicago Property   *D1245*
"Chick" or Myrtle Ferns   *C144*
The Chief Instrument of Freedom   *D1865*
Chief Shaking Spear Rides Again   *D821*
The Child   *D2220*
Children of Nazareth   *D1326*
Children of the Year   *D353*
The Chinese Joss   *D60*
Chinook   *D332*
Choosing a Model   *D1327*
Christmas   *D51*
Christmas at the Circle A   *D572*
Christmas Bells and Fairies   *D1181*
Christmas Candles   *D646*
Christmas Capers   *D200*
A Christmas Carol   *D1838*
The Christmas Committee   *D573*
A Christmas Dream   *D2219*
Christmas Eve in Santa Claus Land   *D1115*
A Christmas Eve in the Forest   *D1182*
A Christmas Festival of Play   *D1634*
Christmas Guests   *D1328*
Christmas in Skunk's Misery   *D629*
Christmas in the Village   *D652*
The Christmas Log   *D574*
Christmas Music   *D465*
Christmas, 1940   *D2015*
The Christmas Ship   *D461*
A Christmas Story   *D463*
Christmas Time   *D267*
The Christmas Tree Bluebird   *D598*
A Christmas Tree for Mother Goose's Children   *D2108*
The Christmas Tree Forest   *D380*
Christmas Wonders   *D2096*
Cinderella   *D653, D2111*
The Citizens of Calais   *D1498*
City Street   *D1554*
La Claire Fontaine   *D504*

348

The Clam Made A Face *D1499*
Classroom Theatre *D1163*
Claws *D904*
The Clean End *D1594*
Clear Light *D952*
The Clever Cobbler *D633*
The Clever One *D1030*
The Cleverest Woman in the World *D2001*
Clontarf *D580*
Close Friends *D925*
The Coal Miner *D1935*
Cobbler, Stick To Thy Last *D936*
Cod Fishing *D1936*
Coercion *D1639*
Coffee at 12:30 *D1048*
Coffee Break *D2122*
Coffee House *D1616*
Coincidence *D1447*
A Cold Beer With a Warm Friend *D1164*
Cold Flame *D451*
The Cold Water Army *D1866*
A Cold Winter and a Dead Spring *D1132*
Colour the Flesh the Colour of Dust *D418*
Colours in the Dark *D1649*
The Columbiad *C135*
Columbus *D1937*
Come Away, Come Away *D1424*
Come True *D534*
A Comedy in One Act *C5*
The Comedy of Trade *C56*
The Coming of Spring *D775*
The Coming of Susan *D1230*
The Coming of the Pale-Face *D599*
The Commissioner and the Injun *C6*
Common Sense and Moonshine *D1867*
Company *D1296*
Company or Voices *D2035*
Complicated Courtship *D110*
Compulsory Option *D1601*
Concerning a Temporary Permit *D1282*
Confederation *D796, D1938*
Conflict and Triumph *D724*
The Conquest of Canada *B2*
The Conscript's Return *D743*
The Conspiracy of Spring *D600*
Consquamcook to the Micmacs *D2242*
The Consumer *D1435*

The Continuous Dream of the Former Prime Minister *D788*
The Contract *D767*
Conversations with Shakespeare *D372*
The Conversion of a Dishonest Tax-Collector *D1909*
The Cool Constable *D1233*
Coom-Na-Goppel *D349*
The Copetown City Kite Crisis *D562*
Copper Mountain *D2019*
Cornflowers *D1231*
The Cornplanter *D836A, D1898*
A Coronation Pageant *D1373*
Counsellor Extraordinary *D225*
Count Filippo *C127*
Countdown to Armageddon *D387*
The Count's Bride *C136*
Courage Mr. Green *D649*
Course for Collision *D862*
The Courting of Marie Jenvrin *D1688*
Cousin Charlotte's Visit *D673*
The Coward *D460*
Cowboy Island *D1830*
Crabdance *D1845*
The Cradle *D314*
The Cradle in the Hills *D2151*
The Cratchits' Christmas Dinner *D168*
Crazy Horse Suite *D1514*
Creeps *D712*
Cressida *D226*
The Crickets Must Sing *D1291*
The Crime and Punishment Show *D903*
The Crime of Louis Riel *D436*
The Critics *D1773*
Crocus Bulbs *D61*
The Crooked Tree *C7*
The Cross *D1744*
Cross and Chrysanthemum *D1329*
The Crowning of Canada *D1378*
The Crowning Test *C117*
Crows *D1795*
The Crucifixion *D1471*
Cruel Tears *D1410*
The Cruise *D227*
The Crusader *D1846*
Cubistique *D402*
Culture *C8*
Cupid on the Wire *D1118*

Curiosity Rewarded *D1227*
The Curse of ChirraPoonje *D277*
The Curse of the Lost Lemon Mine *D2101*
Customs *D1425*
Cyclone Jack *D208*
Cynicism and Seclusion *D290*

D

The Dada Show *D1186*
Daft Danny *D1990*
Daft Dream Adyin' *D806*
Daily News from the Whole World *D522*
Dairying *D1939*
Damnation of Vancouver *D189*
Damned Souls *D1170*
Dance Diurnal *D354*
Dance for My Father *D948*
The Dancers of Colbek *D912*
Dandelion *D1980*
The Dandy Lion *D1541, D1702*
Dark Days of Ancient Hate *D437*
Dark Harvest *D1689*
D'Artagnan *D1839*
Daughters of the Dawn *D355, D1105*
Daulac *C75*
David and Abigail *D1141*
David at Aunt Betsy's *D1737*
A Day at Mother Nature's Court *D1116*
The Day of Redemption *D934*
Day of Victory *D1868*
A Day with Peggy *D1330*
De Roberval *C131*
Dead Heat *D368*
A Dead Woman Bites Not *D577*
Deadline F.L.Q. *D871*
Dealer's Choice *D218*
Death *D660*
The Death and Execution *D1650*
The Death Cup *D2002*
Death Minus One *D863*
The Death of Pierrot *D834*
The Death of Sappho *D308*
Death Seat *D999*
Deep Sea *D1748*
Defunctive Music *D939*
Deirdre *D438*
Deirdre of the Sorrows *D439*

The Departures *D1149*
Dermot McMurrough *C125A, C164*
Des Deux Choses L'Une *D1171*
Desert Soliloquy *D1568*
Despair *D905*
The Deviates *D1372*
Devil Mas' *D259*
The Devil's Instrument *D1417*
Dialogue *C185*
A Dialogue at M'Killaway-Lodge *C189*
Dialogue Between the Client and the Lambton Ghost *C146*
Dialogue—Columbus and his Men *D6*
A Dialogue in Spring *D2003*
A Dialogue On the State of Theatre in Canada *D508*
Dialogues Between Two Methodists *C63*
Dialogues on Canadian History *D375*
Dialogues on English History *D376*
Diamond Cutters *D2062*
Diary of a Nurse *D864*
Dinner Party *D1796*
The Dinosaurs *D926*
Dirty Work At the Crosswalks *D1370*
The Disciple of the Night *D1910*
The Discovery of Canada *D1940*
The Dismissal *D1651*
Dismissal Leading to Lustfulness *D2199*
Displaced Affections *D990*
Dispossessed *D1642*
The Divine Guest *D1331*
Divinity in Montreal *D1300*
A Division Court and County Court Case *C147*
Do You Remember *D2160*
Doctor Umlaut's Earthly Kingdom *D768*
Dodo *D1891*
Does Anybody Here Know Denny? *D1879*
Dollard *D177*
Dolorsolatio *C172*
The Domestics at Glenholme *D111*
Dominion Day Pageant *D7*
The Donnellys *D397*
Don't Touch That Phone *D2210*
The Door *D1670, D1993*
Double *D2032*
Double Image *D58*
A Double Life *C181*

350

Doukhobors   *D2036, D2050*
Down by the Sea   *D526*
Down on Your Knees   *D1066*
Down the Years   *D1746*
Down There   *D807*
Down to the Sea   *D362*
Dragon Lady   *D1064*
The Dragons of Kent   *D1689A*
Drake's Drum   *D160*
Dramatic Scene   *C87*
Dramatic Sketch   *C88, C89, C178*
Dramatic Sketch from Scripture History   *C90*
Dramatic Sketch. The Intercepted Letter   *C91*
Dramatization of Civics Lesson   *D1374*
The Dream   *D253, D2102*
The Dream of Glooscap   *D1117*
A Dream of Sky People   *D683*
The Dream of the Months   *D1463*
The Dream Unwinds   *D893*
The Dreambook   *D913*
A Dreamer in Moab   *D1243*
Dreams   *D2211*
The Dress   *D170*
The Dressmaker and the Queen   *D634*
The Drums Are Out   *D440*
The Drunkard   *D986*
La Duchesse de Langeais   *D2082*
Duet for a Schizophrenic   *D1044*
Duet for Three   *D1707*
The Dumbfounding   *D1453*
During the Tea Hour   *D87*
The Dybbuk   *D940*

E

Earth Deities   *D356, D1105*
Earth Song   *D2113*
The Easter Egg   *D1652*
Easter Week at Rome   *D352*
Ebb-Tide   *D615*
Echoes of Other Things   *D975*
Economy   *C190*
The Ecstasy of Rita Joe   *D1764*
The Edison Doll   *C61*
The Education of Phyllistine   *D1782*
Eight Men Speak   *D363A, D762, D1215, D1761*

1837: The Farmers' Revolt   *D1790, D2037*
Eithne   *C142*
Electric Gunfighters   *D2123*
The Electrical Man   *D1187, D1614*
The Elephant and the Jewish Question   *D1847*
Elephant Dust   *D2247*
Elevator   *D1981*
The Eleventh Hour   *D935*
Elise Le Beau   *D595*
The Elixir   *D531*
Emmanuel Xoc   *D828*
The Empire Calls   *D1159*
The Empress Helena   *D1332*
The Empress of China   *D1379*
The Empty Cornucopia   *D452*
En Pièces Détachées   *D2083*
The Enamorado   *C132*
The End   *D1531*
The End of a Dream   *D691*
The English Essay   *D1038*
Enough Rope   *D736*
Enter the Prince   *D1479*
An Entertainment at the Cafe Terminus   *D1831*
The Epic of Toad and Heron   *D1089*
The Episode of the Quarrel Between Titania and Oberon   *C97*
Epitaph on a War of Liberation   *D1869*
Eros at Breakfast   *D509*
The Error of Our Ways   *D1266*
The Escape   *D1818*
Esker Mike and His Wife Agiluk   *D879*
The Eskimo People   *D2265*
Esther   *C92, D2114*
Eve   *D661, D1129A*
Even Our Faith   *D941*
An Evening in a Loyalist Household   *D1941*
An Evening in August   *D47*
Evening Meeting   *D1723*
An Evening on Innell and Auden   *D494*
Ever Onward   *D161*
Everlasting Salvation Machine   *D340*
Everybody's Troubles   *D295*
Everyfreshette   *D8*
Everygirl   *D9, D601*
Everywoman's Road   *D725*
Evidence   *D2004*

The Execution   *D196*
The Execution of William Abel   *D38*
The Exile   *D808*
Exit Columbine   *D1527*
Exit Muttering   *D1020*
Exit Son   *D2197*
The Experiment   *D228*
Explosion   *D468*
Express   *D1671*
Extract From an Original and Unpublished Play   *C8A*
The Extraverted Suicide   *D1982*
The Eyewash Indians   *D183*

F

The Face of Life   *D199*
Facts Are Stubborn Things   *D1911*
The Failure   *D1403*
The Fair Country   *D955, D1538*
The Fair Grit   *C96*
Fair Rosamond   *C9*
A Fairy Play   *D150*
Faith   *D1086*
Faithful   *D1588*
The Faithful Heart   *D1870*
The Fall of Man   *D1983*
The False Face Legend   *D1905*
Family Circle   *D2267*
The Family Portrait   *D441*
Famous People   *D146, D257A*
Famous Women   *D726*
Fantasy, Flight and Feathers   *D1080*
Far As the Eye Can See   *D2038, D2202*
Far Garden   *D1893*
The Farm Show   *D2039*
The Farmer and the Birds   *D1544*
Farmer Maxwell's City Niece   *D1610*
The Fat Clown   *D998*
The Fatal Quest   *D10*
The Fatal Ring   *C93*
Fate   *C154, D877*
Father Christmas   *D722*
Father Lacombe   *D2052*
Father Malachy's Miracle   *D579*
The Favours of My Lady Leone   *D610*
The Feast of Belshazzar   *D222*
February 25, 1972   *D1583*
The Female Consistory of Brockville   *C79*

A Festival of Carol's   *D908*
Festival of the Arts   *D1213*
The Festival of the Wheat   *D1437*
A Festival Pageant   *D361*
A Few Hills Away   *D240*
Fifine, the Fisher-Maid   *C98*
Fifteen Miles of Broken Glass   *D915*
15 U.B.   *D2231*
Fifty Faces Spring   *D626*
52 North by 21 West   *D1463*
Final Chorus From "Ill-Met By Moonlight"   *D1871*
Final Edition   *D1294*
Final Rehearsal   *D1821*
Find the Thief   *D2073*
Fine Feathers   *D464*
Fire In the North   *D1246*
The Firebrand   *D2005*
A Fireside Drama   *C163*
Fireweed   *D1081*
The Fireworshippers   *C125A, C165*
The First Christmas   *D547, D700*
A First Death   *D2156*
The First Falls on Monday   *D1464*
First Job   *D2157*
Fish Bowl   *D2033*
The Fishery Commission at Halifax   *C10*
5BX in History   *D1519*
Five Fugues for Isaac Newton   *D523*
Five Thousand Years Mortgage   *D277*
A Flag of Empire   *D1157*
The Flight   *D1805*
Flight into Danger   *D865*
Floating Homeland   *D1741*
Flood   *D1274*
Flower of the Storm   *D832*
Flowers   *D1251*
Flowers in the City   *D1222*
Flowers of Paradise   *D995*
The Folks Next Door   *D1495*
Follow the Leader   *D1199*
Following the Star   *D701*
Following Up a Clue   *C11*
Food for Thought   *D747*
Fools and Masters   *D532*
For All Eternity   *D1819*
For Crying Out Loud   *D151*

For Love & Chicken Soup *D1192*
For the Empire *D578*
For the Love of a Horse *D2071*
For the Red Cross *D622*
A Foretaste of Hindsight *D2103*
Forever till Friday *D1708*
Forever Yours, Marie-Lou *D2084*
Forfeits *D906*
Forging the Fifteenth Amendment *D1172*
Forgotten Heritage *D2072*
Fort Beausejour *D1315*
Forte Fortissimo *D1607*
Forthcoming Wedding *D81*
Fortune *D268*
Fortune and Men's Eyes *D927*
Fortune My Foe *D510*
Fortunes *D1067*
42 Seconds from Broadway *D538*
Foul Play *D1749*
The Fountain *D1011*
Four to Four *D729*
The Fourth Monkey *D1500*
The Fourth of July in Albany, 1831 *D1872*
Fox of a Thousand Faces *D319*
Fragment of a Comedy on Prohibition *D2238*
François Bigot *D442*
Frankenstein *D1180, D1510*
Free Beer *D2200*
The Freedom of Jean Guichet *D1260*
The Freedom of the House *D692*
French and Langlais of Wakanda *D1620*
French Chaos *C166*
Fresh Water from the Sea *D1122*
Friedhof *D2161*
Friends and Lovers *D917*
Friends and Relations *D957*
The Frog Galliard *D477*
From A to V *D787*
From Their Own Place *D548*
From Wilderness to Wonderland *D251*
Frosted Icing *D383*
Frugal Repast *D1728*
The Fruit Rancher *D1942*
Fugue for Female Voices *D1000*
The Fur Coat *D434*
The Future *D719*

G

Gabe *D209*
Gabriel Dumont and the Northwest Rebellion *D2234*
Gabriel Lajeunesse *D122*
Galarian *D412A*
The Gallant Soldiers *D776*
The Gallows *D1150*
A Garden for Recompense *D1224*
Garden Varieties *D769*
Gardens of the Wind *D1509*
Gargoyles *D1406*
The Gayden Chronicles *D419*
The General *D1556*
General Confession *D511*
General Wolfe *D347*
Gentlemen Adventurers *D498*
Geography Match *D1653*
George and Margaret Fox *D123*
George, Gertie and the Garbage Grabbers *D1316*
George Johnson is a Son-of-a-Bitch *D1894*
Gesture of Concern *D1104*
Get Away Somewhere Quiet *D1001*
Getting In *D1426*
Getting Rid of an Agent *D11*
The Ghost *D1478*
Ghosts *D112*
A Gift for Benjamin *D695*
The Gift of the Drum *D777*
The Gift of the Nile *D1823*
The Gift of the Sun *D1540*
Gilliam *D1210, D1460, D2227A*
Gimme Yeast *D1623*
A Glass Darkly *D752*
Gloria Star *D2085*
Gloriana *D426*
Goblin Gold *D1255*
God Caesar *D1621*
God-Forsaken *D358*
The God-Intoxicated Man *D837*
The God of Gods *D45*
God Save McQueen *D1309*
God So Loved the World *D2186*
God's Plenty *D2152*
Goglu *D137*
Going to the North Pole *D113*

Gold   *D591*
Gold-Mad   *D1452*
The Golden Age   *D478*
Golden Secrets   *D874*
Good-By   *D12*
Good-bye Books   *D1545*
The Good Life   *D740*
Good Morning Dear   *D2043*
Good Morning, Mr. Bell!   *D1440*
The Good of the Sun   *D1134*
The Gook   *D1613*
The Goose's Sauce   *D1228*
Gordon Paul McCray   *D364*
The Governor in the Boarding House   *D1873*
Goya   *D152*
The Gracchi   *D2189*
The Grand Duchess   *D763*
The Grand Hysteric   *D1729*
Grande Finale   *D187*
The Grandmother   *D1002*
Granite and Oak   *D1626*
Grantly Granville   *C137*
Grass and Wild Strawberries   *D1765*
Gravediggers of 1942   *D916*
The Greasewood Tree   *D1292*
The Great Company   *D162*
The Great Grunbaum   *D809*
The Great Hunger   *D1569*
The Great Land Bubble   *C12*
The Great Religious Stir   *D2190*
The Great Wave of Civilization   *D880*
The Greater Sacrifice   *D1619*
The Greatest Realistic Burlesque Farce   *C13*
The Green Glass Beads   *D2016*
Green Lawn Rest Home   *D1848*
Greta, the Divine   *D2090*
The Grey Cup Murder Trial   *D1009*
The Grin on the Moon   *D1570*
Grip in Council   *C14*
The Groanin' Board   *D320*
Ground Zero   *D1832*
Growth   *D820*
The Guest   *D1107*
Guilty or Not Guilty   *D1589*
Gunner's Rope   *D175*
Gwendoline   *D1486*

H

H.M. Canadian Ship Blunderbore   *C15*
H.M.S. "Parliament"   *C113*
The Habitant   *D1943*
Hacta Nicotiana   *D2067*
Hail   *D1528*
Haliburton Farmer   *D339*
Halibut Fishing   *D1944*
The Hamesick Wife   *C167*
Hand & Teale's Pyro-Spectacular Drama   *C124*
Hand & Teale's Spectacular Drama   *C125*
The Hand That Cradles The Rock   *D822*
Handcuffs   *D1654*
The Hangashore   *D1756*
The Hanged Man   *D857*
Hannah, Come Back   *D1638*
Hansel and Gretel   *D18*
The Happiest Place   *D2057*
A Happy Mistake   *D1333*
The Happy Republic   *D1874*
The Happy Return   *C16*
The Hardhead   *D1640*
Harriott!   *D232*
Hasid   *D1735*
The Haskill House   *D92*
Hatching Eggs   *D583*
The Haunted House   *D2191*
Haven of the Spirit   *D549*
He Didn't Even Say Goodbye   *D2212*
He Passed Through Samaria   *D278*
A Head for Peppino   *D1388*
The Head, Guts and Sound Bone Dance   *D420*
Health Hints   *D14*
The Hearing   *D1922*
Hearing Committee   *D872*
The Heart Specialist   *D321*
Hearts   *D858*
The Heavenly Prison   *D1875*
Helene of New France   *D959*
Hell   *D149*
Hell's Bells   *D1906*
The Helper   *D810*
Henrik Ibsen   *D1532*
Henry Hudson   *D550, D1945*
Her Affairs in Order   *D219*
Heracles   *D678*

Here Will I Nest   *D960*
Hero at Hatch's Mill   *D1791*
Heroes   *D1411*
Heroes of Health   *D1598*
Heroes of History   *D128*
Herringbone   *D403*
Hershel of Ostropol   *D1112*
Hey, Mister   *D1512*
Hiawatha or Manabozho   *D91*
The Hiders   *D2227*
Higher Entrance Exam   *D184*
The Highland Heart in Nova Scotia   *D2195*
Hildebrand   *C76, D350*
Him   *D1487*
His Majesty's Pie   *D191*
Hit and Run   *D1194*
Hoarse Muse   *D333*
Hob's Heaven   *D710*
The Holdin' Ground   *D1757*
Holed Up   *D1068*
The Holy Crown   *D102*
The Holy Grail   *D246*
Holy Manhattan   *D443*
The Home for Heroes   *D236*
Home from Young Ladies' College   *D15*
Home Sweet Home   *D1571*
The Homesteaders   *D1946*
Hoodman Blind   *D596*
Hope   *D662*
Hope Deferred   *D512*
Horns   *D1643*
Horseshoe House   *D282*
The Horticulturist   *D1895*
Hosanna   *D2086*
The Hottest Bet in Town   *D486*
The House in the Quiet Glen   *D444*
The House of Laval   *D2196*
The House of Oedipus   *D2006*
The House on Chestnut Street   *D1488, D1489*
How Are Things With the Walking Wounded?   *D918*
How History Is Made   *D2112*
How I Met My Husband   *D1459*
How Long   *D942*
How St. Nicholas Came to the Academy   *D1334*
How the Song Was Made   *C62*

How to Get Your Man   *D42*
How to Make a Decent Revolution   *D2268*
How To Run the Country   *D1783*
How We Hear   *D1123*
How We Killed the Moose   *D1165*
Human Remains   *D663*
Hunting Stuart   *D513*
Hurray for Johnny Canuck!   *D738*
Hydro-Electric   *D1947*
Hypothetical Meeting   *D39*

I

I Can't Afford It   *D1559*
I Can't Go On   *D283*
I Don't Care What It Looks Like   *D684*
I Have to Call My Father   *D260*
I Love You   *D1421*
I Love You, Baby Blue   *D2040*
I Love You, Billy Striker   *D341*
I Remember Dali   *D1750*
I Thank You   *D435*
I Wish   *D210, D1043*
The Ice-Box Speaks   *D647*
If You Meet a Leprechaun   *D635*
Iggy Makes an End   *D1383*
Ignoramus   *D1655*
Il Penseroso   *D291*
I'll Remember You Love   *D1082*
The Imaginary Line   *D1308*
Imperial Britain   *C155*
The Impressionists   *D654*
In a Lifetime   *D1197*
In a Lumber Camp   *D1948*
In a Venetian Garden   *D1714*
In Arizona the Air is Clean   *D811*
In County Mayo   *D400*
In Search of the Last Paradiddle   *D342*
In the Blood   *D2178*
In the Middle of the Night   *D1069*
In the Mood   *D2162*
In the Oil Fields   *D1949*
An Incident   *D1268*
An Incident at Hornsdale Park   *D408*
Incident at the Poseidon   *D1627*
The Incredible Murder of Cardinal Tosca   *D1180, D1510A*
Indian   *D1766*

The Indian Huntresses   *D16*
The Injured   *D812*
The Inmates   *D491*
Innocent Bigamy   *C68*
Innocent in Zion   *D707*
Inook and the Sun   *D153*
Inside Out   *D1427*
The Intelligence Office   *D17*
Interrupted Plans   *D1367*
The Interview   *D489*
The Investigator   *D1835*
The Invisible Dogs   *D1129*
The Invisible Line   *D367*
The Invisible Urge   *D932*
The Invisible Worm   *D301*
The Invitation   *D563*
Ireneo   *D479*
Irish Grannie   *D1211*
The Irish Philosopher   *D18*
Irish Plays Cupid   *D1039*
An Irish Princess   *D1335*
Isabel   *D788*
Isadora and G.B.   *D82*
The Island Abode of Bliss   *D275*
Island of Demons   *D2235*
Islands   *D949*
It Happened In September   *D145*
It Happened Only Yesterday   *D1816*
It's Great to Be Single   *D613*

J

Jack and Jill   *D1021*
The Jack and the Joker   *D1690*
Jake Hayseed in the City   *D19*
Jacob's Wake   *D421*
The Jade Heart   *D392*
James and the Ogre   *D881*
Jassoket and Anemon   *C118*
Jerome   *D1900*
Jessie   *D1289*
Jesus Christ, Rabble Rouser   *D2068*
A Jig for the Gypsy   *D514*
Jim Barber's Spite Fence   *D2042*
The Jingo Ring   *D338*
Joan of Arc's Violin   *D176*
Joe Christ   *D373*
Joe Derry   *D1204*
Joe's Lunch   *D1517*

The Joggsville Convention   *D70*
John and the Missus   *D1586*
John Bull and Jonathan   *C17*
Johnny Dunn   *D728*
Johnny Mangano and His Astonishing Dogs   *D2087*
Joker in the Pack   *D395*
Jonah   *D148, D1301*
Joseph the Dreamer   *D1912*
Joseph, the Interpreter of Dreams   *D1913*
Joseph's Dreams Come True   *D1914*
Jour Ouvert   *D261*
Judas Iscariot   *D1402*
Judith of Bethulia   *D1774*
Jumping Rope Drill   *D20*
Junior Hero   *D778*
Junkyard   *D685*
Just Johnny   *D105*

K

Kafka   *D1833*
Kaleidoscope   *D281*
Kate   *D1275*
Katy Did   *D1336*
Kee Kee   *D48*
Keeper of the Gold   *D1465*
Keillor House Dialogue   *D764, D1314*
Keyhole   *D1151*
The Key of Jack Canuck's Treasure-House   *D851*
The Key of Life   *D1812*
The Key That Unlocks   *D1715*
The Kibitzer   *D981*
The Kidnappers   *C141, D970*
The Kill   *D813*
Kill Them   *D1188*
Killarney's Return   *D1579*
The Killdeer   *D1656*
The King   *D1553*
The King Decides   *D2213*
King Grumbletum and the Magic Pie   *D1087*
The King of New Albion   *D1950*
The King of the Beavers   *C173*
The King of the Golden Mountain   *D1262*
King Phoenix   *D515*
The King, the Sword and the Dragon   *D625*
Kingdom of Kinkapoo   *D2153*

The Kingdom of the Sun *D388*
A King's Girl *D2239*
The King's Girls *D2053*
The King's Ugly Bride *D305*
Kingsayer *D2245*
The Klondike *C161*
A Knife to Thy Throat *D1628*
The Knights and the Dragon *D21*
Knud Iverson *C119*
The Komagata Maru Incident *D1602*
Krokodile *D1724*

L

Labor and Capital *C18*
The Labyrinth *D1018*
Laddie Boy *D1767*
The Ladies *D1800*
The Ladies of Camelot *D1276*
The Lady of Lodore *D954*
The Lady Sees Red *D1606*
Ladybug, Ladybug *D1418*
The Lake *D789*
Lake Dore *D1391*
The Lake of Killearny by Moonlight *C158*
Lamech *C120*
Lament for Harmonica *D1691*
The Lampshade *D1404*
The Land *D1297*
The Land of Ephranor *D1801*
The Land of Liberty *C19*
Land of Magic Spell *D2263*
The Land Swap *C20*
The Landlord and Tenant Act *D264*
A Language Game in Limbo *D1786*
The Lantern of Magellan *D163*
The Last Cache *D1256*
The Last Chapter *D956*
The Last Days of Paul Bunyan *D678A*
The Last Death of Abraham Schurmann *D814*
The Last of the Order *D172*
The Last of the Tsars *D144*
The Last of the Vestals *D1337*
The Last Riding *D1298*
The Last Spike *D1951*
Laura Secord *D499, D551, D1952*
Laura Secord, the Heroine of 1812 *C83*

Lavender Gloves *D412*
The Leather Medal *D178*
Leave It To Beaver Is Dead *D1223*
Leaving Home *D714*
Leela Means to Play *D1849*
A Legal Puzzle *D2074*
The Legend of Echo and Narcissus *D1236*
The Legend of the Light *D93*
Legend of the Long House *D1876*
The Legend of the Roses *C185*
Lemons and Hieroglyphs *D735*
Lenore Nevermore *D129*
Leo and Venetia *C59*
Leo, the Royal Cadet *C73*
Let Mary Lou Do It *D71*
Let My People Go *D1108*
Let Swords Slash for Freedom *D1699*
Let There Be Farce *D2148*
The Letellier Drama *C21*
Let's Make A Carol *D1657*
Let's Make A World *D1572*
Let's Play Fish *D1456*
Liberation *D2181*
The Liberator *D480*
The Lie *D841*
Lief the Lucky *D1953*
The Life and Death of Adolf Hitler *D991*
Life Burns On *D391*
The Life of a Toy *D346*
The Life of Jackson Piper *D378*
Lifeguard *D2124*
The Light *D2259*
Like as Two P's *D2179*
Like Death Warmed Over *D2088*
Like Father, Like Fun *D1501*
Like It or Not *D676*
The Line *D1472*
The Lion and the Unicorn *D1482*
Listen to the Drum *D2175*
Listen to the Tall Wheat Singing *D717*
Listen to the Wind *D1658*
A Little Bit Left *D1384*
A Little Child Shall Lead Them *D575*
Little Chipmunk and the Owl Woman *D1677*
Little Cinderella *D1338*
The Little Fir Tree *D702*

Little Guy Napoleon *D1597*
Little Legion *D1100*
Little Monsters *D322*
Little Nobody *C99*
The Little People *D1827*
Little Saint Teresa *D1339*
Little Steps to Heaven *D1061*
Little Taras *D1777*
Little Theatre *D1394*
A Living Thing *D873, D1219*
Local *C22*
Locals *C23*
The Lodge *D1692*
Loggerheads *D1083*
The Long Illness of Ex-Chief Kiti *D755*
The Long Leather Bag *D636*
Looking for a Job *D1740*
Looking Forward *D1216*
Lord Fitz Fraud *C69*
Lord Selkirk *D500*
Lord Ullin's Daughter *D611*
Lost a Smallish Brown Dog *D882*
Lost—a Temper! *D1824*
The Lost Queen *D86*
Louis Riel *D1152, D1428*
Love and Libel *D516*
The Love Feast *D173*
The Love Gift *D1549*
Love-Making for Profit and Taxes *D1319*
Love Me, Love My Children *D2020*
Love Mime #5 *D492*
Love Mouse *D1730*
The Love Potion *D323*
Love Scene: Dominic and Sadie *D1070*
Love's Pilgrimage *D844*
Low Life *D535*
The Loyalists *D955, D1539*
Le Lucciole *C111*
The Luck of Ginger Coffey *D869*
Lucky Dollars *D431*
Ludwig, the Emigrant *C170*
Lulu Street *D922*

M

Maada and Ulke *D592*
A Mad Philosopher *C66*
Mad Shelley *D2150*
Madam Fou-Fou *D2047*

Madam Leclaire *D2221*
Madam Verite at Bath *D1529*
Madeleine de Vercheres *D1954*
Madeline de Vercheres *D501*
Maestro *D797*
The Magic Candlestick *D648*
The Magic Donkey *D1058*
The Magic Nugget *D1267*
The Magician *D1896*
Magic Juice *D1751*
The Magnet *D730*
The Magnificent Slowpoke *D1133*
The Maid *D88*
Maiden Mona the Mermaid *C100*
The Maire of St. Brieux *C101*
Making Maple Sugar *D1955*
The Making of Canada's Flag *D852*
The Making of Our Flag *D2109*
A Man at Westminster *D1102*
The Man Comes Down From the Moon *D749*
A Man for Mathilde *D1010*
The Man from Inner Space *D1502*
The Man from Wulfshausen *D815*
Man in the Basement *D2192*
The Man in the Moon *D1398*
The Man in the Winter Catalogue *D1130*
The Man of Kerioth *D1507, D1915*
A Man Was Killed *D393, D1160*
The Man Who Played Judas *D2243*
The Man Who Read the Stars *D1956*
The Man Who Wanted to Sing *D409*
The Man Who Went *D2075*
The Man Who Would Like to Forget *D242*
The Man With the Red Hat *D1037*
Manitou Portage *D1448*
Manon Lastcall *D138*
Man's World *D1031*
Many Days and Holidays *D1226*
Marco Polo *D481*
Margaret McLeod *D1234*
Margo *D1408*
Marie Hebert *D2054*
Marigold *D889, D1635*
Marina, The Fisherman's Daughter *C148*
Marjorie's Wedding Dress *D1247*
Marmion *C138*

Marrying Anne? *D72*
Marsh Hay *D552*
Martha Made Over *D73*
Martha's Looking Glass *D221*
Mary *D2107*
Mary and the Holy Thorn *D861*
Mary Magdalen *D1340*
Mary Midnight *D1312*
Mary Stuart and her Friends *D1341*
Mary Tudor *D1503B*
Maskerman *D2236*
Masque *D313*
A Masque Entitled "Canada's Welcome" *C102*
A Masque of Aesop *D517*
The Masque of Learning *D1505*
A Masque of Mr. Punch *D518*
The Master Cat or Puss in Boots *D779*
Mathematics *D52*
A Matter of Curious Chemistry *D488*
A Matter of Life and Death *D2269*
Maurice *D211*
Maximilian Beetle *D2264*
A May Festival *D1342*
Maybe We Could Get Some Bach *D539*
The Mayor *C103*
Me? *D1101*
The Meal Club Plot *C183*
The Measures *D315*
Medea *D664*
The Medicine Line *D1412*
A Medieval Hun *D351*
The Meeting *D262*
The Member from Trois-Rivieres *D396*
Memoir *D1478*
Memories for My Brother *D1533*
Men Were Deceivers Ever *D987*
Mercedes Bends *D993*
The Mercenary *D1907*
Metamorphosis *D1474*
The Metaphysical White Cat *D530*
Mettawamkeag *D1173*
Meyer's Room *D1731*
Midashasassesears *D324*
Middleman *D1261*
Midnight and Christmas Eve *D371*
Midnight Burial *D937*
The Midnight of Monsieur St. Jean *D142*

Midway Priest *D343*
The Mighty Mr. Samson *D1119*
The Millionaire's Daughter *D1343*
Millions for Her *C130*
The Mind Cure *C108*
The Miner *D1957*
A Miner's Wife *D270*
The Minister's Bride *D74*
A Minister's Mistake *D22*
Minnie *D1071*
Minnie Trail *C193*
The Miracle of Roses *D2229*
The Mirrored Countenance *D1759*
Mirrors *D1045*
Miss Canada's Reception *D1239*
Miss Pebble (of New York) *D198*
Miss Pebble's Retreat *D374*
A Mission School *D1958*
The Missionary Position *D919*
Mrs. Jones' Conversion *D23*
Mrs. Tactician's Triumph *C70*
Mr. and Mrs. *D1254*
Mr. Bumble's Proposal *D902*
Mr. Bunch's Toys *D780*
Mr. Excelsior *D1072*
Mr. Huntington, F.R.G.S. *D114*
Mr. Mackenzie at Buckingham *C25*
Mr. Miggles *D1049*
Mr. Scrooge *D1443*
Mr. Scrooge on Main Street *D284*
Mr. Thompson Retires *D188*
The Mod at Grand Pre *D1109*
The Moderate Drinker *C24*
A Modern Romeo and Juliet *C145*
A Modest Proposal *D792*
A Moment of Existence *D1310*
Monday, the Thirteenth *D723*
Money and Mud *D1560*
Money for Jam *D891*
Monomania *D1380*
Mons Angelorum *D1584*
Monster *D1752*
Montcalm *D553*
Montgomery *C112*
The Moon for a Candle *D1745*
The Moonless Nights *D1629*
The Moon-Tree *D99*
Mordred *C77*

More Sinned Against Than Sinning   C80
More Things in Heaven   D961
Morning   C78
Morning Glory   D2014
Mortier   D746
The Most Lamentable Tragedy   D1040
Mother Canada's Christmas Tree   D971
Mother Country   D950
The Mother Lode   D1098
Mother's Birthday   D1344
Motors That Pass in the Night   D2218
The Mountain   D2214
Mountjoy and the Flower Children   D2025
The Mouse Trap   D24
The Movers   D1220
Moving Day   D237
Muffler   D524
The Mulgrove Road Show   D1457
The Mumberley Inheritance   D823
The Mummer's Play   D781
Murder in the Empress   D2134
Murder in the University   D974
Murder Pattern   D2115
Museum of Man   D1877
The Music Box   D529
My Best Friend Is Twelve Feet High   D212
My Eyes Were Opened   D363
My Father Was a Doctor   D1451
My Mother's House Has Too Many Rooms   D2163
My Sister's Keeper   D59
The Mystery of Meaux   D348
The Mystery of the Nile   D164
Mystery of the Pig Killer's Daughter   D1753
A Mystery Play   D1806
The Myth Includes   D1636

N

Names and Nicknames   D1659
Narrow Passage   D56
National Service   D721
The Nativity   D782
Nativity Play   D466
Nature In the Raw Is Seldom   D130
Ned and Jack   D1732
Neighbours' Business   D1736

Nellie McNabb   D1093
Neptune's Theatre   A1
The Net   D2252
Nets of Silver   D1995
The New Canada   D1878
The New Deal   D244
The New Dumbells Play   D1596
The New Gentle Shepherd   B1
The New Governess   D1345
New Horizons for Rolling Prairie   D1269
The New House   D1299
New Laff-Tested Dialogues   D1225
New Maurry's Lunch   D1283
The New Minister   C26
The New Step   D394
New Year's Eve   D1346
The Newcomer   D89
A Nice Girl Like You   D410
Nice Mice   D325
The Night Before   D718A
Night-Blooming Cereus   D1660
Night Freight   D2253
Night Mail   D311
The Night No One Yelled   D1306
Night of Betrothal   D1580
Night of Storm   D2215
The Night They Raided Truxx   D1154, D1189
A Night With a Stranger   D1599
Nightjar   D593
Nightshift   D2125
Nina   C82
The 90th on Active Service   C64
No Certain Harbour   D1617
No Longer At Ease   D1618
No Moon - No Son   D1709
No More Octobers   D833
No Red Carpet   D248
No Reporters Please   D1094
No Scandal in Spain   D1879
No Trouble at All   D992
Noel in Old Quebec   D165
None But the Brave   D883
Noot-chee and the Paddle   D1712
The Norsemen in America   D166
North Mountain Breakdown   D1190
Not All Who Grieve   D195
Not Dead Yet   C174

Not Only the Guppy   *D1034*
Not to Hong Kong   *D276*
Nothing But a Man   *D1768*
Nothing to Lose   *D642*
Number Five Cheyne Row   *D459*
Number One   *D2149*
Nunc Dimittis   *D185*
Nuts & Bolts & Rusty Things   *D724A, D2059*

O

O Woman   *D1095*
The Oasis   *D1369*
The Ocean   *D197*
October Stranger   *D1090*
Oedipus the King   *D1880*
Of Course I Never Get Excited   *D1143*
Of the Fields Lately   *D715*
Off the Freeway   *D2126*
Offense and Defense   *D2262*
Old Friends and New   *D1347*
The Old Lady and the Pig   *D783*
Old Master   *D1121*
An Old Time Ladies' Aid Business Meeting   *D75*
Old Times and Old Timers   *D115*
The Old Woman and the Pedlar   *D2246*
Oliver Twist   *D1840*
The Olympic Banquet   *C191*
Omphale and the Hero   *D928*
On Christmas Night   *D554*
On Streisand   *D1158*
On the Job   *D643*
On the King's Birthday   *D962*
On the Lee Shore   *D909*
On the Rim of the Curve   *D422*
On the Roof   *D2007*
Once a Giant   *D298*
Once Burnt, Twice Shy   *D1135*
Once in a Blue Moon   *D2017*
One Act is Plenty   *D1781*
One Crack Out   *D716*
One Crowded Hour   *D655*
One Day's Fun   *D429*
The One-Eyed Jack   *D790*
One Hundred Feet Up   *D1084*
One Hundred Years Ago   *C143*
One-Man Masque   *D1661*

One Night Stand   *D213*
One Plus One   *D1441*
One's a Heifer   *D582*
One Spring Morning   *D1984*
One Wish Too Many   *D637*
One Who Looks at the Stars   *D798*
Ooomerahgi Oh   *D2099*
Open Doors   *D1096*
The Opera of the Machine   *D312*
Operators   *D951*
Operetta-Dinner   *D1439*
The Optimistic Dollar   *D326*
Oratorio for Sasquatch   *D100*
The Order of Good Cheer   *D750*
The Organizer   *D404, D839*
Original Child Bomb   *D360*
The Original Version of The Curse of ChirraPoonje   *D277*
Origins   *D141*
Orpheus and Eurydice   *C175*
Oscar Remembered   *D1377*
The Other Half   *D302*
The Ottawa Man   *D1429*
An Ounce of Prevention   *D25*
Our Boys in the Riel Rebellion   *C105A*
Our Dream House   *D705, D1444*
Our Flags   *D1183*
Our House   *D1555*
Our Japanese Cousin   *D1348*
Our Lady of the Moon   *D97*
Our Own Particular Jane   *D1003*
Our Poet in the Council Chamber   *C27*
Out Flew the Web and Floated Wide   *D996*
Out of the Past   *D1721*
Outport   *D243*
Over Prairie Trails   *D2171*
Overcrowding in the Desert   *D1059*
Overlaid   *D519*
The Oyster   *D2008*

P

The P.B.I.   *D1814*
A Pacific Coast Tragedy   *D616*
Pagan Magic   *D784*
A Pageant of Bethlehem   *D285*
A Pageant of Canadian History   *D310, D1458, D1815*

A Pageant of Nursing in Canada *D1392*
Pageant of the Years *D1375*
Paid in Full *D1590*
Pair of Rubbers *D1518*
Pa-Ke-Noh-Ka, The Winner *D630*
The Panel *D2254*
Pan's Damn Lamb *D2060*
Paper Making *D1959*
Paper Wheat *D2104*
Par for the Course *D2049*
Paracelsus *D1769*
Parallels *D1758*
Pardon *D1802*
Parents' Day *D1004*
The Park *D2106*
Parting of Boabdil and Morayma *C94*
The Partition *D1153*
Party Day *D2231A*
Pas de Trois *D357*
Pasque Flower *D1693*
Pass the Salt Peter *D1985*
Passacaglia *D1005*
Passage *D1557*
The Passing Hours *D1828*
The Passing of the Red Man *D1960*
Passion and Sin *D53*
Passport Please *D272*
Patches *D2176*
The Paths of Glory *D179*
The Patriot *D180*
A Patriotic Auction *D853*
The Patriots *D469*
A Patriot's Daughter *D1349*
Pause *D1419*
The Pawnshop *D870*
Peace with Pontiac *D1961*
Peach *D679*
Pearl Divers *D929*
The Pearl Without Price *D1798*
Pearls for the Missions *D1350*
Peepshow *D1198A*
The Pencil *D1778*
Penetration *D1754*
Penicillin *D1124*
A Penny's Worth of Power *D453*
Peppercorn's Magic *D689*
Perambulance *D233*
Perfect Perley *D1073*

The Perilous Dream *D1710*
Perseus and Andromeda *D884*
Pete Goes Home *D1511*
Peter & John *D1024*
A Phantom Born of Song *D896*
The Philosopher's Stone *D1799*
The Photograph *D973*
The Photographic Moment *D125*
Pickles and Puppets *D2117, D2260*
The Pied Piper *D43*
Pierre *D1807*
Pierre LaPorte *D365*
Pierre Radisson *D555*
A Pig in a Poke *D249*
Pig Tales *D1804, D2013*
Piggy Back *D1006*
The Pile *D1430*
Pilgrims and Strangers *D1393*
Pillar of Sand *D1503*
Pinocchio *D44*
Pipandor *C104*
Pipe Dream *D234*
Pipistrelle of Aquitaine *D1271*
Pirates!! *D785*
A Place of Refuge *D26*
Placida, The Christian Martyr *C81*
Plans for the Holidays *D1351*
Play *D1920*
A Play About Bread and Roses *D690*
A Play About How the Greeks *D83*
Play and By Play *D1007*
A Play for Labour Day *D1962*
The Play Is The Thing, Tra La! *D327*
A Play on Words *D1881*
The Play-Room Closet Door *D900*
A Plea of Judas *D385*
Please Don't Sneeze *D2204*
The Pleasures of the World *D296*
Plen-An-Guary *D2164*
Ploughmen of the Glacier *D1770*
Plus One Minus One Equals *D473*
The Pobble People *D1722*
The Poet *D62*
Poet of the Plains *D2055*
Poets for Lunch *D1454*
The Point of View *D1522*
Politics of Passion *D307*
Ponteach *B3*

The Poor Man's Clever Daughter   D638
The Popcorn Man   D1541, D1703
Pope John VIII   D1284
The Popish Plot   C28
Pot of Gold   D1546
The Potter's Dream   D708
A Poulterer In Hell   D300
Preparations   D1368
Preparing   D1850
Presbyterian General Assembly   C29
Press Release   D454
The Prime Minister's Golden Wig   D1303
Prince Charlie and Flora   D751
Prince Edward Island   D1185
A Prince in Egypt   D286
The Prince of Naples   D2138
Prince Pedro   C115
Princess Mignon   D923
The Princess of the Snows   D963
The Princess Who Dreamed Too Much   D799
Private Turvey's War   D898
The Prizewinner   D556
Pro and Con   C30, C31
The Prodigal Son   D417
The Professionals   D588
Professor Fuddle's Fantastic Fairy-Tale Machine   D127, D241
Prologue   D273, D1808, D1809, D1851
A Promethean Trilogy   D482
Prometheus Rebound   D235
Prometheus, the Fire Giver   D483
The Promise   D1591
The Proper Perspective   D824
The Prospector   D1963
Protest   D2216
The Proud One   D1400
Provincial Drama Called The Family Compact   C171
Ptarmigan   C152
The Pump and the Tavern   C32
The Pumpkinhead Family   D116
The Purple Seal   D1248
Purr   D1490
Puss in Boots   D657
Pussy's in the Well   D2093
Put On the Spot   D1278
Pygmalion, Prince of Cyprus   C57
Pyramus and Thisbe   D484

Q

Q   D901, D1174
The Quarrelling Quails   D2048
Quebec   D1144
Queen Eleanor and Fair Rosamond   C71
Queen Esther   D1352
The Queen of Sheba   D1353
A Queen Who Saved A Nation From Death   D1916
The Queen's Oak   C33
A Question of Clothes   D2076
A Question of Perspective   D274
Question Time   D520
Quick-Witted Jack   D639
Quid et Quare   D1536
Quiet Day in Belfast   D487
A Quiet Half-Hour   D606
Quiller   D423
The Quilt   D336

R

Radio Script   D1705
Radisson   D1964
The Raft   D1175
Raft Baby   D679A
Rag Doll   D1191
The Rain Falls Harder   D474
The Rainmaker   D1694
The Rainstone   D2177
Ramona and the White Slaves   D2139
Ravlan   C186
Rayon   C121
Ready, Steady, Go   D1053
Real Christmas Gifts   D257
Rear View   D1264
Rebel and Patriot   D1965
The Recognition   D1743
The Recoil   D983
Recollections of a Civilized Man   D1503A
Recompense   D1023
The Red Cross Badge   D1184
The Red Cross Helpers   D1354
Red Emma   D214
Red Flag at Evening   D1694A
Red Hand   D445, D1249
Red Riding-Hood   C179, D1541, D1704
Red Riding Hood Up to Date   D1176
The Red Shawl   D772

Reformation and Reward *D1250*
The Rehearsal *D1488*
Rehearsal II *D399*
Reindeer at Christmas *D269*
Release *D1991*
The Release of Allen Danvers *D2222*
Relief *D186*
The Reluctant Hero *D1200*
Reluctantly Last Summer *D1103*
Remember the Good Old Days *D650*
Remembrance Day *D1196*
Remorse *D279*
Rendezvous *D2193*
Report of Mr. Bull's Jury *C116, C165A*
Requiem for a Mensh *D982*
Requiem for a Small Boy *D1442*
Rest Home *D131*
A Restoration Show for Strumpet and Fruit *D84*
The Resurrection of Philip Jerome Michaels *D475*
Retribution *D1923*
Return of the Emigrant *D536*
Return to an Early Home *C95*
Return to Colonus *D1882*
Reverberations of Erostratus *D42A*
A Revised Experiment *D1407*
The Revolt of the Puppets *D1992*
Revolutions *D1986*
Rewrite *D382*
Rex Morgan, M.D. *D1834*
The Rich Young Ruler *D1917*
The Riddle Machine *D1136*
Ride to the Hill *D2029*
Ridiculous and Sublime *D1035*
Riel *D446*
Rinse Cycle *D470, D1155*
Rise and Shine *D303*
Rites of Passage *D976*
The Ritual *D1013*
The River of White Flowers *D1966*
Riz Flowers *D1313*
The Road *D1672*
The Road to Charlottetown *D40*
The Roads of Learning *D46*
Roast Pig *D988*
Robin Hood *D1841*
Robin Hood and Friar Tobias *D885*

Rocky Mountain Bill *D117*
Rolling Stone *D432*
A Roman Drama in Five Acts *C59*
The Romance of a Princess *D1716*
The Romance of Canada *D2208*
Romantic Royalty *D886*
The Roncarelli Affair *D1431*
Roommates *D245*
A Rope Against the Sun *D1593*
Rosa *D2069*
Rose Latulippe *D570*
Roundabout *D816*
Roundhouse *D1195*
Routine *D1099*
The Rowley Band *D2244*
A Royal Romance *D1237*
Royal Suspect *D670*
The Royal Touch *D800*
The Ruby of Melchoir *D607*
A Run for His Money *D398*
The Runaway *D620*
A Runaway Couple *D2077*
The Russian Drama *D1177*
The Rusting Heart *D1996*
Ruth *D1290*

S

Sacktown Rag *D2140*
Sacred and Secular *D2165*
The Sacrifice *D229, D1504*
The Sad Story of Billy Max *D1285*
The Safety Court *D27*
The Saint *D935*
Saint Bartholomew's Day in Canada *C55*
The St. Nicholas Hotel *D1662*
St. Paul's Defence *D386*
Sainte-Marie Among the Hurons *D1491*
St. Ursula *D1717*
Salmon Fishing *D1967*
Salt in the Blood *D1581*
The Salvage Play *D28*
Sam Weller Visits *D1921*
Sam Weller's Valentine *D1050*
The Same Old Santa Claus *D1547*
Samuel de Champlain *D2230*
Santiago *C67*
Sappho and Phaon *D1523*
Sappho in Leucadia *D2010, D2011*

Sarah's Play   *D564*
Saturday Night   *D1694B*
Saul   *C128*
The Savage Dream   *D2027*
Sawdust   *D2173*
The Sawmill   *D1968*
Say Hi to Owsley   *D686*
Say What You Will   *D539*
Scar Tissue   *D2166*
The Scarlet Knight   *D602*
Scarlet Slippers   *D49*
Scene at Ottawa   *C34, C35*
Scene—City Hall   *C36*
Scene in Ottawa   *C37*
Scenes from 'The Old Curiosity Shop'   *D169*
Scenes from Unpublished Dramas   *C40*
Scenes in Court   *C38*
Scenes in Court—The Deaf Female Witness   *C39*
Scenes of World Fellowship   *D2097*
A School for Backwards   *D118*
School of Darkness   *D230*
Schoolgirl Visions   *D1355*
Scientific Socialism   *D238*
Score/Score   *D770*
Screwaround   *D1166*
The Scribleromania   *C192*
Sea Legend   *D1386*
Search for the Tse Tse Fly   *D2255*
Season of the Witch   *D309*
Sebastian   *C150*
The Second Duchess   *D1630*
The Second Lie   *D1257*
The Secret of the Spyglass   *D1550*
The Seedling   *D1008*
The Seekers   *D1718*
The Seigneur   *D1969*
Selkirk   *D1371*
The Senate   *D252*
The Senator's Sensitive Daughter   *C41*
Sense and Sentiment   *D1356*
Seven Caesar's Ransoms   *D1272*
Seven Hours to Sundown   *D1771*
Seven Oaks   *D557*
72 Under the 0   *D1997*
Sewing Seams with Steel   *D1125*
Sex, Cold Cans, and a Coffin   *D1046*

Sex Education   *D1573*
Shadow of Suspicion   *D866*
The Shadow of the Nile   *D280*
A Shakespeare Pageant   *D1357*
Shakespeare Revises a Play   *D182*
Shakespeare's Skull and Falstaff's Nose   *C162*
Shaman   *D687*
Shellgame   *D132*
Shelter   *D215*
The Shinbone General Store Caper   *D565*
The Ship of Dreams   *D984*
Ships That Pass   *D155*
Shipwreck   *D2167*
Shootup   *D133*
The Shop in Toad Lane   *D801*
Short Drama   *C42*
The Shortest Distance   *D1739*
Shortshrift   *D566*
Shoulder Pads   *D1644*
Showdown at Sand Valley   *D1413*
The Shrievalty of Lynden   *C140*
The Sickle   *D427*
The Signature   *D1779*
The Silent Customer   *D1506*
Silent Movie Days   *D771*
The Silver Chief   *D1970*
The Silver Jubilee   *D1253*
Simon Black   *C159*
Simon's Reason   *D174*
Simple Activities   *D525*
Simple Dramatization of History   *D2143*
Sinbad and the Mermaid   *D2205*
Sir Isaac Brock   *D502*
Sir John and Sir Charles   *C43*
Sis   *D2223*
Sister Balonika   *D1784*
Sisters of Mercy   *D1025*
Sitting Bill   *D1516*
Sitting in the Audience   *D1381*
Six Dry Cakes for the Hunted   *D2237*
The Six Queens of Henry   *D1622*
Sixteen Decades of Parsonages   *D1110*
Sixteen Ninety   *D845*
'67   *D2142*
Skit   *D29*
Slane   *D817*
Slang   *D754*

The Sleeping Bag   *D1466*
The Sleeping Beauty   *C44, D887, D1695, D2206*
Small Potatoes   *D2018*
Smith Broadens Out   *D1366*
Smokestack in the Desert   *D2256*
The Snake   *D1145*
Snow Birds   *D2063*
Snow White and Rose Red   *D658*
So Who's Goldberg?   *D540*
Social Idolatry   *D1526*
Society Idyls   *C72*
Socrates   *D1883*
Socrates and Xantippe   *C45*
Soft Voices   *D1645*
Solange   *D139*
Soldiers Acting at Christmas   *D30*
Some Are So Lucky   *D731*
A Somersault to Love   *D1826*
Something Red   *D2144*
Something Suitable for Him   *D31*
Something Wrong Somewhere   *D1217*
Sometime Every Summertime   *D1317*
A Song for Sara   *D542*
The Song of James and John   *D1829*
The Song of Louise in the Morning   *D1055*
The Song of Songs   *D560*
The Song of the Serpent   *D1137*
Songs for the Bible Belt   *D668*
Songs for the Coal Forest Children   *D1680*
Sophie   *D1074*
Spanish Conquistadores   *D167*
Speak for Life   *D471, D1305*
Spirit and Flesh   *D1810*
The Spirit of Giving   *D969*
The Spirit of the Thing   *D507*
The Splits   *D1700*
The Spotted Veil   *D2011*
Spratt   *D2203*
The Spratts   *D1241*
A Spring Fantasy   *D853A*
A Spring Flower Garden   *D943*
Spring Tea   *D328*
Sqrieux-De-Dieu   *D1138*
Stampede   *D1696*
The Stamp Lady's Miracle   *D910*
Stand   *D2194*

Stand-in For a Murderer   *D1574*
Star Quality   *D216*
Starborn the Conjurer   *C122*
Stargazing   *D404A*
The States   *D413*
The Station   *D1147*
The Statue and the Bust   *D2061*
Statues   *D369*
Stephen Truscott   *D366*
The Step-Sisters   *D1358*
The Stick Men   *D1477*
Stick With Molasses   *D1279*
Sticks and Stones   *D1575, D1663*
Still Stands the House   *D1697*
The Stone Cross   *D1780*
Stonehenge   *D131, D665*
Stonehenge Trilogy   *D666*
The Store   *D1432*
The Story of Canada   *D119, D672*
Straight Man   *D946*
The Strange Disappearance of Princess Gloriana   *D1209*
Strawberry Fields   *D953*
The Streamlined Madonna   *D964*
The Street Cleaner   *D1054*
The Strength of Love   *D1631*
The Striker   *D390*
Striker Schneiderman   *D829*
Striking for Higher Wages   *D287*
Strobe   *D2127*
The Strong People   *D1785*
Strong Wind's Choice   *D1825*
Struggle   *D1205*
The Sub-Contractor   *D1178*
Subjunction   *D2257*
The Subsidiary Vice-President   *D2022*
Success of a Mission   *D1128, D1797, D2070*
Such Harmony   *D894*
Such Is Life   *C109*
The Suicide Meet   *D126*
Sulfa Drugs   *D1126*
Summer Hotel   *D1097*
Summer Solstice   *D57*
Summer's Rehearsal   *D875*
Summit Conference   *D329*
The Sun and The Moon   *D1664*
Sunrise on Sarah   *D1772*

Sunshine in Mariposa   *D1179*
Sure of a Fourth   *D627*
Surprise, Surprise   *D2089*
Survival   *D868*
Susannah, Agnes and Ruth   *D830*
The Sweet Girl Graduate   *C84*
Sweet Home Sweet   *D1492*
The Sweets of Office   *C46*
Sword/Play   *D1725*
Symbols   *D201*
Syrinx   *D1706*

T

Take Away My Shadow   *D703*
Take to the Trees   *D2217*
Take Me Where the Water's Warm   *D533*
The Taking of the Holy City   *D1359*
A Tale of a Tub   *D202*
Tales from a Prairie Drifter   *D1148*
Talking Dirty   *D1902*
Talleyrand   *D147*
Tamerlane   *D2133*
Tancred, Prince of Salerno   *D485*
Tangleflags   *D217*
Tanned   *D2128*
Tantramar   *D765*
Tantrums   *D54*
Tattered Roses   *D1525*
Tea for Two   *D1270*
Tea Party   *D1075, D1548*
The Tea Party at the Shoe   *D1252*
Teach Me How to Cry   *D1056*
The Tearful and Tragical Tale of the Tricky Troubadour   *C65*
Tecumseh   *C157*
The Telegram   *D931*
Telemachus   *D1409*
Temperance Dialogue   *C47*
The Tempest   *D527*
Ten Years   *C133*
The Ten Virgins   *D288*
Terror and Erebus   *D1242*
The Test   *D614*
Tharbis   *D1719*
That Boy, Call Him Back   *D920*
That Time of the Month   *D2201*
Thayendanegea   *C153*
Le Théâtre de Neptune   *A1*

The Theatre of Neptune   *A1*
Theatre of War   *D2258*
Theatre Our Weapon   *D32*
Theatricals at the Theatre   *C48*
Their Class Motto   *D1360*
There   *D405*
There Go I   *D192*
There Little Girl   *D2198*
Therese's Creed   *D424*
These Precious Promises   *D1884*
They Meet Again   *D628*
They Were All Deceived   *D709*
They're Burning Down the House   *D594*
The Thirty Dollar Wreath   *D836*
This, Gentlemen, is Justice   *D1311*
This Glittering Dust   *D447*
This Side of the Rockies   *D2129*
This Train   *D1414*
This Was London   *D1397*
Thomas, the Twin   *D1918*
Those Shamrocks From Ireland   *D1361*
Three Cabbagetown Plays   *D2064*
Three Desks   *D1665*
Three Dramatic Objects   *D741*
Three Rings for Michelle   *D1057*
Three Sheets in the Wind   *D1582*
Three to Get Married   *D938*
Three Weddings of a Hunchback   *D223*
Three Women   *D732*
Through the Glass   *D1513*
Throw Sand Against the Wind   *D2154*
Thunder on a Distant Mountain   *D760*
Thy Sons Command   *D1467*
The Tiger from Zanzibar   *D1106*
Tiln   *D425*
Time Lock   *D867*
A Time of Minor Miracles   *D194*
A Time of Winter   *D914*
Time Running Out   *D455*
Time Warp   *D1755*
The Times Were Different   *D1206*
Timewatch   *D761*
Tiny's Story   *D1263*
Tit-Coq   *D744*
To Become a Drummer   *D344*
To Get Off the Street   *D907*
To Meet the Chinooks   *D706*
To-Night of all Nights   *D1637*

To the Dead Man   *D604*
To the Hollow   *D1026*
To What Purpose   *D206, D370A*
To Write a Poem of Walter Patterson   *D41*
Togetherness   *D1433*
The Token   *D85*
The Toll Gate   *D384*
Tom and the Leprechaun   *D640*
The Tomahawk   *D1720*
Tommy and His Grandfather   *D2024*
Tomorrow and Tomorrow   *D1844*
Tom's Dream   *D496*
Tony Weller's Benificence   *D1051*
Too Late   *D1295*
Too Many Kings   *D334*
Too Much Plum Pudding   *D1395*
A Toronto Hotel Room   *D1286*
Toronto—London—One Way   *D370*
The Totem   *D1198*
A Touch of God in the Golden Age   *D1534*
A Tower for Tommy   *D1673*
A Toy Mutiny   *D818*
The Toy Shop   *D671, D1396*
Trading in Innocence   *D2168*
A Tragedy Entitled Cantamantaloedis   *D587*
The Tragedy of St. George   *D33*
The Tragedy of Tanoo   *D617*
The Tragedy of Wallace   *D1817*
Train Town   *D1449*
The Traitor   *D143*
Tramp's Progress   *D597*
Trans-Canada Highway   *D2026*
Transit Through Fire   *D448*
The Translation of John Snaith   *D428*
Transport Survey   *D791*
Trapping   *D1971*
The Travesty and the Fruit Fly   *D2065*
Treasure   *D1258*
Treasure Island   *D1019*
Trespassers   *D1669*
Trial of a City   *D190*
The Trial of Jean-Baptiste M.   *D859*
The Trial of John Jasper   *D1052*
The Trial of Karl Von Bunker   *D120*
The Trial of Louis Riel   *D449, D2147*
The Trial of the Weather   *D1362*

Triangle   *D1852*
The Tribulations of N.F.D.   *C49*
Trick Doors   *D1076*
Trilogy in a Garden   *D1232*
The Trinity of Four   *D263*
A Trip for Mrs. Taylor   *D733*
The Triple Goddess   *D101*
Trips   *D1047*
Triptych   *D1062, D1668*
The Triumph of Intrigue   *C50*
The Trouble With the Women's Movement   *D977*
The Troublemaker   *D103*
Truants   *D297*
The True Believer   *D1901*
The True North Blueprint   *D345*
The True Romantic Love-Story of Col. and Mrs. Hutchinson   *C58*
A Truly Great Offer   *D567*
A Trumpet for Nap   *D154*
Tub   *D1493*
The Tubtown Orchestra   *D121*
The Tuggers and the Toll-Gate   *C110*
Tulip Talks   *D203*
Turkish Delight   *D1558*
The Turn of the Road   *D379*
Turnabout   *D608*
The Turning Tide   *D693*
Turns Home Again   *D414*
12 1/2 Cents   *D2240*
Twenty Years   *D2224*
Twenty-five Cents   *D895*
Twenty-one Trolls and a Dragon   *D1208*
The Twin Sinks of Allan Sammy   *D978*
The Twins' Santa Claus   *D34*
The Twisted Loaf   *D1646*
Twisted Roots   *D1726, D1853*
The Two Elders   *C184*
The Two Offerings   *C123*
Two Pollution Sketches   *D1111*
The Two Premiers   *C51*
Two Sides of Darkness   *D1632*
Two Sisters/The Scream   *D911*
Two Together   *D381*
Two Too Many   *D1259*
Two Tricks in Diamonds   *D2058*
The Tyranny of the Majority   *D1885*
The Tyrants of Toronto   *D967*

Tzinquaw *D1445*

U

The U.S. vs. Susan B. Anthony *D558*
An Unanswerable Collage *D135*
Uncle Jerry's Silver Jubilee *D1363*
Under the Arch *D335*
Undercover *D94*
Underground *D2130*
The Underground Lake *D568*
Underground Theology *C139*
Unemployed *D181*
Unemployment *D1307*
United Church of Canada *D35*
United to Serve *D1687*
Unity *D1760*
The Unmuzzled Max *D651*
The Unreasonable Act of Julian Waterman *D2030*
The Unreluctant Hostage *D696*
The Unspecific Scandal *C114*
Untitled *D2021*
The Up-Hill Revival *D569*
Upon a Midnight Clear *D63*
The Usual Three *D1036*

V

The V.P. *D1211*
Vacation *D134*
Vacuum *D2131*
Val and Tyne *D36*
The Valedictorian *D1897*
The Valentine *D456*
The Valiant Tailor *D2261*
The Valiant Woman *D846*
Vancouver and Quadra *D1972*
Variations on a Schizoid Interview *D930*
Variations on a Seventeenth Century Theme *D1811*
Veils *D406*
The Velvet Rut *D1711*
Verbrennte Soup *D2270*
A Very Desirable Residence *D584*
A Very Small Rebellion *D2100*
The Vestal Virgin *D1207*
Via Vitae *D1376*
The Vice President *D1803*
The Viceroy's Dream *C176*

Vicky *D2241*
The Victim *D1077*
Victoria 412 *D95*
Vignette #5 *D1674*
Vignette #1 *D1675*
A Virus Called Clarence *D1468*
A Visitor from Charleston *D1701*
Voices *D254*
Voices of Desire *D1633*
The Voice of the People *D521*
Vol. One *C52*

W

Wagging Their Tails Behind Them *D2094*
Wail for Two Pedestals *D2172*
Waiting *D98*
Waiting for Gaudreault *D1842*
Waiting to Go *D1733*
A Wake *D1142*
A Walk in Dark Places *D1092*
Walk Into Our Parlour *D239*
A Walk Through the Valley *D193*
Walking Back *D1078*
Walls *D266*
Walsh *D1603*
Wanted—A Chauffeur *D1611*
Wanted—A Radio *D462*
Wanted—A Wife *D76, D2225*
The War Drums of Skedans *D618*
War in the East *D1762*
The War on the Western Front *D854*
Wardle's Christmas Party *D1738*
Was She Sown or Was She Reaped? *D330*
Waterfall *D667*
Wawa *D680*
The Waxen Man *D1683*
The Way of Lacross *D140*
The Way Out *D1085*
The Way They Manage It *C53*
The Wayside Piper *D603*
We All Hate Toronto *D1886*
We Are Coming *D1612*
We Three, You and I *D840*
We've Won *D878*
The Weather Breeder *D559*
Weathered Oak *D2012*
Wedded to a Villain *D989*
Wedding in White *D720*

Week End *D1494*
Welcome, Baby Dear *D704*
Welcome, Stranger *D1387*
We're All Here Except Mike Casey's Horse *D979*
Westbound 12:01 *D1837*
Western *D55*
The Western Hero *D2180*
Westward to Canaan *D694*
Whaling *D1973*
What A Good Boy Am I *D2095*
What Do You Save From a Burning Building? *D624*
What Glorious Times They Had *D819*
What Next! And Next!! And Next!!! *C54*
What Price *D1277*
What Price Love *D1592*
What to Do After *D1469*
Whatever the Guise *D2155*
The Wheel *D1676*
Wheelchair *D1551*
Wheels and Friction *D1127*
When at Unawares *D1202A*
When Everybody Cares *D1280*
When George the Third Was King *C160*
When Greek Meets Greek *D1887*
When Half Gods Go *D945*
When I Hear *D256*
When Santa Needed Help *D2110*
When Sin Rides High *D1063*
When the Bough Bends *D457*
When the Cock Crows *D697*
When the King Smiled *D619*
When the Winds Stopped Blowing *D609*
Where Are You When We Need You? *D1481*
Where Could I Be Better Off? *D1888*
Where is Betsy? *D576*
Where the Buffalo Roam *D968*
Where There's a Will *D96*
Where Wheat Is King *D1974*
Where's That Happy Ending? *D411*
Which? *D2207*
Which Witch is Which? *D1281*
While I Live *D450*
Whirr of Wings *D255*
Whisper to Mendelsohn *D407*
The Whispering Time *D1903*
The Whistler in the Whirlwind *D1793*

The White Geese *D589*
The White Night *D1600*
The White Peaks *D1975*
Whiteoaks *D537*
Who Am I? *D2232*
Who Governs Canada? *D337*
Who is Strongest? *D641*
Who's Looking After the Atlantic? *D825*
Who's Pauline? *D1987*
Who's Who? *D1434*
Why Can't Men Cry? *D803*
Why Mice Leave Home *D331*
Why the Ant's Waist is Small *D1293, D1678*
Why the Chipmunk's Coat Is Striped *D1293, D1679*
Wickanninish Memory *D2169*
Widger's Way *D1698*
Widows Learn Fast *D430*
Widow's Scarlet *D965*
A Wife in the Hand *D467*
A Wig for My Lady *D698*
The Wild Animal Play for Children *D1820*
Wild Goose Chase *D2056*
The Wild Plum *D758*
Wild West Circus *D688*
Wilderness *D2116*
Willie and the Watchers *D1988*
Wind of Power *D1114*
The Wind on the Heath *D892, D1405*
The Windigo *D681*
The Window *D753*
Winds of Life *D415*
The Winged Victory *C151*
The Wings of the Dove *D2028*
Winnifred and Grace *D1079*
Winter Offensive *D739*
Winter Scene *D299*
The Wisdom Tooth *D1515*
The Wishing Well *D888*
Wisp in the Wind *D476*
Witch Doctor *D1470*
The Witch House of Baldoon *D966*
The Witch of Endor *D1508*
The Witch of Plum Hollow *D1438*
With the Seal Hunters *D1976*
Woman Called "X" *D433*
Woman Suffrage *C168*

Woman, the Masterpiece *D838*
A Woman's Heart *D1577*
A Woman's Wager *D2078*
Women and War *D1455*
The Women Haters' Club *D2226*
Women in the Attic *D1576*
The Wonderful World of William Bends *D1734*
The Woodcarver's Wife *D1585*
The Wooing of Miss Canada *D855*
The Woolen Mill *D1977*
The Woolly Lamb of God *D220*
Word From an Ambassador of Dreams *D265*
A Word in Your Ear *D1889*
Words for an Imaginary Future *D1320*
The Workingman *D2146*
The Worm *D1788*
Worth's Burlesque Ritual *C194*
Wozzeck *D1684*
The Wrecked Blackship *D2233*
The Wringing of Hearts *D1382*
Writing Poetry *D37*
Wu-feng *D1813*

Y

Ye Gunne Pouder Plott *D1214*
Ye Last Sweet Thing in Corners *C105*
The Yellow Bag *D306*
Yes, Dear *D826*
Yesterday the Children Were Dancing *D745*
Yea, Though I Walk *D1273*
Years Afterward *D1399*
Yet Shall He Live *D1484*
You Are Not Alone *D1792*
You Are the Only WASP I Know *D1685*
You Can't Do That *D802, D1016*
You Can't Stop Now *D1890*
You Remind Me of Me *D1167*
You Smell Good to Me *D921*
The Young Country Schoolm'am *D77*
Young Hunting *D997*
The Young Professor *D1364*
The Young Village Doctor *D69*
You're Gonna Be Alright, Jamie Boy *D713*
Youth Goes West *D1120*

Z

Zanorin *D250*
Zastrozzi *D2141*
Zuma, the Peruvian Maid *D1365*

Resource List

English-Canadian Drama Bibliographies:
- Watters, Reginald Eyre. *A Checklist of Canadian Literature and Background Materials 1628-1960.* Toronto, University of Toronto Press, 1972.
- Milne, W.S. "Letters In Canada: Drama", *University of Toronto Quarterly,* 1935-1942.
- Canadian Association for Adult Education. *Canadian Plays and Playwrights.* Toronto, C.A.A.E., 1957.
- Cummings, Richard, et. al. *The Brock Bibliography of Published Canadian Stage Plays in English 1900-1972.* St. Catharines, Ont., Brock University, 1972.
- Bryan, Bonita J. Orosz, et. al. *The First Supplement to the Brock Bibliography of Published Canadian Plays.* St. Catharines, Ont., Brock University, 1973.
- Sedgwick, Dorothy. *A Bibliography of English-Language Theatre and Drama in Canada 1800-1914.* Edmonton, Nineteenth Century Theatre Research, 1976.
- O'Neill, Patrick B. *Canadian Plays—A Supplementary Checklist to 1945.* Halifax, Dalhousie University, School of Library Science, 1978.

Canadian Drama Catalogues and Finding Aids:
- *A Directory of Canadian Plays and Playwrights.* Toronto, Playwrights Co-op, 1977.
- *The Catalogue: B.C. Playwrights.* Vancouver, New Play Centre, 1977.
- *Our Plays First.* Halifax, Dramatists Co-op of Nova Scotia, 1979.
- *Canadiana.* Vol. 1- 1951-. Ottawa, National Library of Canada.
- *Canadian Books in Print:* Subject Index, Author and Title Index. Toronto, University of Toronto Press, 1967-.
- *Canadian Periodical Index.* Vol. 1- 1948-. Ottawa, Canadian Library Association.

- *The National Union Catalog, Pre-1956 Imprints*: A Cumulative Author List Representing Library of Congress Printed Cards and Titles Reported by Other American Libraries. London, Mansell, 1968-.
- *Dictionary Catalog of the Harris Collection of American Poetry and Plays.* Boston, G.K. Hall, 1972. *First Supplement,* 1977.
- *The New York Public Library Catalog of the Theatre and Drama Collections*: Author Listing, Listing by Cultural Origin. Boston, G.K. Hall, 1967. *First Supplement,* 1973.
- *An Index to One Act Plays.* Boston, F.W. Faxon, 1924-.
- *Cumulated Dramatic Index 1909-1949.* Boston, G.K. Hall, 1965.
- Keller, Dean H. *Index to Plays in Periodicals.* Metuchen, N.J., Scarecrow Press, 1971. *Supplement,* 1973.
- Patterson, Charlotte A. *Plays in Periodicals: An Index to English Language Scripts in Twentieth Century Journals.* Boston, G.K. Hall, 1970.
- *Union List of Serials in Libraries of the United States and Canada.* New York, H.W. Wilson, 1965.
- *New Serial Titles.* Washington, D.C., 1973-.

Canadian Publishers and Playwrights Associations:
- Association of Canadian Publishers, 70 the Esplanade, Toronto, Ont., M5E 1A6.
- The Canadian Book Information Centre, 70 the Esplanade, Toronto, Ont., M5E 1A6. Issues annual catalogues.
- *Canadian Publishers' Directory.* Greey de Pencier Publications, 59 Front Street East, Toronto, Ont., M5E 1B3. Semi-annual.
- Canadian Periodical Publishers' Association, 54 Wolseley St., Toronto, Ont., M5T 1A5. Regularly issues catalogues listing its member publications.
- *Quill & Quire,* 59 Front Street East, Toronto, Ont., M5E 1B3. Vol. 1- 1935-. Provides the most comprehensive monthly survey of publishing in Canada in addition to book reviews and the semi-annual *New and Forthcoming Books.*
- Playwrights Canada (formerly Playwrights Co-op), 8 York Street, Toronto, Ont., M5J 1R2. The national association of professional playwrights; regularly issues catalogues of Canadian plays and theatre reference books.
- The New Play Centre, Box 46568, Vancouver, B.C., V6R 4G8. Issues catalogues of scripts circulated by the Centre.
- The Dramatists Co-op, Writers' Federation, P.O. Box 3606, South Halifax, N.S., B3J 3K6. Issues catalogues of scripts circulated by the Co-op.
- The Guild of Canadian Playwrights, The Writers' Centre, 24 Ryerson Ave., Toronto, Ont., M5T 2P3.

French-Canadian Drama Bibliographies:
- Hare, John E. "Bibliographie du théâtre canadien-francais (des origines à 1973)", *Le Théâtre Canadien-Francais.* Montreal, Fidès, 1976. pp. 951-999.
- Rinfret, Gabriel-Edouard. *Le Théâtre canadien d'expression francaise: répertoire analytique des origines à nos jours.* 3 vols. Montreal, Leméac, 1975-1977.
- Pagé, Pierre, et al. *Répertoire des oeuvres de la littérature radiophonique québécoise, 1930-1970.* Montreal, Fidès, 1975.
- Pagé, Pierre and Renée Legris. *Répertoire des dramatiques québécoises à la télévision, 1952-1977.* Montreal, Fidès, 1977.

Canadian Theatre History Bibliographies:
- Ball, John and Richard Plant. *A Bibliography of Canadian Theatre History 1583-1975.* Toronto, Playwrights Co-op, 1976. *First Supplement,* 1979.
- *Canada On Stage: Canadian Theatre Review Yearbook.* Vol.1- 1974-. Don Rubin, ed. Toronto, Canadian Theatre Review. Annual. Provides detailed production information on plays produced in Canada.
- Fink, Howard and Brian Morrison. *Bibliography of Canadian Radio Drama in English 1925-1961.* Radio Drama Project, Concordia University, Montreal, 1980.

Anton Wagner is a theatre critic and Canadian theatre historian. He served as dramaturge and general editor for Playwrights Co-op from 1975 to 1977. He is also series editor of *Canada's Lost Plays* published by Canadian Theatre Review Publications.

Other bibliographies from Playwrights Canada:

A Bibliography of Canadian Theatre History 1583-1975
Edited by John Ball and Richard Plant

The Bibliography of Canadian Theatre History Supplement 1975-1976
Edited by John Ball and Richard Plant

Write for our current Directory of Canadian Plays and Playwrights. It includes synopses of more than 300 plays (many of which are included in this bibliography) as well as biographies of the authors and production photographs.